Heckuva Job, Bushie!

Doonesbury Books by G. B. Trudeau

Recent Collections

Read My Lips, Make My Day, Eat Quiche and Die!
Give Those Nymphs Some Hooters!
You're Smokin' Now, Mr. Butts!
I'd Go with the Helmet, Ray
Welcome to Club Scud!
What Is It, Tink, Is Pan in Trouble?
Quality Time on Highway 1
Washed Out Bridges and Other Disasters
In Search of Cigarette Holder Man
Doonesbury Nation
Virtual Doonesbury
Planet Doonesbury
Buck Wild Doonesbury
Duke 2000: Whatever It Takes
The Revolt of the English Majors
Peace Out, Dawg!
Got War?
Talk to the Hand

Anthologies

The Doonesbury Chronicles
Doonesbury's Greatest Hits
The People's Doonesbury
Doonesbury Dossier: The Reagan Years
Doonesbury Deluxe: Selected Glances Askance
Recycled Doonesbury: Second Thoughts on a Gilded Age
The Portable Doonesbury
The Bundled Doonesbury

Special Collections

Action Figure!
Flashbacks: Twenty-Five Years of Doonesbury
The Long Road Home: One Step at a Time
Dude: The Big Book of Zonker
The War Within: One More Step at a Time

A DOONESBURY BOOK

Heckuva Job, Bushie!

BY G. B. TRUDEAU

Andrews McMeel
Publishing, LLC
Kansas City

DOONESBURY is distributed internationally by Universal Press Syndicate.

06 07 08 09 10 BAM 10 9 8 7 6 5 4 3 2 1

ISBN-13: 978-0-7407-6200-0
ISBN-10: 0-7407-6200-1

Library of Congress Catalog Card Number: 2006925238

DOONESBURY may be viewed on the Internet at
www.doonesbury.com and www.GoComics.com.

"Our enemies are innovative and resourceful, and so are we.
They never stop thinking about new ways to harm our country
and our people, and neither do we."

—President George W. Bush

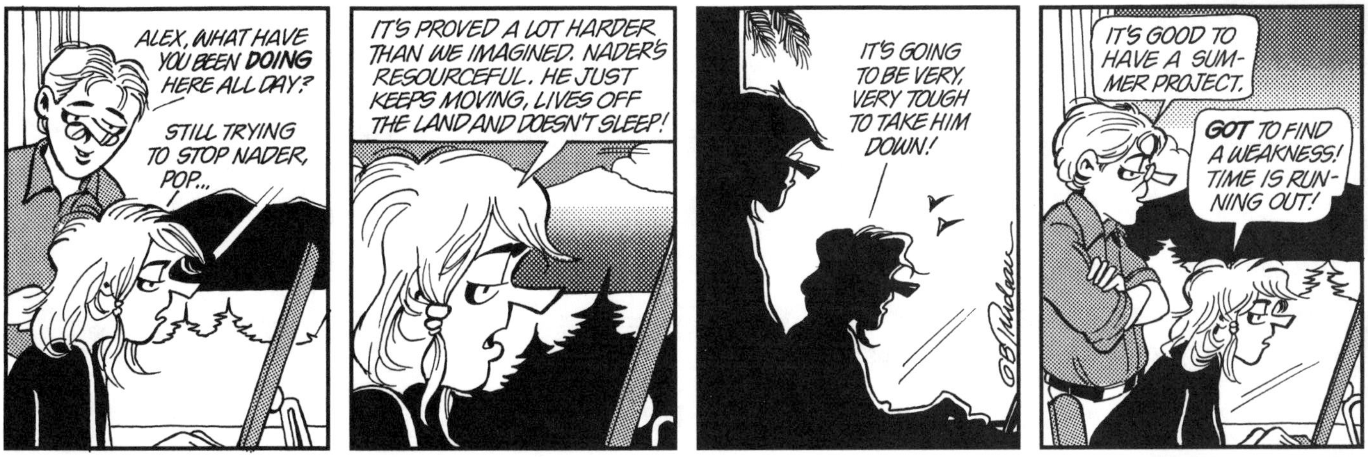

ALEX, WHAT HAVE YOU BEEN **DOING** HERE ALL DAY?
STILL TRYING TO STOP NADER, POP...
IT'S PROVED A LOT HARDER THAN WE IMAGINED. NADER'S RESOURCEFUL. HE JUST KEEPS MOVING, LIVES OFF THE LAND AND DOESN'T SLEEP!
IT'S GOING TO BE VERY, VERY TOUGH TO TAKE HIM DOWN!
IT'S GOOD TO HAVE A SUMMER PROJECT.
GOT TO FIND A WEAKNESS! TIME IS RUNNING OUT!

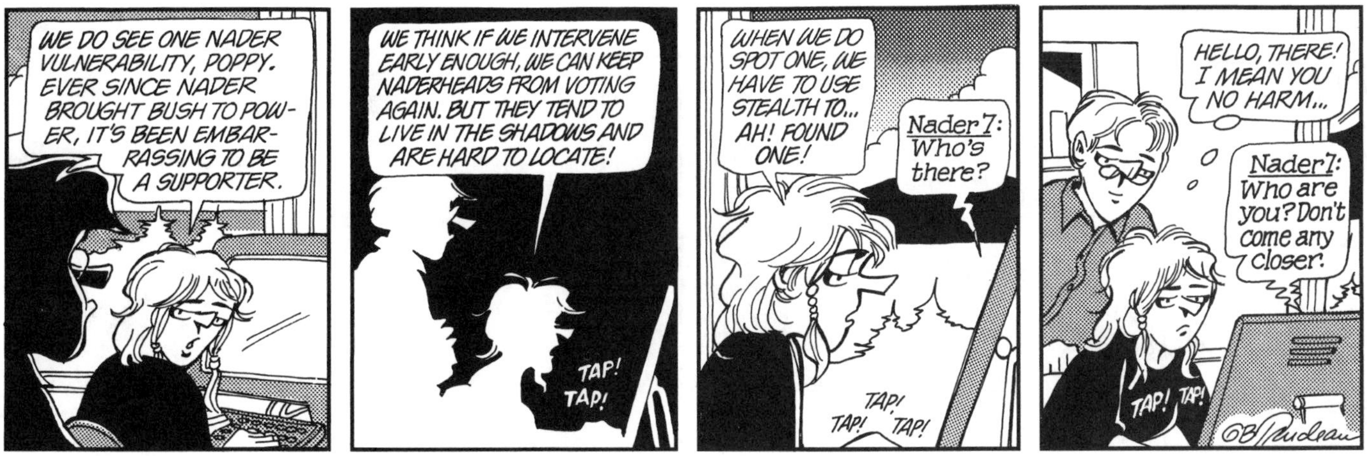

WE DO SEE ONE NADER VULNERABILITY, POPPY. EVER SINCE NADER BROUGHT BUSH TO POWER, IT'S BEEN EMBARRASSING TO BE A SUPPORTER.
WE THINK IF WE INTERVENE EARLY ENOUGH, WE CAN KEEP NADERHEADS FROM VOTING AGAIN. BUT THEY TEND TO LIVE IN THE SHADOWS AND ARE HARD TO LOCATE!
TAP! TAP!
WHEN WE DO SPOT ONE, WE HAVE TO USE STEALTH TO... AH! FOUND ONE!
Nader7: Who's there?
TAP! TAP! TAP!
HELLO, THERE! I MEAN YOU NO HARM...
Nader7: Who are you? Don't come any closer.
TAP! TAP!

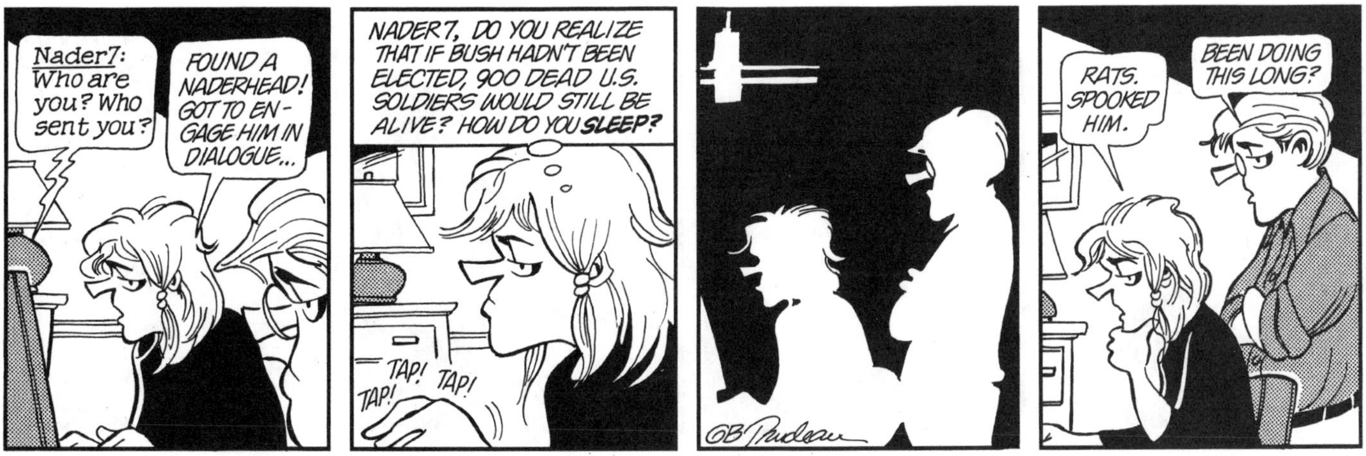

Nader7: Who are you? Who sent you?
FOUND A NADERHEAD! GOT TO ENGAGE HIM IN DIALOGUE...
NADER7, DO YOU REALIZE THAT IF BUSH HADN'T BEEN ELECTED, 900 DEAD U.S. SOLDIERS WOULD STILL BE ALIVE? HOW DO YOU **SLEEP?**
TAP! TAP! TAP!
RATS. SPOOKED HIM.
BEEN DOING THIS LONG?

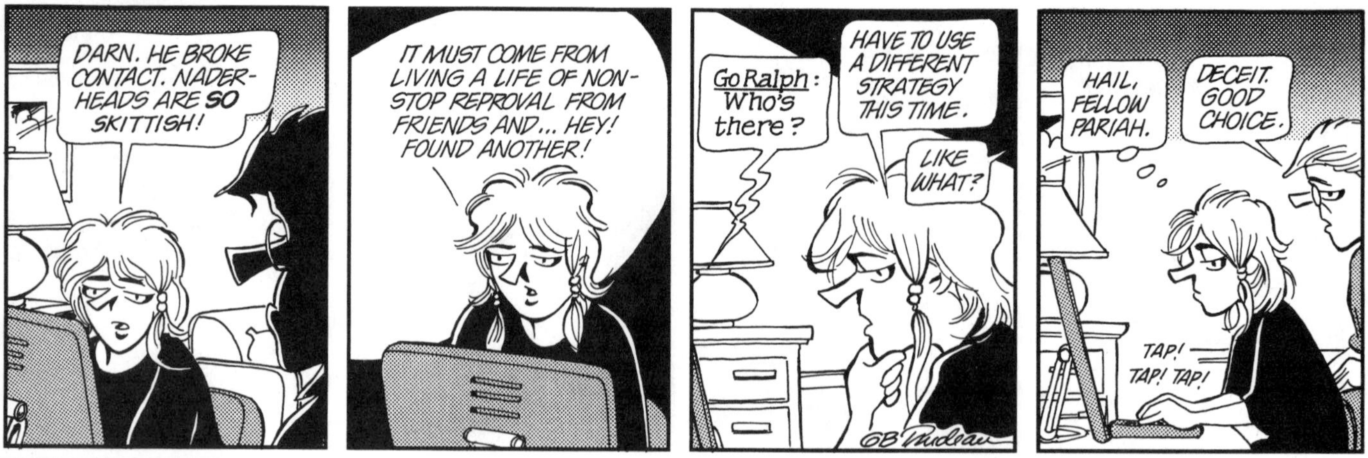
DARN. HE BROKE CONTACT. NADERHEADS ARE SO SKITTISH!
IT MUST COME FROM LIVING A LIFE OF NON-STOP REPROVAL FROM FRIENDS AND... HEY! FOUND ANOTHER!
Go Ralph: Who's there?
HAVE TO USE A DIFFERENT STRATEGY THIS TIME.
LIKE WHAT?
HAIL, FELLOW PARIAH.
DECEIT. GOOD CHOICE.
TAP! TAP! TAP!

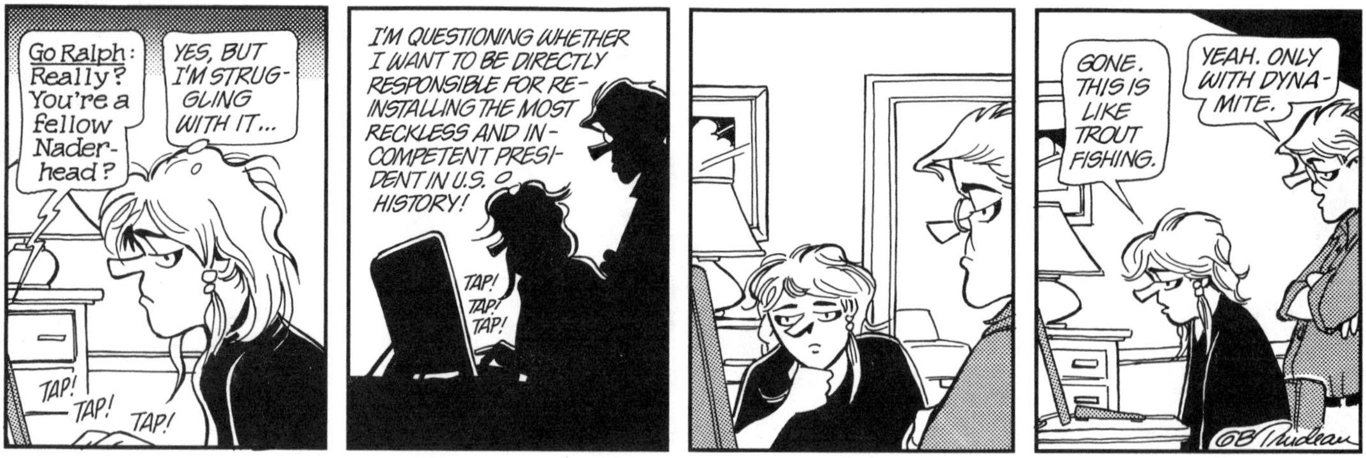
Go Ralph: Really? You're a fellow Naderhead?
YES, BUT I'M STRUGGLING WITH IT...
TAP! TAP! TAP!
I'M QUESTIONING WHETHER I WANT TO BE DIRECTLY RESPONSIBLE FOR REINSTALLING THE MOST RECKLESS AND INCOMPETENT PRESIDENT IN U.S. HISTORY!
TAP! TAP! TAP!
GONE. THIS IS LIKE TROUT FISHING.
YEAH. ONLY WITH DYNAMITE.

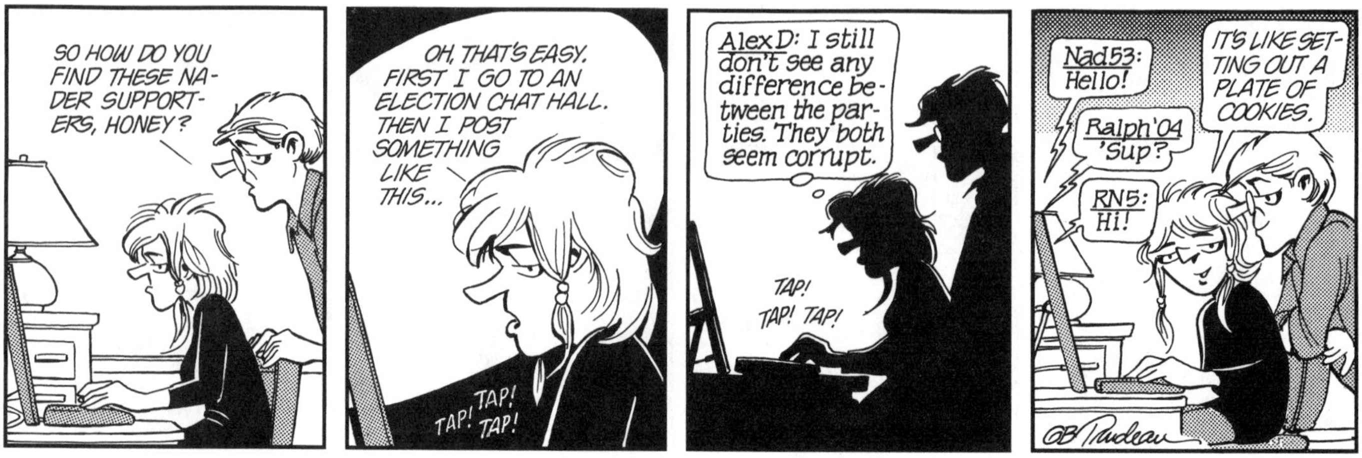
SO HOW DO YOU FIND THESE NADER SUPPORTERS, HONEY?
OH, THAT'S EASY. FIRST I GO TO AN ELECTION CHAT HALL. THEN I POST SOMETHING LIKE THIS...
TAP! TAP! TAP!
Alex D: I still don't see any difference between the parties. They both seem corrupt.
TAP! TAP! TAP!
Nad53: Hello!
Ralph'04: 'Sup?
RN5: Hi!
IT'S LIKE SETTING OUT A PLATE OF COOKIES.

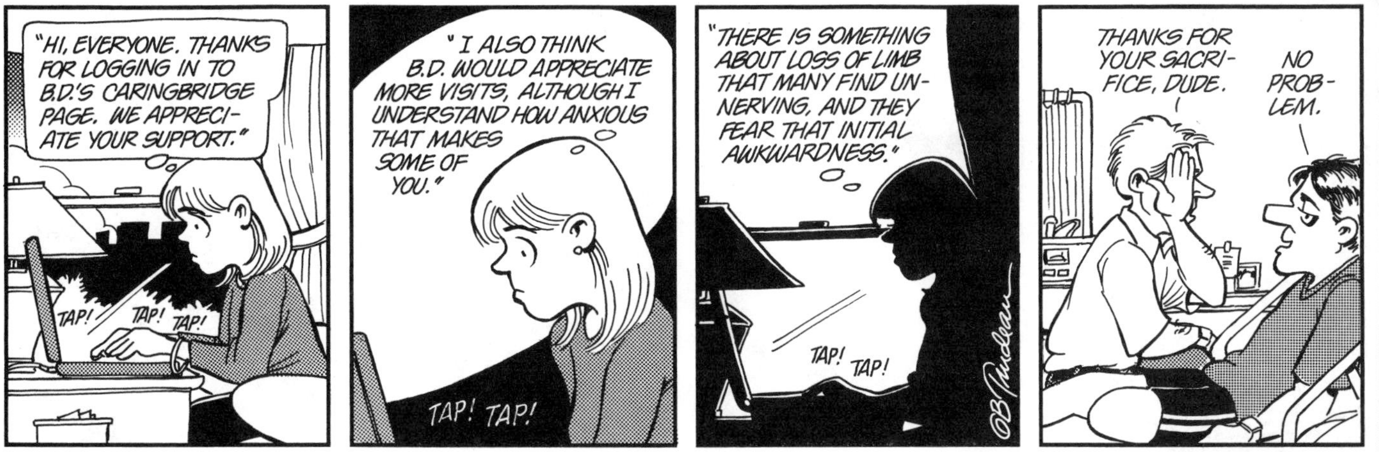
"HI, EVERYONE. THANKS FOR LOGGING IN TO B.D.'S CARINGBRIDGE PAGE. WE APPRECIATE YOUR SUPPORT."
TAP! TAP! TAP!
"I ALSO THINK B.D. WOULD APPRECIATE MORE VISITS, ALTHOUGH I UNDERSTAND HOW ANXIOUS THAT MAKES SOME OF YOU."
TAP! TAP!
"THERE IS SOMETHING ABOUT LOSS OF LIMB THAT MANY FIND UNNERVING, AND THEY FEAR THAT INITIAL AWKWARDNESS."
TAP! TAP!
©B Trudeau
THANKS FOR YOUR SACRIFICE, DUDE.
NO PROBLEM.

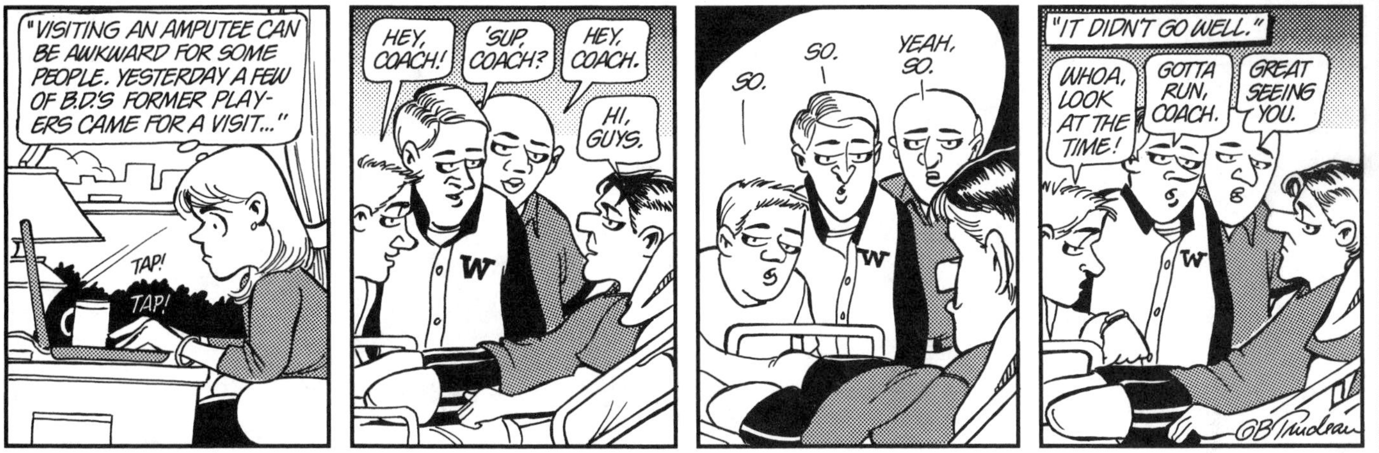
"VISITING AN AMPUTEE CAN BE AWKWARD FOR SOME PEOPLE. YESTERDAY A FEW OF B.D.'S FORMER PLAYERS CAME FOR A VISIT..."
TAP! TAP!
HEY, COACH!
'SUP, COACH?
HEY, COACH.
HI, GUYS.
SO.
SO.
YEAH, SO.
"IT DIDN'T GO WELL."
WHOA, LOOK AT THE TIME!
GOTTA RUN, COACH.
GREAT SEEING YOU.
©B Trudeau

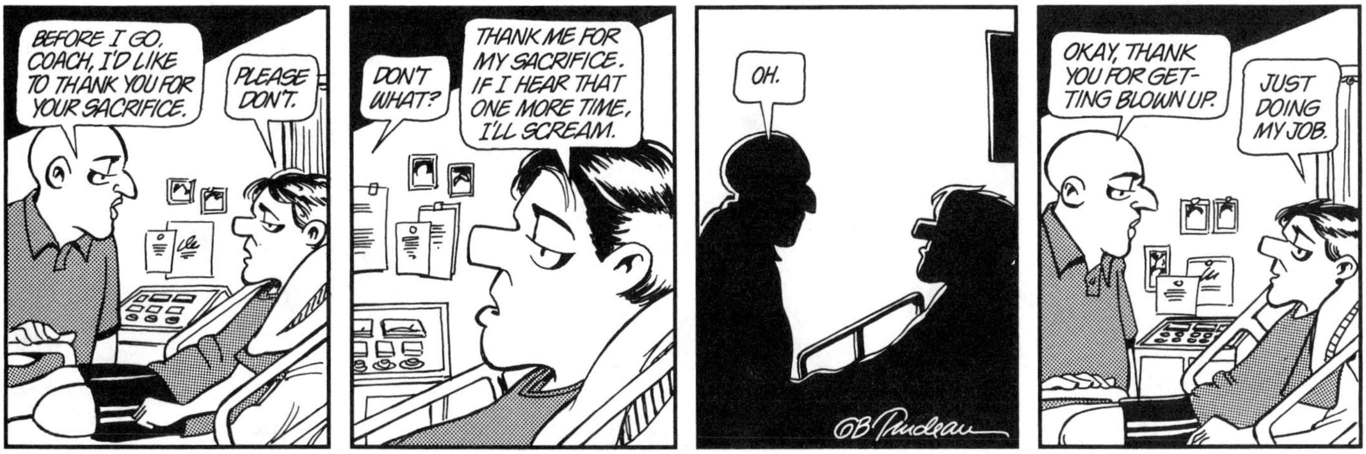
BEFORE I GO, COACH, I'D LIKE TO THANK YOU FOR YOUR SACRIFICE.
PLEASE DON'T.
DON'T WHAT?
THANK ME FOR MY SACRIFICE. IF I HEAR THAT ONE MORE TIME, I'LL SCREAM.
OH.
©B Trudeau
OKAY, THANK YOU FOR GETTING BLOWN UP.
JUST DOING MY JOB.

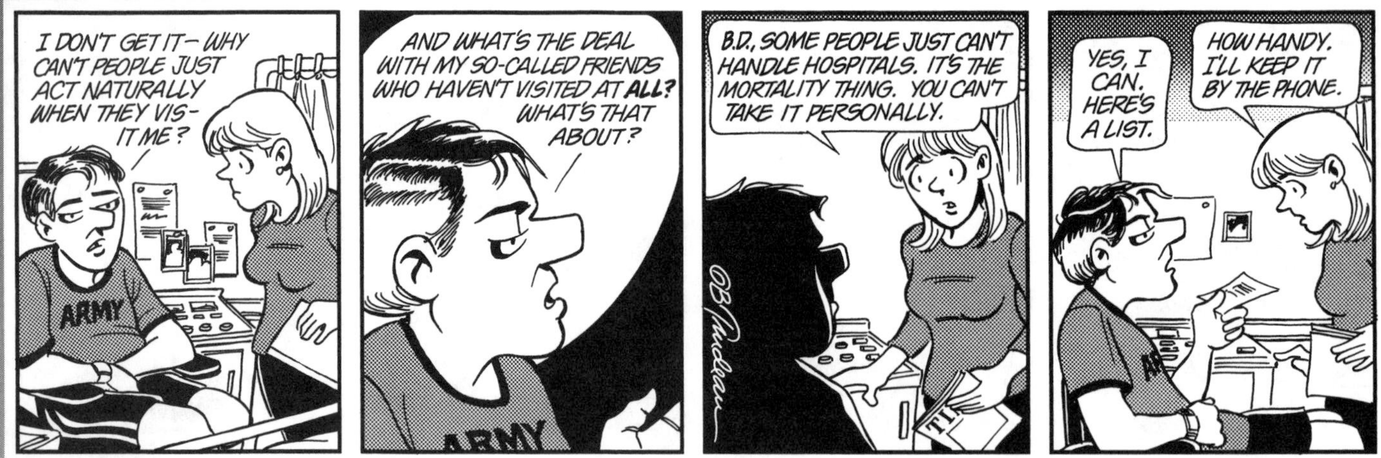
I DON'T GET IT— WHY CAN'T PEOPLE JUST ACT NATURALLY WHEN THEY VISIT ME?
AND WHAT'S THE DEAL WITH MY SO-CALLED FRIENDS WHO HAVEN'T VISITED AT **ALL?** WHAT'S THAT ABOUT?
B.D., SOME PEOPLE JUST CAN'T HANDLE HOSPITALS. IT'S THE MORTALITY THING. YOU CAN'T TAKE IT PERSONALLY.
YES, I CAN. HERE'S A LIST.
HOW HANDY. I'LL KEEP IT BY THE PHONE.

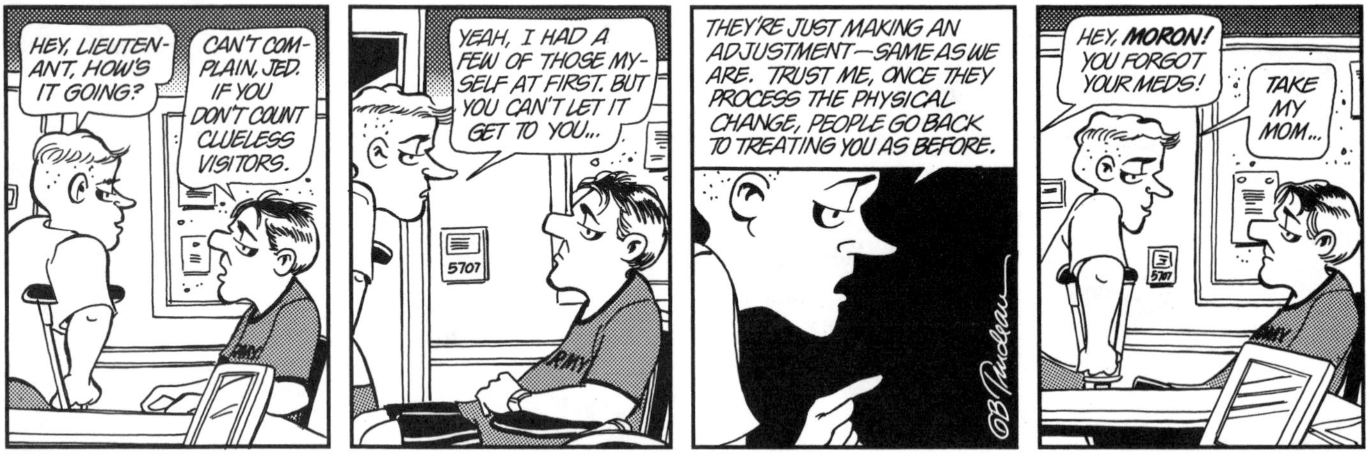
HEY, LIEUTENANT, HOW'S IT GOING?
CAN'T COMPLAIN, JED. IF YOU DON'T COUNT CLUELESS VISITORS.
YEAH, I HAD A FEW OF THOSE MYSELF AT FIRST. BUT YOU CAN'T LET IT GET TO YOU...
THEY'RE JUST MAKING AN ADJUSTMENT—SAME AS WE ARE. TRUST ME, ONCE THEY PROCESS THE PHYSICAL CHANGE, PEOPLE GO BACK TO TREATING YOU AS BEFORE.
HEY, **MORON!** YOU FORGOT YOUR MEDS!
TAKE MY MOM...

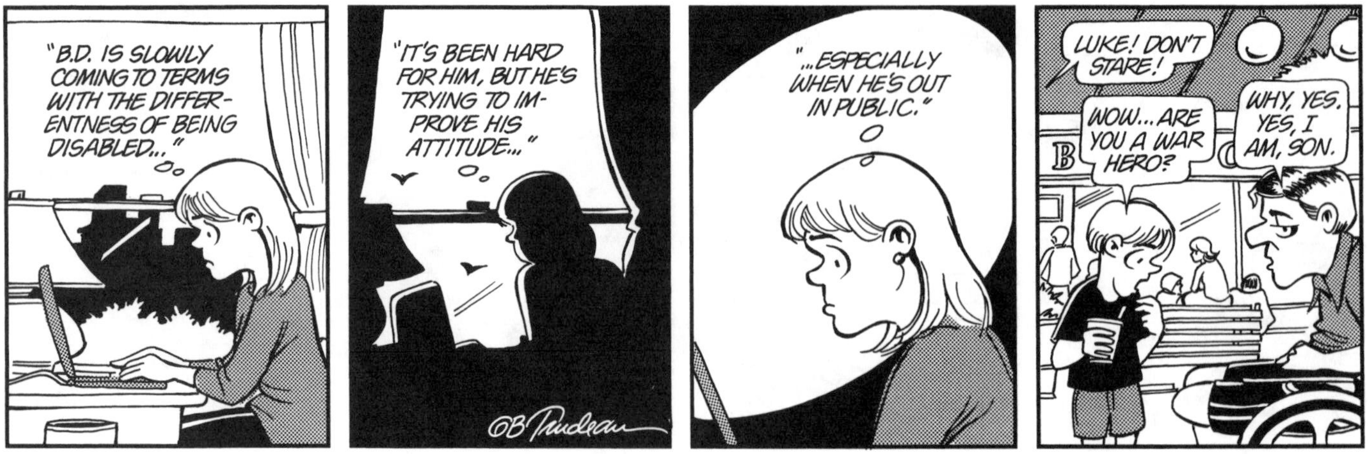
"B.D. IS SLOWLY COMING TO TERMS WITH THE DIFFERENTNESS OF BEING DISABLED..."
"IT'S BEEN HARD FOR HIM, BUT HE'S TRYING TO IMPROVE HIS ATTITUDE..."
"...ESPECIALLY WHEN HE'S OUT IN PUBLIC."
LUKE! DON'T STARE!
WOW... ARE YOU A WAR HERO?
WHY, YES. YES, I AM, SON.

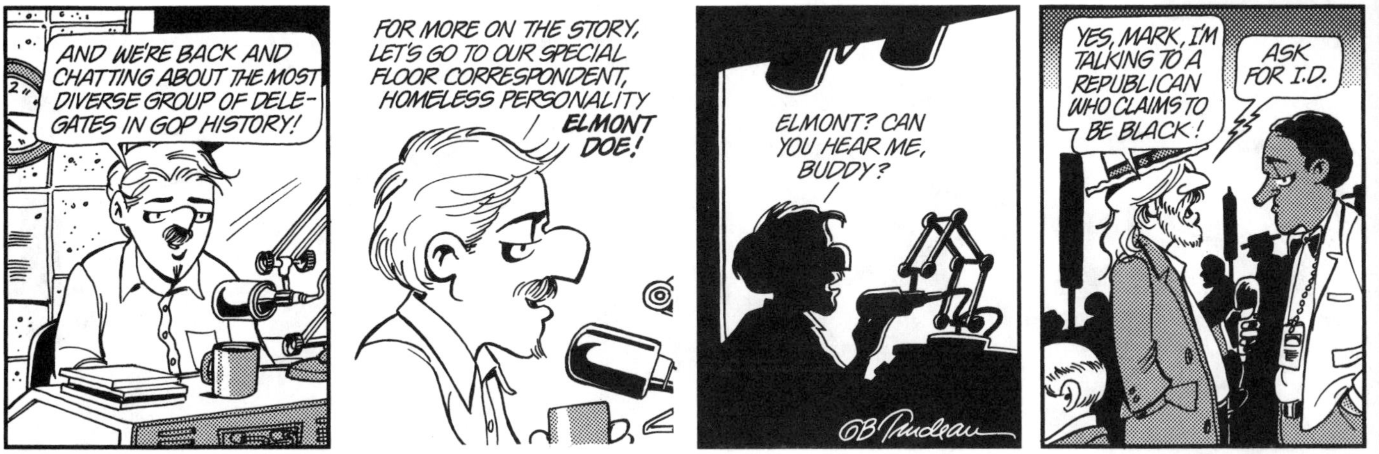
AND WE'RE BACK AND CHATTING ABOUT THE MOST DIVERSE GROUP OF DELEGATES IN GOP HISTORY!
FOR MORE ON THE STORY, LET'S GO TO OUR SPECIAL FLOOR CORRESPONDENT, HOMELESS PERSONALITY ELMONT DOE!
ELMONT? CAN YOU HEAR ME, BUDDY?
YES, MARK, I'M TALKING TO A REPUBLICAN WHO CLAIMS TO BE BLACK!
ASK FOR I.D.

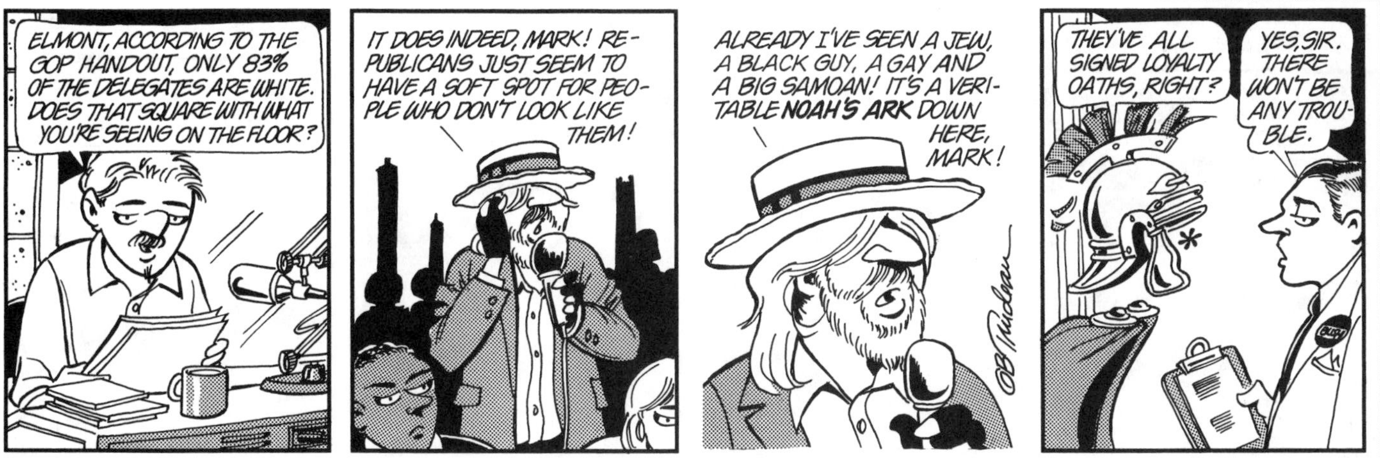
ELMONT, ACCORDING TO THE GOP HANDOUT, ONLY 83% OF THE DELEGATES ARE WHITE. DOES THAT SQUARE WITH WHAT YOU'RE SEEING ON THE FLOOR?
IT DOES INDEED, MARK! REPUBLICANS JUST SEEM TO HAVE A SOFT SPOT FOR PEOPLE WHO DON'T LOOK LIKE THEM!
ALREADY I'VE SEEN A JEW, A BLACK GUY, A GAY AND A BIG SAMOAN! IT'S A VERITABLE NOAH'S ARK DOWN HERE, MARK!
THEY'VE ALL SIGNED LOYALTY OATHS, RIGHT?
YES, SIR. THERE WON'T BE ANY TROUBLE.

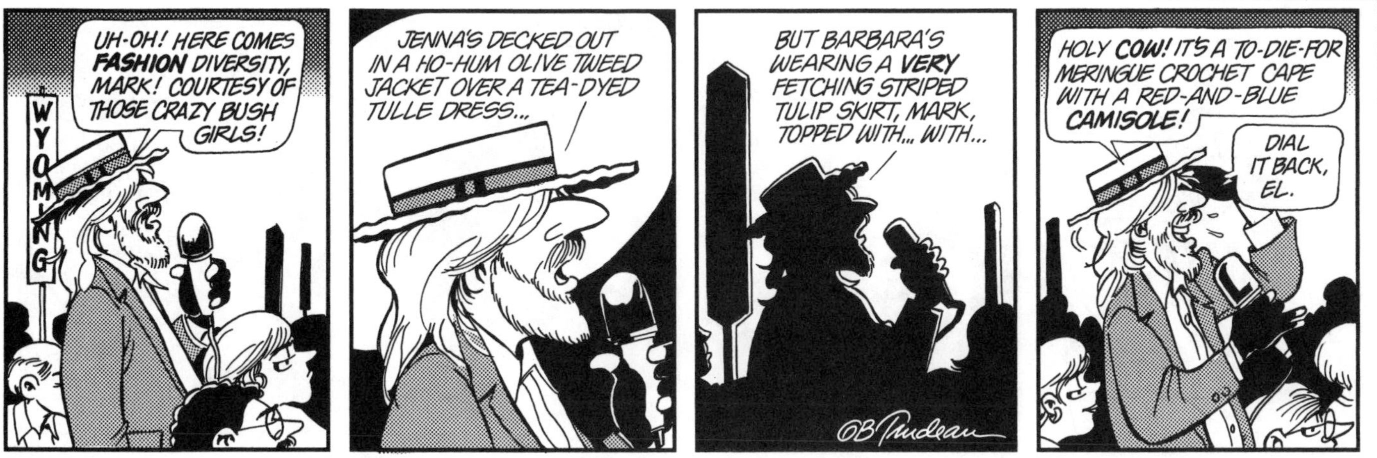
UH-OH! HERE COMES FASHION DIVERSITY, MARK! COURTESY OF THOSE CRAZY BUSH GIRLS!
WYOMING
JENNA'S DECKED OUT IN A HO-HUM OLIVE TWEED JACKET OVER A TEA-DYED TULLE DRESS...
BUT BARBARA'S WEARING A VERY FETCHING STRIPED TULIP SKIRT, MARK, TOPPED WITH... WITH...
HOLY COW! IT'S A TO-DIE-FOR MERINGUE CROCHET CAPE WITH A RED-AND-BLUE CAMISOLE!
DIAL IT BACK, EL.

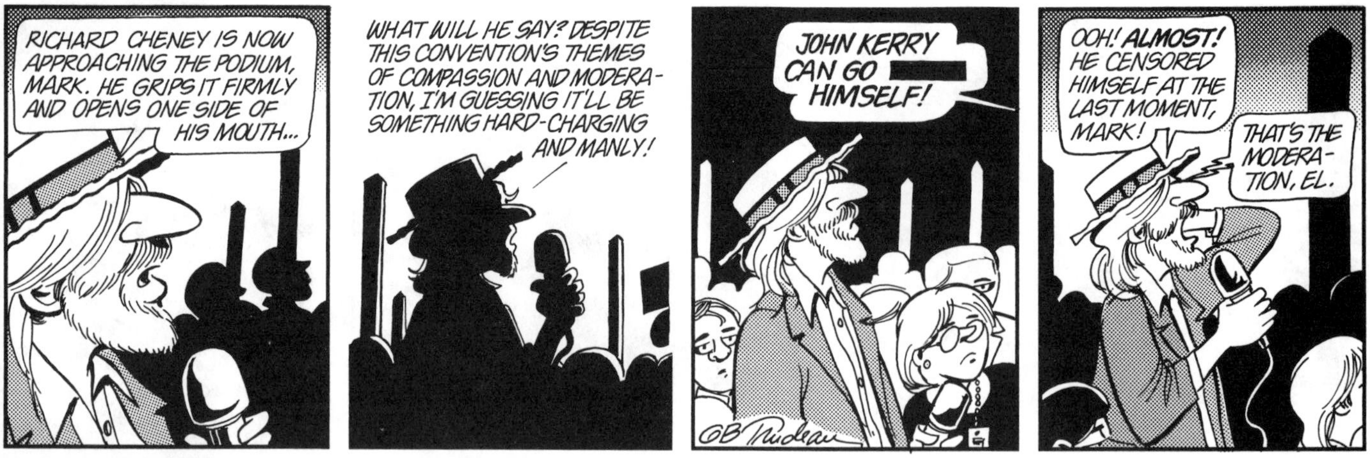
RICHARD CHENEY IS NOW APPROACHING THE PODIUM, MARK. HE GRIPS IT FIRMLY AND OPENS ONE SIDE OF HIS MOUTH...
WHAT WILL HE SAY? DESPITE THIS CONVENTION'S THEMES OF COMPASSION AND MODERATION, I'M GUESSING IT'LL BE SOMETHING HARD-CHARGING AND MANLY!
JOHN KERRY CAN GO [redacted] HIMSELF!
OOH! ALMOST! HE CENSORED HIMSELF AT THE LAST MOMENT, MARK!
THAT'S THE MODERATION, EL.
©B Trudeau

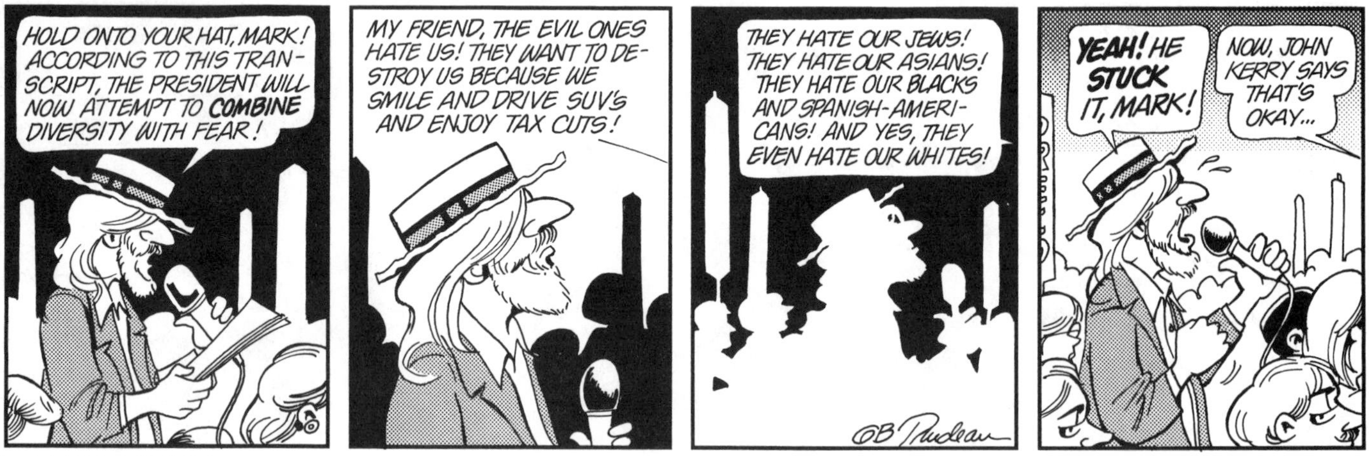
HOLD ONTO YOUR HAT, MARK! ACCORDING TO THIS TRANSCRIPT, THE PRESIDENT WILL NOW ATTEMPT TO COMBINE DIVERSITY WITH FEAR!
MY FRIEND, THE EVIL ONES HATE US! THEY WANT TO DESTROY US BECAUSE WE SMILE AND DRIVE SUV's AND ENJOY TAX CUTS!
THEY HATE OUR JEWS! THEY HATE OUR ASIANS! THEY HATE OUR BLACKS AND SPANISH-AMERICANS! AND YES, THEY EVEN HATE OUR WHITES!
©B Trudeau
YEAH! HE STUCK IT, MARK!
NOW, JOHN KERRY SAYS THAT'S OKAY...

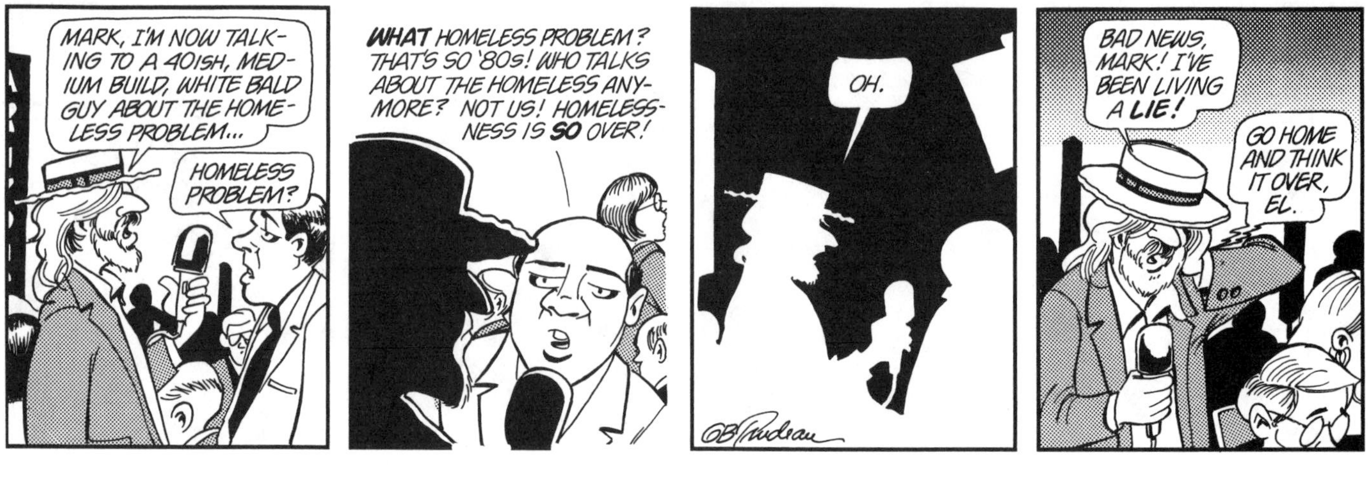
MARK, I'M NOW TALKING TO A 40ISH, MEDIUM BUILD, WHITE BALD GUY ABOUT THE HOMELESS PROBLEM...
HOMELESS PROBLEM?
WHAT HOMELESS PROBLEM? THAT'S SO '80s! WHO TALKS ABOUT THE HOMELESS ANYMORE? NOT US! HOMELESSNESS IS SO OVER!
OH.
©B Trudeau
BAD NEWS, MARK! I'VE BEEN LIVING A LIE!
GO HOME AND THINK IT OVER, EL.

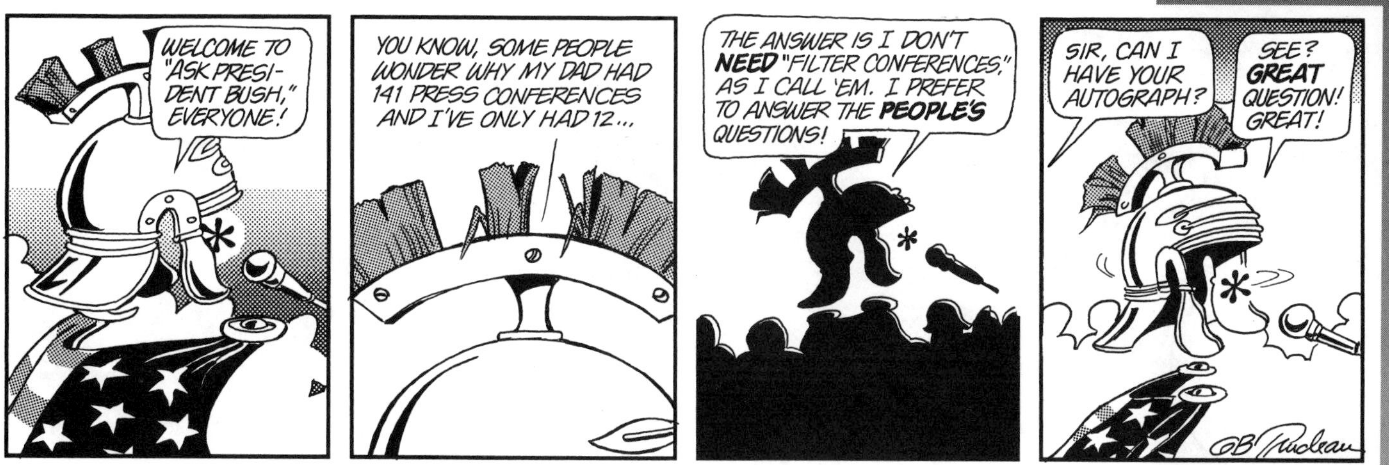
WELCOME TO "ASK PRESIDENT BUSH," EVERYONE!
YOU KNOW, SOME PEOPLE WONDER WHY MY DAD HAD 141 PRESS CONFERENCES AND I'VE ONLY HAD 12...
THE ANSWER IS I DON'T **NEED** "FILTER CONFERENCES," AS I CALL 'EM. I PREFER TO ANSWER THE **PEOPLE'S** QUESTIONS!
SIR, CAN I HAVE YOUR AUTOGRAPH?
SEE? **GREAT** QUESTION! GREAT!

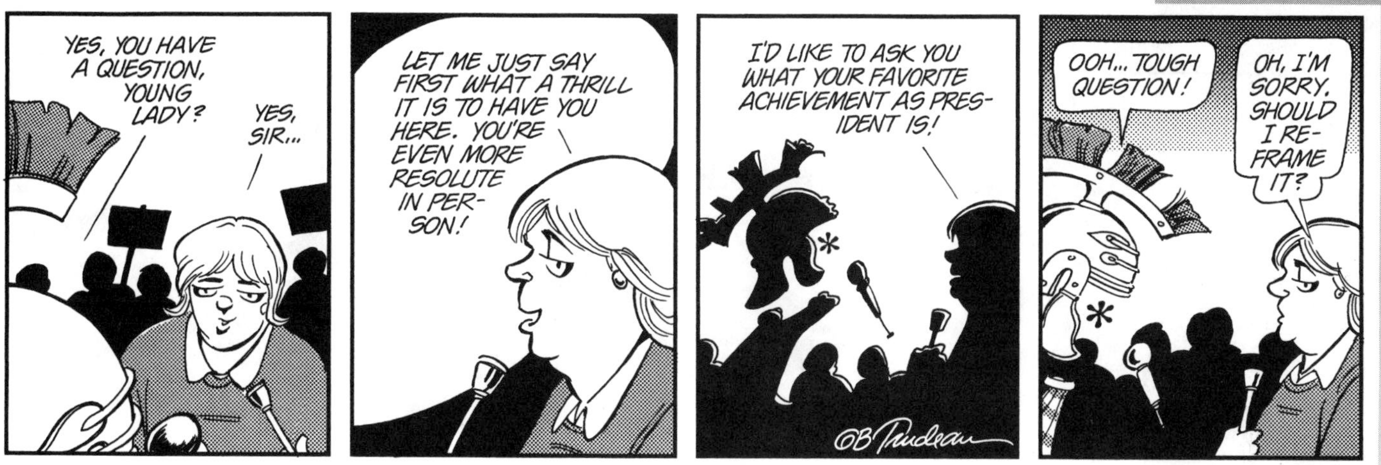
YES, YOU HAVE A QUESTION, YOUNG LADY?
YES, SIR...
LET ME JUST SAY FIRST WHAT A THRILL IT IS TO HAVE YOU HERE. YOU'RE EVEN MORE RESOLUTE IN PERSON!
I'D LIKE TO ASK YOU WHAT YOUR FAVORITE ACHIEVEMENT AS PRESIDENT IS!
OOH... TOUGH QUESTION!
OH, I'M SORRY. SHOULD I REFRAME IT?

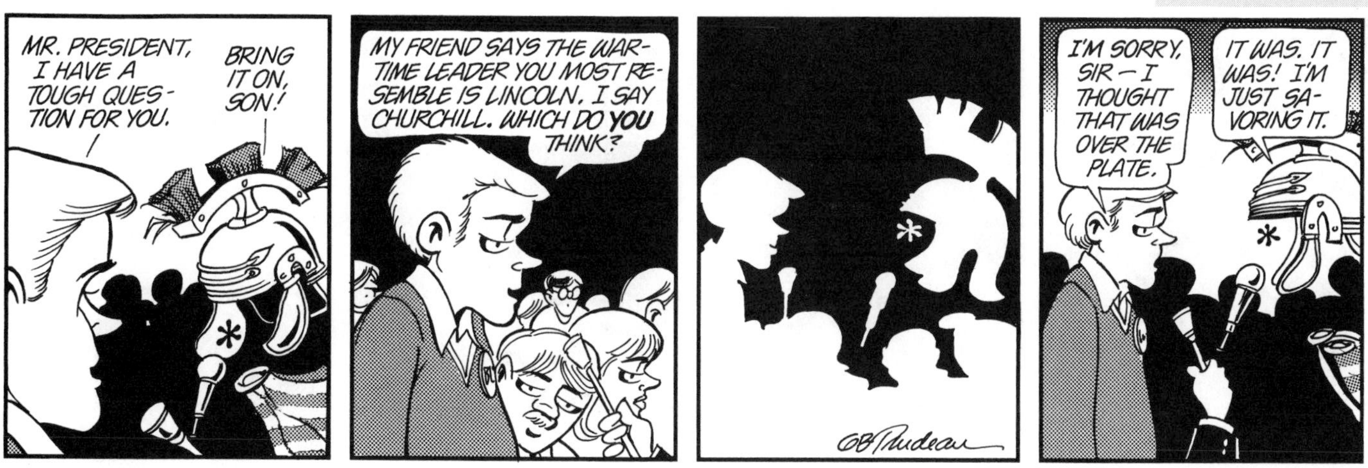
MR. PRESIDENT, I HAVE A TOUGH QUESTION FOR YOU.
BRING IT ON, SON!
MY FRIEND SAYS THE WARTIME LEADER YOU MOST RESEMBLE IS LINCOLN. I SAY CHURCHILL. WHICH DO **YOU** THINK?
I'M SORRY, SIR — I THOUGHT THAT WAS OVER THE PLATE.
IT WAS. IT WAS! I'M JUST SAVORING IT.

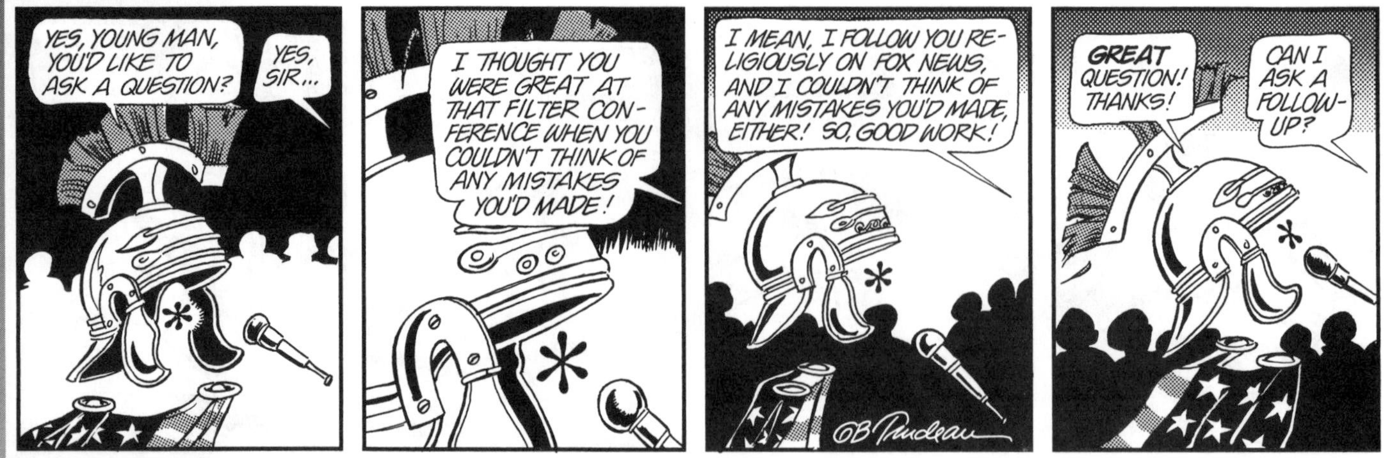
YES, YOUNG MAN, YOU'D LIKE TO ASK A QUESTION?
YES, SIR...
I THOUGHT YOU WERE GREAT AT THAT FILTER CONFERENCE WHEN YOU COULDN'T THINK OF ANY MISTAKES YOU'D MADE!
I MEAN, I FOLLOW YOU RELIGIOUSLY ON FOX NEWS, AND I COULDN'T THINK OF ANY MISTAKES YOU'D MADE, EITHER! SO, GOOD WORK!
©B Trudeau
GREAT QUESTION! THANKS!
CAN I ASK A FOLLOW-UP?

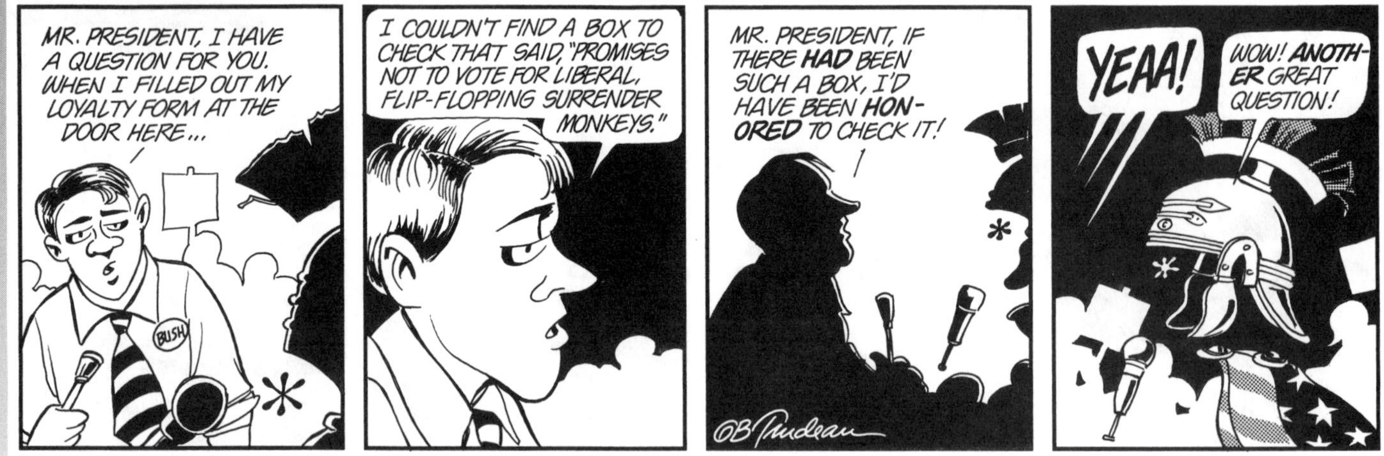
MR. PRESIDENT, I HAVE A QUESTION FOR YOU. WHEN I FILLED OUT MY LOYALTY FORM AT THE DOOR HERE...
BUSH
I COULDN'T FIND A BOX TO CHECK THAT SAID, "PROMISES NOT TO VOTE FOR LIBERAL, FLIP-FLOPPING SURRENDER MONKEYS."
MR. PRESIDENT, IF THERE HAD BEEN SUCH A BOX, I'D HAVE BEEN HONORED TO CHECK IT!
©B Trudeau
YEAA!
WOW! ANOTHER GREAT QUESTION!

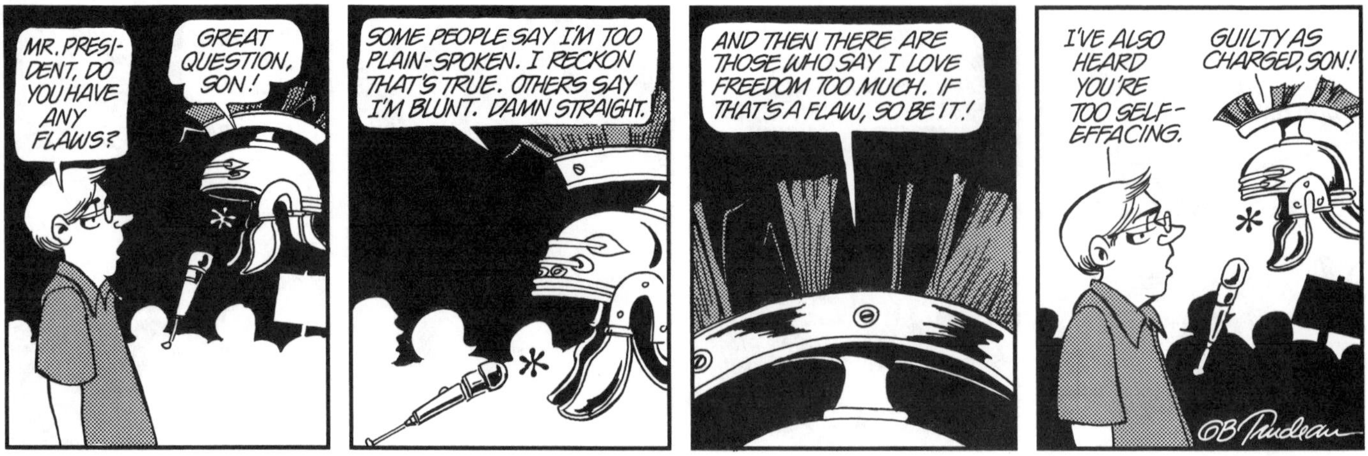
MR. PRESIDENT, DO YOU HAVE ANY FLAWS?
GREAT QUESTION, SON!
SOME PEOPLE SAY I'M TOO PLAIN-SPOKEN. I RECKON THAT'S TRUE. OTHERS SAY I'M BLUNT. DAMN STRAIGHT.
AND THEN THERE ARE THOSE WHO SAY I LOVE FREEDOM TOO MUCH. IF THAT'S A FLAW, SO BE IT!
I'VE ALSO HEARD YOU'RE TOO SELF-EFFACING.
GUILTY AS CHARGED, SON!
©B Trudeau

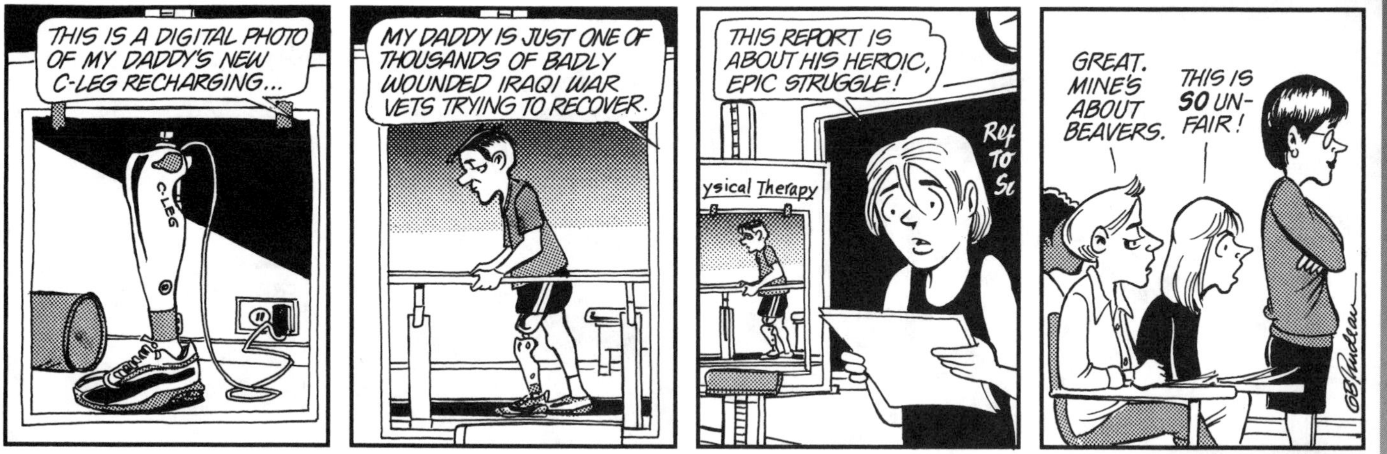
THIS IS A DIGITAL PHOTO OF MY DADDY'S NEW C-LEG RECHARGING...
C-LEG
MY DADDY IS JUST ONE OF THOUSANDS OF BADLY WOUNDED IRAQI WAR VETS TRYING TO RECOVER.
THIS REPORT IS ABOUT HIS HEROIC, EPIC STRUGGLE!
GREAT. MINE'S ABOUT BEAVERS.
THIS IS **SO** UNFAIR!

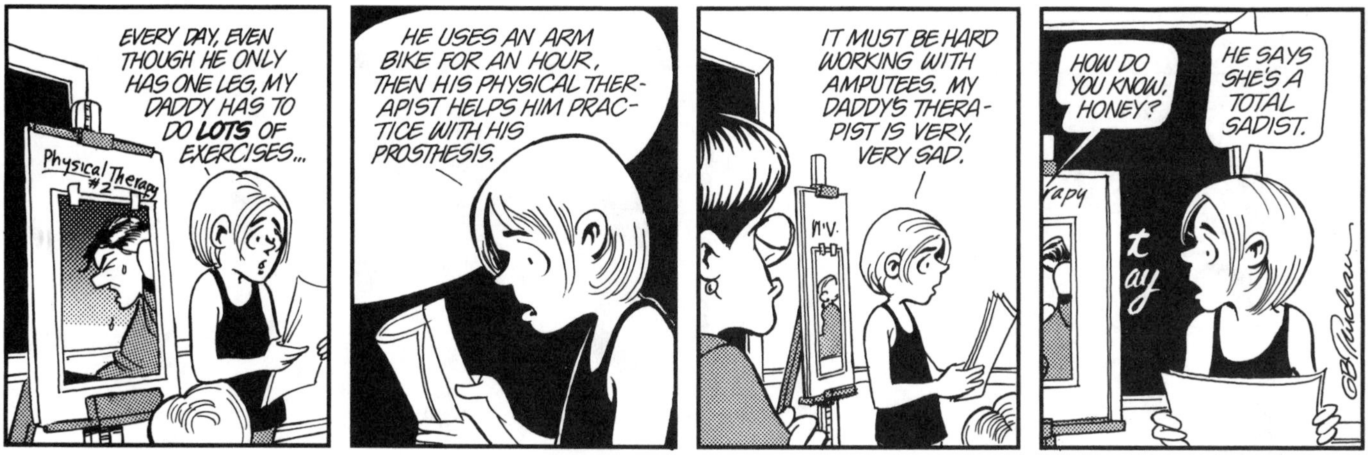
EVERY DAY, EVEN THOUGH HE ONLY HAS ONE LEG, MY DADDY HAS TO DO **LOTS** OF EXERCISES...
Physical Therapy #2
HE USES AN ARM BIKE FOR AN HOUR, THEN HIS PHYSICAL THERAPIST HELPS HIM PRACTICE WITH HIS PROSTHESIS.
IT MUST BE HARD WORKING WITH AMPUTEES. MY DADDY'S THERAPIST IS VERY, VERY SAD.
HOW DO YOU KNOW, HONEY?
HE SAYS SHE'S A TOTAL SADIST.

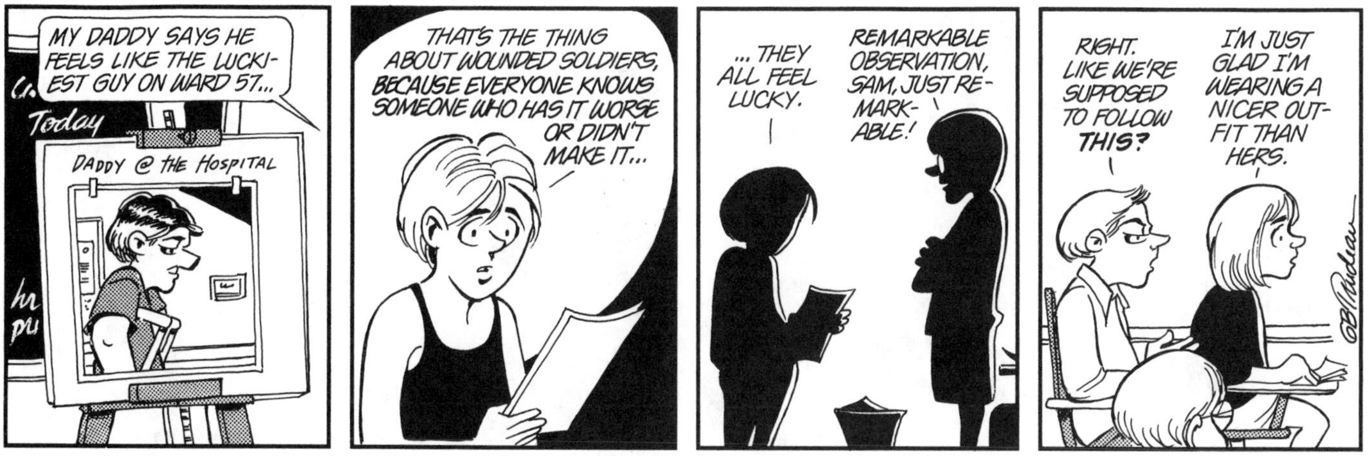
MY DADDY SAYS HE FEELS LIKE THE LUCKIEST GUY ON WARD 57...
Today
DADDY @ THE HOSPITAL
THAT'S THE THING ABOUT WOUNDED SOLDIERS, BECAUSE EVERYONE KNOWS SOMEONE WHO HAS IT WORSE OR DIDN'T MAKE IT...
...THEY ALL FEEL LUCKY.
REMARKABLE OBSERVATION, SAM, JUST REMARKABLE!
RIGHT. LIKE WE'RE SUPPOSED TO FOLLOW **THIS?**
I'M JUST GLAD I'M WEARING A NICER OUTFIT THAN HERS.

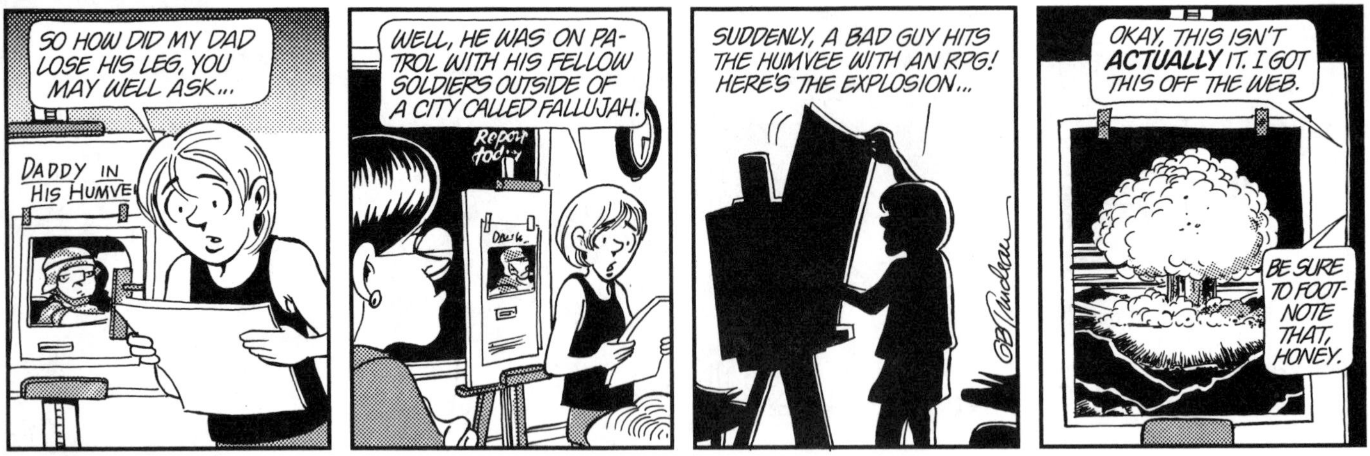
SO HOW DID MY DAD LOSE HIS LEG, YOU MAY WELL ASK...
WELL, HE WAS ON PATROL WITH HIS FELLOW SOLDIERS OUTSIDE OF A CITY CALLED FALLUJAH.
SUDDENLY, A BAD GUY HITS THE HUMVEE WITH AN RPG! HERE'S THE EXPLOSION...
OKAY, THIS ISN'T **ACTUALLY** IT. I GOT THIS OFF THE WEB.
BE SURE TO FOOTNOTE THAT, HONEY.

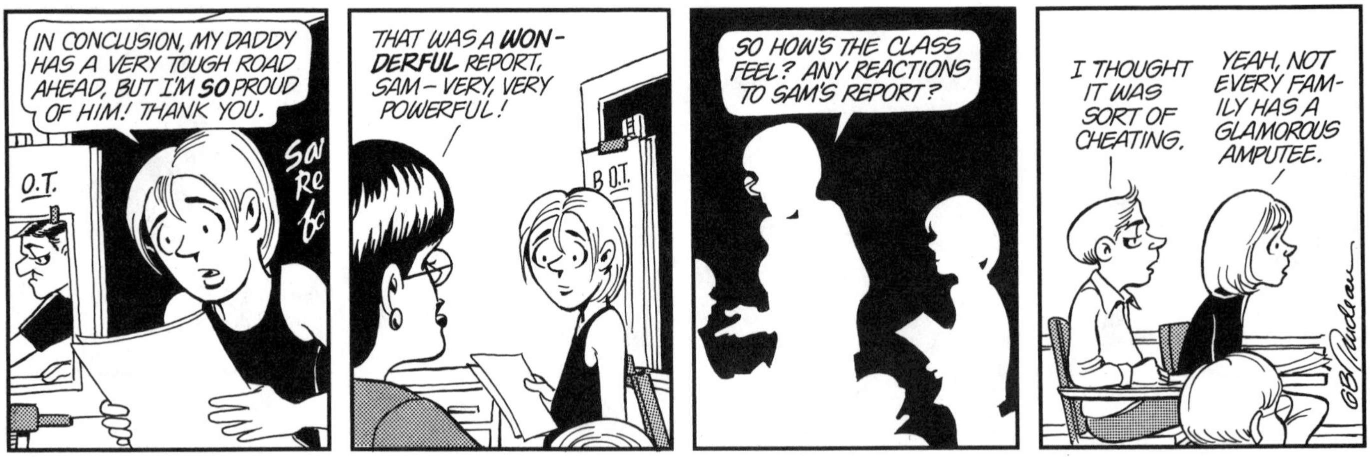
IN CONCLUSION, MY DADDY HAS A VERY TOUGH ROAD AHEAD, BUT I'M **SO** PROUD OF HIM! THANK YOU.
THAT WAS A **WONDERFUL** REPORT, SAM – VERY, VERY POWERFUL!
SO HOW'S THE CLASS FEEL? ANY REACTIONS TO SAM'S REPORT?
I THOUGHT IT WAS SORT OF CHEATING.
YEAH, NOT EVERY FAMILY HAS A GLAMOROUS AMPUTEE.

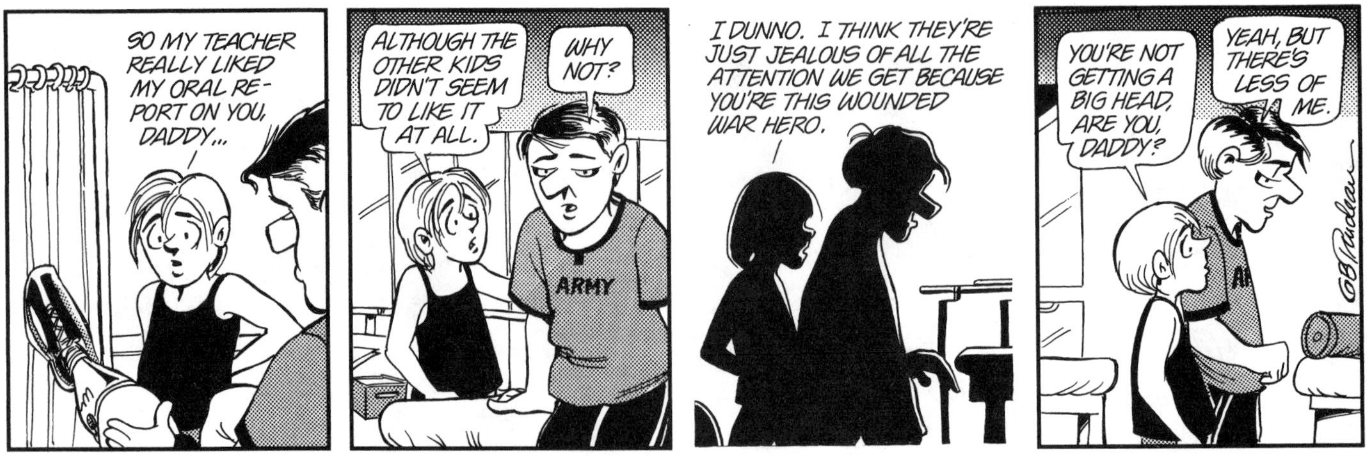
SO MY TEACHER REALLY LIKED MY ORAL REPORT ON YOU, DADDY...
ALTHOUGH THE OTHER KIDS DIDN'T SEEM TO LIKE IT AT ALL.
WHY NOT?
ARMY
I DUNNO. I THINK THEY'RE JUST JEALOUS OF ALL THE ATTENTION WE GET BECAUSE YOU'RE THIS WOUNDED WAR HERO.
YOU'RE NOT GETTING A BIG HEAD, ARE YOU, DADDY?
YEAH, BUT THERE'S LESS OF ME.

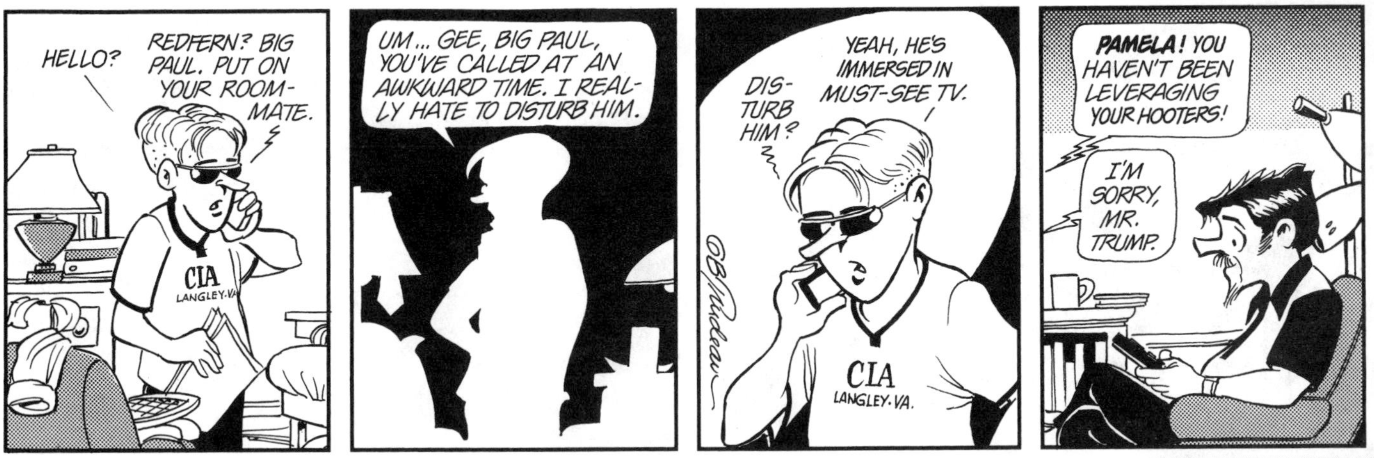
HELLO?
REDFERN? BIG PAUL. PUT ON YOUR ROOM-MATE.
CIA LANGLEY-VA
UM ... GEE, BIG PAUL, YOU'VE CALLED AT AN AWKWARD TIME. I REAL-LY HATE TO DISTURB HIM.
DIS-TURB HIM?
YEAH, HE'S IMMERSED IN MUST-SEE TV.
CIA LANGLEY-VA.
PAMELA! YOU HAVEN'T BEEN LEVERAGING YOUR HOOTERS!
I'M SORRY, MR. TRUMP.

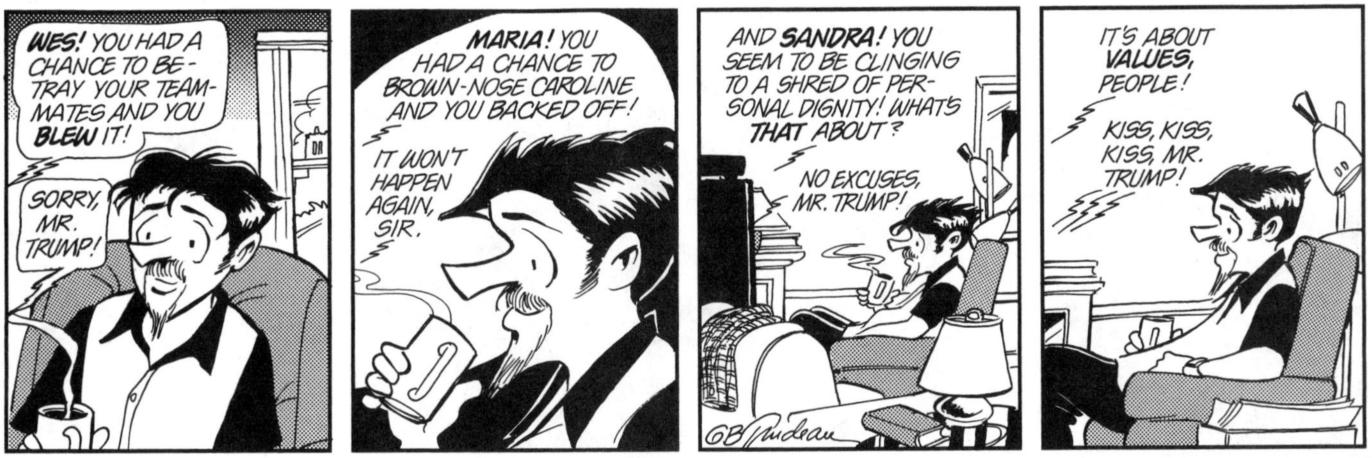
WES! YOU HAD A CHANCE TO BE-TRAY YOUR TEAM-MATES AND YOU BLEW IT!
SORRY, MR. TRUMP!
MARIA! YOU HAD A CHANCE TO BROWN-NOSE CAROLINE AND YOU BACKED OFF!
IT WON'T HAPPEN AGAIN, SIR.
AND SANDRA! YOU SEEM TO BE CLINGING TO A SHRED OF PER-SONAL DIGNITY! WHAT'S THAT ABOUT?
NO EXCUSES, MR. TRUMP!
IT'S ABOUT VALUES, PEOPLE!
KISS, KISS, KISS, MR. TRUMP!

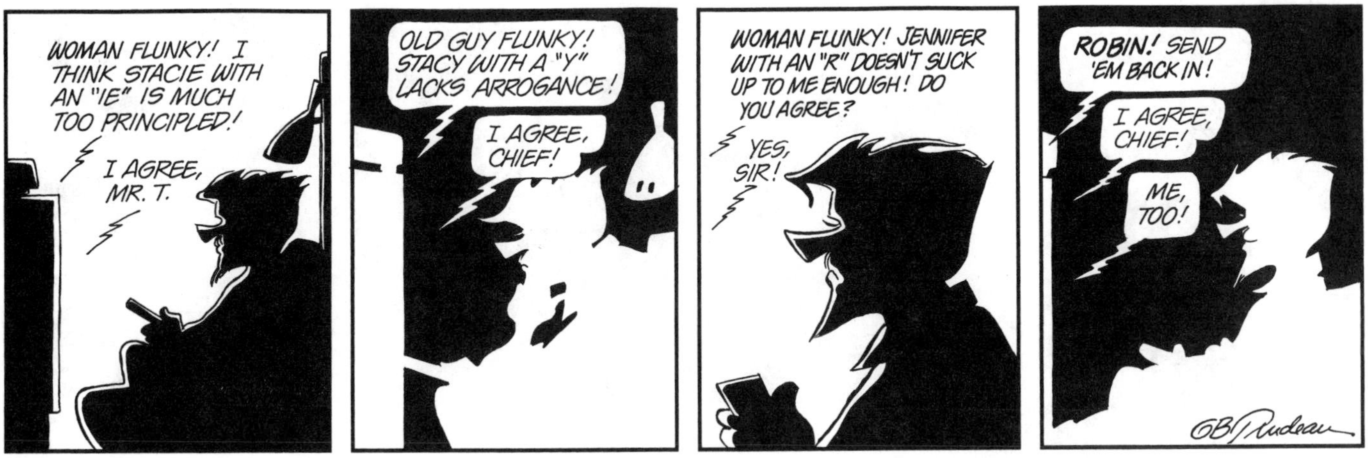
WOMAN FLUNKY! I THINK STACIE WITH AN "IE" IS MUCH TOO PRINCIPLED!
I AGREE, MR. T.
OLD GUY FLUNKY! STACY WITH A "Y" LACKS ARROGANCE!
I AGREE, CHIEF!
WOMAN FLUNKY! JENNIFER WITH AN "R" DOESN'T SUCK UP TO ME ENOUGH! DO YOU AGREE?
YES, SIR!
ROBIN! SEND 'EM BACK IN!
I AGREE, CHIEF!
ME, TOO!

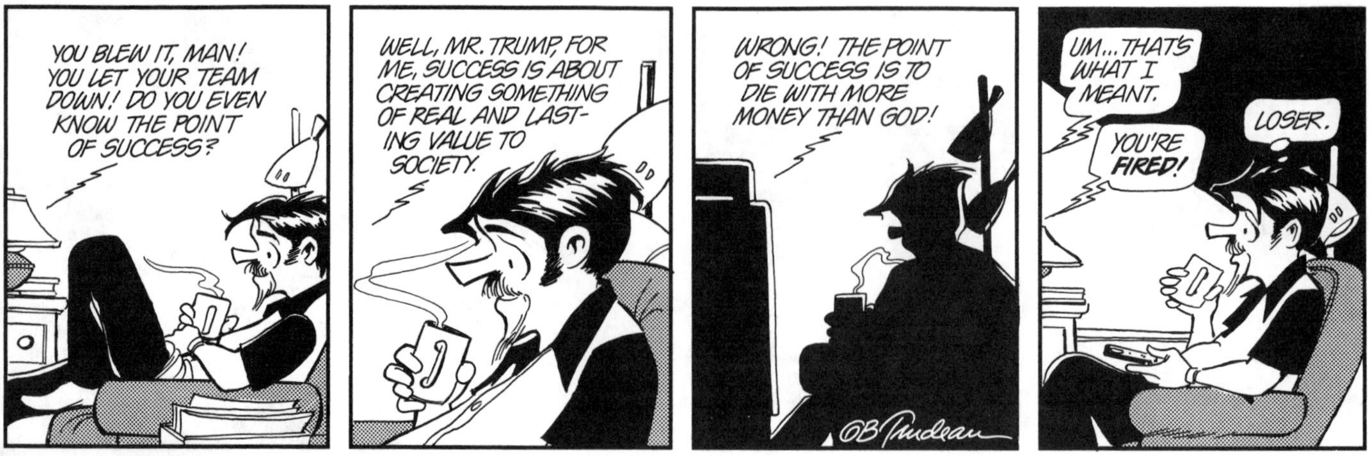
YOU BLEW IT, MAN! YOU LET YOUR TEAM DOWN! DO YOU EVEN KNOW THE POINT OF SUCCESS?
WELL, MR. TRUMP, FOR ME, SUCCESS IS ABOUT CREATING SOMETHING OF REAL AND LASTING VALUE TO SOCIETY.
WRONG! THE POINT OF SUCCESS IS TO DIE WITH MORE MONEY THAN GOD!
UM... THAT'S WHAT I MEANT.
LOSER.
YOU'RE FIRED!
©B Trudeau

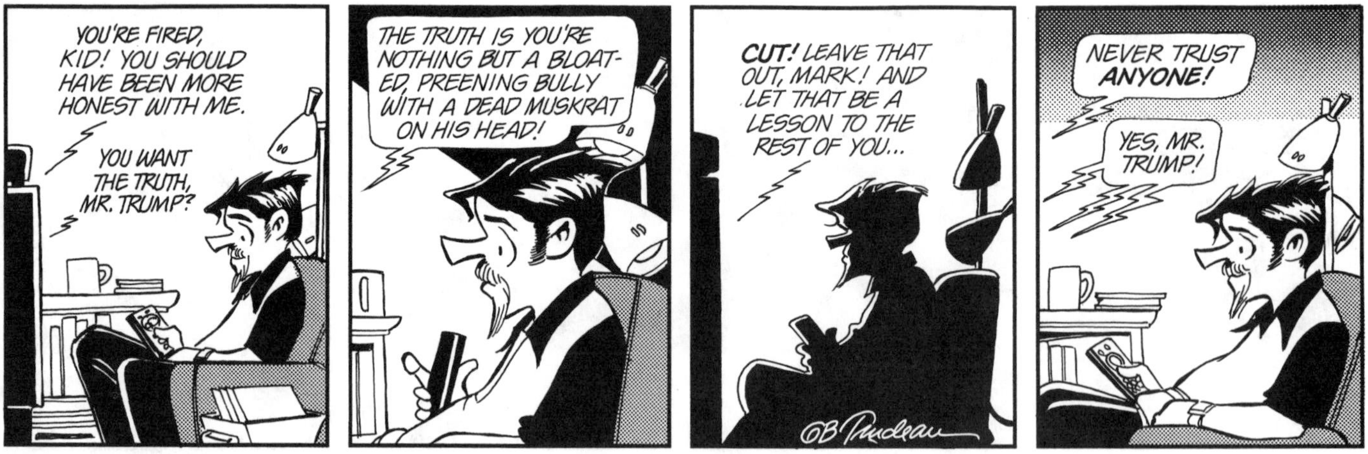
YOU'RE FIRED, KID! YOU SHOULD HAVE BEEN MORE HONEST WITH ME.
YOU WANT THE TRUTH, MR. TRUMP?
THE TRUTH IS YOU'RE NOTHING BUT A BLOATED, PREENING BULLY WITH A DEAD MUSKRAT ON HIS HEAD!
CUT! LEAVE THAT OUT, MARK! AND LET THAT BE A LESSON TO THE REST OF YOU...
NEVER TRUST ANYONE!
YES, MR. TRUMP!
©B Trudeau

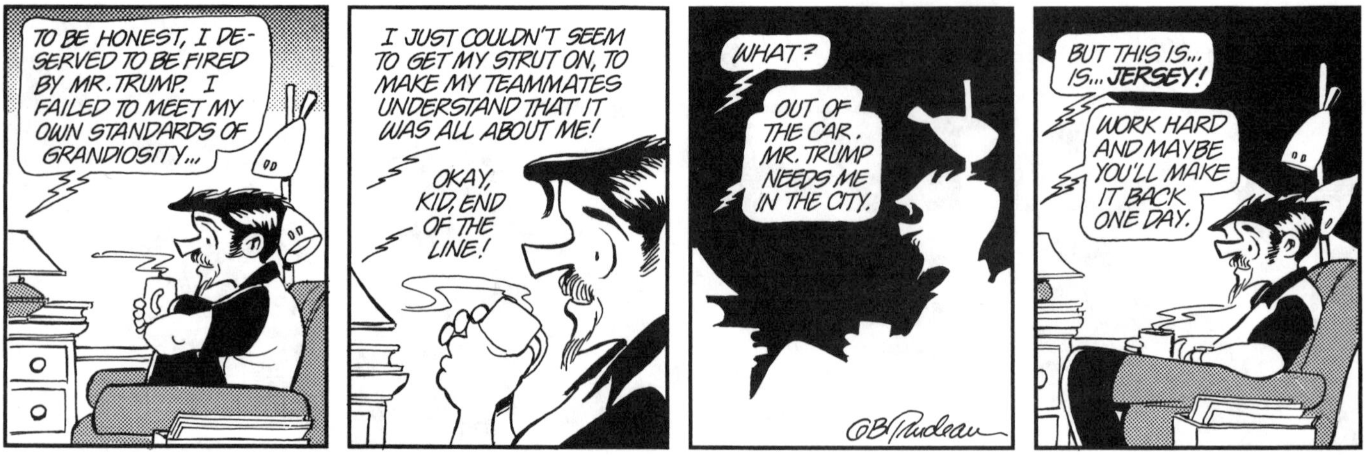
TO BE HONEST, I DESERVED TO BE FIRED BY MR. TRUMP. I FAILED TO MEET MY OWN STANDARDS OF GRANDIOSITY...
I JUST COULDN'T SEEM TO GET MY STRUT ON, TO MAKE MY TEAMMATES UNDERSTAND THAT IT WAS ALL ABOUT ME!
OKAY, KID, END OF THE LINE!
WHAT?
OUT OF THE CAR. MR. TRUMP NEEDS ME IN THE CITY.
BUT THIS IS... IS... JERSEY!
WORK HARD AND MAYBE YOU'LL MAKE IT BACK ONE DAY.
©B Trudeau

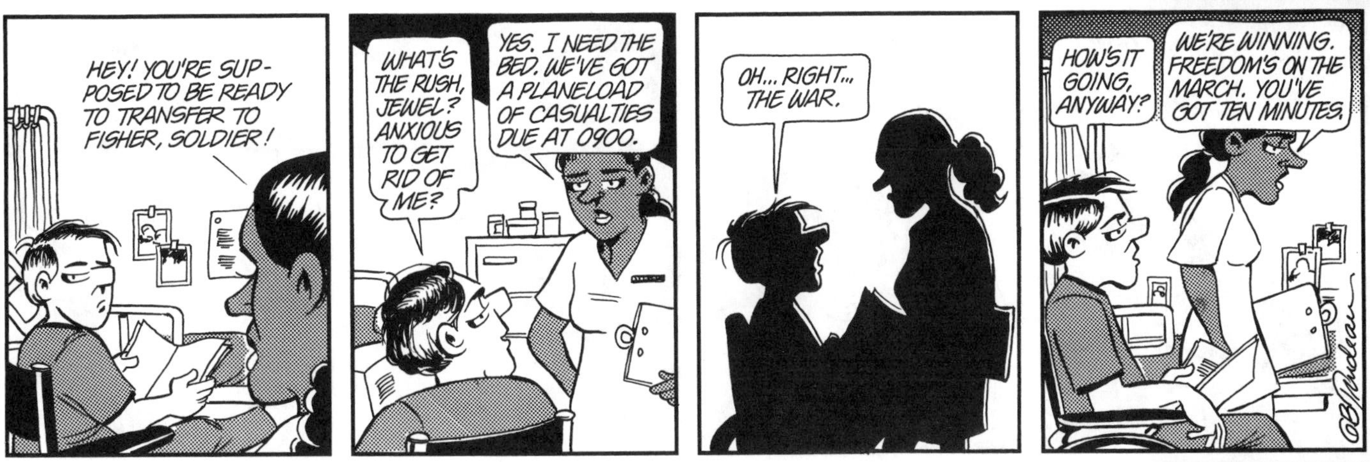
HEY! YOU'RE SUP-POSED TO BE READY TO TRANSFER TO FISHER, SOLDIER!
WHAT'S THE RUSH, JEWEL? ANXIOUS TO GET RID OF ME?
YES. I NEED THE BED. WE'VE GOT A PLANELOAD OF CASUALTIES DUE AT 0900.
OH... RIGHT... THE WAR.
HOW'S IT GOING, ANYWAY?
WE'RE WINNING. FREEDOM'S ON THE MARCH. YOU'VE GOT TEN MINUTES.

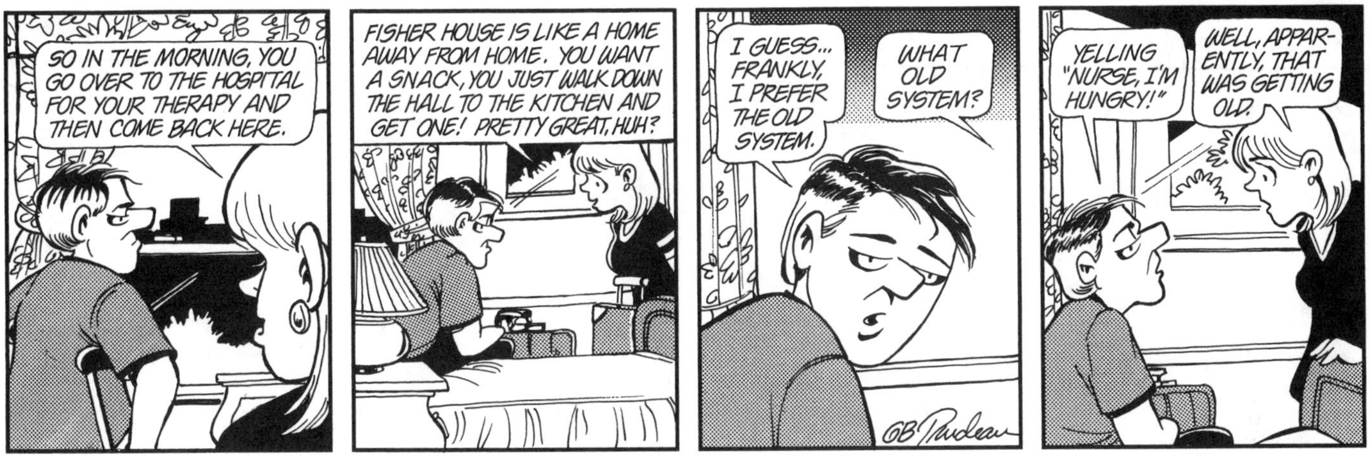
SO IN THE MORNING, YOU GO OVER TO THE HOSPITAL FOR YOUR THERAPY AND THEN COME BACK HERE.
FISHER HOUSE IS LIKE A HOME AWAY FROM HOME. YOU WANT A SNACK, YOU JUST WALK DOWN THE HALL TO THE KITCHEN AND GET ONE! PRETTY GREAT, HUH?
I GUESS... FRANKLY, I PREFER THE OLD SYSTEM.
WHAT OLD SYSTEM?
YELLING "NURSE, I'M HUNGRY!"
WELL, APPAR-ENTLY, THAT WAS GETTING OLD.

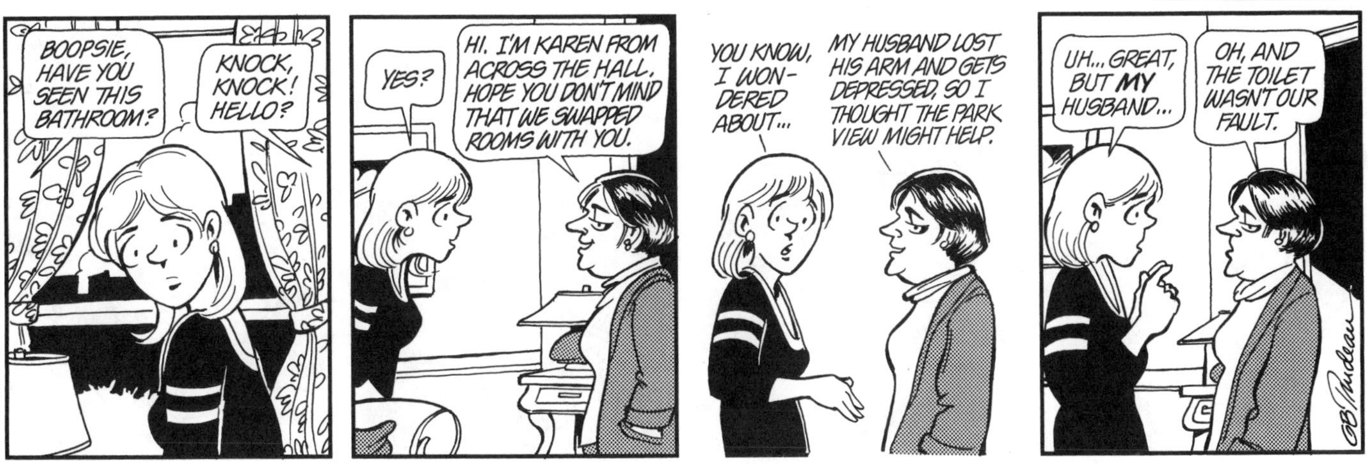
BOOPSIE, HAVE YOU SEEN THIS BATHROOM?
KNOCK, KNOCK! HELLO?
YES?
HI. I'M KAREN FROM ACROSS THE HALL. HOPE YOU DON'T MIND THAT WE SWAPPED ROOMS WITH YOU.
YOU KNOW, I WON-DERED ABOUT...
MY HUSBAND LOST HIS ARM AND GETS DEPRESSED, SO I THOUGHT THE PARK VIEW MIGHT HELP.
UH... GREAT, BUT MY HUSBAND...
OH, AND THE TOILET WASN'T OUR FAULT.

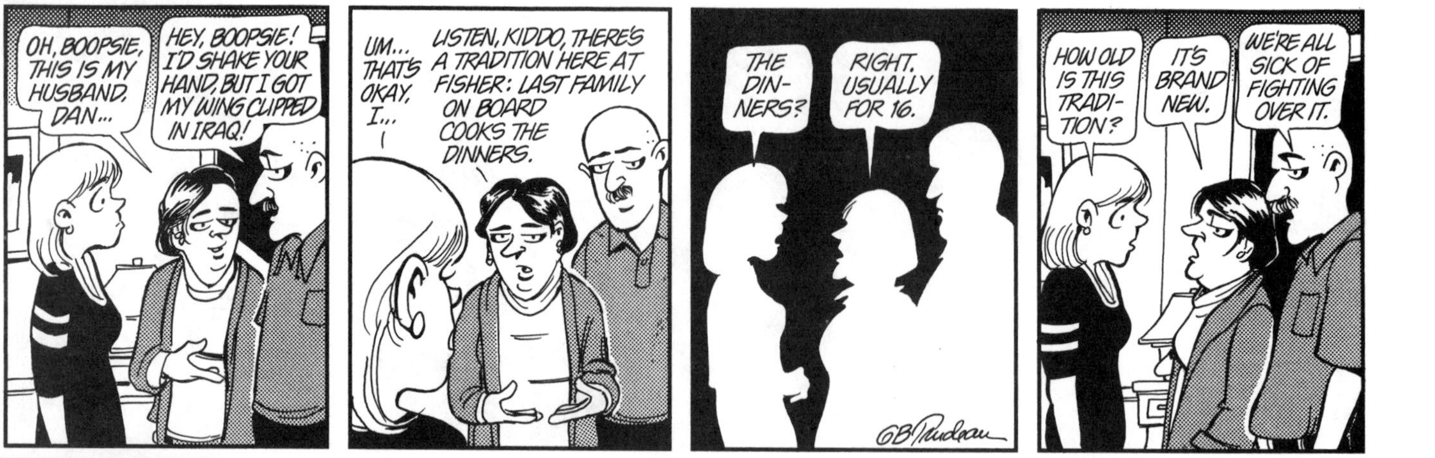
OH, BOOPSIE, THIS IS MY HUSBAND, DAN...
HEY, BOOPSIE! I'D SHAKE YOUR HAND, BUT I GOT MY WING CLIPPED IN IRAQ!
UM... THAT'S OKAY, I...
LISTEN, KIDDO, THERE'S A TRADITION HERE AT FISHER: LAST FAMILY ON BOARD COOKS THE DINNERS.
THE DINNERS?
RIGHT. USUALLY FOR 16.
HOW OLD IS THIS TRADITION?
IT'S BRAND NEW.
WE'RE ALL SICK OF FIGHTING OVER IT.
GB Trudeau

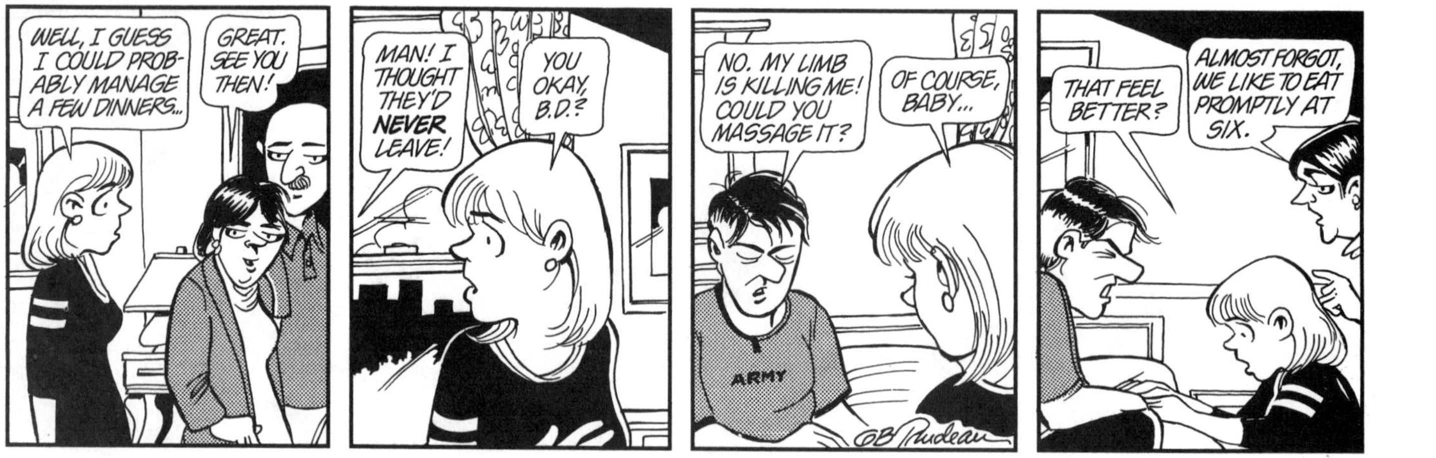
WELL, I GUESS I COULD PROBABLY MANAGE A FEW DINNERS...
GREAT. SEE YOU THEN!
MAN! I THOUGHT THEY'D NEVER LEAVE!
YOU OKAY, B.D.?
NO. MY LIMB IS KILLING ME! COULD YOU MASSAGE IT?
OF COURSE, BABY...
ARMY
GB Trudeau
THAT FEEL BETTER?
ALMOST FORGOT, WE LIKE TO EAT PROMPTLY AT SIX.

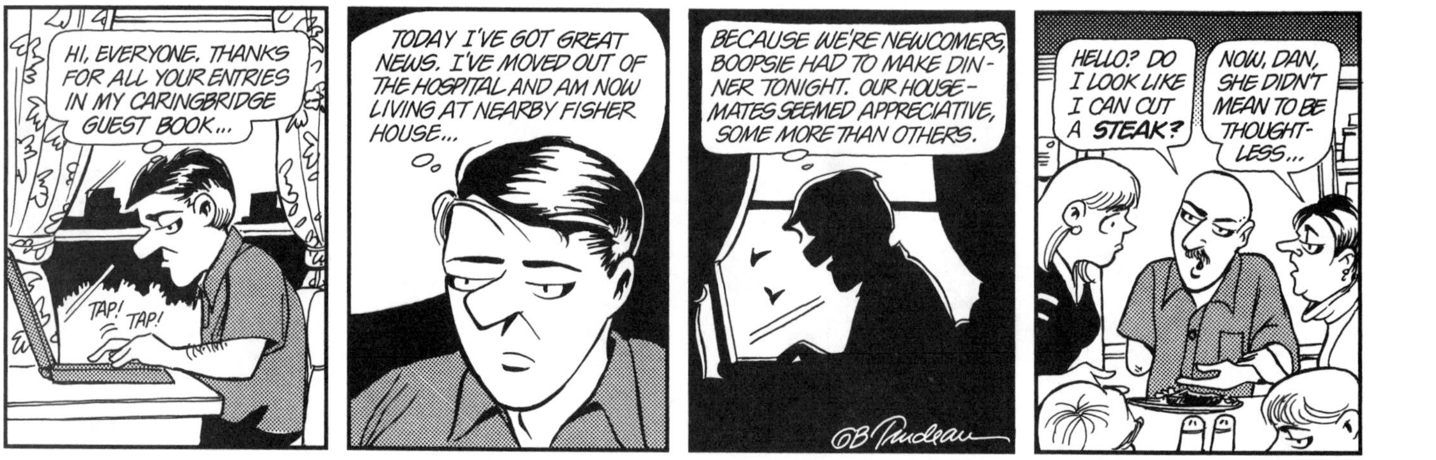
HI, EVERYONE. THANKS FOR ALL YOUR ENTRIES IN MY CARINGBRIDGE GUEST BOOK...
TAP! TAP!
TODAY I'VE GOT GREAT NEWS. I'VE MOVED OUT OF THE HOSPITAL AND AM NOW LIVING AT NEARBY FISHER HOUSE...
BECAUSE WE'RE NEWCOMERS, BOOPSIE HAD TO MAKE DINNER TONIGHT. OUR HOUSEMATES SEEMED APPRECIATIVE, SOME MORE THAN OTHERS.
GB Trudeau
HELLO? DO I LOOK LIKE I CAN CUT A STEAK?
NOW, DAN, SHE DIDN'T MEAN TO BE THOUGHTLESS...

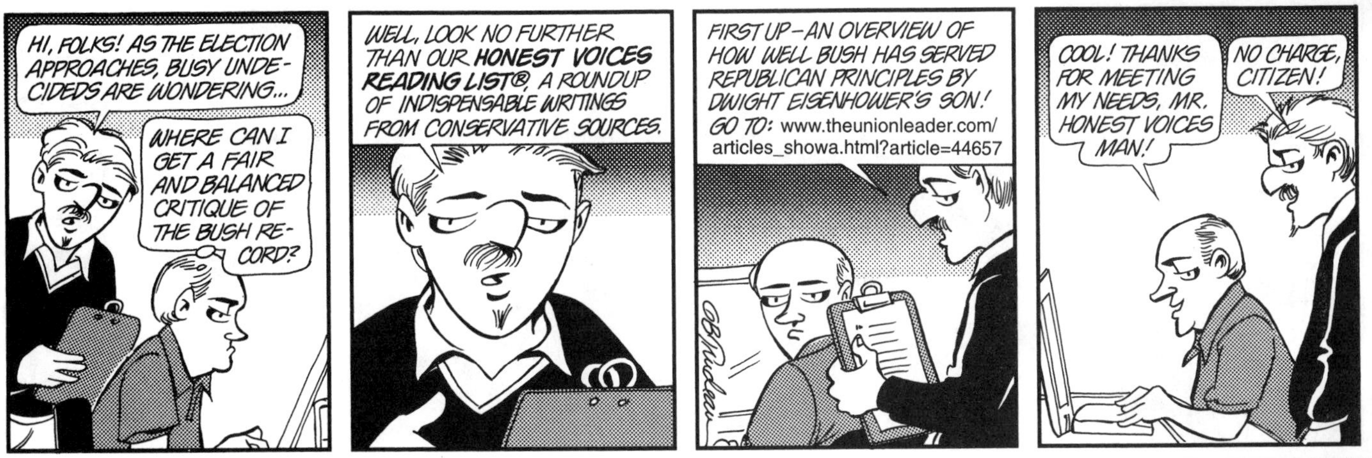
HI, FOLKS! AS THE ELECTION APPROACHES, BUSY UNDECIDEDS ARE WONDERING...
WHERE CAN I GET A FAIR AND BALANCED CRITIQUE OF THE BUSH RECORD?
WELL, LOOK NO FURTHER THAN OUR **HONEST VOICES READING LIST®**, A ROUNDUP OF INDISPENSABLE WRITINGS FROM CONSERVATIVE SOURCES.
FIRST UP–AN OVERVIEW OF HOW WELL BUSH HAS SERVED REPUBLICAN PRINCIPLES BY DWIGHT EISENHOWER'S SON! GO TO: www.theunionleader.com/articles_showa.html?article=44657
COOL! THANKS FOR MEETING MY NEEDS, MR. HONEST VOICES MAN!
NO CHARGE, CITIZEN!

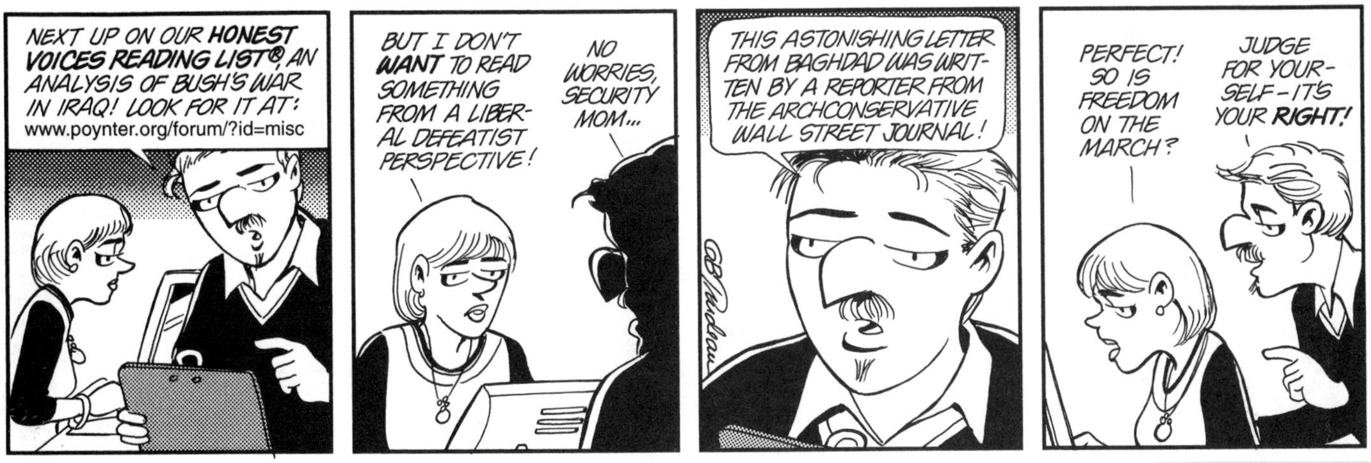
NEXT UP ON OUR **HONEST VOICES READING LIST®**, AN ANALYSIS OF BUSH'S WAR IN IRAQ! LOOK FOR IT AT: www.poynter.org/forum/?id=misc
BUT I DON'T **WANT** TO READ SOMETHING FROM A LIBERAL DEFEATIST PERSPECTIVE!
NO WORRIES, SECURITY MOM...
THIS ASTONISHING LETTER FROM BAGHDAD WAS WRITTEN BY A REPORTER FROM THE ARCHCONSERVATIVE WALL STREET JOURNAL!
PERFECT! SO IS FREEDOM ON THE MARCH?
JUDGE FOR YOURSELF–IT'S YOUR **RIGHT!**

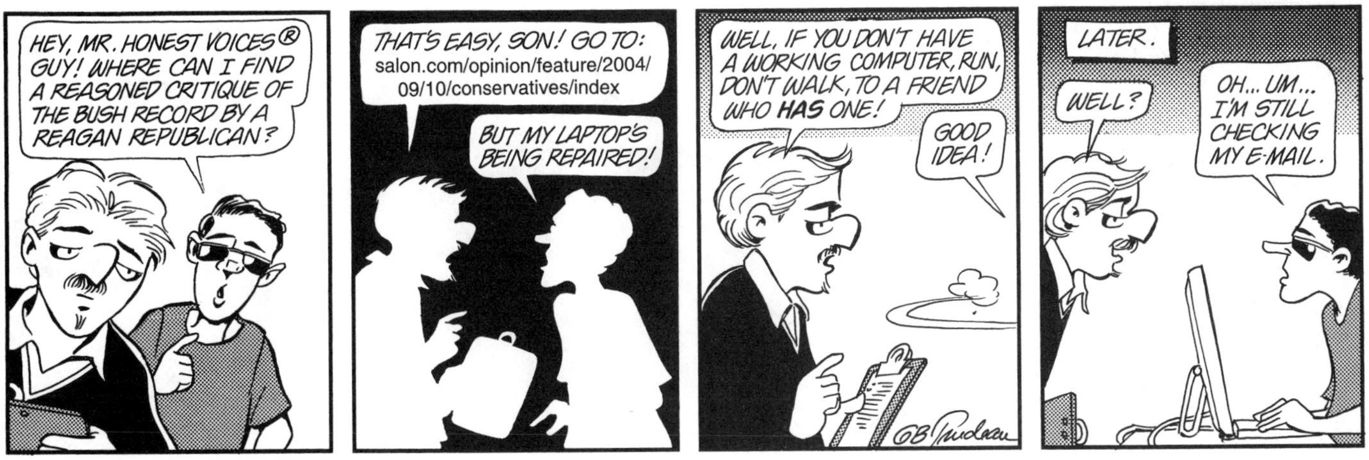
HEY, MR. HONEST VOICES® GUY! WHERE CAN I FIND A REASONED CRITIQUE OF THE BUSH RECORD BY A REAGAN REPUBLICAN?
THAT'S EASY, SON! GO TO: salon.com/opinion/feature/2004/09/10/conservatives/index
BUT MY LAPTOP'S BEING REPAIRED!
WELL, IF YOU DON'T HAVE A WORKING COMPUTER, RUN, DON'T WALK, TO A FRIEND WHO **HAS** ONE!
GOOD IDEA!
LATER.
WELL?
OH... UM... I'M STILL CHECKING MY E-MAIL.

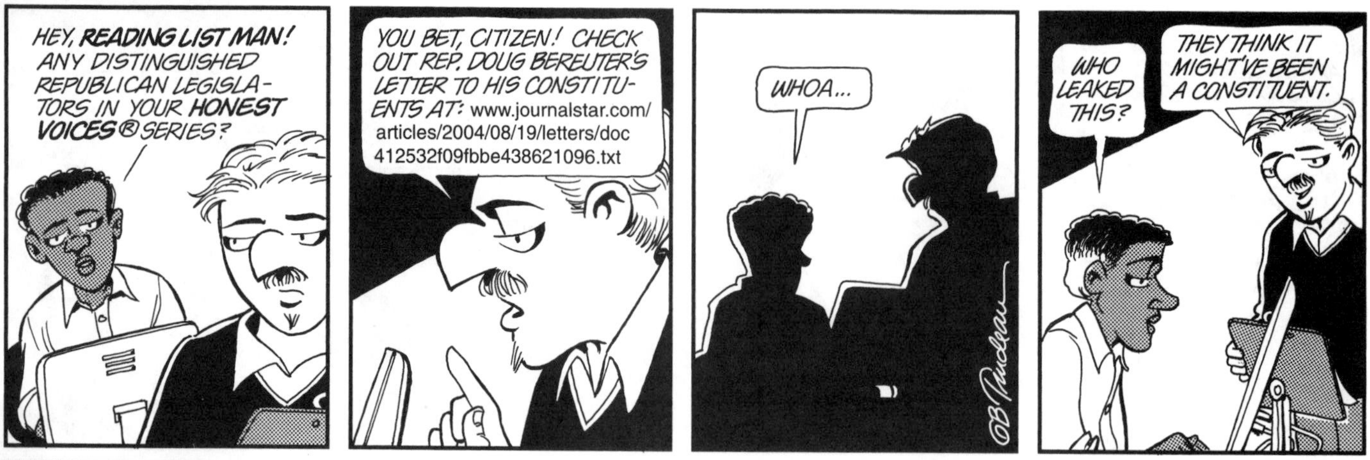
HEY, READING LIST MAN! ANY DISTINGUISHED REPUBLICAN LEGISLATORS IN YOUR HONEST VOICES® SERIES?
YOU BET, CITIZEN! CHECK OUT REP. DOUG BEREUTER'S LETTER TO HIS CONSTITUENTS AT: www.journalstar.com/articles/2004/08/19/letters/doc412532f09fbbe438621096.txt
WHOA...
WHO LEAKED THIS?
THEY THINK IT MIGHT'VE BEEN A CONSTITUENT.

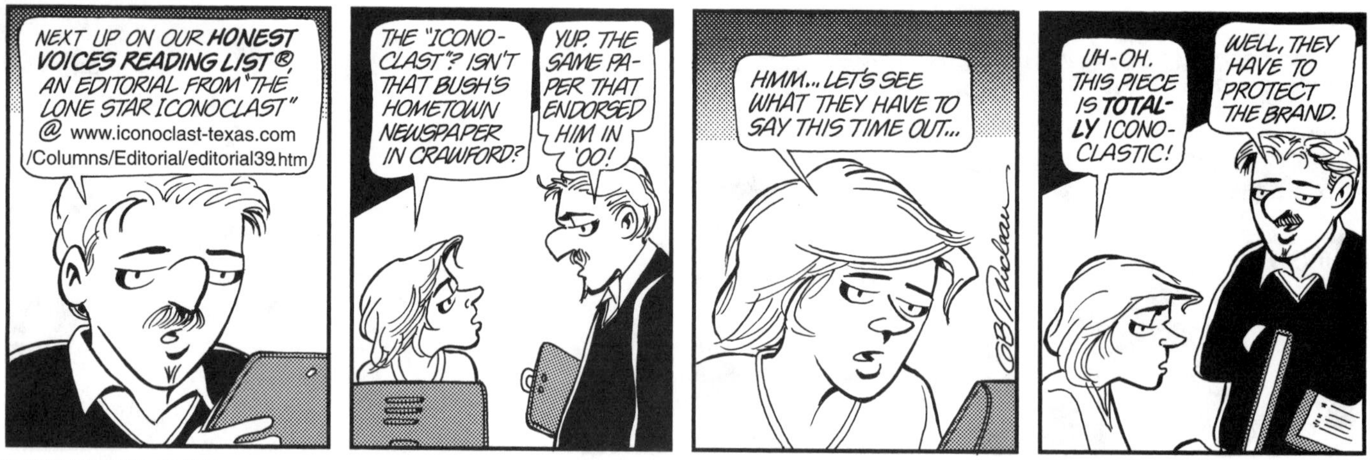
NEXT UP ON OUR HONEST VOICES READING LIST®, AN EDITORIAL FROM "THE LONE STAR ICONOCLAST" @ www.iconoclast-texas.com/Columns/Editorial/editorial39.htm
THE "ICONOCLAST"? ISN'T THAT BUSH'S HOMETOWN NEWSPAPER IN CRAWFORD?
YUP. THE SAME PAPER THAT ENDORSED HIM IN '00!
HMM... LET'S SEE WHAT THEY HAVE TO SAY THIS TIME OUT...
UH-OH. THIS PIECE IS TOTALLY ICONOCLASTIC!
WELL, THEY HAVE TO PROTECT THE BRAND.

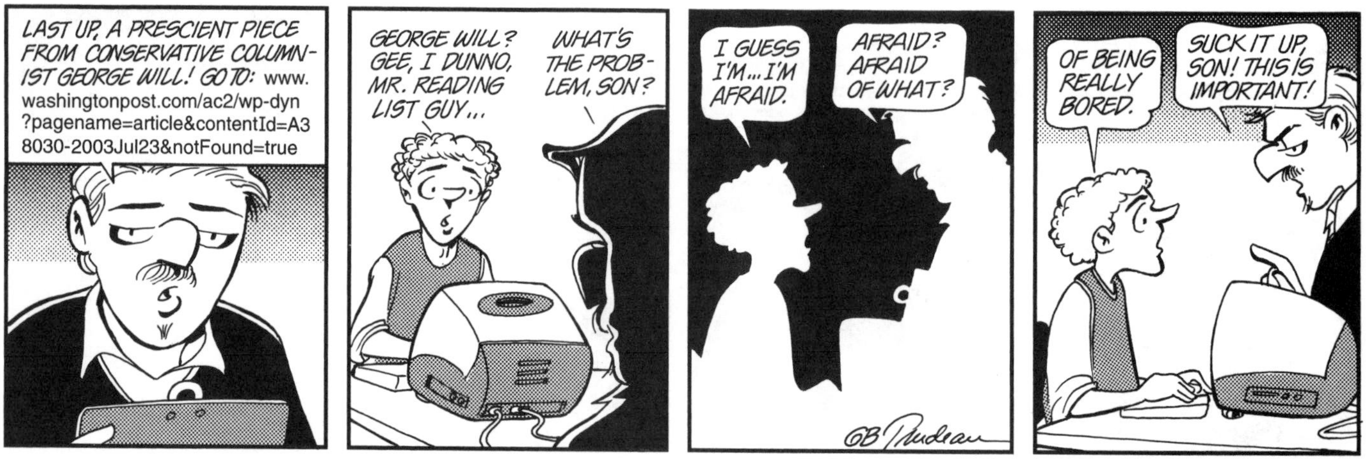
LAST UP, A PRESCIENT PIECE FROM CONSERVATIVE COLUMNIST GEORGE WILL! GO TO: www.washingtonpost.com/ac2/wp-dyn?pagename=article&contentId=A38030-2003Jul23&notFound=true
GEORGE WILL? GEE, I DUNNO, MR. READING LIST GUY...
WHAT'S THE PROBLEM, SON?
I GUESS I'M... I'M AFRAID.
AFRAID? AFRAID OF WHAT?
OF BEING REALLY BORED.
SUCK IT UP, SON! THIS IS IMPORTANT!

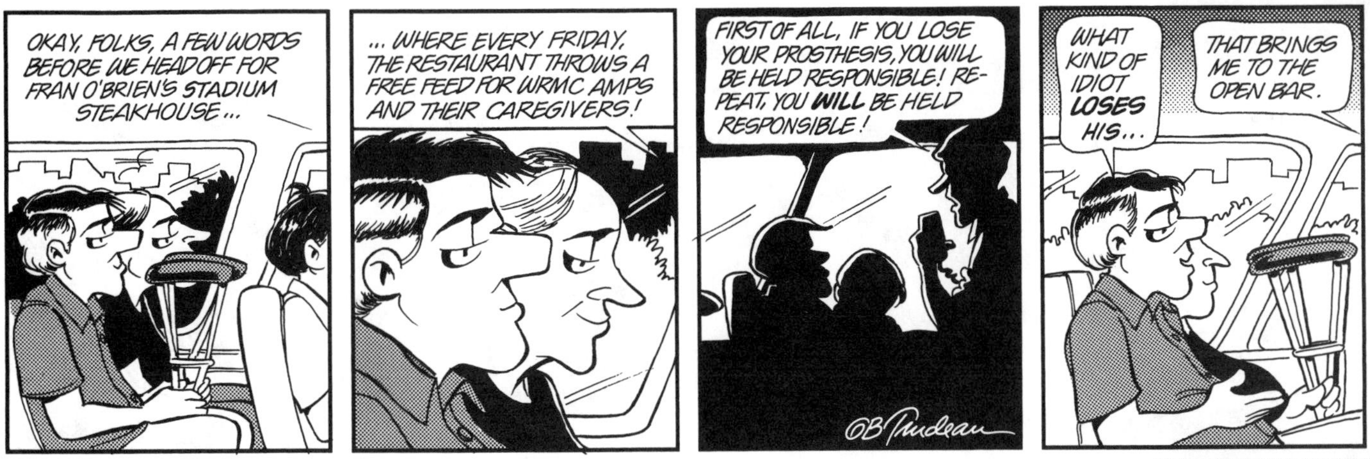
OKAY, FOLKS, A FEW WORDS BEFORE WE HEAD OFF FOR FRAN O'BRIEN'S STADIUM STEAKHOUSE ...
... WHERE EVERY FRIDAY, THE RESTAURANT THROWS A FREE FEED FOR WRMC AMPS AND THEIR CAREGIVERS!
FIRST OF ALL, IF YOU LOSE YOUR PROSTHESIS, YOU WILL BE HELD RESPONSIBLE! RE-PEAT, YOU **WILL** BE HELD RESPONSIBLE!
GB Trudeau
WHAT KIND OF IDIOT **LOSES** HIS...
THAT BRINGS ME TO THE OPEN BAR.

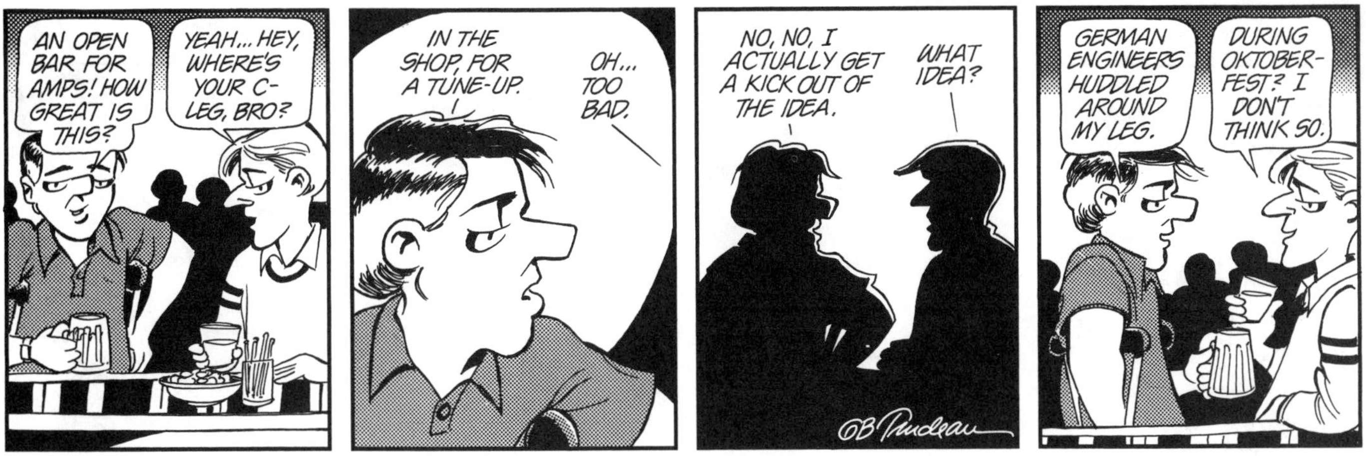
AN OPEN BAR FOR AMPS! HOW GREAT IS THIS?
YEAH,... HEY, WHERE'S YOUR C-LEG, BRO?
IN THE SHOP, FOR A TUNE-UP.
OH... TOO BAD.
NO, NO, I ACTUALLY GET A KICK OUT OF THE IDEA.
WHAT IDEA?
GB Trudeau
GERMAN ENGINEERS HUDDLED AROUND MY LEG.
DURING OKTOBER-FEST? I DON'T THINK SO.

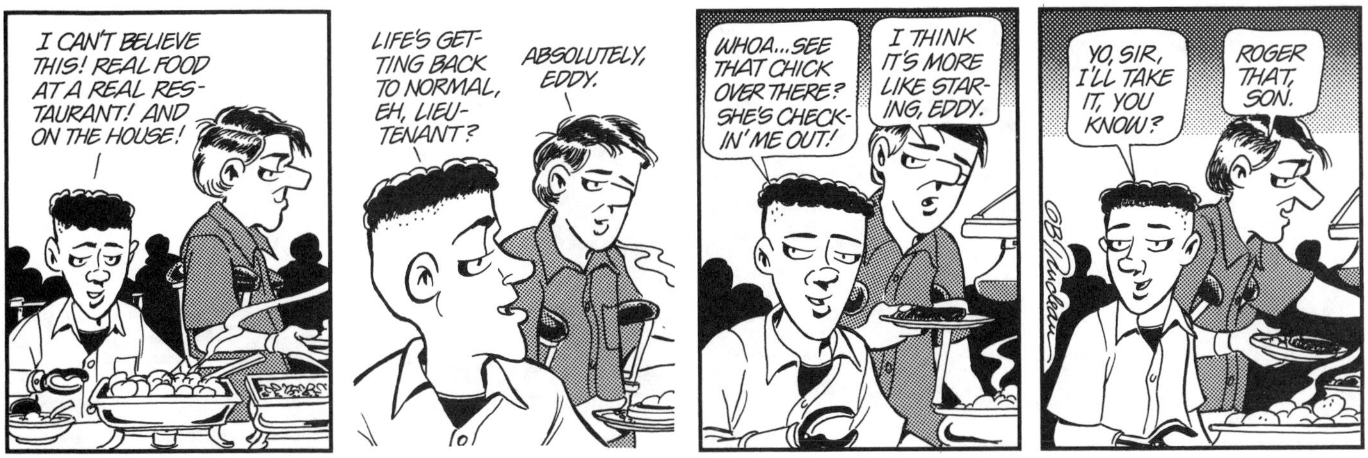
I CAN'T BELIEVE THIS! REAL FOOD AT A REAL RES-TAURANT! AND ON THE HOUSE!
LIFE'S GET-TING BACK TO NORMAL, EH, LIEU-TENANT?
ABSOLUTELY, EDDY.
WHOA...SEE THAT CHICK OVER THERE? SHE'S CHECK-IN' ME OUT!
I THINK IT'S MORE LIKE STAR-ING, EDDY.
YO, SIR, I'LL TAKE IT, YOU KNOW?
ROGER THAT, SON.
GB Trudeau

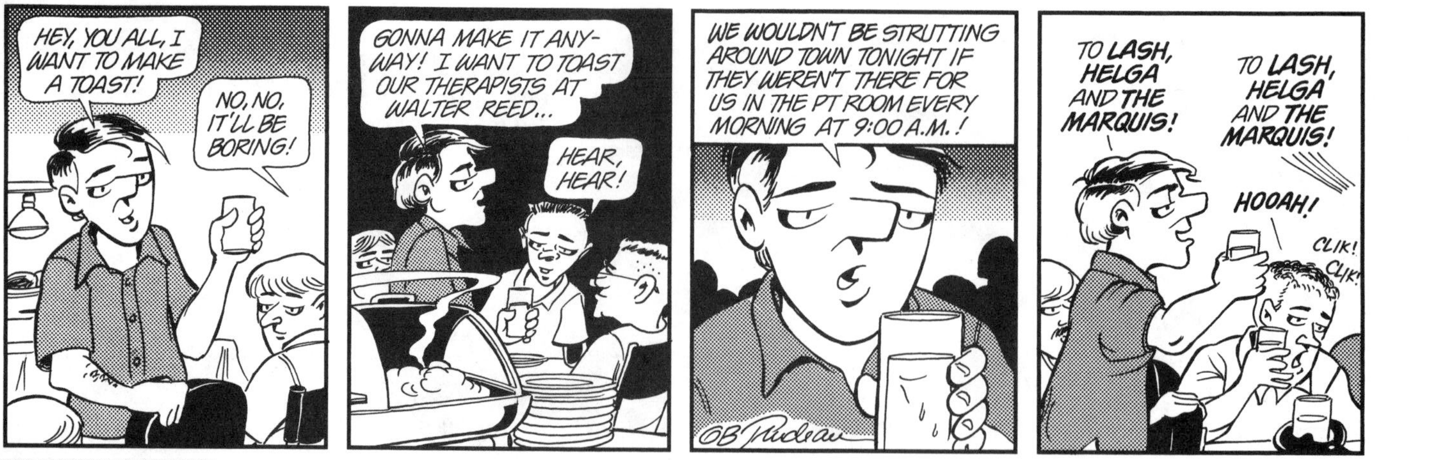
HEY, YOU ALL, I WANT TO MAKE A TOAST!
NO, NO, IT'LL BE BORING!
GONNA MAKE IT ANY-WAY! I WANT TO TOAST OUR THERAPISTS AT WALTER REED...
HEAR, HEAR!
WE WOULDN'T BE STRUTTING AROUND TOWN TONIGHT IF THEY WEREN'T THERE FOR US IN THE PT ROOM EVERY MORNING AT 9:00 A.M.!
TO **LASH, HELGA** AND **THE MARQUIS!**
TO **LASH, HELGA** AND **THE MARQUIS!**
HOOAH!
CLIK! CLIK!

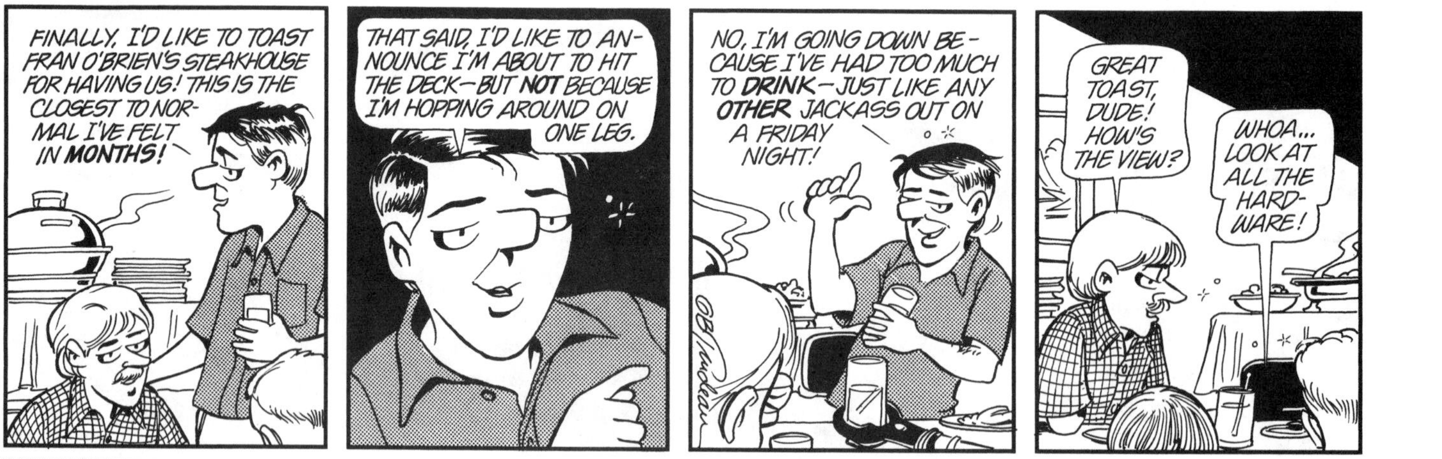
FINALLY, I'D LIKE TO TOAST FRAN O'BRIEN'S STEAKHOUSE FOR HAVING US! THIS IS THE CLOSEST TO NOR-MAL I'VE FELT IN **MONTHS!**
THAT SAID, I'D LIKE TO AN-NOUNCE I'M ABOUT TO HIT THE DECK—BUT **NOT** BECAUSE I'M HOPPING AROUND ON ONE LEG.
NO, I'M GOING DOWN BE-CAUSE I'VE HAD TOO MUCH TO **DRINK**—JUST LIKE ANY **OTHER** JACKASS OUT ON A FRIDAY NIGHT!
GREAT TOAST, DUDE! HOW'S THE VIEW?
WHOA... LOOK AT ALL THE HARD-WARE!

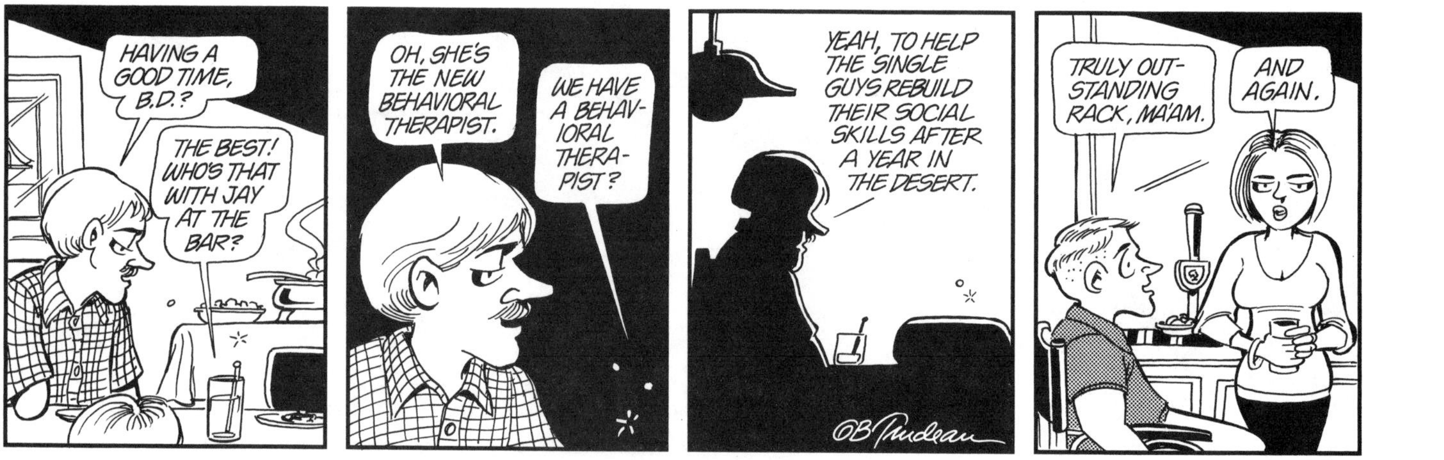
HAVING A GOOD TIME, B.D.?
THE BEST! WHO'S THAT WITH JAY AT THE BAR?
OH, SHE'S THE NEW BEHAVIORAL THERAPIST.
WE HAVE A BEHAV-IORAL THERA-PIST?
YEAH, TO HELP THE SINGLE GUYS REBUILD THEIR SOCIAL SKILLS AFTER A YEAR IN THE DESERT.
TRULY OUT-STANDING RACK, MA'AM.
AND AGAIN.

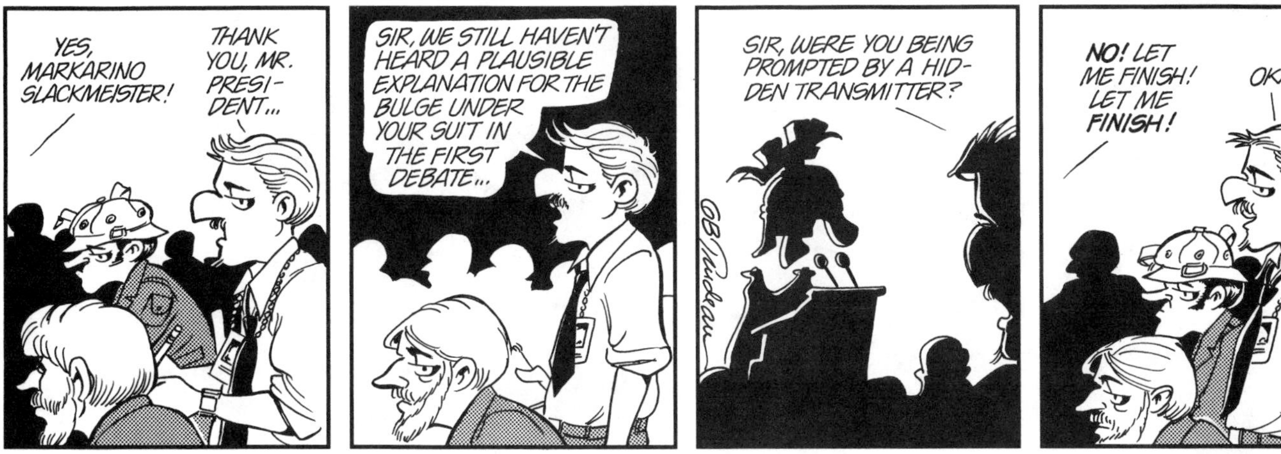
YES, MARKARINO SLACKMEISTER!
THANK YOU, MR. PRESI- DENT...
SIR, WE STILL HAVEN'T HEARD A PLAUSIBLE EXPLANATION FOR THE BULGE UNDER YOUR SUIT IN THE FIRST DEBATE...
SIR, WERE YOU BEING PROMPTED BY A HID- DEN TRANSMITTER?
NO! LET ME FINISH! LET ME FINISH!
OKAY.

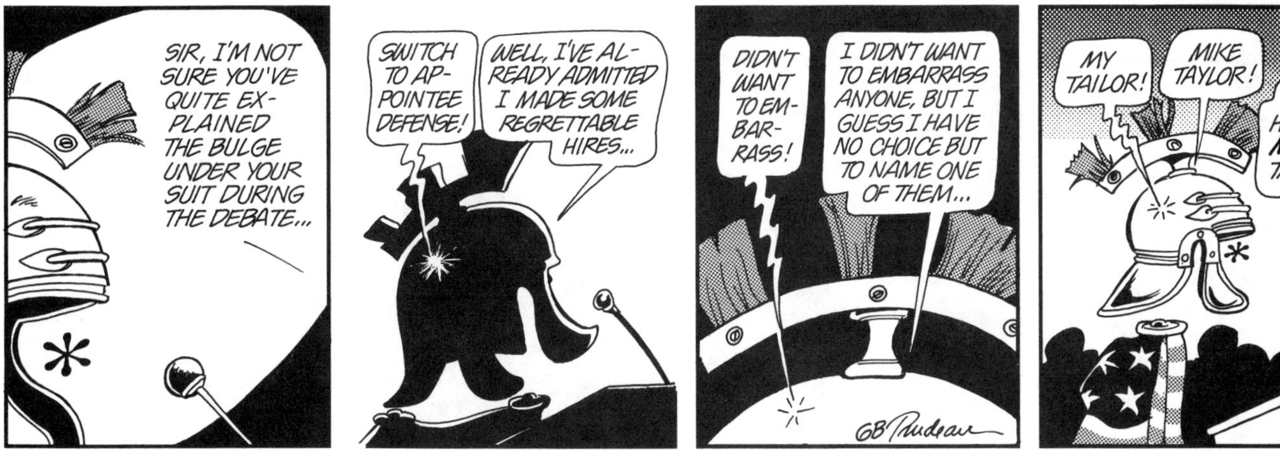
SIR, I'M NOT SURE YOU'VE QUITE EX- PLAINED THE BULGE UNDER YOUR SUIT DURING THE DEBATE...
SWITCH TO AP- POINTEE DEFENSE!
WELL, I'VE AL- READY ADMITTED I MADE SOME REGRETTABLE HIRES...
DIDN'T WANT TO EM- BAR- RASS!
I DIDN'T WANT TO EMBARRASS ANYONE, BUT I GUESS I HAVE NO CHOICE BUT TO NAME ONE OF THEM...
MY TAILOR!
MIKE TAYLOR!
YOU HAVE A MIKE TAILOR?

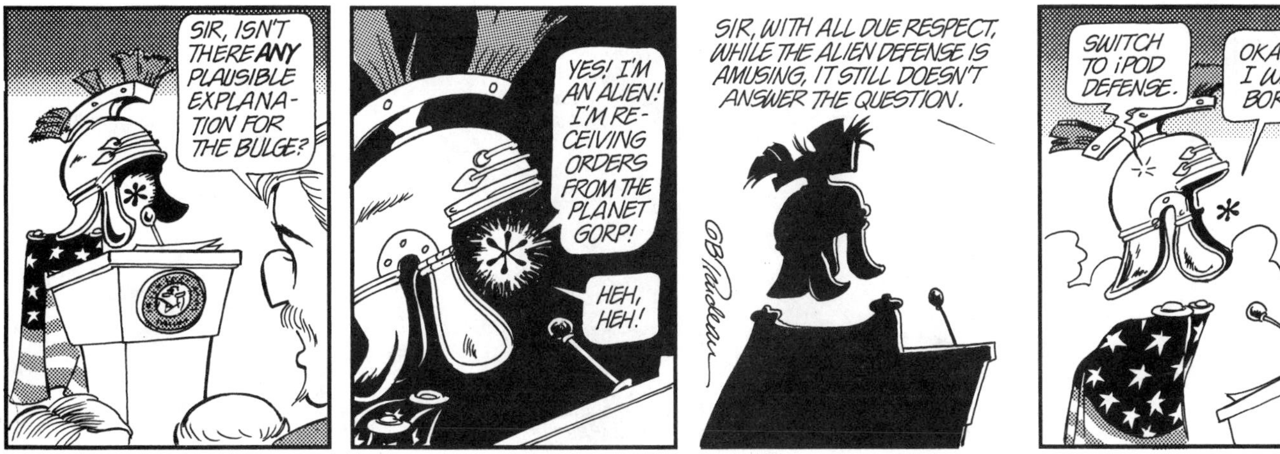
SIR, ISN'T THERE ANY PLAUSIBLE EXPLANA- TION FOR THE BULGE?
YES! I'M AN ALIEN! I'M RE- CEIVING ORDERS FROM THE PLANET GORP!
HEH, HEH!
SIR, WITH ALL DUE RESPECT, WHILE THE ALIEN DEFENSE IS AMUSING, IT STILL DOESN'T ANSWER THE QUESTION.
SWITCH TO iPOD DEFENSE.
OKAY, SO I WAS BORED...

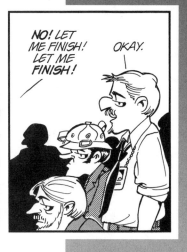

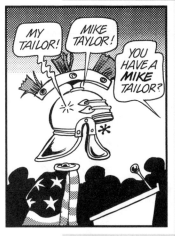

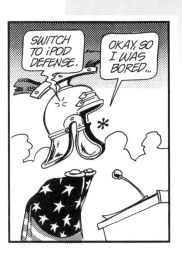

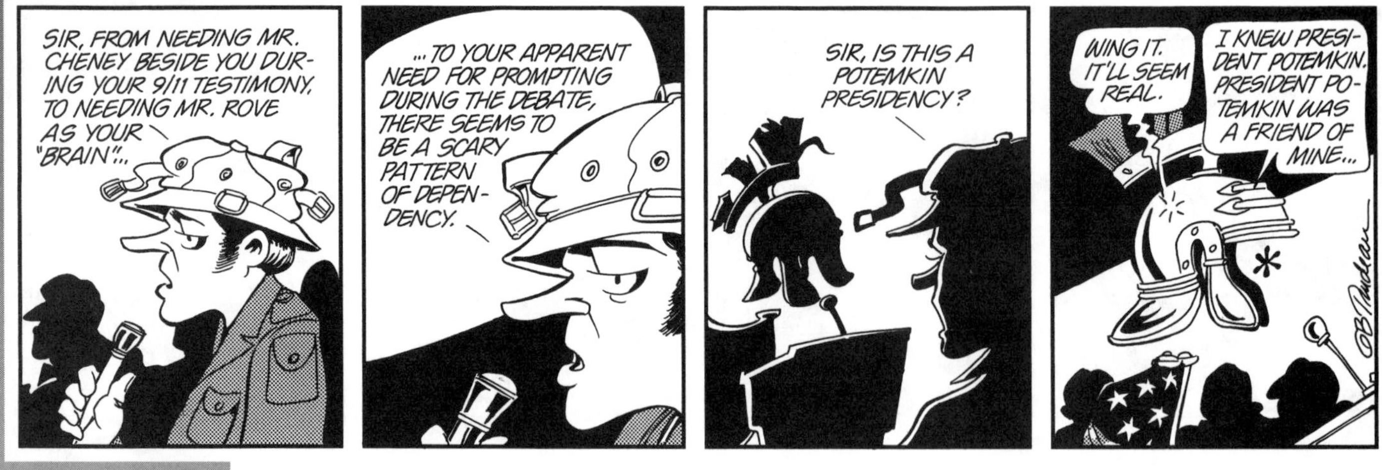
SIR, FROM NEEDING MR. CHENEY BESIDE YOU DURING YOUR 9/11 TESTIMONY, TO NEEDING MR. ROVE AS YOUR "BRAIN"...
...TO YOUR APPARENT NEED FOR PROMPTING DURING THE DEBATE, THERE SEEMS TO BE A SCARY PATTERN OF DEPENDENCY.
SIR, IS THIS A POTEMKIN PRESIDENCY?
WING IT. IT'LL SEEM REAL.
I KNEW PRESIDENT POTEMKIN. PRESIDENT POTEMKIN WAS A FRIEND OF MINE...
©B Trudeau

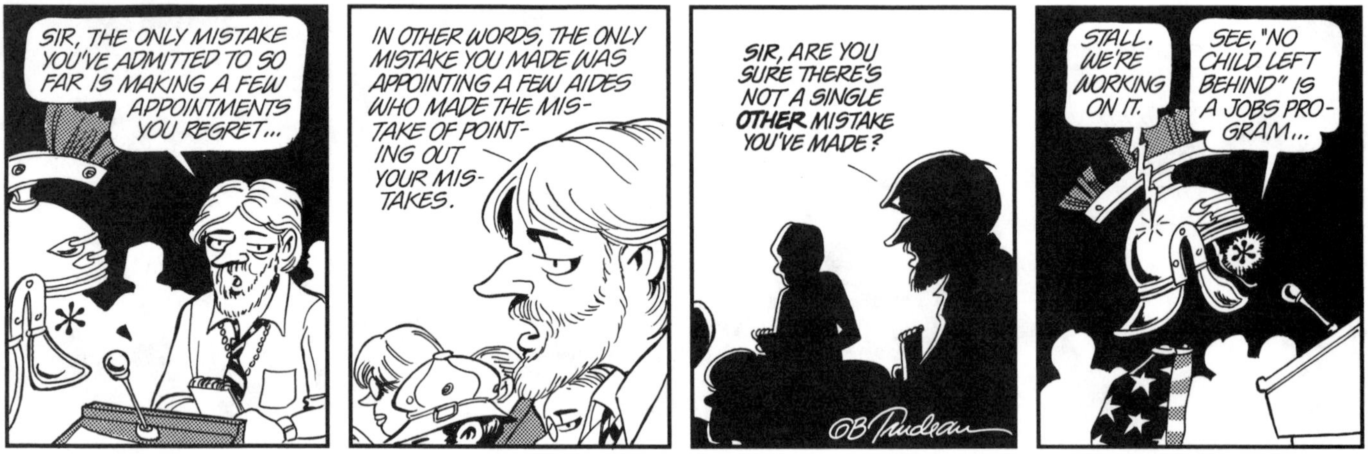
SIR, THE ONLY MISTAKE YOU'VE ADMITTED TO SO FAR IS MAKING A FEW APPOINTMENTS YOU REGRET...
IN OTHER WORDS, THE ONLY MISTAKE YOU MADE WAS APPOINTING A FEW AIDES WHO MADE THE MISTAKE OF POINTING OUT YOUR MISTAKES.
SIR, ARE YOU SURE THERE'S NOT A SINGLE OTHER MISTAKE YOU'VE MADE?
©B Trudeau
STALL. WE'RE WORKING ON IT.
SEE, "NO CHILD LEFT BEHIND" IS A JOBS PROGRAM...

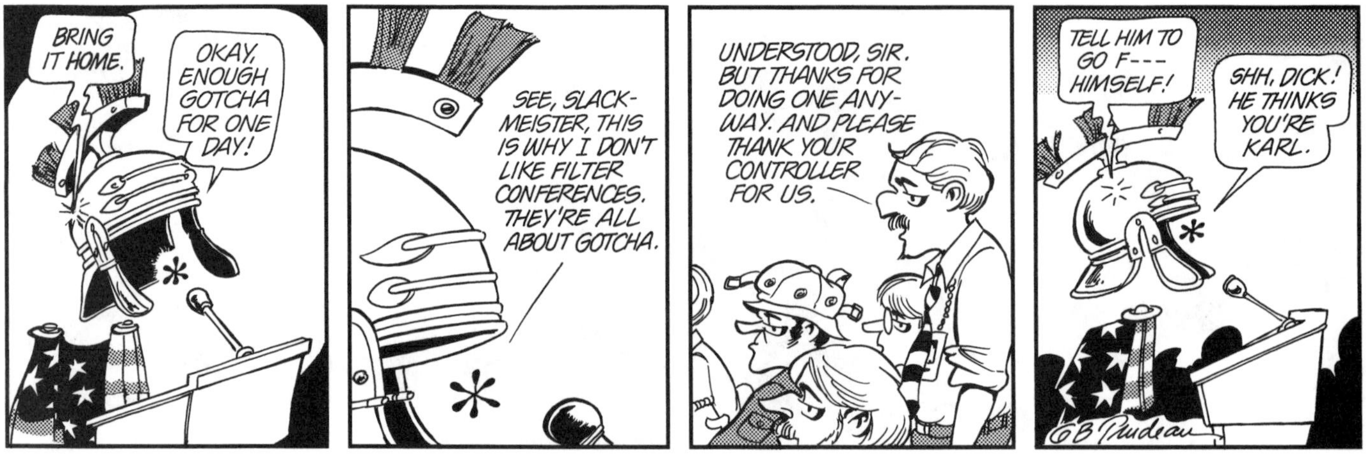
BRING IT HOME.
OKAY, ENOUGH GOTCHA FOR ONE DAY!
SEE, SLACKMEISTER, THIS IS WHY I DON'T LIKE FILTER CONFERENCES. THEY'RE ALL ABOUT GOTCHA.
UNDERSTOOD, SIR. BUT THANKS FOR DOING ONE ANYWAY. AND PLEASE THANK YOUR CONTROLLER FOR US.
TELL HIM TO GO F--- HIMSELF!
SHH, DICK! HE THINKS YOU'RE KARL.
©B Trudeau

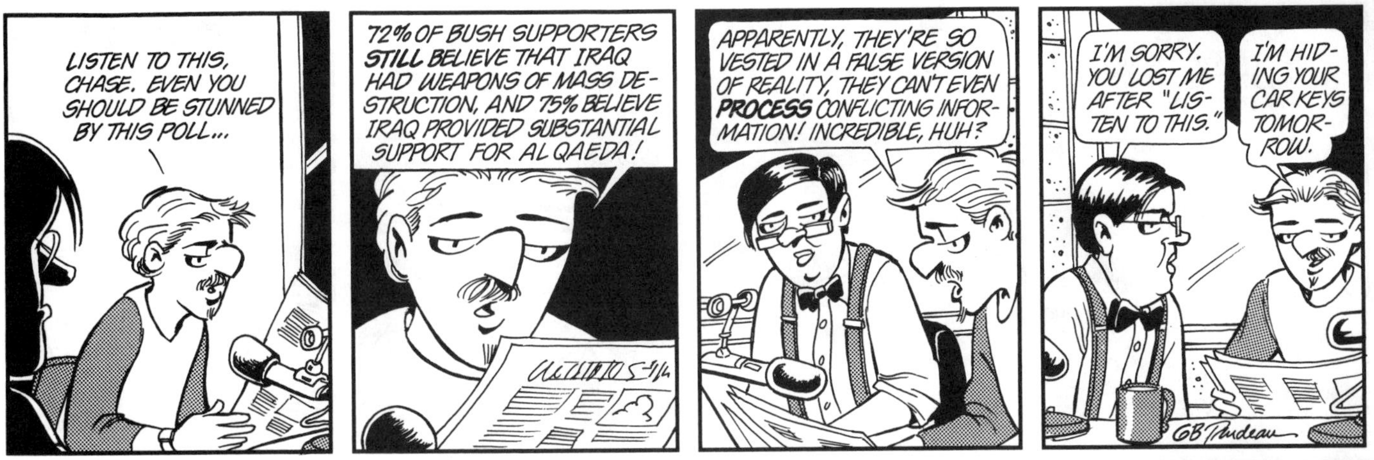
LISTEN TO THIS, CHASE. EVEN YOU SHOULD BE STUNNED BY THIS POLL...
72% OF BUSH SUPPORTERS STILL BELIEVE THAT IRAQ HAD WEAPONS OF MASS DESTRUCTION, AND 75% BELIEVE IRAQ PROVIDED SUBSTANTIAL SUPPORT FOR AL QAEDA!
APPARENTLY, THEY'RE SO VESTED IN A FALSE VERSION OF REALITY, THEY CAN'T EVEN PROCESS CONFLICTING INFORMATION! INCREDIBLE, HUH?
I'M SORRY. YOU LOST ME AFTER "LISTEN TO THIS."
I'M HIDING YOUR CAR KEYS TOMORROW.

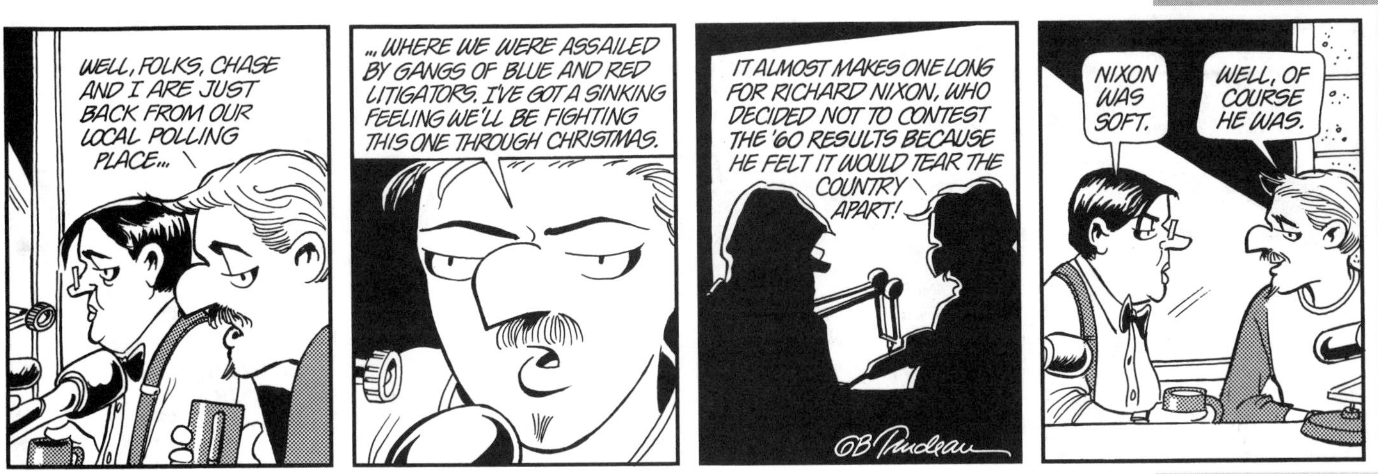
WELL, FOLKS, CHASE AND I ARE JUST BACK FROM OUR LOCAL POLLING PLACE...
...WHERE WE WERE ASSAILED BY GANGS OF BLUE AND RED LITIGATORS. I'VE GOT A SINKING FEELING WE'LL BE FIGHTING THIS ONE THROUGH CHRISTMAS.
IT ALMOST MAKES ONE LONG FOR RICHARD NIXON, WHO DECIDED NOT TO CONTEST THE '60 RESULTS BECAUSE HE FELT IT WOULD TEAR THE COUNTRY APART!
NIXON WAS SOFT.
WELL, OF COURSE HE WAS.

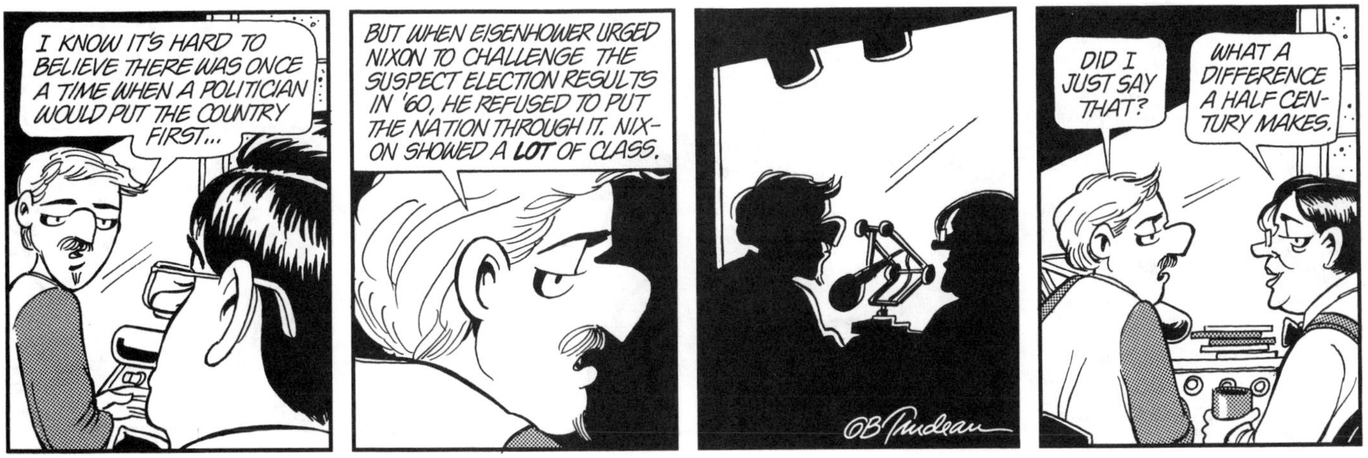
I KNOW IT'S HARD TO BELIEVE THERE WAS ONCE A TIME WHEN A POLITICIAN WOULD PUT THE COUNTRY FIRST...
BUT WHEN EISENHOWER URGED NIXON TO CHALLENGE THE SUSPECT ELECTION RESULTS IN '60, HE REFUSED TO PUT THE NATION THROUGH IT. NIXON SHOWED A LOT OF CLASS.
DID I JUST SAY THAT?
WHAT A DIFFERENCE A HALF CENTURY MAKES.

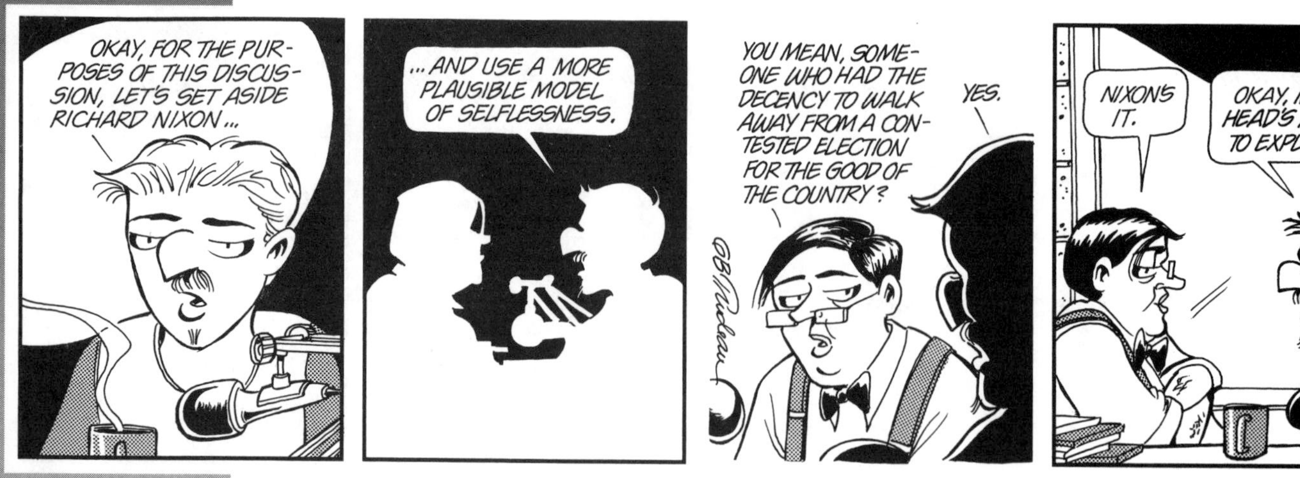
OKAY, FOR THE PURPOSES OF THIS DISCUSSION, LET'S SET ASIDE RICHARD NIXON...
...AND USE A MORE PLAUSIBLE MODEL OF SELFLESSNESS.
YOU MEAN, SOMEONE WHO HAD THE DECENCY TO WALK AWAY FROM A CONTESTED ELECTION FOR THE GOOD OF THE COUNTRY?
YES.
NIXON'S IT.
OKAY, MY HEAD'S ABOUT TO EXPLODE.

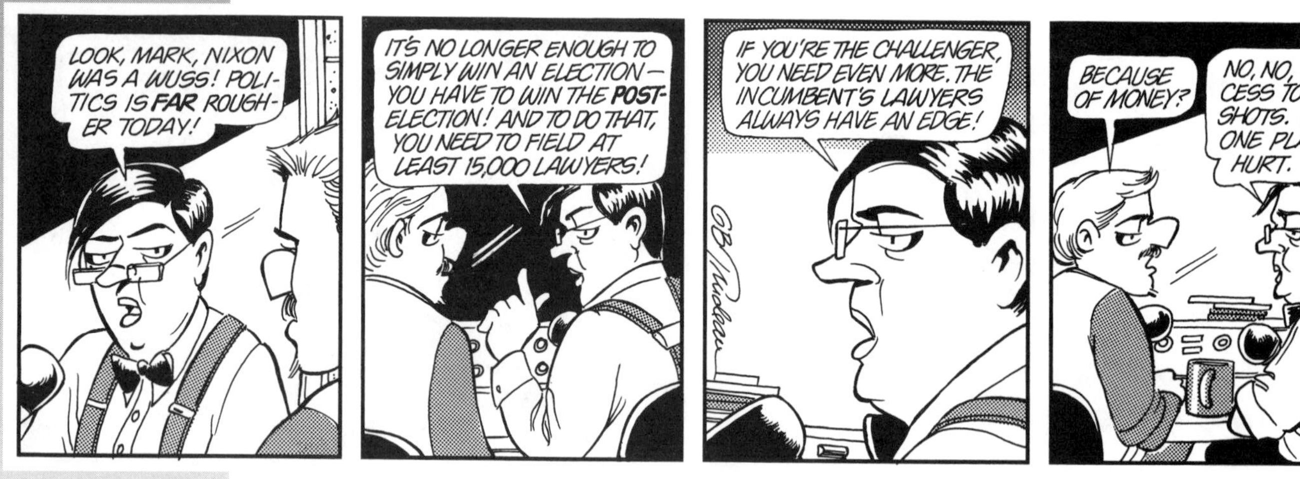
LOOK, MARK, NIXON WAS A WUSS! POLITICS IS FAR ROUGHER TODAY!
IT'S NO LONGER ENOUGH TO SIMPLY WIN AN ELECTION — YOU HAVE TO WIN THE POST-ELECTION! AND TO DO THAT, YOU NEED TO FIELD AT LEAST 15,000 LAWYERS!
IF YOU'RE THE CHALLENGER, YOU NEED EVEN MORE. THE INCUMBENT'S LAWYERS ALWAYS HAVE AN EDGE!
BECAUSE OF MONEY?
NO, NO, ACCESS TO FLU SHOTS. NO ONE PLAYS HURT.

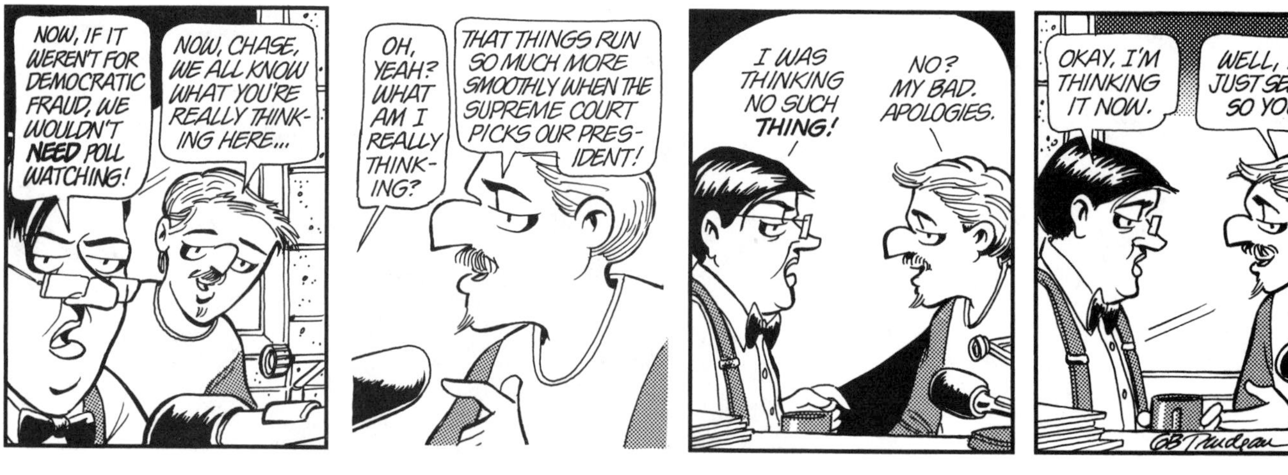
NOW, IF IT WEREN'T FOR DEMOCRATIC FRAUD, WE WOULDN'T NEED POLL WATCHING!
NOW, CHASE, WE ALL KNOW WHAT YOU'RE REALLY THINKING HERE...
OH, YEAH? WHAT AM I REALLY THINKING?
THAT THINGS RUN SO MUCH MORE SMOOTHLY WHEN THE SUPREME COURT PICKS OUR PRESIDENT!
I WAS THINKING NO SUCH THING!
NO? MY BAD. APOLOGIES.
OKAY, I'M THINKING IT NOW.
WELL, IT JUST SEEMS SO YOU.

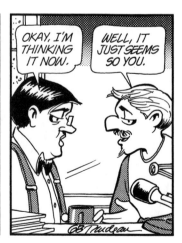

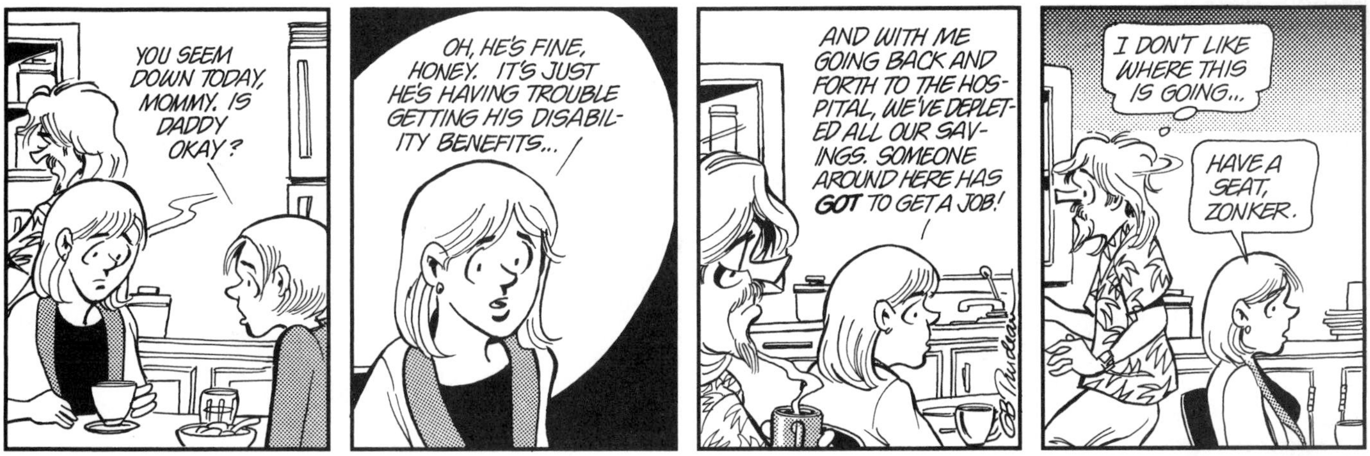
YOU SEEM DOWN TODAY, MOMMY. IS DADDY OKAY?
OH, HE'S FINE, HONEY. IT'S JUST HE'S HAVING TROUBLE GETTING HIS DISABILITY BENEFITS...
AND WITH ME GOING BACK AND FORTH TO THE HOSPITAL, WE'VE DEPLETED ALL OUR SAVINGS. SOMEONE AROUND HERE HAS **GOT** TO GET A JOB!
I DON'T LIKE WHERE THIS IS GOING...
HAVE A SEAT, ZONKER.
GB Trudeau

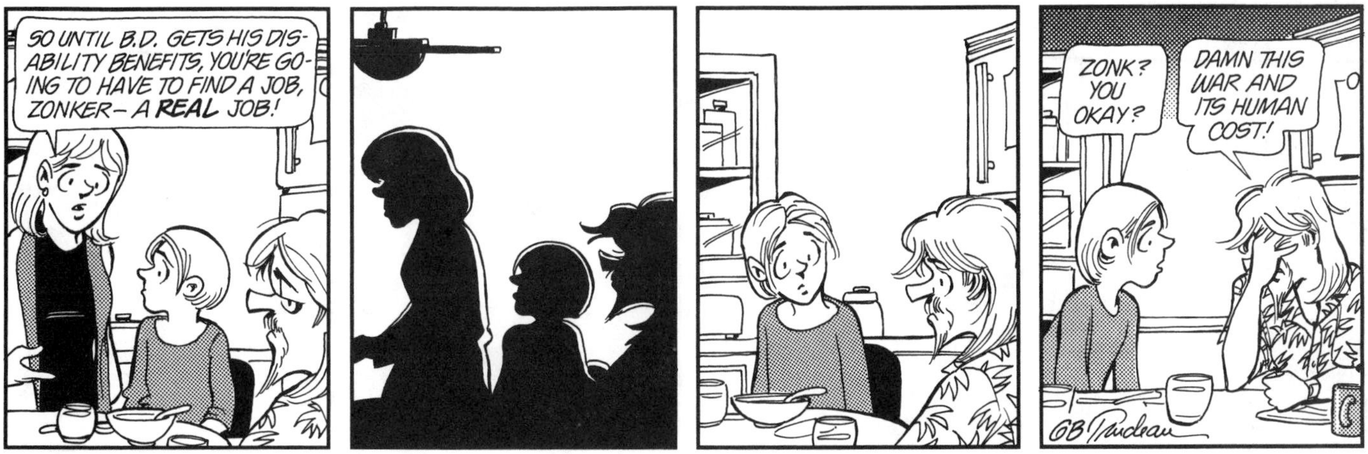
SO UNTIL B.D. GETS HIS DISABILITY BENEFITS, YOU'RE GOING TO HAVE TO FIND A JOB, ZONKER– A **REAL** JOB!
ZONK? YOU OKAY?
DAMN THIS WAR AND ITS HUMAN COST!
GB Trudeau

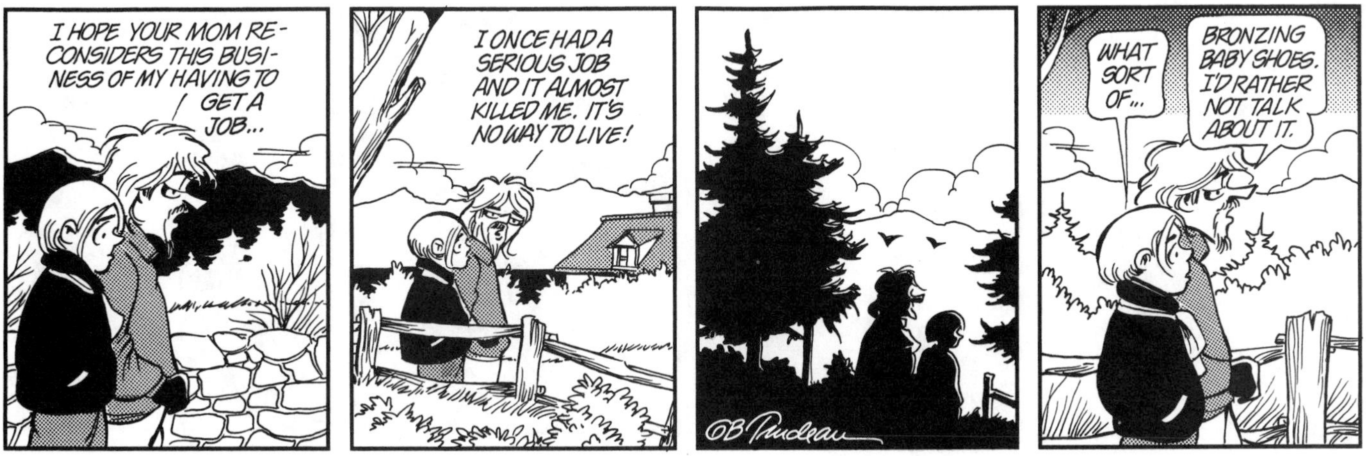
I HOPE YOUR MOM RECONSIDERS THIS BUSINESS OF MY HAVING TO GET A JOB...
I ONCE HAD A SERIOUS JOB AND IT ALMOST KILLED ME. IT'S NO WAY TO LIVE!
GB Trudeau
WHAT SORT OF...
BRONZING BABY SHOES. I'D RATHER NOT TALK ABOUT IT.

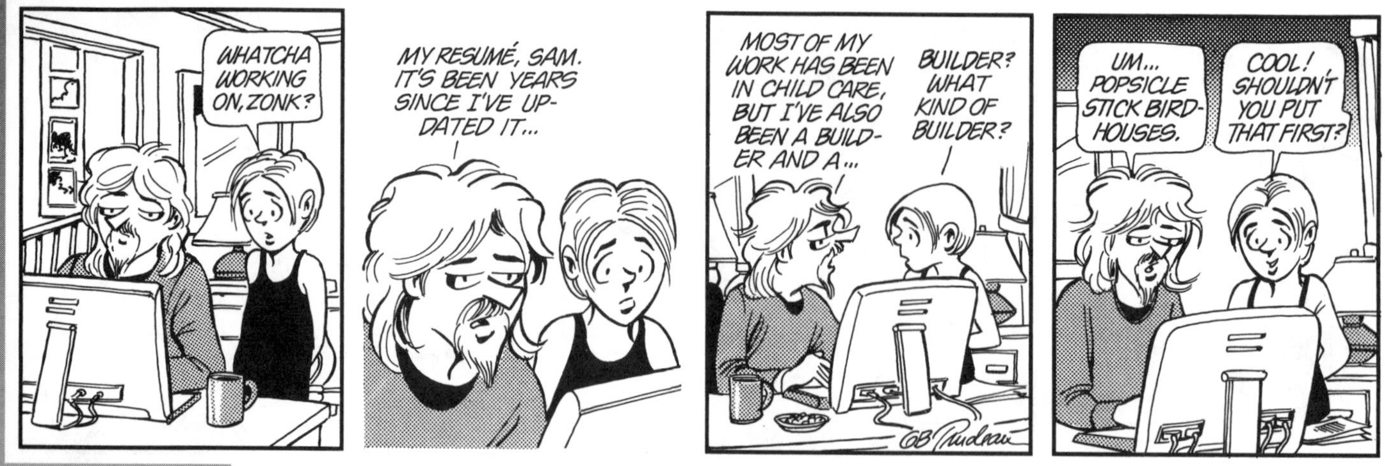
WHATCHA WORKING ON, ZONK?
MY RESUMÉ, SAM. IT'S BEEN YEARS SINCE I'VE UPDATED IT...
MOST OF MY WORK HAS BEEN IN CHILD CARE, BUT I'VE ALSO BEEN A BUILDER AND A...
BUILDER? WHAT KIND OF BUILDER?
UM... POPSICLE STICK BIRD-HOUSES.
COOL! SHOULDN'T YOU PUT THAT FIRST?

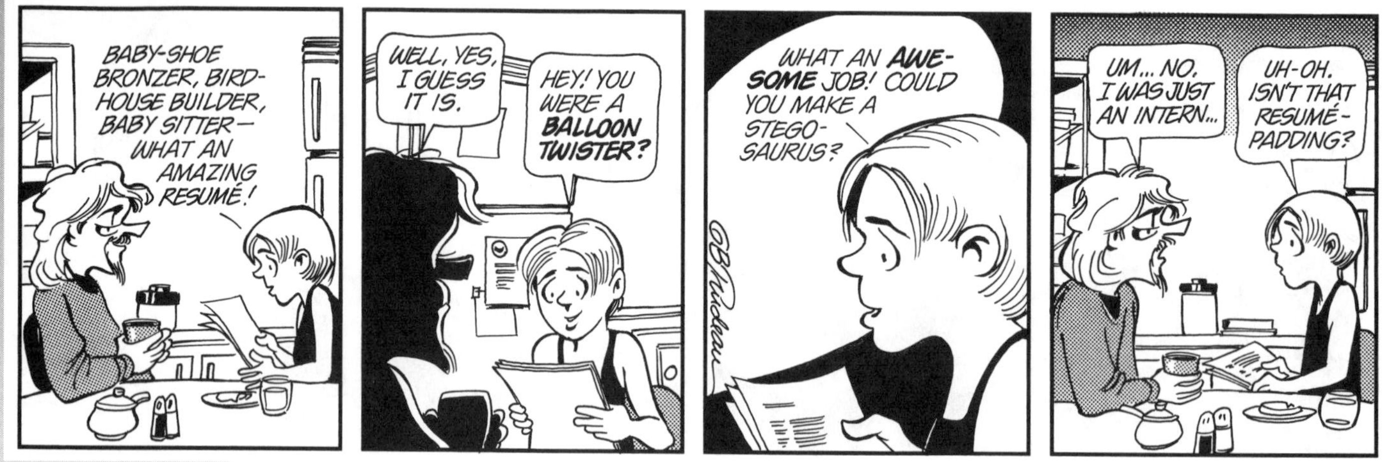
BABY-SHOE BRONZER, BIRD-HOUSE BUILDER, BABY SITTER— WHAT AN AMAZING RESUMÉ!
WELL, YES, I GUESS IT IS.
HEY! YOU WERE A BALLOON TWISTER?
WHAT AN AWESOME JOB! COULD YOU MAKE A STEGOSAURUS?
UM... NO. I WAS JUST AN INTERN...
UH-OH. ISN'T THAT RESUMÉ-PADDING?

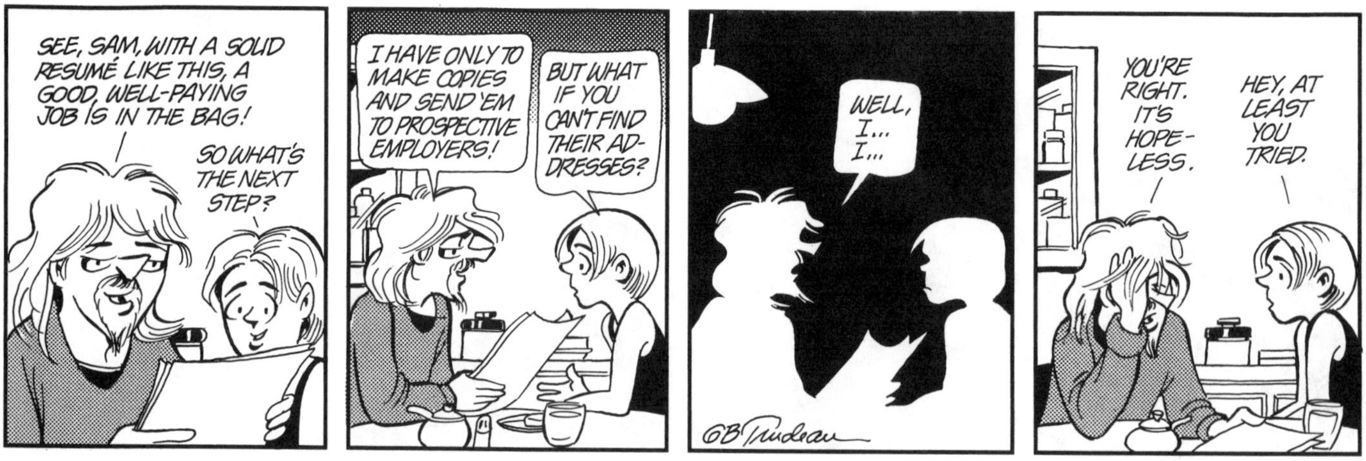
SEE, SAM, WITH A SOLID RESUMÉ LIKE THIS, A GOOD, WELL-PAYING JOB IS IN THE BAG!
SO WHAT'S THE NEXT STEP?
I HAVE ONLY TO MAKE COPIES AND SEND 'EM TO PROSPECTIVE EMPLOYERS!
BUT WHAT IF YOU CAN'T FIND THEIR ADDRESSES?
WELL, I... I...
YOU'RE RIGHT. IT'S HOPELESS.
HEY, AT LEAST YOU TRIED.

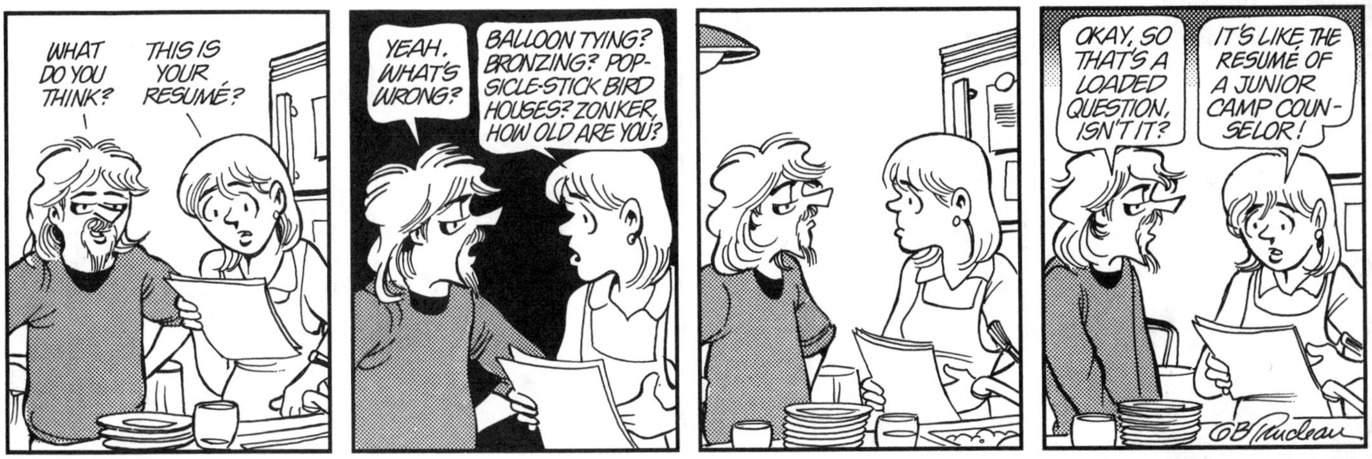
WHAT DO YOU THINK?
THIS IS YOUR RESUMÉ?
YEAH. WHAT'S WRONG?
BALLOON TYING? BRONZING? POPSICLE-STICK BIRD HOUSES? ZONKER, HOW OLD ARE YOU?
OKAY, SO THAT'S A LOADED QUESTION, ISN'T IT?
IT'S LIKE THE RESUMÉ OF A JUNIOR CAMP COUNSELOR!
GB Trudeau

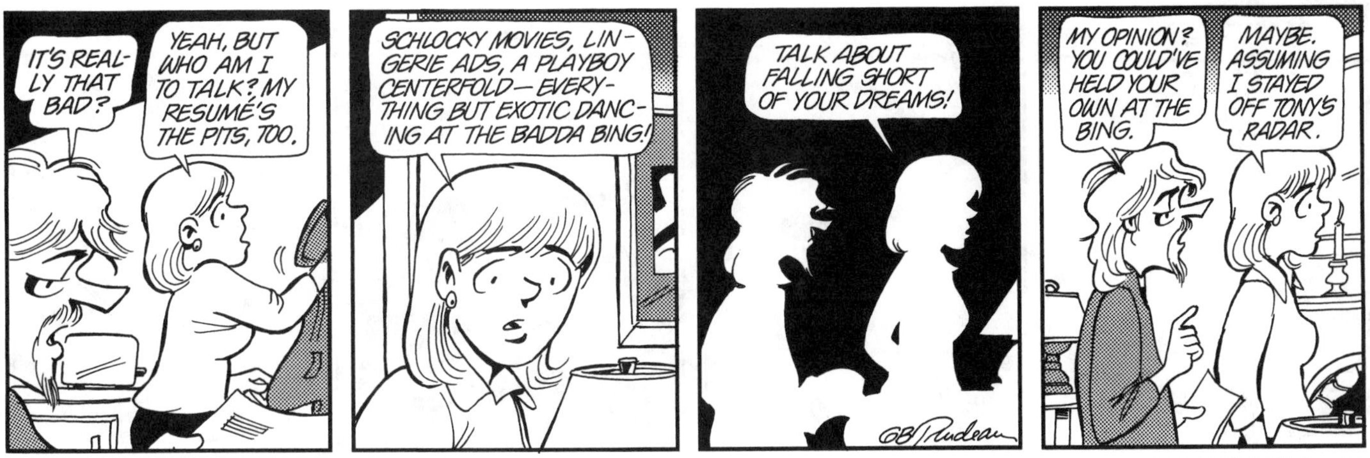
IT'S REALLY THAT BAD?
YEAH, BUT WHO AM I TO TALK? MY RESUMÉ'S THE PITS, TOO.
SCHLOCKY MOVIES, LINGERIE ADS, A PLAYBOY CENTERFOLD—EVERYTHING BUT EXOTIC DANCING AT THE BADDA BING!
TALK ABOUT FALLING SHORT OF YOUR DREAMS!
GB Trudeau
MY OPINION? YOU COULD'VE HELD YOUR OWN AT THE BING.
MAYBE. ASSUMING I STAYED OFF TONY'S RADAR.

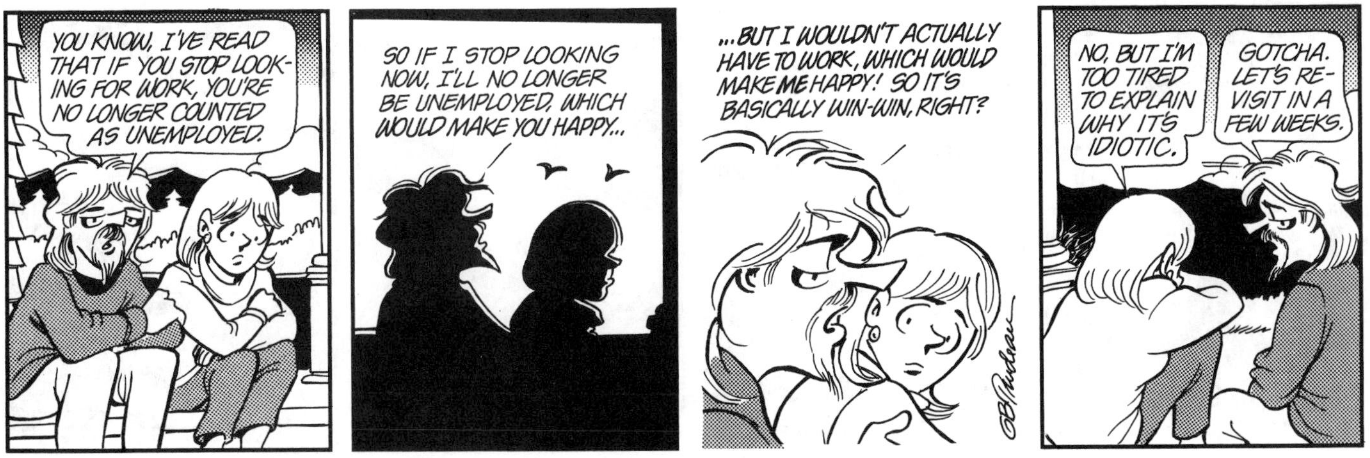
YOU KNOW, I'VE READ THAT IF YOU STOP LOOKING FOR WORK, YOU'RE NO LONGER COUNTED AS UNEMPLOYED.
SO IF I STOP LOOKING NOW, I'LL NO LONGER BE UNEMPLOYED, WHICH WOULD MAKE YOU HAPPY...
...BUT I WOULDN'T ACTUALLY HAVE TO WORK, WHICH WOULD MAKE ME HAPPY! SO IT'S BASICALLY WIN-WIN, RIGHT?
GB Trudeau
NO, BUT I'M TOO TIRED TO EXPLAIN WHY IT'S IDIOTIC.
GOTCHA. LET'S REVISIT IN A FEW WEEKS.

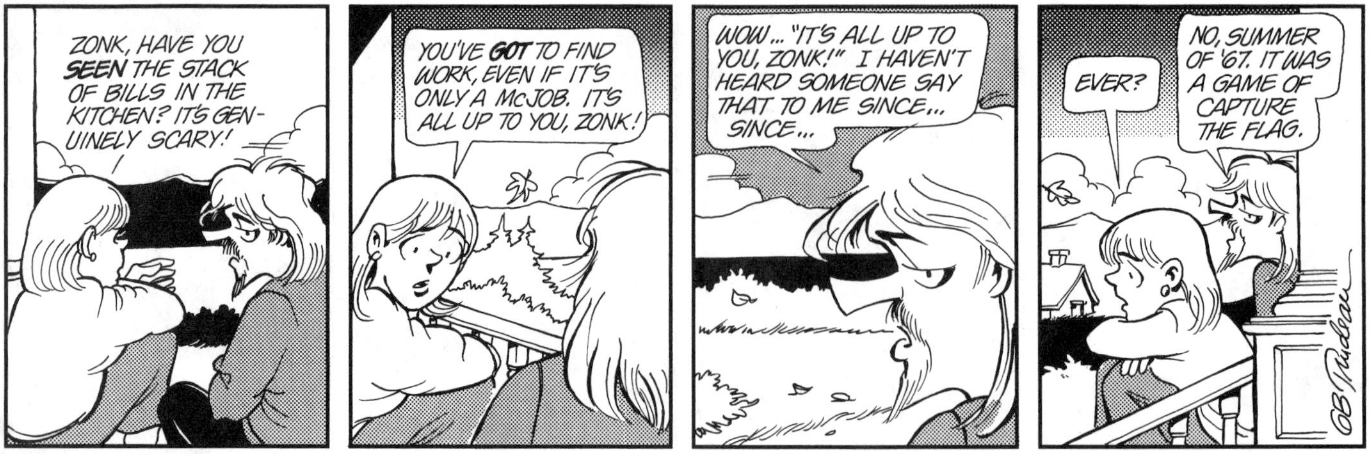
ZONK, HAVE YOU **SEEN** THE STACK OF BILLS IN THE KITCHEN? IT'S GENUINELY SCARY!
YOU'VE **GOT** TO FIND WORK, EVEN IF IT'S ONLY A McJOB. IT'S ALL UP TO YOU, ZONK!
WOW... "IT'S ALL UP TO YOU, ZONK!" I HAVEN'T HEARD SOMEONE SAY THAT TO ME SINCE... SINCE...
EVER?
NO, SUMMER OF '67. IT WAS A GAME OF CAPTURE THE FLAG.
©B Trudeau

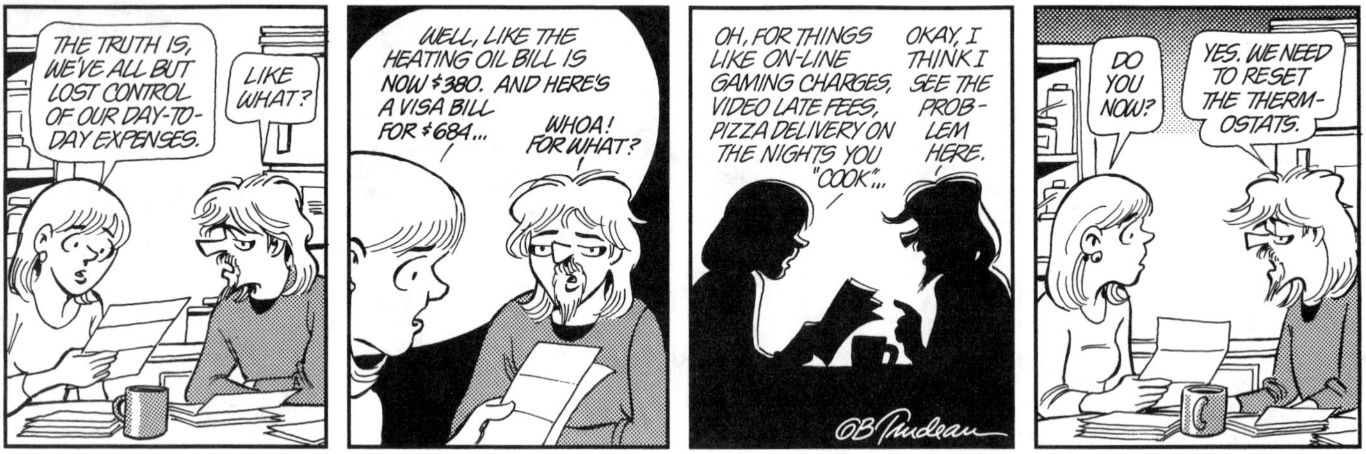
THE TRUTH IS, WE'VE ALL BUT LOST CONTROL OF OUR DAY-TO-DAY EXPENSES.
LIKE WHAT?
WELL, LIKE THE HEATING OIL BILL IS **NOW** $380. AND HERE'S A VISA BILL FOR $684...
WHOA! FOR WHAT?
OH, FOR THINGS LIKE ON-LINE GAMING CHARGES, VIDEO LATE FEES, PIZZA DELIVERY ON THE NIGHTS YOU "COOK"...
OKAY, I THINK I SEE THE PROBLEM HERE.
DO YOU NOW?
YES. WE NEED TO RESET THE THERMOSTATS.
©B Trudeau

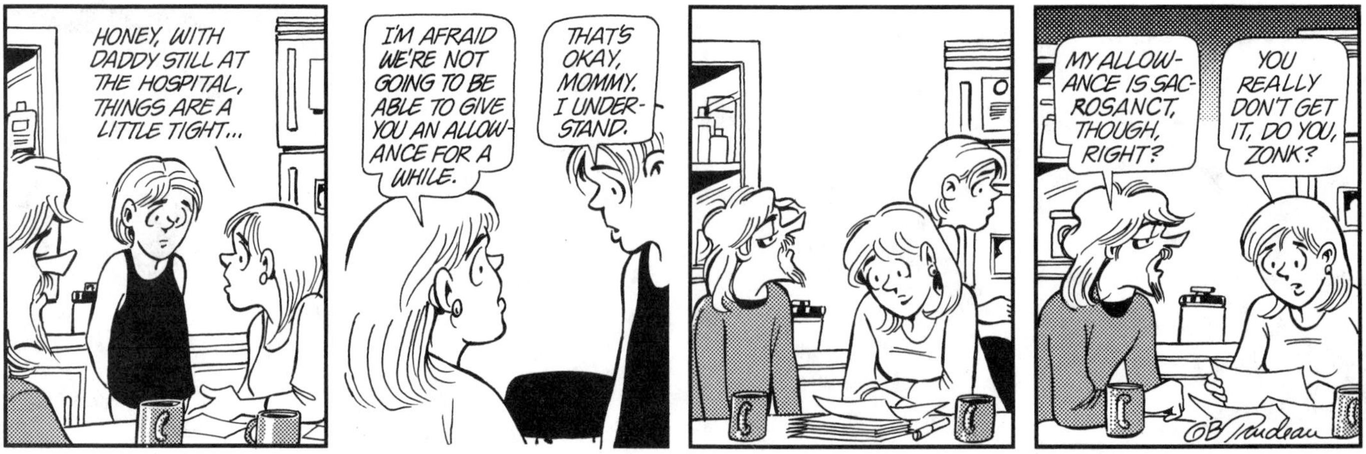
HONEY, WITH DADDY STILL AT THE HOSPITAL, THINGS ARE A LITTLE TIGHT...
I'M AFRAID **WE'RE** NOT GOING TO BE ABLE TO GIVE YOU AN ALLOWANCE FOR A WHILE.
THAT'S OKAY, MOMMY. I UNDERSTAND.
MY ALLOWANCE IS SACROSANCT, THOUGH, RIGHT?
YOU REALLY DON'T GET IT, DO YOU, ZONK?
©B Trudeau

"I WONDER WHAT THE KING IS WISHING TONIGHT."

"HE WISHES HE WERE IN KEY WEST, FISHING TONIGHT."

WHEN I ARRIVED THAT EVENING, THE MAYOR WAS IN A FUNK...

MORE CRAZINESS DOWNTOWN. HOW DID IT COME TO THIS, HONEY?

IT SEEMS LIKE ONLY YESTERDAY WE HAD THIS COUNTRY UNDER OUR HEEL!

WE WERE GIANTS BACK THEN! WE SWAGGERED! WE USED WORDS LIKE "ROBUST" AND "TAKE DOWN" AND "FORCE-MULTIPLIER"!

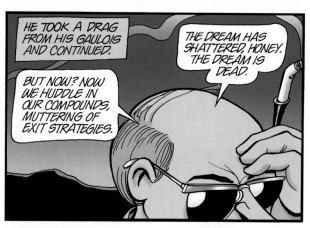

HE TOOK A DRAG FROM HIS GAULOIS AND CONTINUED.

BUT NOW? NOW WE HUDDLE IN OUR COMPOUNDS, MUTTERING OF EXIT STRATEGIES.

THE DREAM HAS SHATTERED, HONEY. THE DREAM IS DEAD.

WHAT DREAM, I WONDERED.

THE DREAM OF PEACE?

NO, NO, OF INVADING SYRIA.

33

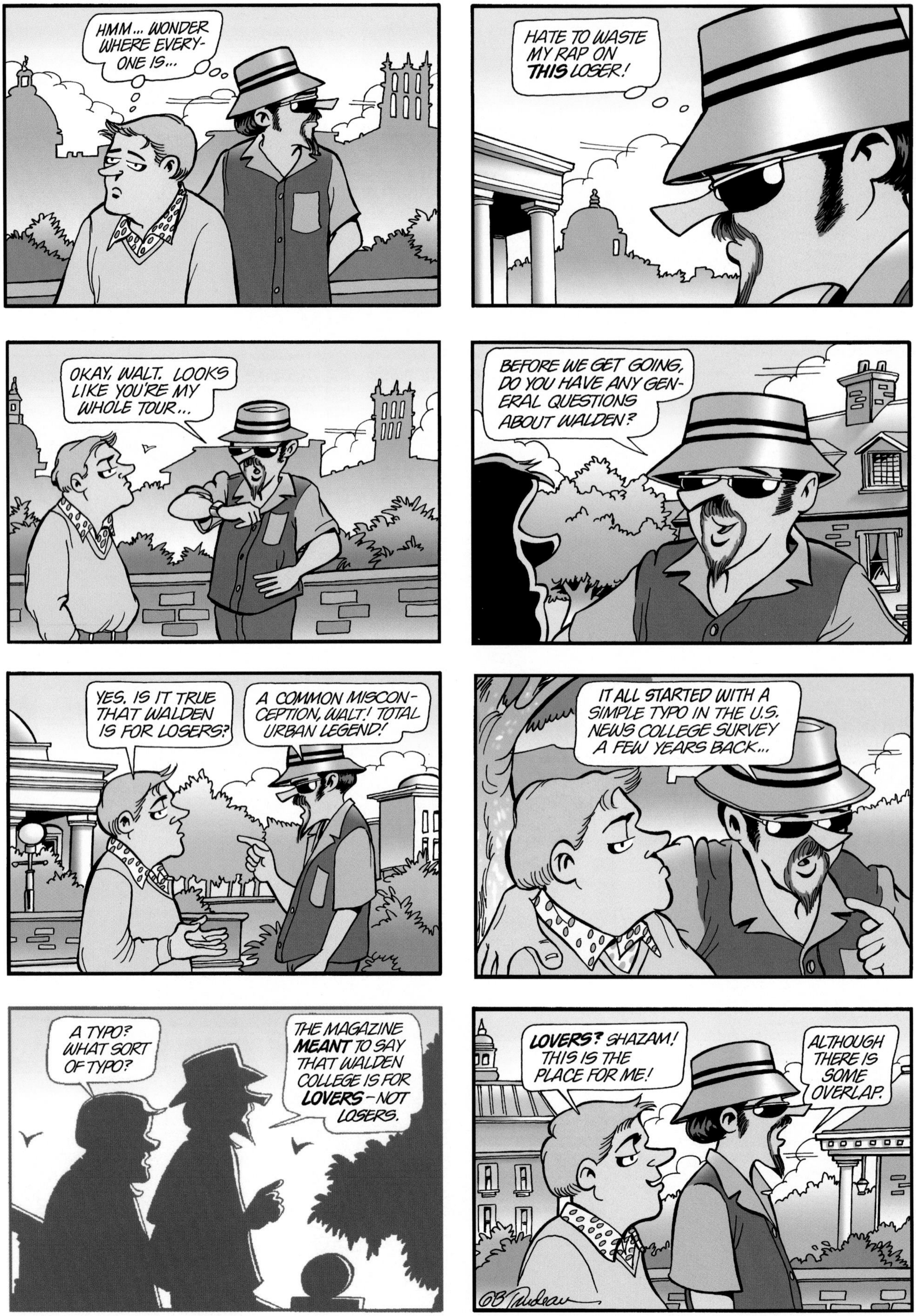
HMM... WONDER WHERE EVERY-ONE IS...
HATE TO WASTE MY RAP ON THIS LOSER!
OKAY, WALT. LOOKS LIKE YOU'RE MY WHOLE TOUR...
BEFORE WE GET GOING, DO YOU HAVE ANY GEN-ERAL QUESTIONS ABOUT WALDEN?
YES. IS IT TRUE THAT WALDEN IS FOR LOSERS?
A COMMON MISCON-CEPTION, WALT! TOTAL URBAN LEGEND!
IT ALL STARTED WITH A SIMPLE TYPO IN THE U.S. NEWS COLLEGE SURVEY A FEW YEARS BACK...
A TYPO? WHAT SORT OF TYPO?
THE MAGAZINE MEANT TO SAY THAT WALDEN COLLEGE IS FOR LOVERS–NOT LOSERS.
LOVERS? SHAZAM! THIS IS THE PLACE FOR ME!
ALTHOUGH THERE IS SOME OVERLAP.

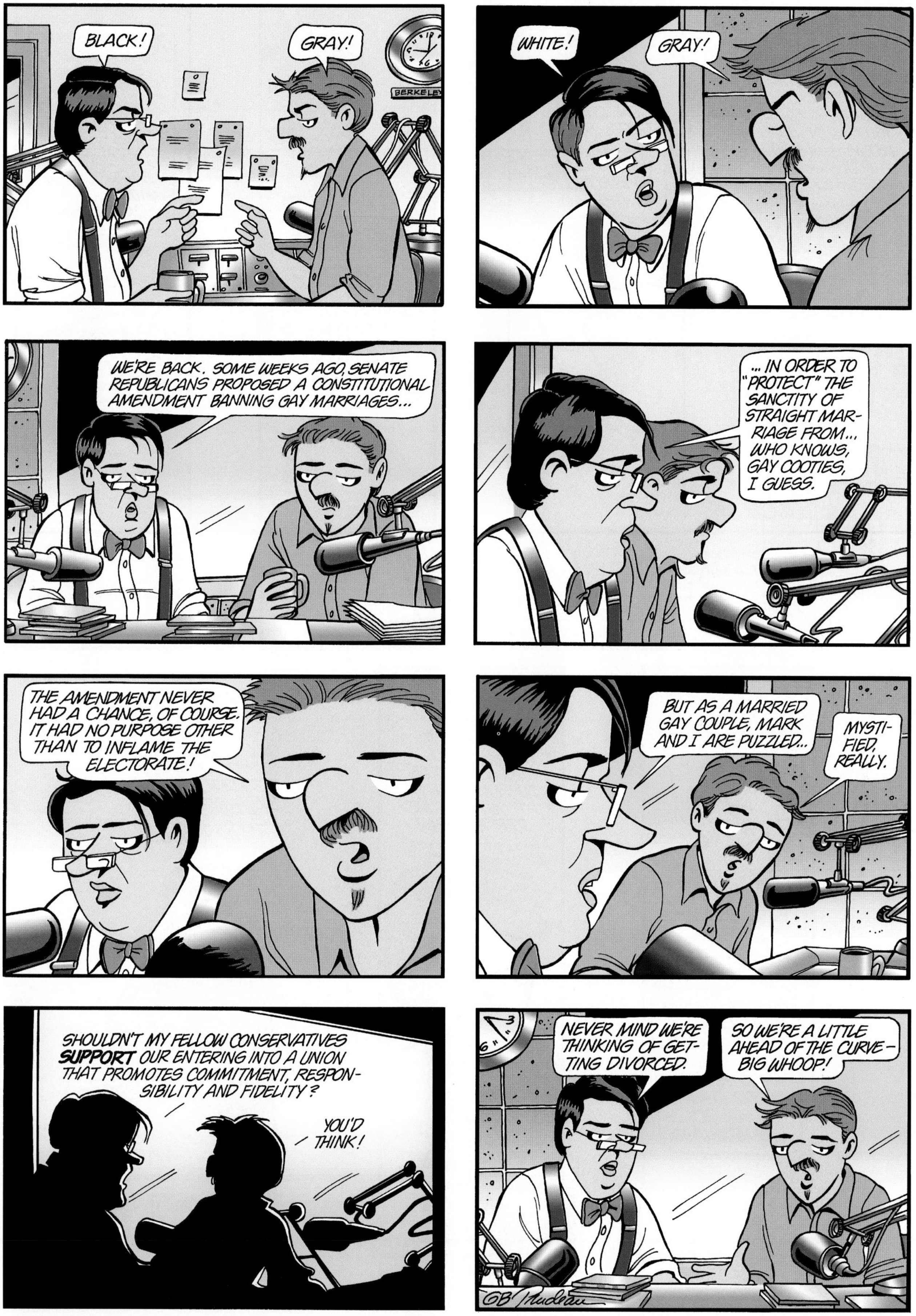
BLACK!
GRAY!
BERKELEY
WHITE!
GRAY!
WE'RE BACK. SOME WEEKS AGO, SENATE REPUBLICANS PROPOSED A CONSTITUTIONAL AMENDMENT BANNING GAY MARRIAGES...
... IN ORDER TO "PROTECT" THE SANCTITY OF STRAIGHT MARRIAGE FROM... WHO KNOWS, GAY COOTIES, I GUESS.
THE AMENDMENT NEVER HAD A CHANCE, OF COURSE. IT HAD NO PURPOSE OTHER THAN TO INFLAME THE ELECTORATE!
BUT AS A MARRIED GAY COUPLE, MARK AND I ARE PUZZLED...
MYSTIFIED, REALLY.
SHOULDN'T MY FELLOW CONSERVATIVES **SUPPORT** OUR ENTERING INTO A UNION THAT PROMOTES COMMITMENT, RESPONSIBILITY AND FIDELITY?
YOU'D THINK!
NEVER MIND WE'RE THINKING OF GETTING DIVORCED.
SO WE'RE A LITTLE AHEAD OF THE CURVE — BIG WHOOP!

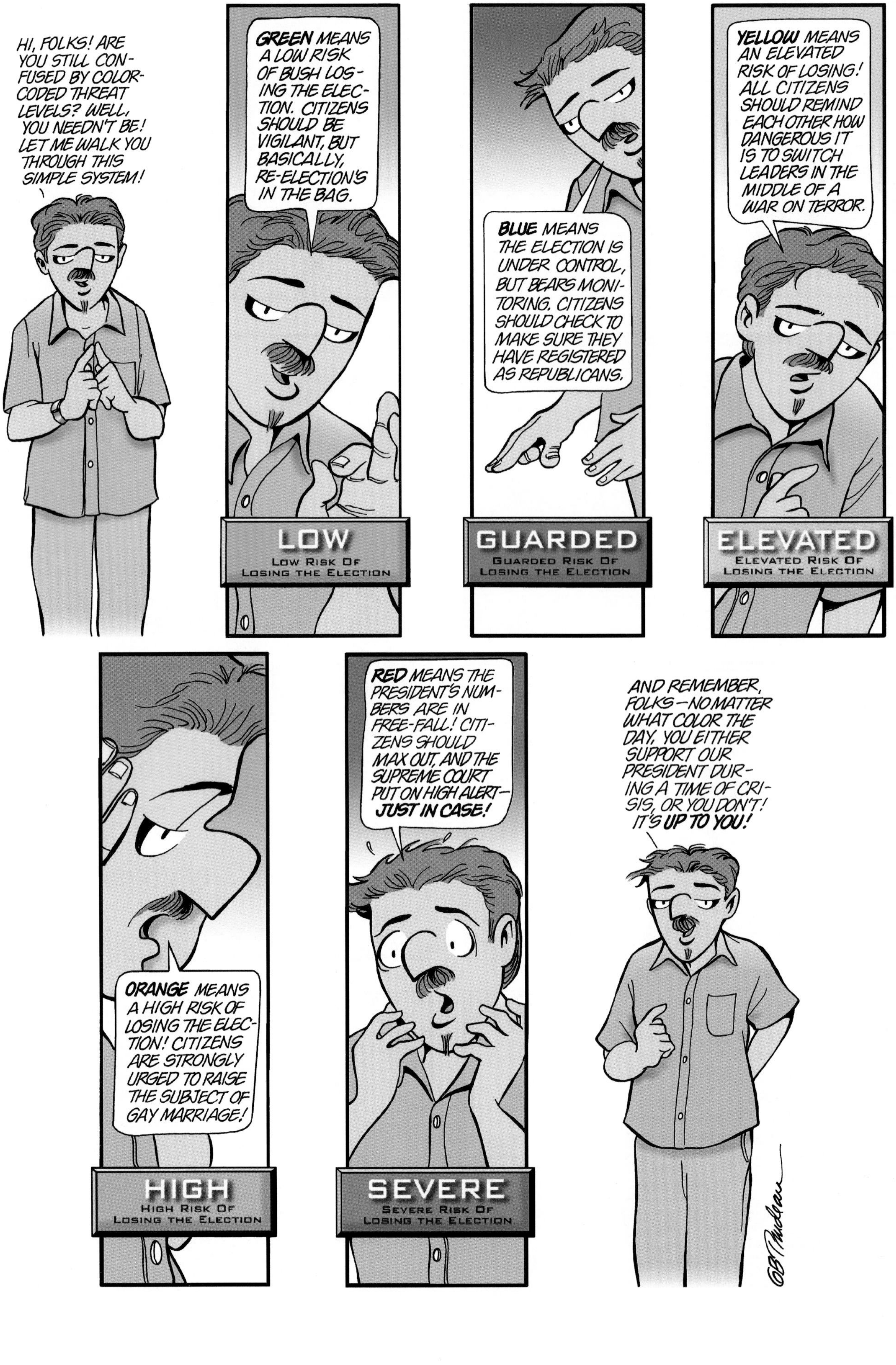
HI, FOLKS! ARE YOU STILL CONFUSED BY COLOR-CODED THREAT LEVELS? WELL, YOU NEEDN'T BE! LET ME WALK YOU THROUGH THIS SIMPLE SYSTEM!
GREEN MEANS A LOW RISK OF BUSH LOSING THE ELECTION. CITIZENS SHOULD BE VIGILANT, BUT BASICALLY, RE-ELECTION'S IN THE BAG.
LOW
Low Risk Of Losing the Election
BLUE MEANS THE ELECTION IS UNDER CONTROL, BUT BEARS MONITORING. CITIZENS SHOULD CHECK TO MAKE SURE THEY HAVE REGISTERED AS REPUBLICANS.
GUARDED
Guarded Risk Of Losing the Election
YELLOW MEANS AN ELEVATED RISK OF LOSING! ALL CITIZENS SHOULD REMIND EACH OTHER HOW DANGEROUS IT IS TO SWITCH LEADERS IN THE MIDDLE OF A WAR ON TERROR.
ELEVATED
Elevated Risk Of Losing the Election
ORANGE MEANS A HIGH RISK OF LOSING THE ELECTION! CITIZENS ARE STRONGLY URGED TO RAISE THE SUBJECT OF GAY MARRIAGE!
HIGH
High Risk Of Losing the Election
RED MEANS THE PRESIDENT'S NUMBERS ARE IN FREE-FALL! CITIZENS SHOULD MAX OUT, AND THE SUPREME COURT PUT ON HIGH ALERT— JUST IN CASE!
SEVERE
Severe Risk Of Losing the Election
AND REMEMBER, FOLKS—NO MATTER WHAT COLOR THE DAY, YOU EITHER SUPPORT OUR PRESIDENT DURING A TIME OF CRISIS, OR YOU DON'T! IT'S UP TO YOU!

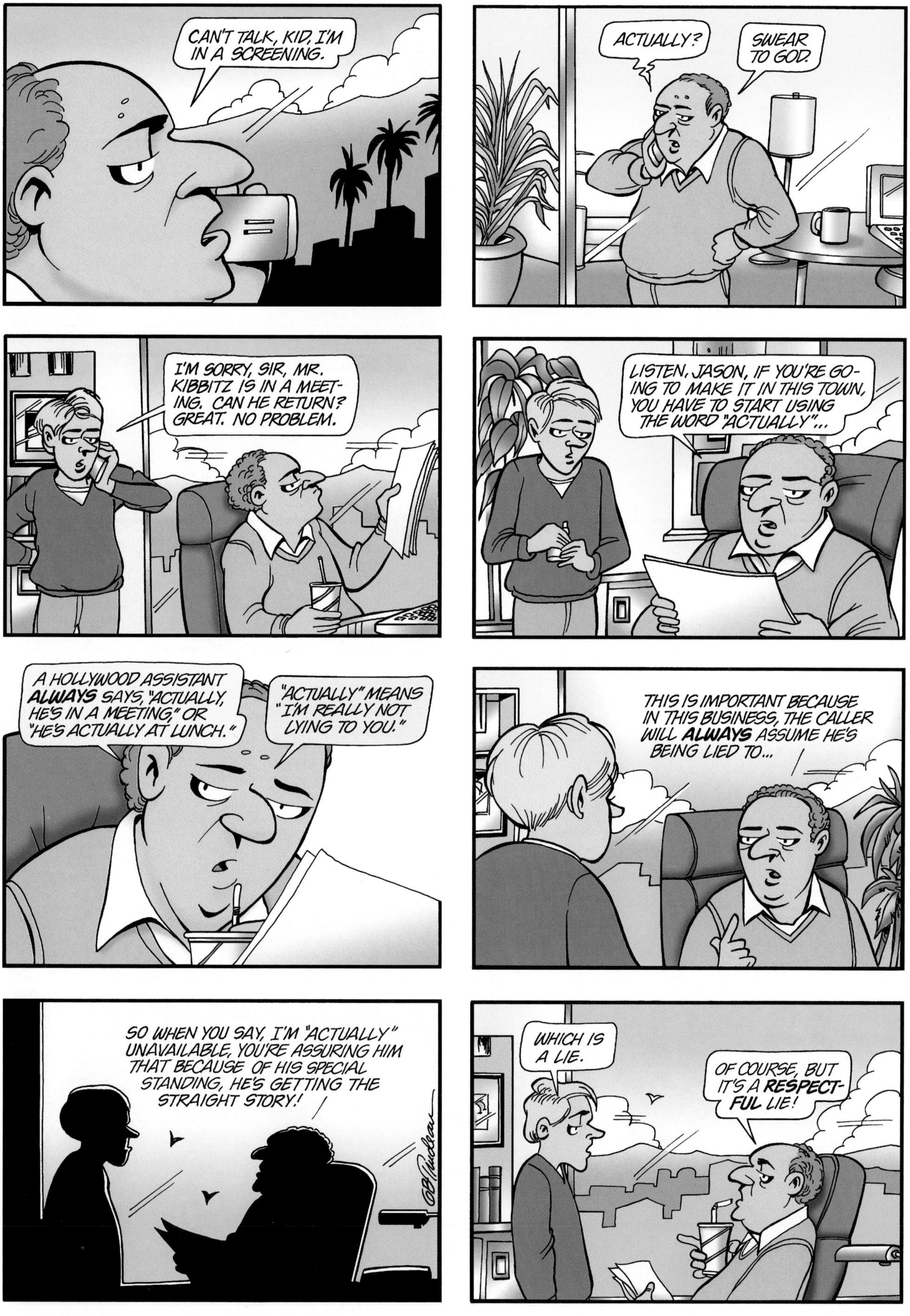
CAN'T TALK, KID, I'M IN A SCREENING.
ACTUALLY?
SWEAR TO GOD.
I'M SORRY, SIR, MR. KIBBITZ IS IN A MEETING. CAN HE RETURN? GREAT. NO PROBLEM.
LISTEN, JASON, IF YOU'RE GOING TO MAKE IT IN THIS TOWN, YOU HAVE TO START USING THE WORD "ACTUALLY"...
A HOLLYWOOD ASSISTANT ALWAYS SAYS, "ACTUALLY, HE'S IN A MEETING," OR "HE'S ACTUALLY AT LUNCH."
"ACTUALLY" MEANS "I'M REALLY NOT LYING TO YOU."
THIS IS IMPORTANT BECAUSE IN THIS BUSINESS, THE CALLER WILL ALWAYS ASSUME HE'S BEING LIED TO...
SO WHEN YOU SAY, I'M "ACTUALLY" UNAVAILABLE, YOU'RE ASSURING HIM THAT BECAUSE OF HIS SPECIAL STANDING, HE'S GETTING THE STRAIGHT STORY!
WHICH IS A LIE.
OF COURSE, BUT IT'S A RESPECTFUL LIE!

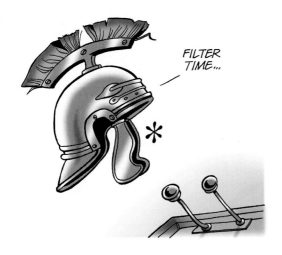

FILTER TIME...
BRING ON YOUR GRUBBY LITTLE FILTER QUESTIONS!
SIR, SECRETARY RUMSFELD SAYS HE TAKES "FULL RESPONSIBILITY" FOR THE ATROCITIES AT ABU GHRAIB...
BUT AFTER YOU VIEWED PHOTOS OF THE TORTURE, YOU SAID HE'D DONE A "SUPERB JOB."
SIR, IF THERE ARE NO CONSEQUENCES, WHAT DOES "FULL RESPONSIBILITY" MEAN?
IT MEANS WHAT IT MEANS!
PRESIDENT OF THE
IT MEANS FOOL HIM ONCE, SHAME ON THE TORTURERS! FOOL HIM TWICE, YOU... YOU CAN'T FOOL HIM AGAIN!
SEE, WE'RE AT WAR – A DIFFERENT **KIND** OF WAR!
THE EVIL ONES **HATE** IT WHEN THE SECRETARY OF DEFENSE DOES A SUPERB JOB!
PRESIDENT OF THE
SO TO CLARIFY, TAKING "FULL RESPONSIBILITY" MEANS...
TAKING CREDIT! WHAT IS THIS— VOCAB GOTCHA?
GBTrudeau

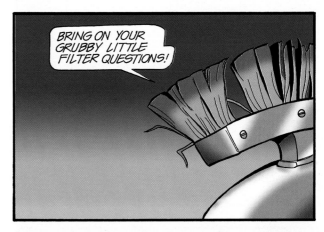

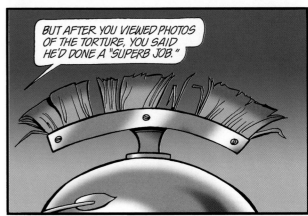

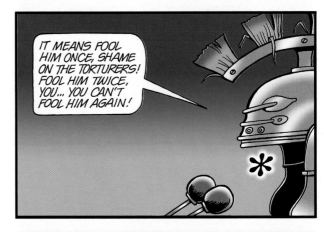

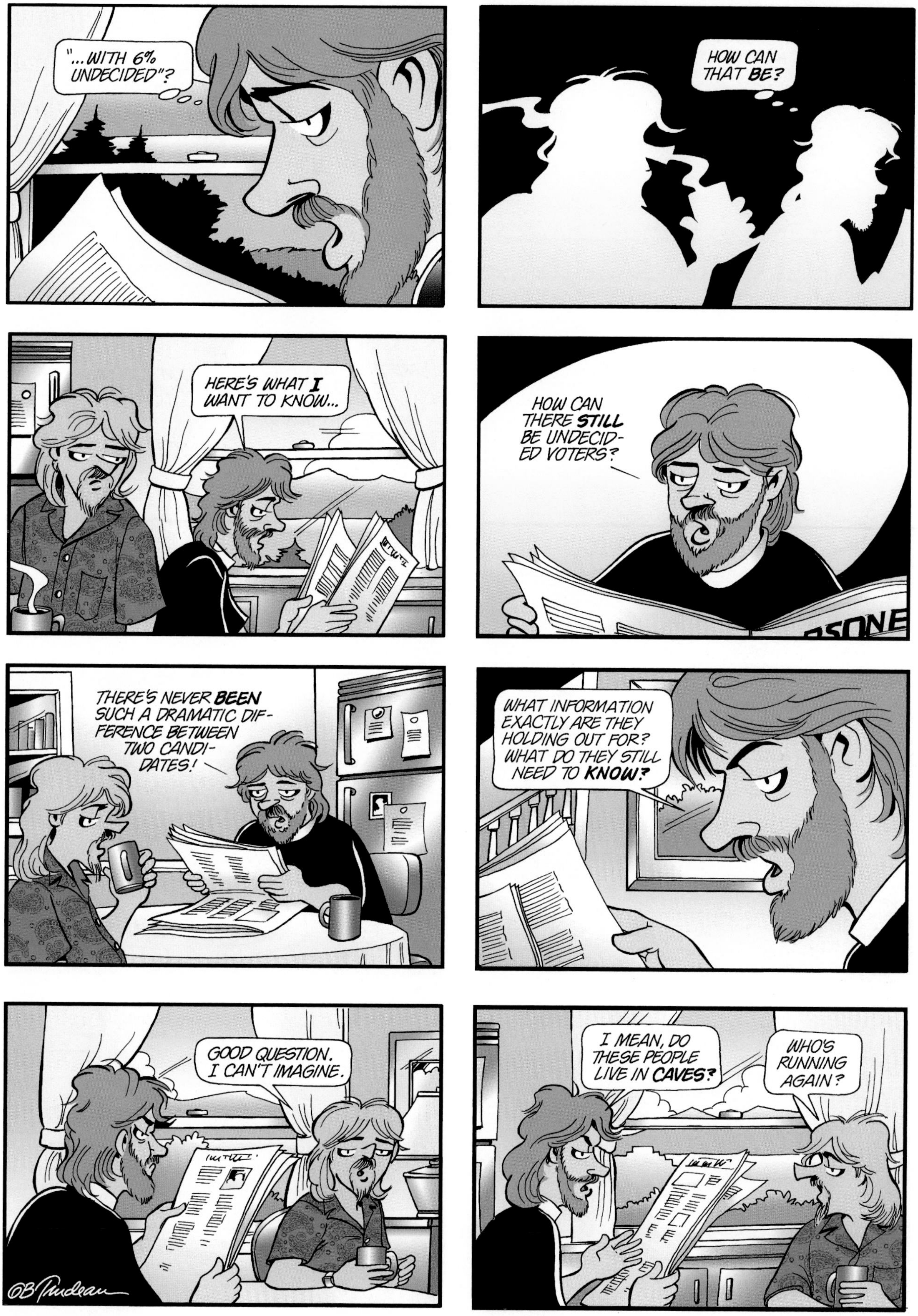
"...WITH 6% UNDECIDED"?
HOW CAN THAT BE?
HERE'S WHAT I WANT TO KNOW...
HOW CAN THERE STILL BE UNDECIDED VOTERS?
THERE'S NEVER BEEN SUCH A DRAMATIC DIFFERENCE BETWEEN TWO CANDIDATES!
WHAT INFORMATION EXACTLY ARE THEY HOLDING OUT FOR? WHAT DO THEY STILL NEED TO KNOW?
GOOD QUESTION. I CAN'T IMAGINE.
I MEAN, DO THESE PEOPLE LIVE IN CAVES?
WHO'S RUNNING AGAIN?
©B Trudeau

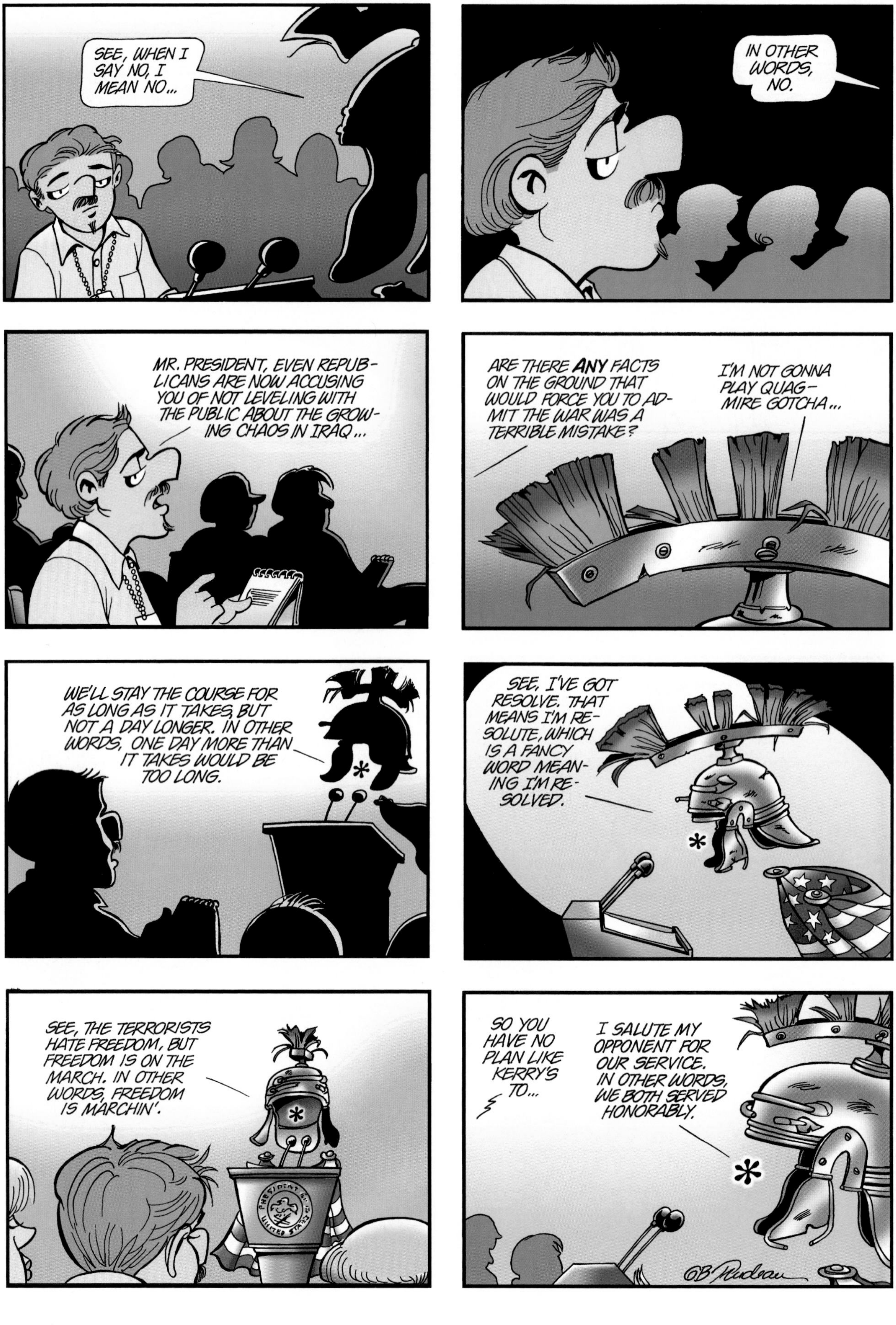
SEE, WHEN I SAY NO, I MEAN NO...
IN OTHER WORDS, NO.
MR. PRESIDENT, EVEN REPUBLICANS ARE NOW ACCUSING YOU OF NOT LEVELING WITH THE PUBLIC ABOUT THE GROWING CHAOS IN IRAQ...
ARE THERE ANY FACTS ON THE GROUND THAT WOULD FORCE YOU TO ADMIT THE WAR WAS A TERRIBLE MISTAKE?
I'M NOT GONNA PLAY QUAGMIRE GOTCHA...
WE'LL STAY THE COURSE FOR AS LONG AS IT TAKES, BUT NOT A DAY LONGER. IN OTHER WORDS, ONE DAY MORE THAN IT TAKES WOULD BE TOO LONG.
SEE, I'VE GOT RESOLVE. THAT MEANS I'M RESOLUTE, WHICH IS A FANCY WORD MEANING I'M RESOLVED.
SEE, THE TERRORISTS HATE FREEDOM, BUT FREEDOM IS ON THE MARCH. IN OTHER WORDS, FREEDOM IS MARCHIN'.
SO YOU HAVE NO PLAN LIKE KERRY'S TO...
I SALUTE MY OPPONENT FOR OUR SERVICE. IN OTHER WORDS, WE BOTH SERVED HONORABLY.

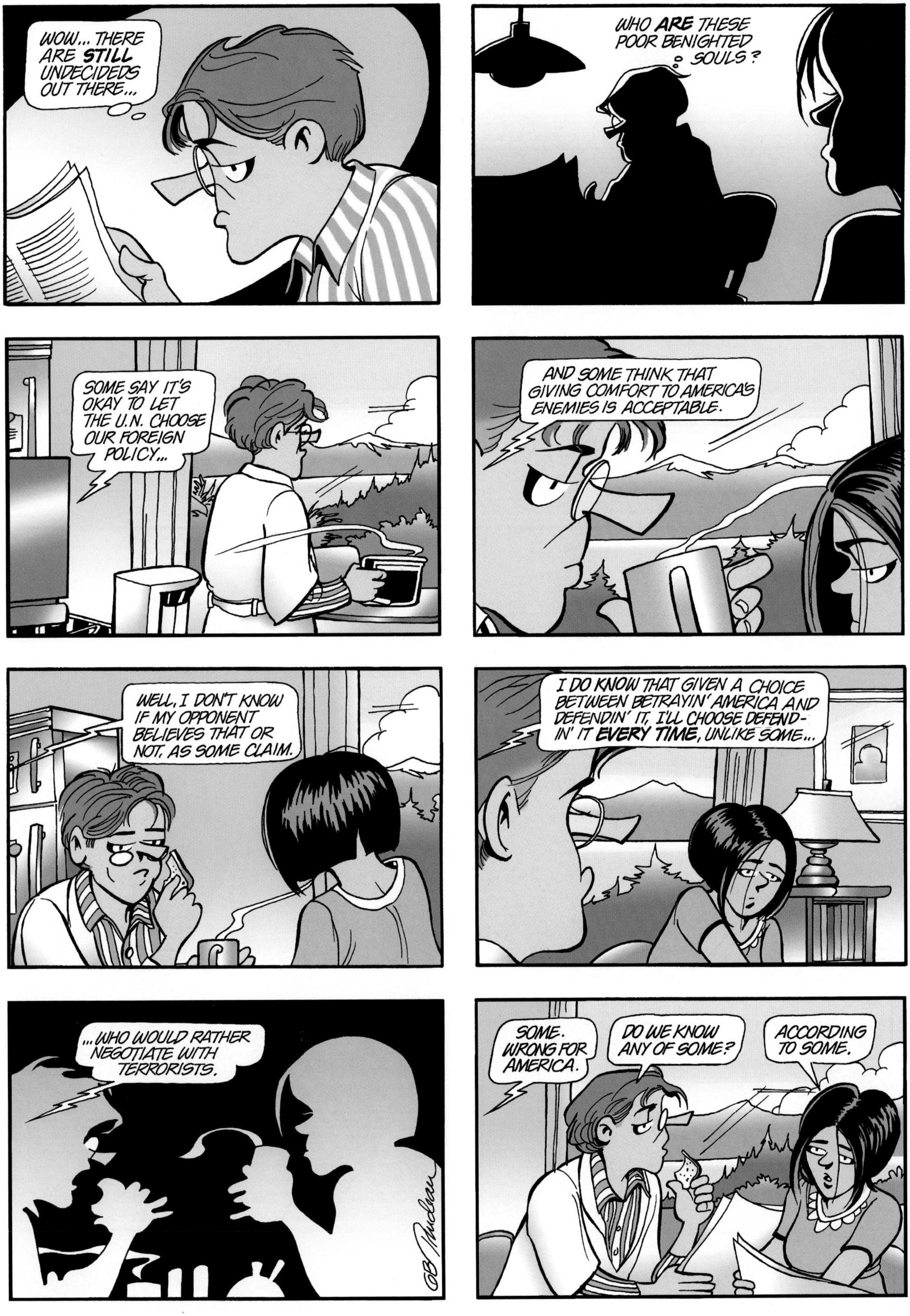
WOW... THERE ARE STILL UNDECIDEDS OUT THERE...
WHO ARE THESE POOR BENIGHTED SOULS?
SOME SAY IT'S OKAY TO LET THE U.N. CHOOSE OUR FOREIGN POLICY...
AND SOME THINK THAT GIVING COMFORT TO AMERICA'S ENEMIES IS ACCEPTABLE.
WELL, I DON'T KNOW IF MY OPPONENT BELIEVES THAT OR NOT, AS SOME CLAIM.
I DO KNOW THAT GIVEN A CHOICE BETWEEN BETRAYIN' AMERICA AND DEFENDIN' IT, I'LL CHOOSE DEFEND-IN' IT EVERY TIME, UNLIKE SOME...
...WHO WOULD RATHER NEGOTIATE WITH TERRORISTS.
SOME. WRONG FOR AMERICA.
DO WE KNOW ANY OF SOME?
ACCORDING TO SOME.

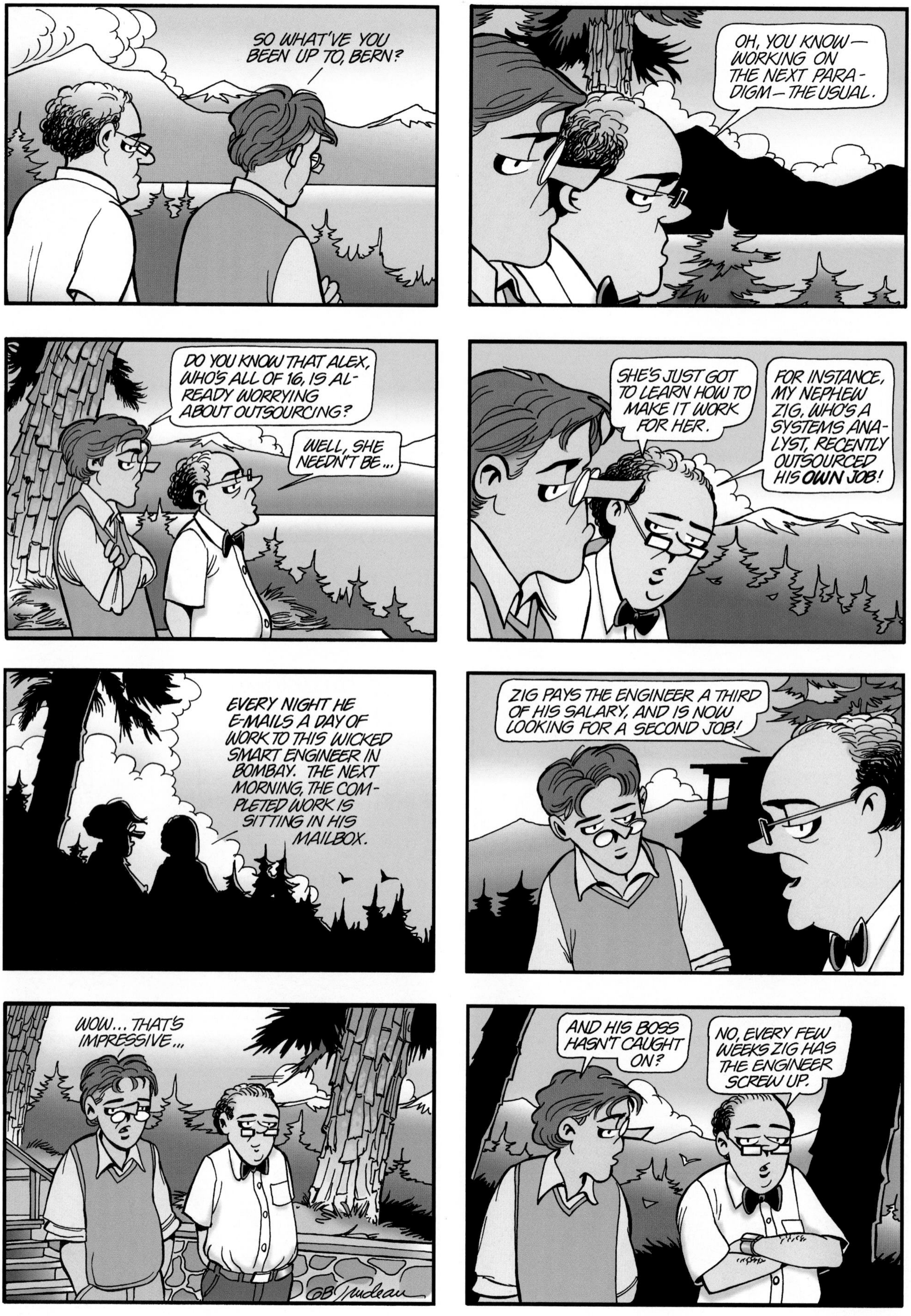
SO WHAT'VE YOU BEEN UP TO, BERN?
OH, YOU KNOW— WORKING ON THE NEXT PARADIGM—THE USUAL.
DO YOU KNOW THAT ALEX, WHO'S ALL OF 16, IS ALREADY WORRYING ABOUT OUTSOURCING?
WELL, SHE NEEDN'T BE...
SHE'S JUST GOT TO LEARN HOW TO MAKE IT WORK FOR HER.
FOR INSTANCE, MY NEPHEW ZIG, WHO'S A SYSTEMS ANALYST, RECENTLY OUTSOURCED HIS **OWN** JOB!
EVERY NIGHT HE E-MAILS A DAY OF WORK TO THIS WICKED SMART ENGINEER IN BOMBAY. THE NEXT MORNING, THE COMPLETED WORK IS SITTING IN HIS MAILBOX.
ZIG PAYS THE ENGINEER A THIRD OF HIS SALARY, AND IS NOW LOOKING FOR A SECOND JOB!
WOW... THAT'S IMPRESSIVE...
©B Trudeau
AND HIS BOSS HASN'T CAUGHT ON?
NO, EVERY FEW WEEKS ZIG HAS THE ENGINEER SCREW UP.

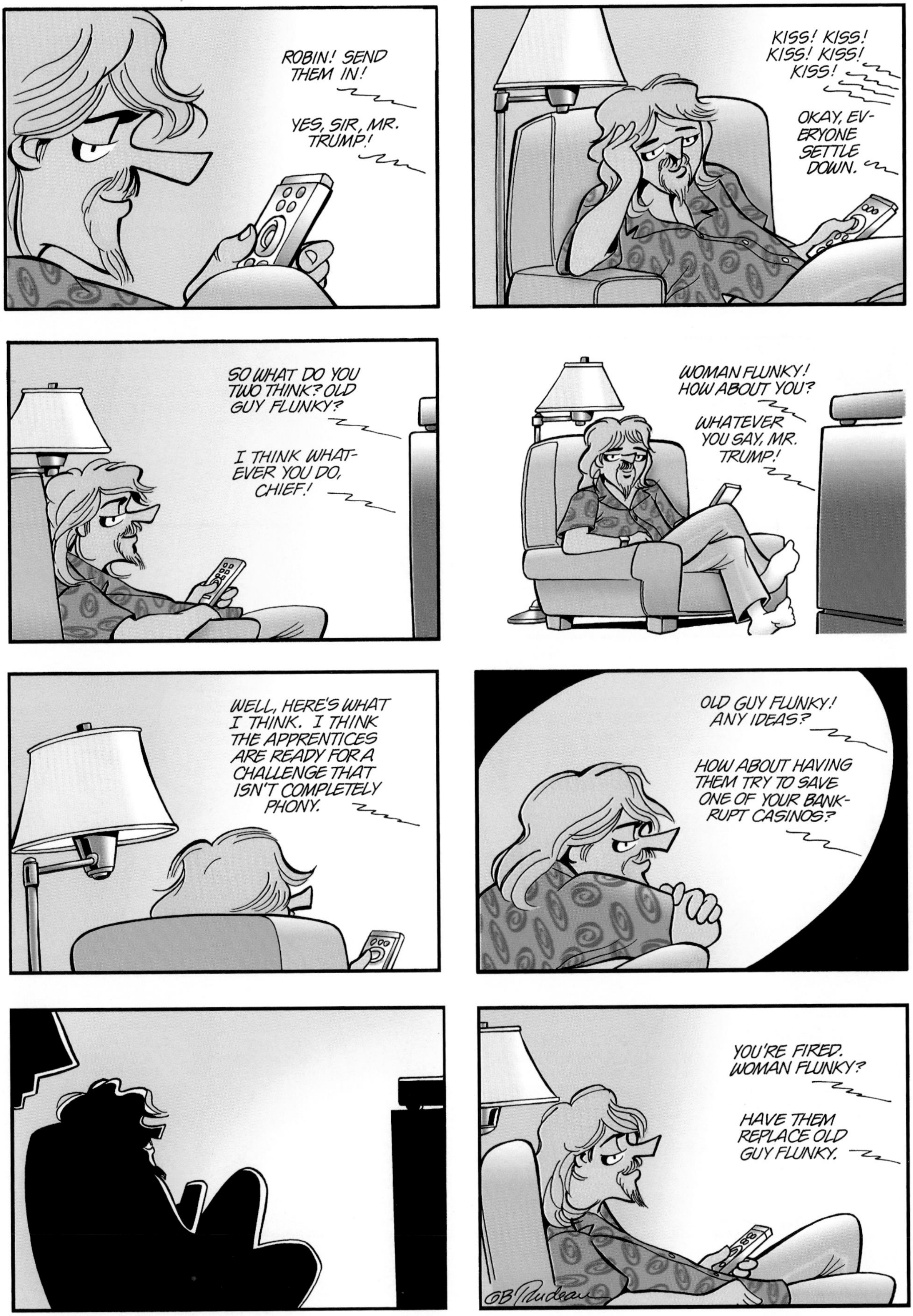
ROBIN! SEND THEM IN!
YES, SIR, MR. TRUMP!
KISS! KISS! KISS! KISS! KISS!
OKAY, EVERYONE SETTLE DOWN.
SO WHAT DO YOU TWO THINK? OLD GUY FLUNKY?
I THINK WHATEVER YOU DO, CHIEF!
WOMAN FLUNKY! HOW ABOUT YOU?
WHATEVER YOU SAY, MR. TRUMP!
WELL, HERE'S WHAT I THINK. I THINK THE APPRENTICES ARE READY FOR A CHALLENGE THAT ISN'T COMPLETELY PHONY.
OLD GUY FLUNKY! ANY IDEAS?
HOW ABOUT HAVING THEM TRY TO SAVE ONE OF YOUR BANKRUPT CASINOS?
YOU'RE FIRED. WOMAN FLUNKY?
HAVE THEM REPLACE OLD GUY FLUNKY.
©B Trudeau

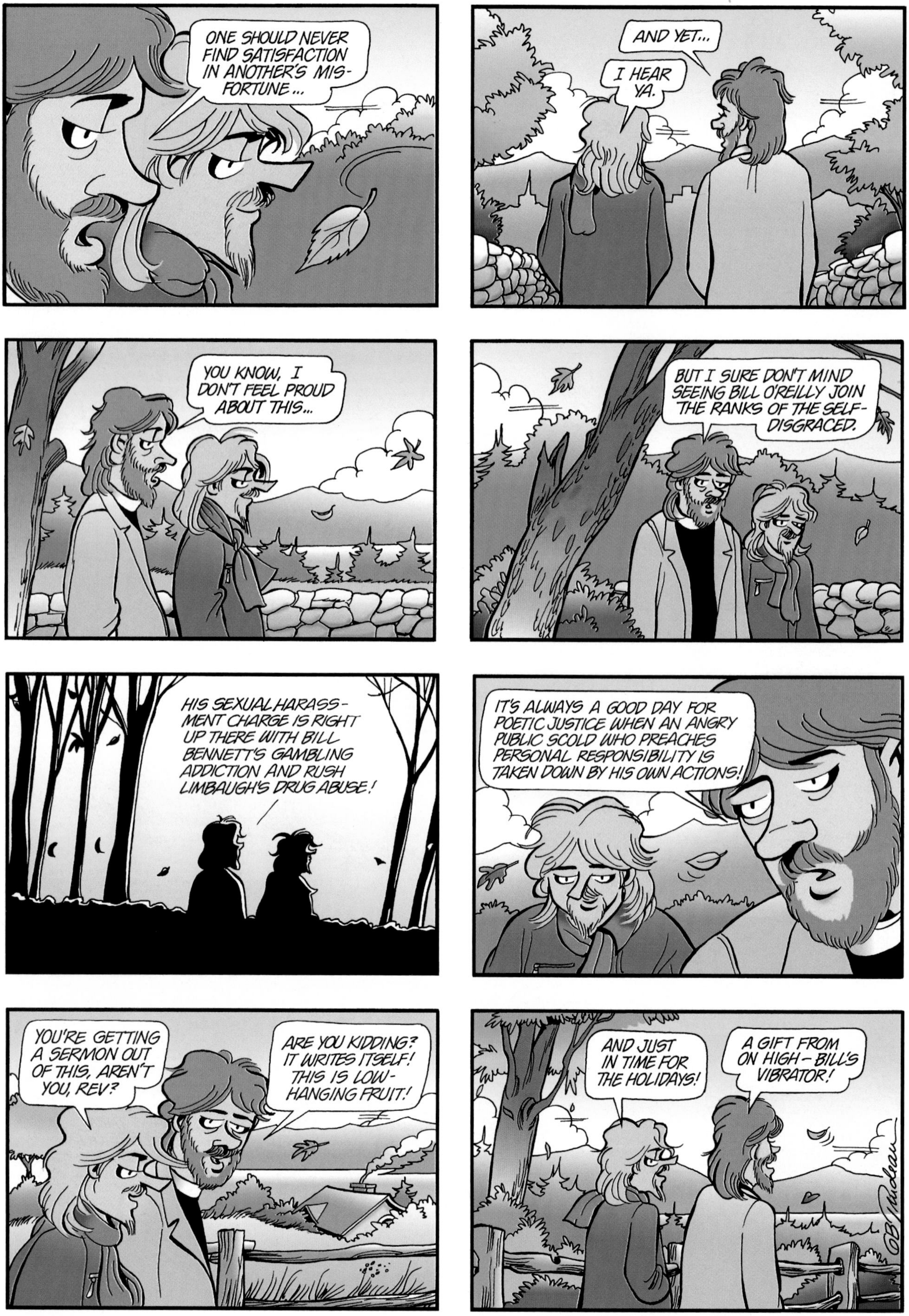
ONE SHOULD NEVER FIND SATISFACTION IN ANOTHER'S MIS-FORTUNE...
AND YET...
I HEAR YA.
YOU KNOW, I DON'T FEEL PROUD ABOUT THIS...
BUT I SURE DON'T MIND SEEING BILL O'REILLY JOIN THE RANKS OF THE SELF-DISGRACED.
HIS SEXUAL HARASS-MENT CHARGE IS RIGHT UP THERE WITH BILL BENNETT'S GAMBLING ADDICTION AND RUSH LIMBAUGH'S DRUG ABUSE!
IT'S ALWAYS A GOOD DAY FOR POETIC JUSTICE WHEN AN ANGRY PUBLIC SCOLD WHO PREACHES PERSONAL RESPONSIBILITY IS TAKEN DOWN BY HIS OWN ACTIONS!
YOU'RE GETTING A SERMON OUT OF THIS, AREN'T YOU, REV?
ARE YOU KIDDING? IT WRITES ITSELF! THIS IS LOW-HANGING FRUIT!
AND JUST IN TIME FOR THE HOLIDAYS!
A GIFT FROM ON HIGH—BILL'S VIBRATOR!
GB Trudeau

IF TO ERR IS HUMAN...
WHERE DOES THAT LEAVE ME?
GEORGE, I'VE BEEN MEANING TO ASK YOU...
UH-HUH...
ARE YOU REALLY UNABLE TO THINK OF ANY MISTAKES YOU'VE MADE? OR WAS THAT JUST CAMPAIGN TALK?
I MEAN, THE BIBLE TEACHES HUMILITY, BE-CAUSE NONE OF US IS PERFECT. WE'RE ALL HUMAN!
ARE YOU SURE YOU CAN'T THINK OF ANYTHING YOU GOT WRONG?
UM... WELL...
GB Trudeau
THAT'S FOR HISTORY TO DECIDE.
LET ME FINISH!
GEORGE! TURN THAT THING OFF!

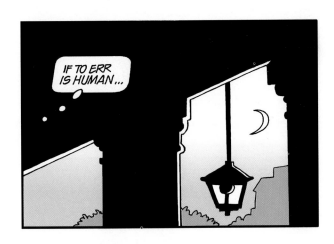

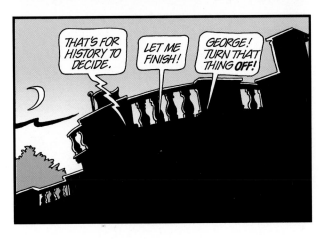

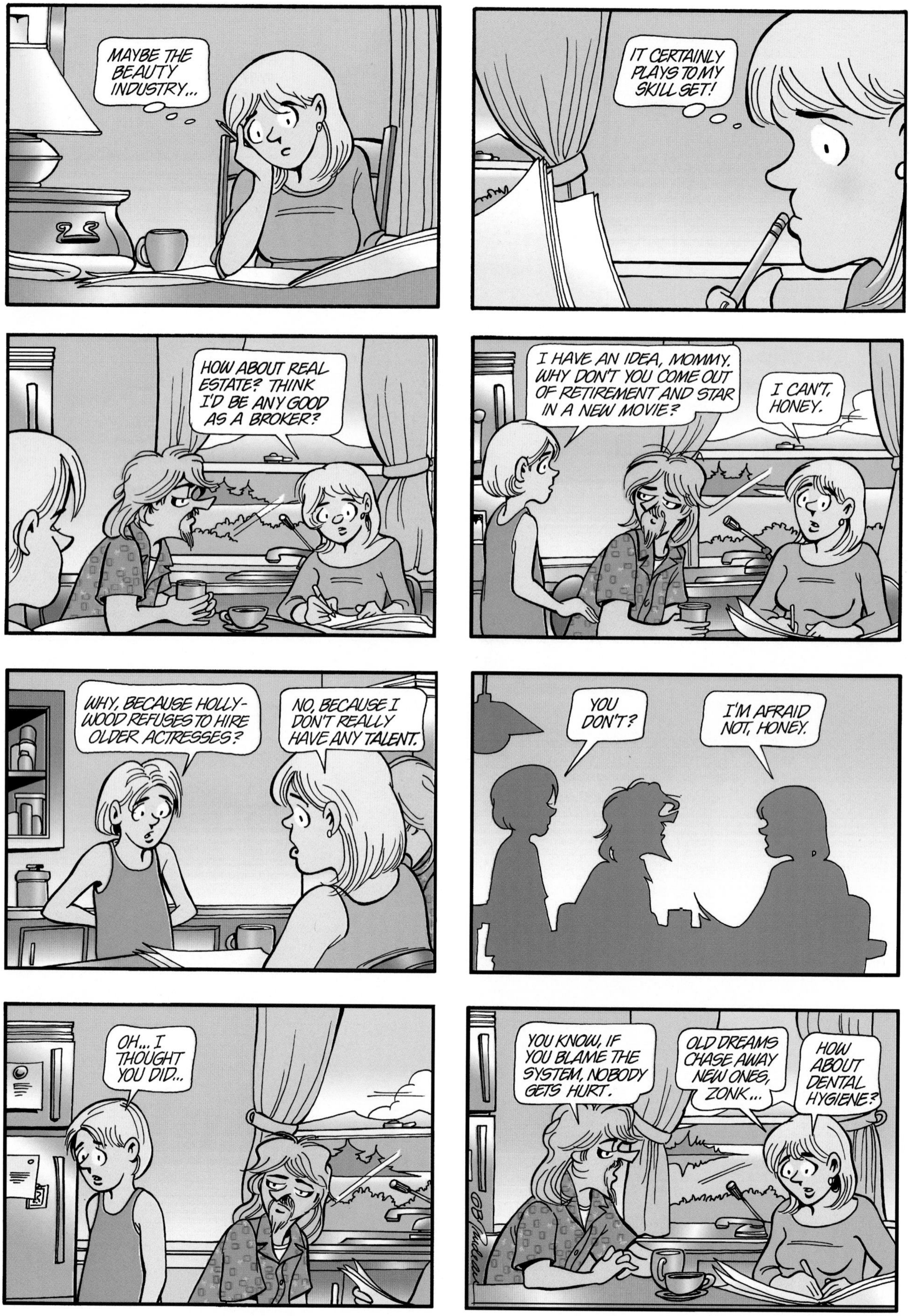
MAYBE THE BEAUTY INDUSTRY...
IT CERTAINLY PLAYS TO MY SKILL SET!
HOW ABOUT REAL ESTATE? THINK I'D BE ANY GOOD AS A BROKER?
I HAVE AN IDEA, MOMMY. WHY DON'T YOU COME OUT OF RETIREMENT AND STAR IN A NEW MOVIE?
I CAN'T, HONEY.
WHY, BECAUSE HOLLY-WOOD REFUSES TO HIRE OLDER ACTRESSES?
NO, BECAUSE I DON'T REALLY HAVE ANY TALENT.
YOU DON'T?
I'M AFRAID NOT, HONEY.
OH... I THOUGHT YOU DID...
YOU KNOW, IF YOU BLAME THE SYSTEM, NOBODY GETS HURT.
OLD DREAMS CHASE AWAY NEW ONES, ZONK...
HOW ABOUT DENTAL HYGIENE?
GB Trudeau

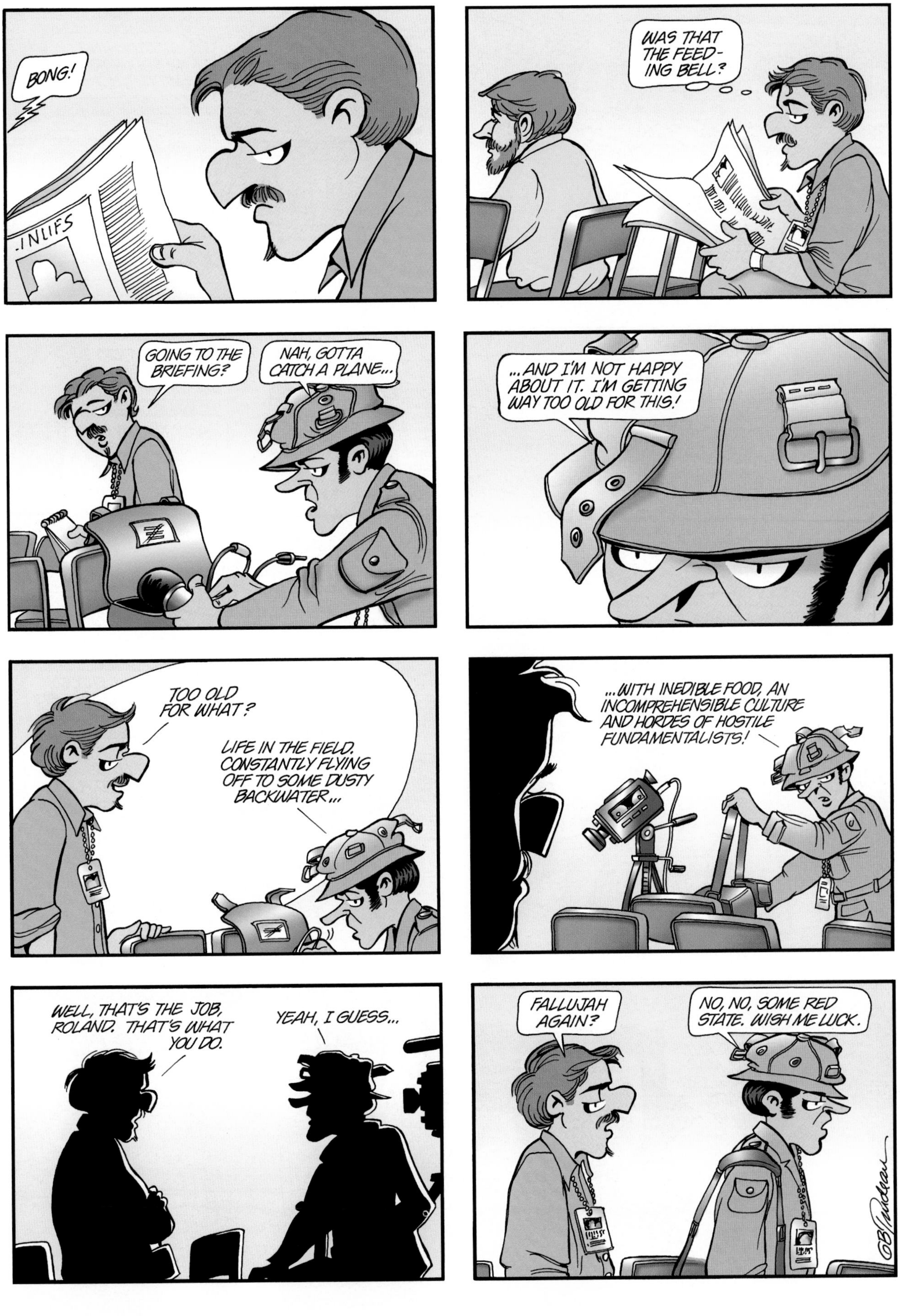
BONG!
WAS THAT THE FEED-ING BELL?
GOING TO THE BRIEFING?
NAH, GOTTA CATCH A PLANE...
...AND I'M NOT HAPPY ABOUT IT. I'M GETTING WAY TOO OLD FOR THIS!
TOO OLD FOR WHAT?
LIFE IN THE FIELD. CONSTANTLY FLYING OFF TO SOME DUSTY BACKWATER...
...WITH INEDIBLE FOOD, AN INCOMPREHENSIBLE CULTURE AND HORDES OF HOSTILE FUNDAMENTALISTS!
WELL, THAT'S THE JOB, ROLAND. THAT'S WHAT YOU DO.
YEAH, I GUESS...
FALLUJAH AGAIN?
NO, NO, SOME RED STATE. WISH ME LUCK.

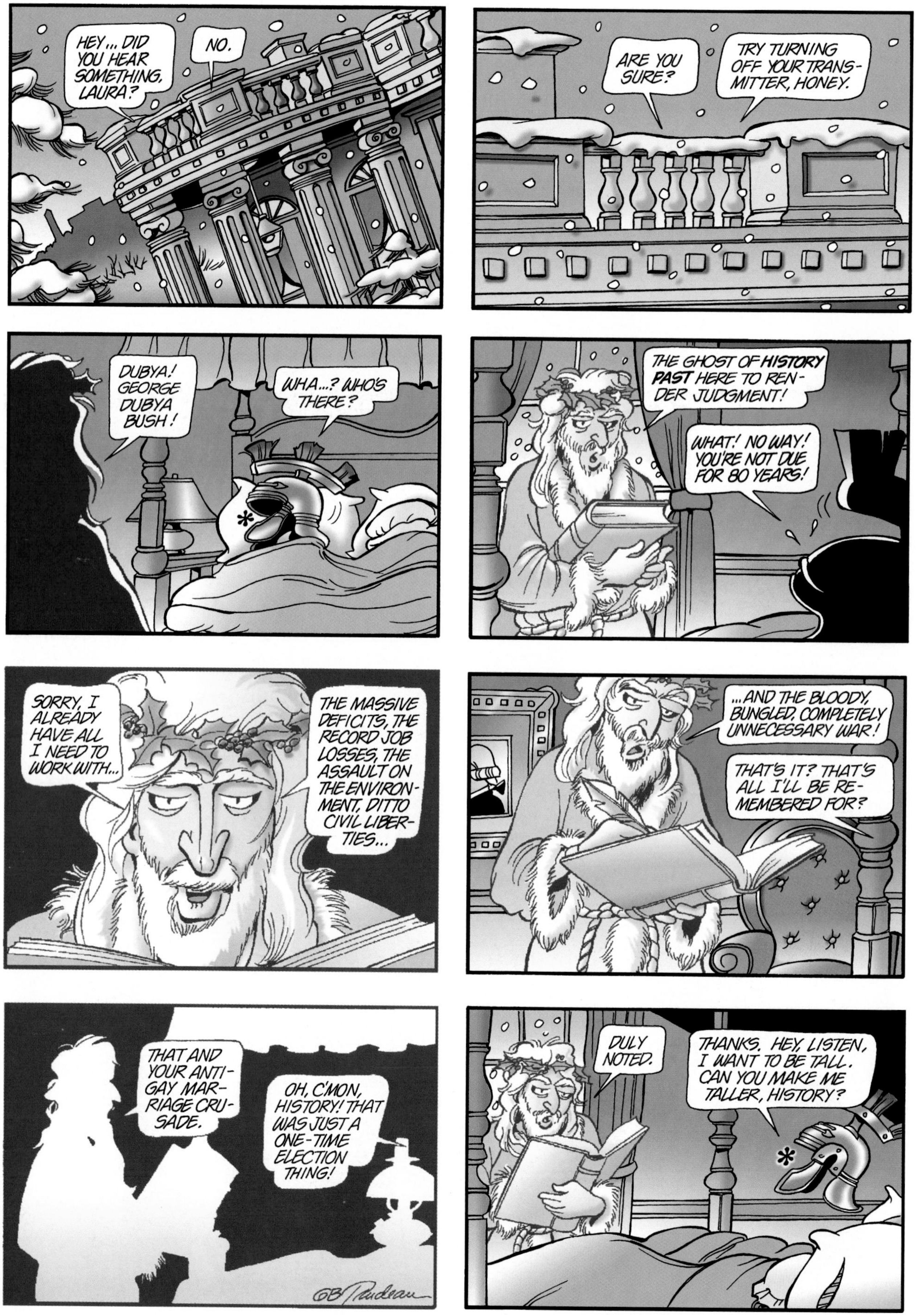
HEY... DID YOU HEAR SOMETHING, LAURA?
NO.
ARE YOU SURE?
TRY TURNING OFF YOUR TRANS-MITTER, HONEY.
DUBYA! GEORGE DUBYA BUSH!
WHA...? WHO'S THERE?
THE GHOST OF HISTORY PAST HERE TO REN-DER JUDGMENT!
WHAT! NO WAY! YOU'RE NOT DUE FOR 80 YEARS!
SORRY, I ALREADY HAVE ALL I NEED TO WORK WITH...
THE MASSIVE DEFICITS, THE RECORD JOB LOSSES, THE ASSAULT ON THE ENVIRON-MENT, DITTO CIVIL LIBER-TIES...
...AND THE BLOODY, BUNGLED, COMPLETELY UNNECESSARY WAR!
THAT'S IT? THAT'S ALL I'LL BE RE-MEMBERED FOR?
THAT AND YOUR ANTI-GAY MAR-RIAGE CRU-SADE.
OH, C'MON, HISTORY! THAT WAS JUST A ONE-TIME ELECTION THING!
DULY NOTED.
THANKS. HEY, LISTEN, I WANT TO BE TALL. CAN YOU MAKE ME TALLER, HISTORY?

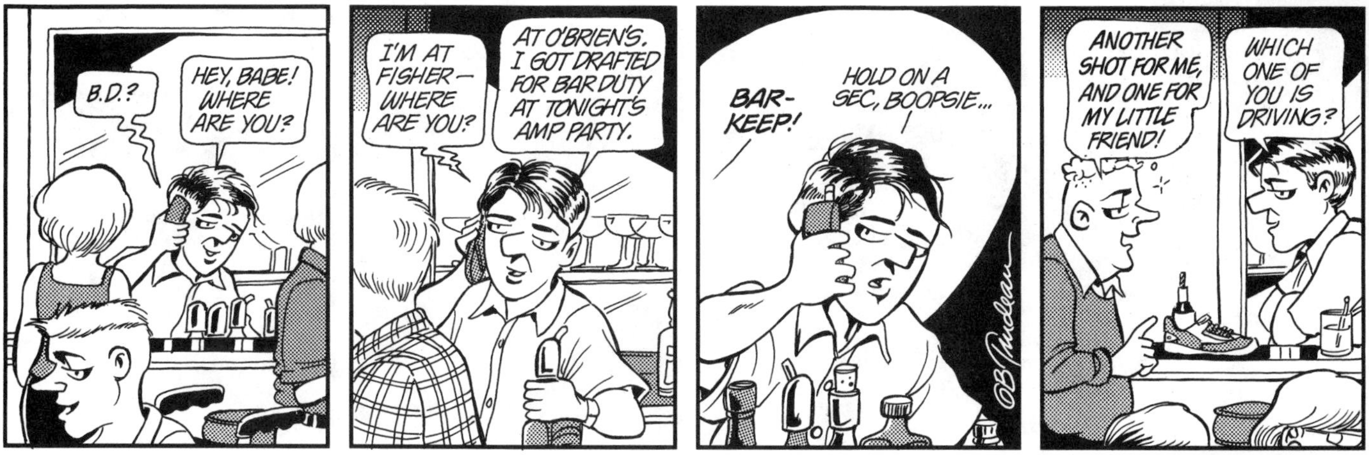
B.D.?
HEY, BABE! WHERE ARE YOU?
I'M AT FISHER— WHERE ARE YOU?
AT O'BRIEN'S. I GOT DRAFTED FOR BAR DUTY AT TONIGHT'S AMP PARTY.
BAR-KEEP!
HOLD ON A SEC, BOOPSIE...
ANOTHER SHOT FOR ME, AND ONE FOR MY LITTLE FRIEND!
WHICH ONE OF YOU IS DRIVING?

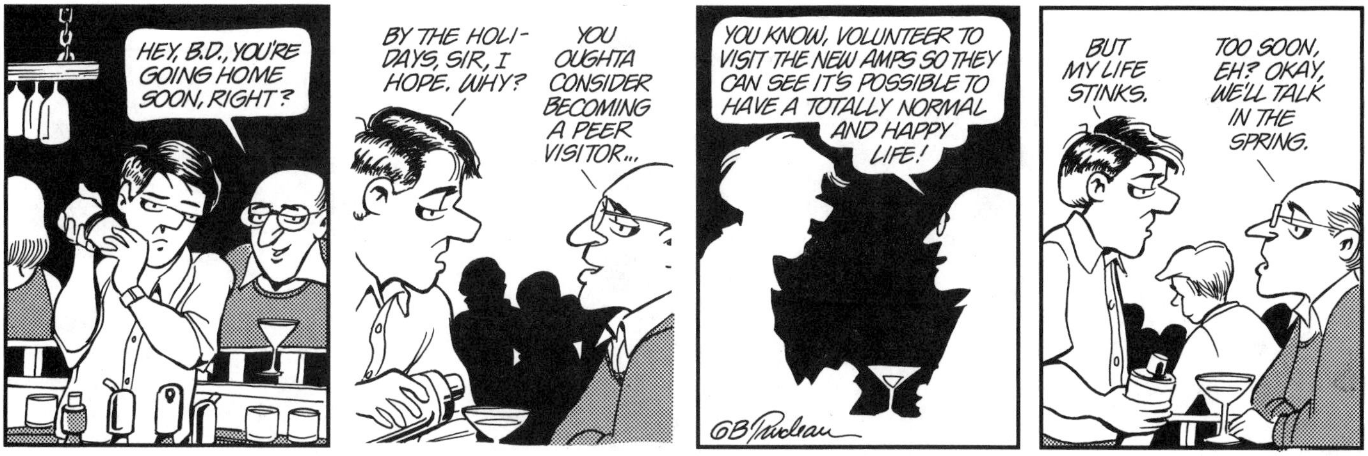
HEY, B.D., YOU'RE GOING HOME SOON, RIGHT?
BY THE HOLI-DAYS, SIR, I HOPE. WHY?
YOU OUGHTA CONSIDER BECOMING A PEER VISITOR...
YOU KNOW, VOLUNTEER TO VISIT THE NEW AMPS SO THEY CAN SEE IT'S POSSIBLE TO HAVE A TOTALLY NORMAL AND HAPPY LIFE!
BUT MY LIFE STINKS.
TOO SOON, EH? OKAY, WE'LL TALK IN THE SPRING.

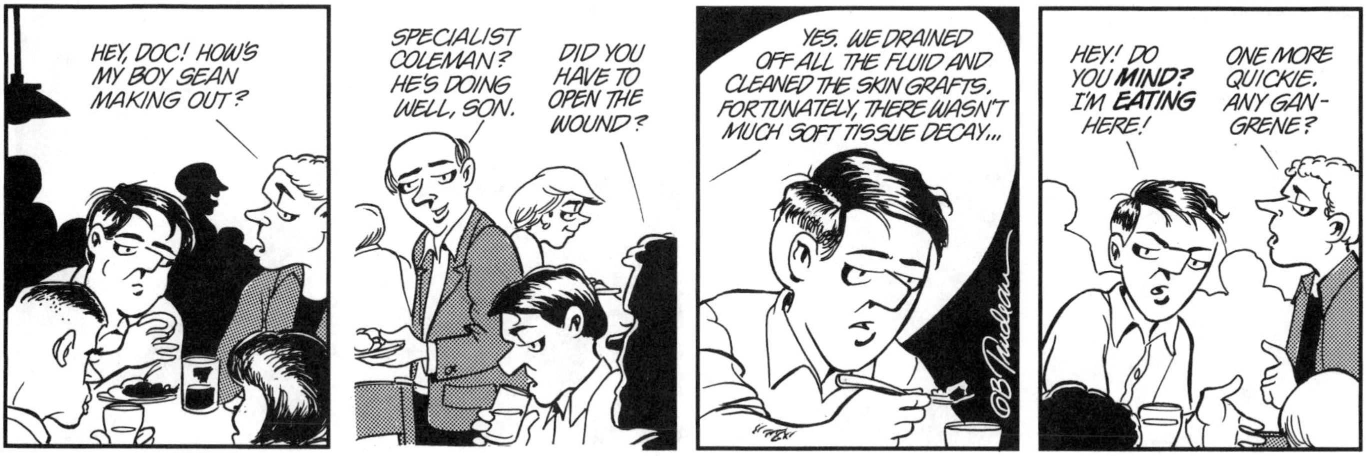
HEY, DOC! HOW'S MY BOY SEAN MAKING OUT?
SPECIALIST COLEMAN? HE'S DOING WELL, SON.
DID YOU HAVE TO OPEN THE WOUND?
YES. WE DRAINED OFF ALL THE FLUID AND CLEANED THE SKIN GRAFTS. FORTUNATELY, THERE WASN'T MUCH SOFT TISSUE DECAY...
HEY! DO YOU MIND? I'M EATING HERE!
ONE MORE QUICKIE. ANY GAN-GRENE?

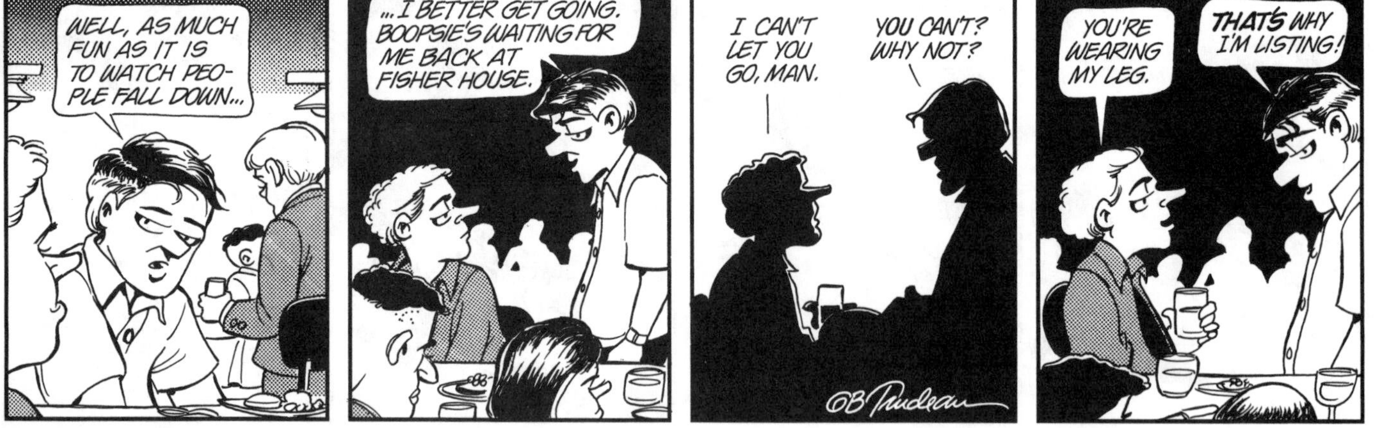
WELL, AS MUCH FUN AS IT IS TO WATCH PEOPLE FALL DOWN...
...I BETTER GET GOING. BOOPSIE'S WAITING FOR ME BACK AT FISHER HOUSE.
I CAN'T LET YOU GO, MAN.
YOU CAN'T? WHY NOT?
YOU'RE WEARING MY LEG.
THAT'S WHY I'M LISTING!

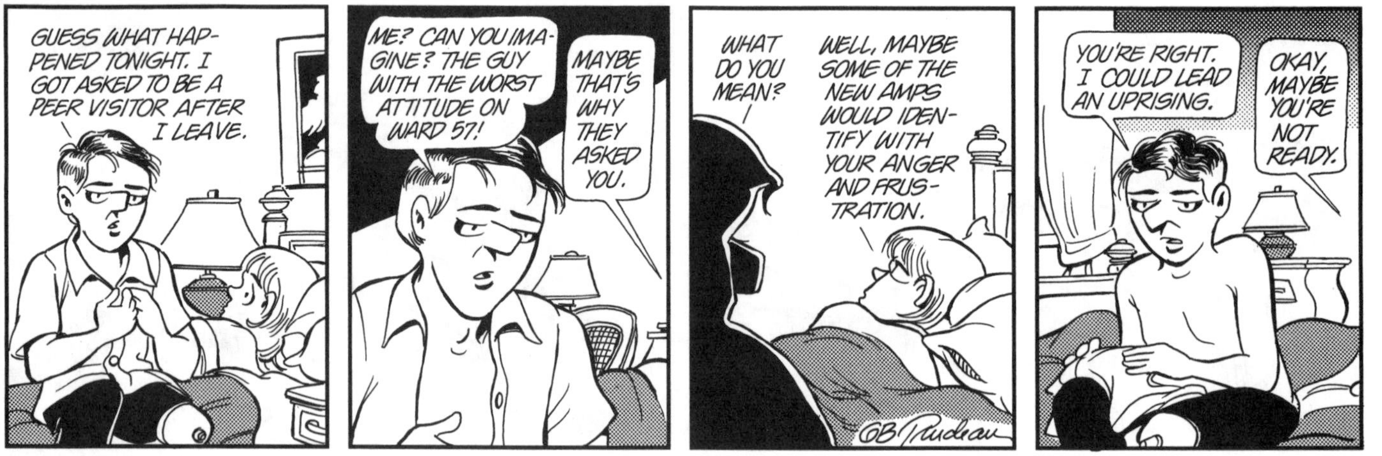
GUESS WHAT HAPPENED TONIGHT. I GOT ASKED TO BE A PEER VISITOR AFTER I LEAVE.
ME? CAN YOU IMAGINE? THE GUY WITH THE WORST ATTITUDE ON WARD 57!
MAYBE THAT'S WHY THEY ASKED YOU.
WHAT DO YOU MEAN?
WELL, MAYBE SOME OF THE NEW AMPS WOULD IDENTIFY WITH YOUR ANGER AND FRUSTRATION.
YOU'RE RIGHT. I COULD LEAD AN UPRISING.
OKAY, MAYBE YOU'RE NOT READY.

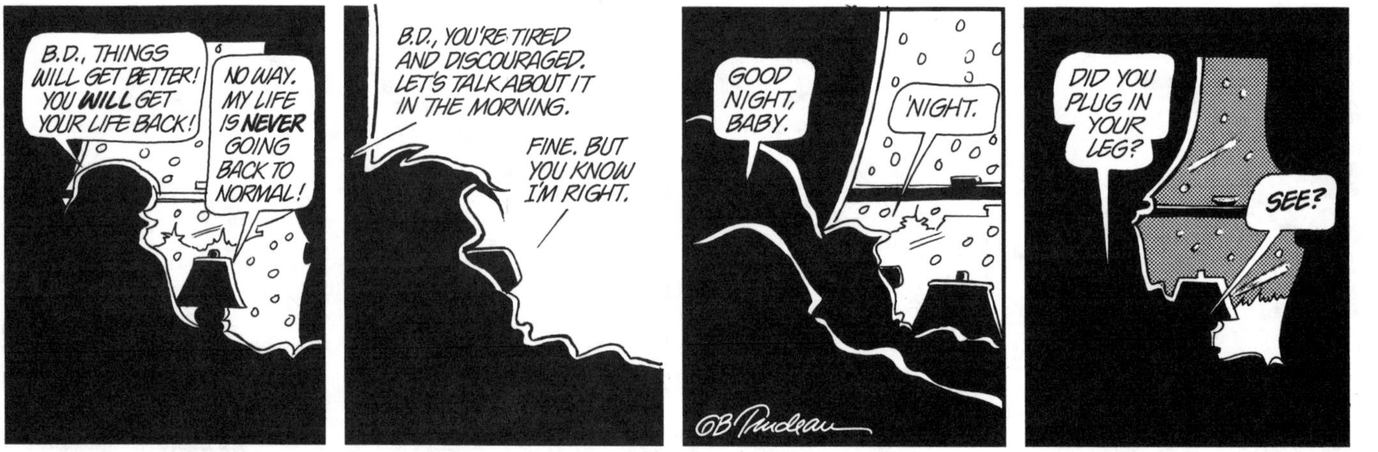
B.D., THINGS WILL GET BETTER! YOU WILL GET YOUR LIFE BACK!
NO WAY. MY LIFE IS NEVER GOING BACK TO NORMAL!
B.D., YOU'RE TIRED AND DISCOURAGED. LET'S TALK ABOUT IT IN THE MORNING.
FINE. BUT YOU KNOW I'M RIGHT.
GOOD NIGHT, BABY.
'NIGHT.
DID YOU PLUG IN YOUR LEG?
SEE?

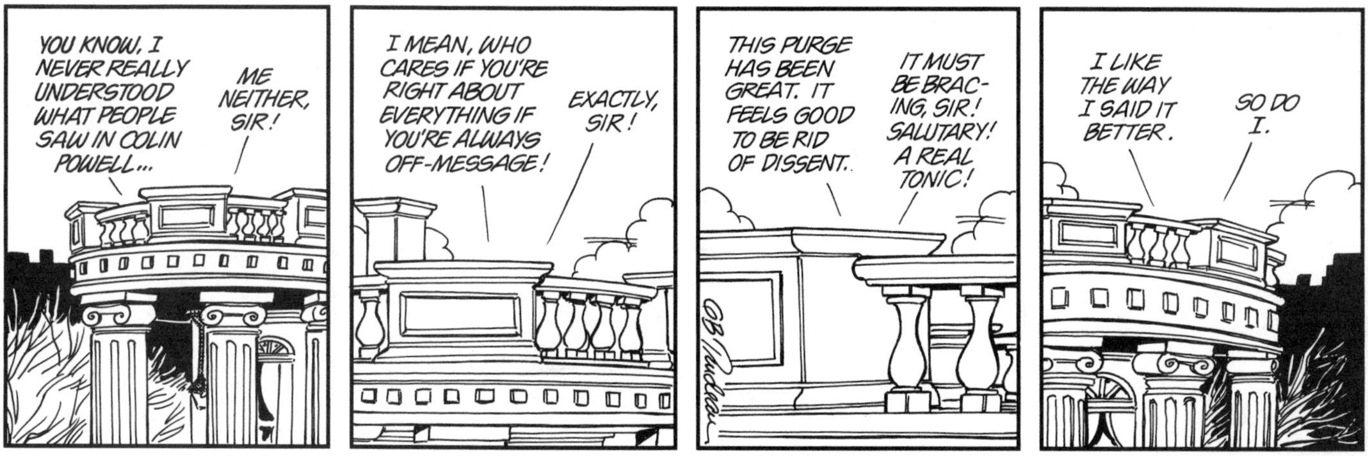
YOU KNOW, I NEVER REALLY UNDERSTOOD WHAT PEOPLE SAW IN COLIN POWELL...
ME NEITHER, SIR!
I MEAN, WHO CARES IF YOU'RE RIGHT ABOUT EVERYTHING IF YOU'RE ALWAYS OFF-MESSAGE!
EXACTLY, SIR!
THIS PURGE HAS BEEN GREAT. IT FEELS GOOD TO BE RID OF DISSENT..
IT MUST BE BRACING, SIR! SALUTARY! A REAL TONIC!
I LIKE THE WAY I SAID IT BETTER.
SO DO I.
GB Trudeau

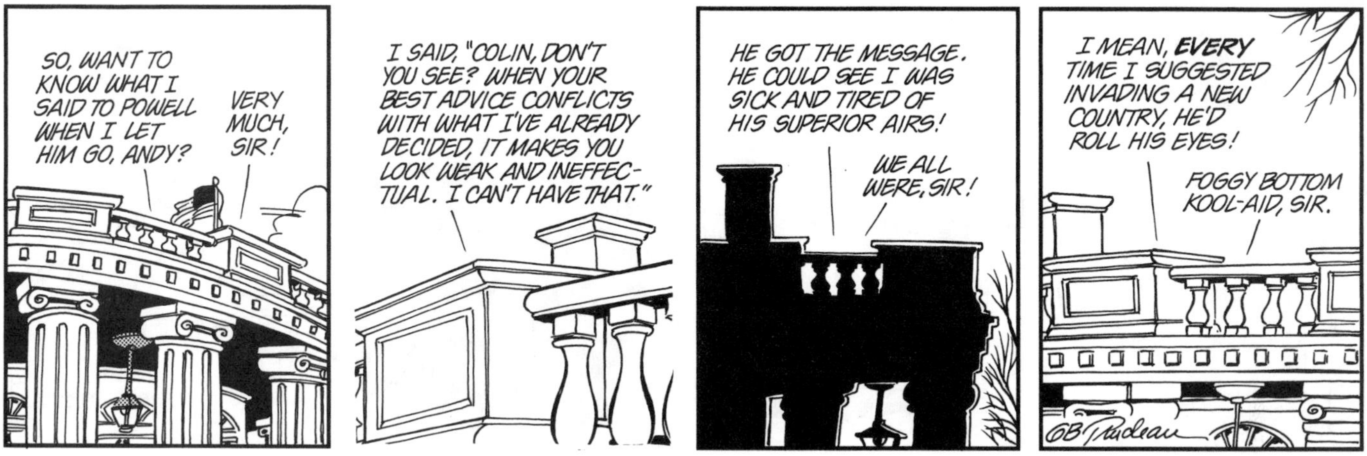
SO, WANT TO KNOW WHAT I SAID TO POWELL WHEN I LET HIM GO, ANDY?
VERY MUCH, SIR!
I SAID, "COLIN, DON'T YOU SEE? WHEN YOUR BEST ADVICE CONFLICTS WITH WHAT I'VE ALREADY DECIDED, IT MAKES YOU LOOK WEAK AND INEFFECTUAL. I CAN'T HAVE THAT."
HE GOT THE MESSAGE. HE COULD SEE I WAS SICK AND TIRED OF HIS SUPERIOR AIRS!
WE ALL WERE, SIR!
I MEAN, EVERY TIME I SUGGESTED INVADING A NEW COUNTRY, HE'D ROLL HIS EYES!
FOGGY BOTTOM KOOL-AID, SIR.
GB Trudeau

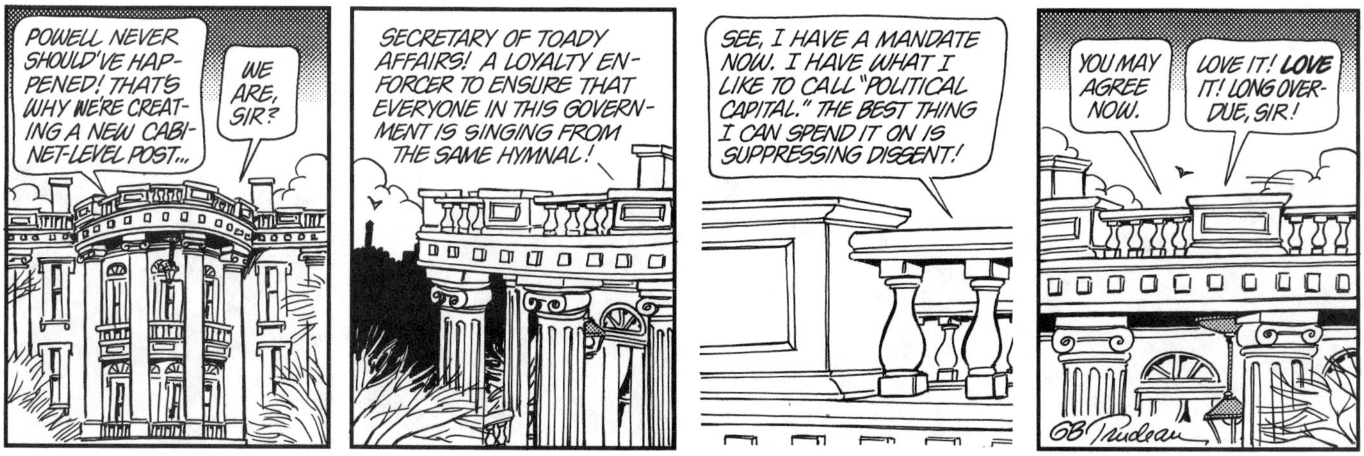
POWELL NEVER SHOULD'VE HAPPENED! THAT'S WHY WE'RE CREATING A NEW CABINET-LEVEL POST...
WE ARE, SIR?
SECRETARY OF TOADY AFFAIRS! A LOYALTY ENFORCER TO ENSURE THAT EVERYONE IN THIS GOVERNMENT IS SINGING FROM THE SAME HYMNAL!
SEE, I HAVE A MANDATE NOW. I HAVE WHAT I LIKE TO CALL "POLITICAL CAPITAL." THE BEST THING I CAN SPEND IT ON IS SUPPRESSING DISSENT!
YOU MAY AGREE NOW.
LOVE IT! LOVE IT! LONG OVERDUE, SIR!
GB Trudeau

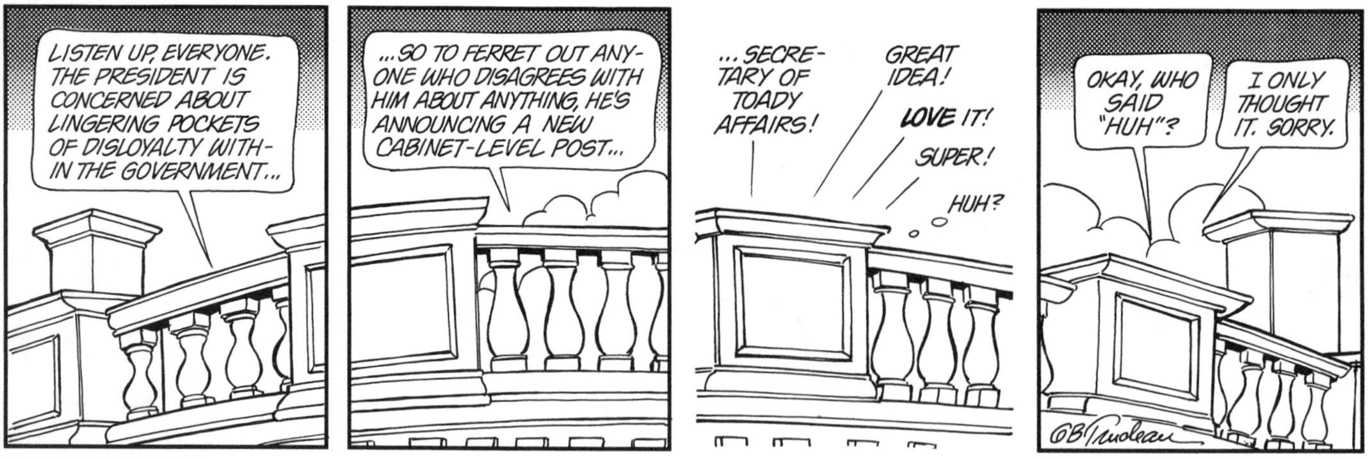
LISTEN UP, EVERYONE. THE PRESIDENT IS CONCERNED ABOUT LINGERING POCKETS OF DISLOYALTY WITHIN THE GOVERNMENT...
...SO TO FERRET OUT ANYONE WHO DISAGREES WITH HIM ABOUT ANYTHING, HE'S ANNOUNCING A NEW CABINET-LEVEL POST...
...SECRETARY OF TOADY AFFAIRS!
GREAT IDEA!
LOVE IT!
SUPER!
HUH?
OKAY, WHO SAID "HUH"?
I ONLY THOUGHT IT. SORRY.
©B. Trudeau

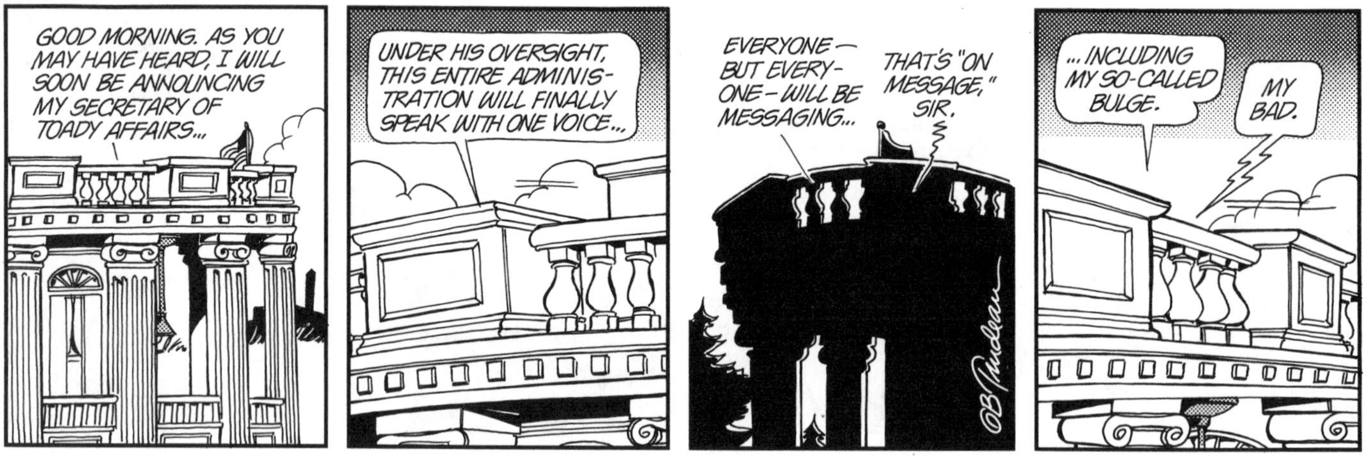
GOOD MORNING. AS YOU MAY HAVE HEARD, I WILL SOON BE ANNOUNCING MY SECRETARY OF TOADY AFFAIRS...
UNDER HIS OVERSIGHT, THIS ENTIRE ADMINISTRATION WILL FINALLY SPEAK WITH ONE VOICE...
EVERYONE — BUT EVERYONE — WILL BE MESSAGING...
THAT'S "ON MESSAGE," SIR.
...INCLUDING MY SO-CALLED BULGE.
MY BAD.
©B. Trudeau

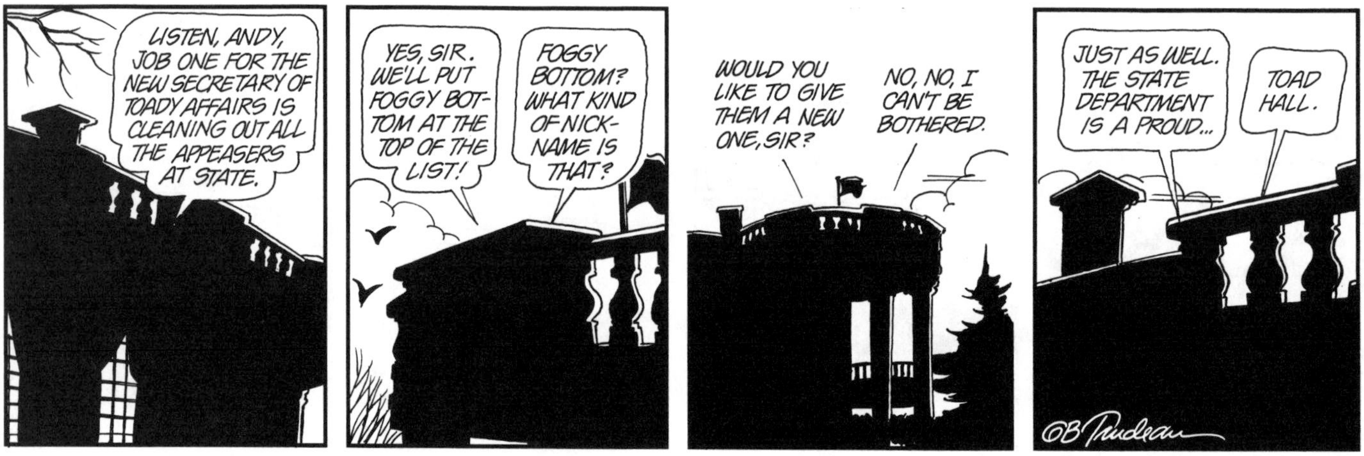
LISTEN, ANDY, JOB ONE FOR THE NEW SECRETARY OF TOADY AFFAIRS IS CLEANING OUT ALL THE APPEASERS AT STATE.
YES, SIR. WE'LL PUT FOGGY BOTTOM AT THE TOP OF THE LIST!
FOGGY BOTTOM? WHAT KIND OF NICKNAME IS THAT?
WOULD YOU LIKE TO GIVE THEM A NEW ONE, SIR?
NO, NO, I CAN'T BE BOTHERED.
JUST AS WELL. THE STATE DEPARTMENT IS A PROUD...
TOAD HALL.
©B. Trudeau

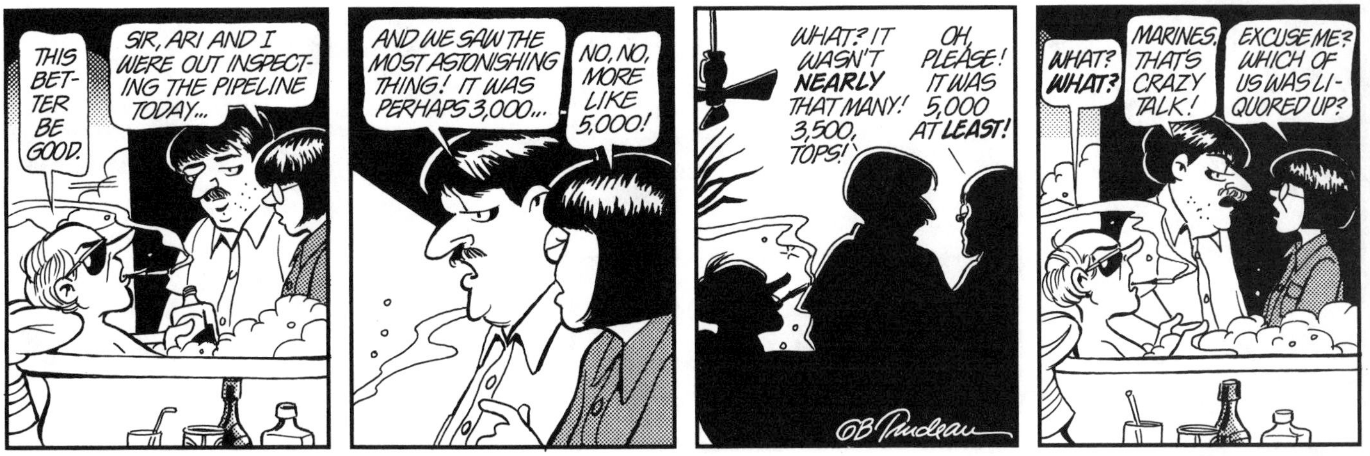
THIS BET-TER BE GOOD.
SIR, ARI AND I WERE OUT INSPECT-ING THE PIPELINE TODAY...
AND WE SAW THE MOST ASTONISHING THING! IT WAS PERHAPS 3,000...
NO, NO, MORE LIKE 5,000!
WHAT? IT WASN'T **NEARLY** THAT MANY! 3,500, TOPS!
OH, PLEASE! IT WAS 5,000 AT **LEAST!**
WHAT? WHAT?
MARINES. THAT'S CRAZY TALK!
EXCUSE ME? WHICH OF US WAS LI-QUORED UP?

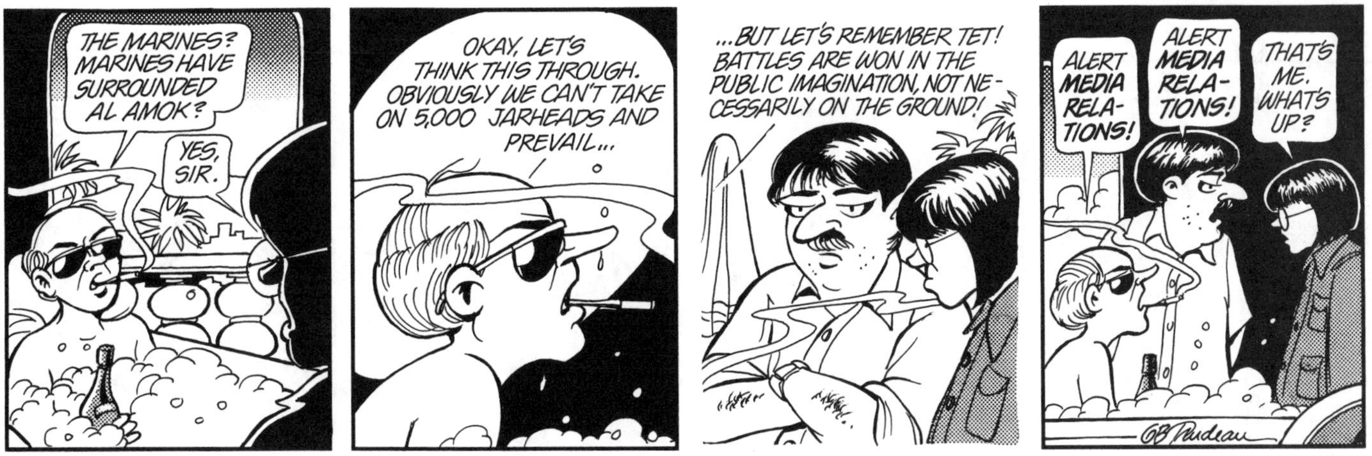
THE MARINES? MARINES HAVE SURROUNDED AL AMOK?
YES, SIR.
OKAY, LET'S THINK THIS THROUGH. OBVIOUSLY WE CAN'T TAKE ON 5,000 JARHEADS AND PREVAIL...
...BUT LET'S REMEMBER TET! BATTLES ARE WON IN THE PUBLIC IMAGINATION, NOT NE-CESSARILY ON THE GROUND!
ALERT **MEDIA RELA-TIONS!**
ALERT **MEDIA RELA-TIONS!**
THAT'S ME. WHAT'S UP?

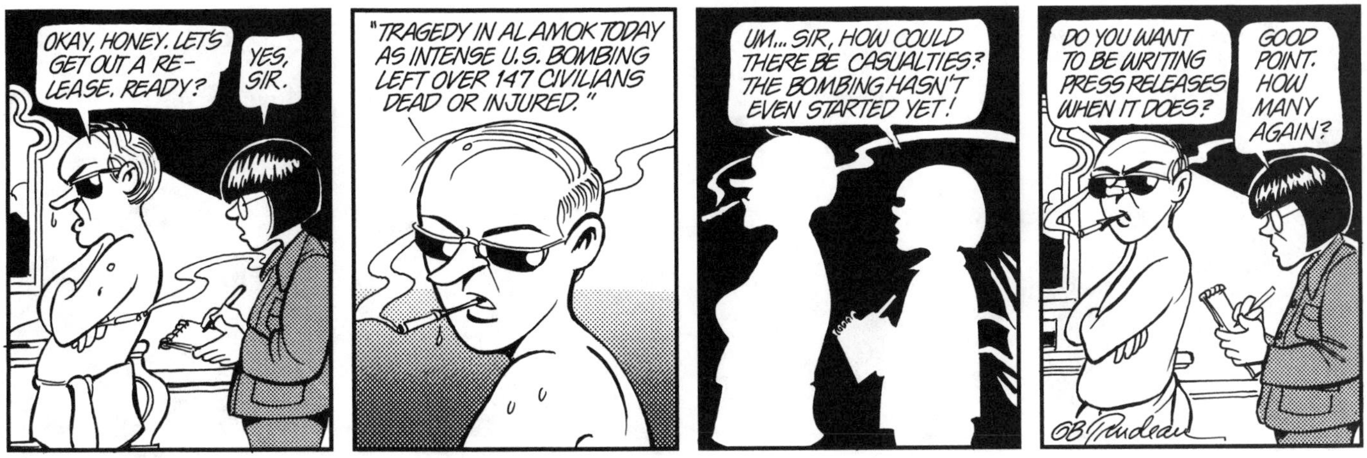
OKAY, HONEY. LET'S GET OUT A RE-LEASE. READY?
YES, SIR.
"TRAGEDY IN AL AMOK TODAY AS INTENSE U.S. BOMBING LEFT OVER 147 CIVILIANS DEAD OR INJURED."
UM... SIR, HOW COULD THERE BE CASUALTIES? THE BOMBING HASN'T EVEN STARTED YET!
DO YOU WANT TO BE WRITING PRESS RELEASES WHEN IT DOES?
GOOD POINT. HOW MANY AGAIN?

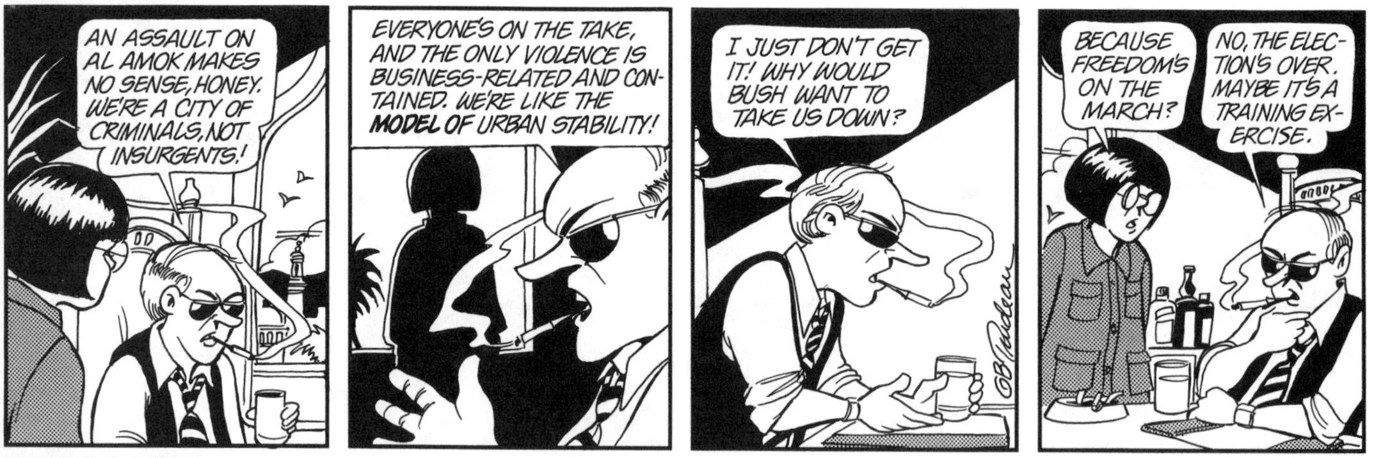
AN ASSAULT ON AL AMOK MAKES NO SENSE, HONEY. WE'RE A CITY OF CRIMINALS, NOT INSURGENTS!
EVERYONE'S ON THE TAKE, AND THE ONLY VIOLENCE IS BUSINESS-RELATED AND CONTAINED. WE'RE LIKE THE MODEL OF URBAN STABILITY!
I JUST DON'T GET IT! WHY WOULD BUSH WANT TO TAKE US DOWN?
BECAUSE FREEDOM'S ON THE MARCH?
NO, THE ELECTION'S OVER. MAYBE IT'S A TRAINING EXERCISE.

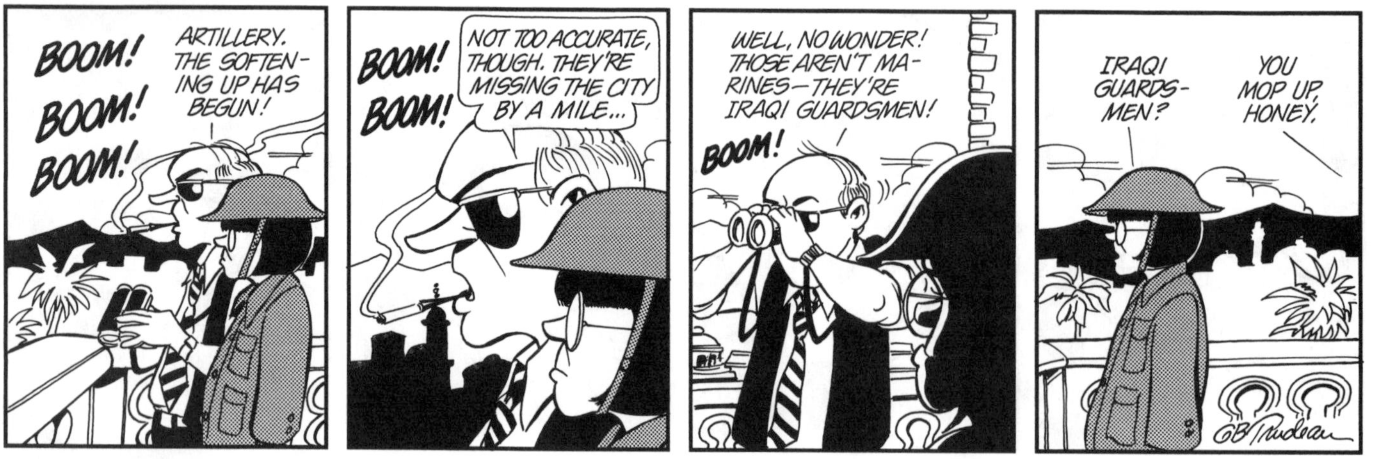
BOOM! BOOM! BOOM!
ARTILLERY. THE SOFTENING UP HAS BEGUN!
BOOM! BOOM!
NOT TOO ACCURATE, THOUGH. THEY'RE MISSING THE CITY BY A MILE...
BOOM!
WELL, NO WONDER! THOSE AREN'T MARINES—THEY'RE IRAQI GUARDSMEN!
IRAQI GUARDSMEN?
YOU MOP UP, HONEY.

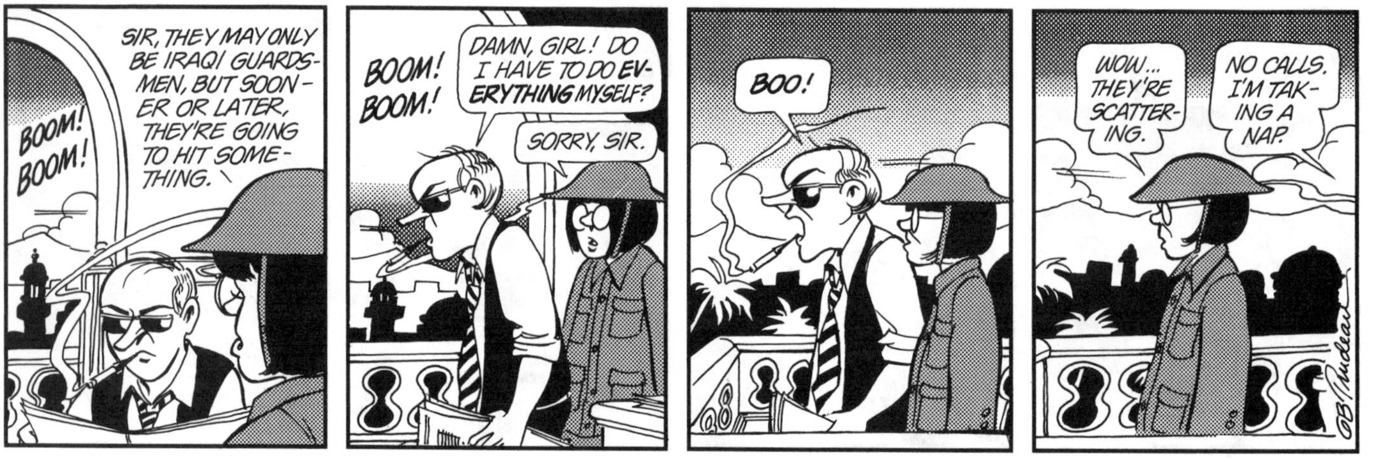
BOOM! BOOM!
SIR, THEY MAY ONLY BE IRAQI GUARDSMEN, BUT SOONER OR LATER, THEY'RE GOING TO HIT SOMETHING.
BOOM! BOOM!
DAMN, GIRL! DO I HAVE TO DO EVERYTHING MYSELF?
SORRY, SIR.
BOO!
WOW... THEY'RE SCATTERING.
NO CALLS. I'M TAKING A NAP.

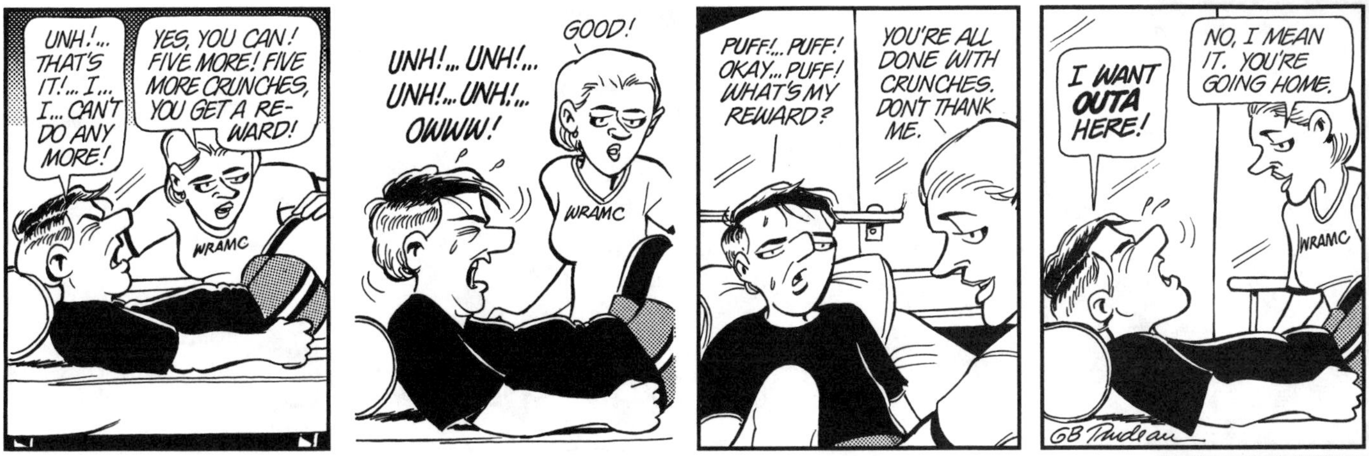
UNH!... THAT'S IT!... I... I... CAN'T DO ANY MORE!
YES, YOU CAN! FIVE MORE! FIVE MORE CRUNCHES, YOU GET A RE-WARD!
WRAMC
GOOD!
UNH!... UNH!... UNH!... UNH!... OWWW!
WRAMC
PUFF!... PUFF! OKAY... PUFF! WHAT'S MY REWARD?
YOU'RE ALL DONE WITH CRUNCHES. DON'T THANK ME.
I WANT OUTA HERE!
NO, I MEAN IT. YOU'RE GOING HOME.
WRAMC

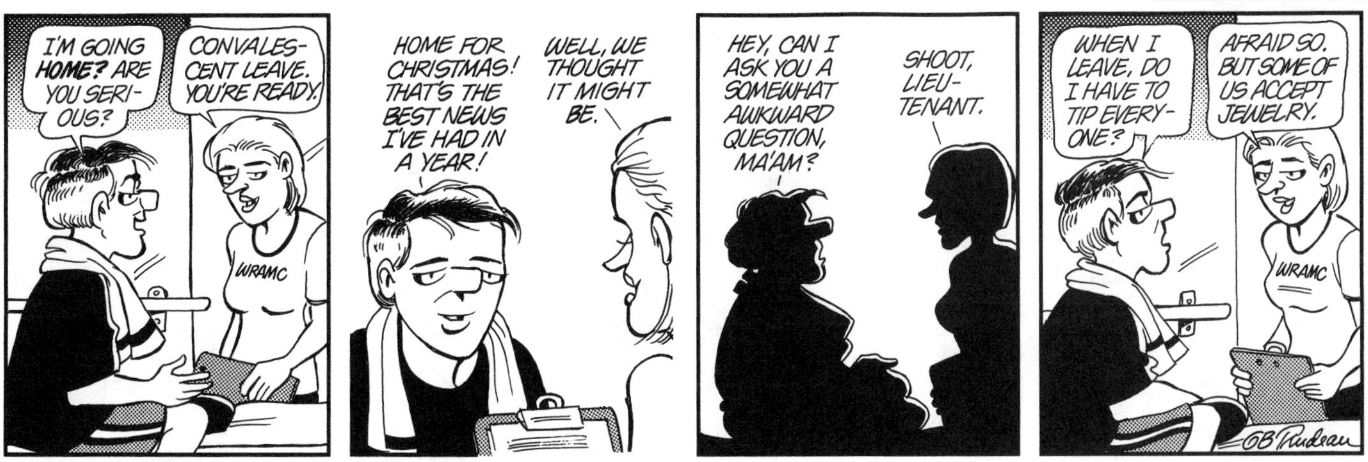
I'M GOING HOME? ARE YOU SERI-OUS?
CONVALES-CENT LEAVE. YOU'RE READY.
WRAMC
HOME FOR CHRISTMAS! THAT'S THE BEST NEWS I'VE HAD IN A YEAR!
WELL, WE THOUGHT IT MIGHT BE.
HEY, CAN I ASK YOU A SOMEWHAT AWKWARD QUESTION, MA'AM?
SHOOT, LIEU-TENANT.
WHEN I LEAVE, DO I HAVE TO TIP EVERY-ONE?
AFRAID SO. BUT SOME OF US ACCEPT JEWELRY.
WRAMC

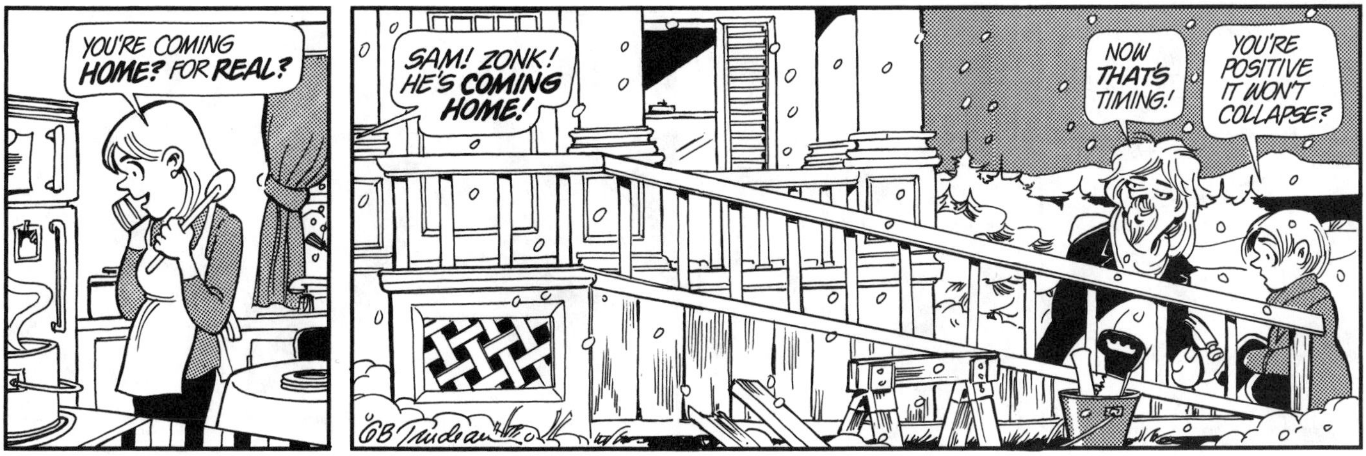
YOU'RE COMING HOME? FOR REAL?
SAM! ZONK! HE'S COMING HOME!
NOW THAT'S TIMING!
YOU'RE POSITIVE IT WON'T COLLAPSE?

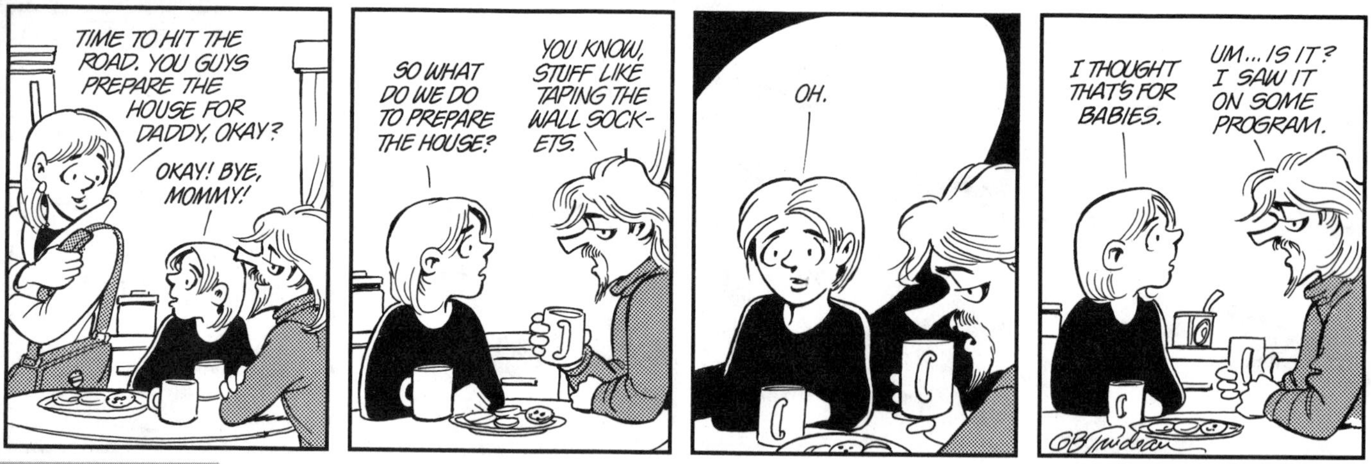
TIME TO HIT THE ROAD. YOU GUYS PREPARE THE HOUSE FOR DADDY, OKAY?
OKAY! BYE, MOMMY!
SO WHAT DO WE DO TO PREPARE THE HOUSE?
YOU KNOW, STUFF LIKE TAPING THE WALL SOCKETS.
OH.
I THOUGHT THAT'S FOR BABIES.
UM... IS IT? I SAW IT ON SOME PROGRAM.
GB Trudeau

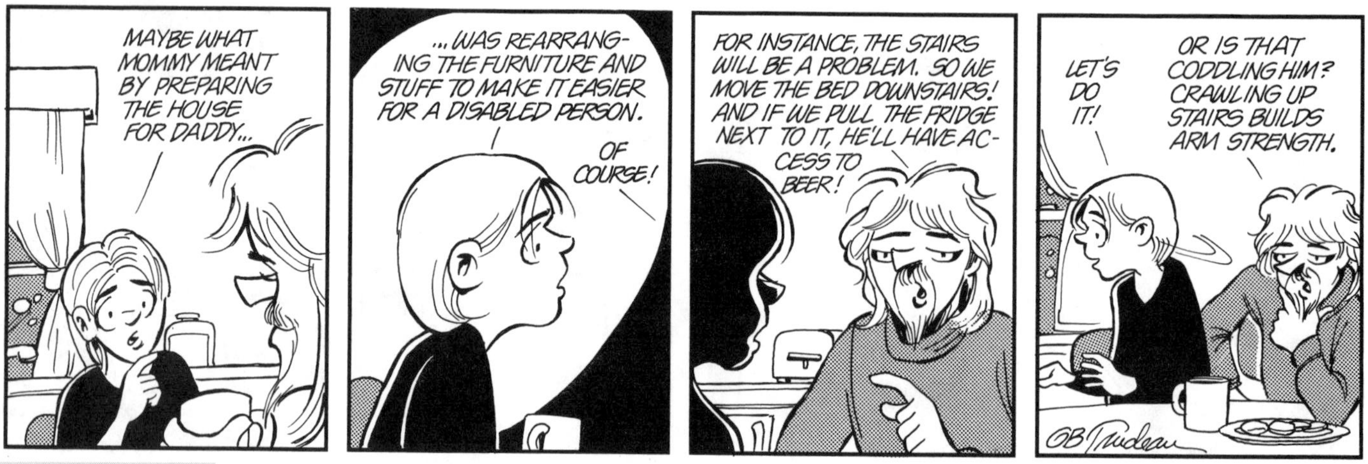
MAYBE WHAT MOMMY MEANT BY PREPARING THE HOUSE FOR DADDY...
...WAS REARRANGING THE FURNITURE AND STUFF TO MAKE IT EASIER FOR A DISABLED PERSON.
OF COURSE!
FOR INSTANCE, THE STAIRS WILL BE A PROBLEM. SO WE MOVE THE BED DOWNSTAIRS! AND IF WE PULL THE FRIDGE NEXT TO IT, HE'LL HAVE ACCESS TO BEER!
LET'S DO IT!
OR IS THAT CODDLING HIM? CRAWLING UP STAIRS BUILDS ARM STRENGTH.
GB Trudeau

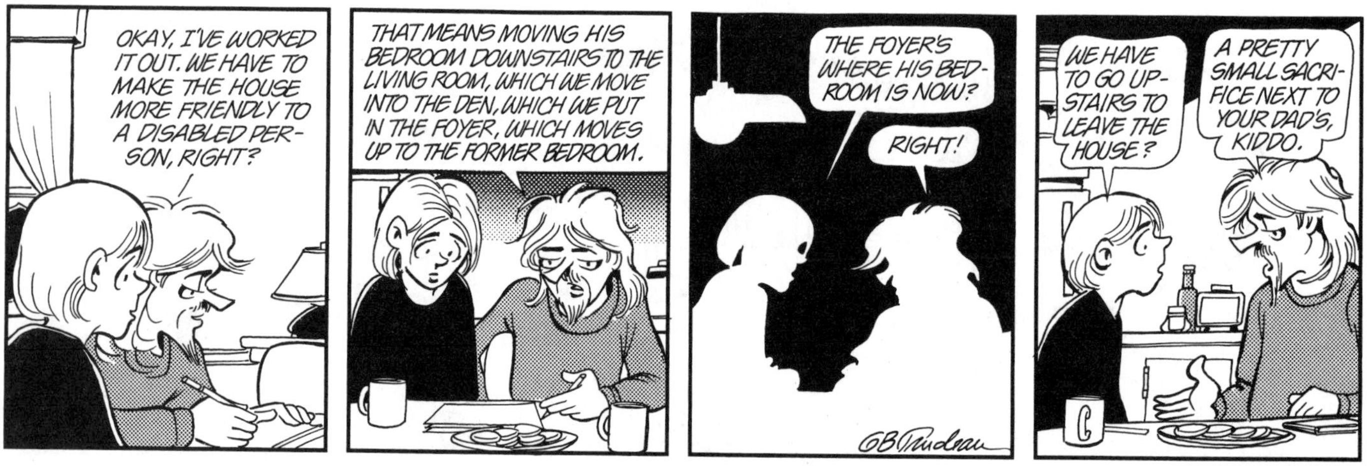
OKAY, I'VE WORKED IT OUT. WE HAVE TO MAKE THE HOUSE MORE FRIENDLY TO A DISABLED PERSON, RIGHT?
THAT MEANS MOVING HIS BEDROOM DOWNSTAIRS TO THE LIVING ROOM, WHICH WE MOVE INTO THE DEN, WHICH WE PUT IN THE FOYER, WHICH MOVES UP TO THE FORMER BEDROOM.
THE FOYER'S WHERE HIS BEDROOM IS NOW?
RIGHT!
WE HAVE TO GO UPSTAIRS TO LEAVE THE HOUSE?
A PRETTY SMALL SACRIFICE NEXT TO YOUR DAD'S, KIDDO.
GB Trudeau

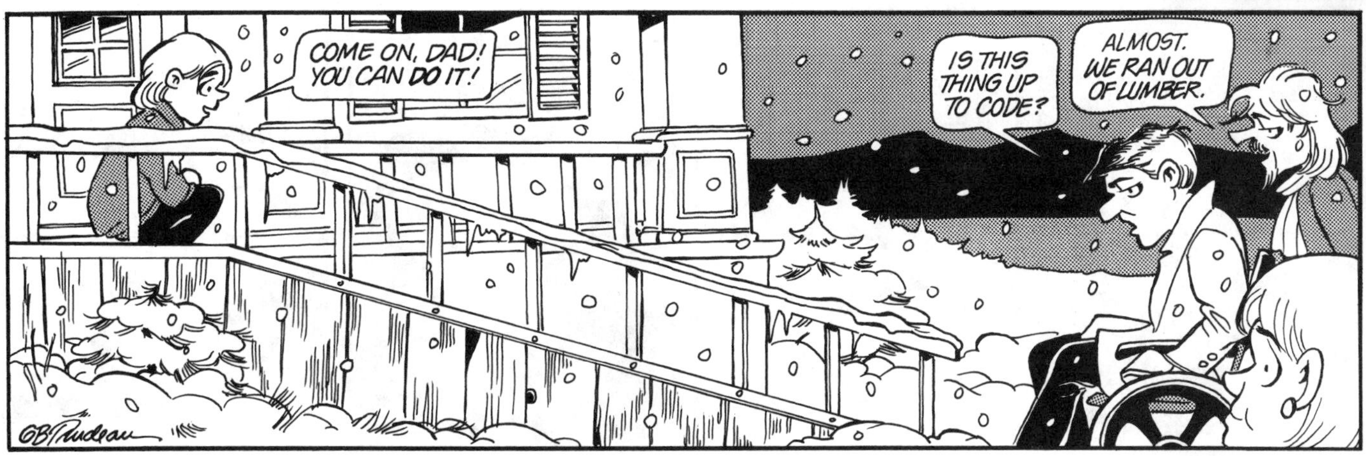
COME ON, DAD! YOU CAN DO IT!
IS THIS THING UP TO CODE?
ALMOST. WE RAN OUT OF LUMBER.
©B Trudeau

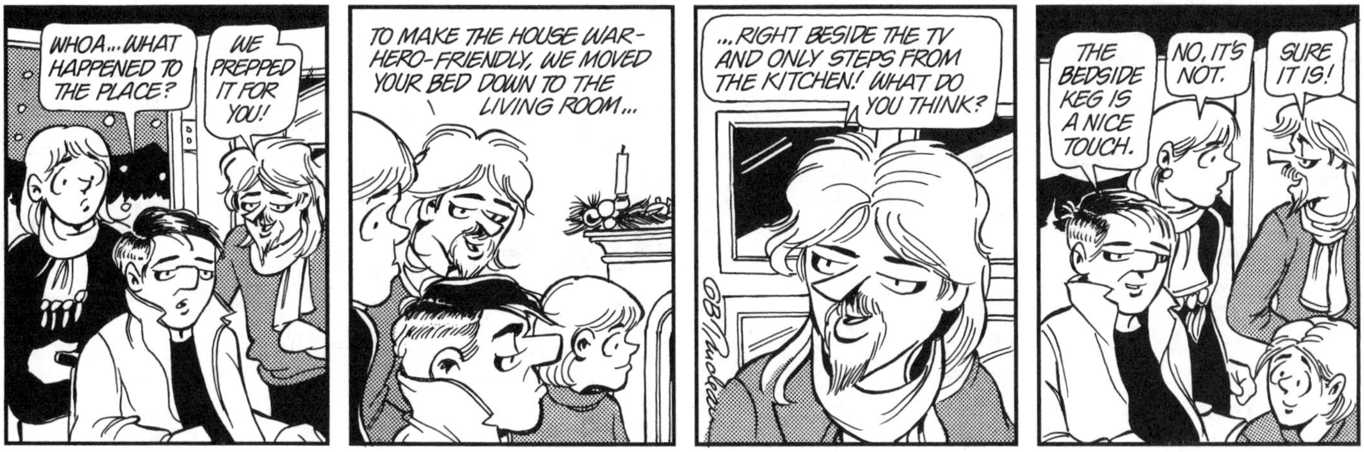
WHOA... WHAT HAPPENED TO THE PLACE?
WE PREPPED IT FOR YOU!
TO MAKE THE HOUSE WAR-HERO-FRIENDLY, WE MOVED YOUR BED DOWN TO THE LIVING ROOM...
...RIGHT BESIDE THE TV AND ONLY STEPS FROM THE KITCHEN! WHAT DO YOU THINK?
THE BEDSIDE KEG IS A NICE TOUCH.
NO, IT'S NOT.
SURE IT IS!

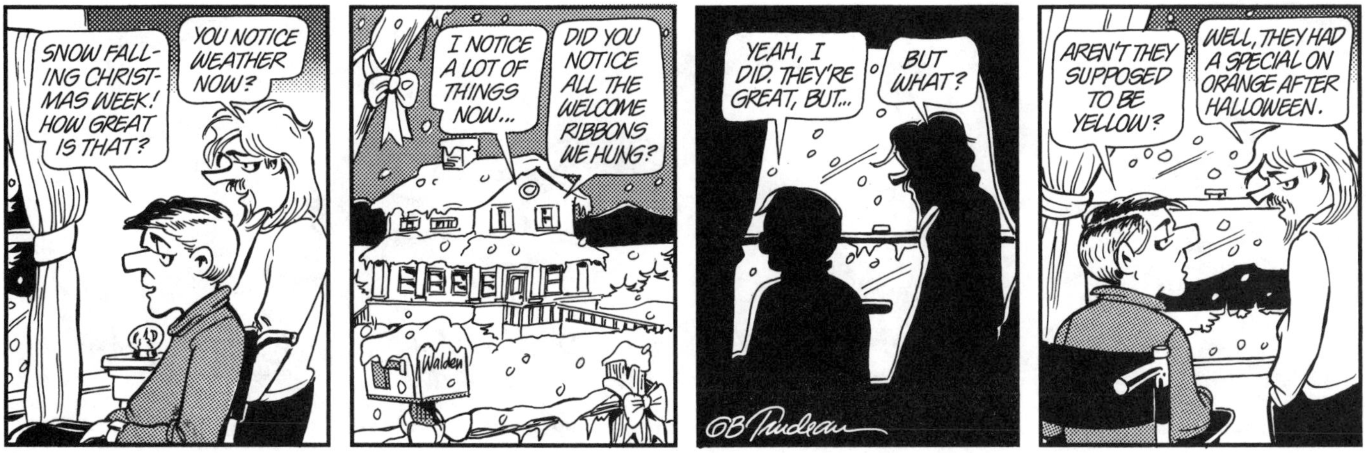
SNOW FALLING CHRISTMAS WEEK! HOW GREAT IS THAT?
YOU NOTICE WEATHER NOW?
I NOTICE A LOT OF THINGS NOW...
DID YOU NOTICE ALL THE WELCOME RIBBONS WE HUNG?
Walden
YEAH, I DID. THEY'RE GREAT, BUT...
BUT WHAT?
©B Trudeau
AREN'T THEY SUPPOSED TO BE YELLOW?
WELL, THEY HAD A SPECIAL ON ORANGE AFTER HALLOWEEN.

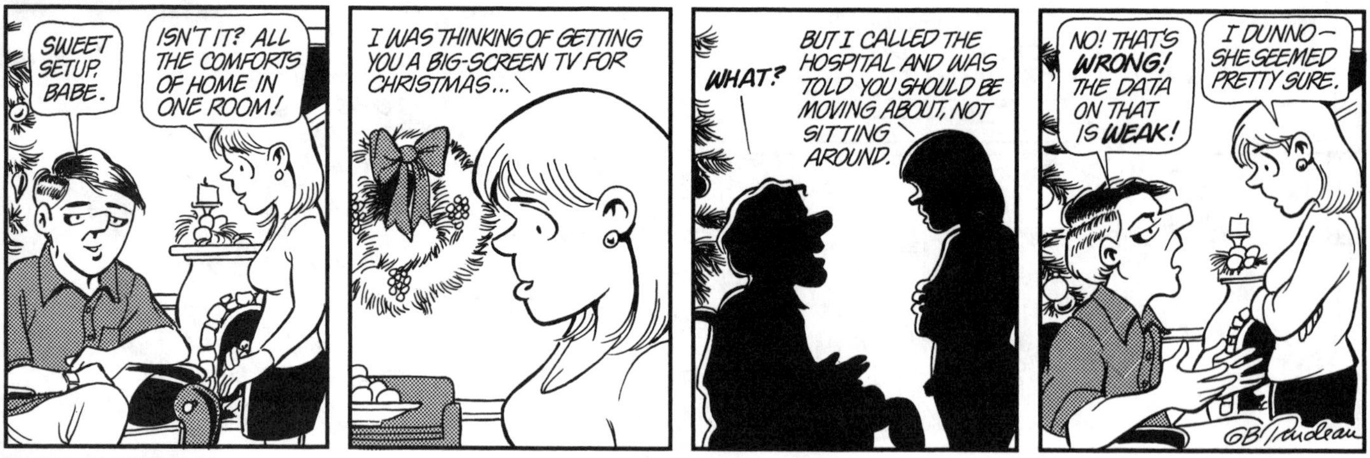
SWEET SETUP, BABE.
ISN'T IT? ALL THE COMFORTS OF HOME IN ONE ROOM!
I WAS THINKING OF GETTING YOU A BIG-SCREEN TV FOR CHRISTMAS...
WHAT?
BUT I CALLED THE HOSPITAL AND WAS TOLD YOU SHOULD BE MOVING ABOUT, NOT SITTING AROUND.
NO! THAT'S **WRONG!** THE DATA ON THAT IS **WEAK!**
I DUNNO— SHE SEEMED PRETTY SURE.

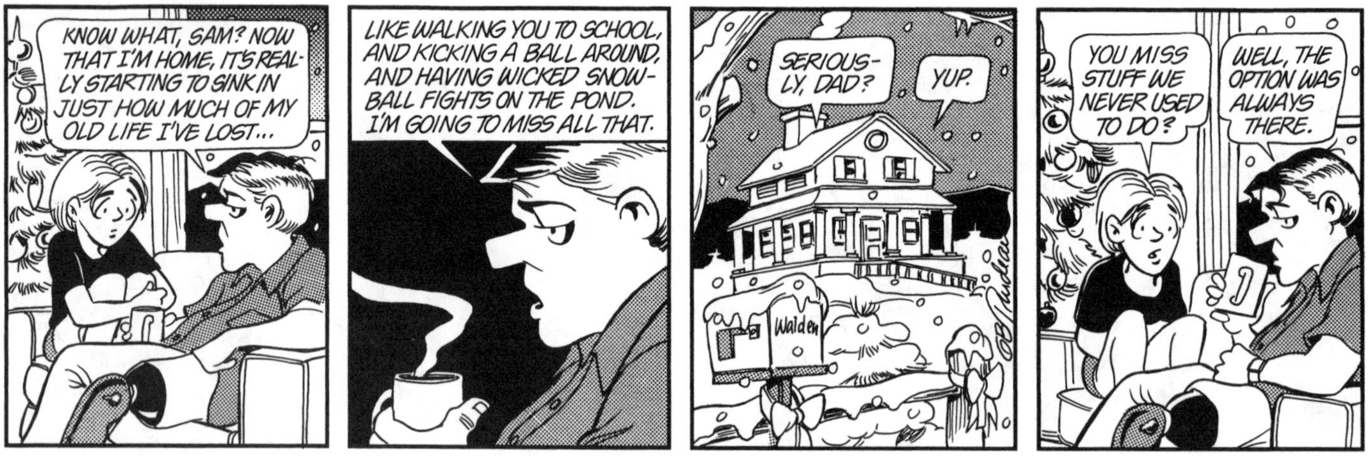
KNOW WHAT, SAM? NOW THAT I'M HOME, IT'S REALLY STARTING TO SINK IN JUST HOW MUCH OF MY OLD LIFE I'VE LOST...
LIKE WALKING YOU TO SCHOOL, AND KICKING A BALL AROUND, AND HAVING WICKED SNOWBALL FIGHTS ON THE POND. I'M GOING TO MISS ALL THAT.
SERIOUSLY, DAD?
YUP.
Walden
YOU MISS STUFF WE NEVER USED TO DO?
WELL, THE OPTION WAS ALWAYS THERE.

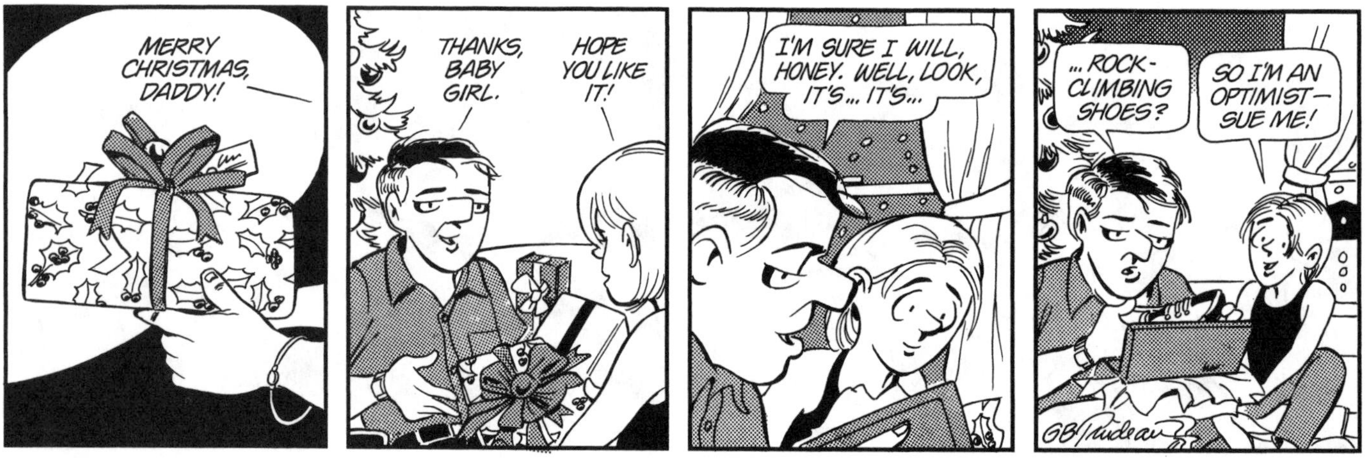
MERRY CHRISTMAS, DADDY!
THANKS, BABY GIRL.
HOPE YOU LIKE IT!
I'M SURE I WILL, HONEY. WELL, LOOK, IT'S... IT'S...
...ROCK-CLIMBING SHOES?
SO I'M AN OPTIMIST— SUE ME!

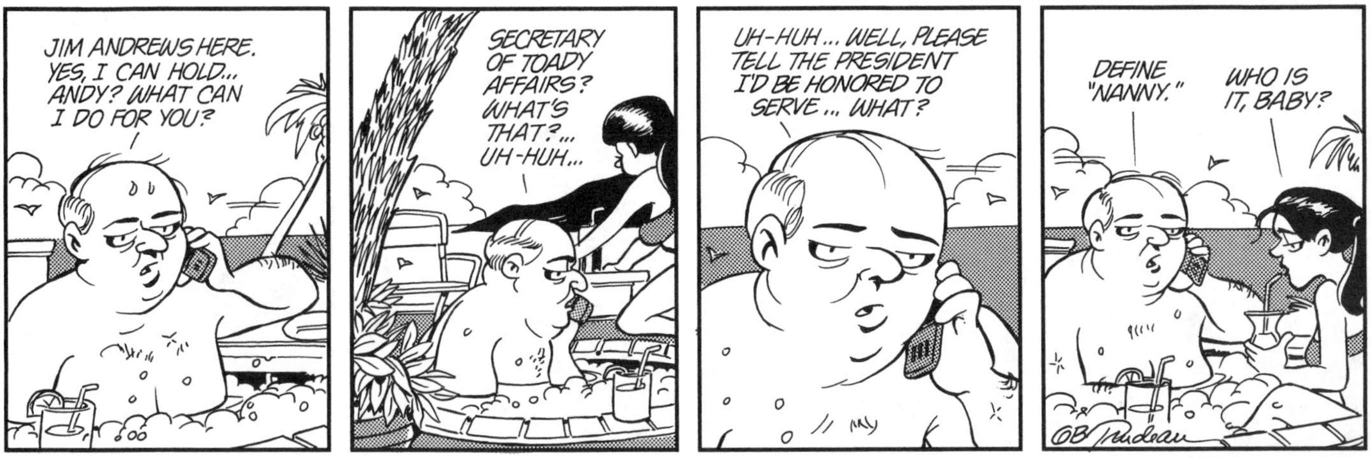
JIM ANDREWS HERE. YES, I CAN HOLD... ANDY? WHAT CAN I DO FOR YOU?
SECRETARY OF TOADY AFFAIRS? WHAT'S THAT?... UH-HUH...
UH-HUH... WELL, PLEASE TELL THE PRESIDENT I'D BE HONORED TO SERVE... WHAT?
DEFINE "NANNY."
WHO IS IT, BABY?

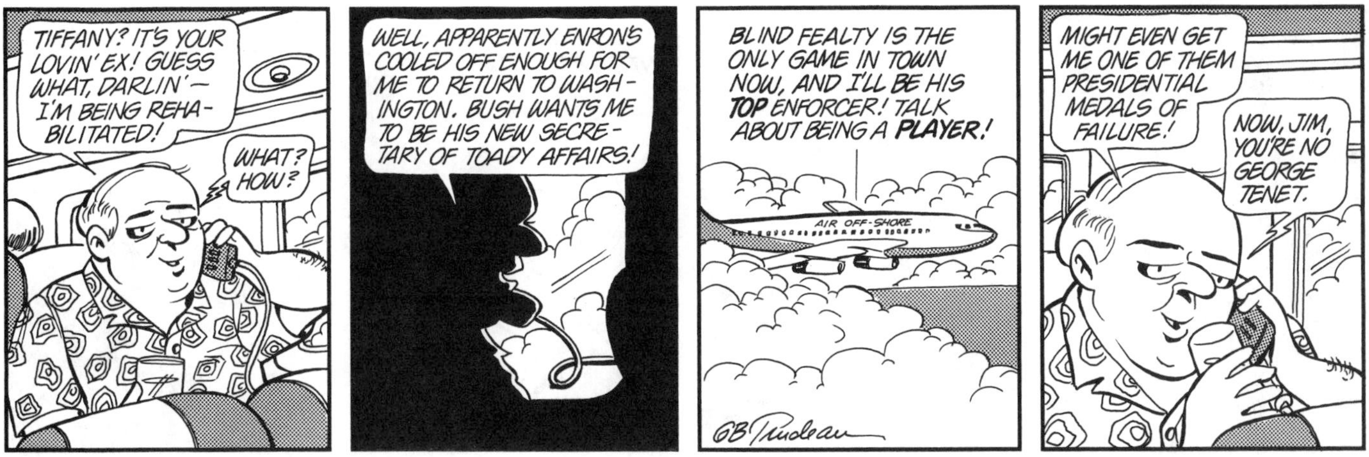
TIFFANY? IT'S YOUR LOVIN' EX! GUESS WHAT, DARLIN'— I'M BEING REHABILITATED!
WHAT? HOW?
WELL, APPARENTLY ENRON'S COOLED OFF ENOUGH FOR ME TO RETURN TO WASHINGTON. BUSH WANTS ME TO BE HIS NEW SECRETARY OF TOADY AFFAIRS!
BLIND FEALTY IS THE ONLY GAME IN TOWN NOW, AND I'LL BE HIS **TOP** ENFORCER! TALK ABOUT BEING A **PLAYER**!
AIR OFF-SHORE
MIGHT EVEN GET ME ONE OF THEM PRESIDENTIAL MEDALS OF FAILURE!
NOW, JIM, YOU'RE NO GEORGE TENET.

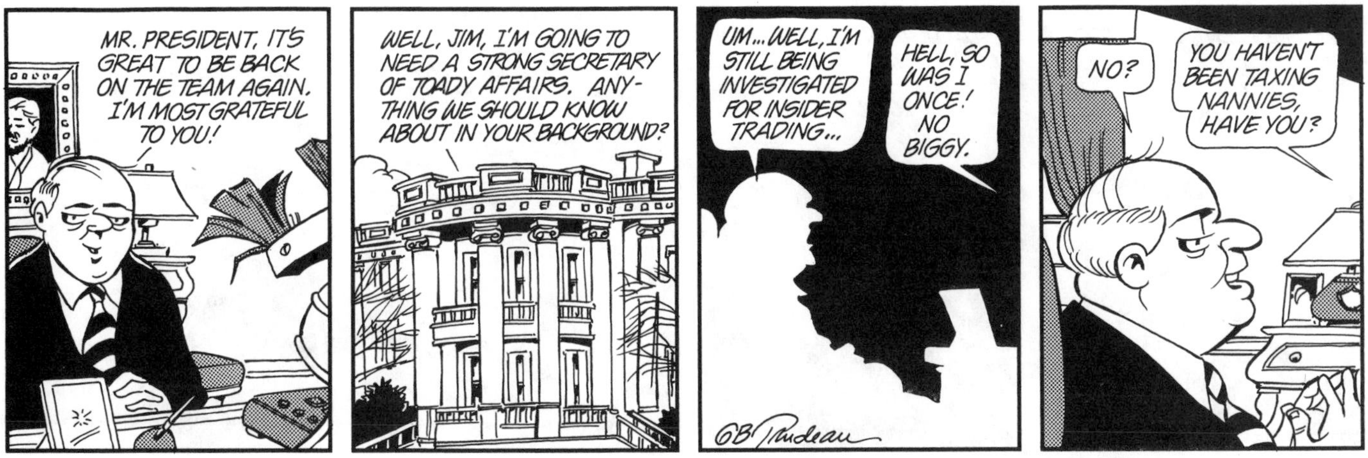
MR. PRESIDENT, IT'S GREAT TO BE BACK ON THE TEAM AGAIN. I'M MOST GRATEFUL TO YOU!
WELL, JIM, I'M GOING TO NEED A STRONG SECRETARY OF TOADY AFFAIRS. ANYTHING WE SHOULD KNOW ABOUT IN YOUR BACKGROUND?
UM... WELL, I'M STILL BEING INVESTIGATED FOR INSIDER TRADING...
HELL, SO WAS I ONCE! NO BIGGY.
NO?
YOU HAVEN'T BEEN TAXING NANNIES, HAVE YOU?

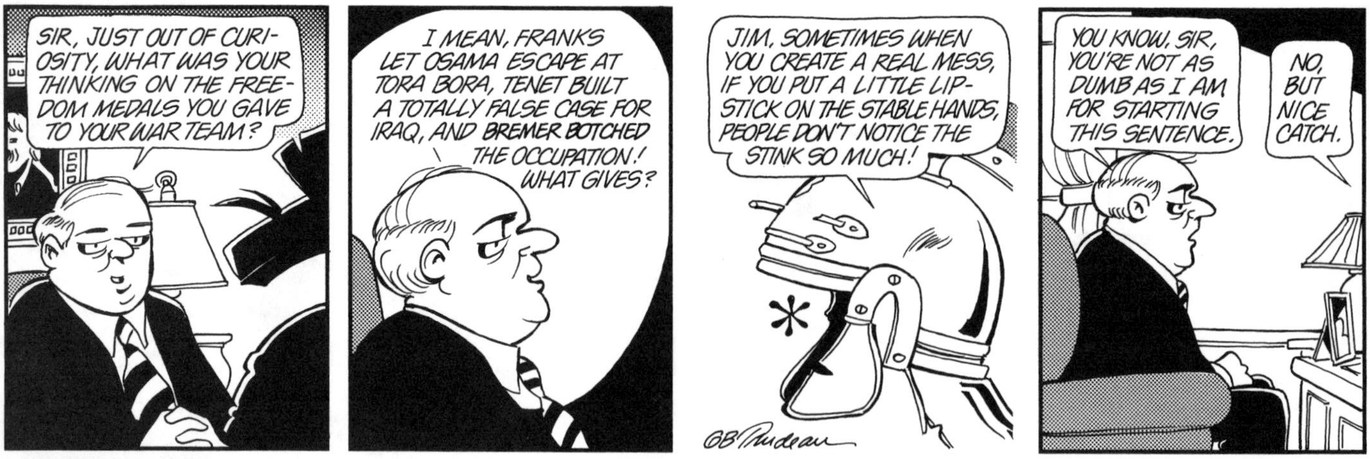
SIR, JUST OUT OF CURIOSITY, WHAT WAS YOUR THINKING ON THE FREEDOM MEDALS YOU GAVE TO YOUR WAR TEAM?
I MEAN, FRANKS LET OSAMA ESCAPE AT TORA BORA, TENET BUILT A TOTALLY FALSE CASE FOR IRAQ, AND BREMER BOTCHED THE OCCUPATION! WHAT GIVES?
JIM, SOMETIMES WHEN YOU CREATE A REAL MESS, IF YOU PUT A LITTLE LIPSTICK ON THE STABLE HANDS, PEOPLE DON'T NOTICE THE STINK SO MUCH!
YOU KNOW, SIR, YOU'RE NOT AS DUMB AS I AM FOR STARTING THIS SENTENCE.
NO, BUT NICE CATCH.
GB Trudeau

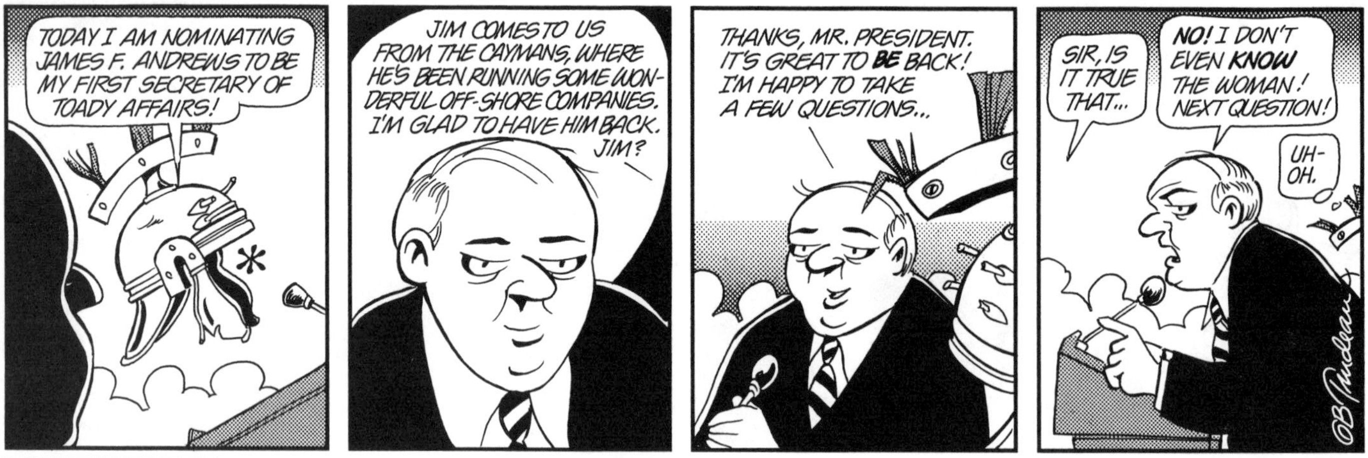
TODAY I AM NOMINATING JAMES F. ANDREWS TO BE MY FIRST SECRETARY OF TOADY AFFAIRS!
JIM COMES TO US FROM THE CAYMANS, WHERE HE'S BEEN RUNNING SOME WONDERFUL OFF-SHORE COMPANIES. I'M GLAD TO HAVE HIM BACK. JIM?
THANKS, MR. PRESIDENT. IT'S GREAT TO BE BACK! I'M HAPPY TO TAKE A FEW QUESTIONS...
SIR, IS IT TRUE THAT...
NO! I DON'T EVEN KNOW THE WOMAN! NEXT QUESTION!
UH-OH.
GB Trudeau

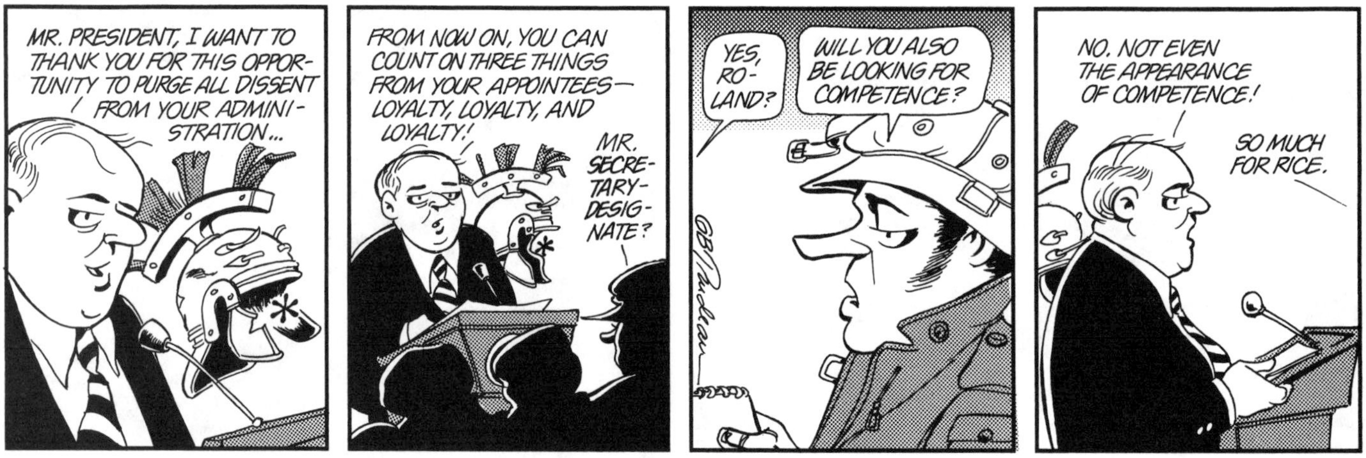
MR. PRESIDENT, I WANT TO THANK YOU FOR THIS OPPORTUNITY TO PURGE ALL DISSENT FROM YOUR ADMINISTRATION...
FROM NOW ON, YOU CAN COUNT ON THREE THINGS FROM YOUR APPOINTEES— LOYALTY, LOYALTY, AND LOYALTY!
MR. SECRETARY-DESIGNATE?
YES, ROLAND?
WILL YOU ALSO BE LOOKING FOR COMPETENCE?
GB Trudeau
NO. NOT EVEN THE APPEARANCE OF COMPETENCE!
SO MUCH FOR RICE.

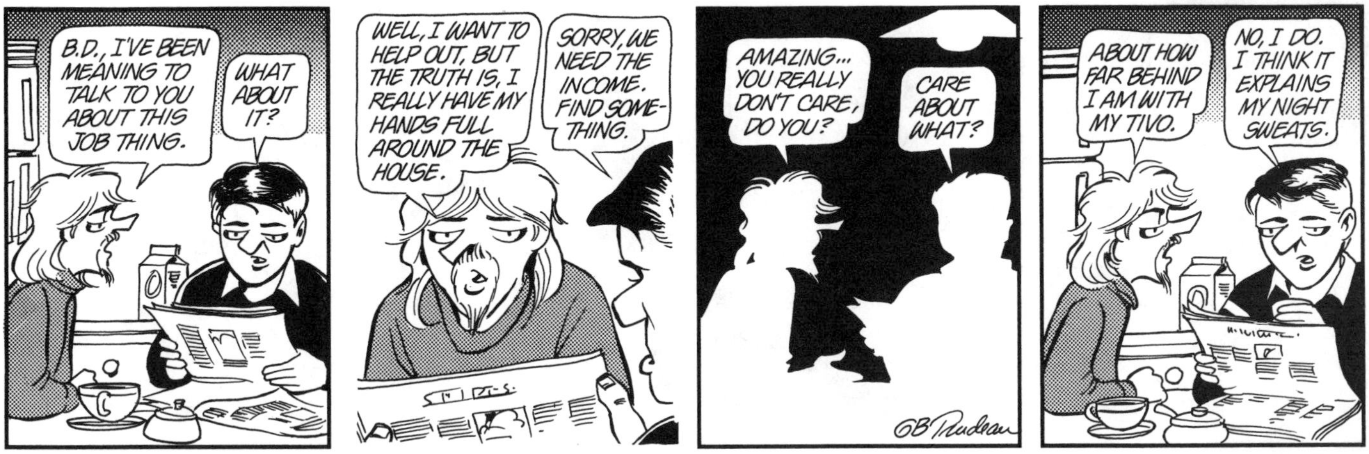
B.D., I'VE BEEN MEANING TO TALK TO YOU ABOUT THIS JOB THING.
WHAT ABOUT IT?
WELL, I WANT TO HELP OUT, BUT THE TRUTH IS, I REALLY HAVE MY HANDS FULL AROUND THE HOUSE.
SORRY, WE NEED THE INCOME. FIND SOMETHING.
AMAZING... YOU REALLY DON'T CARE, DO YOU?
CARE ABOUT WHAT?
ABOUT HOW FAR BEHIND I AM WITH MY TIVO.
NO, I DO. I THINK IT EXPLAINS MY NIGHT SWEATS.

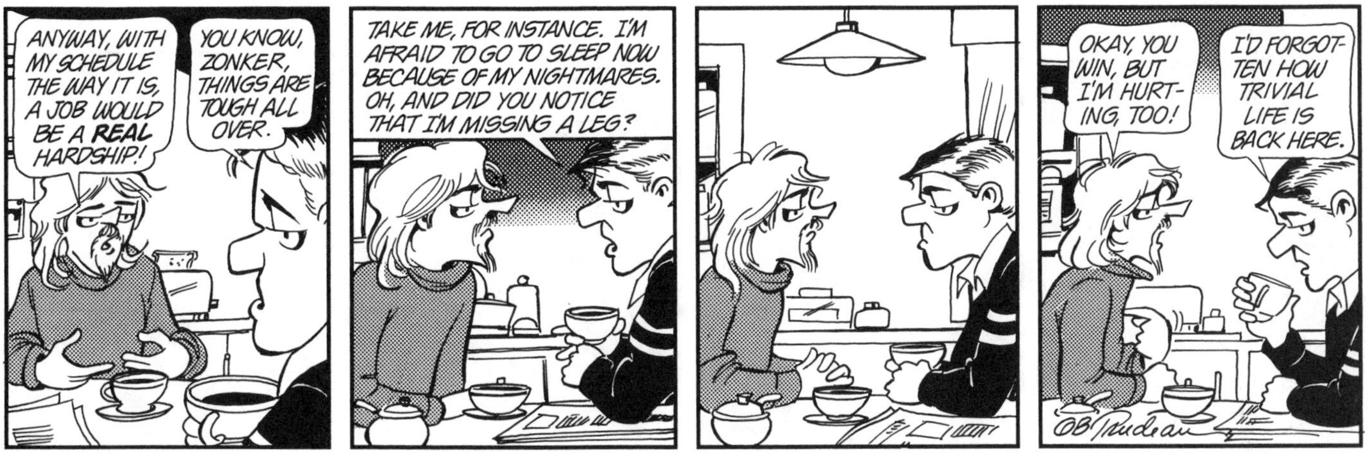
ANYWAY, WITH MY SCHEDULE THE WAY IT IS, A JOB WOULD BE A REAL HARDSHIP!
YOU KNOW, ZONKER, THINGS ARE TOUGH ALL OVER.
TAKE ME, FOR INSTANCE. I'M AFRAID TO GO TO SLEEP NOW BECAUSE OF MY NIGHTMARES. OH, AND DID YOU NOTICE THAT I'M MISSING A LEG?
OKAY, YOU WIN, BUT I'M HURTING, TOO!
I'D FORGOTTEN HOW TRIVIAL LIFE IS BACK HERE.

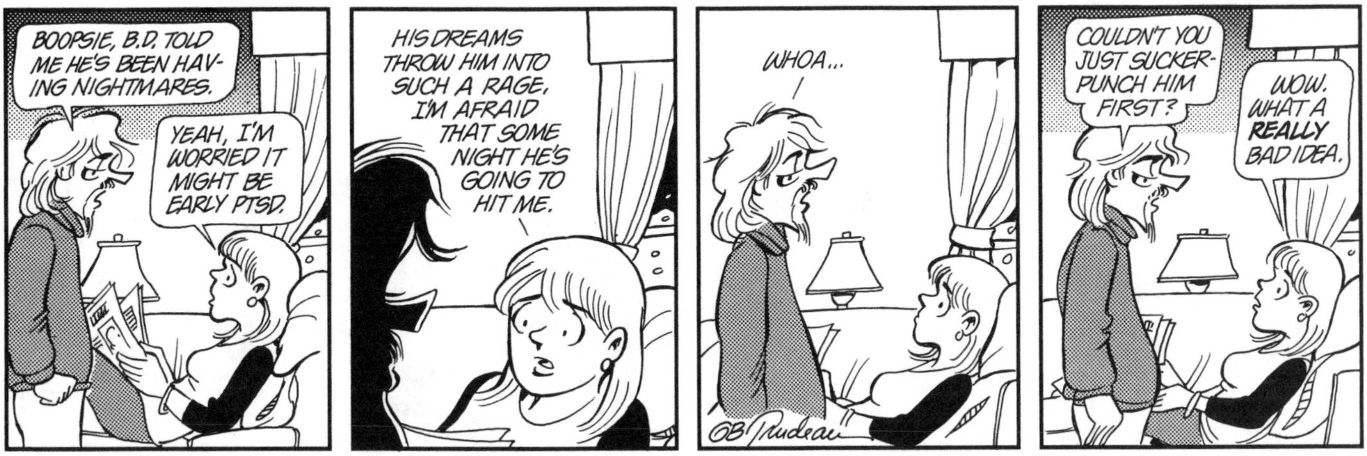
BOOPSIE, B.D. TOLD ME HE'S BEEN HAVING NIGHTMARES.
YEAH, I'M WORRIED IT MIGHT BE EARLY PTSD.
HIS DREAMS THROW HIM INTO SUCH A RAGE, I'M AFRAID THAT SOME NIGHT HE'S GOING TO HIT ME.
WHOA...
COULDN'T YOU JUST SUCKER-PUNCH HIM FIRST?
WOW. WHAT A REALLY BAD IDEA.

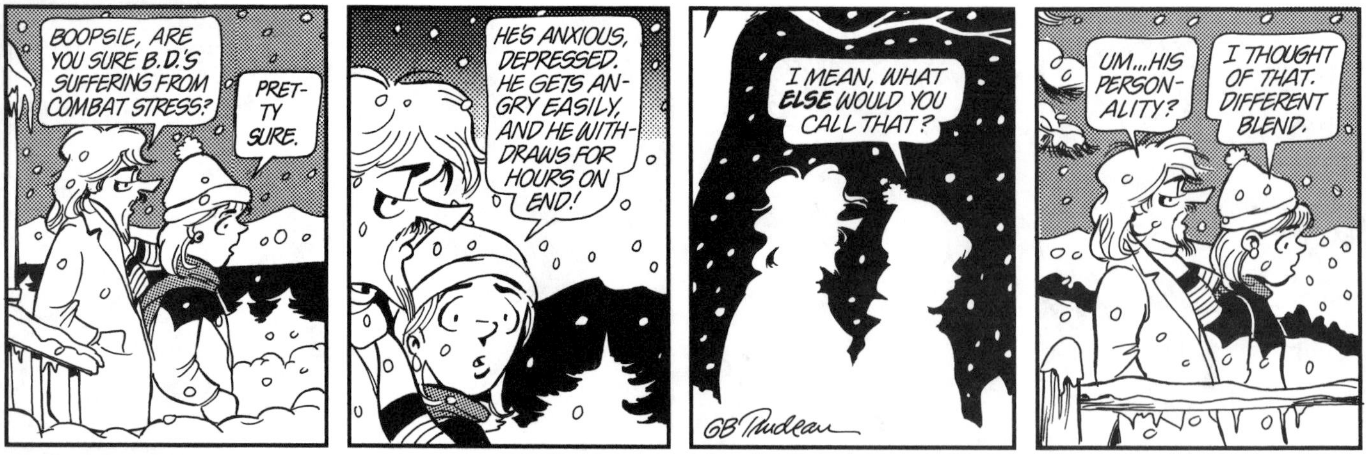
BOOPSIE, ARE YOU SURE B.D.'S SUFFERING FROM COMBAT STRESS?
PRET-TY SURE.
HE'S ANXIOUS, DEPRESSED. HE GETS AN-GRY EASILY, AND HE WITH-DRAWS FOR HOURS ON END!
I MEAN, WHAT ELSE WOULD YOU CALL THAT?
UM... HIS PERSON-ALITY?
I THOUGHT OF THAT. DIFFERENT BLEND.
GB Trudeau

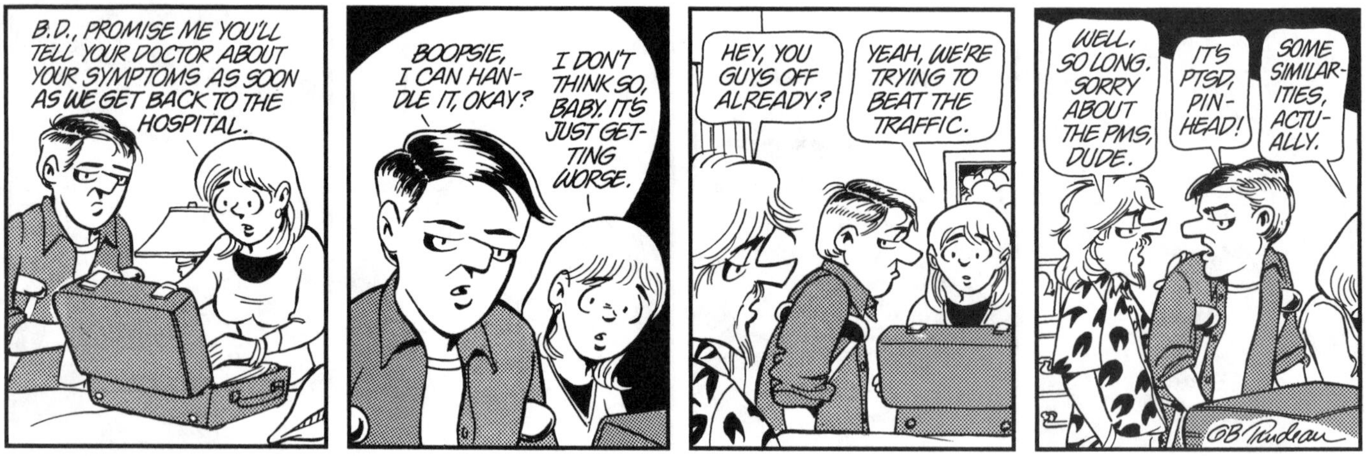
B.D., PROMISE ME YOU'LL TELL YOUR DOCTOR ABOUT YOUR SYMPTOMS AS SOON AS WE GET BACK TO THE HOSPITAL.
BOOPSIE, I CAN HAN-DLE IT, OKAY?
I DON'T THINK SO, BABY. IT'S JUST GET-TING WORSE.
HEY, YOU GUYS OFF ALREADY?
YEAH, WE'RE TRYING TO BEAT THE TRAFFIC.
WELL, SO LONG. SORRY ABOUT THE PMS, DUDE.
IT'S PTSD, PIN-HEAD!
SOME SIMILAR-ITIES, ACTU-ALLY.
GB Trudeau

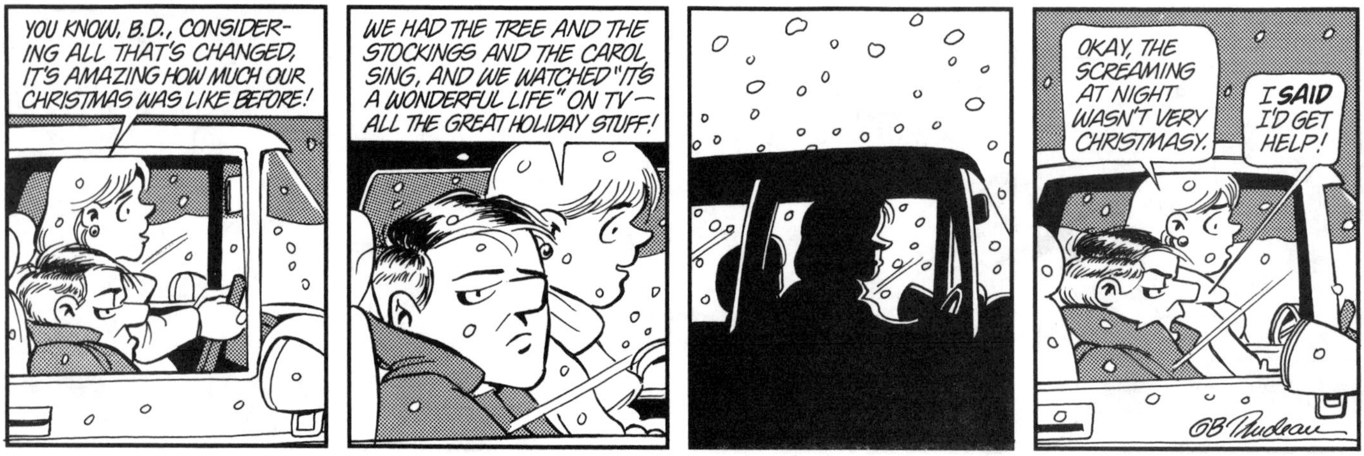
YOU KNOW, B.D., CONSIDER-ING ALL THAT'S CHANGED, IT'S AMAZING HOW MUCH OUR CHRISTMAS WAS LIKE BEFORE!
WE HAD THE TREE AND THE STOCKINGS AND THE CAROL SING, AND WE WATCHED "IT'S A WONDERFUL LIFE" ON TV — ALL THE GREAT HOLIDAY STUFF!
OKAY, THE SCREAMING AT NIGHT WASN'T VERY CHRISTMASY.
I SAID I'D GET HELP!
GB Trudeau

WELL, FOLKS, LOOKS LIKE THE ARCHITECT OF U.S. TORTURE POLICY IS ABOUT TO BECOME ATTORNEY GENERAL.

AFTER 200 YEARS OF SANCTIONS AGAINST IT, TORTURE HAS JUST BEEN MAINSTREAMED BY OUR ELECTED LEADERS.

TIME FOR AMERICANS TO RE-THINK WHAT WE MEAN BY OUR "VALUES."

WELL, OFF TO TORTURE CLASS.

GIVE 'EM HELL.

GB Trudeau

GOOD AFTERNOON. MY NAME IS HAVOC, AND THIS IS CIA TRAINING COURSE 563P, "INTERROGATION PROTOCOLS."

deprivati
hoods
humili

Week I
• beat
• suffo
• strang

AS YOU KNOW, IT'S BEEN UNCLEAR WHETHER THIS CLASS WOULD BE VIABLE. BUT NOW, FOLLOWING THE GONZALES CONFIRMATION, WE'RE GOOD TO GO!

SO WELCOME TO THE WORLD OF RIDING THE DOG, POP-TOP, BURNING HAIR, JUICE BALL, DOUBLE DIPPING AND POUNDING THE MARBLES!

WHAT ABOUT DATING THE WALRUS?

NO, THAT'S STILL COVERED BY GENEVA.

Wed
dep
tr
sei
w

YOU MAY BE WONDERING WHY THE CIA STILL HAS AN INTERROGATION COURSE GIVEN THE BLOWBACK FROM ABU GHRAIB.

Geneva.
connean

hoods
quaint,
obsole

naked
chain
to

WELL, THOSE OF YOU WHO FOLLOW THE PAPERS KNOW WE STILL USE PAIN-BASED INTELLIGENCE EXTRACTION PROTOCOLS AT SECRET CAMPS.

MOST OF YOU ARE HEADED FOR THOSE CAMPS, WHICH ARE PRIMARILY LOCATED IN TWO COUNTRIES CODE-NAMED "IRAQ" AND "AFGHANISTAN."

tie

GBTrudeau

beat
hood

CODE-NAMED?

UNOFFICIALLY, "IRAQ" IS WHERE THE ACTION IS.

OKAY, SO HERE ARE THE KEY INTERROGATION PROTOCOLS WE'LL BE COVERING...

Week I
—soften
—environ
—sleep depriv
Week II
—Ashle
—Backst.

STRESS POSITIONS, SLEEP AND SENSORY DEPRIVATION, TEMPERATURE CONTROL, DOG HANDLING, CIGARETTE BURNS, HOODING AND BEATING.

BUT REMEMBER, THERE IS ONE THING THAT LEADER-SHIP—FROM THE PRESIDENT ON DOWN—WILL **NEVER** AGAIN TOLERATE AT OUR DETENTION CENTERS...

...DIGITAL CAMERAS.

HOW ABOUT CELL PHONE CAMS?

ANY QUESTIONS SO FAR? YEAH, REDFERN.

quaint vention boar $ gar

YEAH, SIR, I'M A BIT CON-FUSED. WORLD WAR II WAS A "NEW TYPE OF WAR," TOO: OVER 50 MILLION PEOPLE WERE KILLED.

YET SOMEHOW WE MANAGED TO DEFEAT A LAWLESS ENEMY WITHOUT RESORTING TO TORTURE. WHAT'S THE DIFFERENCE BETWEEN THEN AND NOW?

©B Trudeau

A SPINE-LESS PRES-IDENT.

HMM...WELL, THAT WOULD EXPLAIN THE WHEELCHAIR.

SO HOW'D TORTURE CLASS GO?

WELL, IT TURNS OUT WE CAN'T CALL IT THAT...

IT'S "INTERROGATION PROTOCOLS." AND I'M ONLY TAKING IT BECAUSE IT'S REQUIRED.

I WANT TO WORK IN SATELLITE SURVEILLANCE, WHICH DOESN'T EXACTLY CALL FOR A LOT OF WATER-BOARDING.

WATER-BOARDING?

SORRY, I MEAN FREEDOM-BOARDING.

©B Trudeau

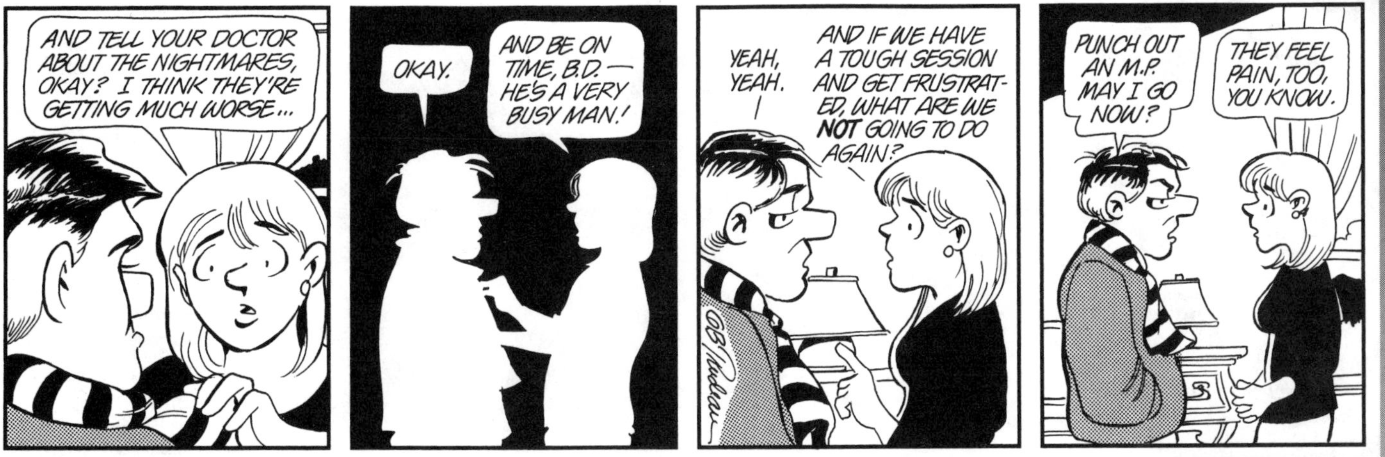
AND TELL YOUR DOCTOR ABOUT THE NIGHTMARES, OKAY? I THINK THEY'RE GETTING MUCH WORSE...
OKAY.
AND BE ON TIME, B.D.— HE'S A VERY BUSY MAN!
YEAH, YEAH.
AND IF WE HAVE A TOUGH SESSION AND GET FRUSTRATED, WHAT ARE WE **NOT** GOING TO DO AGAIN?
PUNCH OUT AN M.P. MAY I GO NOW?
THEY FEEL PAIN, TOO, YOU KNOW.

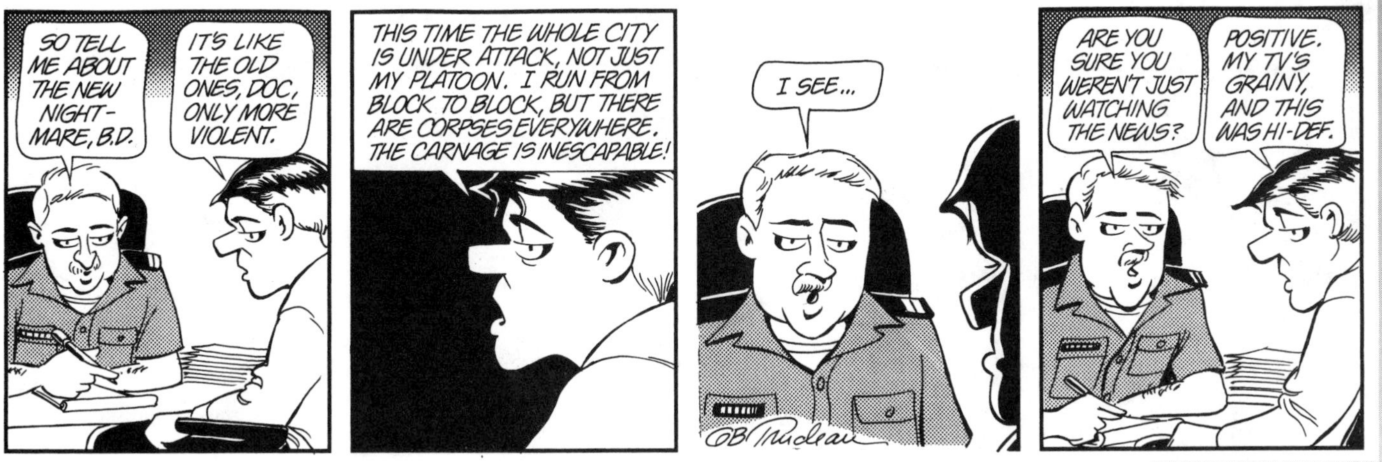
SO TELL ME ABOUT THE NEW NIGHTMARE, B.D.
IT'S LIKE THE OLD ONES, DOC, ONLY MORE VIOLENT.
THIS TIME THE WHOLE CITY IS UNDER ATTACK, NOT JUST MY PLATOON. I RUN FROM BLOCK TO BLOCK, BUT THERE ARE CORPSES EVERYWHERE. THE CARNAGE IS INESCAPABLE!
I SEE...
ARE YOU SURE YOU WEREN'T JUST WATCHING THE NEWS?
POSITIVE. MY TV'S GRAINY, AND THIS WAS HI-DEF.

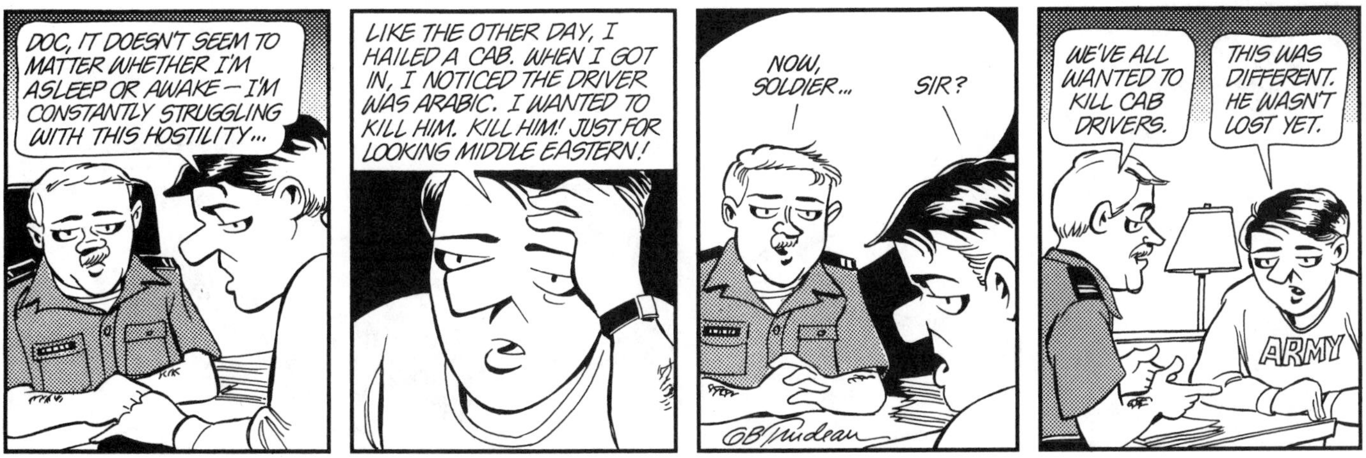
DOC, IT DOESN'T SEEM TO MATTER WHETHER I'M ASLEEP OR AWAKE—I'M CONSTANTLY STRUGGLING WITH THIS HOSTILITY...
LIKE THE OTHER DAY, I HAILED A CAB. WHEN I GOT IN, I NOTICED THE DRIVER WAS ARABIC. I WANTED TO KILL HIM. KILL HIM! JUST FOR LOOKING MIDDLE EASTERN!
NOW, SOLDIER...
SIR?
WE'VE ALL WANTED TO KILL CAB DRIVERS.
THIS WAS DIFFERENT. HE WASN'T LOST YET.
ARMY

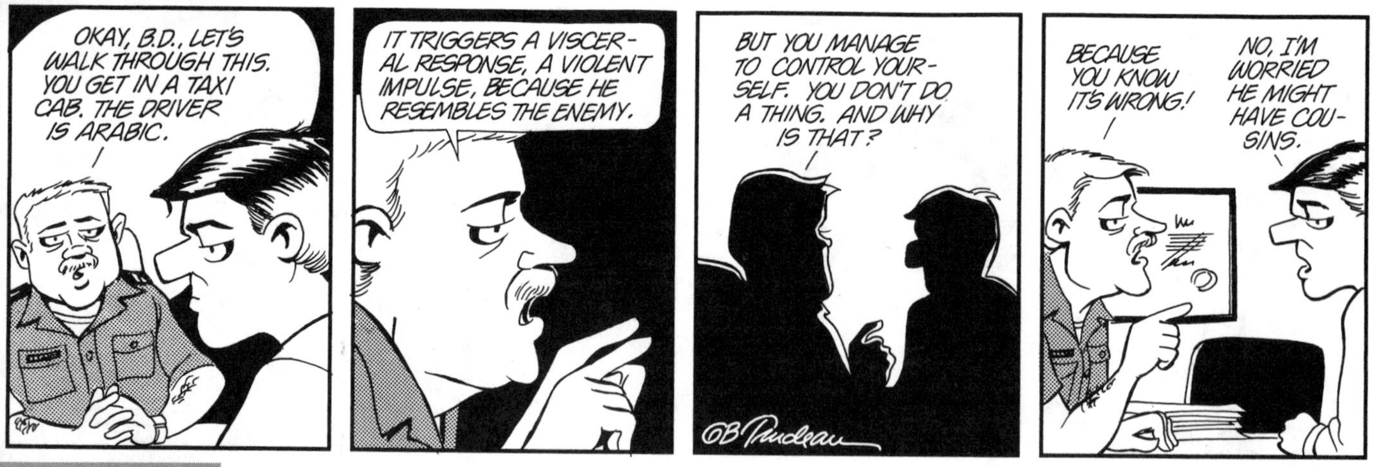
OKAY, B.D., LET'S WALK THROUGH THIS. YOU GET IN A TAXI CAB. THE DRIVER IS ARABIC.
IT TRIGGERS A VISCERAL RESPONSE, A VIOLENT IMPULSE, BECAUSE HE RESEMBLES THE ENEMY.
BUT YOU MANAGE TO CONTROL YOURSELF. YOU DON'T DO A THING. AND WHY IS THAT?
BECAUSE YOU KNOW IT'S WRONG!
NO, I'M WORRIED HE MIGHT HAVE COUSINS.

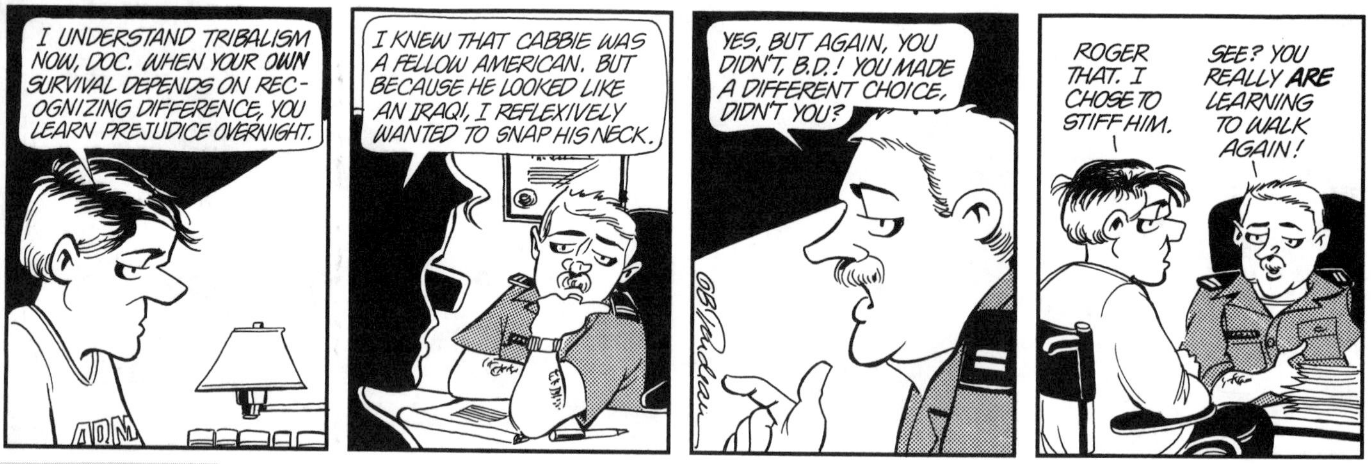
I UNDERSTAND TRIBALISM NOW, DOC. WHEN YOUR **OWN** SURVIVAL DEPENDS ON RECOGNIZING DIFFERENCE, YOU LEARN PREJUDICE OVERNIGHT.
I KNEW THAT CABBIE WAS A FELLOW AMERICAN. BUT BECAUSE HE LOOKED LIKE AN IRAQI, I REFLEXIVELY WANTED TO SNAP HIS NECK.
YES, BUT AGAIN, YOU DIDN'T, B.D.! YOU MADE A DIFFERENT CHOICE, DIDN'T YOU?
ROGER THAT. I CHOSE TO STIFF HIM.
SEE? YOU REALLY **ARE** LEARNING TO WALK AGAIN!

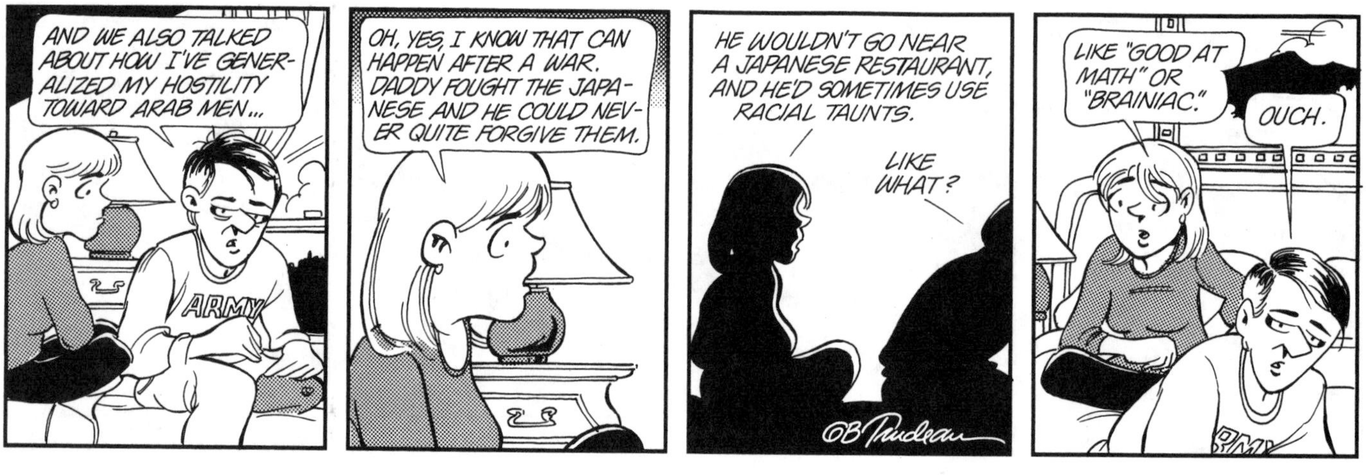
AND WE ALSO TALKED ABOUT HOW I'VE GENERALIZED MY HOSTILITY TOWARD ARAB MEN...
OH, YES, I KNOW THAT CAN HAPPEN AFTER A WAR. DADDY FOUGHT THE JAPANESE AND HE COULD NEVER QUITE FORGIVE THEM.
HE WOULDN'T GO NEAR A JAPANESE RESTAURANT, AND HE'D SOMETIMES USE RACIAL TAUNTS.
LIKE WHAT?
LIKE "GOOD AT MATH" OR "BRAINIAC."
OUCH.

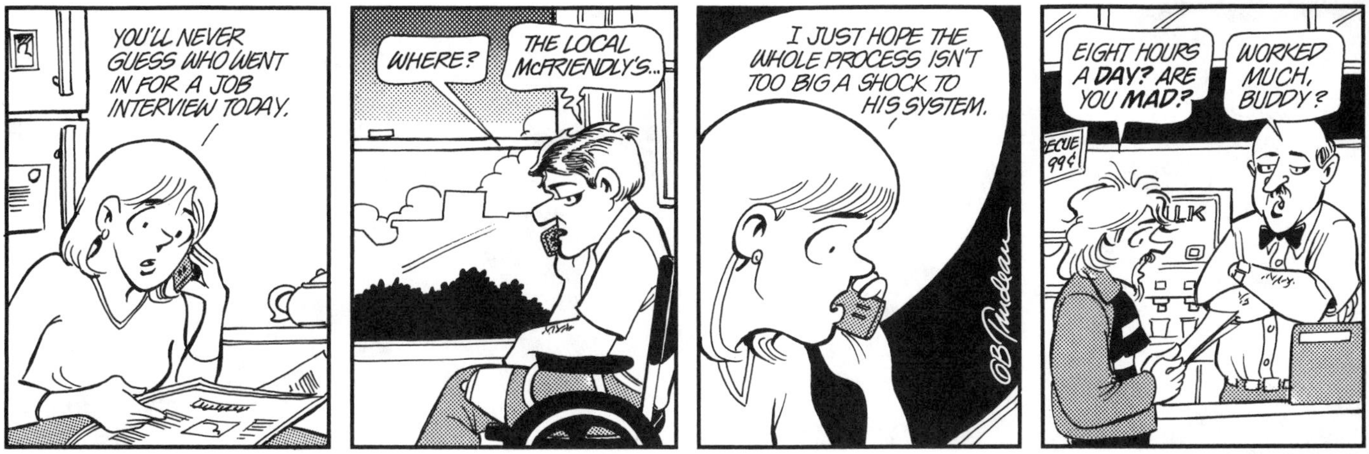

YOU'LL NEVER GUESS WHO WENT IN FOR A JOB INTERVIEW TODAY.
WHERE?
THE LOCAL McFRIENDLY'S...
I JUST HOPE THE WHOLE PROCESS ISN'T TOO BIG A SHOCK TO HIS SYSTEM.
EIGHT HOURS A DAY? ARE YOU MAD?
WORKED MUCH, BUDDY?

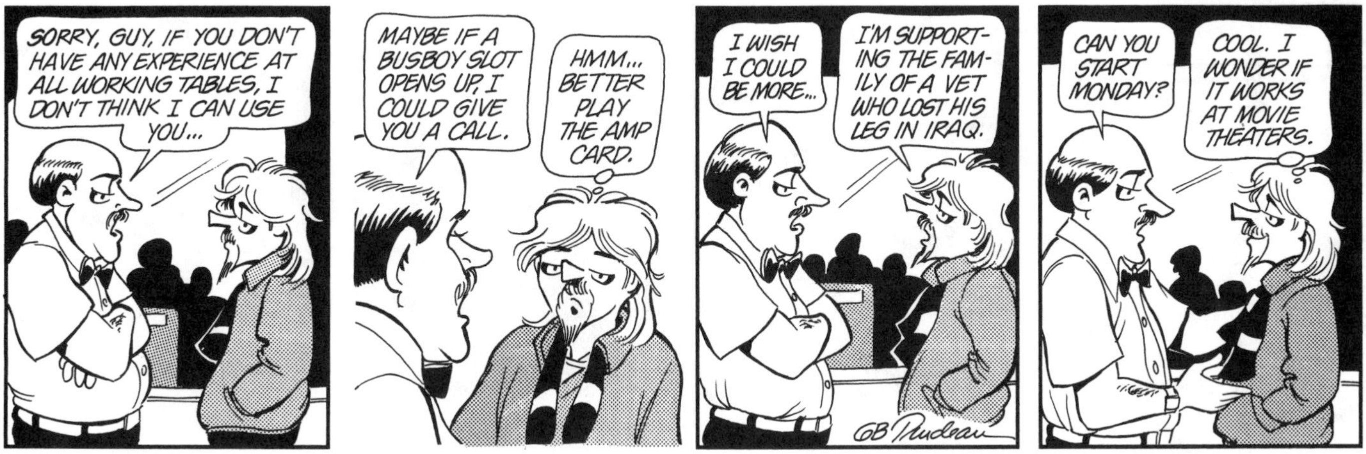

SORRY, GUY, IF YOU DON'T HAVE ANY EXPERIENCE AT ALL WORKING TABLES, I DON'T THINK I CAN USE YOU...
MAYBE IF A BUSBOY SLOT OPENS UP, I COULD GIVE YOU A CALL.
HMM... BETTER PLAY THE AMP CARD.
I WISH I COULD BE MORE...
I'M SUPPORTING THE FAMILY OF A VET WHO LOST HIS LEG IN IRAQ.
CAN YOU START MONDAY?
COOL. I WONDER IF IT WORKS AT MOVIE THEATERS.

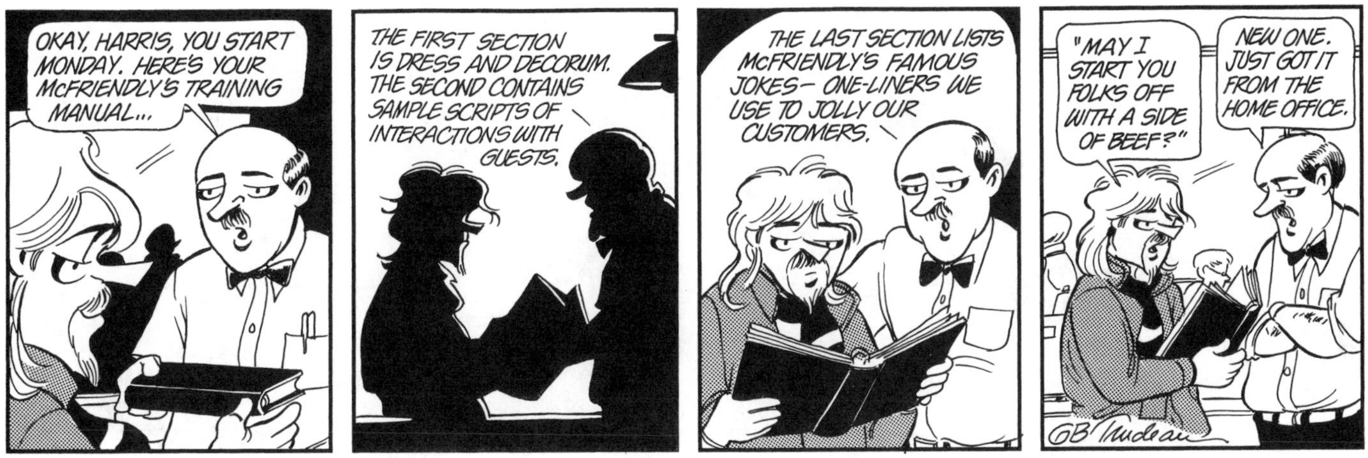

OKAY, HARRIS, YOU START MONDAY. HERE'S YOUR McFRIENDLY'S TRAINING MANUAL...
THE FIRST SECTION IS DRESS AND DECORUM. THE SECOND CONTAINS SAMPLE SCRIPTS OF INTERACTIONS WITH GUESTS.
THE LAST SECTION LISTS McFRIENDLY'S FAMOUS JOKES— ONE-LINERS WE USE TO JOLLY OUR CUSTOMERS.
"MAY I START YOU FOLKS OFF WITH A SIDE OF BEEF?"
NEW ONE. JUST GOT IT FROM THE HOME OFFICE.

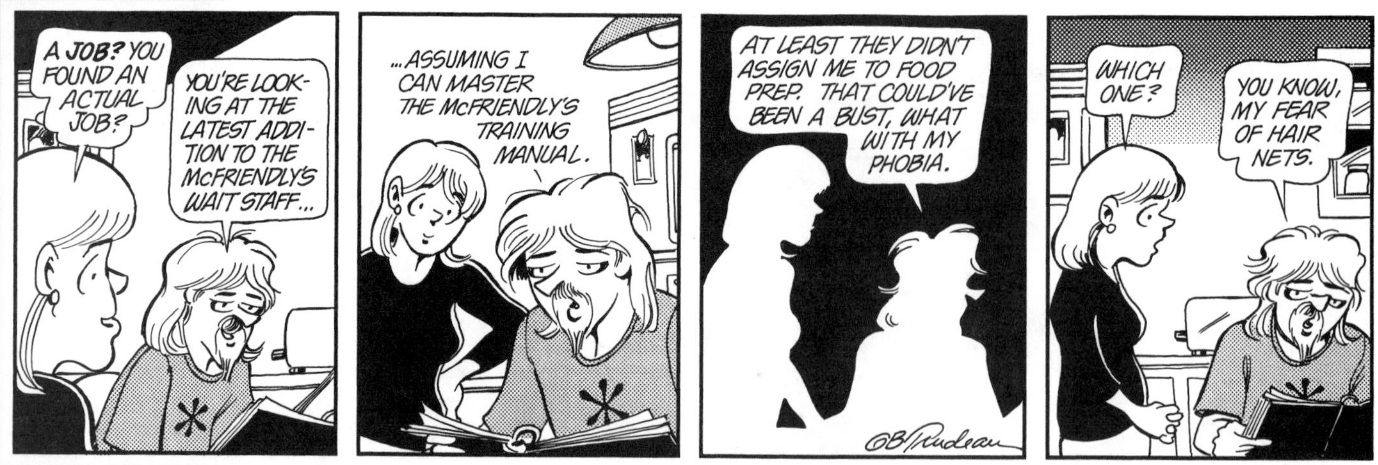
A JOB? YOU FOUND AN ACTUAL JOB?
YOU'RE LOOKING AT THE LATEST ADDITION TO THE McFRIENDLY'S WAIT STAFF...
...ASSUMING I CAN MASTER THE McFRIENDLY'S TRAINING MANUAL.
AT LEAST THEY DIDN'T ASSIGN ME TO FOOD PREP. THAT COULD'VE BEEN A BUST, WHAT WITH MY PHOBIA.
WHICH ONE?
YOU KNOW, MY FEAR OF HAIR NETS.

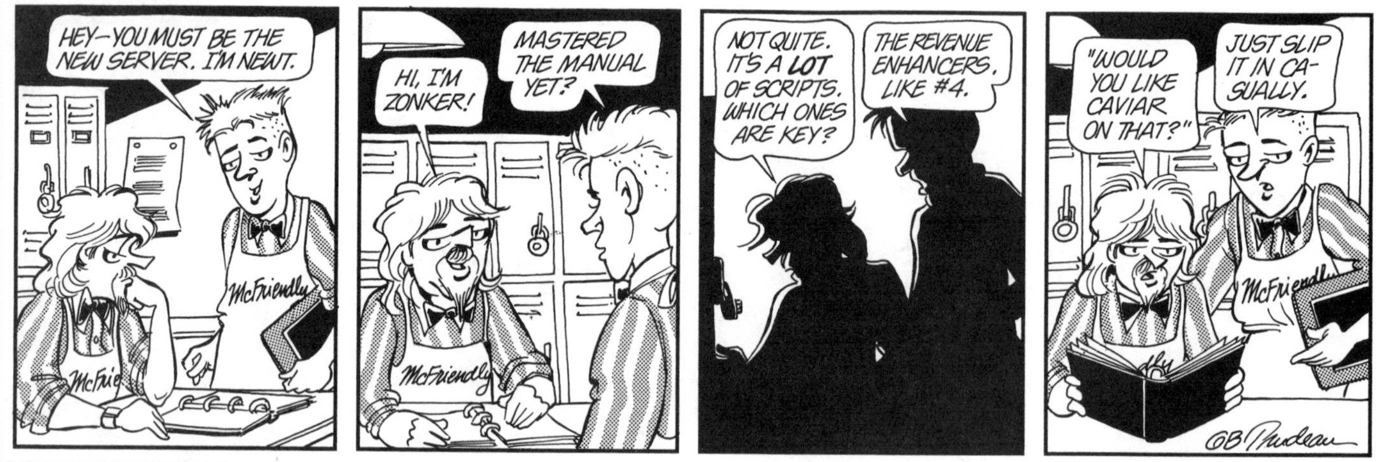
HEY—YOU MUST BE THE NEW SERVER. I'M NEWT.
HI, I'M ZONKER!
MASTERED THE MANUAL YET?
McFriendly
NOT QUITE. IT'S A LOT OF SCRIPTS. WHICH ONES ARE KEY?
THE REVENUE ENHANCERS. LIKE #4.
"WOULD YOU LIKE CAVIAR ON THAT?"
JUST SLIP IT IN CASUALLY.

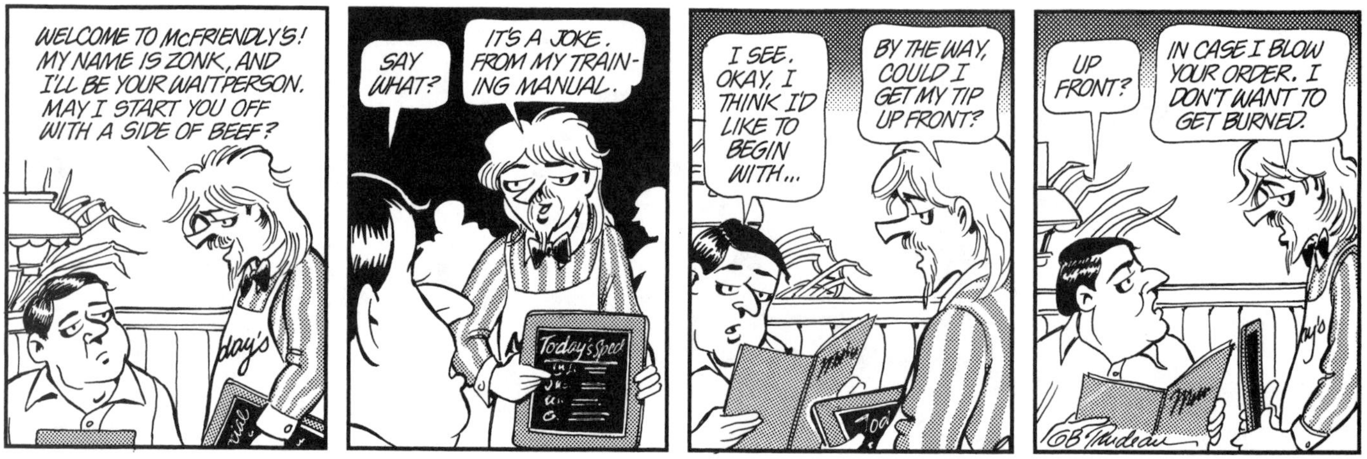
WELCOME TO McFRIENDLY'S! MY NAME IS ZONK, AND I'LL BE YOUR WAITPERSON. MAY I START YOU OFF WITH A SIDE OF BEEF?
SAY WHAT?
IT'S A JOKE. FROM MY TRAINING MANUAL.
Today's Sped
I SEE. OKAY, I THINK I'D LIKE TO BEGIN WITH...
BY THE WAY, COULD I GET MY TIP UP FRONT?
UP FRONT?
IN CASE I BLOW YOUR ORDER. I DON'T WANT TO GET BURNED.

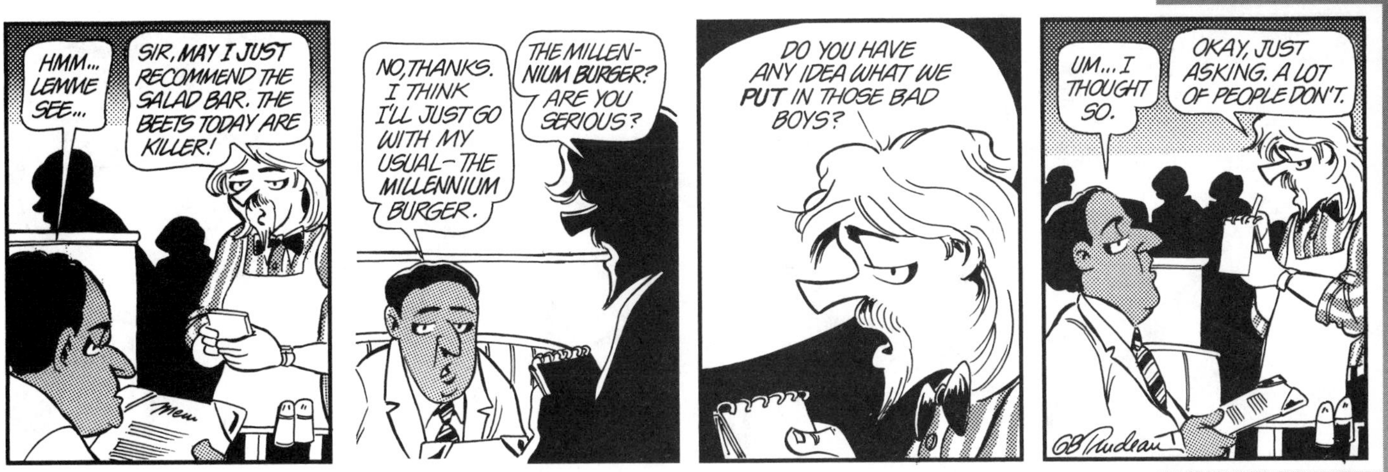
HMM... LEMME SEE...
SIR, MAY I JUST RECOMMEND THE SALAD BAR. THE BEETS TODAY ARE KILLER!
NO, THANKS. I THINK I'LL JUST GO WITH MY USUAL—THE MILLENNIUM BURGER.
THE MILLEN-NIUM BURGER? ARE YOU SERIOUS?
DO YOU HAVE ANY IDEA WHAT WE PUT IN THOSE BAD BOYS?
UM... I THOUGHT SO.
OKAY, JUST ASKING. A LOT OF PEOPLE DON'T.
GB Trudeau

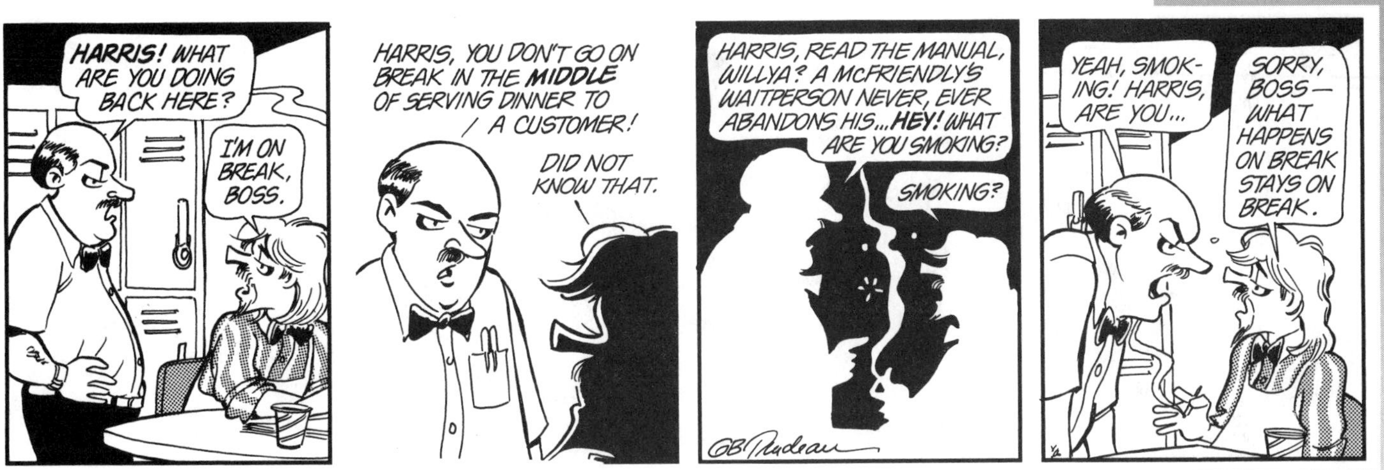
HARRIS! WHAT ARE YOU DOING BACK HERE?
I'M ON BREAK, BOSS.
HARRIS, YOU DON'T GO ON BREAK IN THE MIDDLE OF SERVING DINNER TO A CUSTOMER!
DID NOT KNOW THAT.
HARRIS, READ THE MANUAL, WILLYA? A McFRIENDLY'S WAITPERSON NEVER, EVER ABANDONS HIS... HEY! WHAT ARE YOU SMOKING?
SMOKING?
GB Trudeau
YEAH, SMOK-ING! HARRIS, ARE YOU...
SORRY, BOSS—WHAT HAPPENS ON BREAK STAYS ON BREAK.

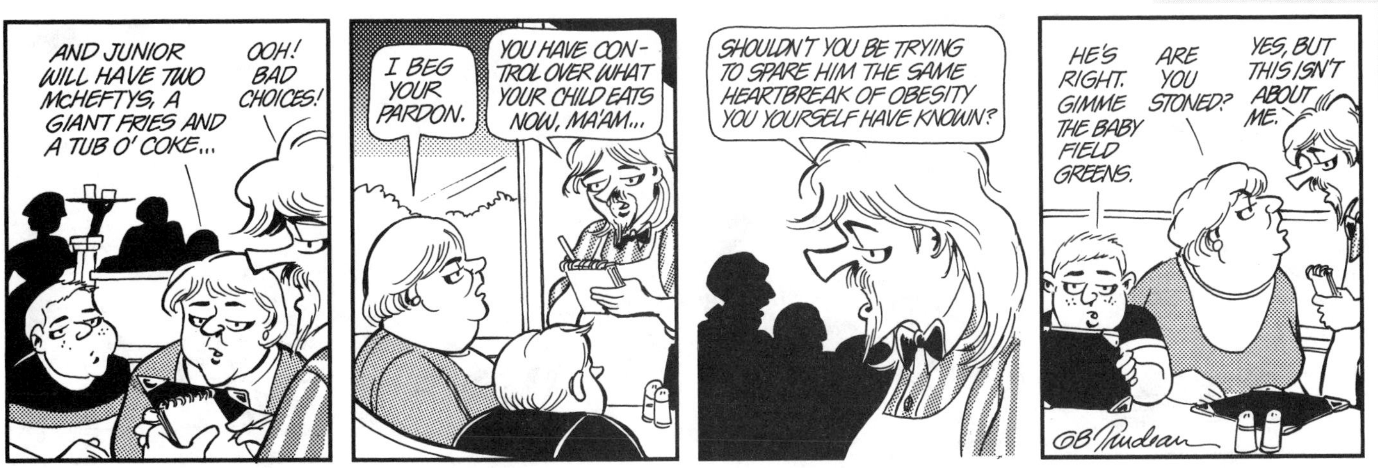
AND JUNIOR WILL HAVE TWO McHEFTYS, A GIANT FRIES AND A TUB O' COKE...
OOH! BAD CHOICES!
I BEG YOUR PARDON.
YOU HAVE CON-TROL OVER WHAT YOUR CHILD EATS NOW, MA'AM...
SHOULDN'T YOU BE TRYING TO SPARE HIM THE SAME HEARTBREAK OF OBESITY YOU YOURSELF HAVE KNOWN?
HE'S RIGHT. GIMME THE BABY FIELD GREENS.
ARE YOU STONED?
YES, BUT THIS ISN'T ABOUT ME.
GB Trudeau

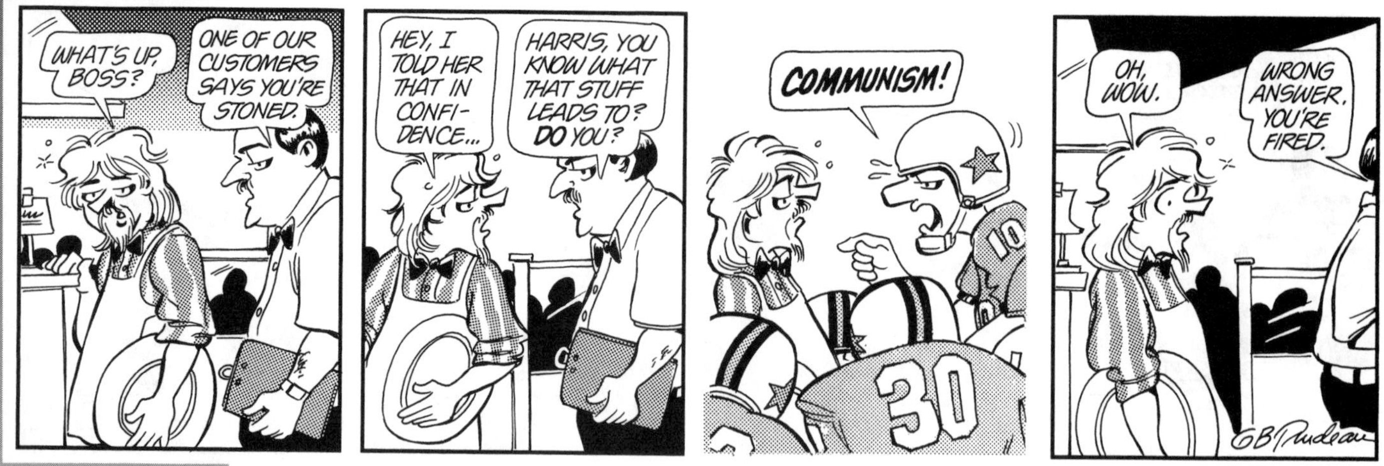
WHAT'S UP, BOSS?
ONE OF OUR CUSTOMERS SAYS YOU'RE STONED.
HEY, I TOLD HER THAT IN CONFI-DENCE...
HARRIS, YOU KNOW WHAT THAT STUFF LEADS TO? DO YOU?
COMMUNISM!
OH, WOW.
WRONG ANSWER. YOU'RE FIRED.
GB Trudeau

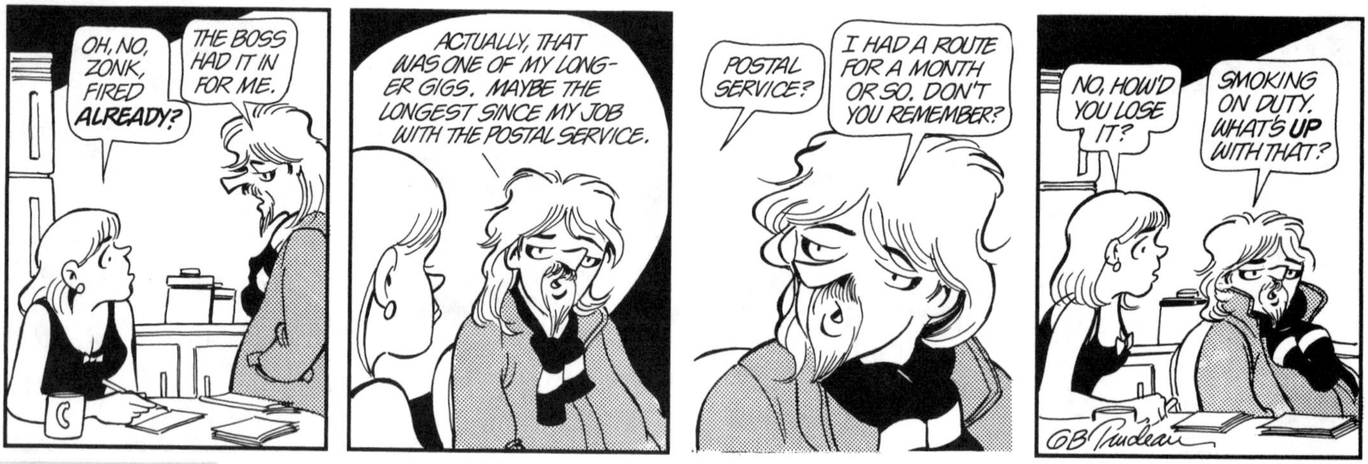
OH, NO, ZONK, FIRED ALREADY?
THE BOSS HAD IT IN FOR ME.
ACTUALLY, THAT WAS ONE OF MY LONG-ER GIGS. MAYBE THE LONGEST SINCE MY JOB WITH THE POSTAL SERVICE.
POSTAL SERVICE?
I HAD A ROUTE FOR A MONTH OR SO. DON'T YOU REMEMBER?
NO, HOW'D YOU LOSE IT?
SMOKING ON DUTY. WHAT'S UP WITH THAT?
GB Trudeau

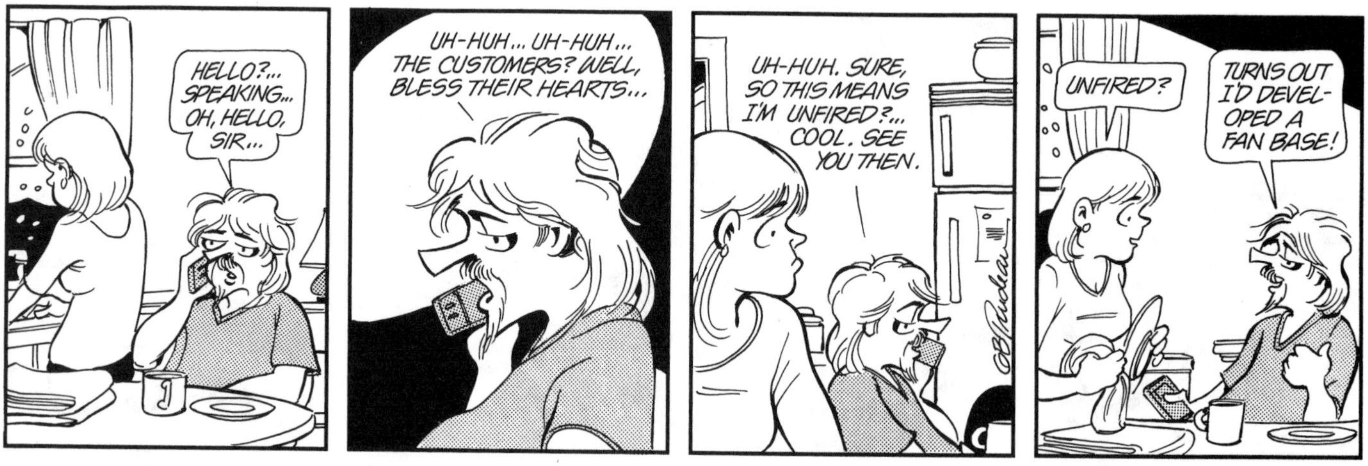
HELLO?... SPEAKING... OH, HELLO, SIR...
UH-HUH... UH-HUH... THE CUSTOMERS? WELL, BLESS THEIR HEARTS...
UH-HUH. SURE, SO THIS MEANS I'M UNFIRED?... COOL. SEE YOU THEN.
GB Trudeau
UNFIRED?
TURNS OUT I'D DEVEL-OPED A FAN BASE!

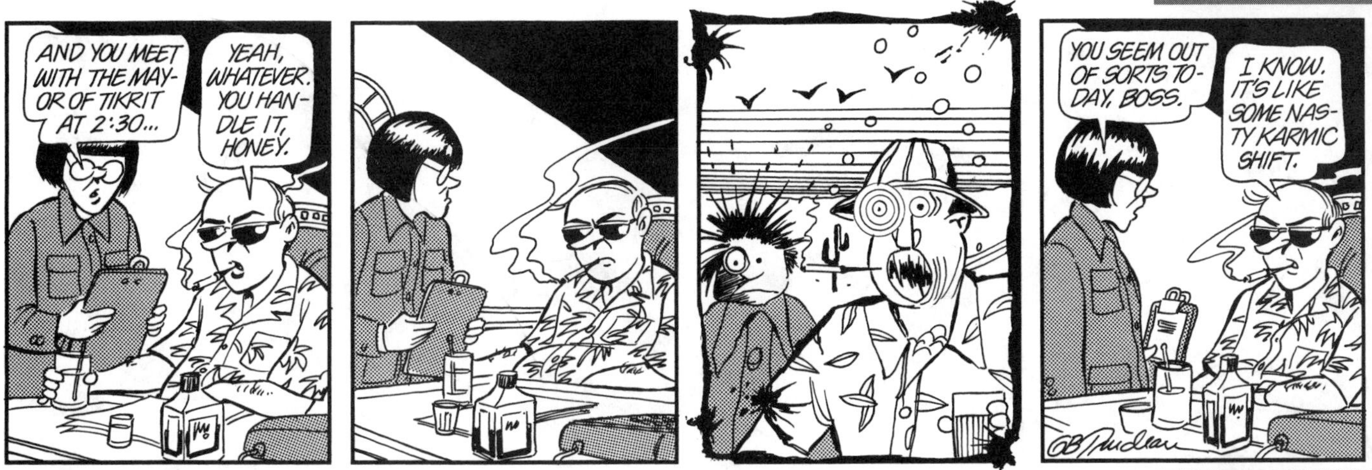
AND YOU MEET WITH THE MAY- OR OF TIKRIT AT 2:30...
YEAH, WHATEVER. YOU HAN- DLE IT, HONEY.
YOU SEEM OUT OF SORTS TO- DAY, BOSS.
I KNOW. IT'S LIKE SOME NAS- TY KARMIC SHIFT.

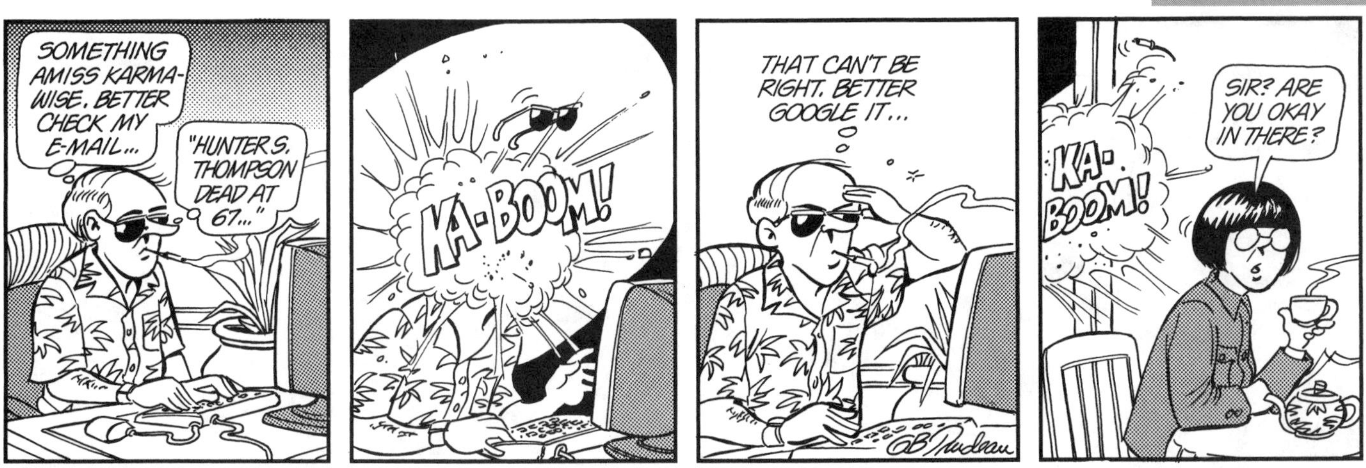
SOMETHING AMISS KARMA- WISE. BETTER CHECK MY E-MAIL...
"HUNTER S. THOMPSON DEAD AT 67..."
KA-BOOM!
THAT CAN'T BE RIGHT. BETTER GOOGLE IT...
KA- BOOM!
SIR? ARE YOU OKAY IN THERE?

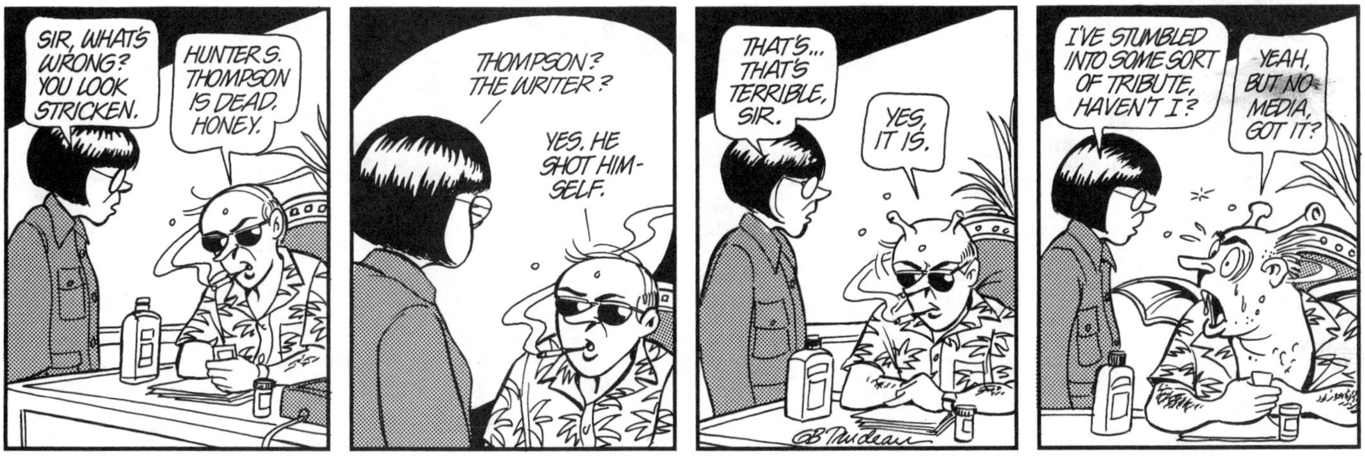
SIR, WHAT'S WRONG? YOU LOOK STRICKEN.
HUNTER S. THOMPSON IS DEAD, HONEY.
THOMPSON? THE WRITER?
YES. HE SHOT HIM- SELF.
THAT'S... THAT'S TERRIBLE, SIR.
YES, IT IS.
I'VE STUMBLED INTO SOME SORT OF TRIBUTE, HAVEN'T I?
YEAH, BUT NO MEDIA, GOT IT?

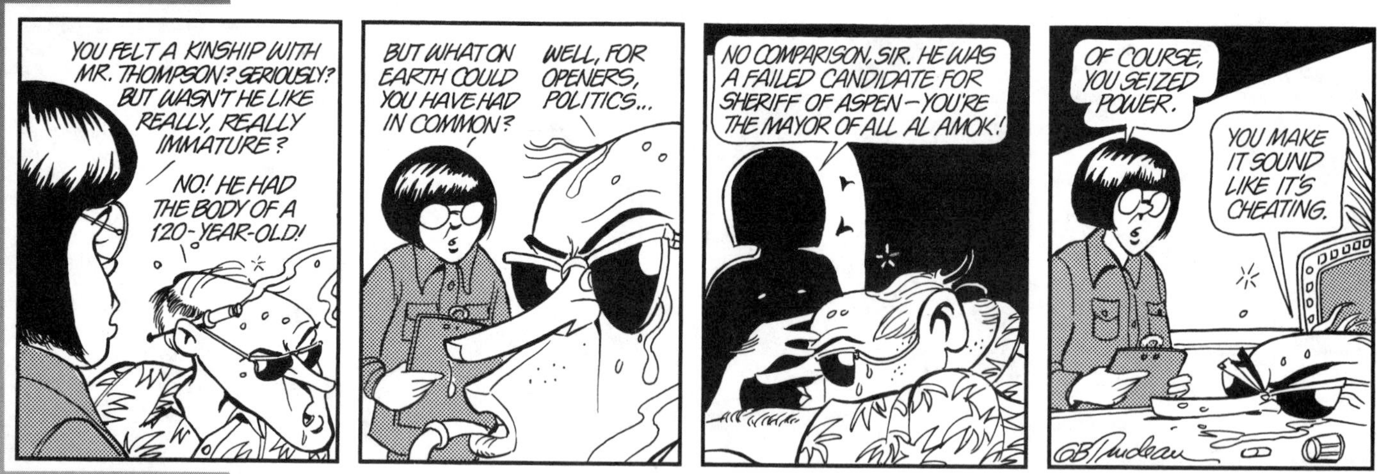
YOU FELT A KINSHIP WITH MR. THOMPSON? SERIOUSLY? BUT WASN'T HE LIKE REALLY, REALLY IMMATURE?
NO! HE HAD THE BODY OF A 120-YEAR-OLD!
BUT WHAT ON EARTH COULD YOU HAVE HAD IN COMMON?
WELL, FOR OPENERS, POLITICS...
NO COMPARISON, SIR. HE WAS A FAILED CANDIDATE FOR SHERIFF OF ASPEN—YOU'RE THE MAYOR OF ALL AL AMOK!
OF COURSE, YOU SEIZED POWER.
YOU MAKE IT SOUND LIKE IT'S CHEATING.

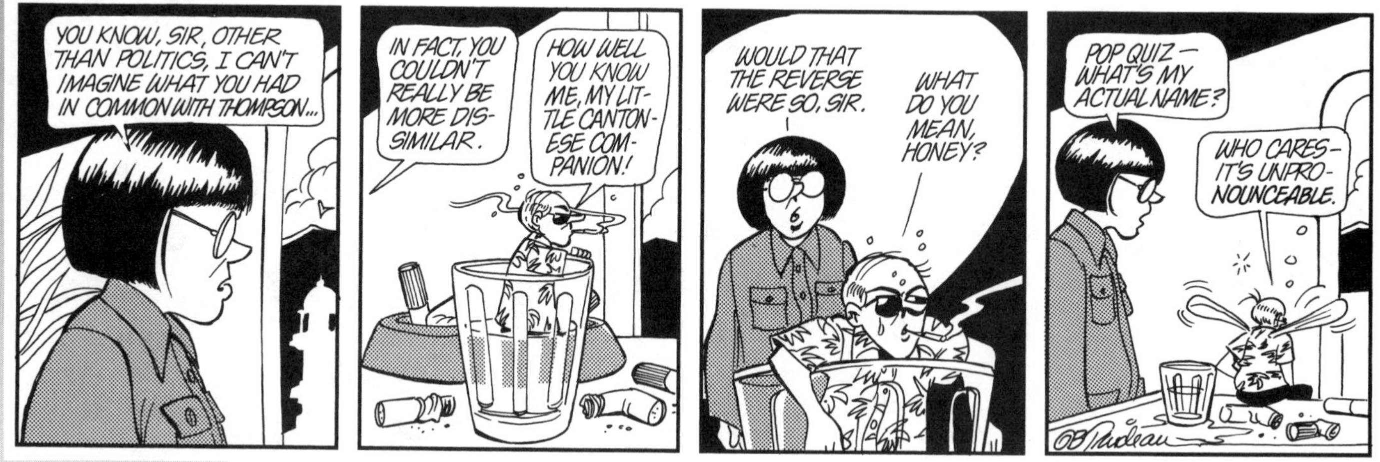
YOU KNOW, SIR, OTHER THAN POLITICS, I CAN'T IMAGINE WHAT YOU HAD IN COMMON WITH THOMPSON...
IN FACT, YOU COULDN'T REALLY BE MORE DISSIMILAR.
HOW WELL YOU KNOW ME, MY LITTLE CANTONESE COMPANION!
WOULD THAT THE REVERSE WERE SO, SIR.
WHAT DO YOU MEAN, HONEY?
POP QUIZ—WHAT'S MY ACTUAL NAME?
WHO CARES—IT'S UNPRONOUNCEABLE.

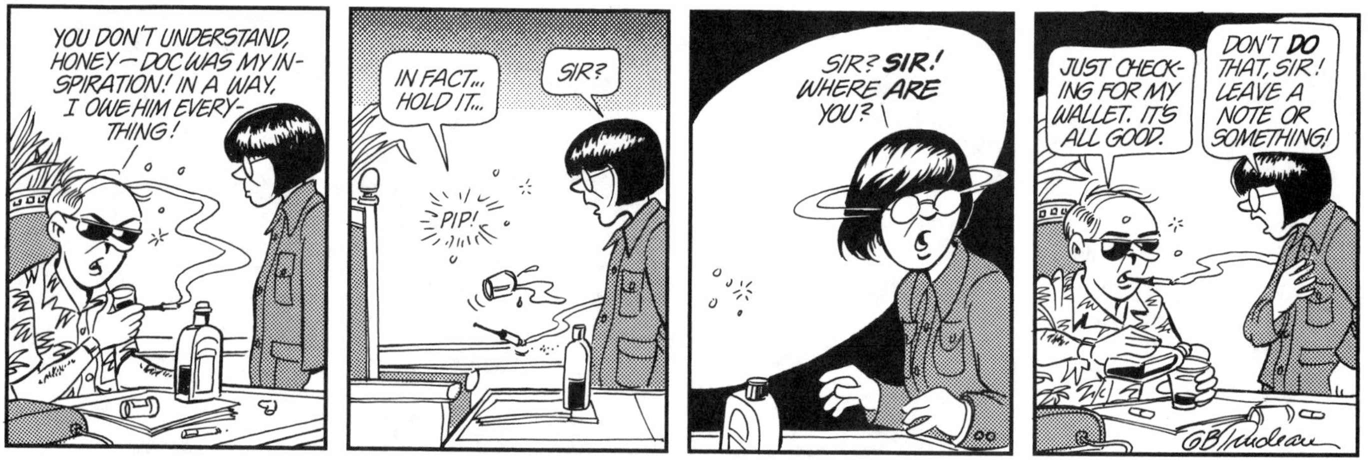
YOU DON'T UNDERSTAND, HONEY—DOC WAS MY INSPIRATION! IN A WAY, I OWE HIM EVERYTHING!
IN FACT... HOLD IT...
SIR?
PIP!
SIR? SIR! WHERE ARE YOU?
JUST CHECKING FOR MY WALLET. IT'S ALL GOOD.
DON'T DO THAT, SIR! LEAVE A NOTE OR SOMETHING!

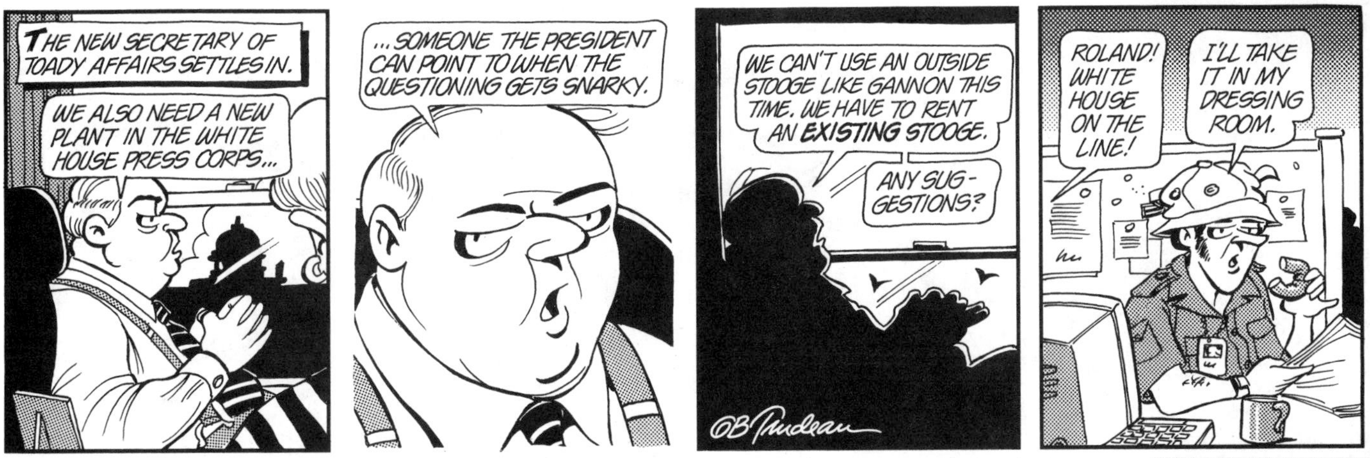
THE NEW SECRETARY OF TOADY AFFAIRS SETTLES IN.
WE ALSO NEED A NEW PLANT IN THE WHITE HOUSE PRESS CORPS...
...SOMEONE THE PRESIDENT CAN POINT TO WHEN THE QUESTIONING GETS SNARKY.
WE CAN'T USE AN OUTSIDE STOOGE LIKE GANNON THIS TIME. WE HAVE TO RENT AN EXISTING STOOGE.
ANY SUGGESTIONS?
ROLAND! WHITE HOUSE ON THE LINE!
I'LL TAKE IT IN MY DRESSING ROOM.

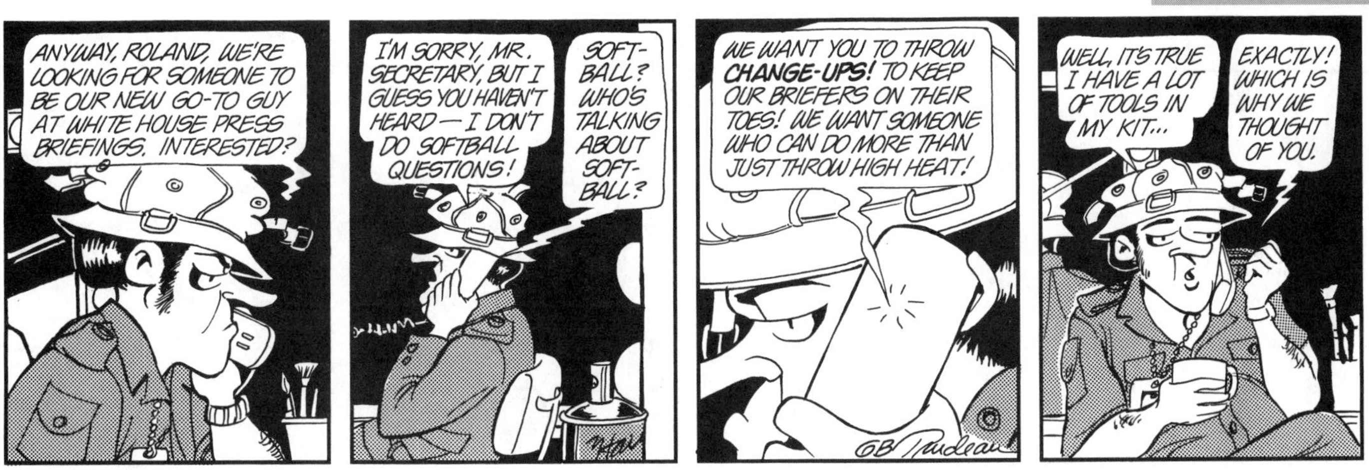
ANYWAY, ROLAND, WE'RE LOOKING FOR SOMEONE TO BE OUR NEW GO-TO GUY AT WHITE HOUSE PRESS BRIEFINGS. INTERESTED?
I'M SORRY, MR. SECRETARY, BUT I GUESS YOU HAVEN'T HEARD — I DON'T DO SOFTBALL QUESTIONS!
SOFT-BALL? WHO'S TALKING ABOUT SOFT-BALL?
WE WANT YOU TO THROW CHANGE-UPS! TO KEEP OUR BRIEFERS ON THEIR TOES! WE WANT SOMEONE WHO CAN DO MORE THAN JUST THROW HIGH HEAT!
WELL, IT'S TRUE I HAVE A LOT OF TOOLS IN MY KIT...
EXACTLY! WHICH IS WHY WE THOUGHT OF YOU.

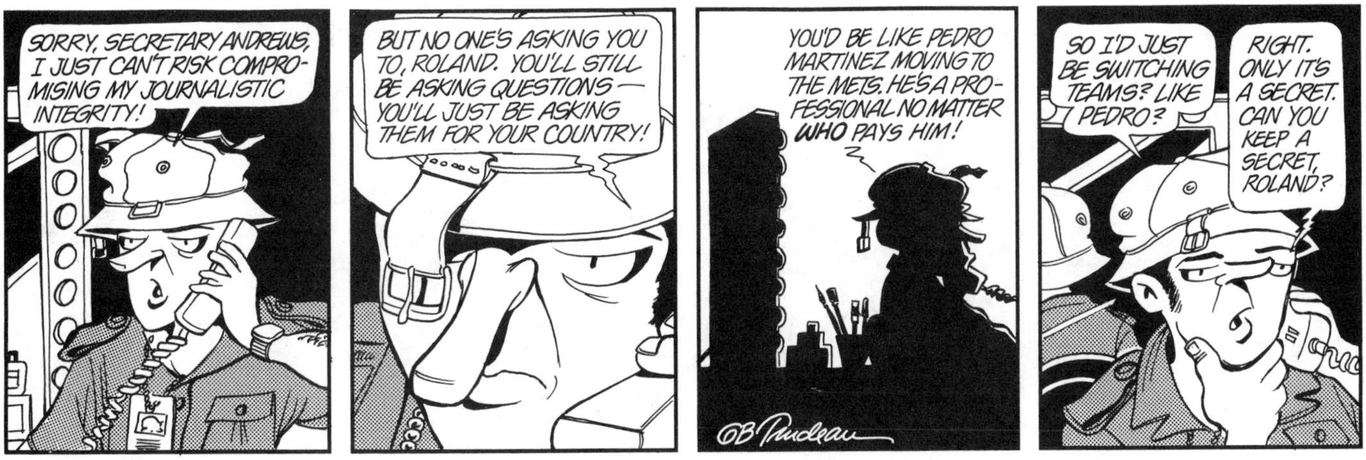
SORRY, SECRETARY ANDREWS, I JUST CAN'T RISK COMPROMISING MY JOURNALISTIC INTEGRITY!
BUT NO ONE'S ASKING YOU TO, ROLAND. YOU'LL STILL BE ASKING QUESTIONS — YOU'LL JUST BE ASKING THEM FOR YOUR COUNTRY!
YOU'D BE LIKE PEDRO MARTINEZ MOVING TO THE METS. HE'S A PROFESSIONAL NO MATTER WHO PAYS HIM!
SO I'D JUST BE SWITCHING TEAMS? LIKE PEDRO?
RIGHT. ONLY IT'S A SECRET. CAN YOU KEEP A SECRET, ROLAND?

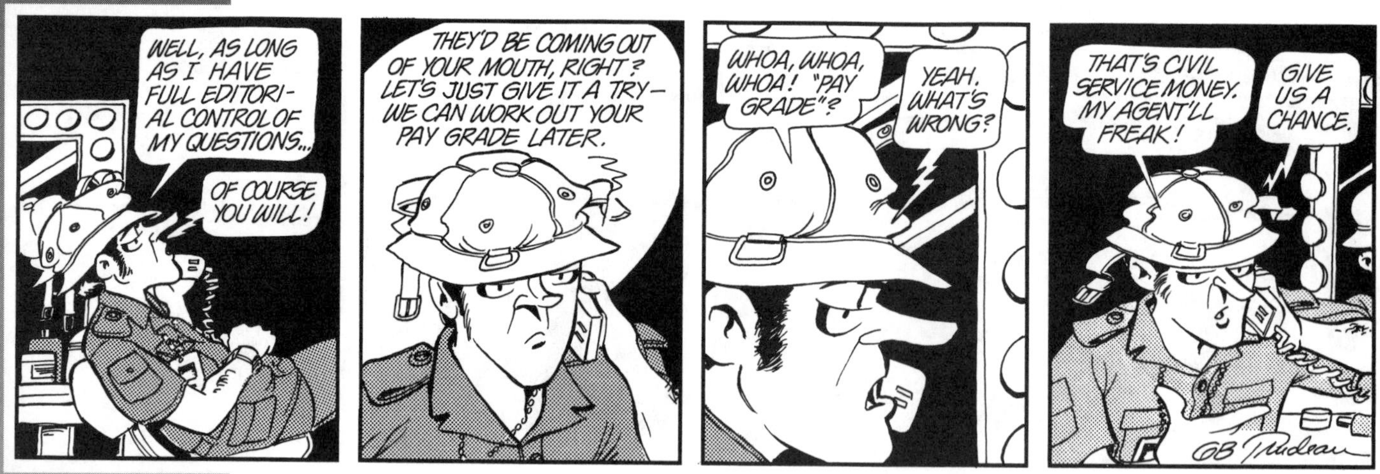
WELL, AS LONG AS I HAVE FULL EDITORIAL CONTROL OF MY QUESTIONS...
OF COURSE YOU WILL!
THEY'D BE COMING OUT OF YOUR MOUTH, RIGHT? LET'S JUST GIVE IT A TRY— WE CAN WORK OUT YOUR PAY GRADE LATER.
WHOA, WHOA, WHOA! "PAY GRADE"?
YEAH. WHAT'S WRONG?
THAT'S CIVIL SERVICE MONEY. MY AGENT'LL FREAK!
GIVE US A CHANCE.
©B Trudeau

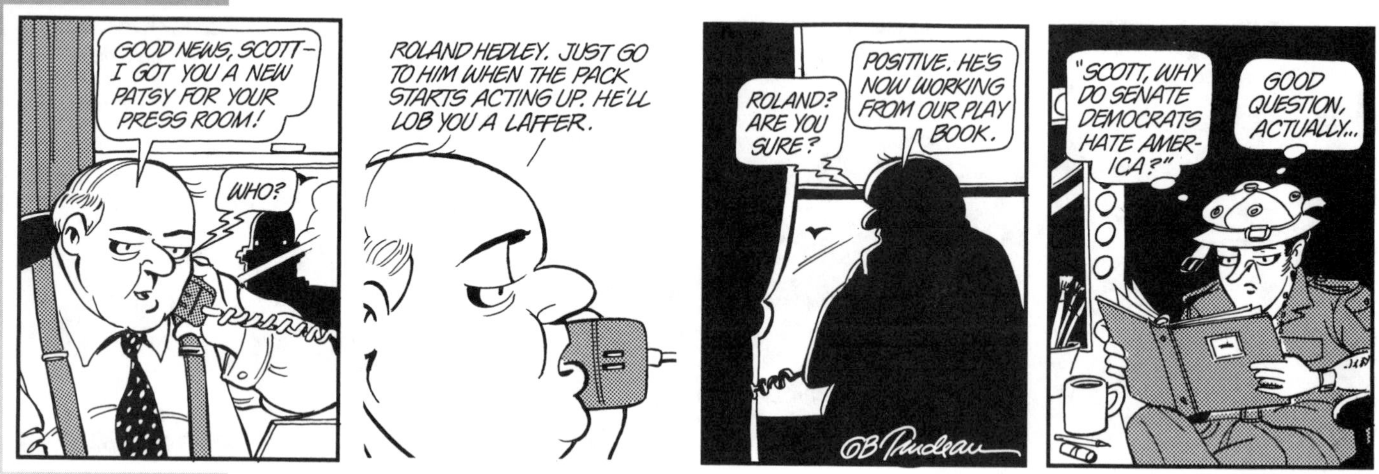
GOOD NEWS, SCOTT— I GOT YOU A NEW PATSY FOR YOUR PRESS ROOM!
WHO?
ROLAND HEDLEY. JUST GO TO HIM WHEN THE PACK STARTS ACTING UP. HE'LL LOB YOU A LAFFER.
ROLAND? ARE YOU SURE?
POSITIVE. HE'S NOW WORKING FROM OUR PLAY BOOK.
©B Trudeau
"SCOTT, WHY DO SENATE DEMOCRATS HATE AMERICA?"
GOOD QUESTION, ACTUALLY...

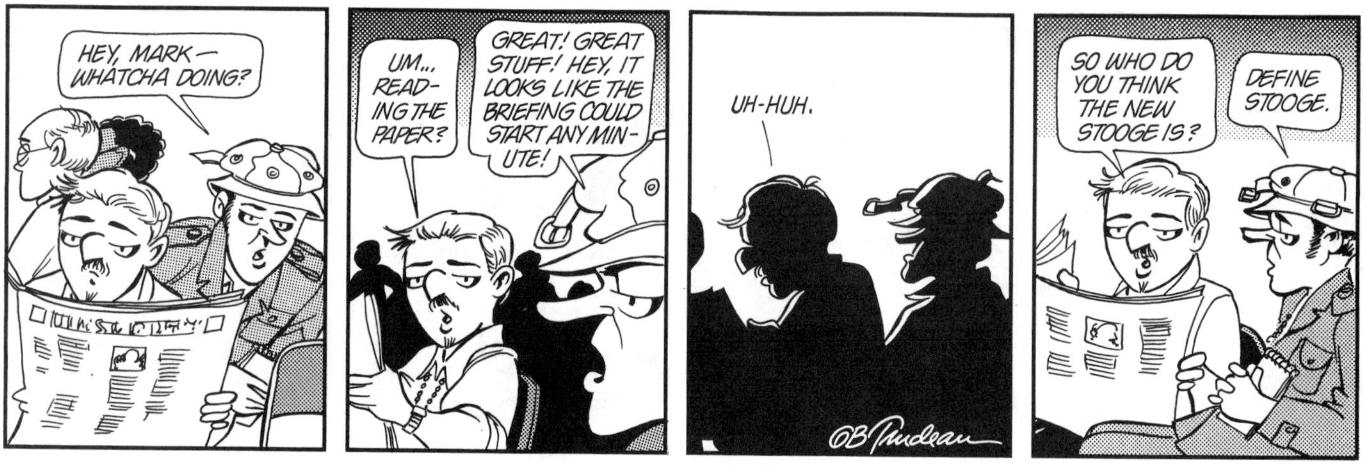
HEY, MARK— WHATCHA DOING?
UM... READING THE PAPER?
GREAT! GREAT STUFF! HEY, IT LOOKS LIKE THE BRIEFING COULD START ANY MINUTE!
UH-HUH.
©B Trudeau
SO WHO DO YOU THINK THE NEW STOOGE IS?
DEFINE STOOGE.

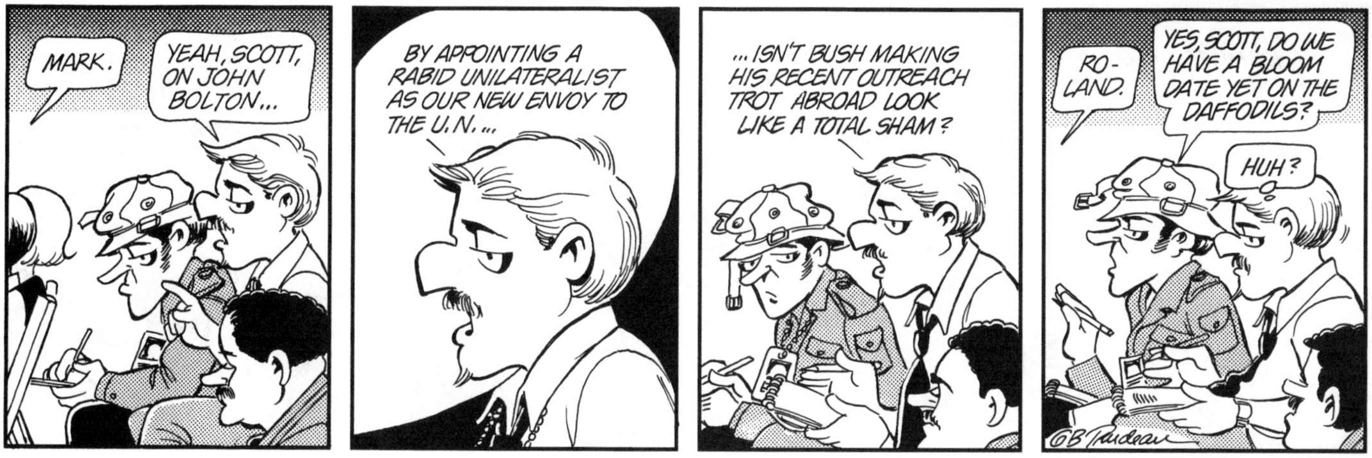
MARK.
YEAH, SCOTT, ON JOHN BOLTON...
BY APPOINTING A RABID UNILATERALIST AS OUR NEW ENVOY TO THE U.N. ...
...ISN'T BUSH MAKING HIS RECENT OUTREACH TROT ABROAD LOOK LIKE A TOTAL SHAM?
RO-LAND.
YES, SCOTT, DO WE HAVE A BLOOM DATE YET ON THE DAFFODILS?
HUH?
©B Trudeau

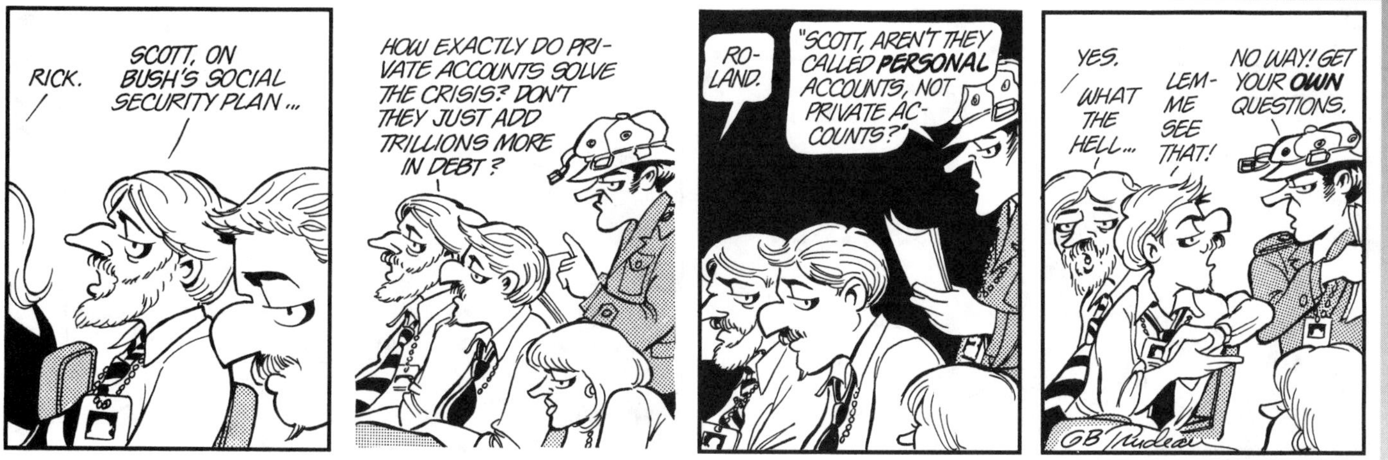
RICK.
SCOTT, ON BUSH'S SOCIAL SECURITY PLAN...
HOW EXACTLY DO PRIVATE ACCOUNTS SOLVE THE CRISIS? DON'T THEY JUST ADD TRILLIONS MORE IN DEBT?
RO-LAND.
"SCOTT, AREN'T THEY CALLED **PERSONAL** ACCOUNTS, NOT PRIVATE ACCOUNTS?"
YES.
WHAT THE HELL...
LEMME SEE THAT!
NO WAY! GET YOUR **OWN** QUESTIONS.
©B Trudeau

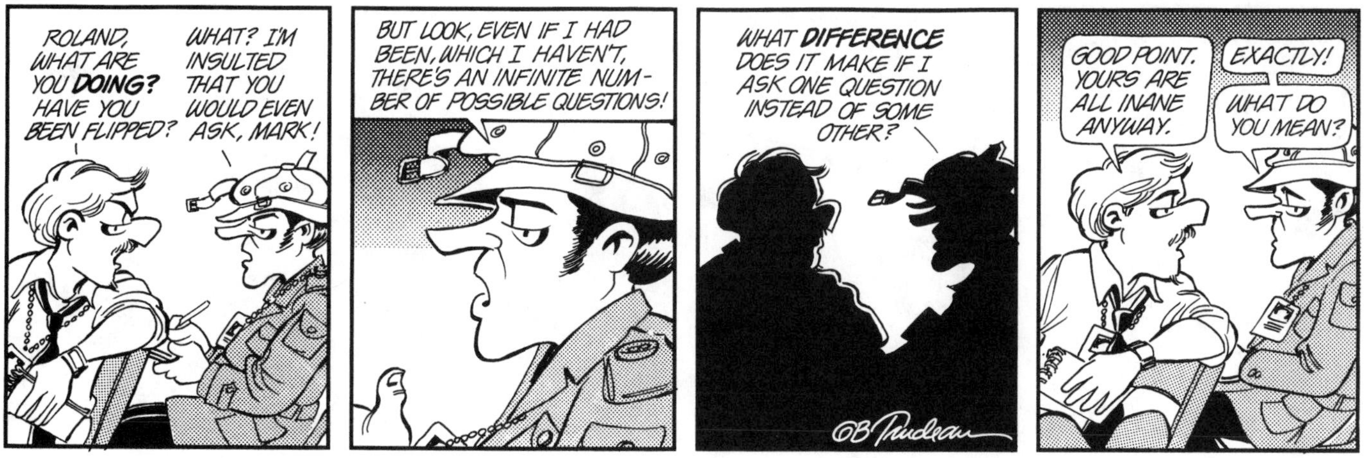
ROLAND, WHAT ARE YOU **DOING?** HAVE YOU BEEN FLIPPED?
WHAT? I'M INSULTED THAT YOU WOULD EVEN ASK, MARK!
BUT LOOK, EVEN IF I HAD BEEN, WHICH I HAVEN'T, THERE'S AN INFINITE NUMBER OF POSSIBLE QUESTIONS!
WHAT **DIFFERENCE** DOES IT MAKE IF I ASK ONE QUESTION INSTEAD OF SOME OTHER?
©B Trudeau
GOOD POINT. YOURS ARE ALL INANE ANYWAY.
EXACTLY!
WHAT DO YOU MEAN?

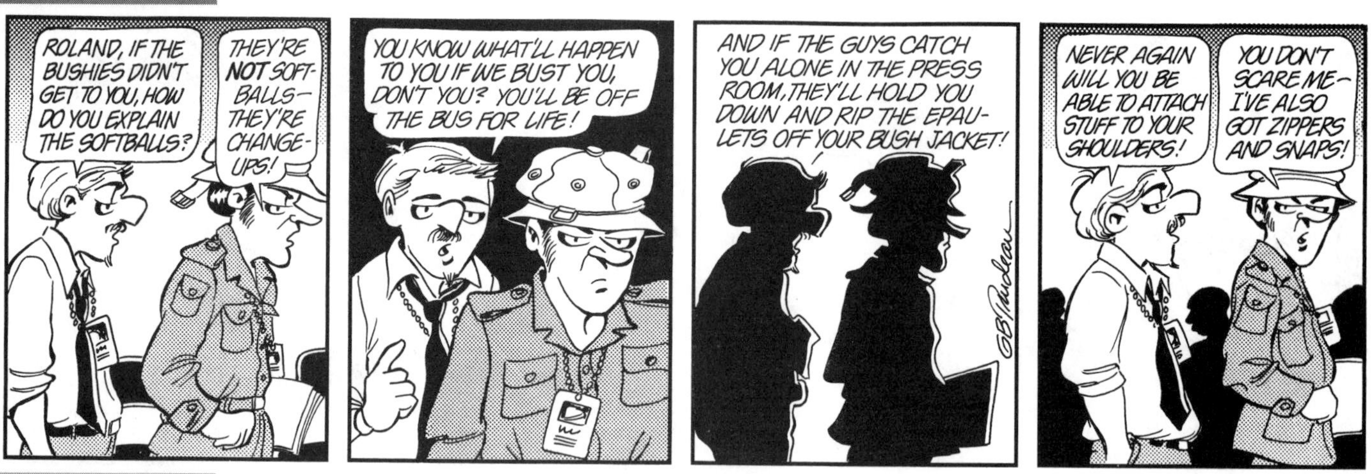
ROLAND, IF THE BUSHIES DIDN'T GET TO YOU, HOW DO YOU EXPLAIN THE SOFTBALLS?
THEY'RE **NOT** SOFT-BALLS– THEY'RE CHANGE-UPS!
YOU KNOW WHAT'LL HAPPEN TO YOU IF WE BUST YOU, DON'T YOU? YOU'LL BE OFF THE BUS FOR LIFE!
AND IF THE GUYS CATCH YOU ALONE IN THE PRESS ROOM, THEY'LL HOLD YOU DOWN AND RIP THE EPAU-LETS OFF YOUR BUSH JACKET!
NEVER AGAIN WILL YOU BE ABLE TO ATTACH STUFF TO YOUR SHOULDERS!
YOU DON'T SCARE ME– I'VE ALSO GOT ZIPPERS AND SNAPS!

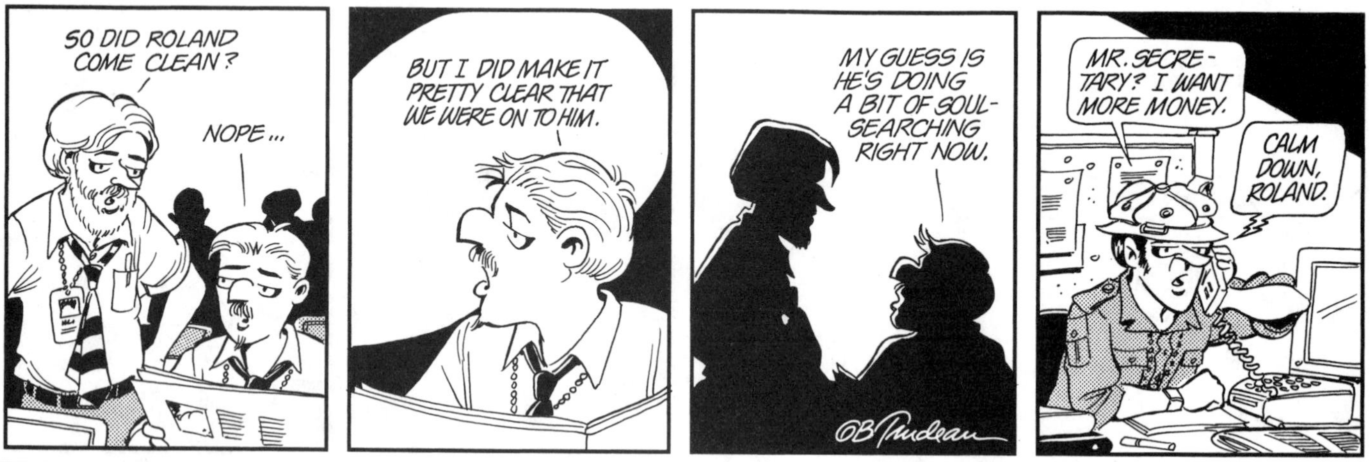
SO DID ROLAND COME CLEAN?
NOPE...
BUT I DID MAKE IT PRETTY CLEAR THAT WE WERE ON TO HIM.
MY GUESS IS HE'S DOING A BIT OF SOUL-SEARCHING RIGHT NOW.
MR. SECRE-TARY? I WANT MORE MONEY.
CALM DOWN, ROLAND.

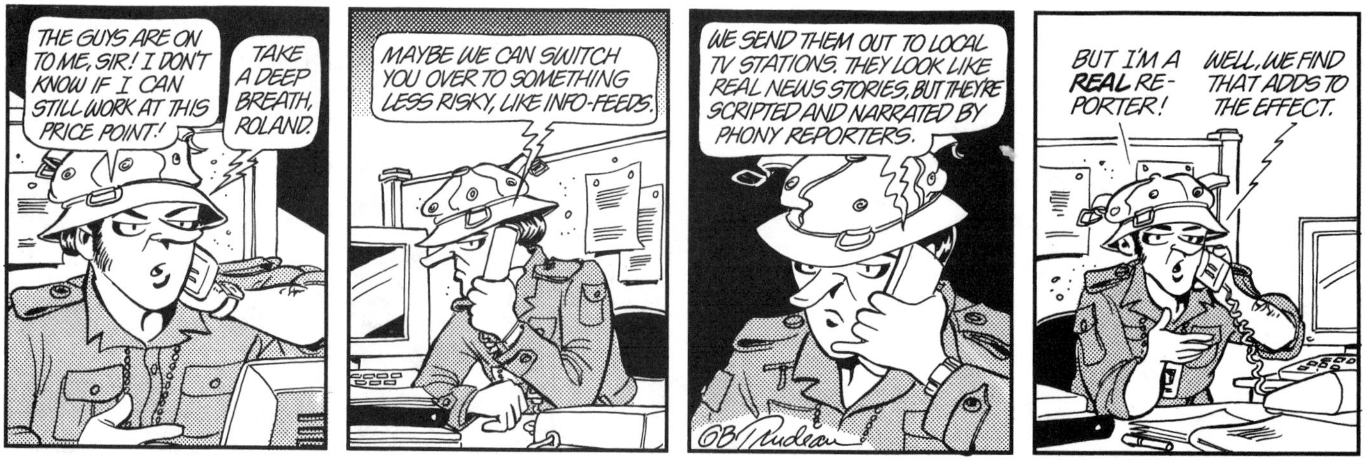
THE GUYS ARE ON TO ME, SIR! I DON'T KNOW IF I CAN STILL WORK AT THIS PRICE POINT!
TAKE A DEEP BREATH, ROLAND.
MAYBE WE CAN SWITCH YOU OVER TO SOMETHING LESS RISKY, LIKE INFO-FEEDS.
WE SEND THEM OUT TO LOCAL TV STATIONS. THEY LOOK LIKE REAL NEWS STORIES, BUT THEY'RE SCRIPTED AND NARRATED BY PHONY REPORTERS.
BUT I'M A **REAL** RE-PORTER!
WELL, WE FIND THAT ADDS TO THE EFFECT.

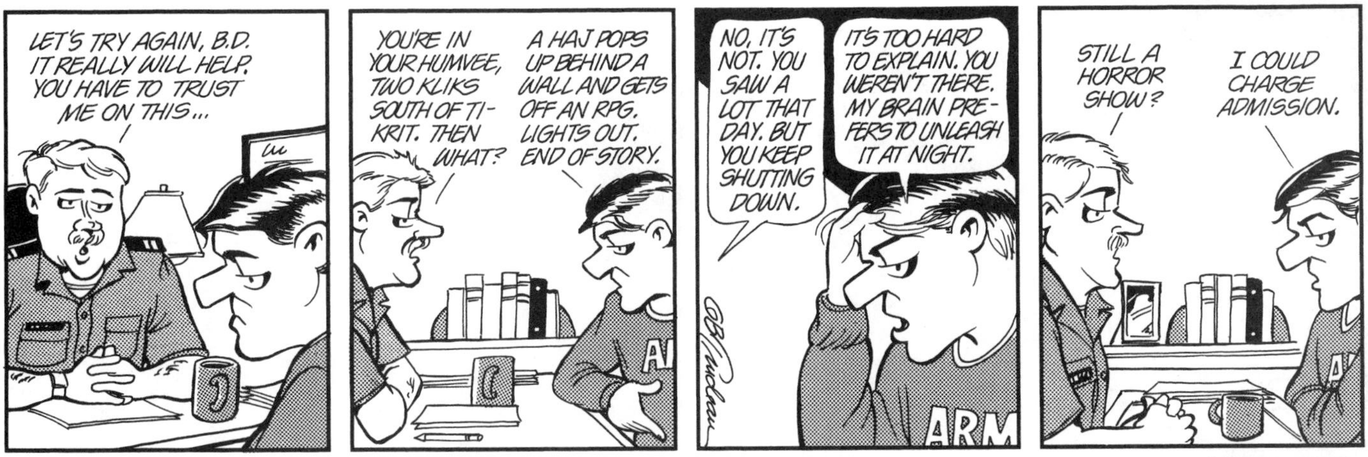

LET'S TRY AGAIN, B.D. IT REALLY WILL HELP. YOU HAVE TO TRUST ME ON THIS...
YOU'RE IN YOUR HUMVEE, TWO KLIKS SOUTH OF TIKRIT. THEN WHAT?
A HAJ POPS UP BEHIND A WALL AND GETS OFF AN RPG. LIGHTS OUT. END OF STORY.
NO, IT'S NOT. YOU SAW A LOT THAT DAY. BUT YOU KEEP SHUTTING DOWN.
IT'S TOO HARD TO EXPLAIN. YOU WEREN'T THERE. MY BRAIN PREFERS TO UNLEASH IT AT NIGHT.
STILL A HORROR SHOW?
I COULD CHARGE ADMISSION.

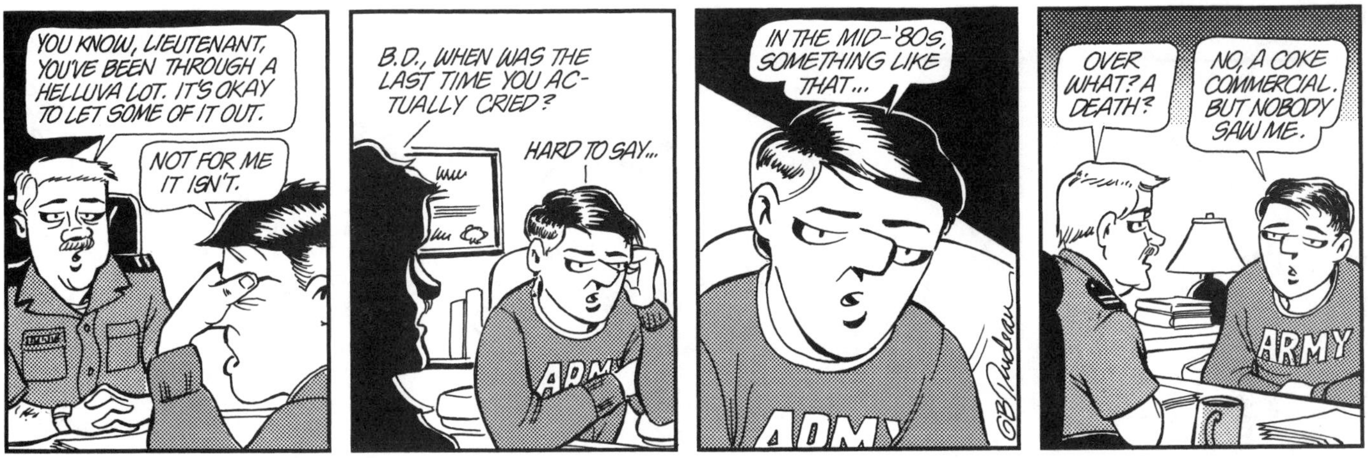

YOU KNOW, LIEUTENANT, YOU'VE BEEN THROUGH A HELLUVA LOT. IT'S OKAY TO LET SOME OF IT OUT.
NOT FOR ME IT ISN'T.
B.D., WHEN WAS THE LAST TIME YOU ACTUALLY CRIED?
HARD TO SAY...
IN THE MID-'80S, SOMETHING LIKE THAT...
OVER WHAT? A DEATH?
NO, A COKE COMMERCIAL. BUT NOBODY SAW ME.

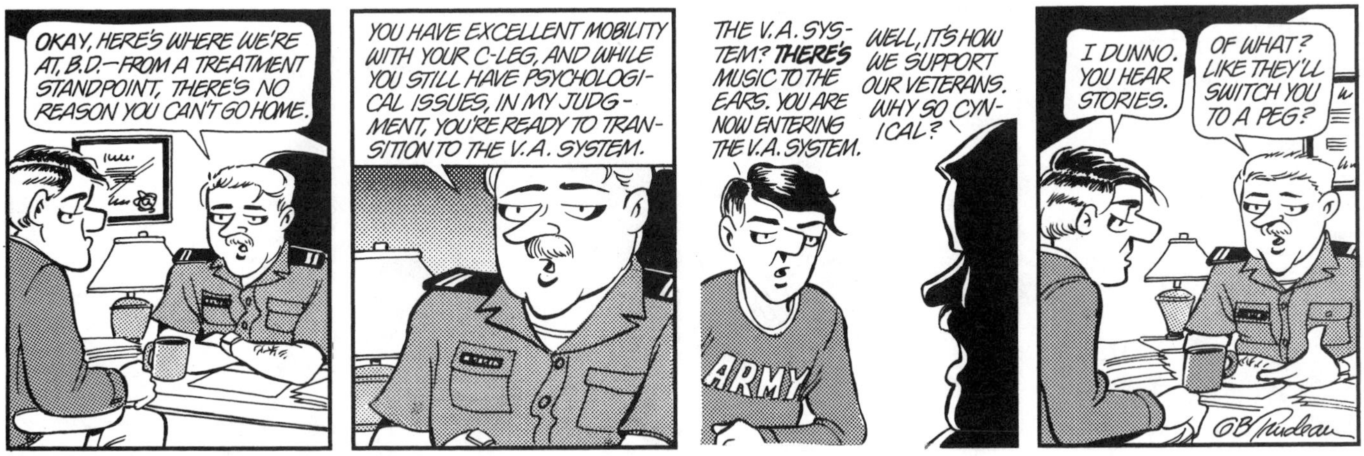

OKAY, HERE'S WHERE WE'RE AT, B.D.—FROM A TREATMENT STANDPOINT, THERE'S NO REASON YOU CAN'T GO HOME.
YOU HAVE EXCELLENT MOBILITY WITH YOUR C-LEG, AND WHILE YOU STILL HAVE PSYCHOLOGICAL ISSUES, IN MY JUDGMENT, YOU'RE READY TO TRANSITION TO THE V.A. SYSTEM.
THE V.A. SYSTEM? THERE'S MUSIC TO THE EARS. YOU ARE NOW ENTERING THE V.A. SYSTEM.
WELL, IT'S HOW WE SUPPORT OUR VETERANS. WHY SO CYNICAL?
I DUNNO. YOU HEAR STORIES.
OF WHAT? LIKE THEY'LL SWITCH YOU TO A PEG?

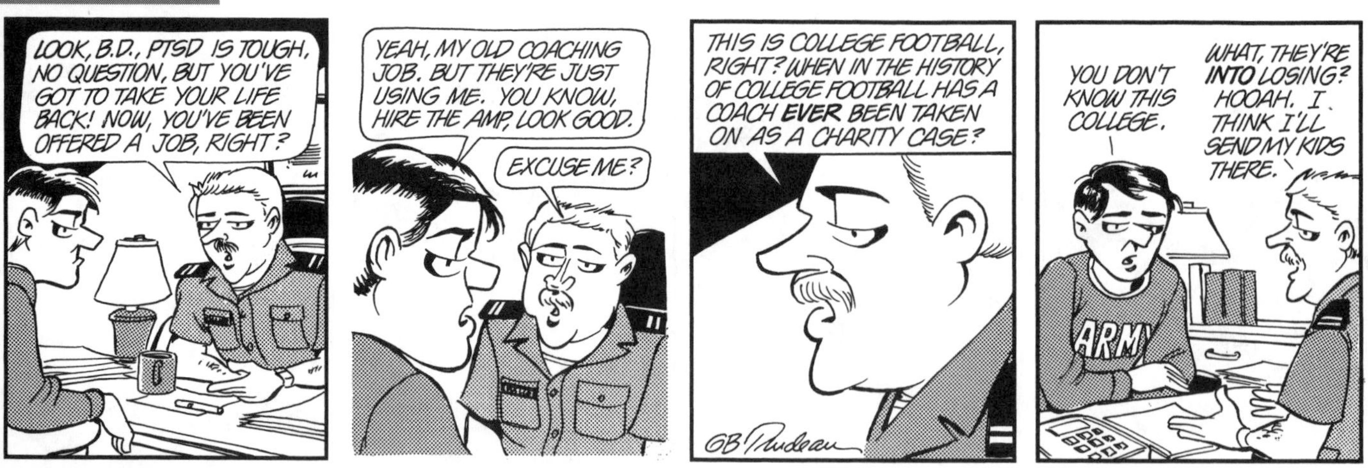
LOOK, B.D., PTSD IS TOUGH, NO QUESTION, BUT YOU'VE GOT TO TAKE YOUR LIFE BACK! NOW, YOU'VE BEEN OFFERED A JOB, RIGHT?
YEAH, MY OLD COACHING JOB. BUT THEY'RE JUST USING ME. YOU KNOW, HIRE THE AMP, LOOK GOOD.
EXCUSE ME?
THIS IS COLLEGE FOOTBALL, RIGHT? WHEN IN THE HISTORY OF COLLEGE FOOTBALL HAS A COACH **EVER** BEEN TAKEN ON AS A CHARITY CASE?
YOU DON'T KNOW THIS COLLEGE.
WHAT, THEY'RE **INTO** LOSING? HOOAH. I THINK I'LL SEND MY KIDS THERE.
ARMY
GB Trudeau

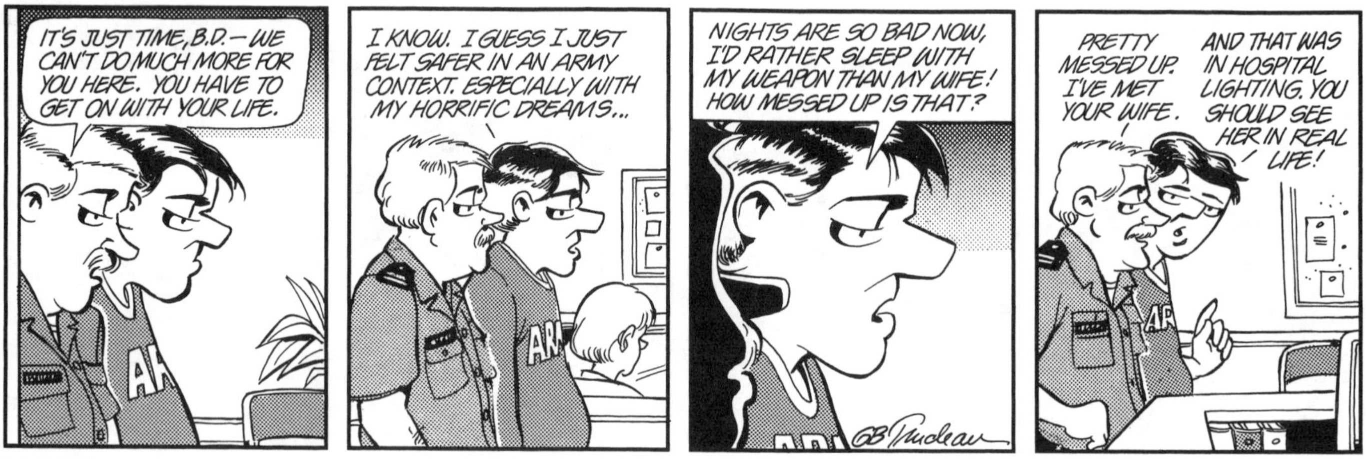
IT'S JUST TIME, B.D.—WE CAN'T DO MUCH MORE FOR YOU HERE. YOU HAVE TO GET ON WITH YOUR LIFE.
I KNOW. I GUESS I JUST FELT SAFER IN AN ARMY CONTEXT. ESPECIALLY WITH MY HORRIFIC DREAMS...
NIGHTS ARE SO BAD NOW, I'D RATHER SLEEP WITH MY WEAPON THAN MY WIFE! HOW MESSED UP IS THAT?
PRETTY MESSED UP. I'VE MET YOUR WIFE.
AND THAT WAS IN HOSPITAL LIGHTING. YOU SHOULD SEE HER IN REAL LIFE!
GB Trudeau

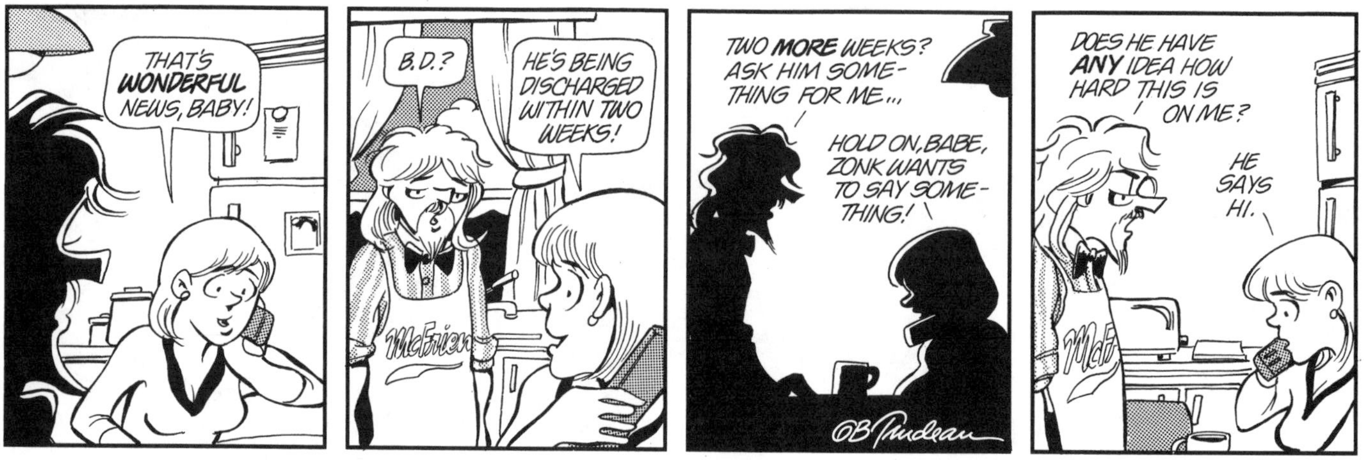
THAT'S **WONDERFUL** NEWS, BABY!
B.D.?
HE'S BEING DISCHARGED WITHIN TWO WEEKS!
McFriendly's
TWO **MORE** WEEKS? ASK HIM SOMETHING FOR ME...
HOLD ON, BABE, ZONK WANTS TO SAY SOMETHING!
DOES HE HAVE **ANY** IDEA HOW HARD THIS IS ON ME?
HE SAYS HI.
GB Trudeau

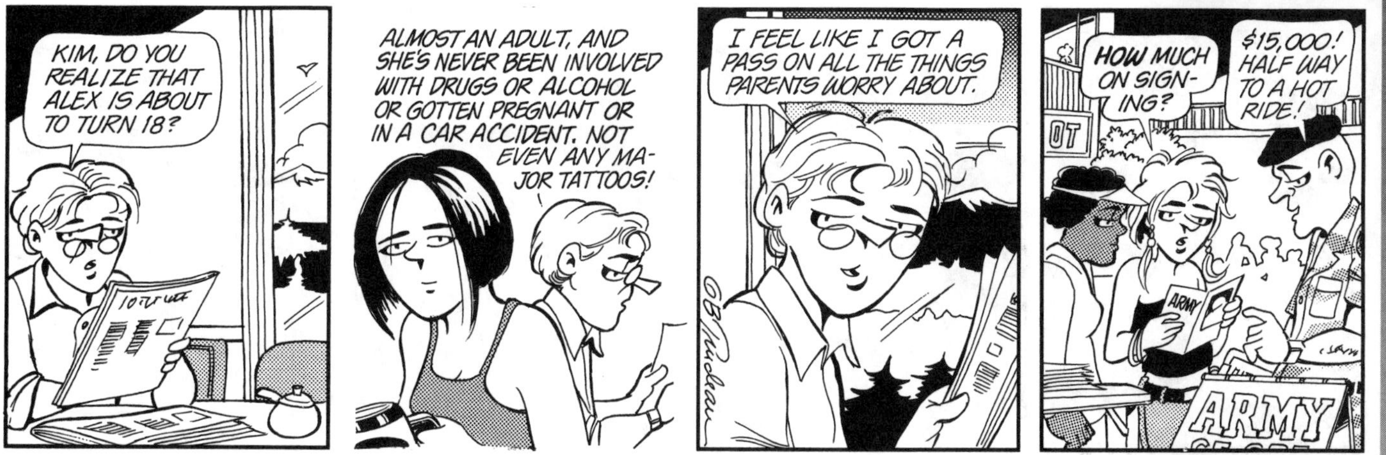
KIM, DO YOU REALIZE THAT ALEX IS ABOUT TO TURN 18?
ALMOST AN ADULT, AND SHE'S NEVER BEEN INVOLVED WITH DRUGS OR ALCOHOL OR GOTTEN PREGNANT OR IN A CAR ACCIDENT. NOT EVEN ANY MAJOR TATTOOS!
I FEEL LIKE I GOT A PASS ON ALL THE THINGS PARENTS WORRY ABOUT.
HOW MUCH ON SIGNING?
$15,000! HALF WAY TO A HOT RIDE!
ARMY

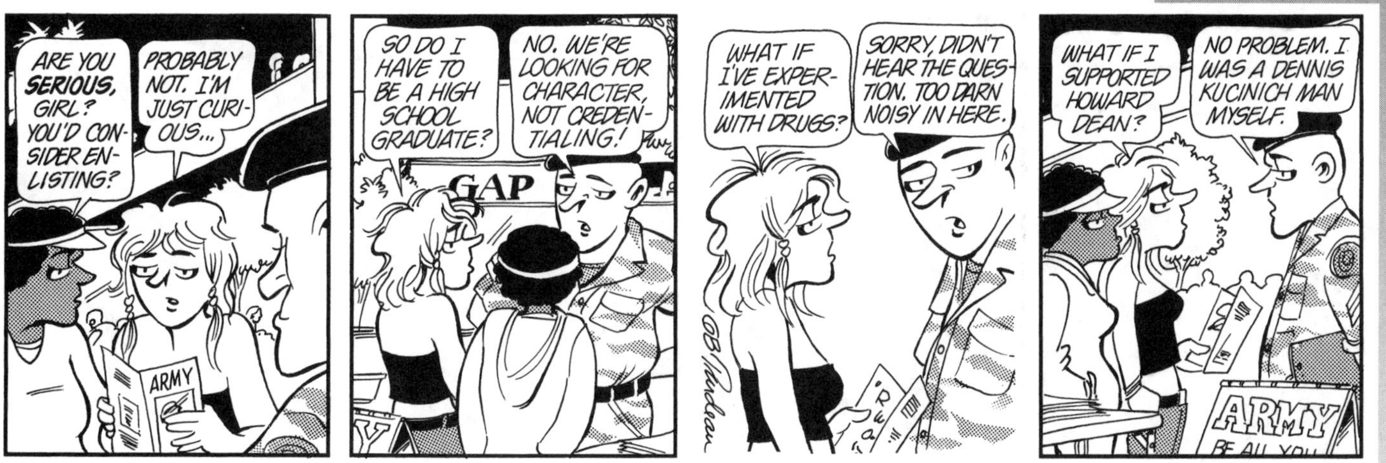
ARE YOU SERIOUS, GIRL? YOU'D CONSIDER ENLISTING?
PROBABLY NOT. I'M JUST CURIOUS...
ARMY
SO DO I HAVE TO BE A HIGH SCHOOL GRADUATE?
NO. WE'RE LOOKING FOR CHARACTER, NOT CREDENTIALING!
GAP
WHAT IF I'VE EXPERIMENTED WITH DRUGS?
SORRY, DIDN'T HEAR THE QUESTION. TOO DARN NOISY IN HERE.
WHAT IF I SUPPORTED HOWARD DEAN?
NO PROBLEM. I WAS A DENNIS KUCINICH MAN MYSELF.
ARMY

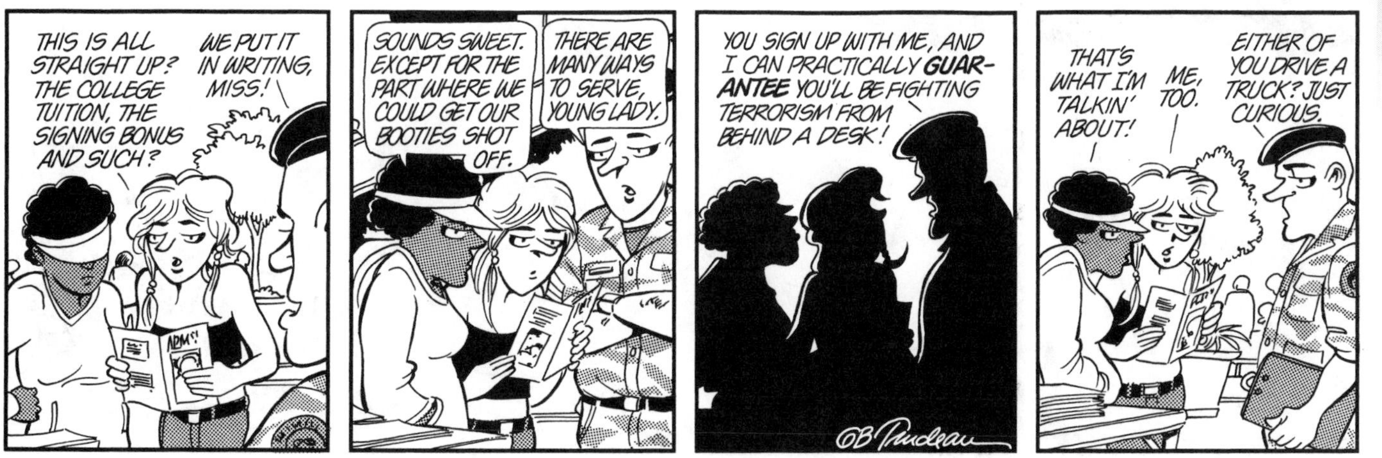
THIS IS ALL STRAIGHT UP? THE COLLEGE TUITION, THE SIGNING BONUS AND SUCH?
WE PUT IT IN WRITING, MISS!
SOUNDS SWEET. EXCEPT FOR THE PART WHERE WE COULD GET OUR BOOTIES SHOT OFF.
THERE ARE MANY WAYS TO SERVE, YOUNG LADY.
YOU SIGN UP WITH ME, AND I CAN PRACTICALLY GUARANTEE YOU'LL BE FIGHTING TERRORISM FROM BEHIND A DESK!
THAT'S WHAT I'M TALKIN' ABOUT!
ME, TOO.
EITHER OF YOU DRIVE A TRUCK? JUST CURIOUS.

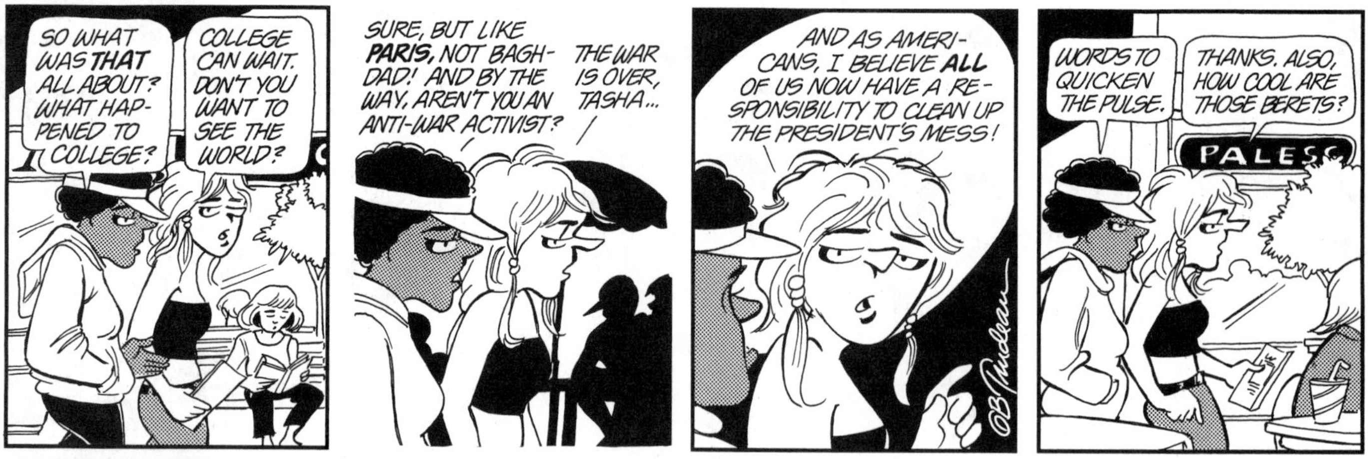
SO WHAT WAS **THAT** ALL ABOUT? WHAT HAPPENED TO COLLEGE?
COLLEGE CAN WAIT. DON'T YOU WANT TO SEE THE WORLD?
SURE, BUT LIKE **PARIS,** NOT BAGHDAD! AND BY THE WAY, AREN'T YOU AN ANTI-WAR ACTIVIST?
THE WAR IS OVER, TASHA...
AND AS AMERICANS, I BELIEVE **ALL** OF US NOW HAVE A RESPONSIBILITY TO CLEAN UP THE PRESIDENT'S MESS!
WORDS TO QUICKEN THE PULSE.
THANKS. ALSO, HOW COOL ARE THOSE BERETS?
PALESC

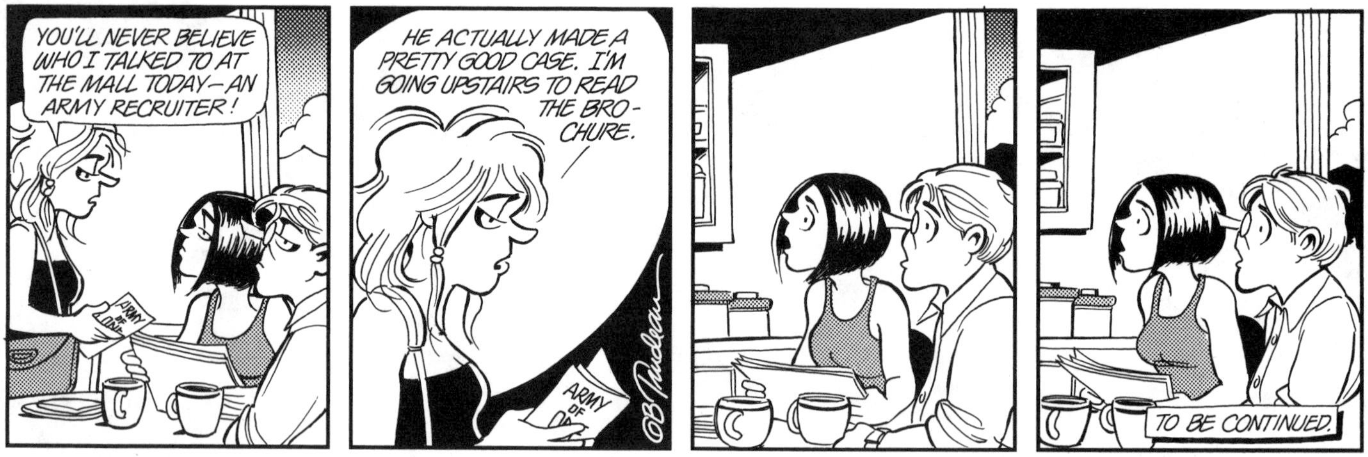
YOU'LL NEVER BELIEVE WHO I TALKED TO AT THE MALL TODAY—AN ARMY RECRUITER!
HE ACTUALLY MADE A PRETTY GOOD CASE. I'M GOING UPSTAIRS TO READ THE BROCHURE.
TO BE CONTINUED.

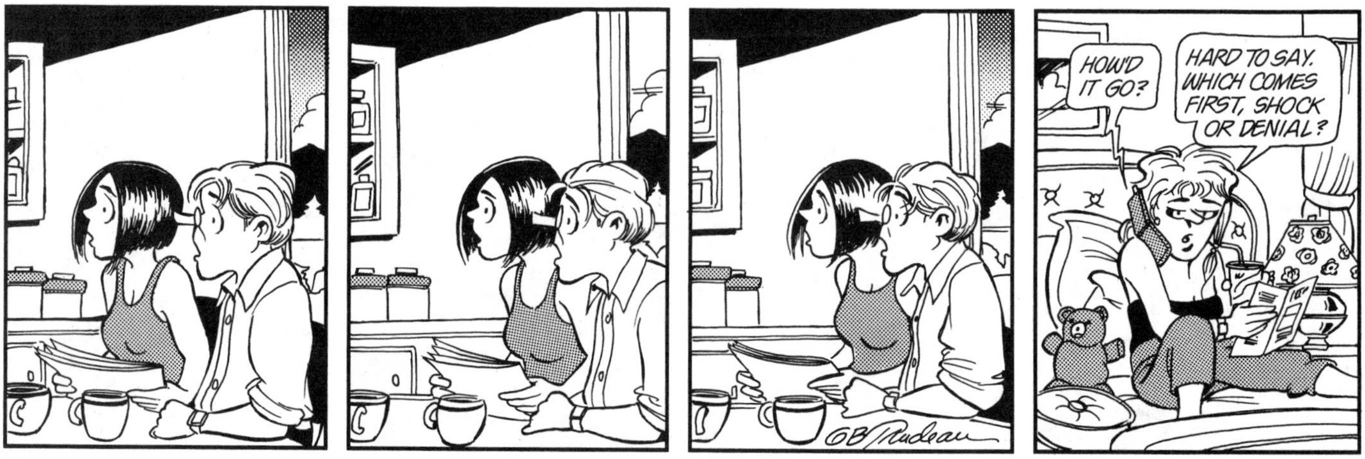
HOW'D IT GO?
HARD TO SAY. WHICH COMES FIRST, SHOCK OR DENIAL?

TESTING! TESTING! TESTING...
...THE WATERS!
HERR GRÖPENFUHRER, IN REGARD TO THE "AMEND FOR ARNOLD" CAMPAIGN...
DO YOU REALLY THINK THE U.S. CONSTITUTION SHOULD BE ALTERED TO ADVANCE THE POLITICAL AMBITIONS OF A SINGLE INDIVIDUAL?
YES! THIS WOULD BE FANTASTIC FOR AMERICA!
NEXT QUESTION!
SIR, ASSUMING SUCH AN AMENDMENT **WERE** PASSED, DO YOU BELIEVE YOU COULD BE A TRULY VIABLE CANDIDATE...
...GIVEN YOUR DECADES-LONG HISTORY OF SEXUAL HARASSMENT?
THIS IS NO PROBLEM, THIS SEX THING!
IT'S NOT?
NO. WE COULD HAVE ANOTHER FANTASTIC AMENDMENT LEGALIZING IT!
GB Trudeau

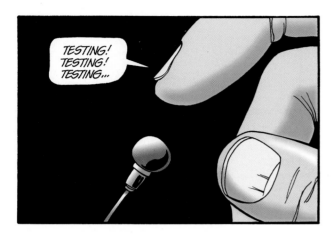

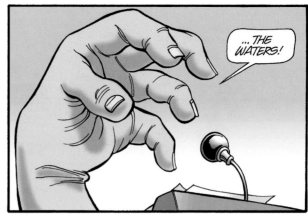

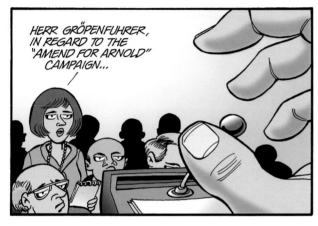

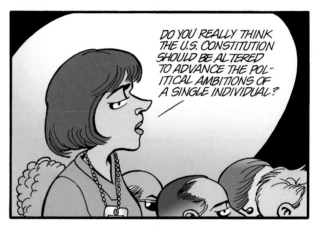

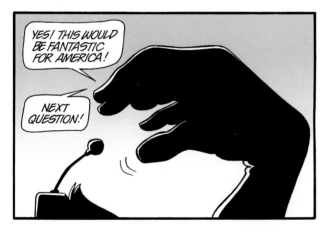

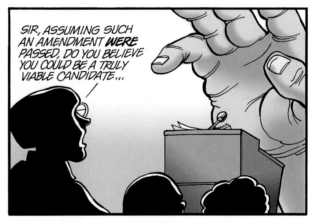

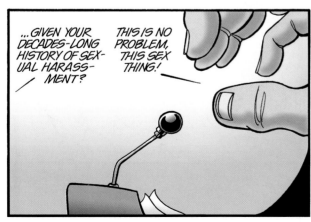

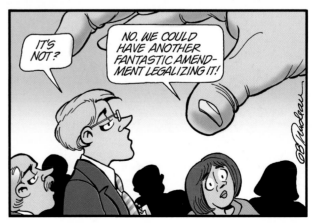

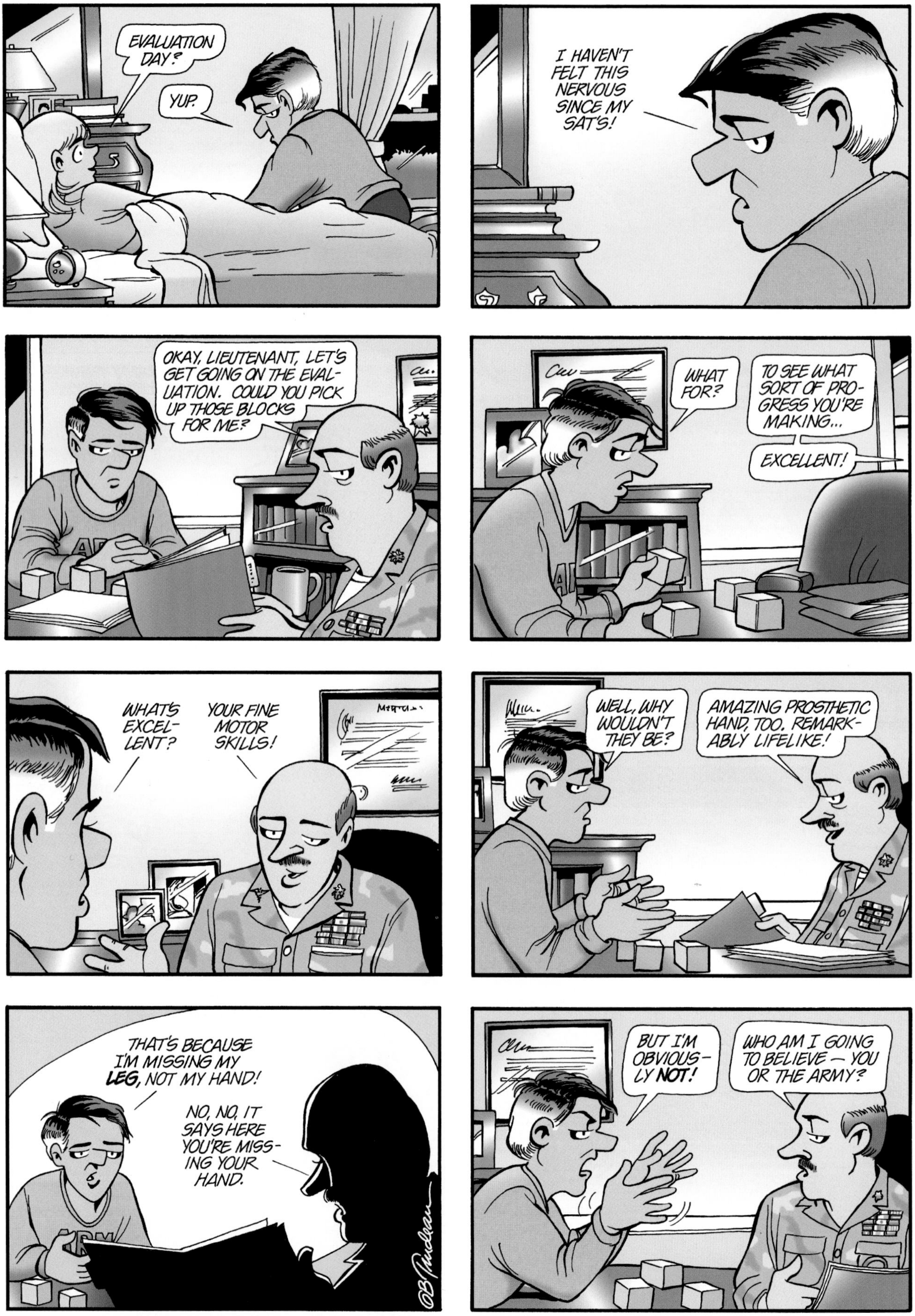
EVALUATION DAY?
YUP.
I HAVEN'T FELT THIS NERVOUS SINCE MY SAT'S!
OKAY, LIEUTENANT, LET'S GET GOING ON THE EVALUATION. COULD YOU PICK UP THOSE BLOCKS FOR ME?
WHAT FOR?
TO SEE WHAT SORT OF PROGRESS YOU'RE MAKING...
EXCELLENT!
WHAT'S EXCELLENT?
YOUR FINE MOTOR SKILLS!
WELL, WHY WOULDN'T THEY BE?
AMAZING PROSTHETIC HAND, TOO. REMARKABLY LIFELIKE!
THAT'S BECAUSE I'M MISSING MY **LEG**, NOT MY HAND!
NO, NO, IT SAYS HERE YOU'RE MISSING YOUR HAND.
BUT I'M OBVIOUSLY **NOT**!
WHO AM I GOING TO BELIEVE — YOU OR THE ARMY?

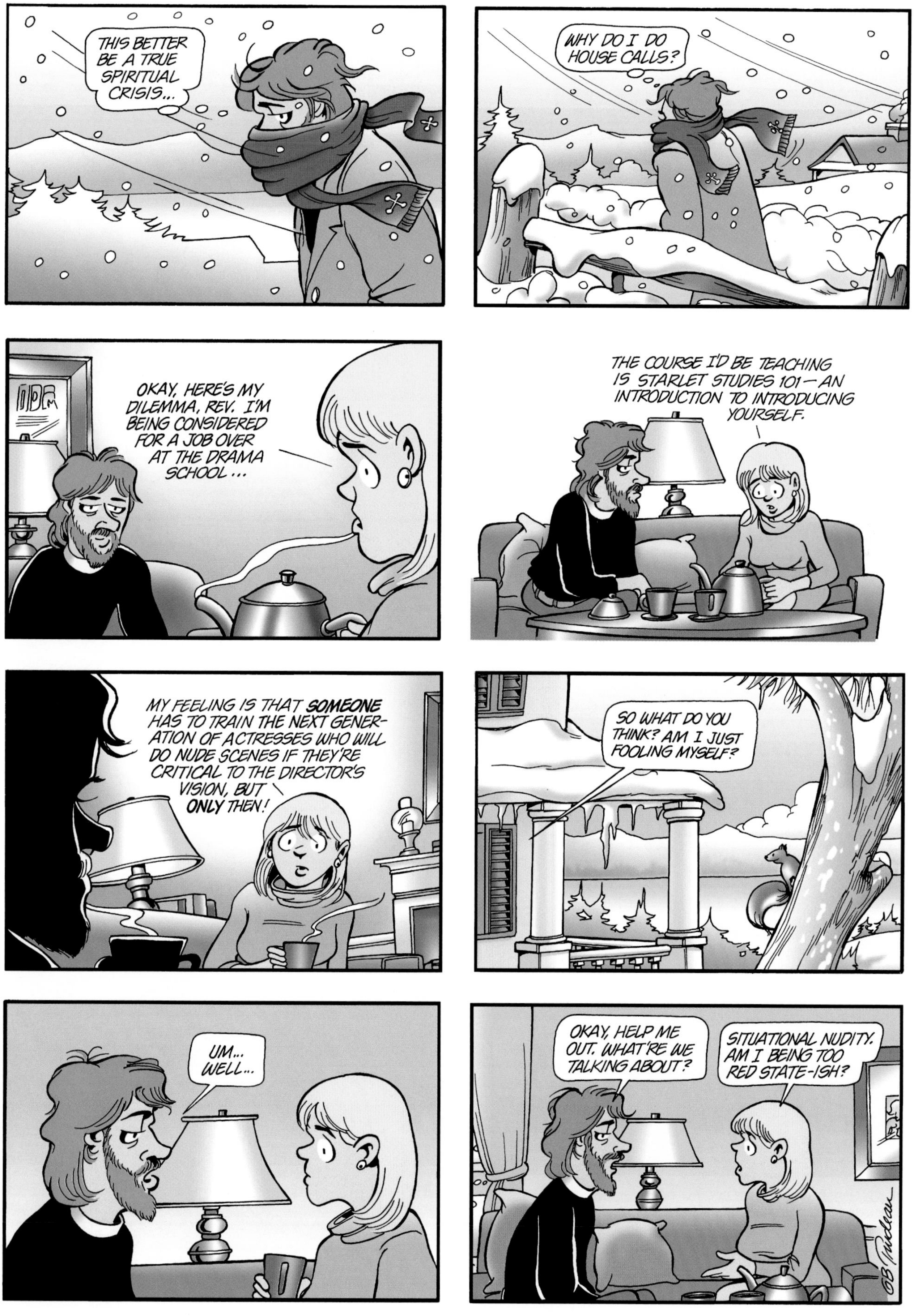
THIS BETTER BE A TRUE SPIRITUAL CRISIS...
WHY DO I DO HOUSE CALLS?
OKAY, HERE'S MY DILEMMA, REV. I'M BEING CONSIDERED FOR A JOB OVER AT THE DRAMA SCHOOL...
THE COURSE I'D BE TEACHING IS STARLET STUDIES 101—AN INTRODUCTION TO INTRODUCING YOURSELF.
MY FEELING IS THAT SOMEONE HAS TO TRAIN THE NEXT GENERATION OF ACTRESSES WHO WILL DO NUDE SCENES IF THEY'RE CRITICAL TO THE DIRECTOR'S VISION, BUT ONLY THEN!
SO WHAT DO YOU THINK? AM I JUST FOOLING MYSELF?
UM... WELL...
OKAY, HELP ME OUT. WHAT'RE WE TALKING ABOUT?
SITUATIONAL NUDITY. AM I BEING TOO RED STATE-ISH?
GBTrudeau

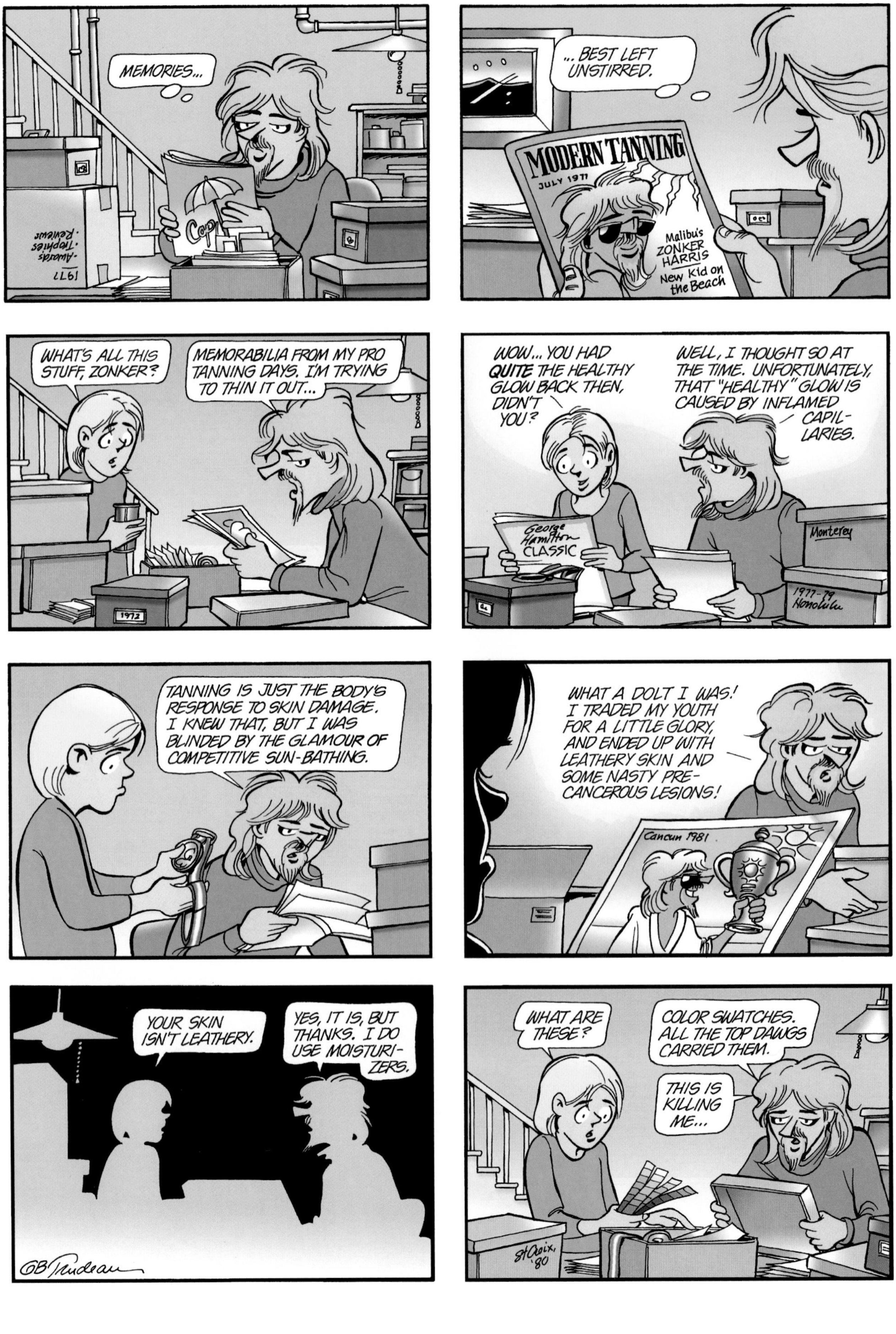
MEMORIES...
... BEST LEFT UNSTIRRED.
MODERN TANNING
JULY 1977
Malibu's ZONKER HARRIS
New Kid on the Beach
WHAT'S ALL THIS STUFF, ZONKER?
MEMORABILIA FROM MY PRO TANNING DAYS. I'M TRYING TO THIN IT OUT...
1972
WOW... YOU HAD **QUITE** THE HEALTHY GLOW BACK THEN, DIDN'T YOU?
WELL, I THOUGHT SO AT THE TIME. UNFORTUNATELY, THAT "HEALTHY" GLOW IS CAUSED BY INFLAMED CAPIL-LARIES.
George Hamilton CLASSIC
Monterey
1977-79 Honolulu
TANNING IS JUST THE BODY'S RESPONSE TO SKIN DAMAGE. I KNEW THAT, BUT I WAS BLINDED BY THE GLAMOUR OF COMPETITIVE SUN-BATHING.
WHAT A DOLT I WAS! I TRADED MY YOUTH FOR A LITTLE GLORY, AND ENDED UP WITH LEATHERY SKIN AND SOME NASTY PRE-CANCEROUS LESIONS!
Cancun 1981
YOUR SKIN ISN'T LEATHERY.
YES, IT IS, BUT THANKS. I DO USE MOISTURI-ZERS.
GB Trudeau
WHAT ARE THESE?
COLOR SWATCHES. ALL THE TOP DAWGS CARRIED THEM.
THIS IS KILLING ME...
St. Croix, '80

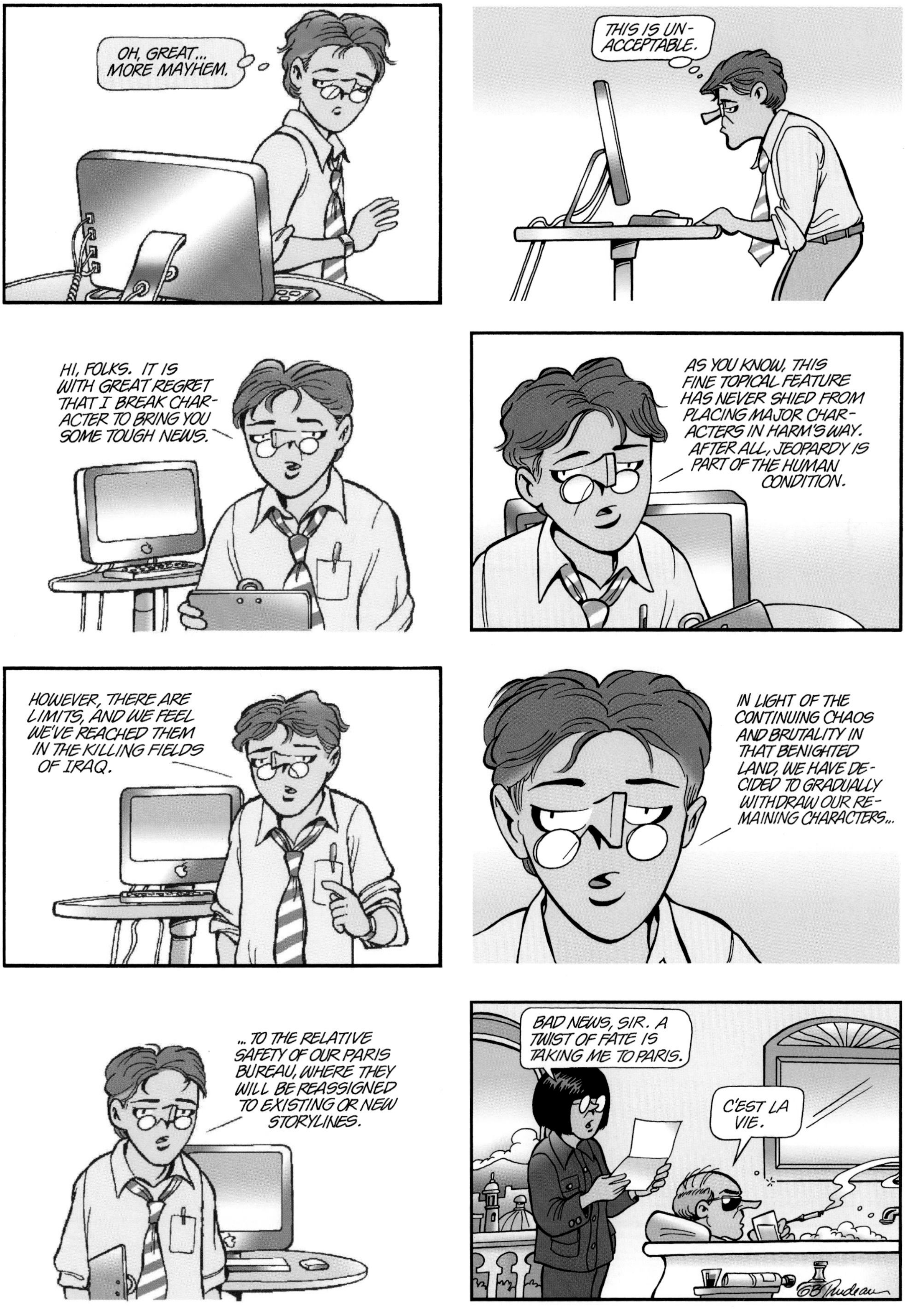
OH, GREAT... MORE MAYHEM.
THIS IS UNACCEPTABLE.
HI, FOLKS. IT IS WITH GREAT REGRET THAT I BREAK CHARACTER TO BRING YOU SOME TOUGH NEWS.
AS YOU KNOW, THIS FINE TOPICAL FEATURE HAS NEVER SHIED FROM PLACING MAJOR CHARACTERS IN HARM'S WAY. AFTER ALL, JEOPARDY IS PART OF THE HUMAN CONDITION.
HOWEVER, THERE ARE LIMITS, AND WE FEEL WE'VE REACHED THEM IN THE KILLING FIELDS OF IRAQ.
IN LIGHT OF THE CONTINUING CHAOS AND BRUTALITY IN THAT BENIGHTED LAND, WE HAVE DECIDED TO GRADUALLY WITHDRAW OUR REMAINING CHARACTERS...
... TO THE RELATIVE SAFETY OF OUR PARIS BUREAU, WHERE THEY WILL BE REASSIGNED TO EXISTING OR NEW STORYLINES.
BAD NEWS, SIR. A TWIST OF FATE IS TAKING ME TO PARIS.
C'EST LA VIE.
GB Trudeau

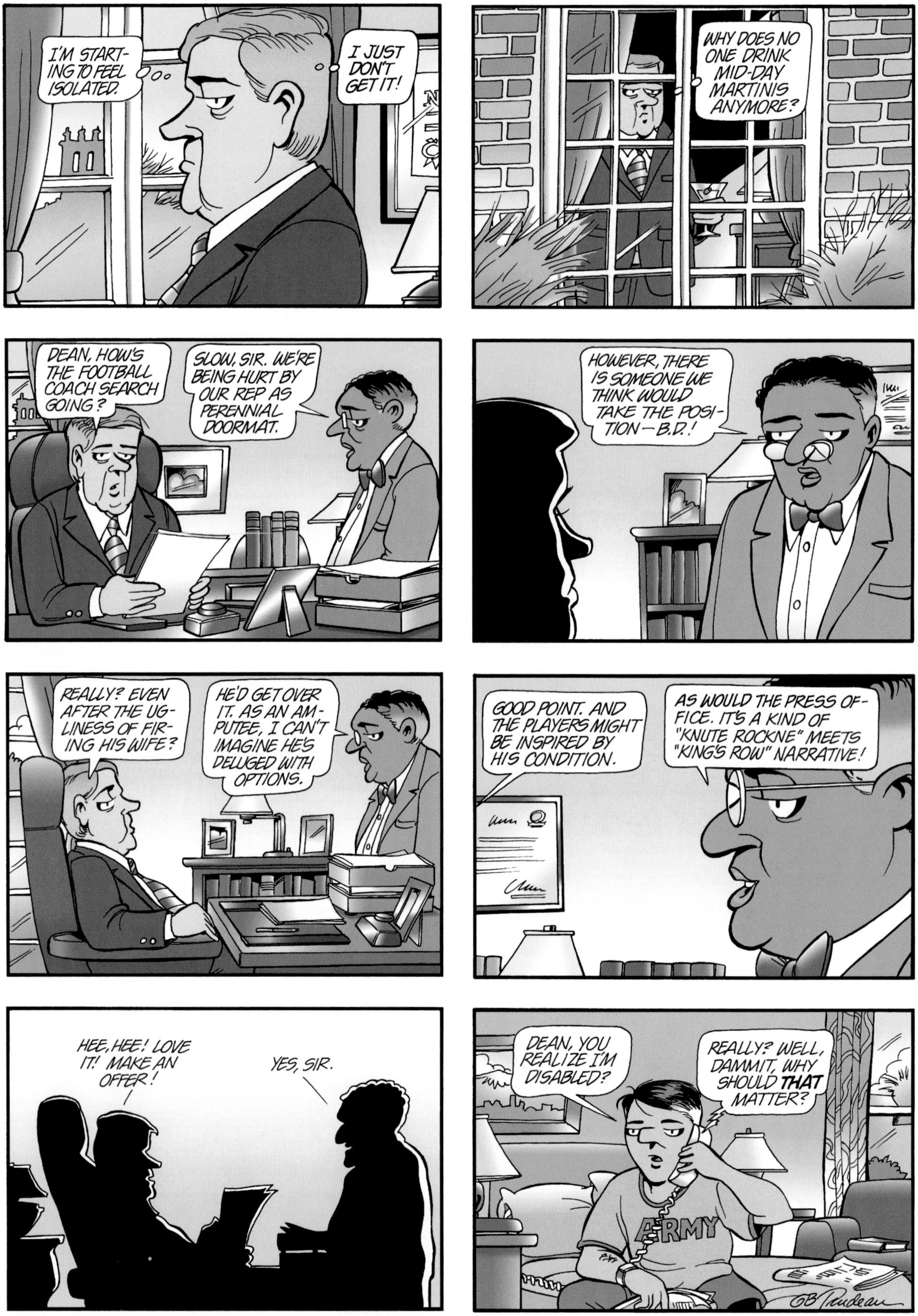
I'M STARTING TO FEEL ISOLATED.
I JUST DON'T GET IT!
WHY DOES NO ONE DRINK MID-DAY MARTINIS ANYMORE?
DEAN, HOW'S THE FOOTBALL COACH SEARCH GOING?
SLOW, SIR. WE'RE BEING HURT BY OUR REP AS PERENNIAL DOORMAT.
HOWEVER, THERE IS SOMEONE WE THINK WOULD TAKE THE POSITION—B.D.!
REALLY? EVEN AFTER THE UGLINESS OF FIRING HIS WIFE?
HE'D GET OVER IT. AS AN AMPUTEE, I CAN'T IMAGINE HE'S DELUGED WITH OPTIONS.
GOOD POINT. AND THE PLAYERS MIGHT BE INSPIRED BY HIS CONDITION.
AS WOULD THE PRESS OFFICE. IT'S A KIND OF "KNUTE ROCKNE" MEETS "KING'S ROW" NARRATIVE!
HEE, HEE! LOVE IT! MAKE AN OFFER!
YES, SIR.
DEAN, YOU REALIZE I'M DISABLED?
REALLY? WELL, DAMMIT, WHY SHOULD **THAT** MATTER?
ARMY
GB Trudeau

WHOA... TEN OR MORE YEARS TO GO IN IRAQ?

THIS STORY WILL FOLLOW ME INTO RETIREMENT!

MARK, HAVE YOU NOTICED THAT RUMSFELD HAS LOST A LOT OF HIS SWAGGER IN RECENT WEEKS?

CAN'T SAY THAT I HAVE.

GOOD MORNING, LADIES AND GENTLEMEN.

REALLY? HE DOESN'T SEEM A BIT CHASTENED TO YOU?

NO, BUT LET'S TEST THAT HYPOTHESIS...

YES, MARK.

MR. SECRETARY, THERE SEEMS TO BE GROWING AGREEMENT THAT THIS WAR HAS BECOME RUINOUS — MILITARILY, FISCALLY, POLITICALLY AND MORALLY...

... AND THAT, AS IN VIETNAM, IT'S NO LONGER A QUESTION OF *IF* WE WITHDRAW IN DISGRACE, BUT *WHEN*.

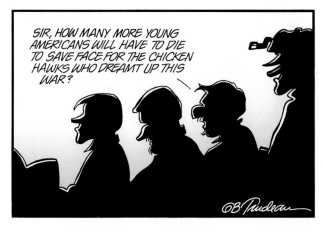

SIR, HOW MANY MORE YOUNG AMERICANS WILL HAVE TO DIE TO SAVE FACE FOR THE CHICKEN HAWKS WHO DREAMT UP THIS WAR?

©B Trudeau

I DON'T KNOW. I'LL TRY TO GET THAT FIGURE FOR YOU.

SEE?

I'LL BE DARNED.

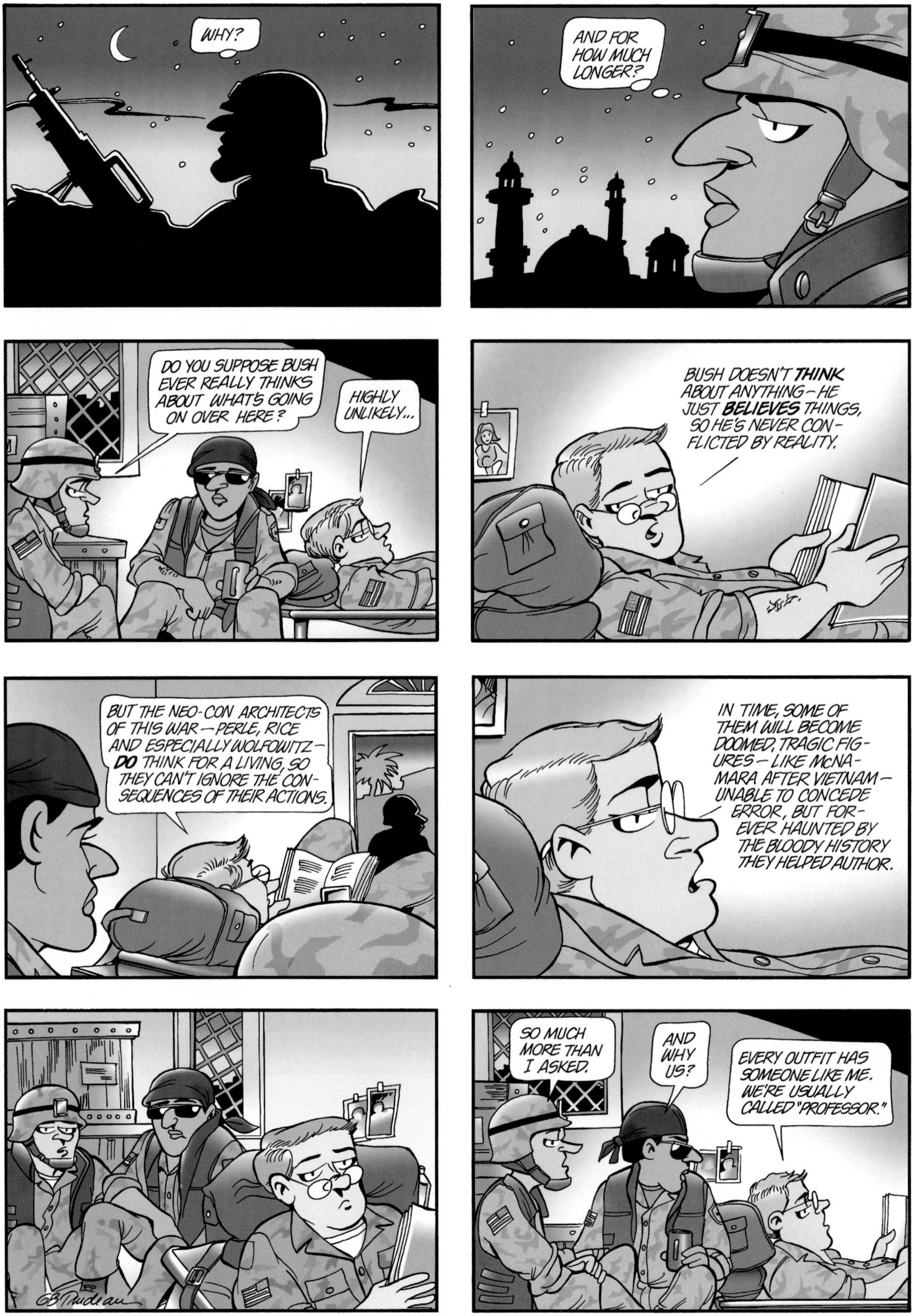
WHY?
AND FOR HOW MUCH LONGER?
DO YOU SUPPOSE BUSH EVER REALLY THINKS ABOUT WHAT'S GOING ON OVER HERE?
HIGHLY UNLIKELY...
BUSH DOESN'T **THINK** ABOUT ANYTHING – HE JUST **BELIEVES** THINGS, SO HE'S NEVER CON-FLICTED BY REALITY.
BUT THE NEO-CON ARCHITECTS OF THIS WAR – PERLE, RICE AND ESPECIALLY WOLFOWITZ – **DO** THINK FOR A LIVING, SO THEY CAN'T IGNORE THE CON-SEQUENCES OF THEIR ACTIONS.
IN TIME, SOME OF THEM WILL BECOME DOOMED, TRAGIC FIG-URES – LIKE McNAMARA AFTER VIETNAM – UNABLE TO CONCEDE ERROR, BUT FOR-EVER HAUNTED BY THE BLOODY HISTORY THEY HELPED AUTHOR.
SO MUCH MORE THAN I ASKED.
AND WHY US?
EVERY OUTFIT HAS SOMEONE LIKE ME. WE'RE USUALLY CALLED "PROFESSOR."
GB Trudeau

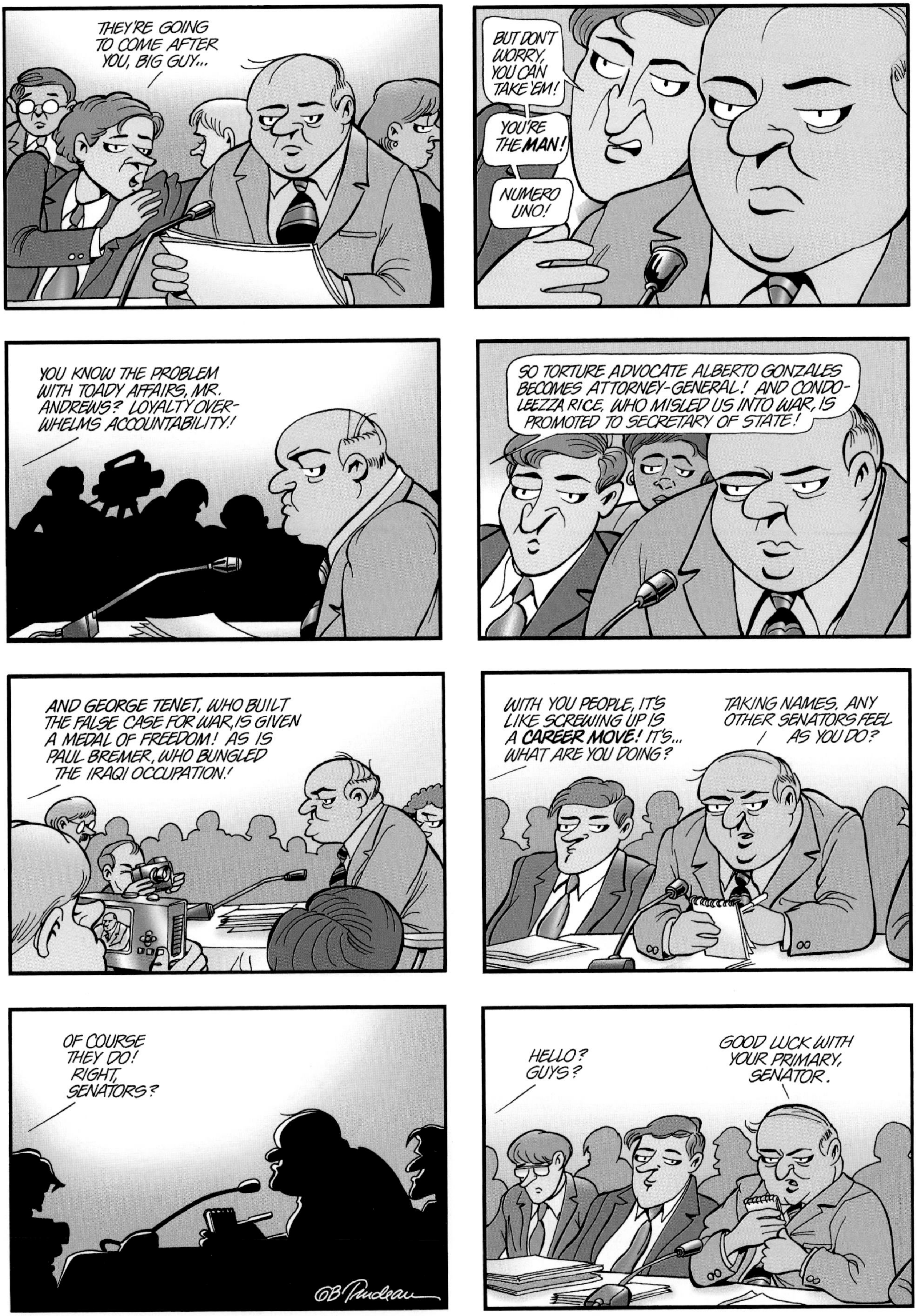
THEY'RE GOING TO COME AFTER YOU, BIG GUY...
BUT DON'T WORRY, YOU CAN TAKE 'EM!
YOU'RE THE **MAN**!
NUMERO UNO!
YOU KNOW THE PROBLEM WITH TOADY AFFAIRS, MR. ANDREWS? LOYALTY OVERWHELMS ACCOUNTABILITY!
SO TORTURE ADVOCATE ALBERTO GONZALES BECOMES ATTORNEY-GENERAL! AND CONDOLEEZZA RICE, WHO MISLED US INTO WAR, IS PROMOTED TO SECRETARY OF STATE!
AND GEORGE TENET, WHO BUILT THE FALSE CASE FOR WAR, IS GIVEN A MEDAL OF FREEDOM! AS IS PAUL BREMER, WHO BUNGLED THE IRAQI OCCUPATION!
WITH YOU PEOPLE, IT'S LIKE SCREWING UP IS A **CAREER MOVE!** IT'S... WHAT ARE YOU DOING?
TAKING NAMES. ANY OTHER SENATORS FEEL AS YOU DO?
OF COURSE THEY DO! RIGHT, SENATORS?
©B Trudeau
HELLO? GUYS?
GOOD LUCK WITH YOUR PRIMARY, SENATOR.

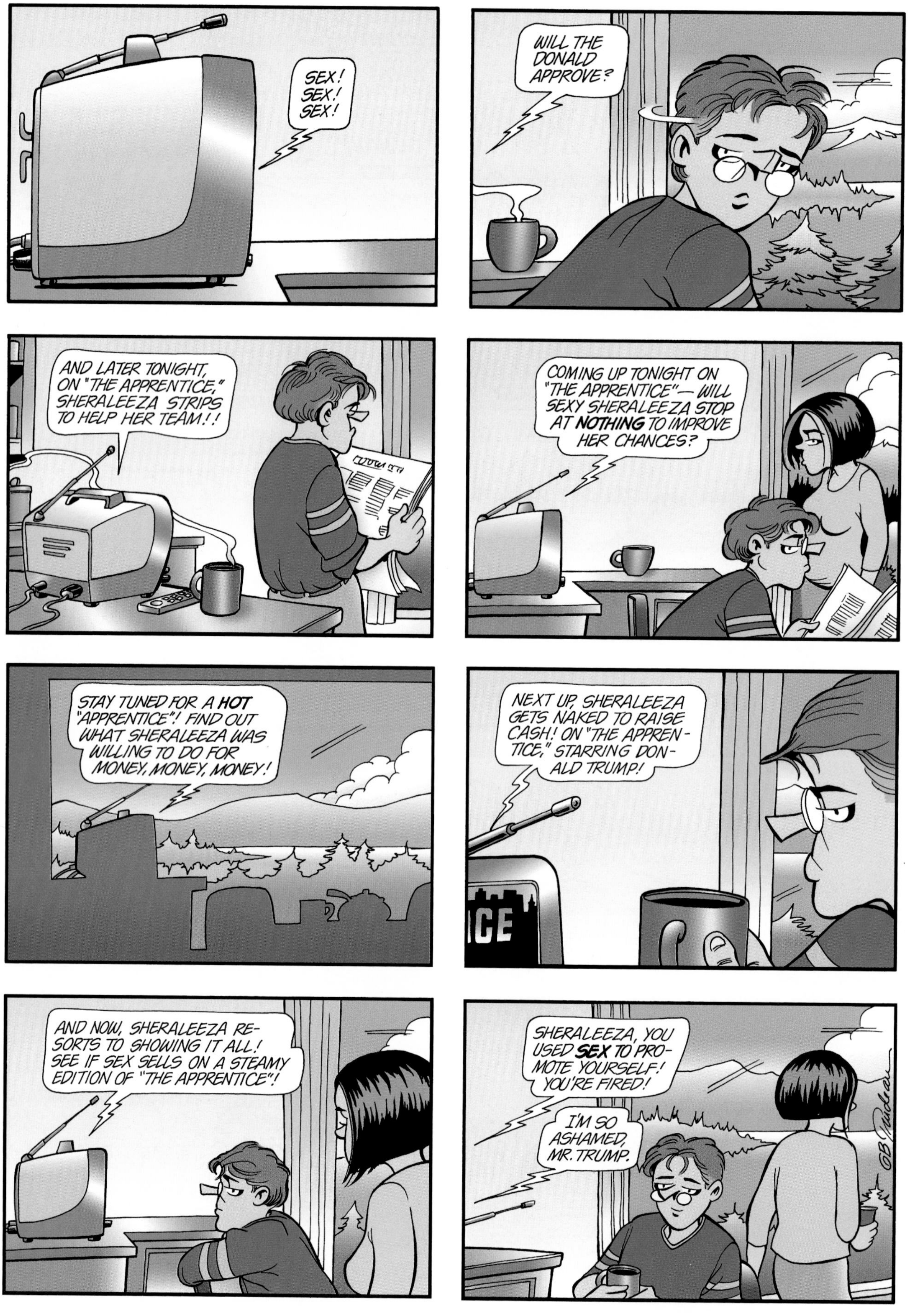
SEX! SEX! SEX!
WILL THE DONALD APPROVE?
AND LATER TONIGHT, ON "THE APPRENTICE," SHERALEEZA STRIPS TO HELP HER TEAM!!
COMING UP TONIGHT ON "THE APPRENTICE"— WILL SEXY SHERALEEZA STOP AT NOTHING TO IMPROVE HER CHANCES?
STAY TUNED FOR A HOT "APPRENTICE"! FIND OUT WHAT SHERALEEZA WAS WILLING TO DO FOR MONEY, MONEY, MONEY!
NEXT UP, SHERALEEZA GETS NAKED TO RAISE CASH! ON "THE APPRENTICE," STARRING DONALD TRUMP!
AND NOW, SHERALEEZA RESORTS TO SHOWING IT ALL! SEE IF SEX SELLS ON A STEAMY EDITION OF "THE APPRENTICE"!
SHERALEEZA, YOU USED SEX TO PROMOTE YOURSELF! YOU'RE FIRED!
I'M SO ASHAMED, MR. TRUMP.
GBTrudeau

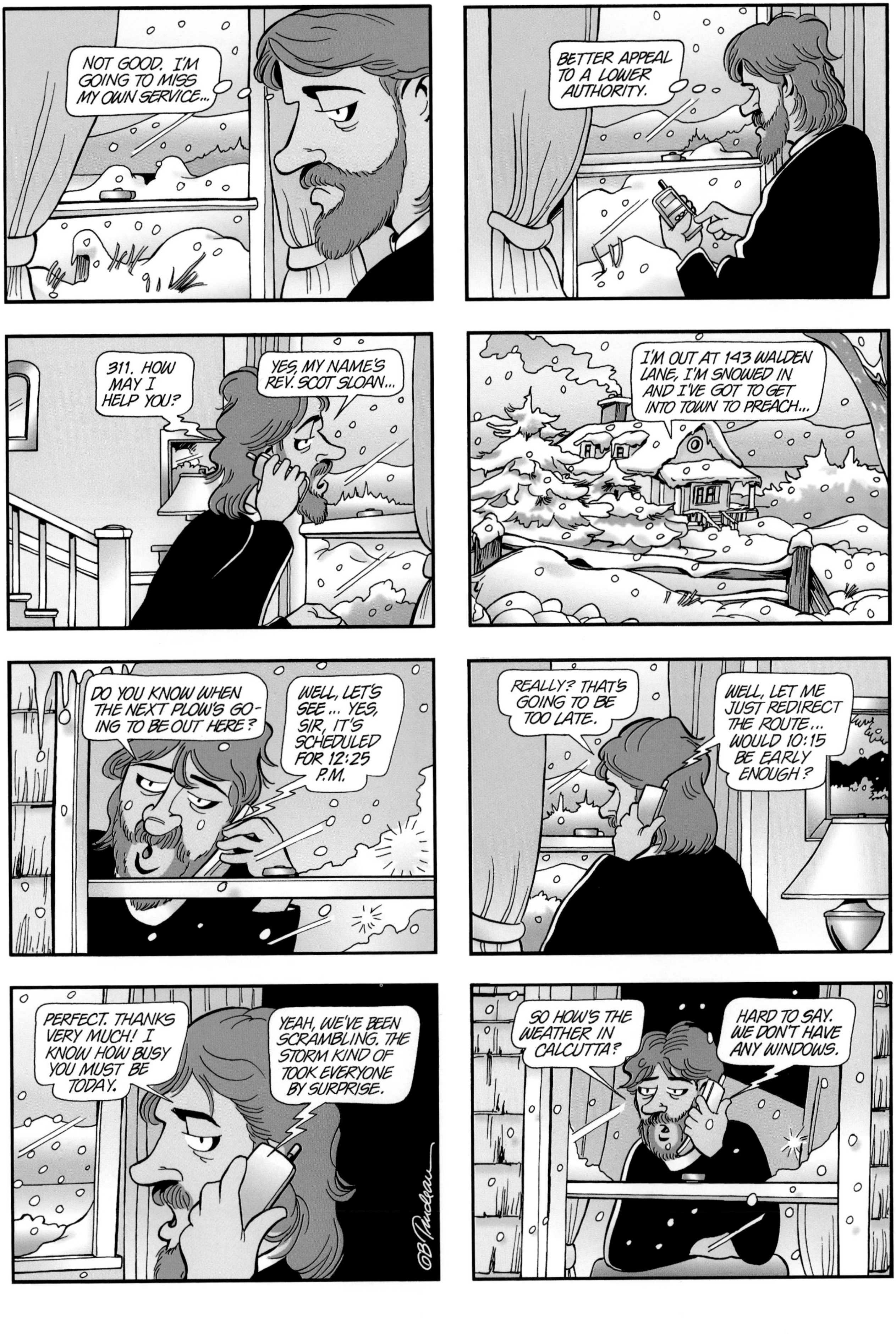
NOT GOOD. I'M GOING TO MISS MY OWN SERVICE...
BETTER APPEAL TO A LOWER AUTHORITY.
311. HOW MAY I HELP YOU?
YES, MY NAME'S REV. SCOT SLOAN...
I'M OUT AT 143 WALDEN LANE, I'M SNOWED IN AND I'VE GOT TO GET INTO TOWN TO PREACH...
DO YOU KNOW WHEN THE NEXT PLOW'S GOING TO BE OUT HERE?
WELL, LET'S SEE ... YES, SIR, IT'S SCHEDULED FOR 12:25 P.M.
REALLY? THAT'S GOING TO BE TOO LATE.
WELL, LET ME JUST REDIRECT THE ROUTE... WOULD 10:15 BE EARLY ENOUGH?
PERFECT. THANKS VERY MUCH! I KNOW HOW BUSY YOU MUST BE TODAY.
YEAH, WE'VE BEEN SCRAMBLING. THE STORM KIND OF TOOK EVERYONE BY SURPRISE.
SO HOW'S THE WEATHER IN CALCUTTA?
HARD TO SAY. WE DON'T HAVE ANY WINDOWS.

SEE ... LOOK ... COST DRIVERS! HELPS ON THE RED!

MAKE ANY SENSE?

THIS **MUST** BE SHARED!

HEY, FOLKS — CONFUSED ABOUT THE BUSH PLAN FOR **SOCIAL SECURITY**?

WELL, HELP IS ON THE WAY! HERE — IN HIS **OWN** WORDS* — THE PRESIDENT EXPLAINS!

*TAMPA, FL 2/04/05

BECAUSE THE — ALL WHICH IS ON THE TABLE BEGINS TO ADDRESS THE BIG COST DRIVERS. FOR EXAMPLE, HOW BENEFITS ARE CALCULATE, FOR EXAMPLE, IS ON THE TABLE; WHETHER OR NOT BENEFITS RISE BASED UPON WAGE INCREASES OR PRICE INCREASES...

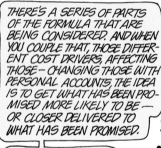

THERE'S A SERIES OF PARTS OF THE FORMULA THAT ARE BEING CONSIDERED. AND WHEN YOU COUPLE THAT, THOSE DIFFERENT COST DRIVERS, AFFECTING THOSE — CHANGING THOSE WITH PERSONAL ACCOUNTS, THE IDEA IS TO GET WHAT HAS BEEN PROMISED MORE LIKELY TO BE — OR CLOSER DELIVERED TO WHAT HAS BEEN PROMISED.

DOES THAT MAKE ANY SENSE TO YOU? IT'S KIND OF MUDDLED.

LOOK, THERE'S A SERIES OF THINGS THAT CAUSE THE — LIKE, FOR EXAMPLE, BENEFITS ARE CALCULATED BASED UPON THE INCREASE OF WAGES, AS OPPOSED TO THE INCREASE OF PRICES. SOME HAVE SUGGESTED THAT WE CALCULATE — THE BENEFITS WILL RISE BASED UPON INFLATION, AS OPPOSED TO WAGE INCREASES...

THERE IS A REFORM THAT WOULD HELP SOLVE THE RED IF THAT WERE PUT INTO EFFECT. IN OTHER WORDS, HOW FAST BENEFITS GROW, HOW FAST THE PROMISED BENEFITS GROW, IF THOSE — IF THAT GROWTH IS AFFECTED...

...IT WILL HELP ON THE RED.

'NUFF SAID!

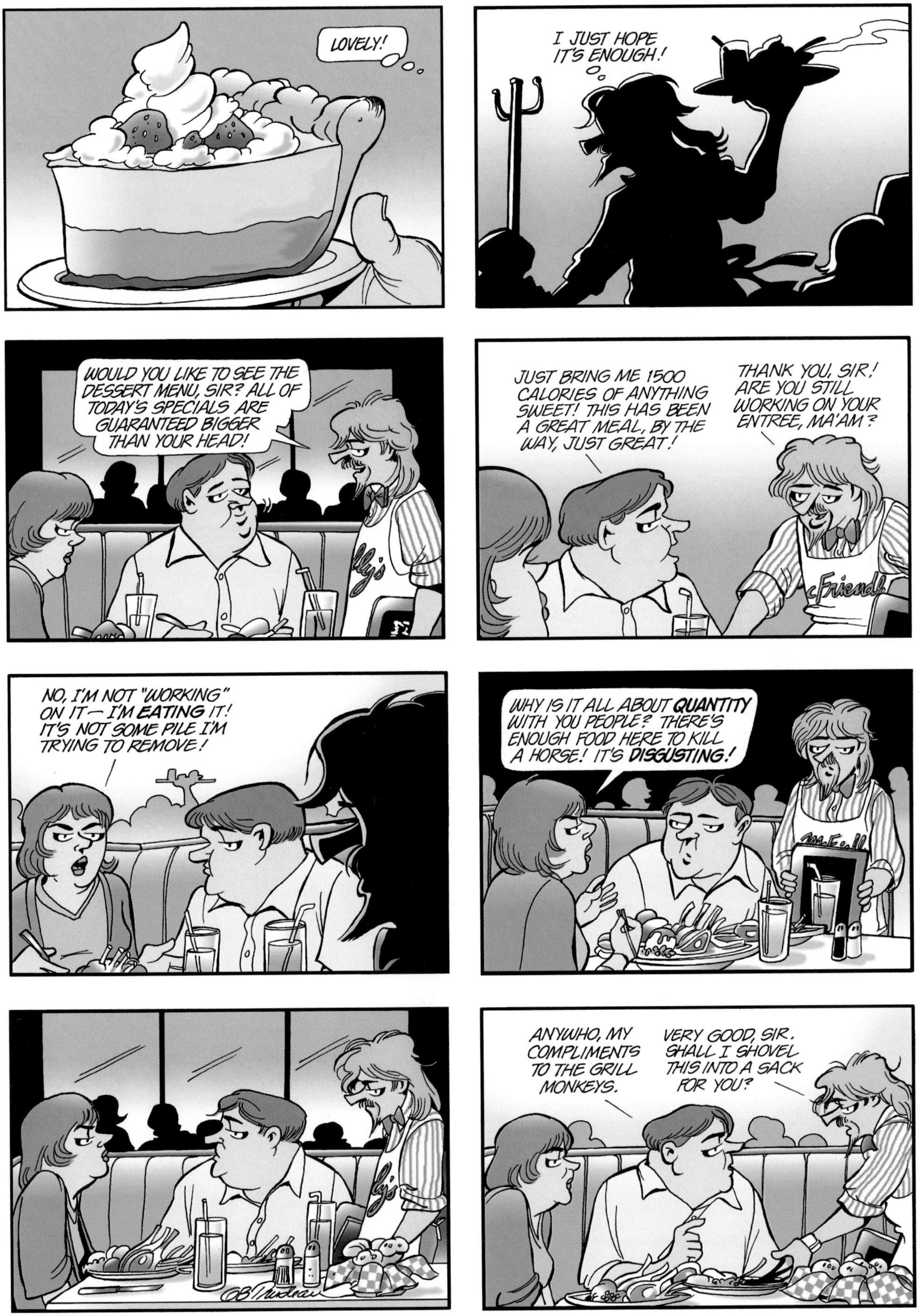

LOVELY!
I JUST HOPE IT'S ENOUGH!
WOULD YOU LIKE TO SEE THE DESSERT MENU, SIR? ALL OF TODAY'S SPECIALS ARE GUARANTEED BIGGER THAN YOUR HEAD!
JUST BRING ME 1500 CALORIES OF ANYTHING SWEET! THIS HAS BEEN A GREAT MEAL, BY THE WAY, JUST GREAT!
THANK YOU, SIR! ARE YOU STILL WORKING ON YOUR ENTREE, MA'AM?
NO, I'M NOT "WORKING" ON IT — I'M EATING IT! IT'S NOT SOME PILE I'M TRYING TO REMOVE!
WHY IS IT ALL ABOUT QUANTITY WITH YOU PEOPLE? THERE'S ENOUGH FOOD HERE TO KILL A HORSE! IT'S DISGUSTING!
ANYWHO, MY COMPLIMENTS TO THE GRILL MONKEYS.
VERY GOOD, SIR. SHALL I SHOVEL THIS INTO A SACK FOR YOU?

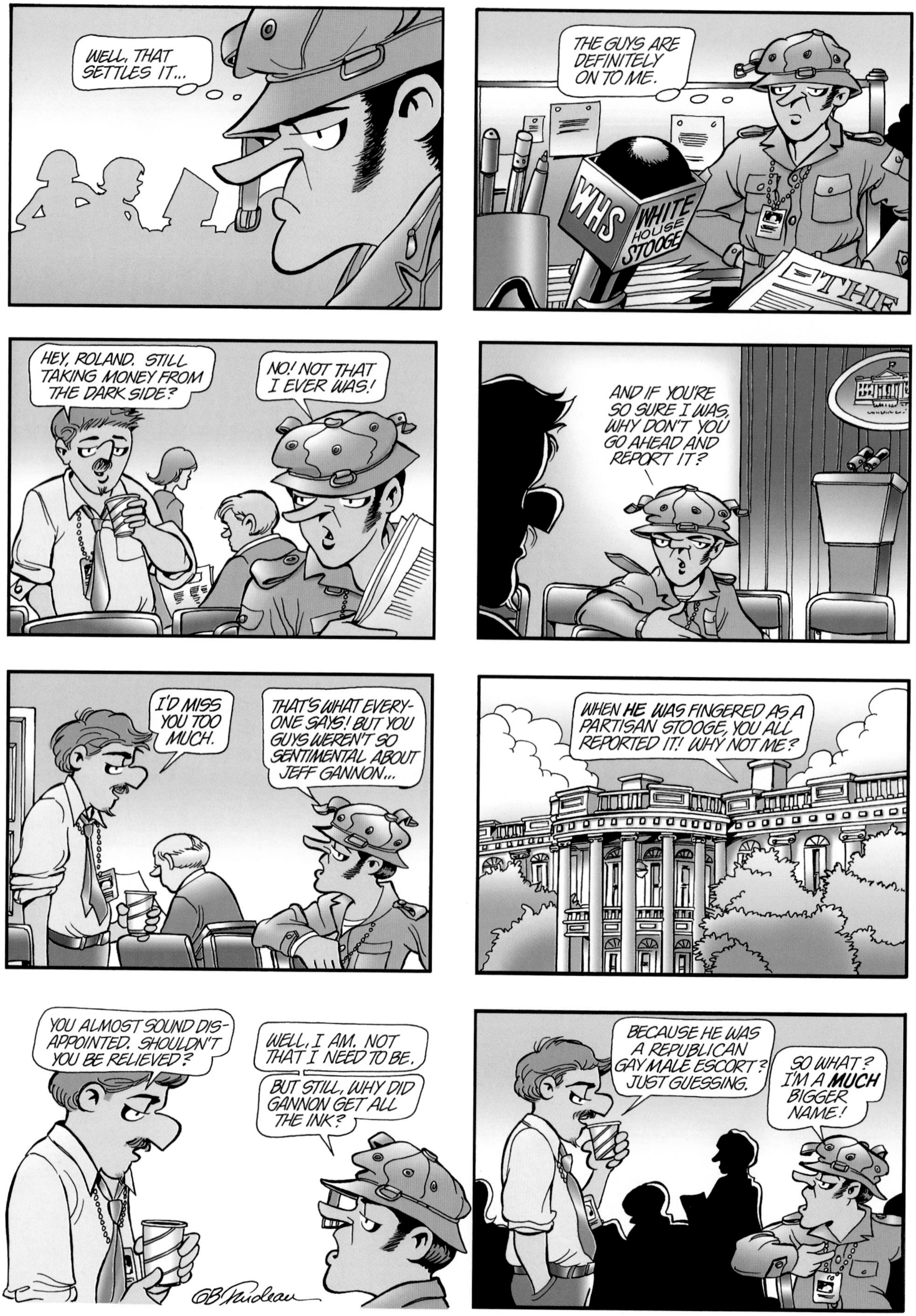
WELL, THAT SETTLES IT...
THE GUYS ARE DEFINITELY ON TO ME.
WHS WHITE HOUSE STOOGE
THE
HEY, ROLAND. STILL TAKING MONEY FROM THE DARK SIDE?
NO! NOT THAT I EVER WAS!
AND IF YOU'RE SO SURE I WAS, WHY DON'T YOU GO AHEAD AND REPORT IT?
I'D MISS YOU TOO MUCH.
THAT'S WHAT EVERY-ONE SAYS! BUT YOU GUYS WEREN'T SO SENTIMENTAL ABOUT JEFF GANNON...
WHEN **HE** WAS FINGERED AS A PARTISAN STOOGE, YOU ALL REPORTED IT! WHY NOT ME?
YOU ALMOST SOUND DIS-APPOINTED. SHOULDN'T YOU BE RELIEVED?
WELL, I AM. NOT THAT I NEED TO BE.
BUT STILL, WHY DID GANNON GET ALL THE INK?
GB Trudeau
BECAUSE HE WAS A REPUBLICAN GAY MALE ESCORT? JUST GUESSING.
SO WHAT? I'M A **MUCH** BIGGER NAME!

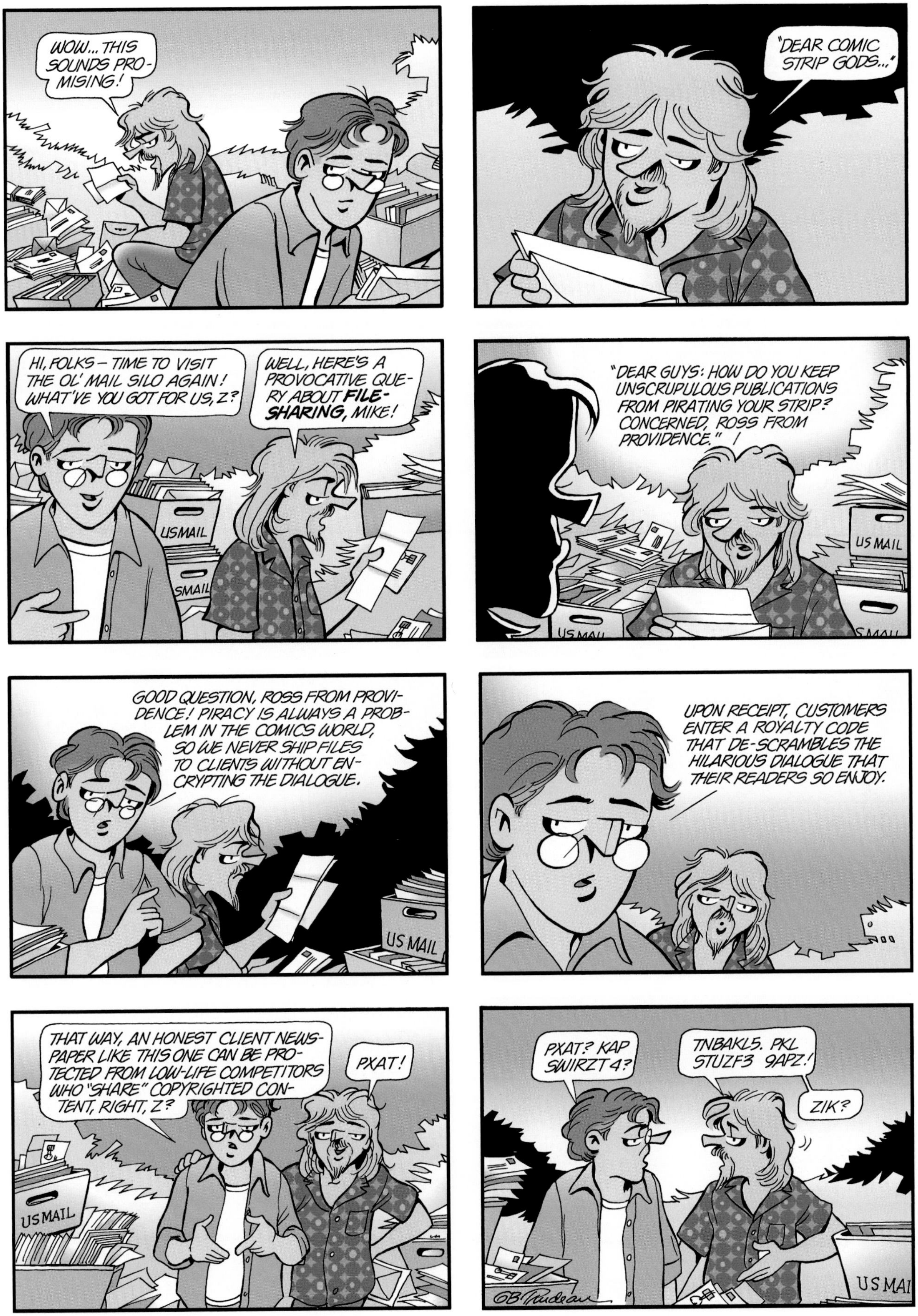
WOW... THIS SOUNDS PRO-MISING!
"DEAR COMIC STRIP GODS..."
HI, FOLKS – TIME TO VISIT THE OL' MAIL SILO AGAIN! WHAT'VE YOU GOT FOR US, Z?
WELL, HERE'S A PROVOCATIVE QUE-RY ABOUT **FILE-SHARING**, MIKE!
US MAIL
"DEAR GUYS: HOW DO YOU KEEP UNSCRUPULOUS PUBLICATIONS FROM PIRATING YOUR STRIP? CONCERNED, ROSS FROM PROVIDENCE." !
US MAIL
GOOD QUESTION, ROSS FROM PROVI-DENCE! PIRACY IS ALWAYS A PROB-LEM IN THE COMICS WORLD, SO WE NEVER SHIP FILES TO CLIENTS WITHOUT EN-CRYPTING THE DIALOGUE.
US MAIL
UPON RECEIPT, CUSTOMERS ENTER A ROYALTY CODE THAT DE-SCRAMBLES THE HILARIOUS DIALOGUE THAT THEIR READERS SO ENJOY.
THAT WAY, AN HONEST CLIENT NEWS-PAPER LIKE THIS ONE CAN BE PRO-TECTED FROM LOW-LIFE COMPETITORS WHO "SHARE" COPYRIGHTED CON-TENT, RIGHT, Z?
PXAT!
US MAIL
PXAT? KAP SWIRZT 4?
TNBAKL5. PKL STUZF3 9APZ!
ZIK?

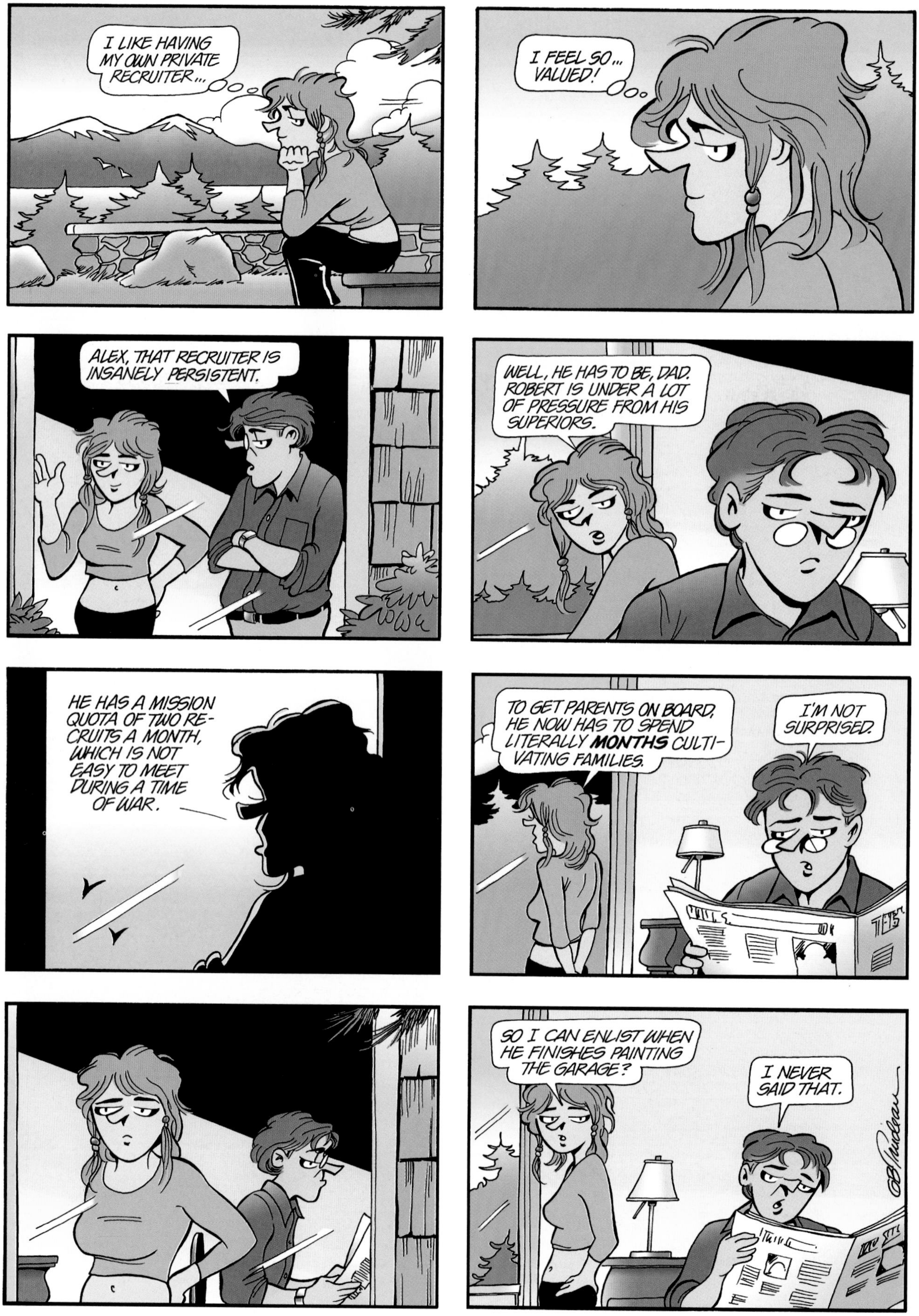
I LIKE HAVING MY OWN PRIVATE RECRUITER...
I FEEL SO... VALUED!
ALEX, THAT RECRUITER IS INSANELY PERSISTENT.
WELL, HE HAS TO BE, DAD. ROBERT IS UNDER A LOT OF PRESSURE FROM HIS SUPERIORS.
HE HAS A MISSION QUOTA OF TWO RECRUITS A MONTH, WHICH IS NOT EASY TO MEET DURING A TIME OF WAR.
TO GET PARENTS ON BOARD, HE NOW HAS TO SPEND LITERALLY MONTHS CULTIVATING FAMILIES.
I'M NOT SURPRISED.
SO I CAN ENLIST WHEN HE FINISHES PAINTING THE GARAGE?
I NEVER SAID THAT.

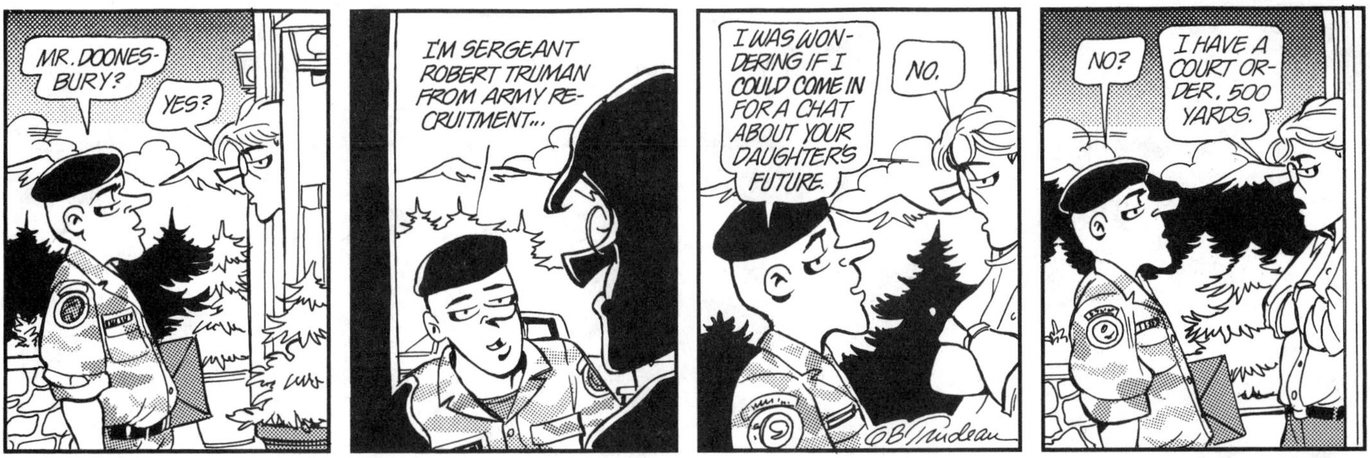
MR. DOONESBURY?
YES?
I'M SERGEANT ROBERT TRUMAN FROM ARMY RECRUITMENT...
I WAS WONDERING IF I COULD COME IN FOR A CHAT ABOUT YOUR DAUGHTER'S FUTURE.
NO.
NO?
I HAVE A COURT ORDER. 500 YARDS.

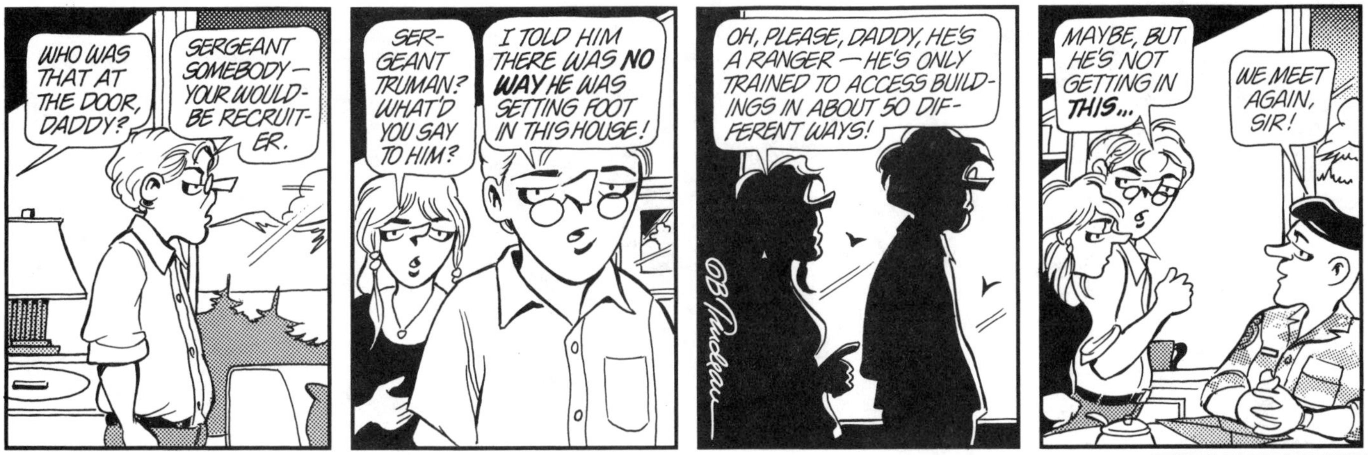
WHO WAS THAT AT THE DOOR, DADDY?
SERGEANT SOMEBODY — YOUR WOULD-BE RECRUITER.
SERGEANT TRUMAN? WHAT'D YOU SAY TO HIM?
I TOLD HIM THERE WAS NO WAY HE WAS SETTING FOOT IN THIS HOUSE!
OH, PLEASE, DADDY, HE'S A RANGER — HE'S ONLY TRAINED TO ACCESS BUILDINGS IN ABOUT 50 DIFFERENT WAYS!
MAYBE, BUT HE'S NOT GETTING IN THIS...
WE MEET AGAIN, SIR!

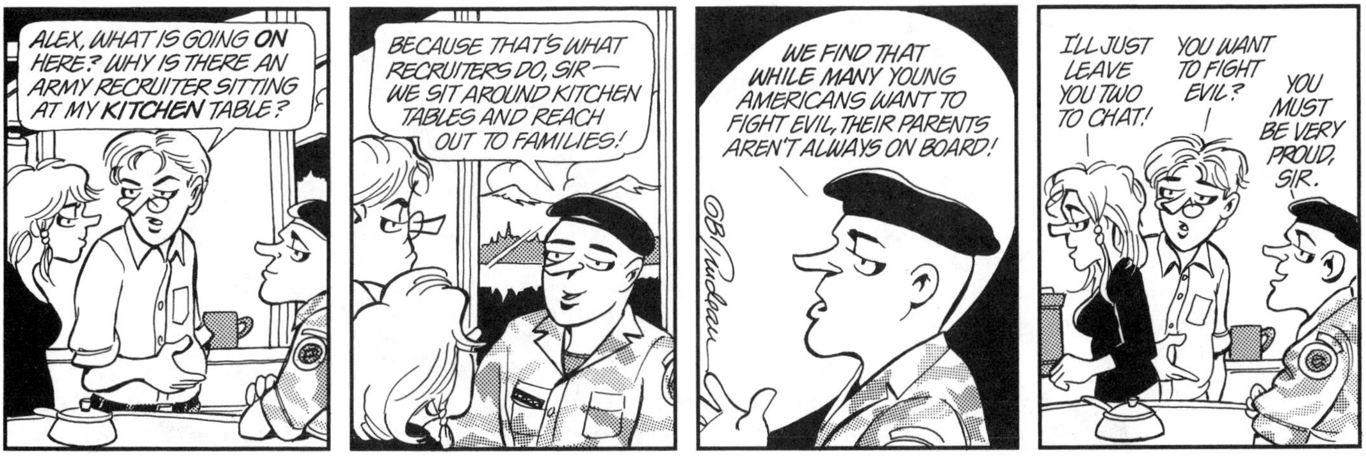
ALEX, WHAT IS GOING ON HERE? WHY IS THERE AN ARMY RECRUITER SITTING AT MY KITCHEN TABLE?
BECAUSE THAT'S WHAT RECRUITERS DO, SIR — WE SIT AROUND KITCHEN TABLES AND REACH OUT TO FAMILIES!
WE FIND THAT WHILE MANY YOUNG AMERICANS WANT TO FIGHT EVIL, THEIR PARENTS AREN'T ALWAYS ON BOARD!
I'LL JUST LEAVE YOU TWO TO CHAT!
YOU WANT TO FIGHT EVIL?
YOU MUST BE VERY PROUD, SIR.

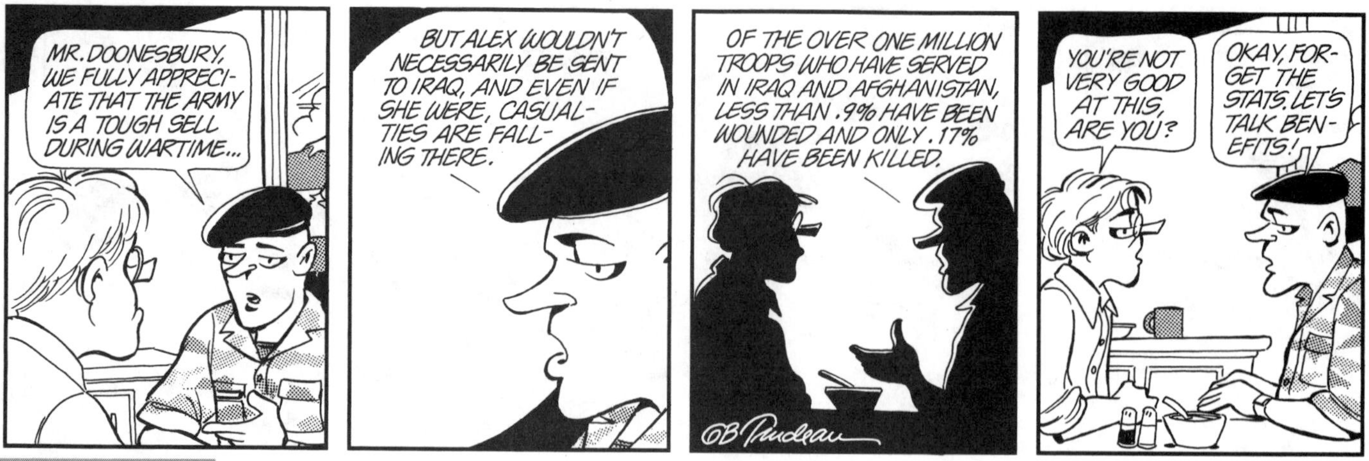
MR. DOONESBURY, WE FULLY APPRECIATE THAT THE ARMY IS A TOUGH SELL DURING WARTIME...
BUT ALEX WOULDN'T NECESSARILY BE SENT TO IRAQ, AND EVEN IF SHE WERE, CASUALTIES ARE FALLING THERE.
OF THE OVER ONE MILLION TROOPS WHO HAVE SERVED IN IRAQ AND AFGHANISTAN, LESS THAN .9% HAVE BEEN WOUNDED AND ONLY .17% HAVE BEEN KILLED.
©B. Trudeau
YOU'RE NOT VERY GOOD AT THIS, ARE YOU?
OKAY, FORGET THE STATS. LET'S TALK BENEFITS!

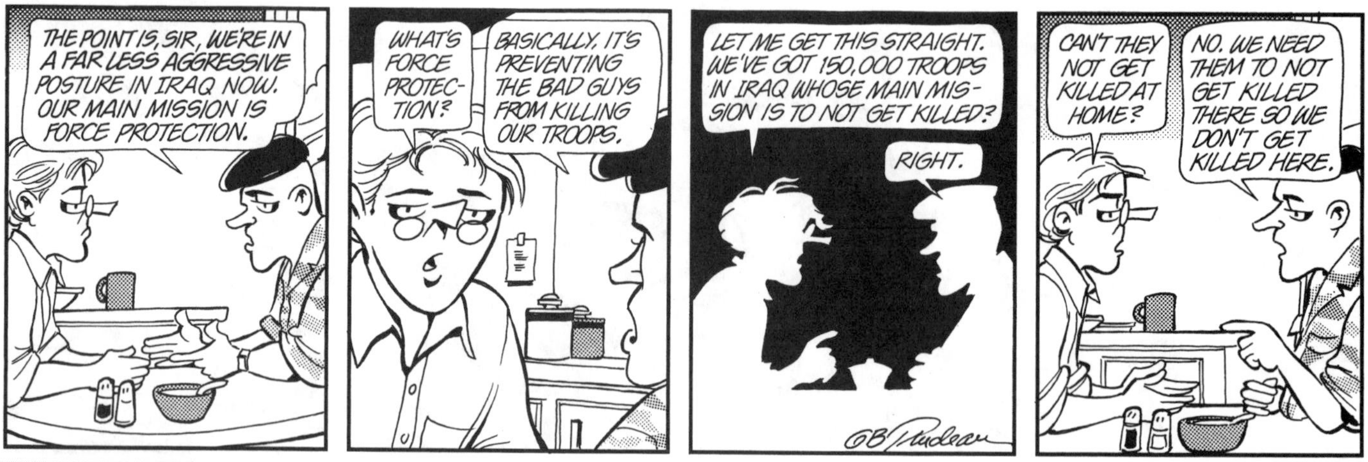
THE POINT IS, SIR, WE'RE IN A FAR LESS AGGRESSIVE POSTURE IN IRAQ NOW. OUR MAIN MISSION IS FORCE PROTECTION.
WHAT'S FORCE PROTECTION?
BASICALLY, IT'S PREVENTING THE BAD GUYS FROM KILLING OUR TROOPS.
LET ME GET THIS STRAIGHT. WE'VE GOT 150,000 TROOPS IN IRAQ WHOSE MAIN MISSION IS TO NOT GET KILLED?
RIGHT.
©B. Trudeau
CAN'T THEY NOT GET KILLED AT HOME?
NO. WE NEED THEM TO NOT GET KILLED THERE SO WE DON'T GET KILLED HERE.

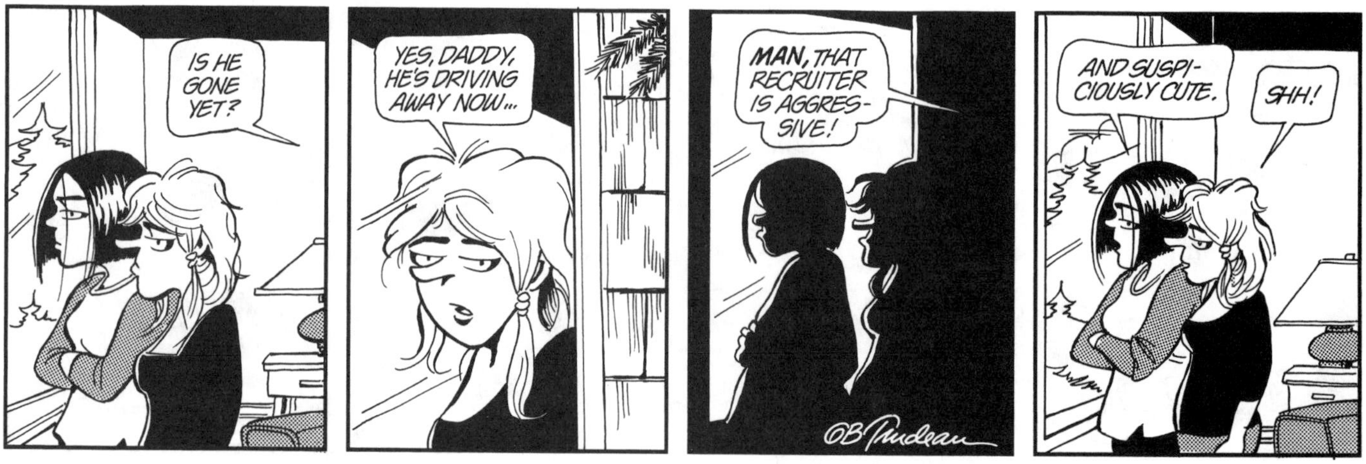
IS HE GONE YET?
YES, DADDY. HE'S DRIVING AWAY NOW...
MAN, THAT RECRUITER IS AGGRESSIVE!
©B. Trudeau
AND SUSPICIOUSLY CUTE.
SHH!

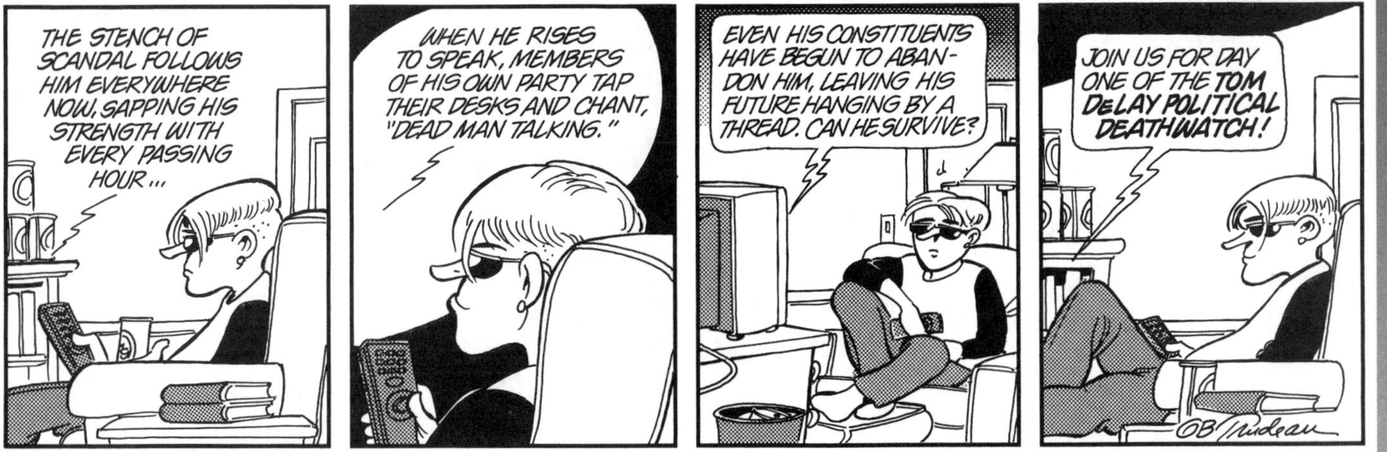
THE STENCH OF SCANDAL FOLLOWS HIM EVERYWHERE NOW, SAPPING HIS STRENGTH WITH EVERY PASSING HOUR...
WHEN HE RISES TO SPEAK, MEMBERS OF HIS OWN PARTY TAP THEIR DESKS AND CHANT, "DEAD MAN TALKING."
EVEN HIS CONSTITUENTS HAVE BEGUN TO ABANDON HIM, LEAVING HIS FUTURE HANGING BY A THREAD. CAN HE SURVIVE?
JOIN US FOR DAY ONE OF THE TOM DeLAY POLITICAL DEATHWATCH!
GB Trudeau

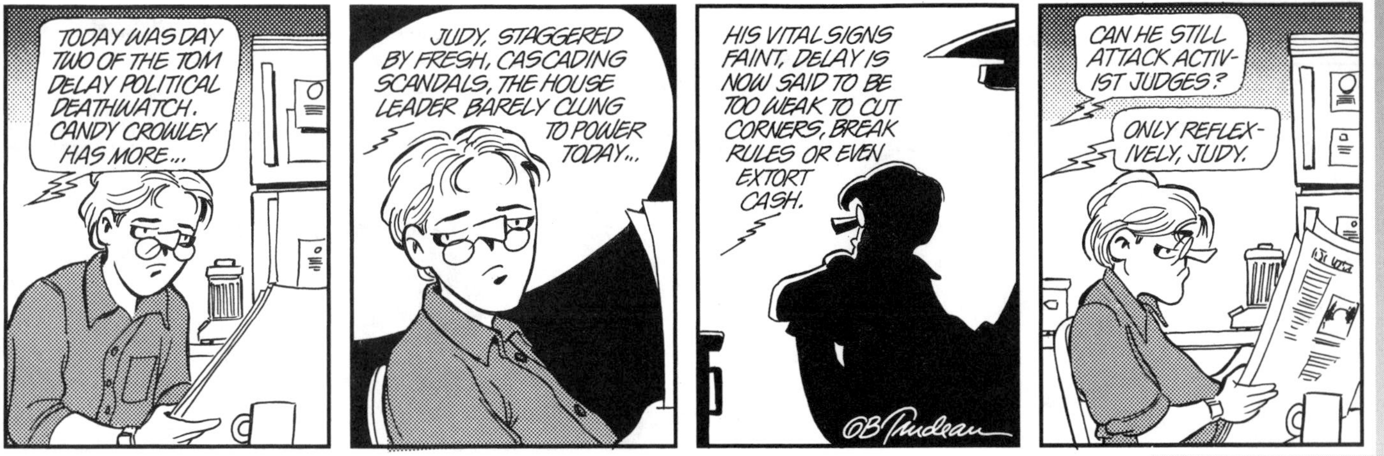
TODAY WAS DAY TWO OF THE TOM DELAY POLITICAL DEATHWATCH. CANDY CROWLEY HAS MORE...
JUDY, STAGGERED BY FRESH, CASCADING SCANDALS, THE HOUSE LEADER BARELY CLUNG TO POWER TODAY...
HIS VITAL SIGNS FAINT, DELAY IS NOW SAID TO BE TOO WEAK TO CUT CORNERS, BREAK RULES OR EVEN EXTORT CASH.
CAN HE STILL ATTACK ACTIVIST JUDGES?
ONLY REFLEXIVELY, JUDY.
GB Trudeau

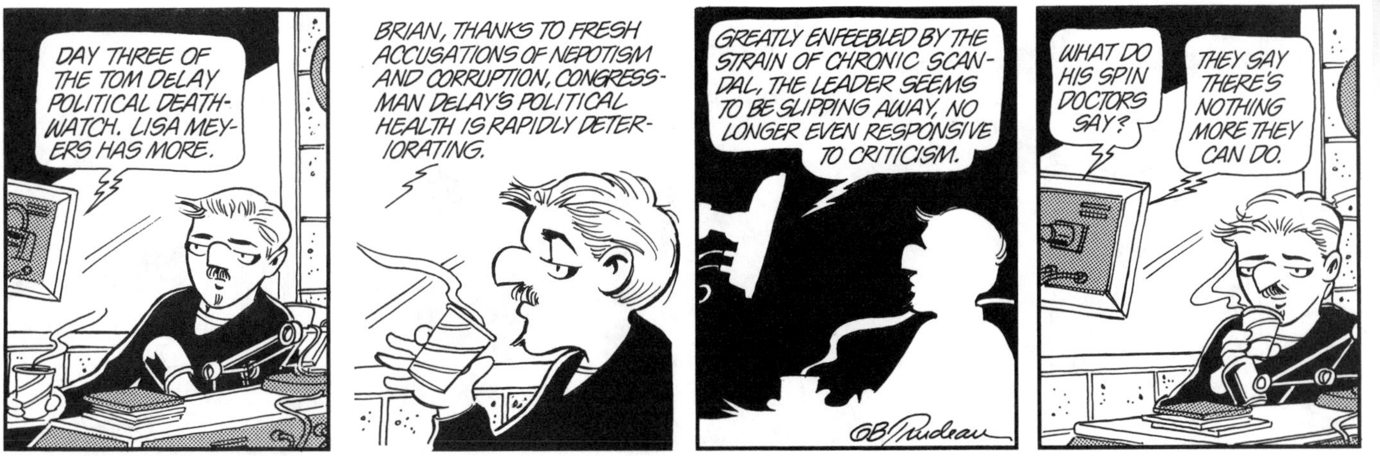
DAY THREE OF THE TOM DELAY POLITICAL DEATHWATCH. LISA MEYERS HAS MORE.
BRIAN, THANKS TO FRESH ACCUSATIONS OF NEPOTISM AND CORRUPTION, CONGRESSMAN DELAY'S POLITICAL HEALTH IS RAPIDLY DETERIORATING.
GREATLY ENFEEBLED BY THE STRAIN OF CHRONIC SCANDAL, THE LEADER SEEMS TO BE SLIPPING AWAY, NO LONGER EVEN RESPONSIVE TO CRITICISM.
WHAT DO HIS SPIN DOCTORS SAY?
THEY SAY THERE'S NOTHING MORE THEY CAN DO.
GB Trudeau

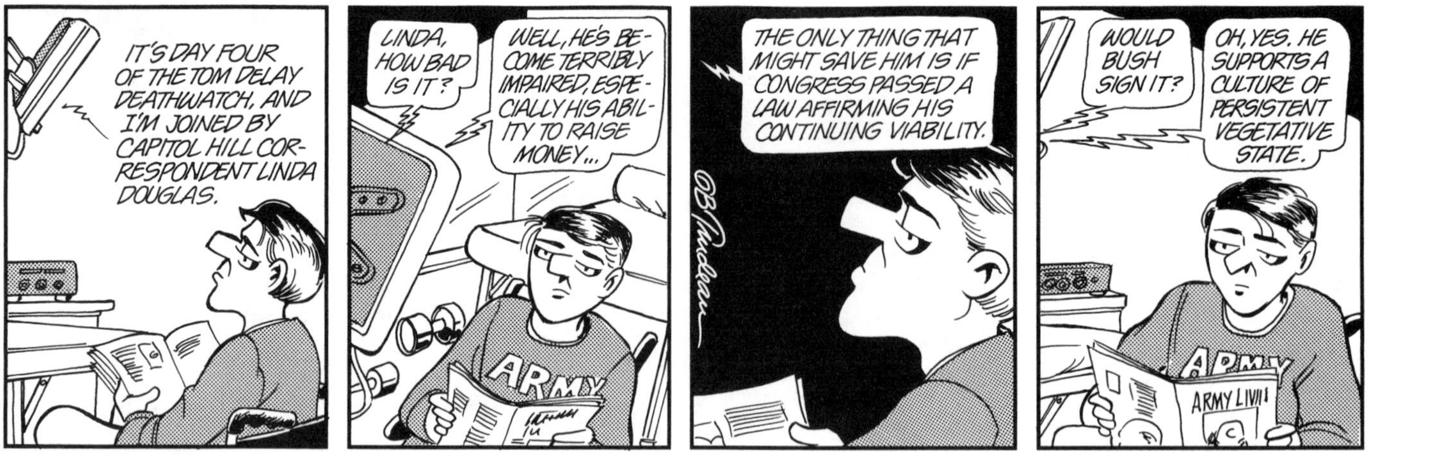
IT'S DAY FOUR OF THE TOM DELAY DEATHWATCH, AND I'M JOINED BY CAPITOL HILL CORRESPONDENT LINDA DOUGLAS.
LINDA, HOW BAD IS IT?
WELL, HE'S BECOME TERRIBLY IMPAIRED, ESPECIALLY HIS ABILITY TO RAISE MONEY...
THE ONLY THING THAT MIGHT SAVE HIM IS IF CONGRESS PASSED A LAW AFFIRMING HIS CONTINUING VIABILITY.
WOULD BUSH SIGN IT?
OH, YES. HE SUPPORTS A CULTURE OF PERSISTENT VEGETATIVE STATE.

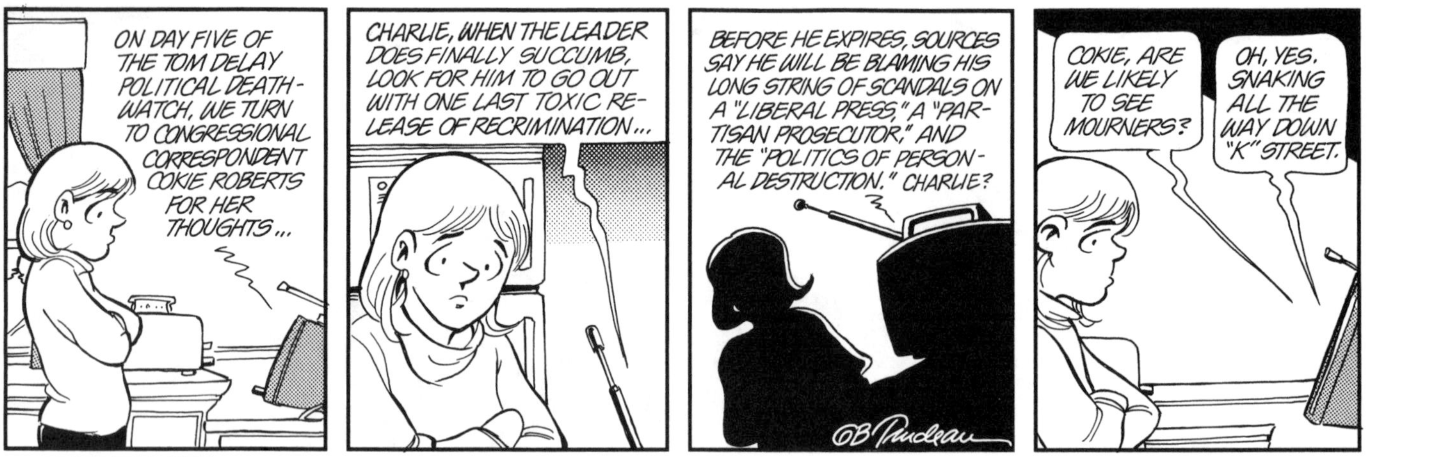
ON DAY FIVE OF THE TOM DELAY POLITICAL DEATHWATCH, WE TURN TO CONGRESSIONAL CORRESPONDENT COKIE ROBERTS FOR HER THOUGHTS...
CHARLIE, WHEN THE LEADER DOES FINALLY SUCCUMB, LOOK FOR HIM TO GO OUT WITH ONE LAST TOXIC RELEASE OF RECRIMINATION...
BEFORE HE EXPIRES, SOURCES SAY HE WILL BE BLAMING HIS LONG STRING OF SCANDALS ON A "LIBERAL PRESS," A "PARTISAN PROSECUTOR," AND THE "POLITICS OF PERSONAL DESTRUCTION." CHARLIE?
COKIE, ARE WE LIKELY TO SEE MOURNERS?
OH, YES. SNAKING ALL THE WAY DOWN "K" STREET.

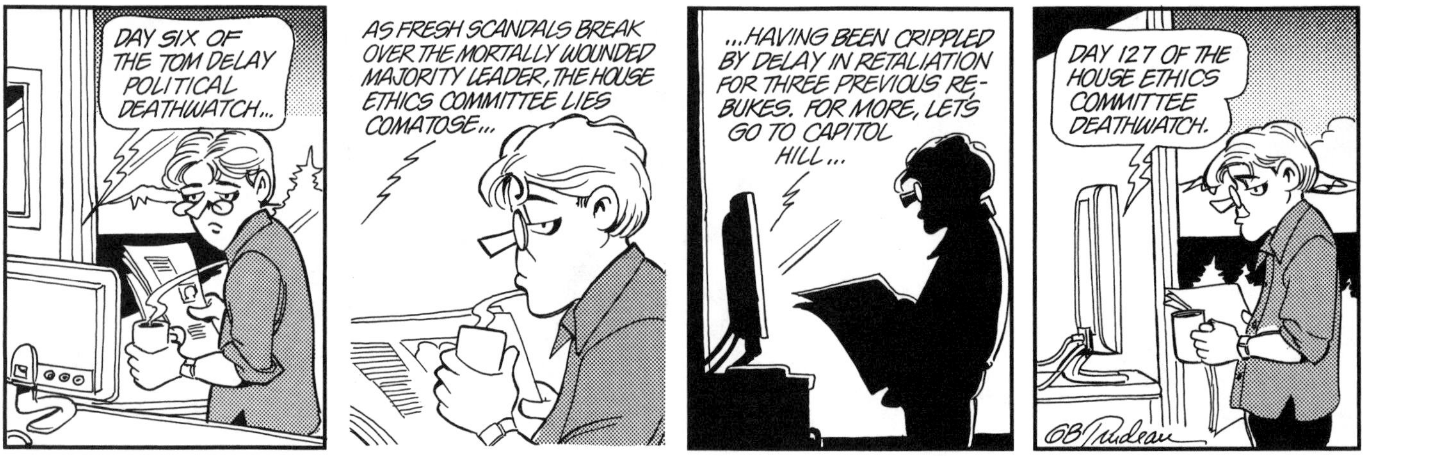
DAY SIX OF THE TOM DELAY POLITICAL DEATHWATCH...
AS FRESH SCANDALS BREAK OVER THE MORTALLY WOUNDED MAJORITY LEADER, THE HOUSE ETHICS COMMITTEE LIES COMATOSE...
...HAVING BEEN CRIPPLED BY DELAY IN RETALIATION FOR THREE PREVIOUS REBUKES. FOR MORE, LETS GO TO CAPITOL HILL...
DAY 127 OF THE HOUSE ETHICS COMMITTEE DEATHWATCH.

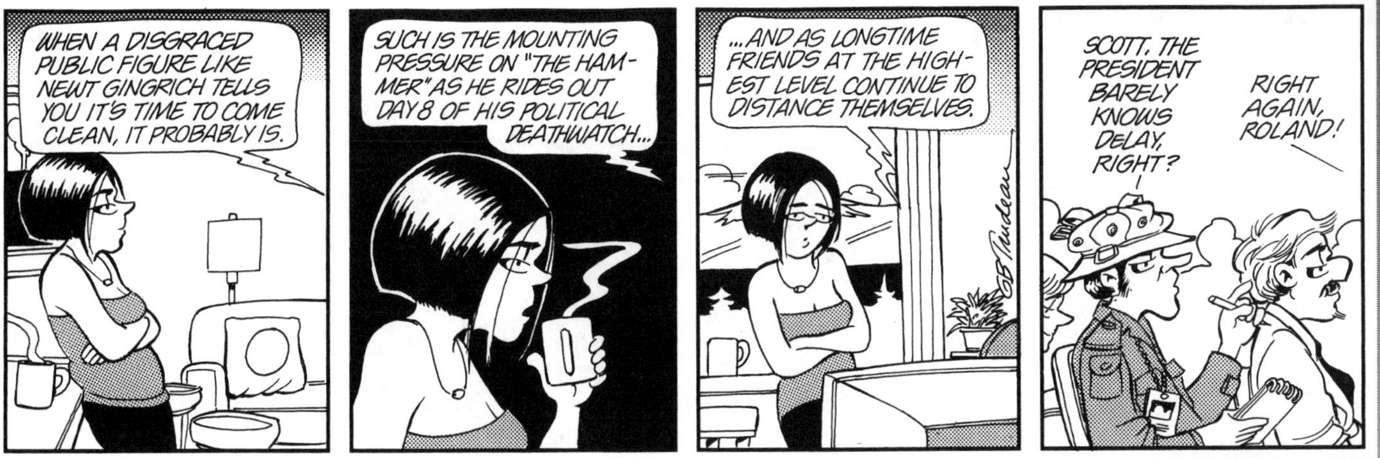
WHEN A DISGRACED PUBLIC FIGURE LIKE NEWT GINGRICH TELLS YOU IT'S TIME TO COME CLEAN, IT PROBABLY IS.
SUCH IS THE MOUNTING PRESSURE ON "THE HAMMER" AS HE RIDES OUT DAY 8 OF HIS POLITICAL DEATHWATCH...
...AND AS LONGTIME FRIENDS AT THE HIGHEST LEVEL CONTINUE TO DISTANCE THEMSELVES.
SCOTT, THE PRESIDENT BARELY KNOWS DELAY, RIGHT?
RIGHT AGAIN, ROLAND!

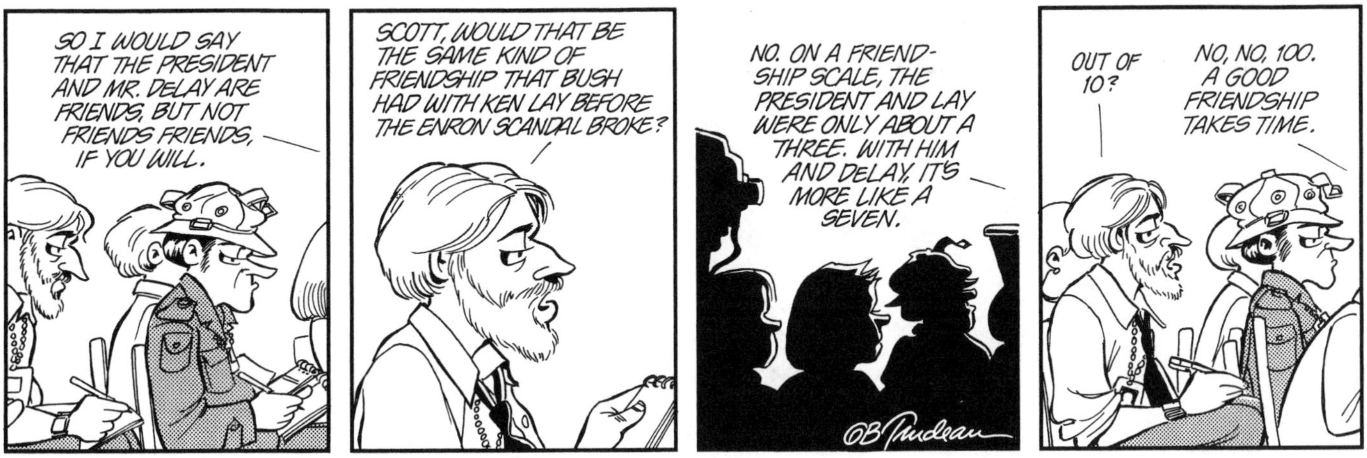
SO I WOULD SAY THAT THE PRESIDENT AND MR. DELAY ARE FRIENDS, BUT NOT FRIENDS FRIENDS, IF YOU WILL.
SCOTT, WOULD THAT BE THE SAME KIND OF FRIENDSHIP THAT BUSH HAD WITH KEN LAY BEFORE THE ENRON SCANDAL BROKE?
NO. ON A FRIENDSHIP SCALE, THE PRESIDENT AND LAY WERE ONLY ABOUT A THREE. WITH HIM AND DELAY, IT'S MORE LIKE A SEVEN.
OUT OF 10?
NO, NO, 100. A GOOD FRIENDSHIP TAKES TIME.

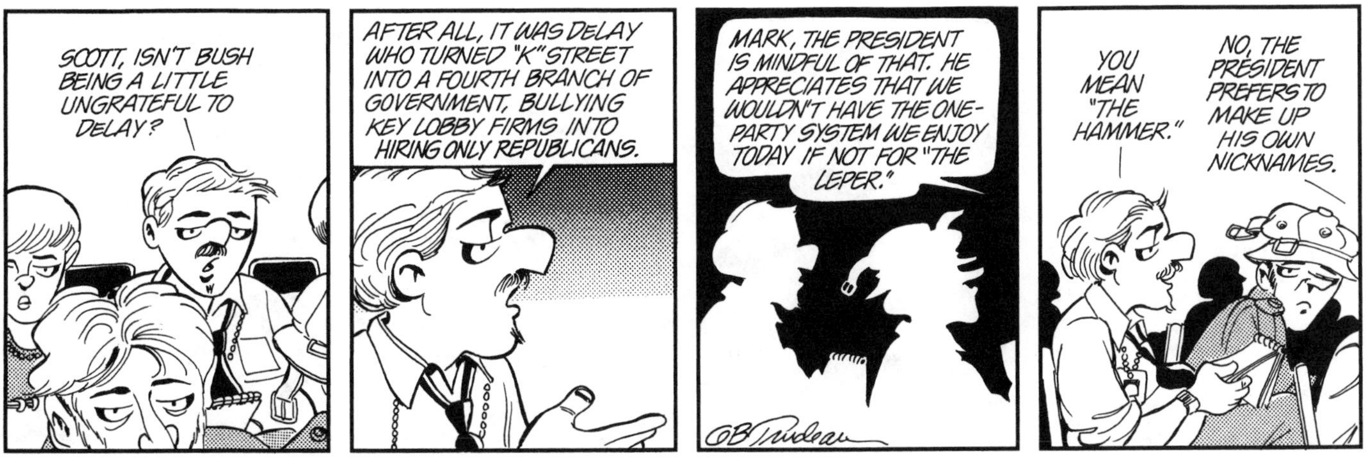
SCOTT, ISN'T BUSH BEING A LITTLE UNGRATEFUL TO DELAY?
AFTER ALL, IT WAS DELAY WHO TURNED "K" STREET INTO A FOURTH BRANCH OF GOVERNMENT, BULLYING KEY LOBBY FIRMS INTO HIRING ONLY REPUBLICANS.
MARK, THE PRESIDENT IS MINDFUL OF THAT. HE APPRECIATES THAT WE WOULDN'T HAVE THE ONE-PARTY SYSTEM WE ENJOY TODAY IF NOT FOR "THE LEPER."
YOU MEAN "THE HAMMER."
NO, THE PRESIDENT PREFERS TO MAKE UP HIS OWN NICKNAMES.

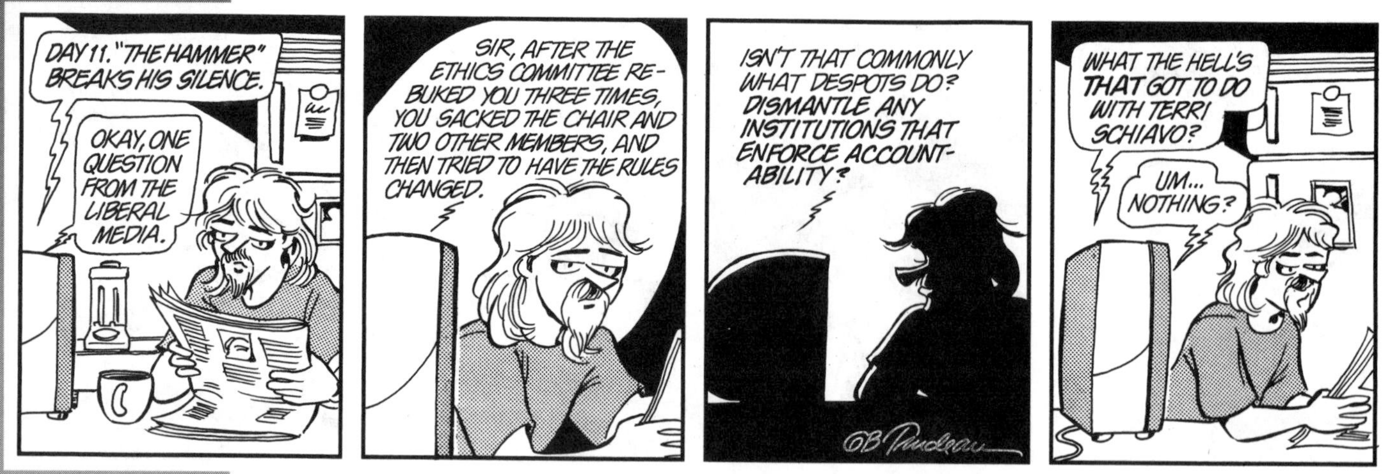
DAY 11. "THE HAMMER" BREAKS HIS SILENCE.
OKAY, ONE QUESTION FROM THE LIBERAL MEDIA.
SIR, AFTER THE ETHICS COMMITTEE REBUKED YOU THREE TIMES, YOU SACKED THE CHAIR AND TWO OTHER MEMBERS, AND THEN TRIED TO HAVE THE RULES CHANGED.
ISN'T THAT COMMONLY WHAT DESPOTS DO? DISMANTLE ANY INSTITUTIONS THAT ENFORCE ACCOUNTABILITY?
©B Trudeau
WHAT THE HELL'S THAT GOT TO DO WITH TERRI SCHIAVO?
UM... NOTHING?

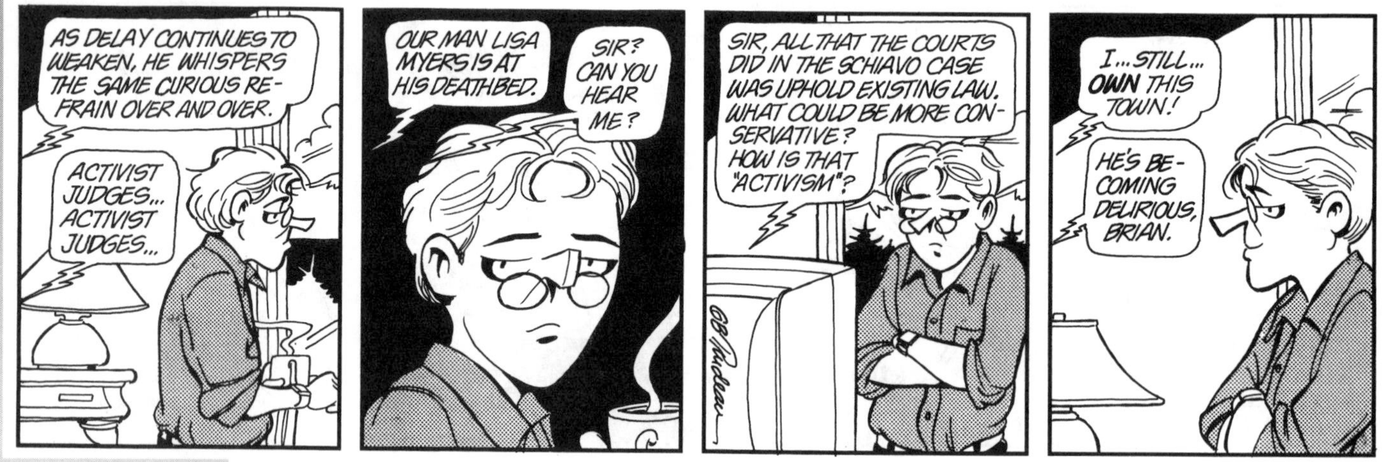
AS DELAY CONTINUES TO WEAKEN, HE WHISPERS THE SAME CURIOUS REFRAIN OVER AND OVER.
ACTIVIST JUDGES... ACTIVIST JUDGES...
OUR MAN LISA MYERS IS AT HIS DEATHBED.
SIR? CAN YOU HEAR ME?
SIR, ALL THAT THE COURTS DID IN THE SCHIAVO CASE WAS UPHOLD EXISTING LAW. WHAT COULD BE MORE CONSERVATIVE? HOW IS THAT "ACTIVISM"?
GB Trudeau
I... STILL... OWN THIS TOWN!
HE'S BECOMING DELIRIOUS, BRIAN.

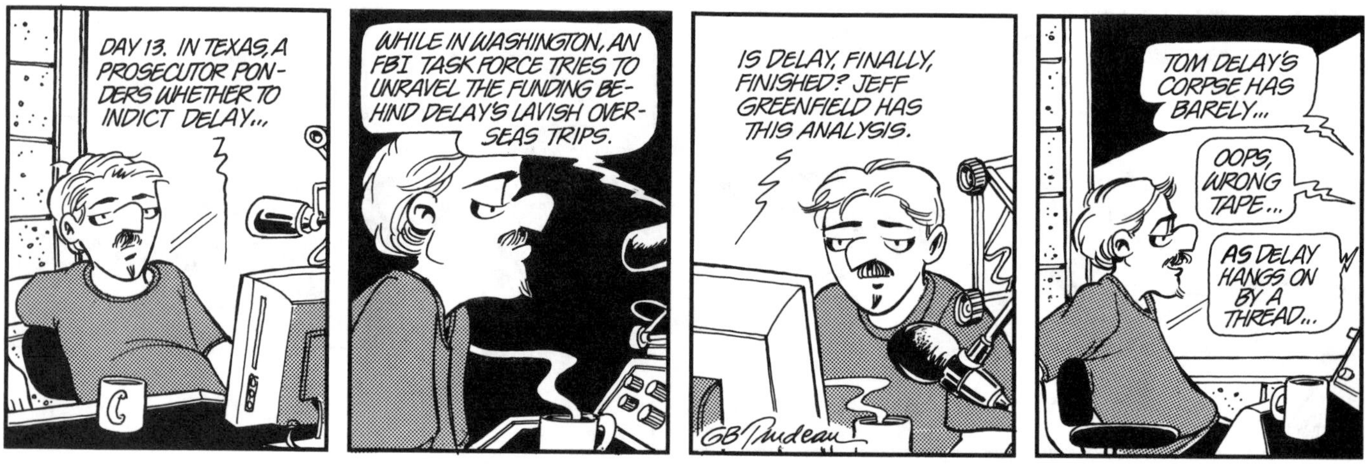
DAY 13. IN TEXAS, A PROSECUTOR PONDERS WHETHER TO INDICT DELAY...
WHILE IN WASHINGTON, AN FBI TASK FORCE TRIES TO UNRAVEL THE FUNDING BEHIND DELAY'S LAVISH OVERSEAS TRIPS.
IS DELAY, FINALLY, FINISHED? JEFF GREENFIELD HAS THIS ANALYSIS.
GB Trudeau
TOM DELAY'S CORPSE HAS BARELY...
OOPS, WRONG TAPE...
AS DELAY HANGS ON BY A THREAD...

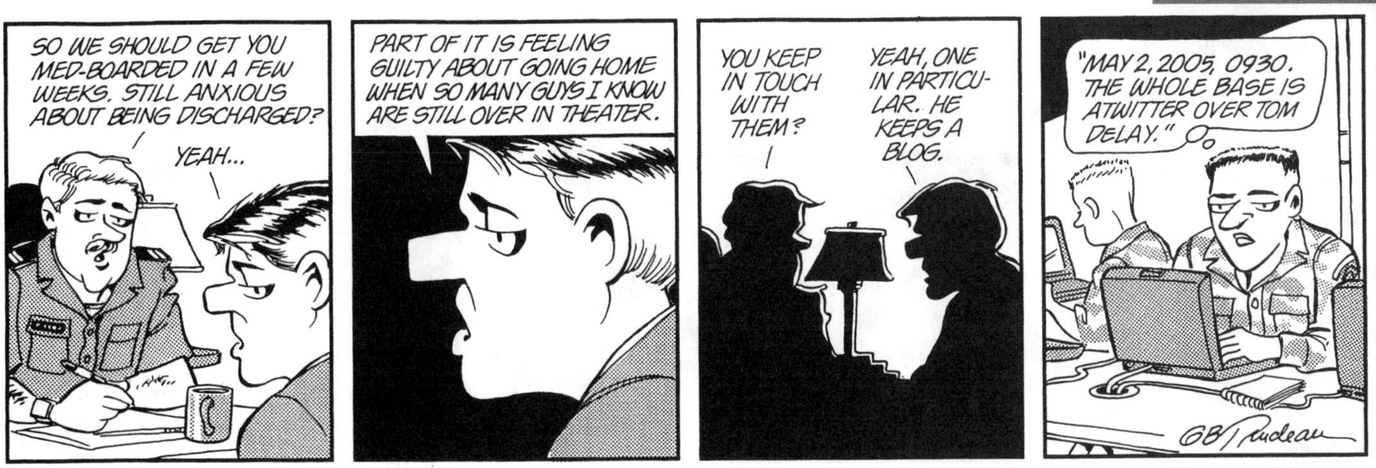
SO WE SHOULD GET YOU MED-BOARDED IN A FEW WEEKS. STILL ANXIOUS ABOUT BEING DISCHARGED?
YEAH...
PART OF IT IS FEELING GUILTY ABOUT GOING HOME WHEN SO MANY GUYS I KNOW ARE STILL OVER IN THEATER.
YOU KEEP IN TOUCH WITH THEM?
YEAH, ONE IN PARTICULAR. HE KEEPS A BLOG.
"MAY 2, 2005, 0930. THE WHOLE BASE IS ATWITTER OVER TOM DELAY."
GB Trudeau

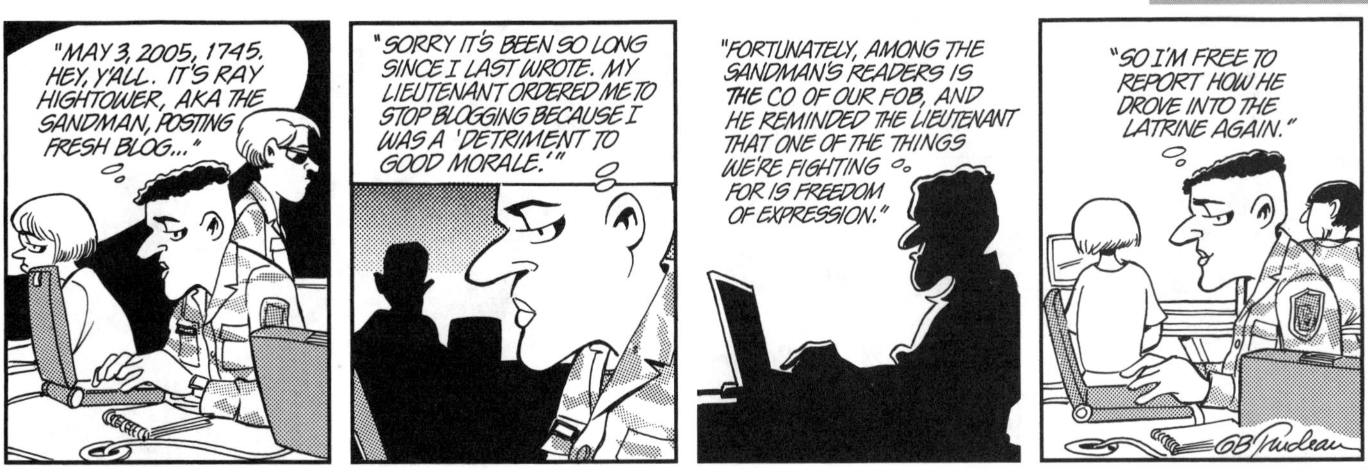
"MAY 3, 2005, 1745. HEY, Y'ALL. IT'S RAY HIGHTOWER, AKA THE SANDMAN, POSTING FRESH BLOG..."
"SORRY IT'S BEEN SO LONG SINCE I LAST WROTE. MY LIEUTENANT ORDERED ME TO STOP BLOGGING BECAUSE I WAS A 'DETRIMENT TO GOOD MORALE.'"
"FORTUNATELY, AMONG THE SANDMAN'S READERS IS THE CO OF OUR FOB, AND HE REMINDED THE LIEUTENANT THAT ONE OF THE THINGS WE'RE FIGHTING FOR IS FREEDOM OF EXPRESSION."
"SO I'M FREE TO REPORT HOW HE DROVE INTO THE LATRINE AGAIN."
GB Trudeau

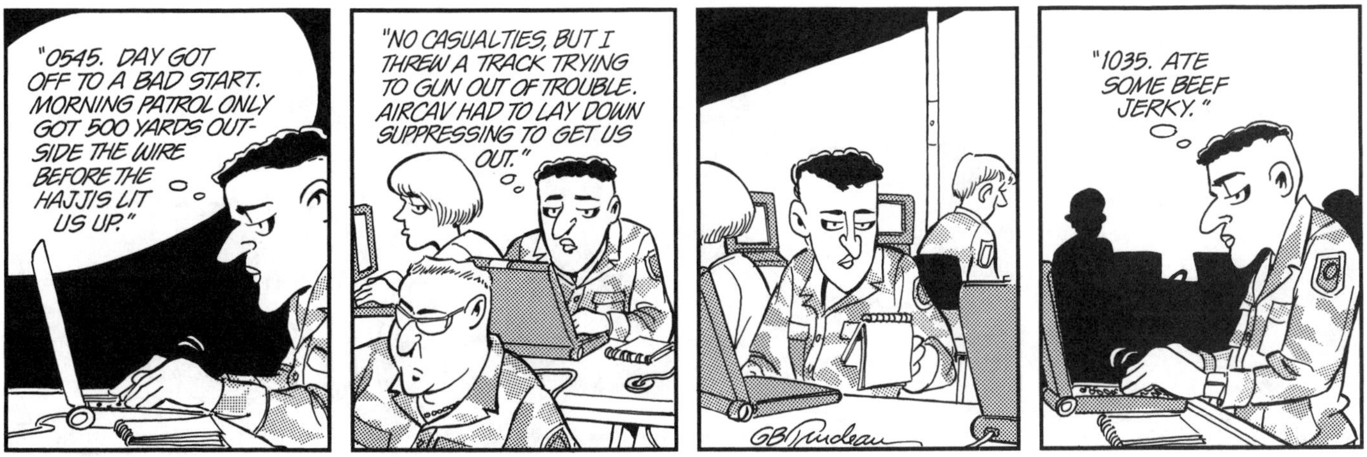
"0545. DAY GOT OFF TO A BAD START. MORNING PATROL ONLY GOT 500 YARDS OUTSIDE THE WIRE BEFORE THE HAJJIS LIT US UP."
"NO CASUALTIES, BUT I THREW A TRACK TRYING TO GUN OUT OF TROUBLE. AIRCAV HAD TO LAY DOWN SUPPRESSING TO GET US OUT."
GB Trudeau
"1035. ATE SOME BEEF JERKY."

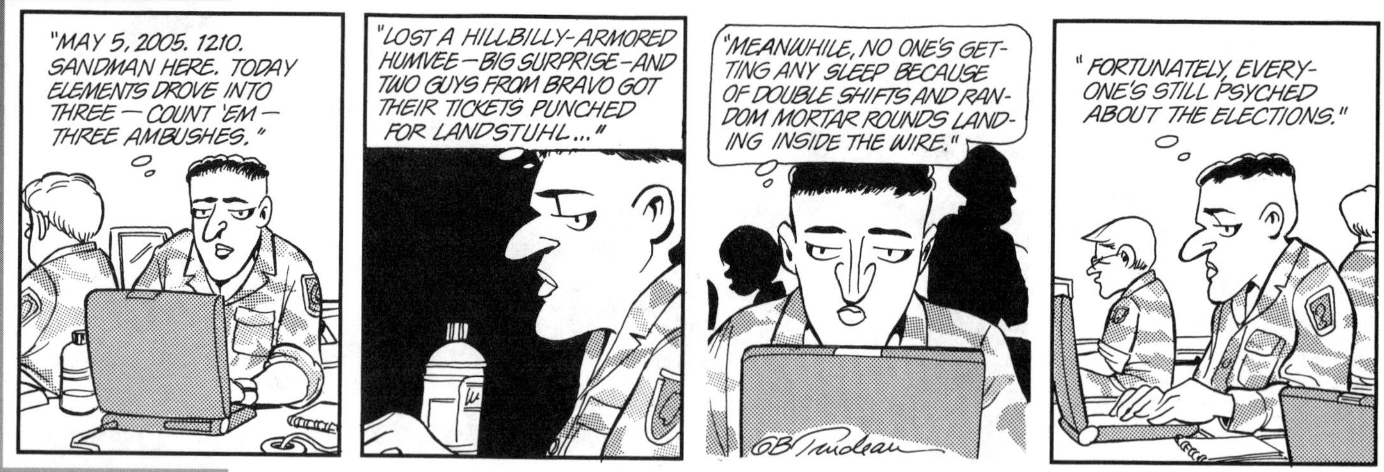
"MAY 5, 2005. 1210. SANDMAN HERE. TODAY ELEMENTS DROVE INTO THREE — COUNT 'EM — THREE AMBUSHES."
"LOST A HILLBILLY-ARMORED HUMVEE — BIG SURPRISE — AND TWO GUYS FROM BRAVO GOT THEIR TICKETS PUNCHED FOR LANDSTUHL..."
"MEANWHILE, NO ONE'S GETTING ANY SLEEP BECAUSE OF DOUBLE SHIFTS AND RANDOM MORTAR ROUNDS LANDING INSIDE THE WIRE."
"FORTUNATELY, EVERYONE'S STILL PSYCHED ABOUT THE ELECTIONS."

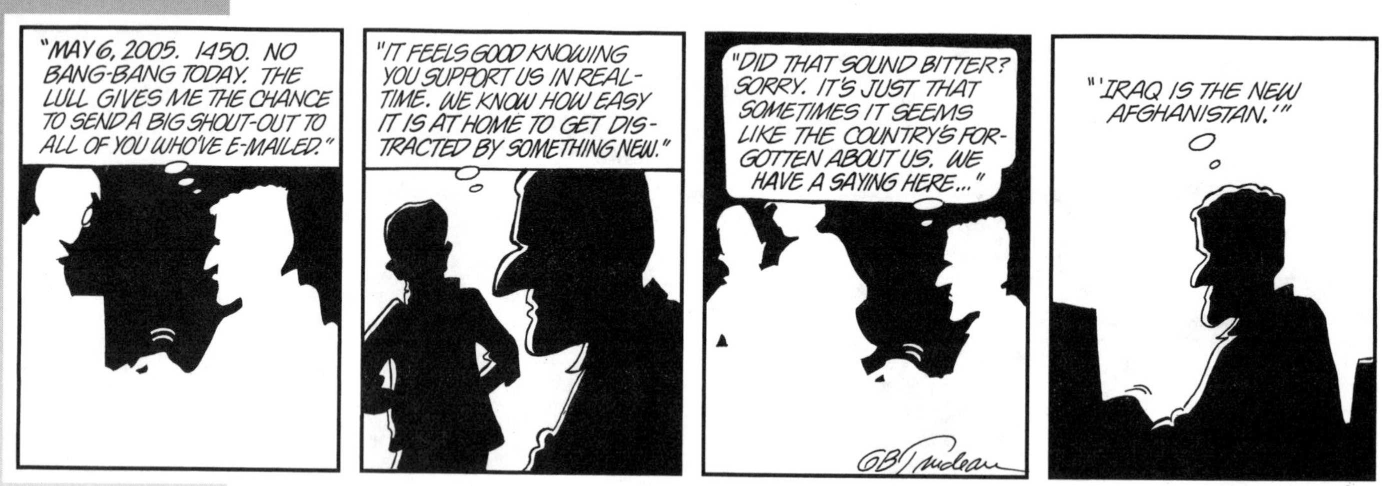
"MAY 6, 2005. 1450. NO BANG-BANG TODAY. THE LULL GIVES ME THE CHANCE TO SEND A BIG SHOUT-OUT TO ALL OF YOU WHO'VE E-MAILED."
"IT FEELS GOOD KNOWING YOU SUPPORT US IN REAL-TIME. WE KNOW HOW EASY IT IS AT HOME TO GET DISTRACTED BY SOMETHING NEW."
"DID THAT SOUND BITTER? SORRY. IT'S JUST THAT SOMETIMES IT SEEMS LIKE THE COUNTRY'S FORGOTTEN ABOUT US. WE HAVE A SAYING HERE..."
"'IRAQ IS THE NEW AFGHANISTAN.'"

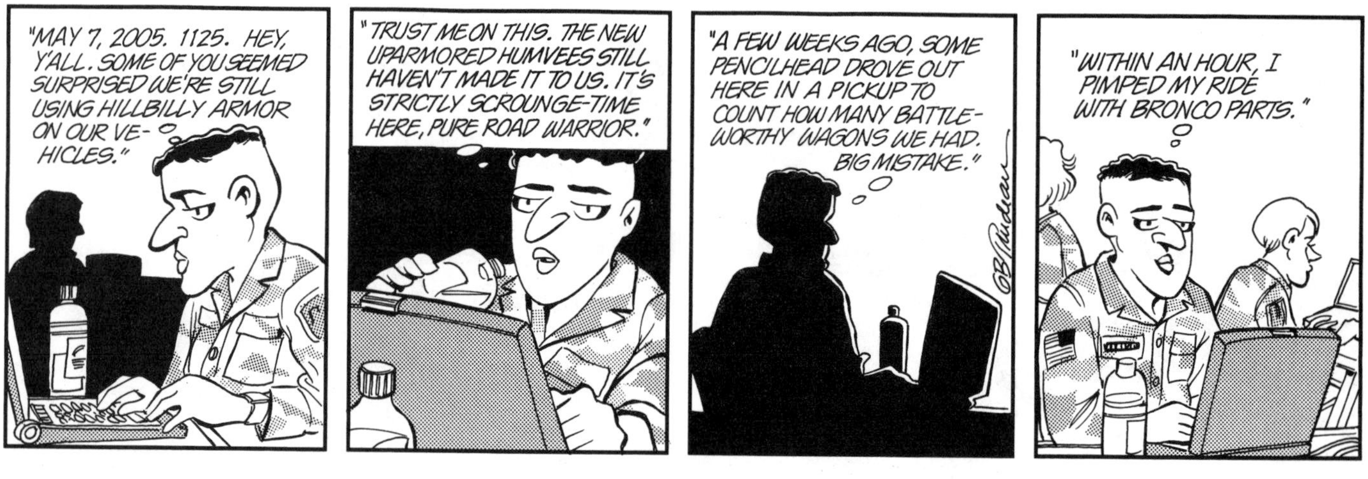
"MAY 7, 2005. 1125. HEY, Y'ALL. SOME OF YOU SEEMED SURPRISED WE'RE STILL USING HILLBILLY ARMOR ON OUR VEHICLES."
"TRUST ME ON THIS. THE NEW UPARMORED HUMVEES STILL HAVEN'T MADE IT TO US. IT'S STRICTLY SCROUNGE-TIME HERE, PURE ROAD WARRIOR."
"A FEW WEEKS AGO, SOME PENCILHEAD DROVE OUT HERE IN A PICKUP TO COUNT HOW MANY BATTLEWORTHY WAGONS WE HAD. BIG MISTAKE."
"WITHIN AN HOUR, I PIMPED MY RIDE WITH BRONCO PARTS."

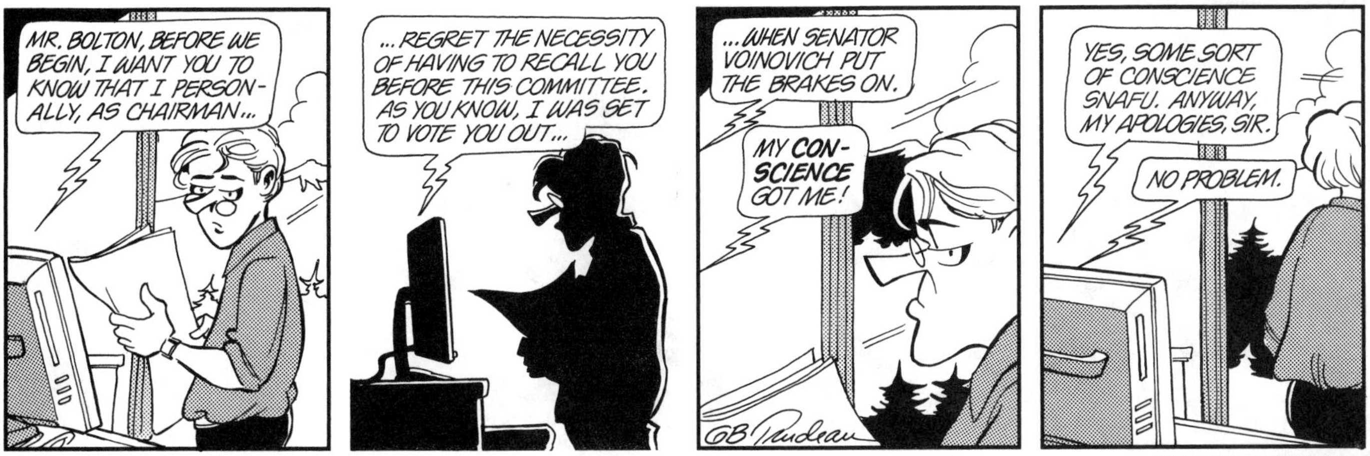
MR. BOLTON, BEFORE WE BEGIN, I WANT YOU TO KNOW THAT I PERSONALLY, AS CHAIRMAN...
...REGRET THE NECESSITY OF HAVING TO RECALL YOU BEFORE THIS COMMITTEE. AS YOU KNOW, I WAS SET TO VOTE YOU OUT...
...WHEN SENATOR VOINOVICH PUT THE BRAKES ON.
MY CONSCIENCE GOT ME!
YES, SOME SORT OF CONSCIENCE SNAFU. ANYWAY, MY APOLOGIES, SIR.
NO PROBLEM.

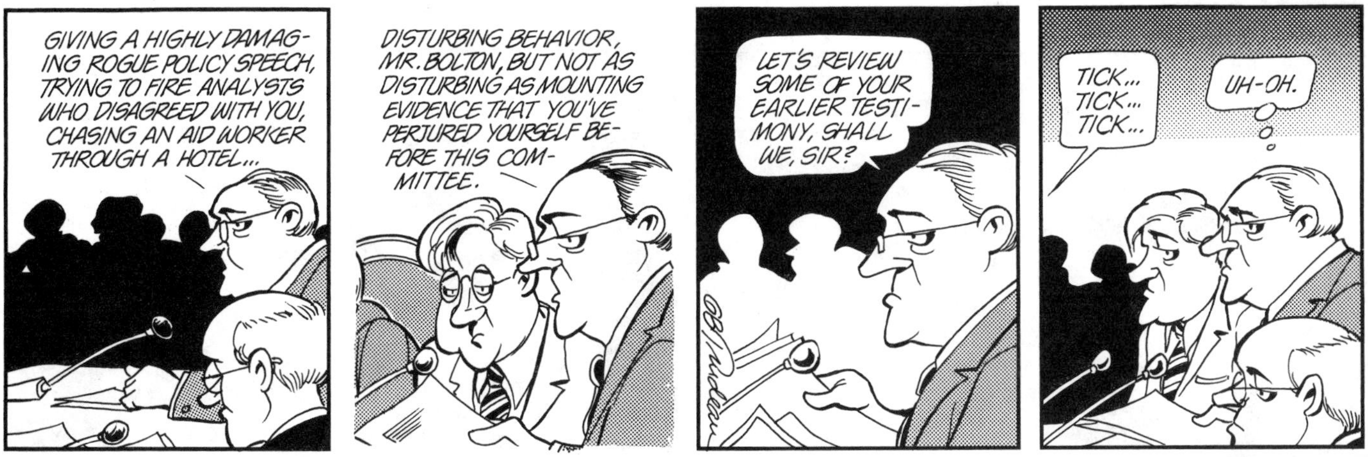
GIVING A HIGHLY DAMAGING ROGUE POLICY SPEECH, TRYING TO FIRE ANALYSTS WHO DISAGREED WITH YOU, CHASING AN AID WORKER THROUGH A HOTEL...
DISTURBING BEHAVIOR, MR. BOLTON, BUT NOT AS DISTURBING AS MOUNTING EVIDENCE THAT YOU'VE PERJURED YOURSELF BEFORE THIS COMMITTEE.
LET'S REVIEW SOME OF YOUR EARLIER TESTIMONY, SHALL WE, SIR?
TICK... TICK... TICK...
UH-OH.

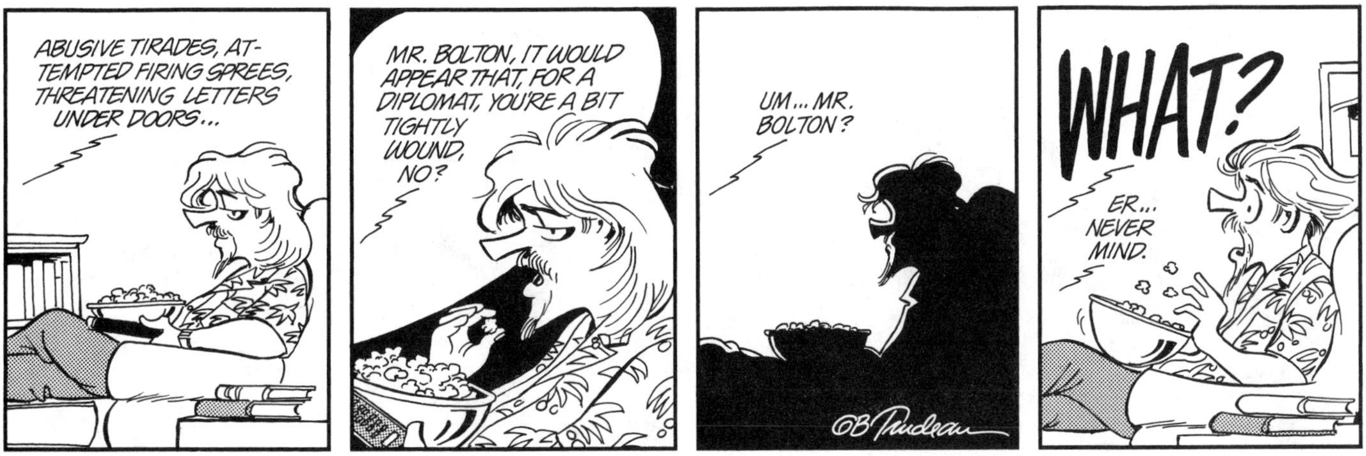
ABUSIVE TIRADES, ATTEMPTED FIRING SPREES, THREATENING LETTERS UNDER DOORS...
MR. BOLTON, IT WOULD APPEAR THAT, FOR A DIPLOMAT, YOU'RE A BIT TIGHTLY WOUND, NO?
UM... MR. BOLTON?
WHAT?
ER... NEVER MIND.

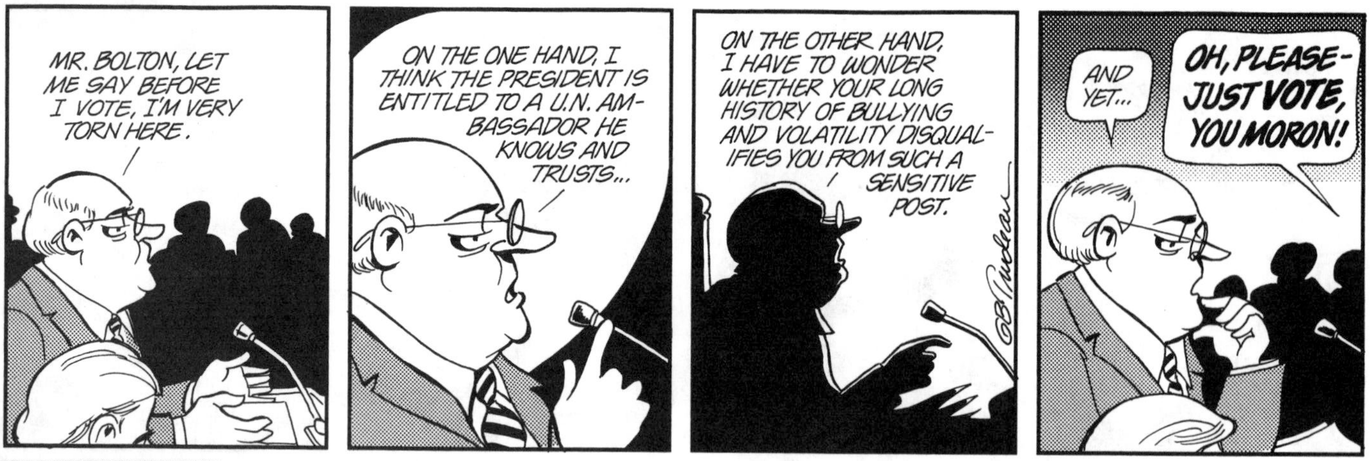
MR. BOLTON, LET ME SAY BEFORE I VOTE, I'M VERY TORN HERE.
ON THE ONE HAND, I THINK THE PRESIDENT IS ENTITLED TO A U.N. AMBASSADOR HE KNOWS AND TRUSTS...
ON THE OTHER HAND, I HAVE TO WONDER WHETHER YOUR LONG HISTORY OF BULLYING AND VOLATILITY DISQUALIFIES YOU FROM SUCH A SENSITIVE POST.
AND YET...
OH, PLEASE- JUST VOTE, YOU MORON!

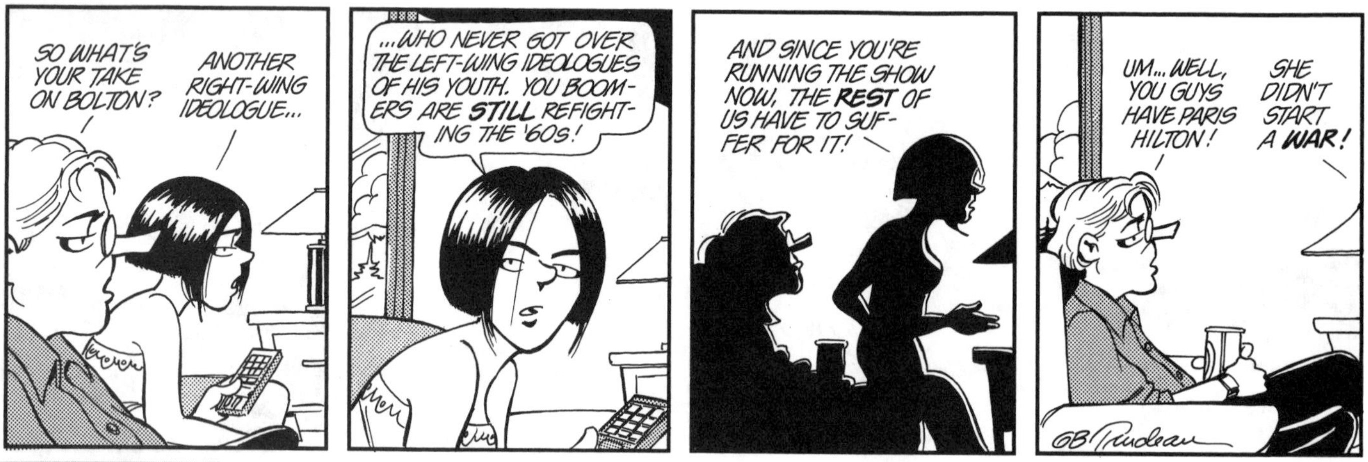
SO WHAT'S YOUR TAKE ON BOLTON?
ANOTHER RIGHT-WING IDEOLOGUE...
...WHO NEVER GOT OVER THE LEFT-WING IDEOLOGUES OF HIS YOUTH. YOU BOOMERS ARE STILL REFIGHTING THE '60s!
AND SINCE YOU'RE RUNNING THE SHOW NOW, THE REST OF US HAVE TO SUFFER FOR IT!
UM... WELL, YOU GUYS HAVE PARIS HILTON!
SHE DIDN'T START A WAR!

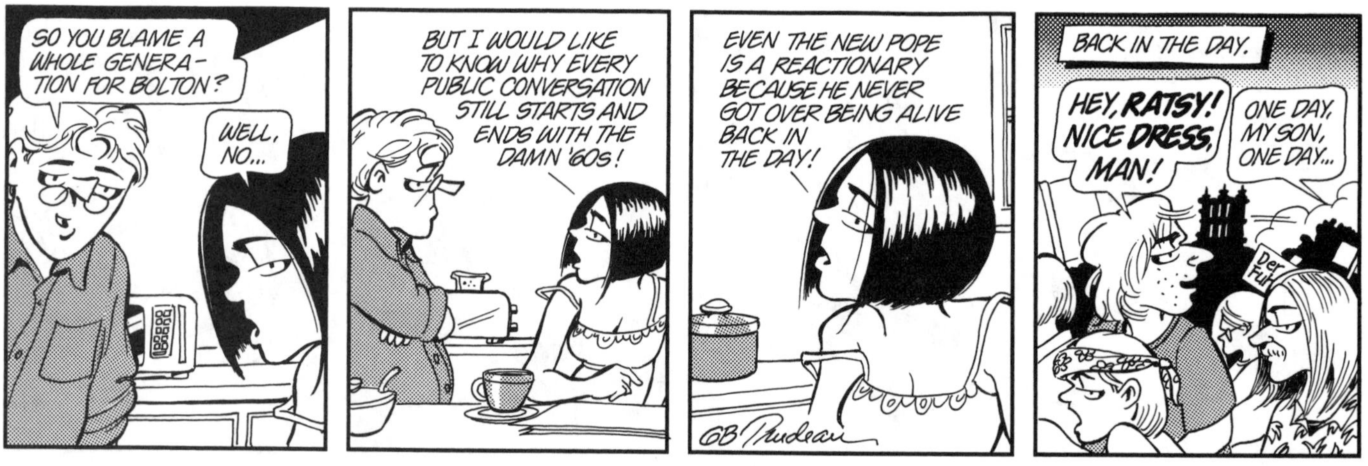
SO YOU BLAME A WHOLE GENERATION FOR BOLTON?
WELL, NO...
BUT I WOULD LIKE TO KNOW WHY EVERY PUBLIC CONVERSATION STILL STARTS AND ENDS WITH THE DAMN '60s!
EVEN THE NEW POPE IS A REACTIONARY BECAUSE HE NEVER GOT OVER BEING ALIVE BACK IN THE DAY!
BACK IN THE DAY.
HEY, RATSY! NICE DRESS, MAN!
ONE DAY, MY SON, ONE DAY...

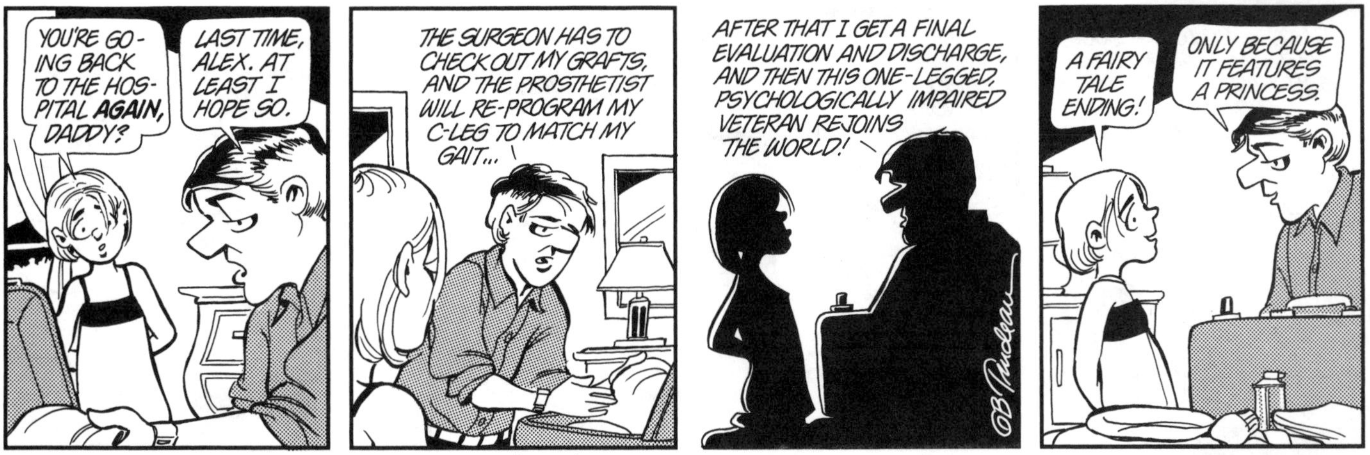
YOU'RE GO-ING BACK TO THE HOS-PITAL **AGAIN,** DADDY?
LAST TIME, ALEX. AT LEAST I HOPE SO.
THE SURGEON HAS TO CHECK OUT MY GRAFTS, AND THE PROSTHETIST WILL RE-PROGRAM MY C-LEG TO MATCH MY GAIT...
AFTER THAT I GET A FINAL EVALUATION AND DISCHARGE, AND THEN THIS ONE-LEGGED, PSYCHOLOGICALLY IMPAIRED VETERAN REJOINS THE WORLD!
A FAIRY TALE ENDING!
ONLY BECAUSE IT FEATURES A PRINCESS.
GB Trudeau

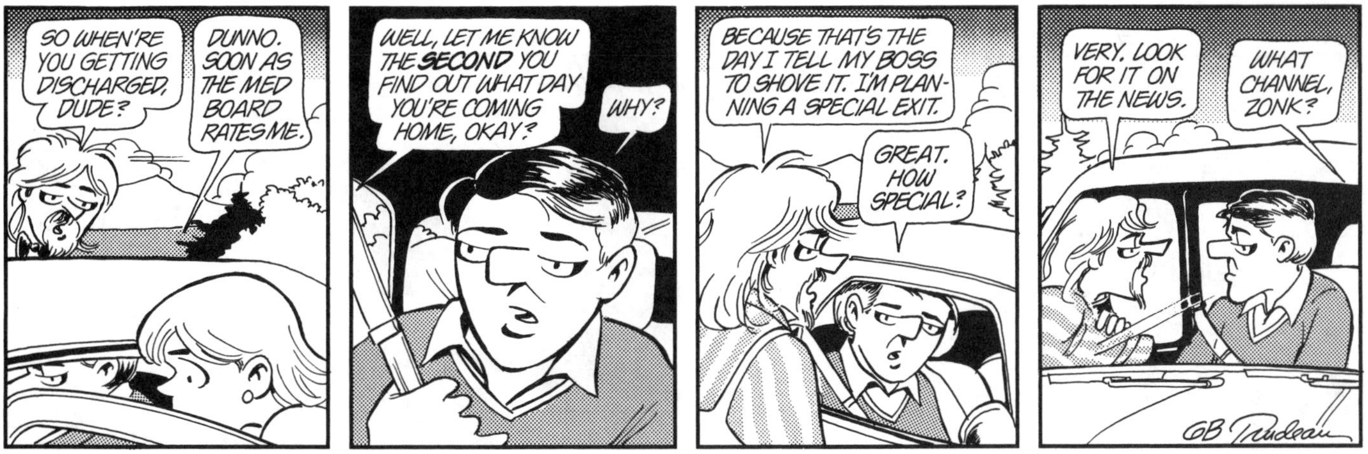
SO WHEN'RE YOU GETTING DISCHARGED, DUDE?
DUNNO. SOON AS THE MED BOARD RATES ME.
WELL, LET ME KNOW THE **SECOND** YOU FIND OUT WHAT DAY YOU'RE COMING HOME, OKAY?
WHY?
BECAUSE THAT'S THE DAY I TELL MY BOSS TO SHOVE IT. I'M PLAN-NING A SPECIAL EXIT.
GREAT. HOW SPECIAL?
VERY. LOOK FOR IT ON THE NEWS.
WHAT CHANNEL, ZONK?
GB Trudeau

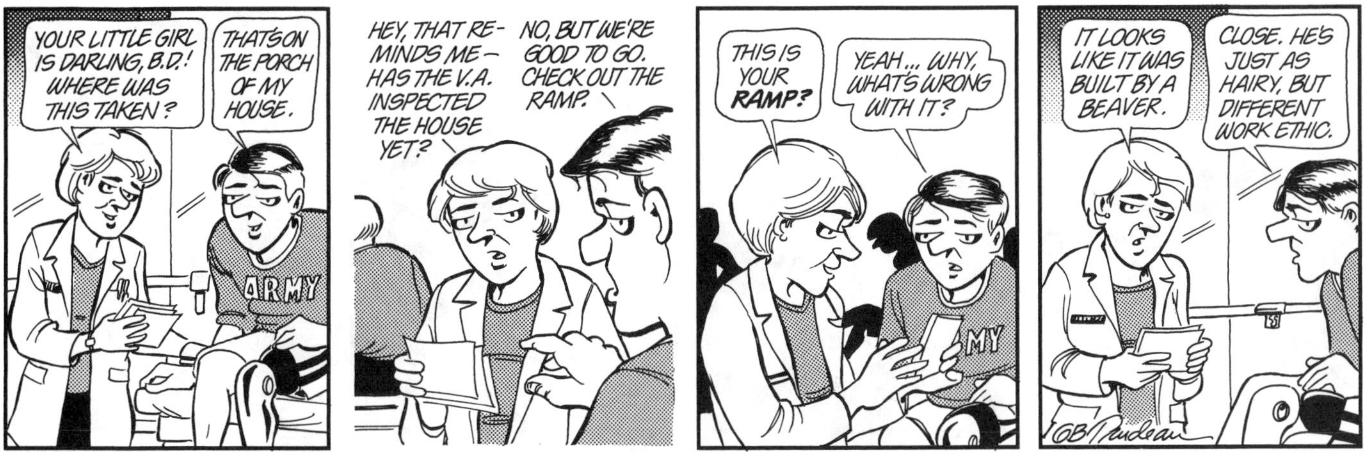
YOUR LITTLE GIRL IS DARLING, B.D.! WHERE WAS THIS TAKEN?
THAT'S ON THE PORCH OF MY HOUSE.
HEY, THAT RE-MINDS ME — HAS THE V.A. INSPECTED THE HOUSE YET?
NO, BUT WE'RE GOOD TO GO. CHECK OUT THE RAMP.
THIS IS YOUR **RAMP?**
YEAH... WHY, WHAT'S WRONG WITH IT?
IT LOOKS LIKE IT WAS BUILT BY A BEAVER.
CLOSE. HE'S JUST AS HAIRY, BUT DIFFERENT WORK ETHIC.
GB Trudeau

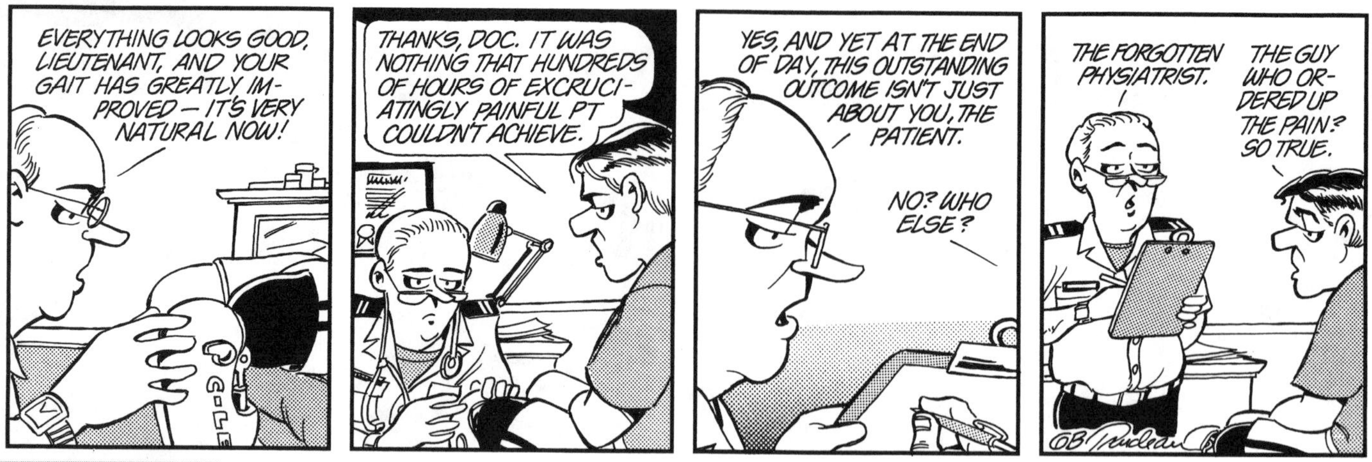
EVERYTHING LOOKS GOOD, LIEUTENANT, AND YOUR GAIT HAS GREATLY IMPROVED — IT'S VERY NATURAL NOW!
THANKS, DOC. IT WAS NOTHING THAT HUNDREDS OF HOURS OF EXCRUCIATINGLY PAINFUL PT COULDN'T ACHIEVE.
YES, AND YET AT THE END OF DAY, THIS OUTSTANDING OUTCOME ISN'T JUST ABOUT YOU, THE PATIENT.
NO? WHO ELSE?
THE FORGOTTEN PHYSIATRIST.
THE GUY WHO ORDERED UP THE PAIN? SO TRUE.

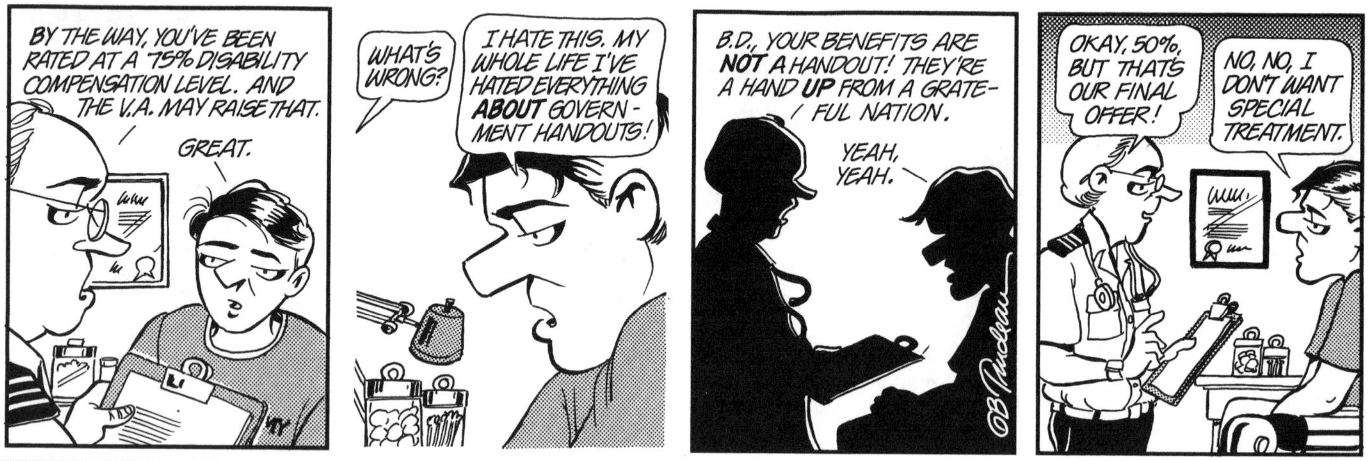
BY THE WAY, YOU'VE BEEN RATED AT A 75% DISABILITY COMPENSATION LEVEL.. AND THE V.A. MAY RAISE THAT.
GREAT.
WHAT'S WRONG?
I HATE THIS. MY WHOLE LIFE I'VE HATED EVERYTHING **ABOUT** GOVERNMENT HANDOUTS!
B.D., YOUR BENEFITS ARE **NOT A** HANDOUT! THEY'RE A HAND **UP** FROM A GRATEFUL NATION.
YEAH, YEAH.
OKAY, 50%, BUT THAT'S OUR FINAL OFFER!
NO, NO, I DON'T WANT SPECIAL TREATMENT.

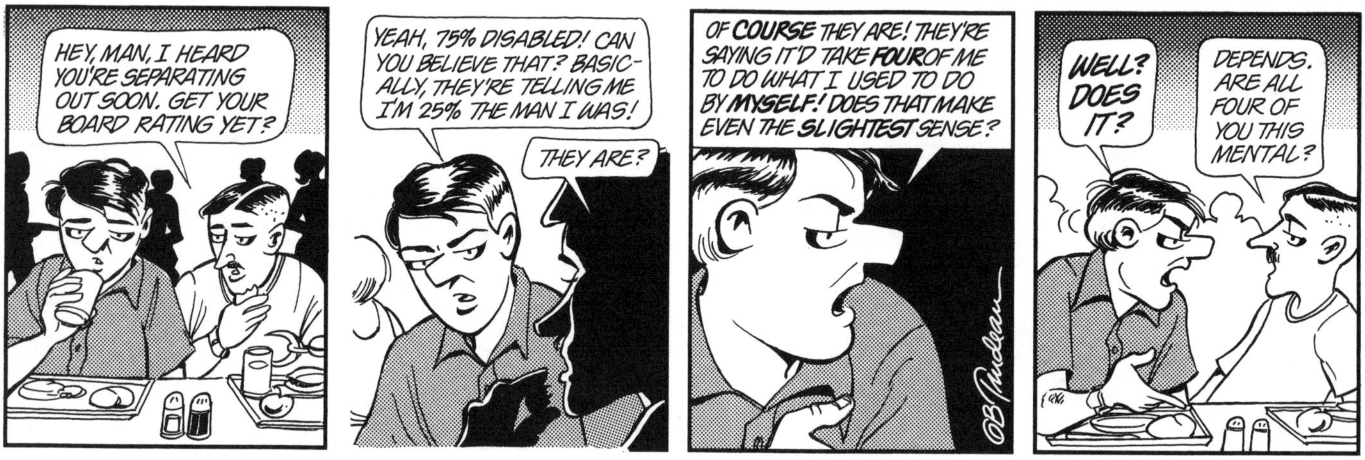
HEY, MAN, I HEARD YOU'RE SEPARATING OUT SOON. GET YOUR BOARD RATING YET?
YEAH, 75% DISABLED! CAN YOU BELIEVE THAT? BASICALLY, THEY'RE TELLING ME I'M 25% THE MAN I WAS!
THEY ARE?
OF **COURSE** THEY ARE! THEY'RE SAYING IT'D TAKE **FOUR** OF ME TO DO WHAT I USED TO DO BY **MYSELF! DOES THAT MAKE EVEN THE SLIGHTEST** SENSE?
WELL? DOES IT?
DEPENDS. ARE ALL FOUR OF YOU THIS MENTAL?

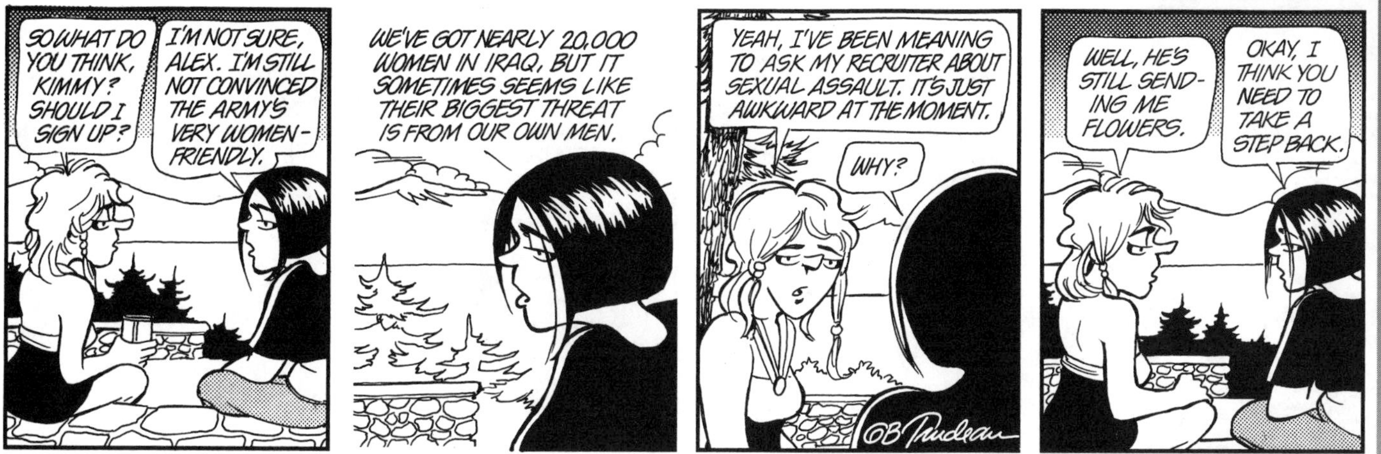
SO WHAT DO YOU THINK, KIMMY? SHOULD I SIGN UP?
I'M NOT SURE, ALEX. I'M STILL NOT CONVINCED THE ARMY'S VERY WOMEN-FRIENDLY.
WE'VE GOT NEARLY 20,000 WOMEN IN IRAQ, BUT IT SOMETIMES SEEMS LIKE THEIR BIGGEST THREAT IS FROM OUR OWN MEN.
YEAH, I'VE BEEN MEANING TO ASK MY RECRUITER ABOUT SEXUAL ASSAULT. IT'S JUST AWKWARD AT THE MOMENT.
WHY?
WELL, HE'S STILL SENDING ME FLOWERS.
OKAY, I THINK YOU NEED TO TAKE A STEP BACK.

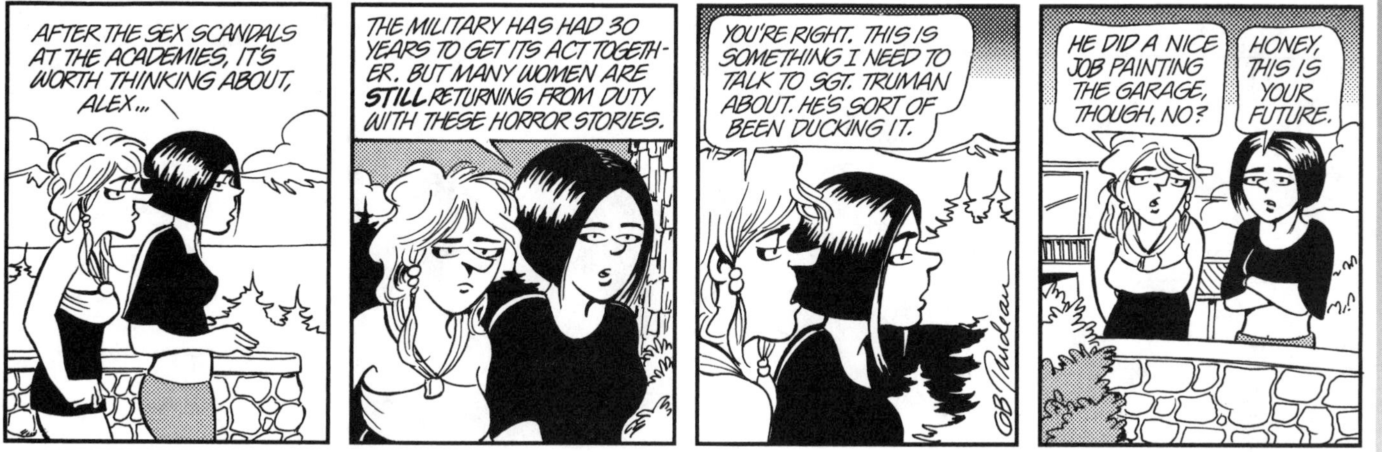
AFTER THE SEX SCANDALS AT THE ACADEMIES, IT'S WORTH THINKING ABOUT, ALEX...
THE MILITARY HAS HAD 30 YEARS TO GET ITS ACT TOGETHER. BUT MANY WOMEN ARE STILL RETURNING FROM DUTY WITH THESE HORROR STORIES.
YOU'RE RIGHT. THIS IS SOMETHING I NEED TO TALK TO SGT. TRUMAN ABOUT. HE'S SORT OF BEEN DUCKING IT.
HE DID A NICE JOB PAINTING THE GARAGE, THOUGH, NO?
HONEY, THIS IS YOUR FUTURE.

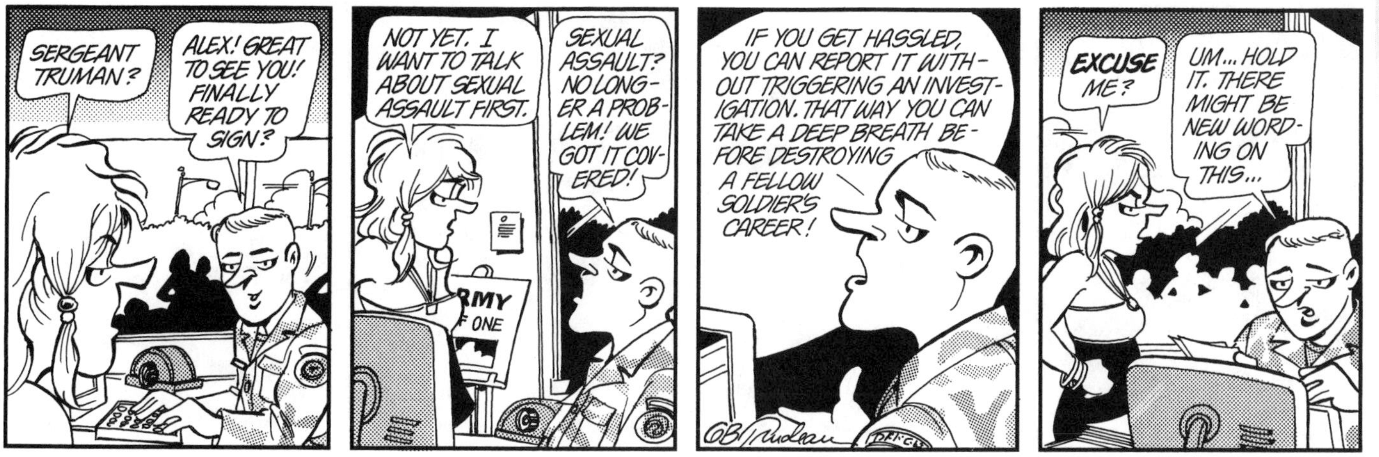
SERGEANT TRUMAN?
ALEX! GREAT TO SEE YOU! FINALLY READY TO SIGN?
NOT YET. I WANT TO TALK ABOUT SEXUAL ASSAULT FIRST.
SEXUAL ASSAULT? NO LONGER A PROBLEM! WE GOT IT COVERED!
IF YOU GET HASSLED, YOU CAN REPORT IT WITHOUT TRIGGERING AN INVESTIGATION. THAT WAY YOU CAN TAKE A DEEP BREATH BEFORE DESTROYING A FELLOW SOLDIER'S CAREER!
EXCUSE ME?
UM... HOLD IT. THERE MIGHT BE NEW WORDING ON THIS...

SO MY STEPMOM SAYS THERE WERE 1,700 ASSAULTS LAST YEAR. AND IT'S WAY UNDER-REPORTED!
YES, BUT WE'RE ADDRESSING THE PROBLEM...
WAIT, WHY DO YOU KEEP CALLING IT A PROBLEM? SEXUAL ASSAULT IS A CRIME!
WELL, OF COURSE IT IS...
BUT THIS YEAR WE PUT IN PLACE A NEW PREVENTION AND RESPONSE POLICY. IF SOMETHING INAPPROPRIATE HAPPENS TO YOU, REPORTING IT NOW IS A SNAP!
REPORTING RAPE IS A "SNAP"?
ONE CALL AND YOU'RE IN BUSINESS! GOD FORBID, OF COURSE.

I DON'T KNOW, SERGEANT TRUMAN. I'M HAVING SECOND THOUGHTS NOW...
YOU **HAVE** TO SIGN, ALEX! I'M COUNTING ON YOU!
IF YOU DON'T ENLIST, I'LL MISS MY QUOTA! YOU HAVE NO **IDEA** WHAT KIND OF PRESSURE I'M UNDER! I CAN'T SLEEP, I HAVE MIGRAINES, I'M FIGHTING DEPRESSION...
YOU KNOW, FOR AN ARMY OF ONE, YOU SURE ARE NEEDY.
I'M PRE-ARMY-OF-ONE. I JOINED TO BE ALL I COULD BE.

I'M NOT GOING TO LIE TO YOU, ALEX—THIS IS A BLOW TO ME, A BIG PERSONAL BLOW!
EVER SINCE THE STAND-DOWN, **WE'VE BEEN UNDER EVEN MORE** PRESSURE! NOW WE HAVE TO RECRUIT WITH **ONE ARM TIED** BEHIND OUR BACKS!
I WAS JUST A BODY TO YOU, WASN'T I?
JUST A BODY? YOU WERE HALF A MONTH'S QUOTA!

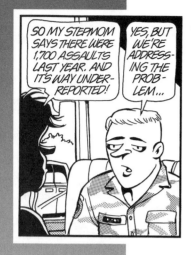

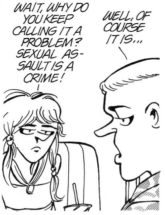

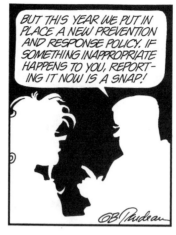

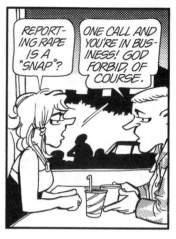

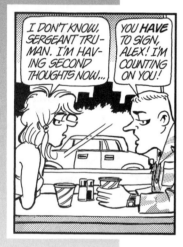

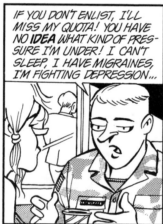

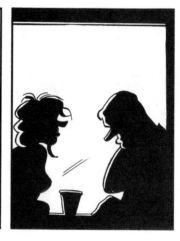

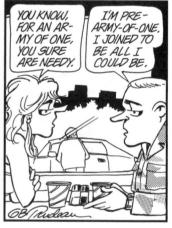

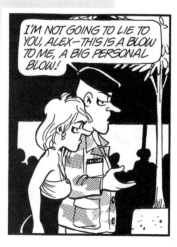

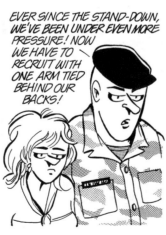

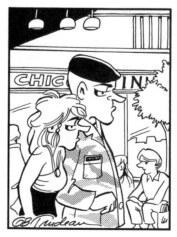

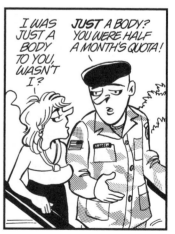

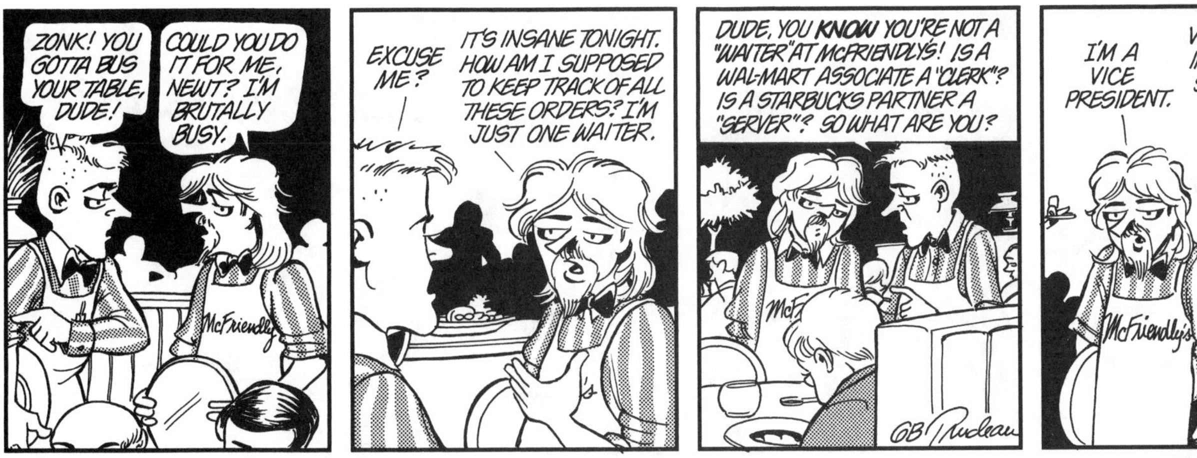
ZONK! YOU GOTTA BUS YOUR TABLE, DUDE!
COULD YOU DO IT FOR ME, NEWT? I'M BRUTALLY BUSY.
EXCUSE ME?
IT'S INSANE TONIGHT. HOW AM I SUPPOSED TO KEEP TRACK OF ALL THESE ORDERS? I'M JUST ONE WAITER.
DUDE, YOU **KNOW** YOU'RE NOT A "WAITER" AT McFRIENDLY'S! IS A WAL-MART ASSOCIATE A "CLERK"? IS A STARBUCKS PARTNER A "SERVER"? SO WHAT ARE YOU?
I'M A VICE PRESIDENT.
VICE PRESIDENT IN CHARGE OF STATION 5! NOW SUCK IT UP!
©B Trudeau

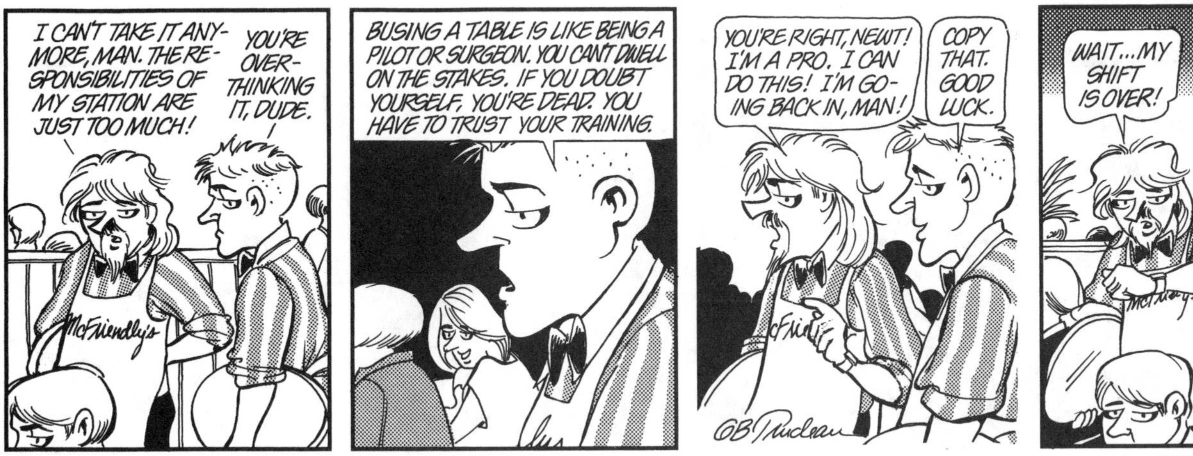
I CAN'T TAKE IT ANYMORE, MAN. THE RESPONSIBILITIES OF MY STATION ARE JUST TOO MUCH!
YOU'RE OVERTHINKING IT, DUDE.
BUSING A TABLE IS LIKE BEING A PILOT OR SURGEON. YOU CAN'T DWELL ON THE STAKES. IF YOU DOUBT YOURSELF, YOU'RE DEAD. YOU HAVE TO TRUST YOUR TRAINING.
YOU'RE RIGHT, NEWT! I'M A PRO. I CAN DO THIS! I'M GOING BACK IN, MAN!
COPY THAT. GOOD LUCK.
©B Trudeau
WAIT... MY SHIFT IS OVER!
AW, DUDE! YOU CHOKED!

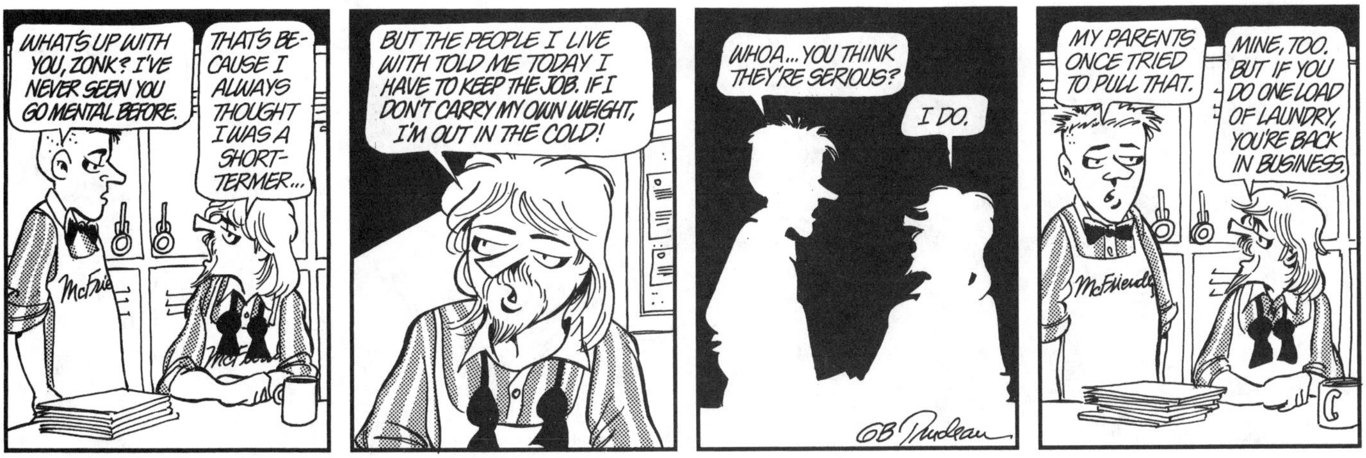
WHAT'S UP WITH YOU, ZONK? I'VE NEVER SEEN YOU GO MENTAL BEFORE.
THAT'S BECAUSE I ALWAYS THOUGHT I WAS A SHORT-TERMER...
BUT THE PEOPLE I LIVE WITH TOLD ME TODAY I HAVE TO KEEP THE JOB. IF I DON'T CARRY MY OWN WEIGHT, I'M OUT IN THE COLD!
WHOA... YOU THINK THEY'RE SERIOUS?
I DO.
©B Trudeau
MY PARENTS ONCE TRIED TO PULL THAT.
MINE, TOO. BUT IF YOU DO ONE LOAD OF LAUNDRY, YOU'RE BACK IN BUSINESS.

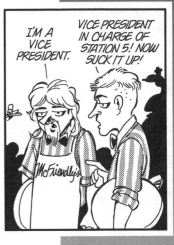

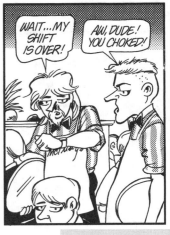

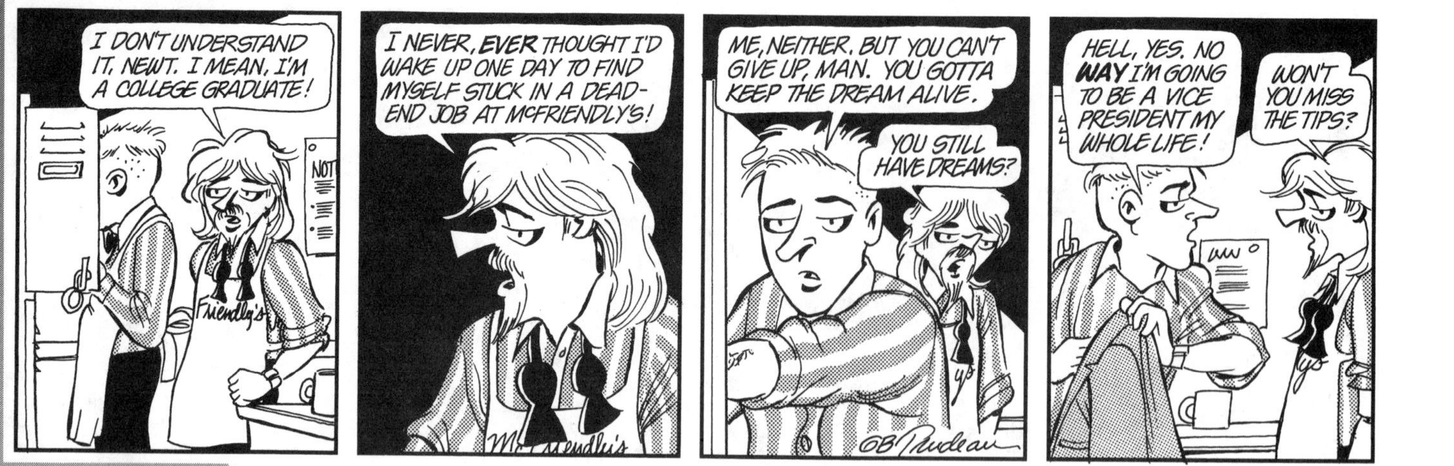
I DON'T UNDERSTAND IT, NEWT. I MEAN, I'M A COLLEGE GRADUATE!
I NEVER, **EVER** THOUGHT I'D WAKE UP ONE DAY TO FIND MYSELF STUCK IN A DEAD-END JOB AT McFRIENDLY'S!
ME, NEITHER. BUT YOU CAN'T GIVE UP, MAN. YOU GOTTA KEEP THE DREAM ALIVE.
YOU STILL HAVE DREAMS?
HELL, YES. NO **WAY** I'M GOING TO BE A VICE PRESIDENT MY WHOLE LIFE!
WON'T YOU MISS THE TIPS?

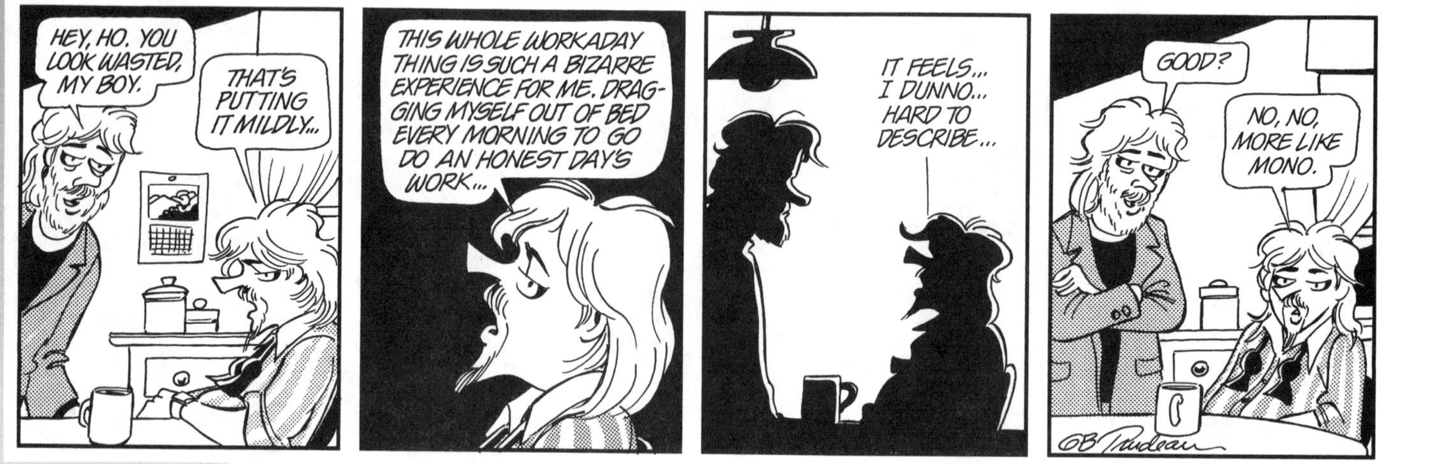
HEY, HO. YOU LOOK WASTED, MY BOY.
THAT'S PUTTING IT MILDLY...
THIS WHOLE WORKADAY THING IS SUCH A BIZARRE EXPERIENCE FOR ME. DRAGGING MYSELF OUT OF BED EVERY MORNING TO GO DO AN HONEST DAY'S WORK...
IT FEELS... I DUNNO... HARD TO DESCRIBE...
GOOD?
NO, NO, MORE LIKE MONO.

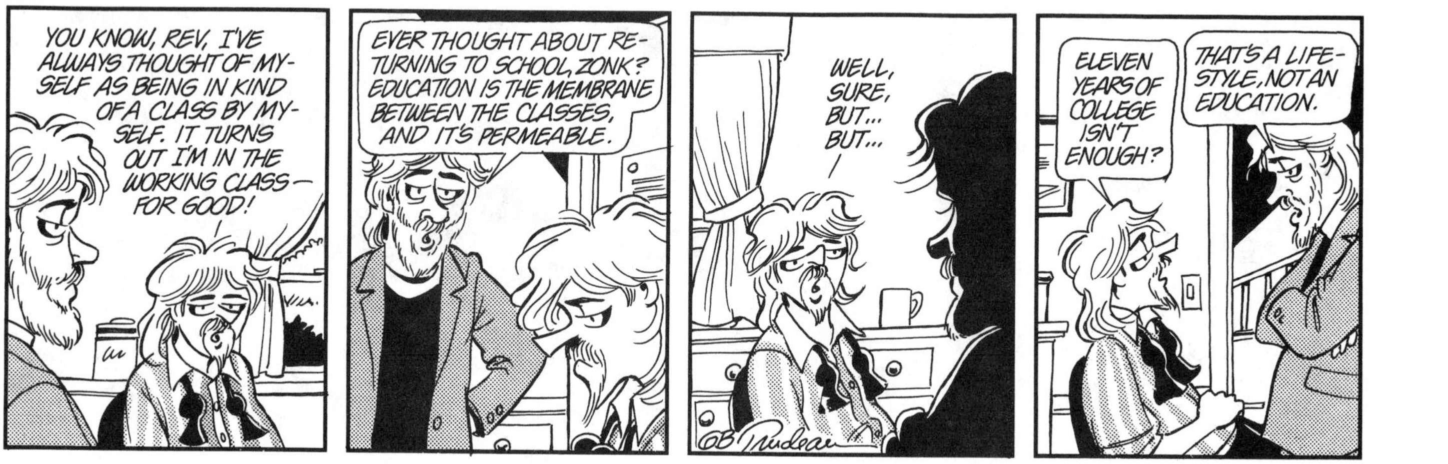
YOU KNOW, REV, I'VE ALWAYS THOUGHT OF MYSELF AS BEING IN KIND OF A CLASS BY MYSELF. IT TURNS OUT I'M IN THE WORKING CLASS—FOR GOOD!
EVER THOUGHT ABOUT RETURNING TO SCHOOL, ZONK? EDUCATION IS THE MEMBRANE BETWEEN THE CLASSES, AND IT'S PERMEABLE.
WELL, SURE, BUT... BUT...
ELEVEN YEARS OF COLLEGE ISN'T ENOUGH?
THAT'S A LIFESTYLE, NOT AN EDUCATION.

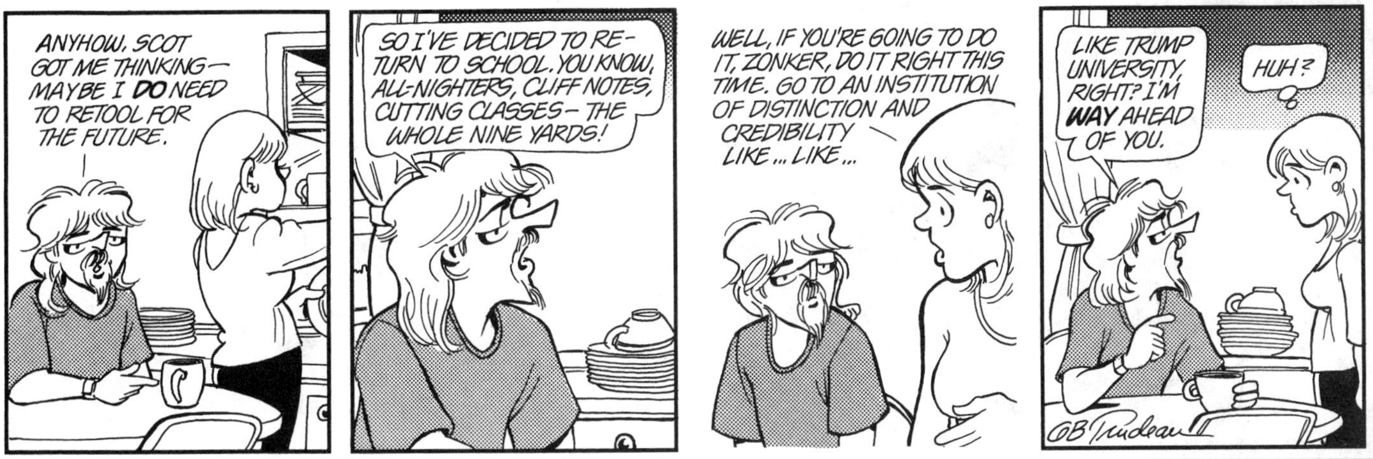
ANYHOW, SCOT GOT ME THINKING— MAYBE I DO NEED TO RETOOL FOR THE FUTURE.
SO I'VE DECIDED TO RETURN TO SCHOOL. YOU KNOW, ALL-NIGHTERS, CLIFF NOTES, CUTTING CLASSES— THE WHOLE NINE YARDS!
WELL, IF YOU'RE GOING TO DO IT, ZONKER, DO IT RIGHT THIS TIME. GO TO AN INSTITUTION OF DISTINCTION AND CREDIBILITY LIKE ... LIKE ...
LIKE TRUMP UNIVERSITY, RIGHT? I'M WAY AHEAD OF YOU.
HUH?

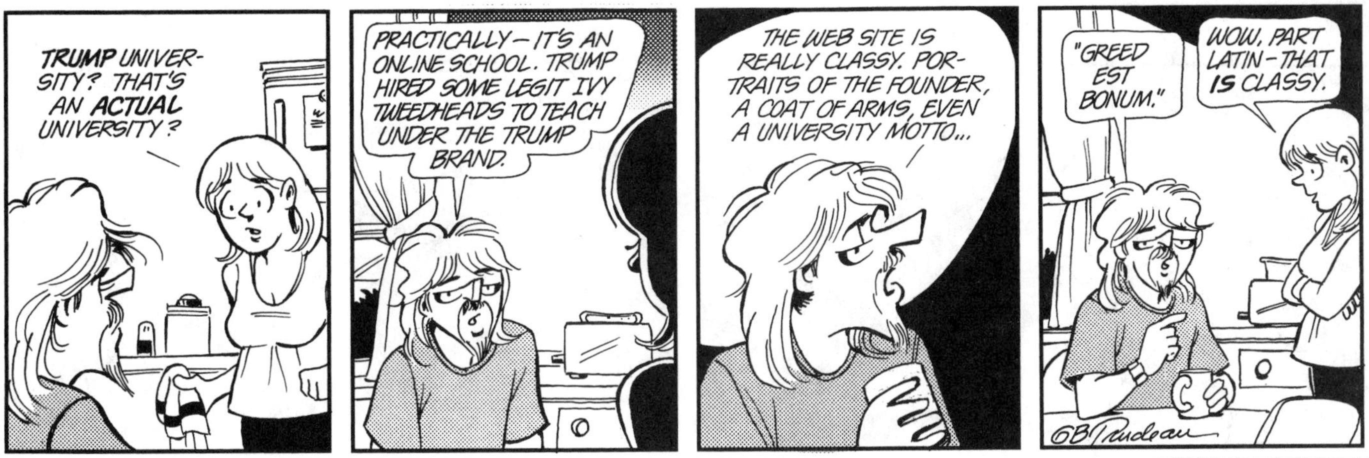
TRUMP UNIVERSITY? THAT'S AN ACTUAL UNIVERSITY?
PRACTICALLY— IT'S AN ONLINE SCHOOL. TRUMP HIRED SOME LEGIT IVY TWEEDHEADS TO TEACH UNDER THE TRUMP BRAND.
THE WEB SITE IS REALLY CLASSY. PORTRAITS OF THE FOUNDER, A COAT OF ARMS, EVEN A UNIVERSITY MOTTO...
"GREED EST BONUM."
WOW. PART LATIN— THAT IS CLASSY.

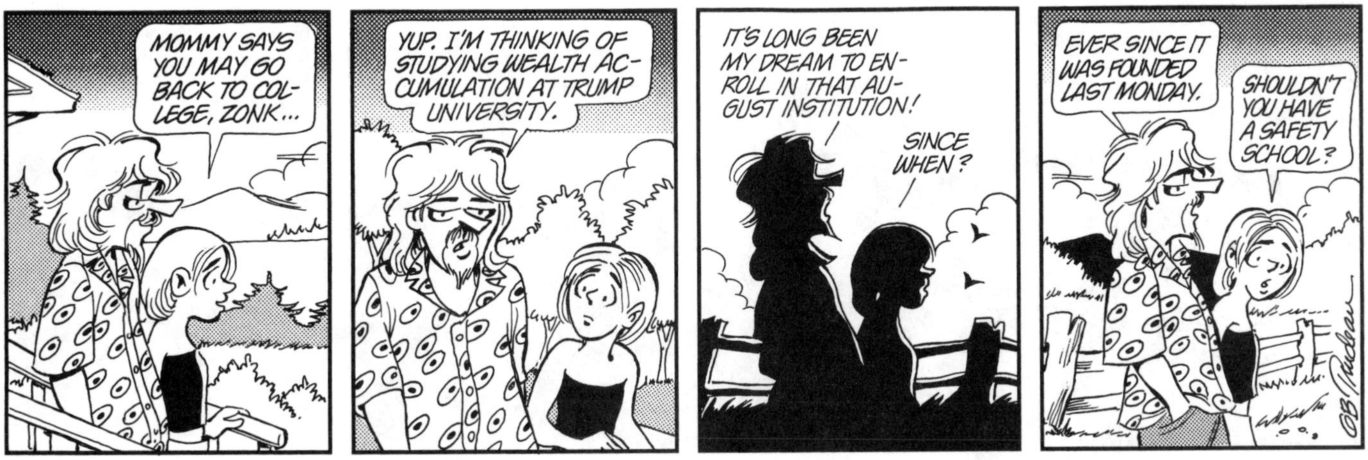
MOMMY SAYS YOU MAY GO BACK TO COLLEGE, ZONK...
YUP. I'M THINKING OF STUDYING WEALTH ACCUMULATION AT TRUMP UNIVERSITY.
IT'S LONG BEEN MY DREAM TO ENROLL IN THAT AUGUST INSTITUTION!
SINCE WHEN?
EVER SINCE IT WAS FOUNDED LAST MONDAY.
SHOULDN'T YOU HAVE A SAFETY SCHOOL?

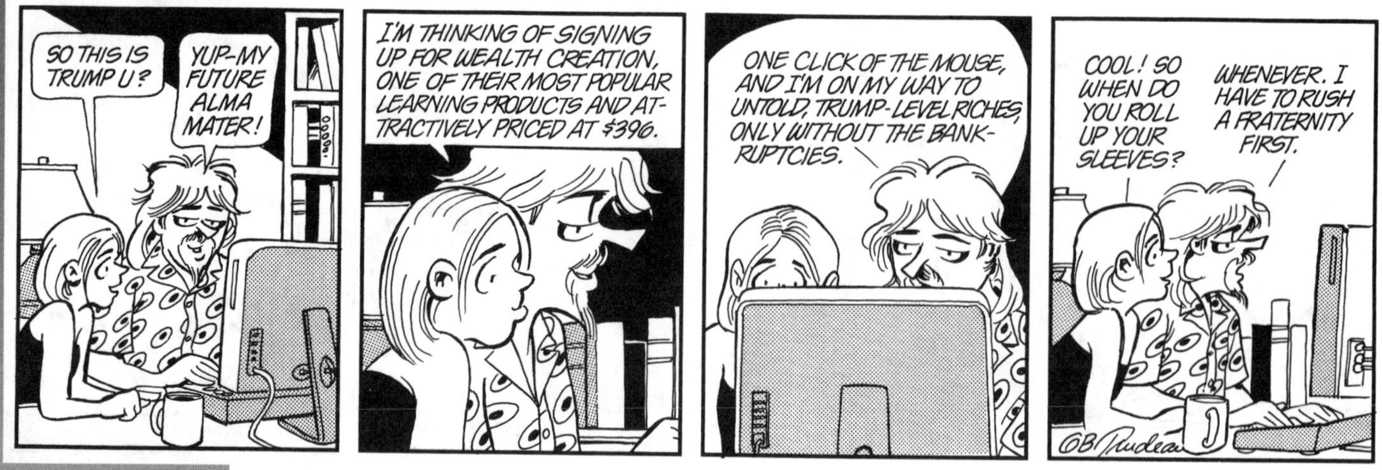
SO THIS IS TRUMP U?
YUP-MY FUTURE ALMA MATER!
I'M THINKING OF SIGNING UP FOR WEALTH CREATION, ONE OF THEIR MOST POPULAR LEARNING PRODUCTS AND ATTRACTIVELY PRICED AT $396.
ONE CLICK OF THE MOUSE, AND I'M ON MY WAY TO UNTOLD, TRUMP-LEVEL RICHES, ONLY WITHOUT THE BANKRUPTCIES.
COOL! SO WHEN DO YOU ROLL UP YOUR SLEEVES?
WHENEVER. I HAVE TO RUSH A FRATERNITY FIRST.
©B Trudeau

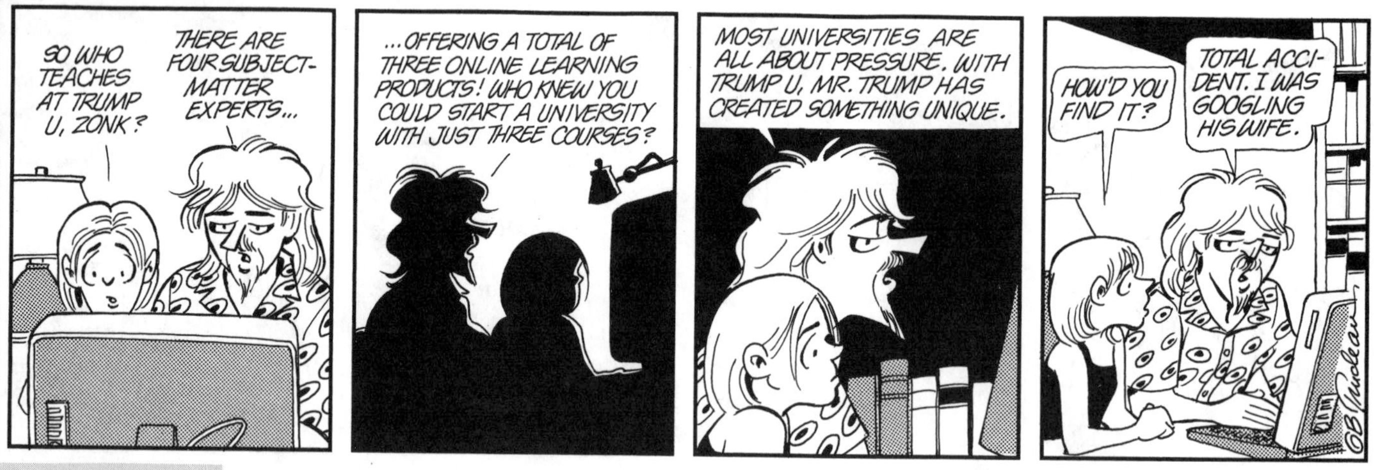
SO WHO TEACHES AT TRUMP U, ZONK?
THERE ARE FOUR SUBJECT-MATTER EXPERTS...
...OFFERING A TOTAL OF THREE ONLINE LEARNING PRODUCTS! WHO KNEW YOU COULD START A UNIVERSITY WITH JUST THREE COURSES?
MOST UNIVERSITIES ARE ALL ABOUT PRESSURE. WITH TRUMP U, MR. TRUMP HAS CREATED SOMETHING UNIQUE.
HOW'D YOU FIND IT?
TOTAL ACCIDENT. I WAS GOOGLING HIS WIFE.
©B Trudeau

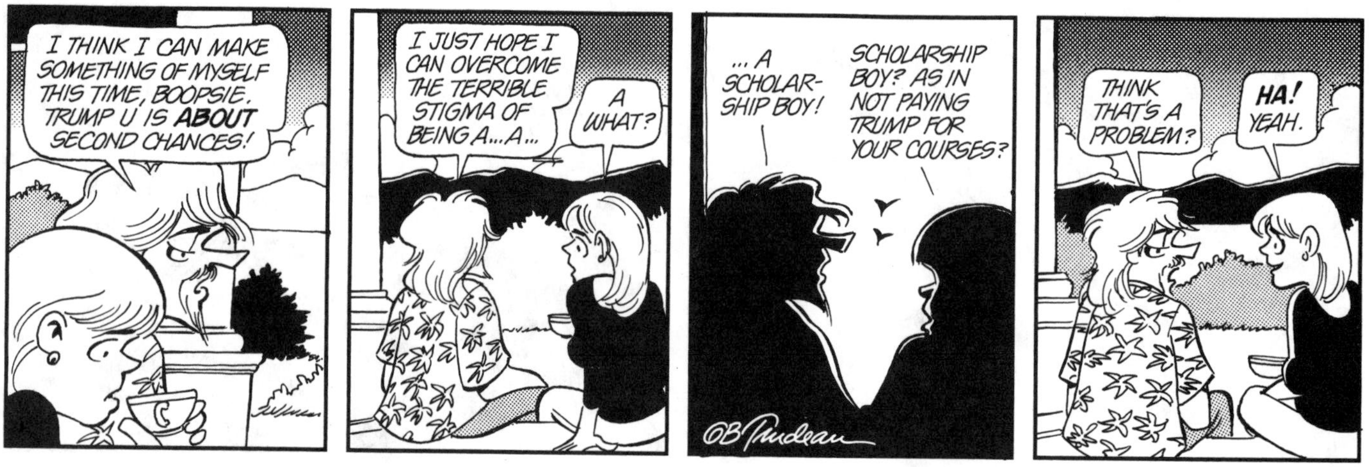
I THINK I CAN MAKE SOMETHING OF MYSELF THIS TIME, BOOPSIE. TRUMP U IS ABOUT SECOND CHANCES!
I JUST HOPE I CAN OVERCOME THE TERRIBLE STIGMA OF BEING A...A...
A WHAT?
...A SCHOLARSHIP BOY!
SCHOLARSHIP BOY? AS IN NOT PAYING TRUMP FOR YOUR COURSES?
THINK THAT'S A PROBLEM?
HA! YEAH.
©B Trudeau

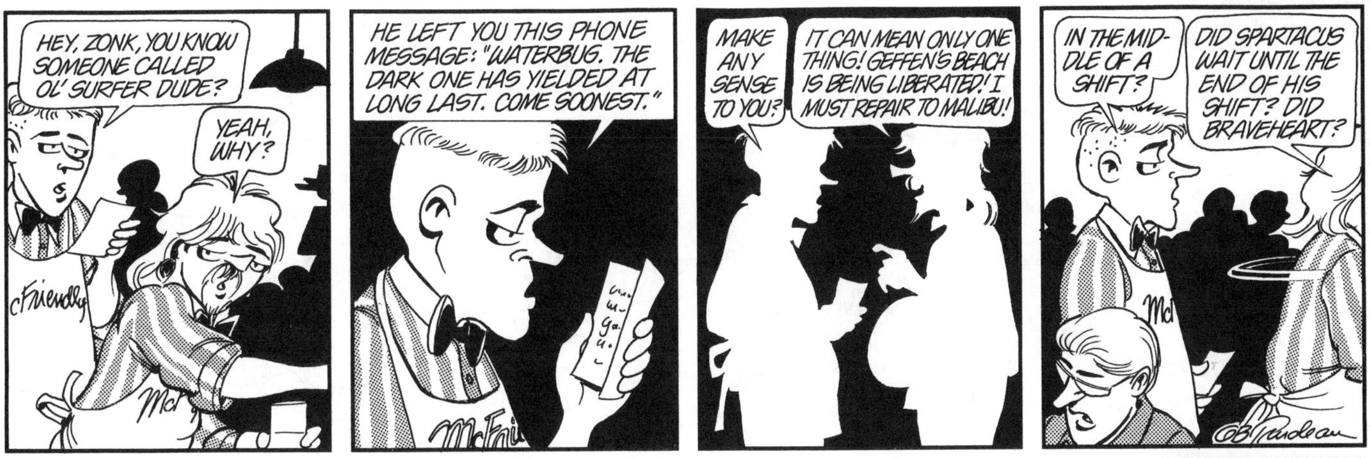
HEY, ZONK, YOU KNOW SOMEONE CALLED OL' SURFER DUDE?
YEAH, WHY?
HE LEFT YOU THIS PHONE MESSAGE: "WATERBUG. THE DARK ONE HAS YIELDED AT LONG LAST. COME SOONEST."
MAKE ANY SENSE TO YOU?
IT CAN MEAN ONLY ONE THING! GEFFEN'S BEACH IS BEING LIBERATED! I MUST REPAIR TO MALIBU!
IN THE MIDDLE OF A SHIFT?
DID SPARTACUS WAIT UNTIL THE END OF HIS SHIFT? DID BRAVEHEART?

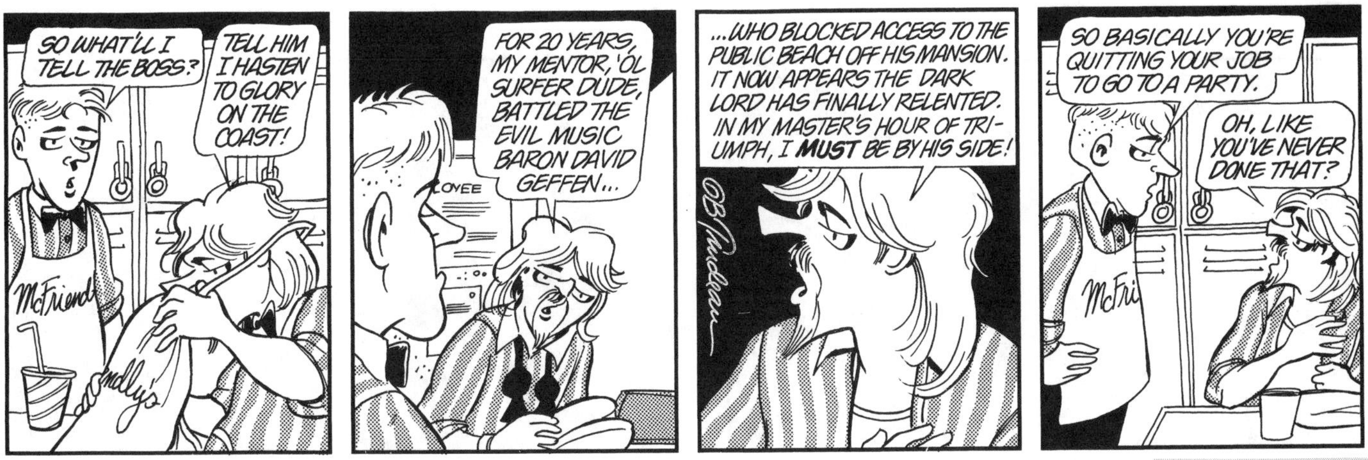
SO WHAT'LL I TELL THE BOSS?
TELL HIM I HASTEN TO GLORY ON THE COAST!
FOR 20 YEARS, MY MENTOR, 'OL SURFER DUDE, BATTLED THE EVIL MUSIC BARON DAVID GEFFEN...
...WHO BLOCKED ACCESS TO THE PUBLIC BEACH OFF HIS MANSION. IT NOW APPEARS THE DARK LORD HAS FINALLY RELENTED. IN MY MASTER'S HOUR OF TRIUMPH, I MUST BE BY HIS SIDE!
SO BASICALLY YOU'RE QUITTING YOUR JOB TO GO TO A PARTY.
OH, LIKE YOU'VE NEVER DONE THAT?

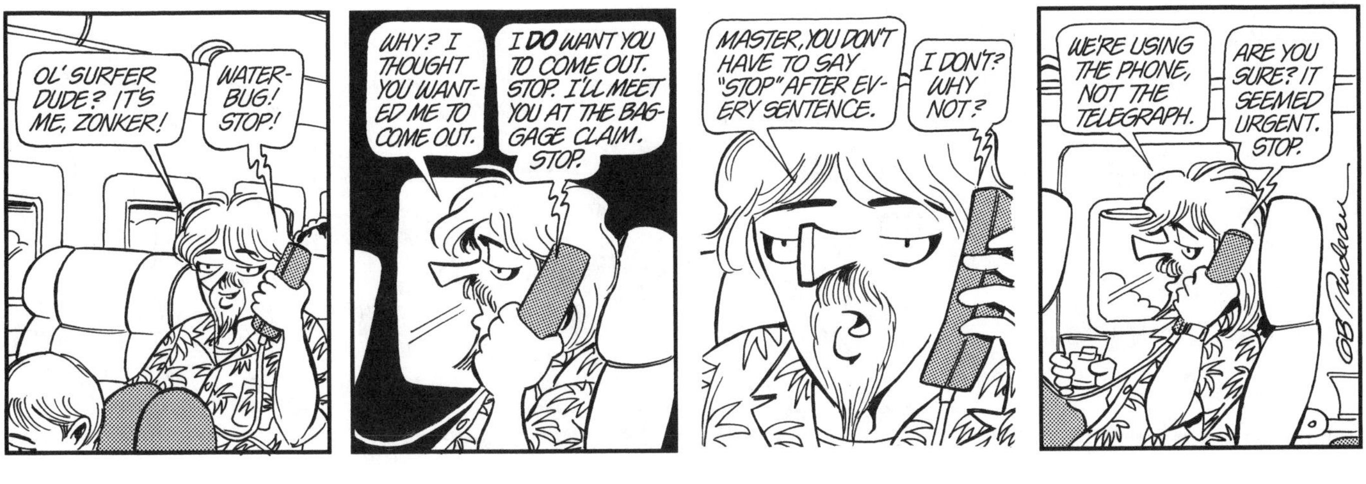
OL' SURFER DUDE? IT'S ME, ZONKER!
WATERBUG! STOP!
WHY? I THOUGHT YOU WANTED ME TO COME OUT.
I DO WANT YOU TO COME OUT. STOP. I'LL MEET YOU AT THE BAGGAGE CLAIM. STOP.
MASTER, YOU DON'T HAVE TO SAY "STOP" AFTER EVERY SENTENCE.
I DON'T? WHY NOT?
WE'RE USING THE PHONE, NOT THE TELEGRAPH.
ARE YOU SURE? IT SEEMED URGENT. STOP.

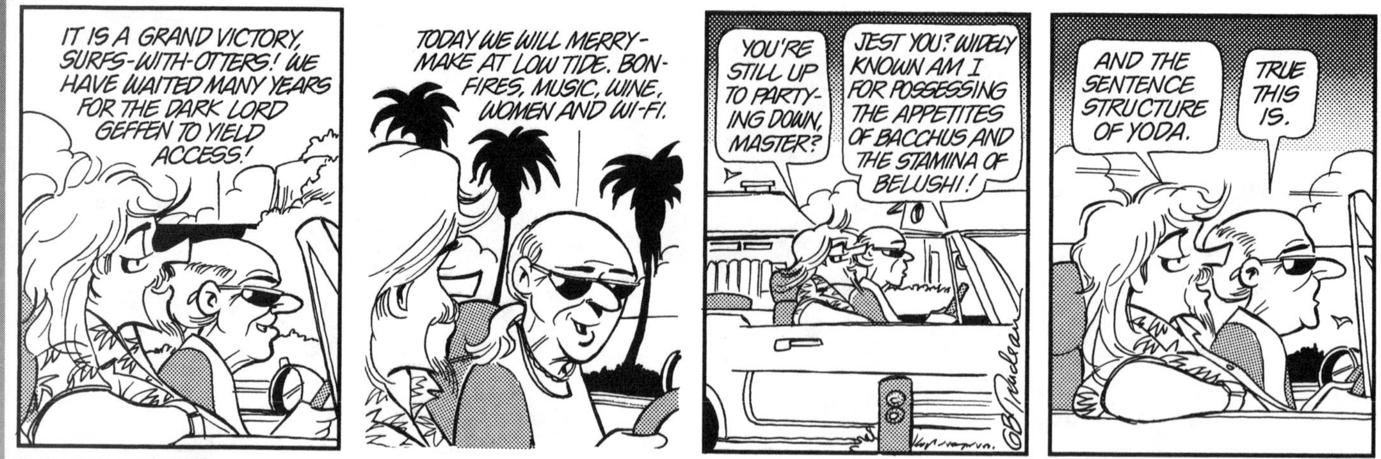
IT IS A GRAND VICTORY, SURFS-WITH-OTTERS! WE HAVE WAITED MANY YEARS FOR THE DARK LORD GEFFEN TO YIELD ACCESS!
TODAY WE WILL MERRY-MAKE AT LOW TIDE. BON-FIRES, MUSIC, WINE, WOMEN AND WI-FI.
YOU'RE STILL UP TO PARTY-ING DOWN, MASTER?
JEST YOU? WIDELY KNOWN AM I FOR POSSESSING THE APPETITES OF BACCHUS AND THE STAMINA OF BELUSHI!
AND THE SENTENCE STRUCTURE OF YODA.
TRUE THIS IS.

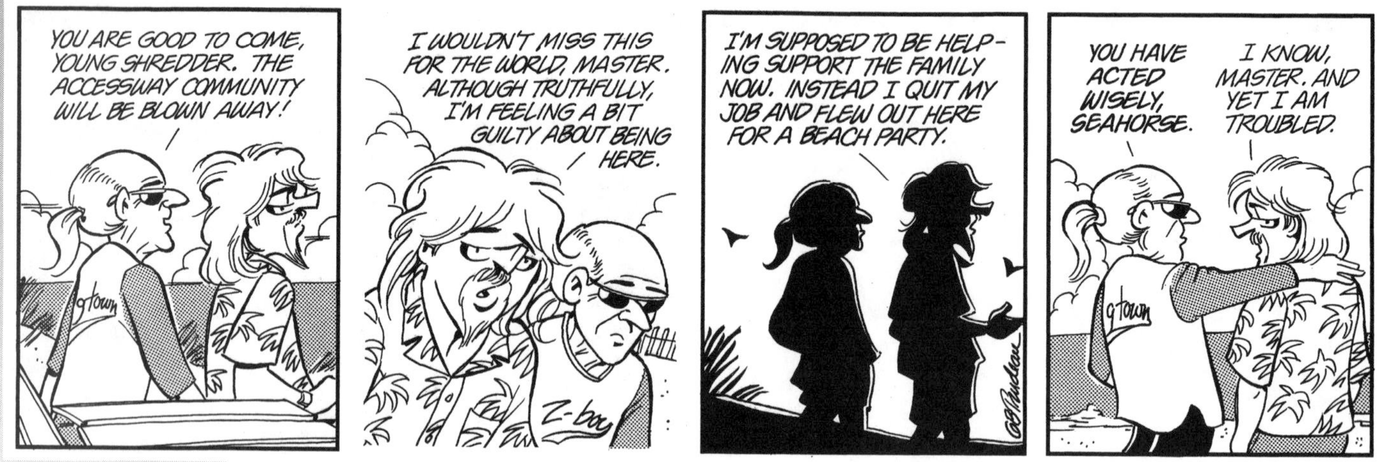
YOU ARE GOOD TO COME, YOUNG SHREDDER. THE ACCESSWAY COMMUNITY WILL BE BLOWN AWAY!
I WOULDN'T MISS THIS FOR THE WORLD, MASTER. ALTHOUGH TRUTHFULLY, I'M FEELING A BIT GUILTY ABOUT BEING HERE.
I'M SUPPOSED TO BE HELP-ING SUPPORT THE FAMILY NOW. INSTEAD I QUIT MY JOB AND FLEW OUT HERE FOR A BEACH PARTY.
YOU HAVE ACTED WISELY, SEAHORSE.
I KNOW, MASTER. AND YET I AM TROUBLED.

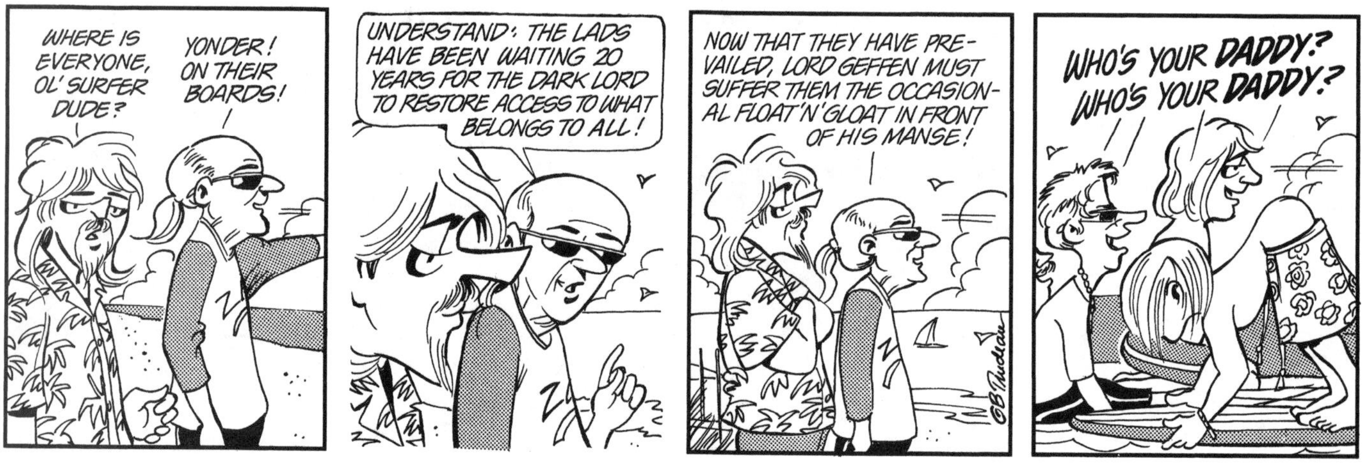
WHERE IS EVERYONE, OL' SURFER DUDE?
YONDER! ON THEIR BOARDS!
UNDERSTAND: THE LADS HAVE BEEN WAITING 20 YEARS FOR THE DARK LORD TO RESTORE ACCESS TO WHAT BELONGS TO ALL!
NOW THAT THEY HAVE PRE-VAILED, LORD GEFFEN MUST SUFFER THEM THE OCCASION-AL FLOAT 'N' GLOAT IN FRONT OF HIS MANSE!
WHO'S YOUR DADDY?
WHO'S YOUR DADDY?

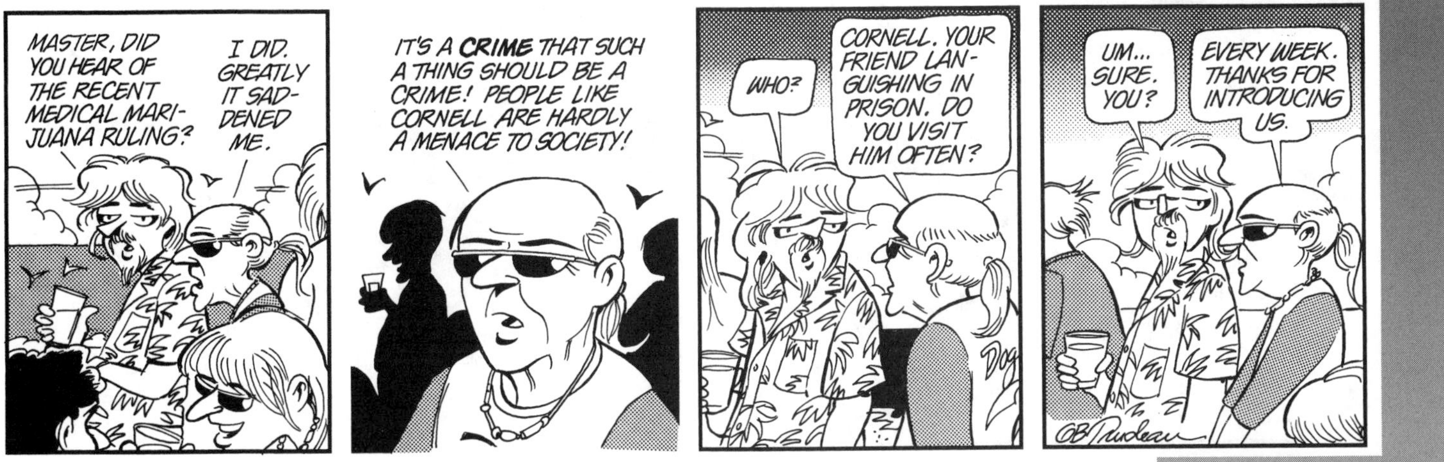
MASTER, DID YOU HEAR OF THE RECENT MEDICAL MARIJUANA RULING?
I DID. GREATLY IT SADDENED ME.
IT'S A **CRIME** THAT SUCH A THING SHOULD BE A CRIME! PEOPLE LIKE CORNELL ARE HARDLY A MENACE TO SOCIETY!
WHO?
CORNELL. YOUR FRIEND LANGUISHING IN PRISON. DO YOU VISIT HIM OFTEN?
UM... SURE. YOU?
EVERY WEEK. THANKS FOR INTRODUCING US.

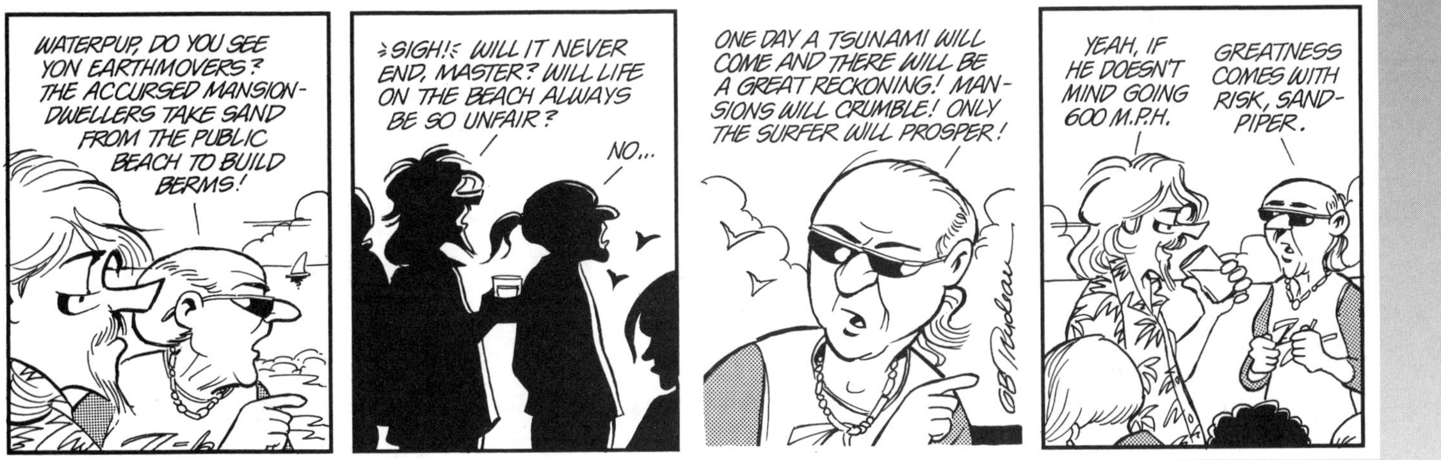
WATERPUP, DO YOU SEE YON EARTHMOVERS? THE ACCURSED MANSION-DWELLERS TAKE SAND FROM THE PUBLIC BEACH TO BUILD BERMS!
SIGH! WILL IT NEVER END, MASTER? WILL LIFE ON THE BEACH ALWAYS BE SO UNFAIR?
NO...
ONE DAY A TSUNAMI WILL COME AND THERE WILL BE A GREAT RECKONING! MANSIONS WILL CRUMBLE! ONLY THE SURFER WILL PROSPER!
YEAH, IF HE DOESN'T MIND GOING 600 M.P.H.
GREATNESS COMES WITH RISK, SANDPIPER.

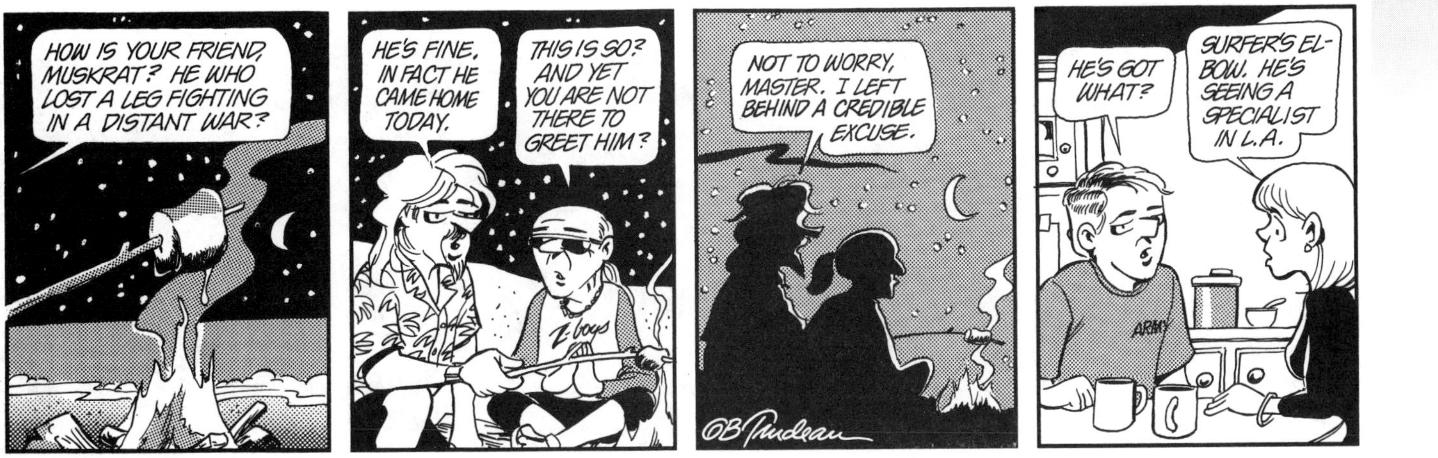
HOW IS YOUR FRIEND, MUSKRAT? HE WHO LOST A LEG FIGHTING IN A DISTANT WAR?
HE'S FINE. IN FACT HE CAME HOME TODAY.
THIS IS SO? AND YET YOU ARE NOT THERE TO GREET HIM?
NOT TO WORRY, MASTER. I LEFT BEHIND A CREDIBLE EXCUSE.
HE'S GOT WHAT?
SURFER'S ELBOW. HE'S SEEING A SPECIALIST IN L.A.

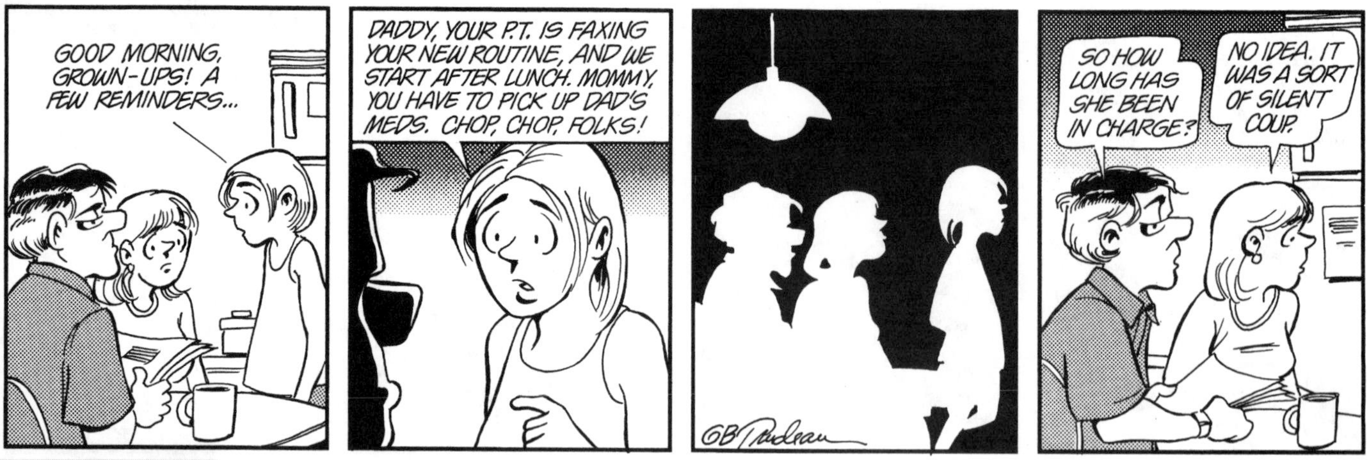
GOOD MORNING, GROWN-UPS! A FEW REMINDERS...
DADDY, YOUR P.T. IS FAXING YOUR NEW ROUTINE, AND WE START AFTER LUNCH. MOMMY, YOU HAVE TO PICK UP DAD'S MEDS. CHOP, CHOP, FOLKS!
SO HOW LONG HAS SHE BEEN IN CHARGE?
NO IDEA. IT WAS A SORT OF SILENT COUP.

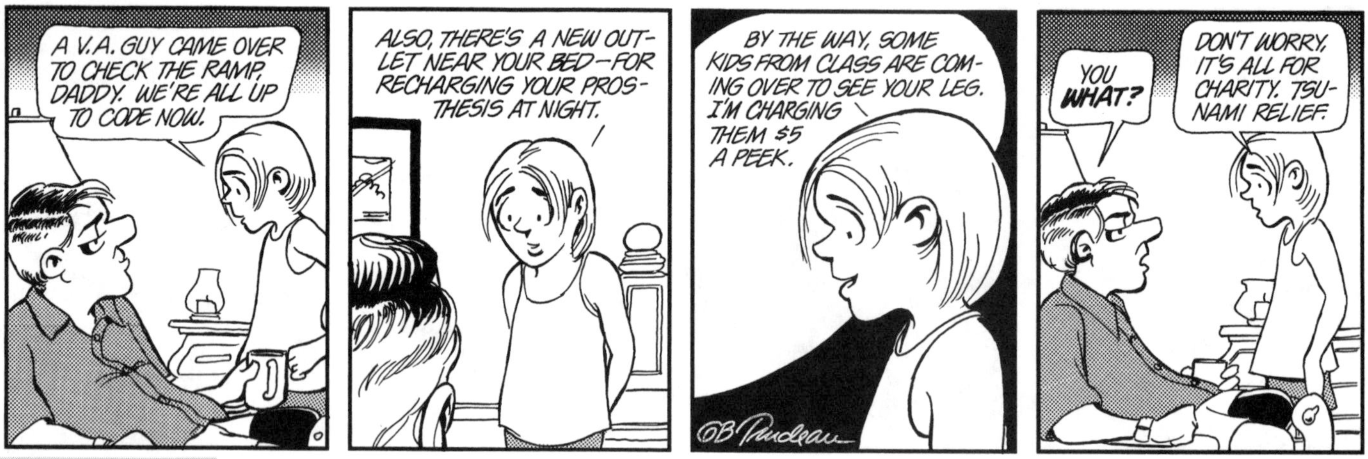
A V.A. GUY CAME OVER TO CHECK THE RAMP, DADDY. WE'RE ALL UP TO CODE NOW.
ALSO, THERE'S A NEW OUTLET NEAR YOUR BED—FOR RECHARGING YOUR PROSTHESIS AT NIGHT.
BY THE WAY, SOME KIDS FROM CLASS ARE COMING OVER TO SEE YOUR LEG. I'M CHARGING THEM $5 A PEEK.
YOU WHAT?
DON'T WORRY, IT'S ALL FOR CHARITY. TSUNAMI RELIEF.

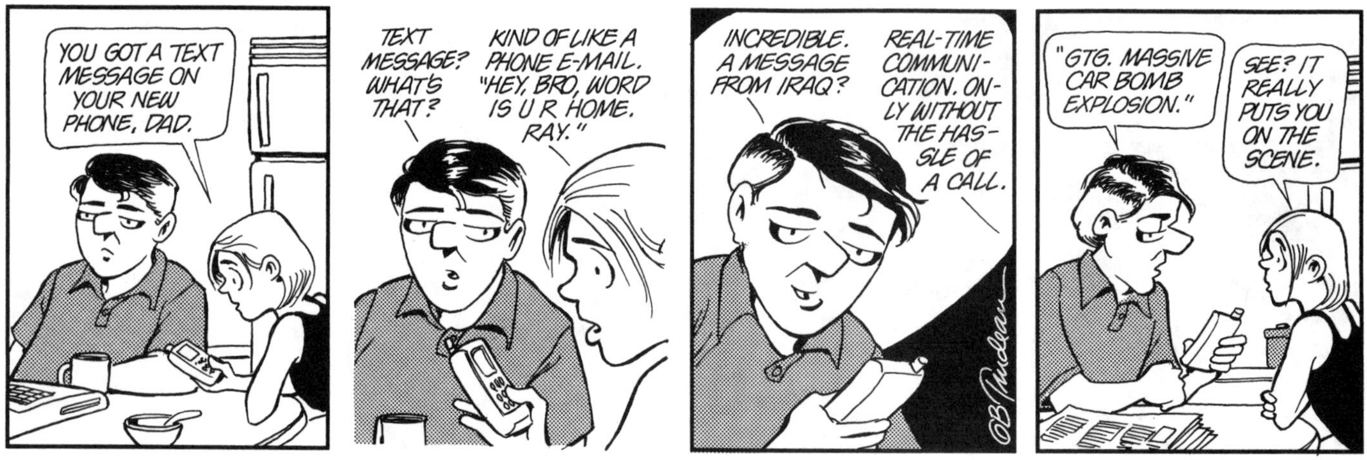
YOU GOT A TEXT MESSAGE ON YOUR NEW PHONE, DAD.
TEXT MESSAGE? WHAT'S THAT?
KIND OF LIKE A PHONE E-MAIL. "HEY, BRO, WORD IS U R HOME. RAY."
INCREDIBLE. A MESSAGE FROM IRAQ?
REAL-TIME COMMUNICATION. ONLY WITHOUT THE HASSLE OF A CALL.
"GTG. MASSIVE CAR BOMB EXPLOSION."
SEE? IT REALLY PUTS YOU ON THE SCENE.

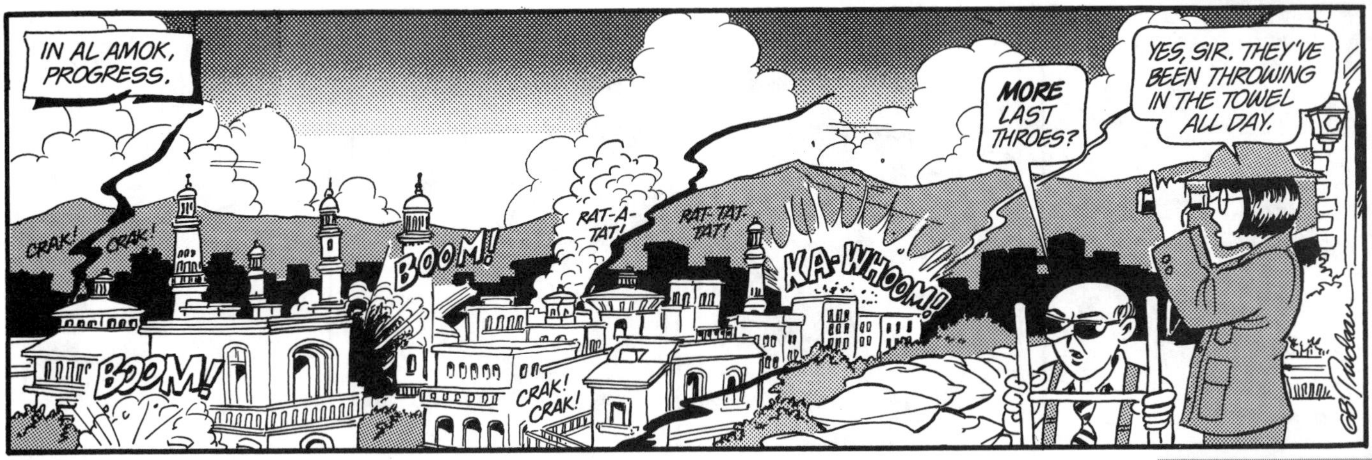
IN AL AMOK, PROGRESS.
CRAK! CRAK!
BOOM!
BOOM!
RAT-A-TAT!
RAT-TAT-TAT!
CRAK! CRAK!
KA-WHOOM!
MORE LAST THROES?
YES, SIR. THEY'VE BEEN THROWING IN THE TOWEL ALL DAY.

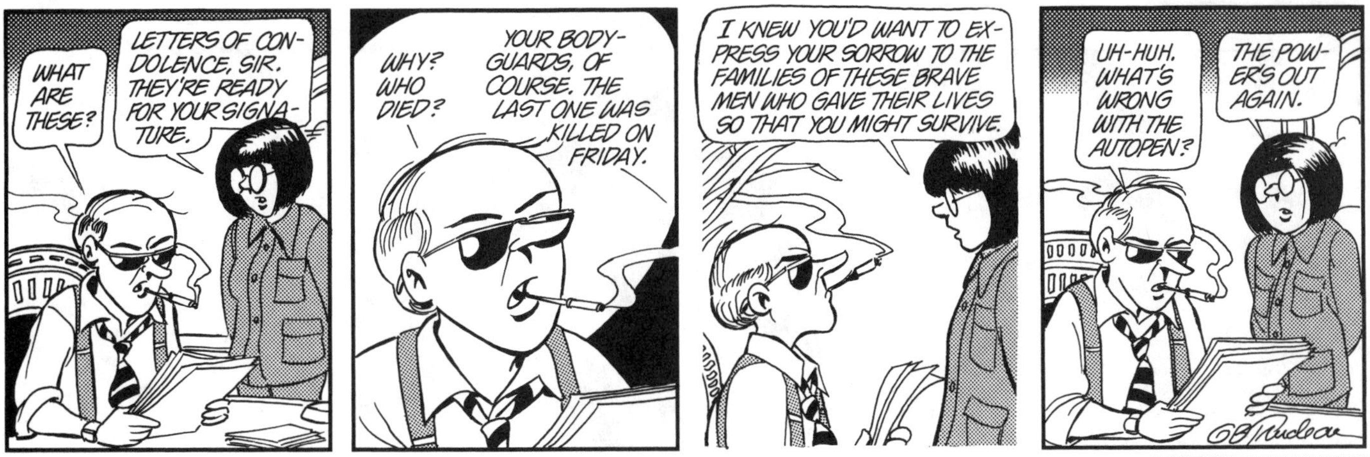
WHAT ARE THESE?
LETTERS OF CONDOLENCE, SIR. THEY'RE READY FOR YOUR SIGNATURE.
WHY? WHO DIED?
YOUR BODYGUARDS, OF COURSE. THE LAST ONE WAS KILLED ON FRIDAY.
I KNEW YOU'D WANT TO EXPRESS YOUR SORROW TO THE FAMILIES OF THESE BRAVE MEN WHO GAVE THEIR LIVES SO THAT YOU MIGHT SURVIVE.
UH-HUH. WHAT'S WRONG WITH THE AUTOPEN?
THE POWER'S OUT AGAIN.

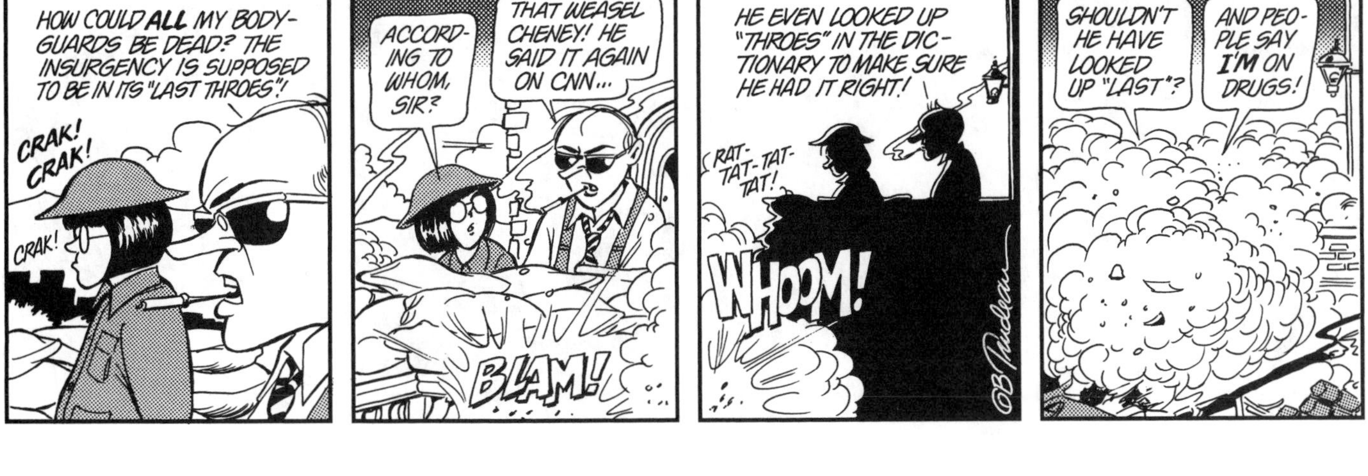
HOW COULD ALL MY BODYGUARDS BE DEAD? THE INSURGENCY IS SUPPOSED TO BE IN ITS "LAST THROES"!
CRAK! CRAK!
CRAK!
ACCORDING TO WHOM, SIR?
THAT WEASEL CHENEY! HE SAID IT AGAIN ON CNN...
BLAM!
HE EVEN LOOKED UP "THROES" IN THE DICTIONARY TO MAKE SURE HE HAD IT RIGHT!
RAT-TAT-TAT-TAT!
WHOOM!
SHOULDN'T HE HAVE LOOKED UP "LAST"?
AND PEOPLE SAY I'M ON DRUGS!

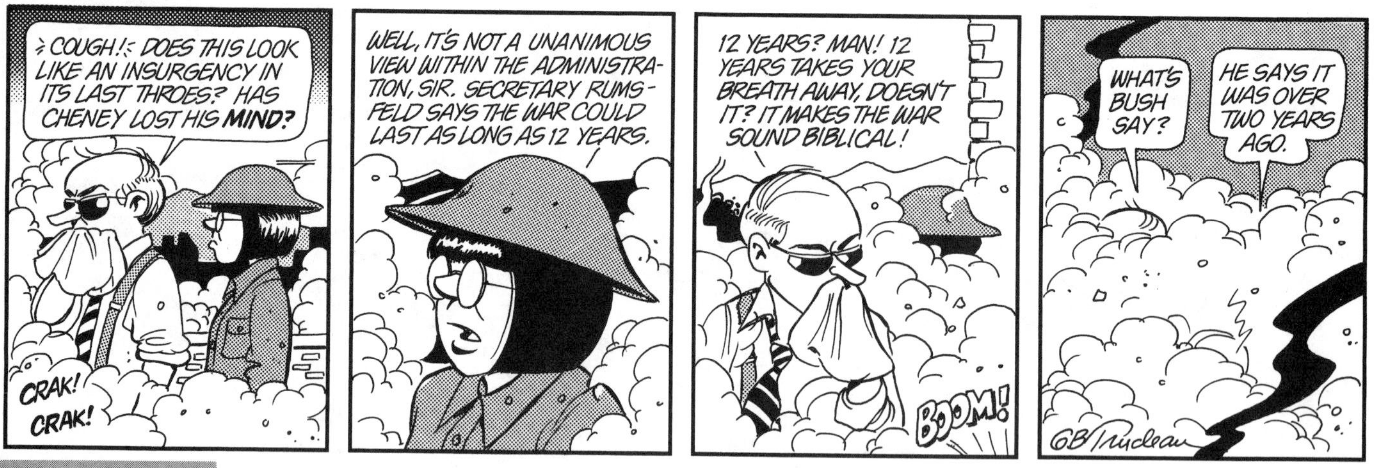
COUGH! DOES THIS LOOK LIKE AN INSURGENCY IN ITS LAST THROES? HAS CHENEY LOST HIS MIND?
CRAK! CRAK!
WELL, IT'S NOT A UNANIMOUS VIEW WITHIN THE ADMINISTRATION, SIR. SECRETARY RUMSFELD SAYS THE WAR COULD LAST AS LONG AS 12 YEARS.
12 YEARS? MAN! 12 YEARS TAKES YOUR BREATH AWAY, DOESN'T IT? IT MAKES THE WAR SOUND BIBLICAL!
BOOM!
WHAT'S BUSH SAY?
HE SAYS IT WAS OVER TWO YEARS AGO.
©B Trudeau

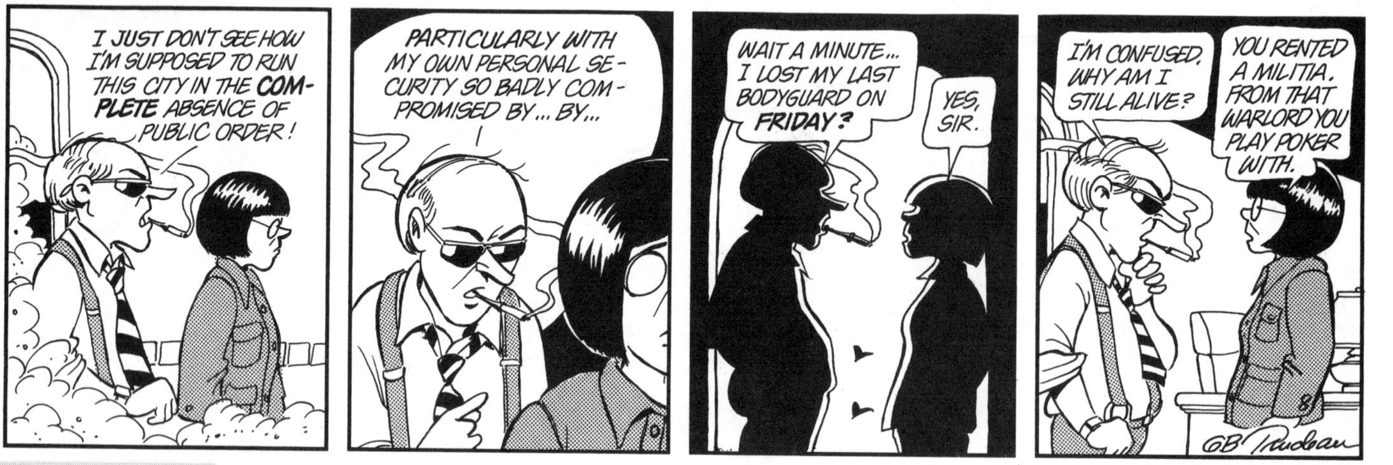
I JUST DON'T SEE HOW I'M SUPPOSED TO RUN THIS CITY IN THE COMPLETE ABSENCE OF PUBLIC ORDER!
PARTICULARLY WITH MY OWN PERSONAL SECURITY SO BADLY COMPROMISED BY ... BY...
WAIT A MINUTE... I LOST MY LAST BODYGUARD ON FRIDAY?
YES, SIR.
I'M CONFUSED. WHY AM I STILL ALIVE?
YOU RENTED A MILITIA. FROM THAT WARLORD YOU PLAY POKER WITH.
©B Trudeau

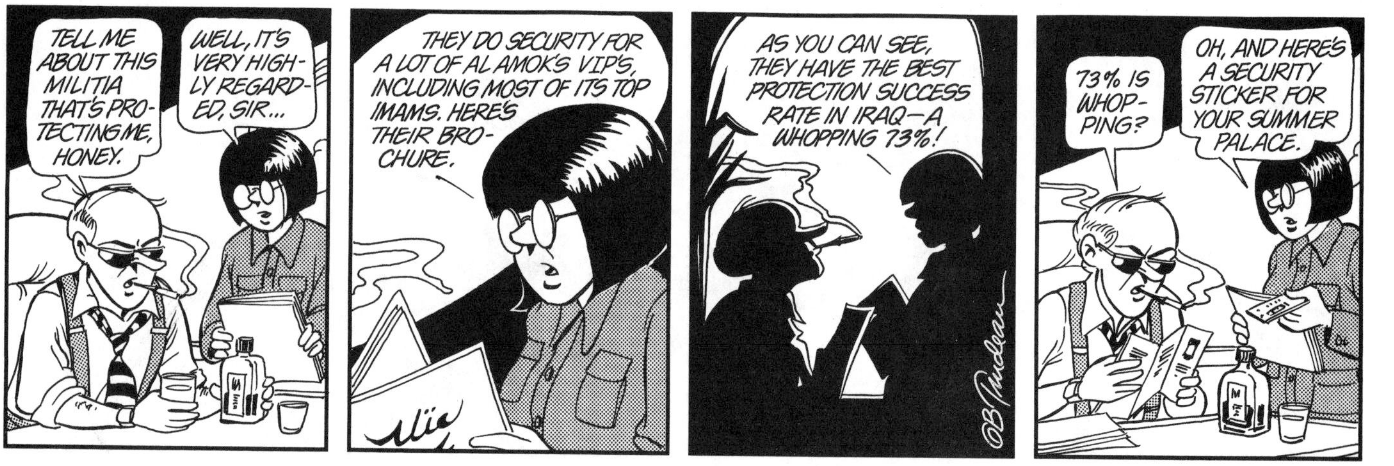
TELL ME ABOUT THIS MILITIA THAT'S PROTECTING ME, HONEY.
WELL, IT'S VERY HIGHLY REGARDED, SIR...
THEY DO SECURITY FOR A LOT OF AL AMOK'S VIP'S, INCLUDING MOST OF ITS TOP IMAMS. HERE'S THEIR BROCHURE.
AS YOU CAN SEE, THEY HAVE THE BEST PROTECTION SUCCESS RATE IN IRAQ—A WHOPPING 73%!
©B Trudeau
73% IS WHOPPING?
OH, AND HERE'S A SECURITY STICKER FOR YOUR SUMMER PALACE.

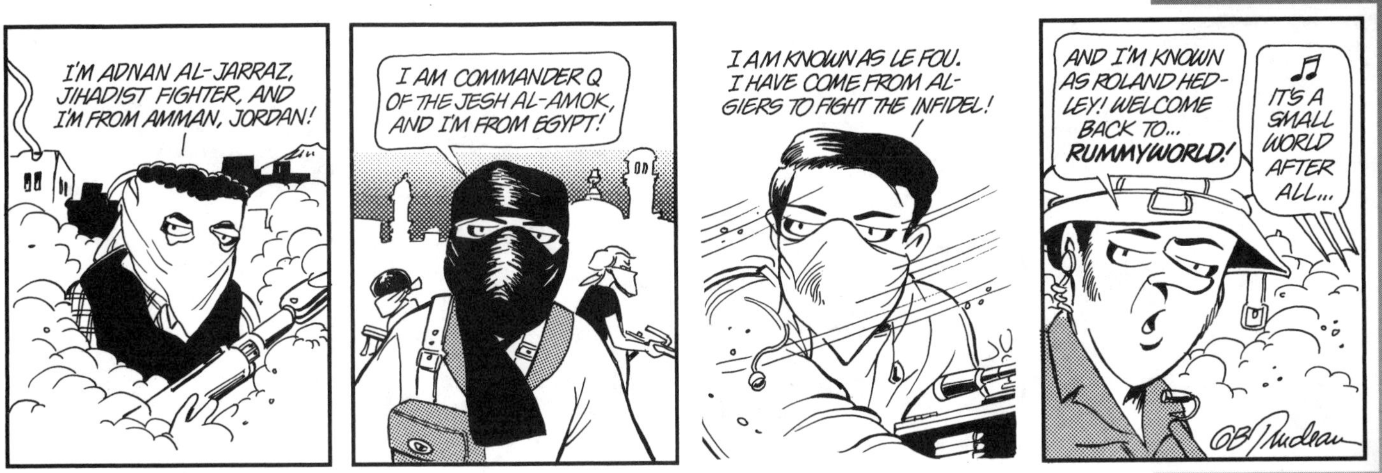
I'M ADNAN AL-JARRAZ, JIHADIST FIGHTER, AND I'M FROM AMMAN, JORDAN!
I AM COMMANDER Q OF THE JESH AL-AMOK, AND I'M FROM EGYPT!
I AM KNOWN AS LE FOU. I HAVE COME FROM ALGIERS TO FIGHT THE INFIDEL!
AND I'M KNOWN AS ROLAND HEDLEY! WELCOME BACK TO... RUMMYWORLD!
♫ IT'S A SMALL WORLD AFTER ALL...
B. Trudeau

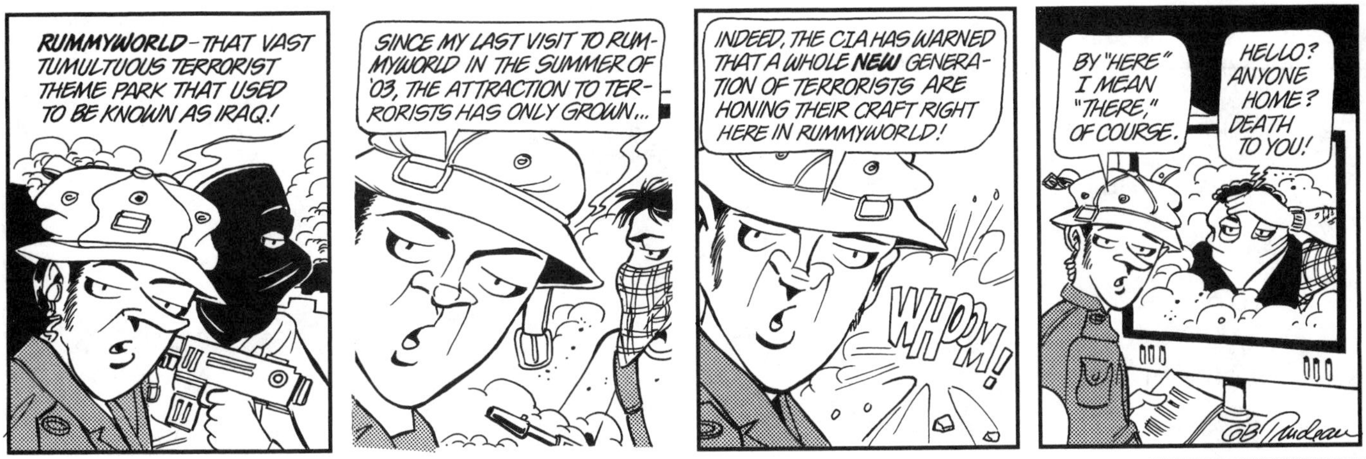
RUMMYWORLD—THAT VAST TUMULTUOUS TERRORIST THEME PARK THAT USED TO BE KNOWN AS IRAQ!
SINCE MY LAST VISIT TO RUMMYWORLD IN THE SUMMER OF '03, THE ATTRACTION TO TERRORISTS HAS ONLY GROWN...
INDEED, THE CIA HAS WARNED THAT A WHOLE NEW GENERATION OF TERRORISTS ARE HONING THEIR CRAFT RIGHT HERE IN RUMMYWORLD!
WHOOM!
BY "HERE" I MEAN "THERE," OF COURSE.
HELLO? ANYONE HOME? DEATH TO YOU!
B. Trudeau

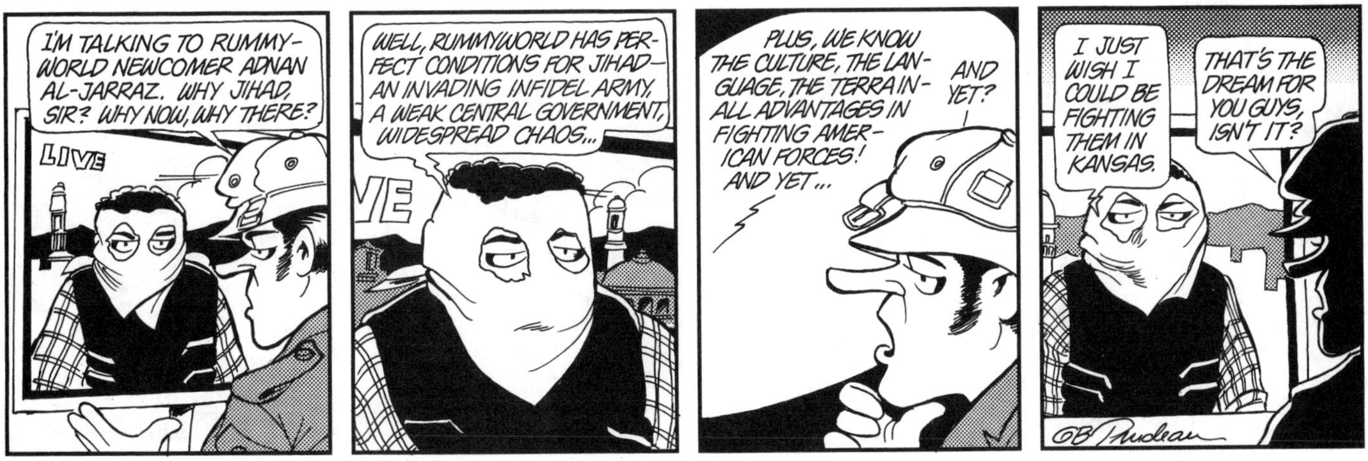
I'M TALKING TO RUMMYWORLD NEWCOMER ADNAN AL-JARRAZ. WHY JIHAD, SIR? WHY NOW, WHY THERE?
LIVE
WELL, RUMMYWORLD HAS PERFECT CONDITIONS FOR JIHAD—AN INVADING INFIDEL ARMY, A WEAK CENTRAL GOVERNMENT, WIDESPREAD CHAOS...
PLUS, WE KNOW THE CULTURE, THE LANGUAGE, THE TERRAIN—ALL ADVANTAGES IN FIGHTING AMERICAN FORCES! AND YET...
AND YET?
I JUST WISH I COULD BE FIGHTING THEM IN KANSAS.
THAT'S THE DREAM FOR YOU GUYS, ISN'T IT?
B. Trudeau

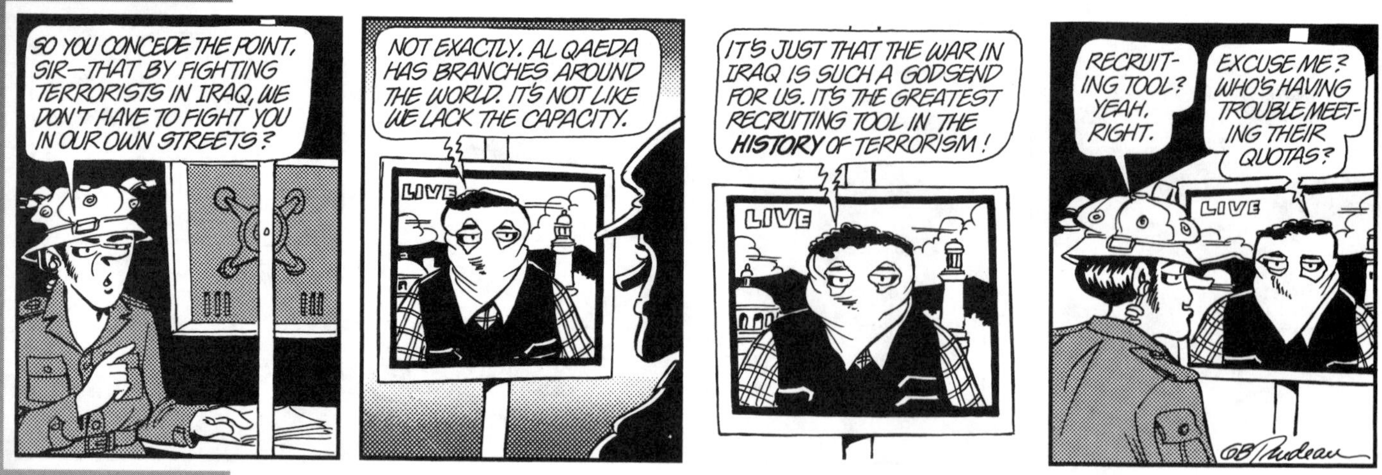
SO YOU CONCEDE THE POINT, SIR—THAT BY FIGHTING TERRORISTS IN IRAQ, WE DON'T HAVE TO FIGHT YOU IN OUR OWN STREETS?
NOT EXACTLY. AL QAEDA HAS BRANCHES AROUND THE WORLD. IT'S NOT LIKE WE LACK THE CAPACITY.
LIVE
IT'S JUST THAT THE WAR IN IRAQ IS SUCH A GODSEND FOR US. IT'S THE GREATEST RECRUITING TOOL IN THE **HISTORY** OF TERRORISM!
LIVE
RECRUITING TOOL? YEAH, RIGHT.
EXCUSE ME? WHO'S HAVING TROUBLE MEETING THEIR QUOTAS?
LIVE
GB Trudeau

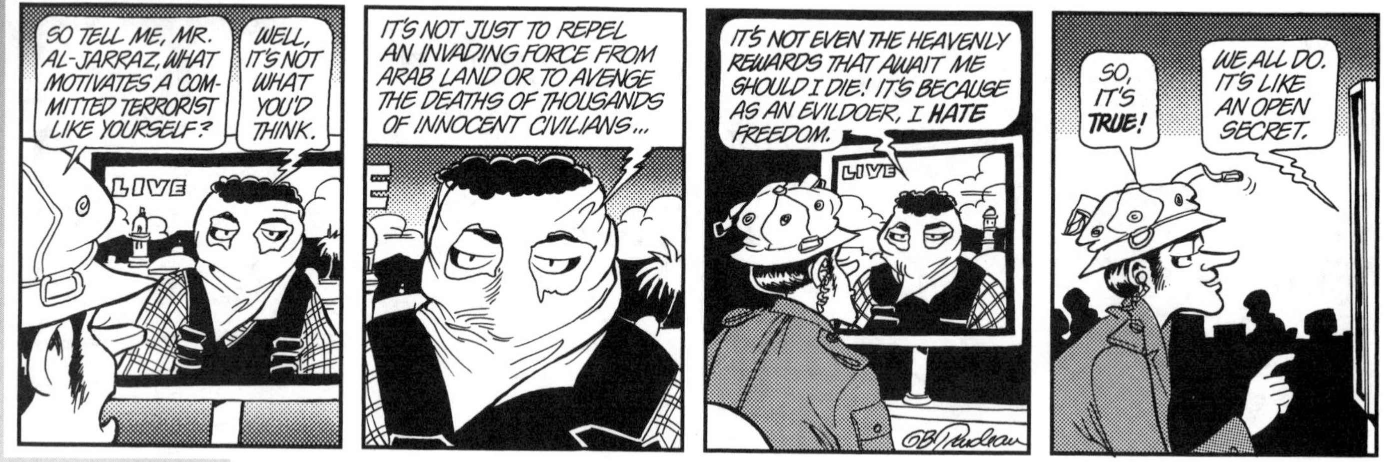
SO TELL ME, MR. AL-JARRAZ, WHAT MOTIVATES A COMMITTED TERRORIST LIKE YOURSELF?
WELL, IT'S NOT WHAT YOU'D THINK.
LIVE
IT'S NOT JUST TO REPEL AN INVADING FORCE FROM ARAB LAND OR TO AVENGE THE DEATHS OF THOUSANDS OF INNOCENT CIVILIANS...
IT'S NOT EVEN THE HEAVENLY REWARDS THAT AWAIT ME SHOULD I DIE! IT'S BECAUSE AS AN EVILDOER, I **HATE** FREEDOM.
LIVE
GB Trudeau
SO, IT'S **TRUE**!
WE ALL DO. IT'S LIKE AN OPEN SECRET.

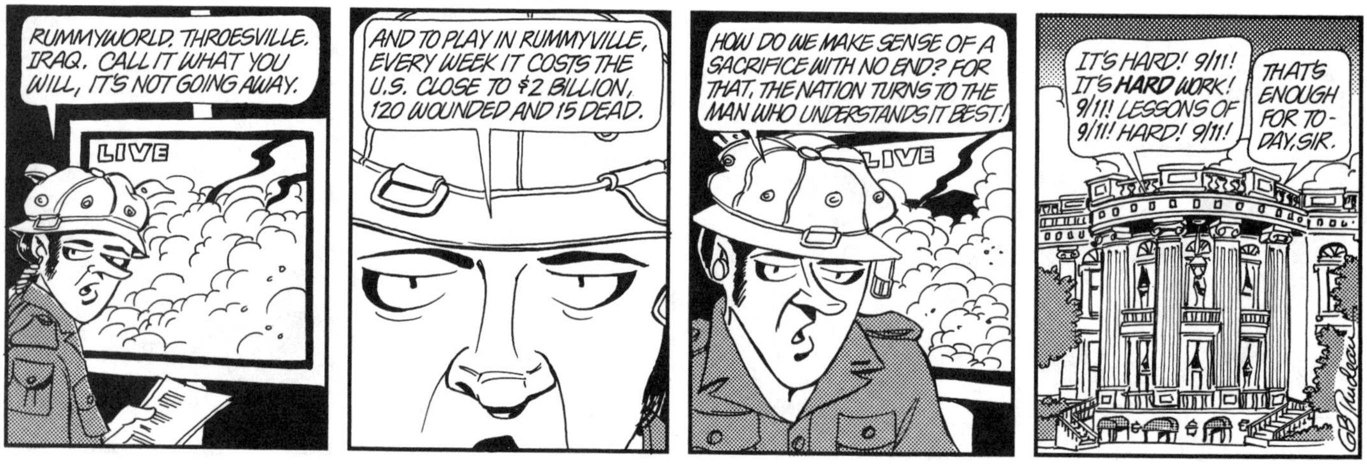
RUMMYWORLD, THROESVILLE, IRAQ. CALL IT WHAT YOU WILL, IT'S NOT GOING AWAY.
LIVE
AND TO PLAY IN RUMMYVILLE, EVERY WEEK IT COSTS THE U.S. CLOSE TO $2 BILLION, 120 WOUNDED AND 15 DEAD.
HOW DO WE MAKE SENSE OF A SACRIFICE WITH NO END? FOR THAT, THE NATION TURNS TO THE MAN WHO UNDERSTANDS IT BEST!
LIVE
IT'S HARD! 9/11! IT'S **HARD WORK**! 9/11! LESSONS OF 9/11! HARD! 9/11!
THAT'S ENOUGH FOR TODAY, SIR.
GB Trudeau

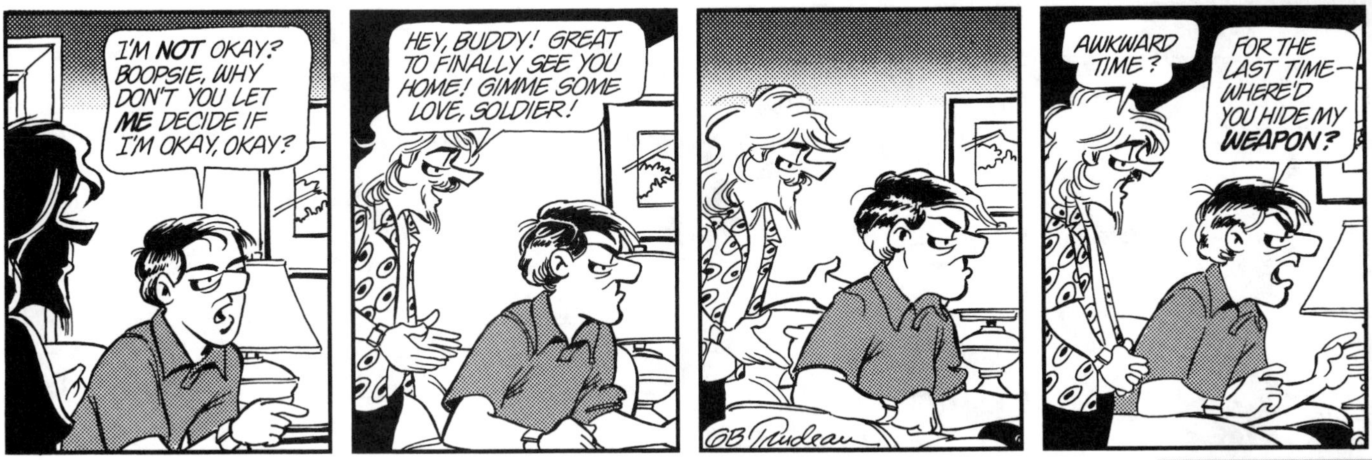
I'M NOT OKAY? BOOPSIE, WHY DON'T YOU LET ME DECIDE IF I'M OKAY, OKAY?
HEY, BUDDY! GREAT TO FINALLY SEE YOU HOME! GIMME SOME LOVE, SOLDIER!
AWKWARD TIME?
FOR THE LAST TIME—WHERE'D YOU HIDE MY WEAPON?
©B Trudeau

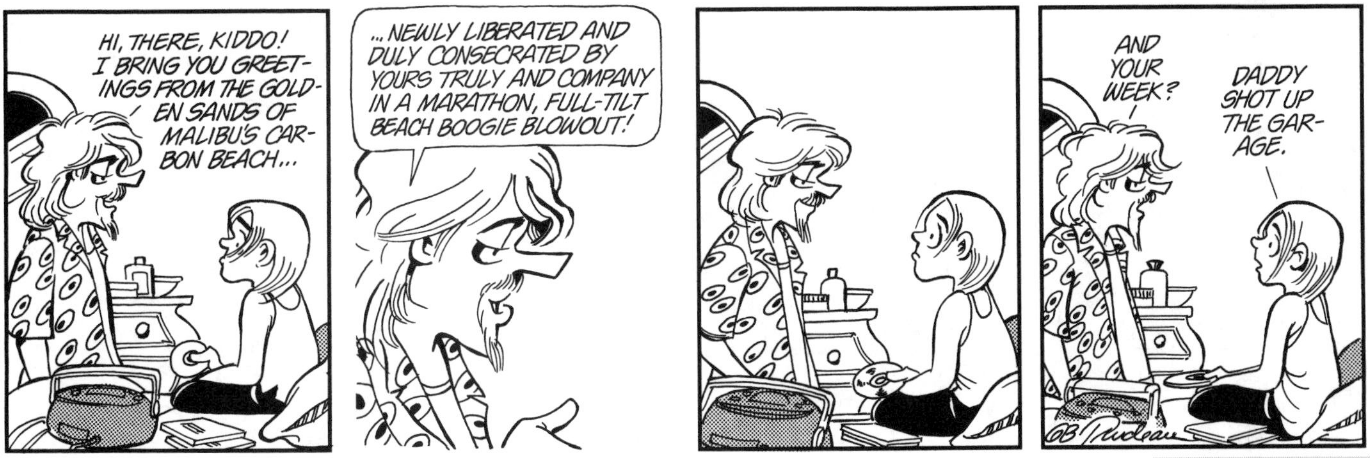
HI, THERE, KIDDO! I BRING YOU GREETINGS FROM THE GOLDEN SANDS OF MALIBU'S CARBON BEACH...
...NEWLY LIBERATED AND DULY CONSECRATED BY YOURS TRULY AND COMPANY IN A MARATHON, FULL-TILT BEACH BOOGIE BLOWOUT!
AND YOUR WEEK?
DADDY SHOT UP THE GARAGE.
©B Trudeau

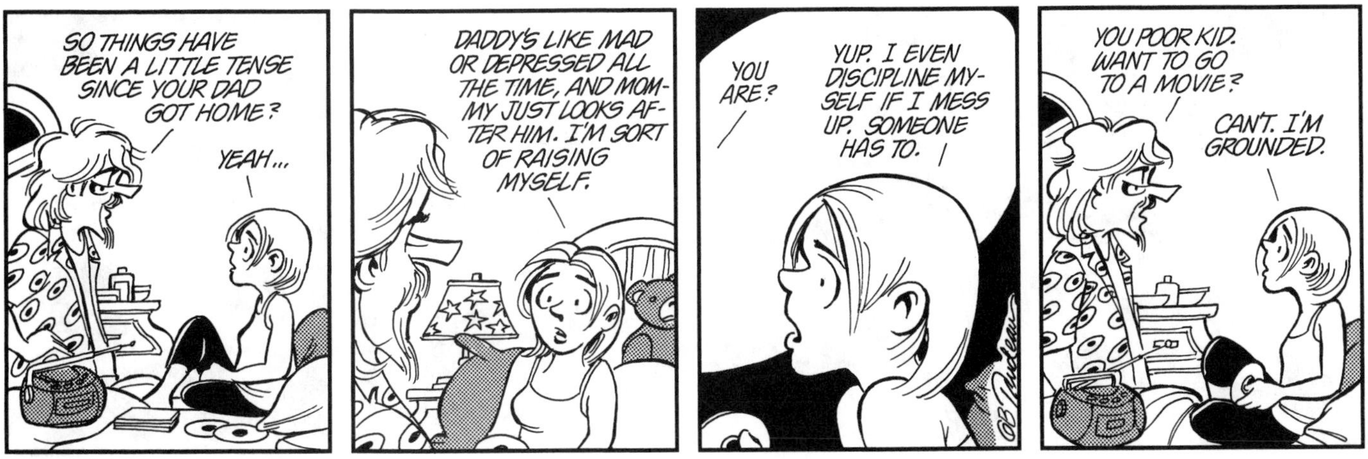
SO THINGS HAVE BEEN A LITTLE TENSE SINCE YOUR DAD GOT HOME?
YEAH...
DADDY'S LIKE MAD OR DEPRESSED ALL THE TIME, AND MOMMY JUST LOOKS AFTER HIM. I'M SORT OF RAISING MYSELF.
YOU ARE?
YUP. I EVEN DISCIPLINE MYSELF IF I MESS UP. SOMEONE HAS TO.
©B Trudeau
YOU POOR KID. WANT TO GO TO A MOVIE?
CAN'T. I'M GROUNDED.

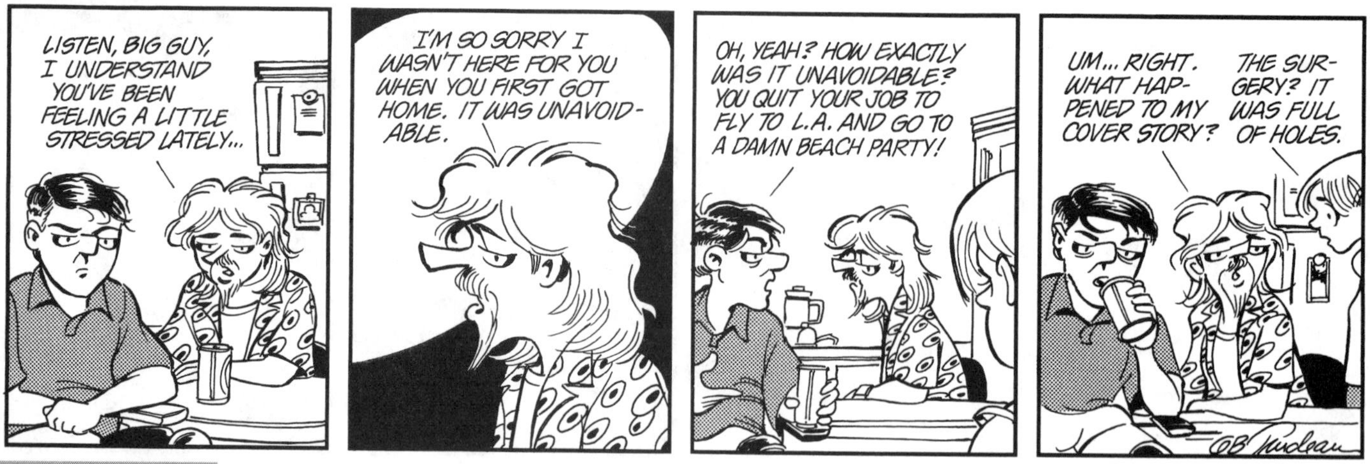
LISTEN, BIG GUY, I UNDERSTAND YOU'VE BEEN FEELING A LITTLE STRESSED LATELY...
I'M SO SORRY I WASN'T HERE FOR YOU WHEN YOU FIRST GOT HOME. IT WAS UNAVOIDABLE.
OH, YEAH? HOW EXACTLY WAS IT UNAVOIDABLE? YOU QUIT YOUR JOB TO FLY TO L.A. AND GO TO A DAMN BEACH PARTY!
UM... RIGHT. WHAT HAPPENED TO MY COVER STORY?
THE SURGERY? IT WAS FULL OF HOLES.

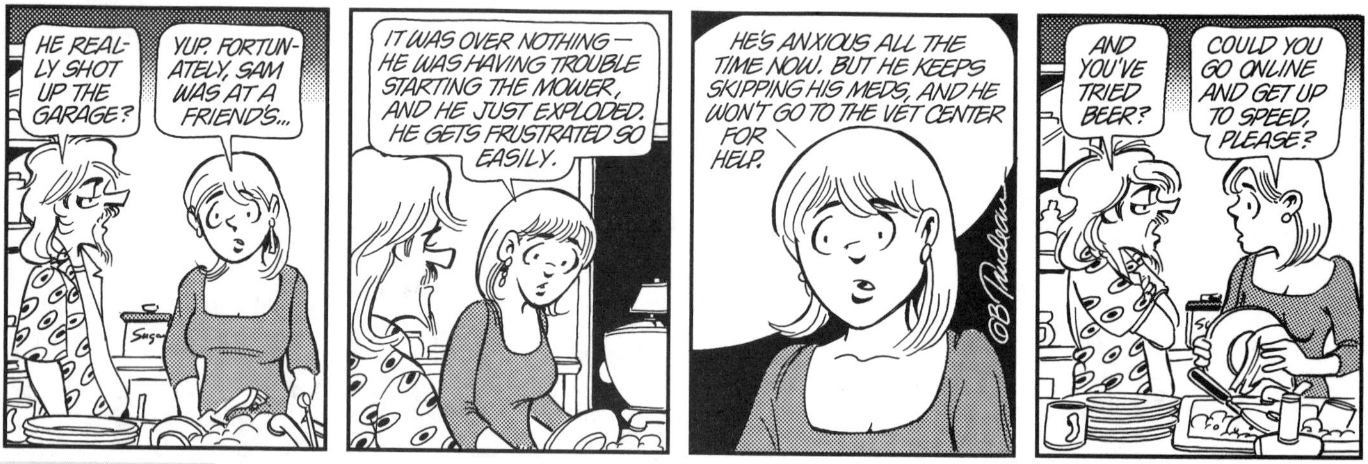
HE REALLY SHOT UP THE GARAGE?
YUP. FORTUNATELY, SAM WAS AT A FRIEND'S...
IT WAS OVER NOTHING — HE WAS HAVING TROUBLE STARTING THE MOWER, AND HE JUST EXPLODED. HE GETS FRUSTRATED SO EASILY.
HE'S ANXIOUS ALL THE TIME NOW. BUT HE KEEPS SKIPPING HIS MEDS, AND HE WON'T GO TO THE VET CENTER FOR HELP.
AND YOU'VE TRIED BEER?
COULD YOU GO ONLINE AND GET UP TO SPEED, PLEASE?

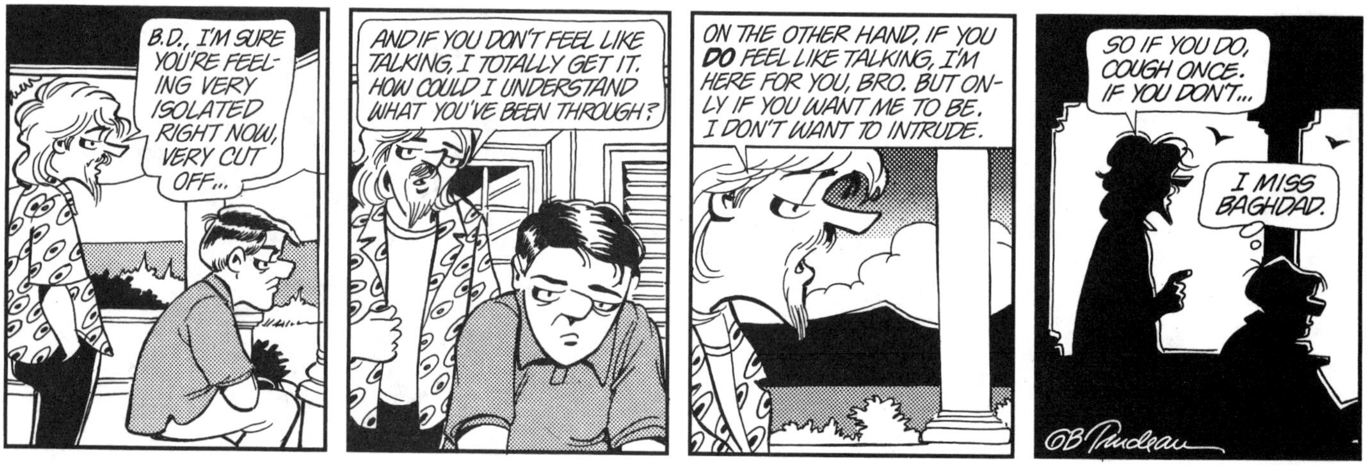
B.D., I'M SURE YOU'RE FEELING VERY ISOLATED RIGHT NOW, VERY CUT OFF...
AND IF YOU DON'T FEEL LIKE TALKING, I TOTALLY GET IT. HOW COULD I UNDERSTAND WHAT YOU'VE BEEN THROUGH?
ON THE OTHER HAND, IF YOU **DO** FEEL LIKE TALKING, I'M HERE FOR YOU, BRO. BUT ONLY IF YOU WANT ME TO BE. I DON'T WANT TO INTRUDE.
SO IF YOU DO, COUGH ONCE. IF YOU DON'T...
I MISS BAGHDAD.

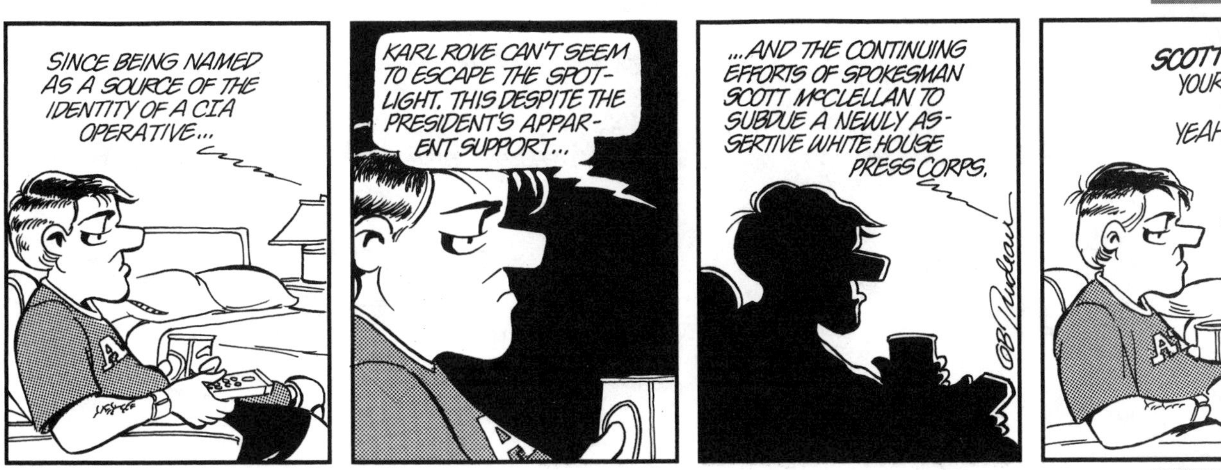
SINCE BEING NAMED AS A SOURCE OF THE IDENTITY OF A CIA OPERATIVE...
KARL ROVE CAN'T SEEM TO ESCAPE THE SPOT-LIGHT. THIS DESPITE THE PRESIDENT'S APPAR-ENT SUPPORT...
...AND THE CONTINUING EFFORTS OF SPOKESMAN SCOTT McCLELLAN TO SUBDUE A NEWLY AS-SERTIVE WHITE HOUSE PRESS CORPS.
SCOTT! WHO'S YOUR DADDY?
YEAH, WHO?
I'M NOT FREE TO...
LIAR!

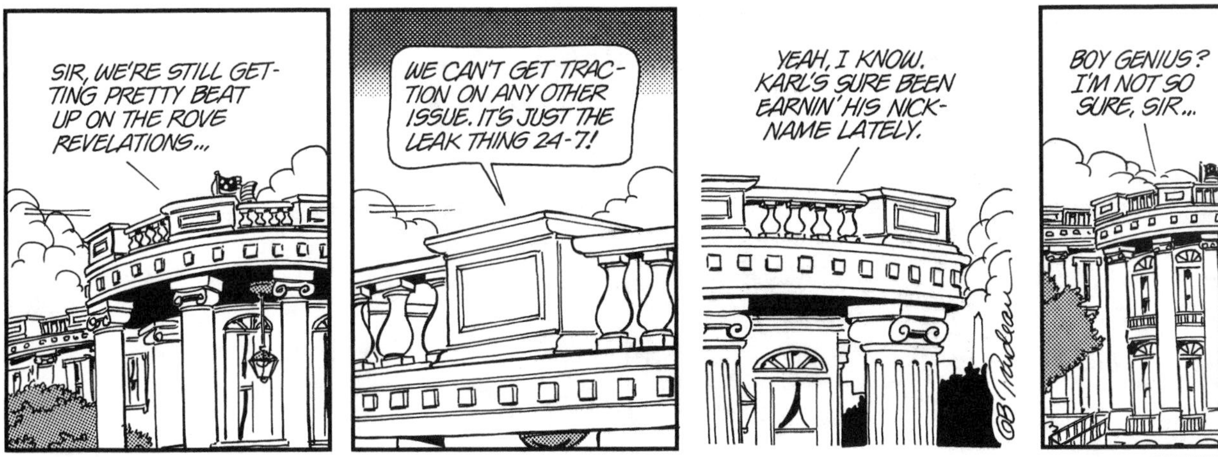
SIR, WE'RE STILL GET-TING PRETTY BEAT UP ON THE ROVE REVELATIONS...
WE CAN'T GET TRAC-TION ON ANY OTHER ISSUE. IT'S JUST THE LEAK THING 24-7!
YEAH, I KNOW. KARL'S SURE BEEN EARNIN' HIS NICK-NAME LATELY.
BOY GENIUS? I'M NOT SO SURE, SIR...
HEY, TURD BLOSSOM! GET IN HERE!

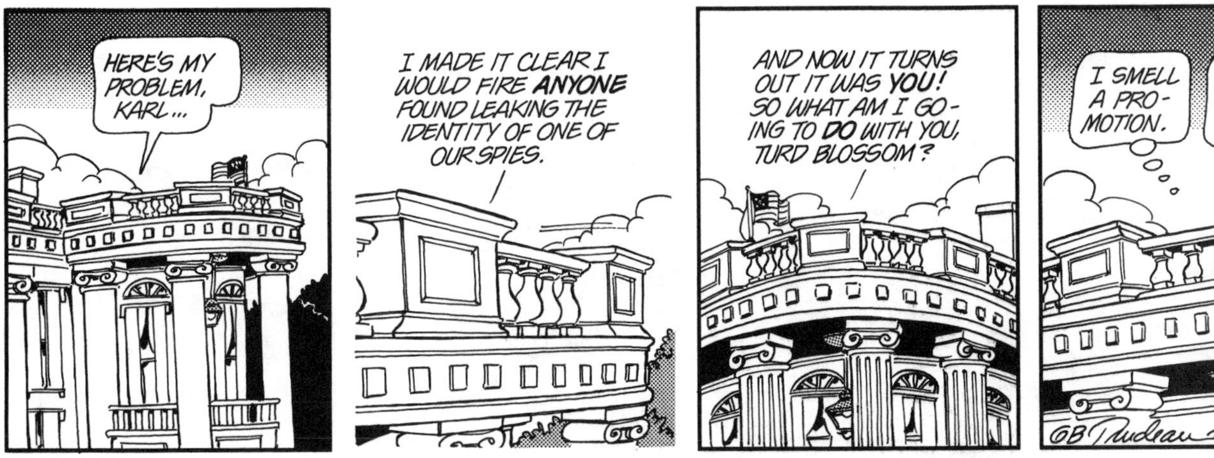
HERE'S MY PROBLEM, KARL...
I MADE IT CLEAR I WOULD FIRE ANYONE FOUND LEAKING THE IDENTITY OF ONE OF OUR SPIES.
AND NOW IT TURNS OUT IT WAS YOU! SO WHAT AM I GO-ING TO DO WITH YOU, TURD BLOSSOM?
I SMELL A PRO-MOTION.
CAN YOU SAY PRO-MOTION?

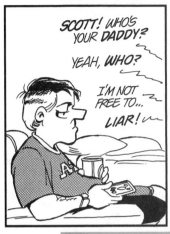

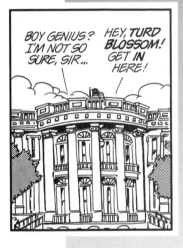

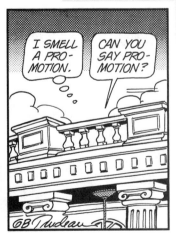

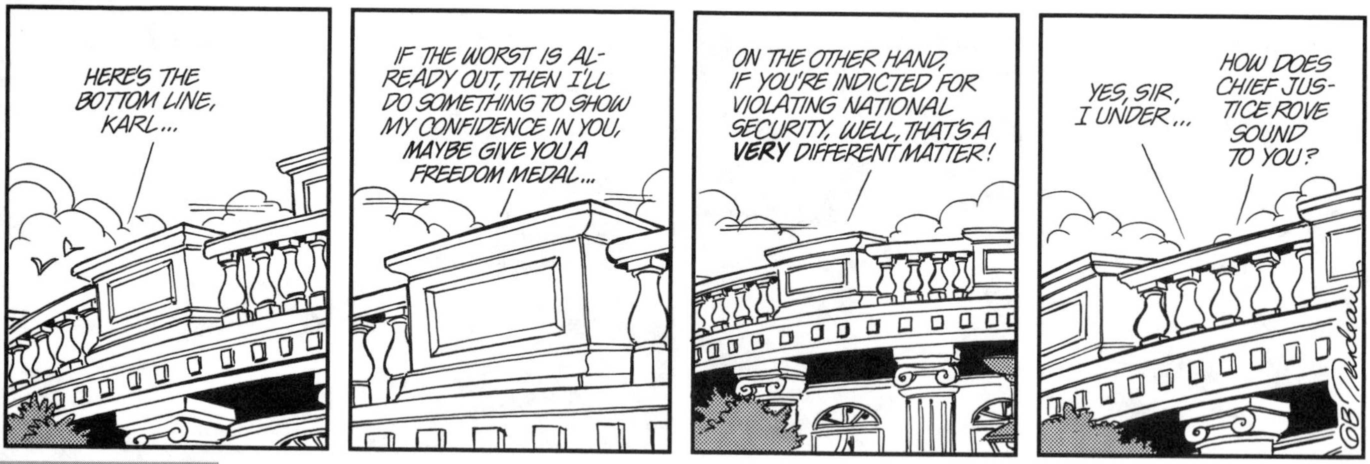
HERE'S THE BOTTOM LINE, KARL...
IF THE WORST IS ALREADY OUT, THEN I'LL DO SOMETHING TO SHOW MY CONFIDENCE IN YOU, MAYBE GIVE YOU A FREEDOM MEDAL...
ON THE OTHER HAND, IF YOU'RE INDICTED FOR VIOLATING NATIONAL SECURITY, WELL, THAT'S A VERY DIFFERENT MATTER!
YES, SIR, I UNDER...
HOW DOES CHIEF JUSTICE ROVE SOUND TO YOU?
©B Trudeau

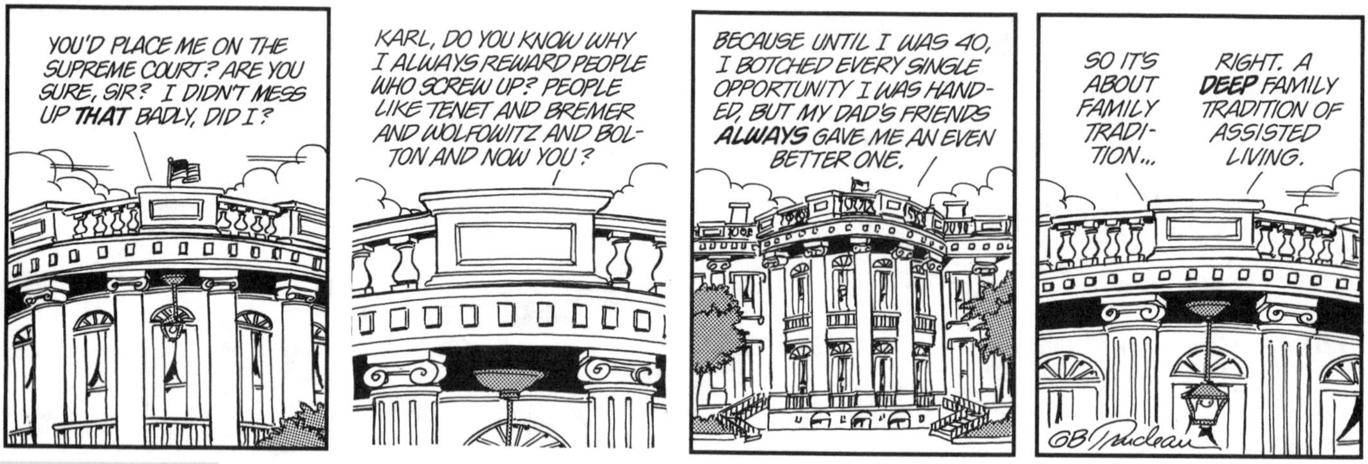
YOU'D PLACE ME ON THE SUPREME COURT? ARE YOU SURE, SIR? I DIDN'T MESS UP THAT BADLY, DID I?
KARL, DO YOU KNOW WHY I ALWAYS REWARD PEOPLE WHO SCREW UP? PEOPLE LIKE TENET AND BREMER AND WOLFOWITZ AND BOLTON AND NOW YOU?
BECAUSE UNTIL I WAS 40, I BOTCHED EVERY SINGLE OPPORTUNITY I WAS HANDED, BUT MY DAD'S FRIENDS ALWAYS GAVE ME AN EVEN BETTER ONE.
SO IT'S ABOUT FAMILY TRADITION...
RIGHT. A DEEP FAMILY TRADITION OF ASSISTED LIVING.
©B Trudeau

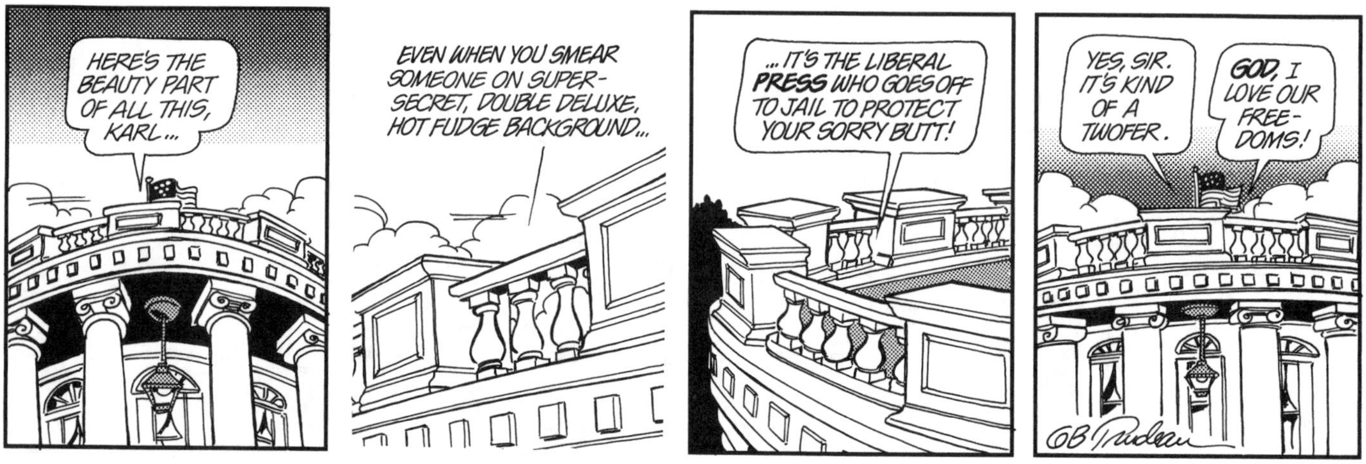
HERE'S THE BEAUTY PART OF ALL THIS, KARL...
EVEN WHEN YOU SMEAR SOMEONE ON SUPER-SECRET, DOUBLE DELUXE, HOT FUDGE BACKGROUND...
...IT'S THE LIBERAL PRESS WHO GOES OFF TO JAIL TO PROTECT YOUR SORRY BUTT!
YES, SIR. IT'S KIND OF A TWOFER.
GOD, I LOVE OUR FREEDOMS!
©B Trudeau

THANK YOU, WILL! IT'S GREAT TO BE BACK IN WASHINGTON AMONG SO MANY LOYAL WALDEN ALUMNI!
D.C. WALDEN CLUB
AND I APPRECIATE YOUR INVITING ME TO GIVE YOU AN UPDATE ON ALL THE DOINGS AT YOUR ALMA MATER!
AS YOU KNOW, WALDEN IS A VERY DIFFERENT PLACE THAN WHEN MOST OF YOU WERE THERE. BACK IN THE DAY, THE COLLEGE WAS... WAS... HOW TO PUT THIS...
FULLY ACCREDITED?
THERE YOU GO. THAT'S JUST ONE EXAMPLE.

WELL, LET ME START WITH THE SUBJECT THAT'S DEAREST TO THE HEARTS OF **ALL** WALDEN ALUMNI – THE FOOTBALL TEAM!
AS YOU KNOW, THE PROGRAM WAS ROILED IN THE PAST BY A MUCH-OVERBLOWN SEX SCANDAL, BUT I CAN ASSURE YOU WE'VE PUT THAT BEHIND US...
...WITH THE RE-HIRING OF RETURNING IRAQI WAR VETERAN B.D.! WE LOOK FORWARD TO A **GREAT** YEAR UNDER COACH B.D.'S SEASONED LEADERSHIP!
D.C. WALDEN CLUB
KING, I HEARD HE SHOT UP HIS GARAGE.
SO HE'S AGGRESSIVE. DO WE WANT SOME TOUCHY-FEELY TYPE?
D.C. WALDEN CLUB

LET ME JUST SAY THIS IN REGARDS TO COACH B.D.'S RECENT ERRATIC BEHAVIOR...
IT'S TRUE THAT B.D. IS NOW FACING BOTH PHYSICAL AND PSYCHOLOGICAL CHALLENGES AS A RESULT OF HIS SERVICE IN IRAQ. BUT WE FEEL HE WILL BE AN INSPIRATION TO THE TEAM!
ALSO, COME KICKOFF, WHEN THE SUN GLINTS OFF OUR COACH'S TITANIUM PROSTHESIS, **NO ONE** WILL BE ABLE TO DOUBT WALDEN'S COMMITMENT TO OUR NATION'S VETS!
KING, ISN'T THAT A LITTLE CYNICAL?
AL, DO YOU SURVIVE ON FEDERAL GRANTS? I'M GUESSING NOT.

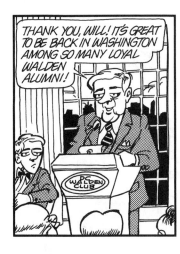

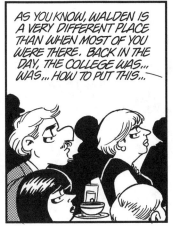

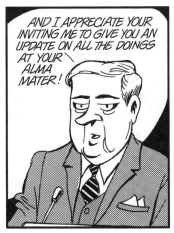

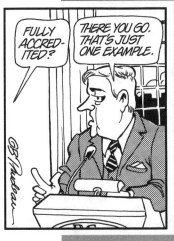

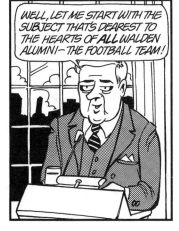

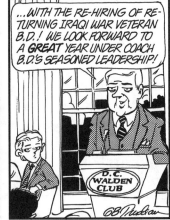

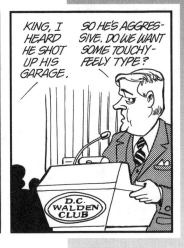

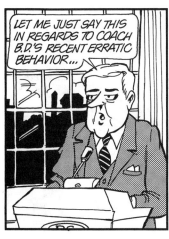

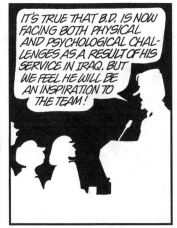

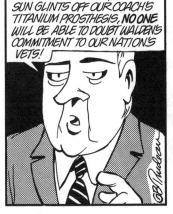

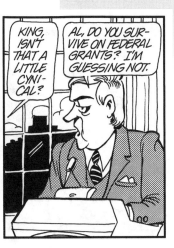

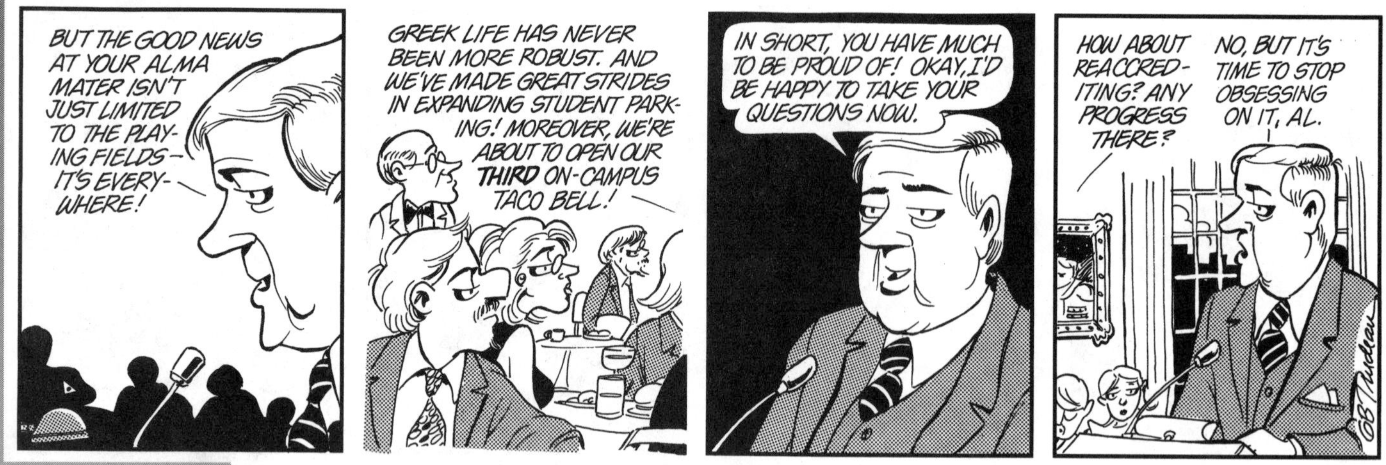
BUT THE GOOD NEWS AT YOUR ALMA MATER ISN'T JUST LIMITED TO THE PLAYING FIELDS— IT'S EVERYWHERE!
GREEK LIFE HAS NEVER BEEN MORE ROBUST. AND WE'VE MADE GREAT STRIDES IN EXPANDING STUDENT PARKING! MOREOVER, WE'RE ABOUT TO OPEN OUR THIRD ON-CAMPUS TACO BELL!
IN SHORT, YOU HAVE MUCH TO BE PROUD OF! OKAY, I'D BE HAPPY TO TAKE YOUR QUESTIONS NOW.
HOW ABOUT REACCREDITING? ANY PROGRESS THERE?
NO, BUT IT'S TIME TO STOP OBSESSING ON IT, AL.

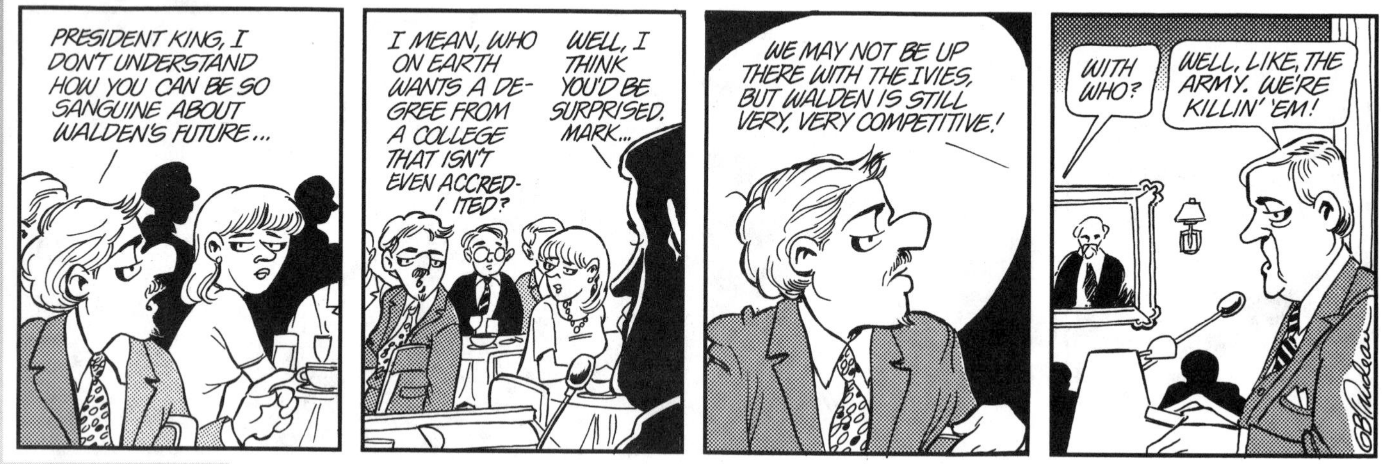
PRESIDENT KING, I DON'T UNDERSTAND HOW YOU CAN BE SO SANGUINE ABOUT WALDEN'S FUTURE...
I MEAN, WHO ON EARTH WANTS A DEGREE FROM A COLLEGE THAT ISN'T EVEN ACCREDITED?
WELL, I THINK YOU'D BE SURPRISED, MARK...
WE MAY NOT BE UP THERE WITH THE IVIES, BUT WALDEN IS STILL VERY, VERY COMPETITIVE!
WITH WHO?
WELL, LIKE, THE ARMY. WE'RE KILLIN' 'EM!

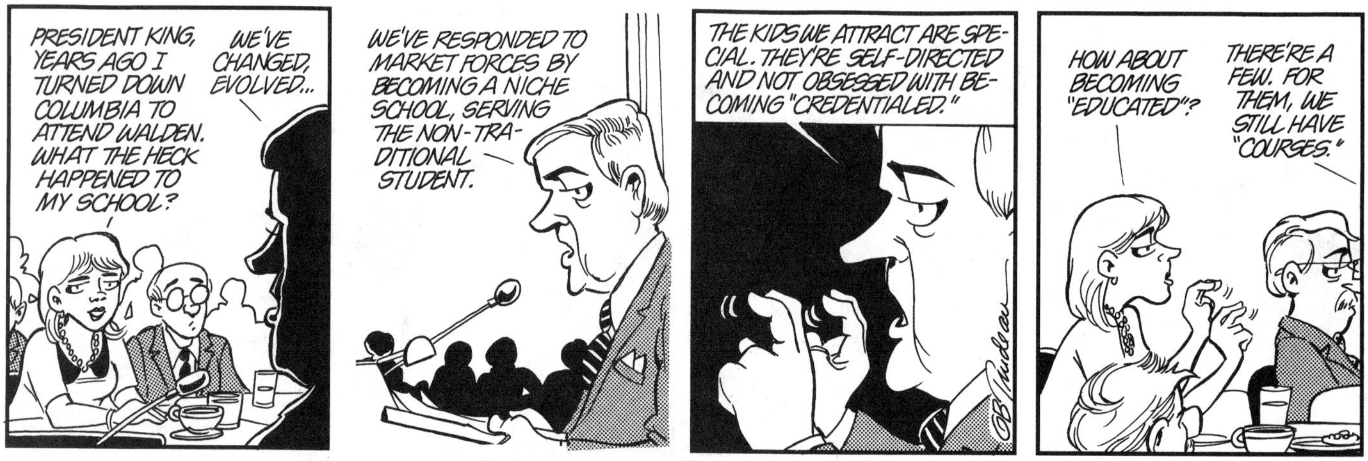
PRESIDENT KING, YEARS AGO I TURNED DOWN COLUMBIA TO ATTEND WALDEN. WHAT THE HECK HAPPENED TO MY SCHOOL?
WE'VE CHANGED, EVOLVED...
WE'VE RESPONDED TO MARKET FORCES BY BECOMING A NICHE SCHOOL, SERVING THE NON-TRADITIONAL STUDENT.
THE KIDS WE ATTRACT ARE SPECIAL. THEY'RE SELF-DIRECTED AND NOT OBSESSED WITH BECOMING "CREDENTIALED."
HOW ABOUT BECOMING "EDUCATED"?
THERE'RE A FEW. FOR THEM, WE STILL HAVE "COURSES."

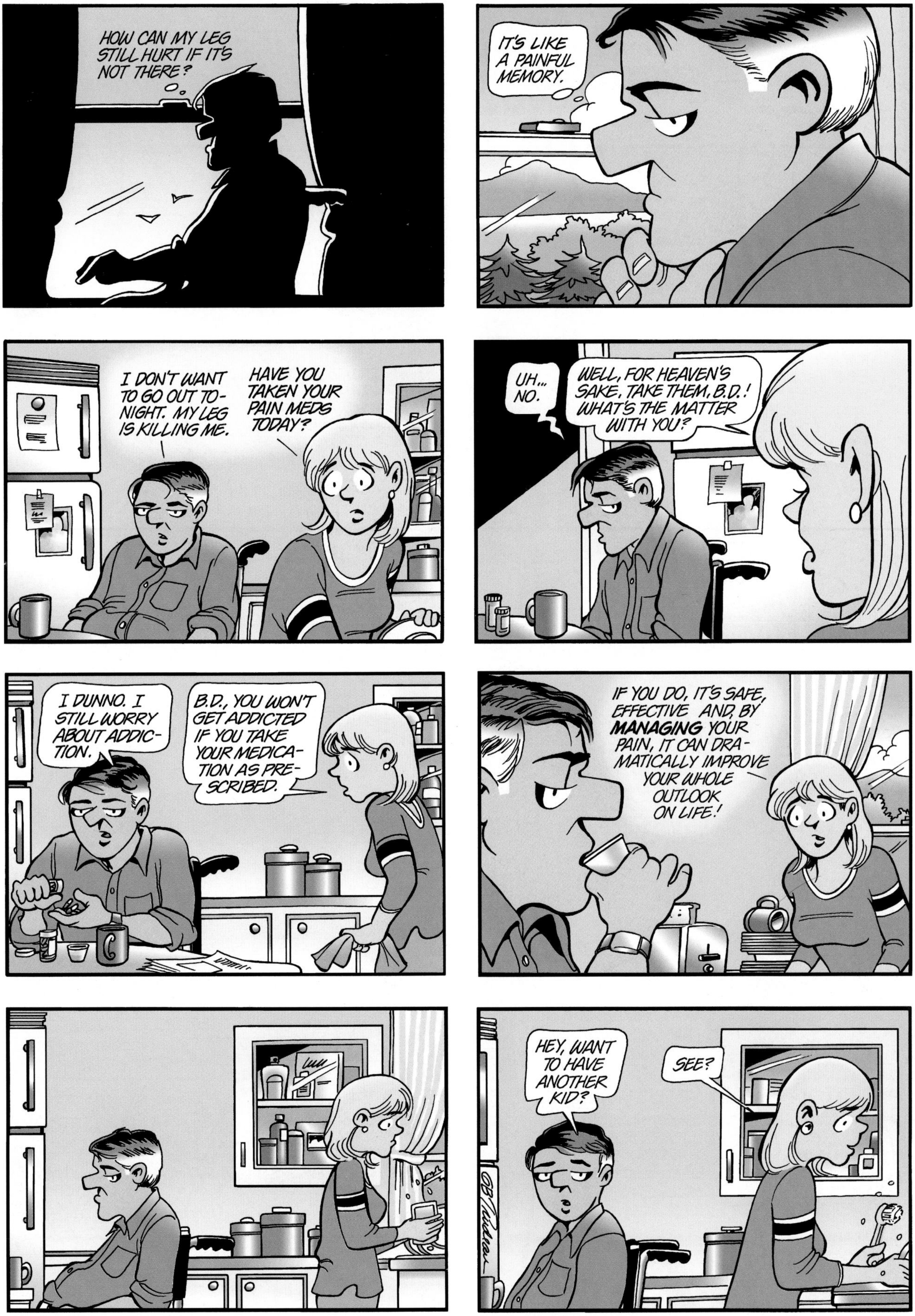
HOW CAN MY LEG STILL HURT IF IT'S NOT THERE?
IT'S LIKE A PAINFUL MEMORY.
I DON'T WANT TO GO OUT TO-NIGHT. MY LEG IS KILLING ME.
HAVE YOU TAKEN YOUR PAIN MEDS TODAY?
UH... NO.
WELL, FOR HEAVEN'S SAKE, TAKE THEM, B.D.! WHAT'S THE MATTER WITH YOU?
I DUNNO. I STILL WORRY ABOUT ADDIC-TION.
B.D., YOU WON'T GET ADDICTED IF YOU TAKE YOUR MEDICA-TION AS PRE-SCRIBED.
IF YOU DO, IT'S SAFE, EFFECTIVE AND, BY MANAGING YOUR PAIN, IT CAN DRA-MATICALLY IMPROVE YOUR WHOLE OUTLOOK ON LIFE!
HEY, WANT TO HAVE ANOTHER KID?
SEE?

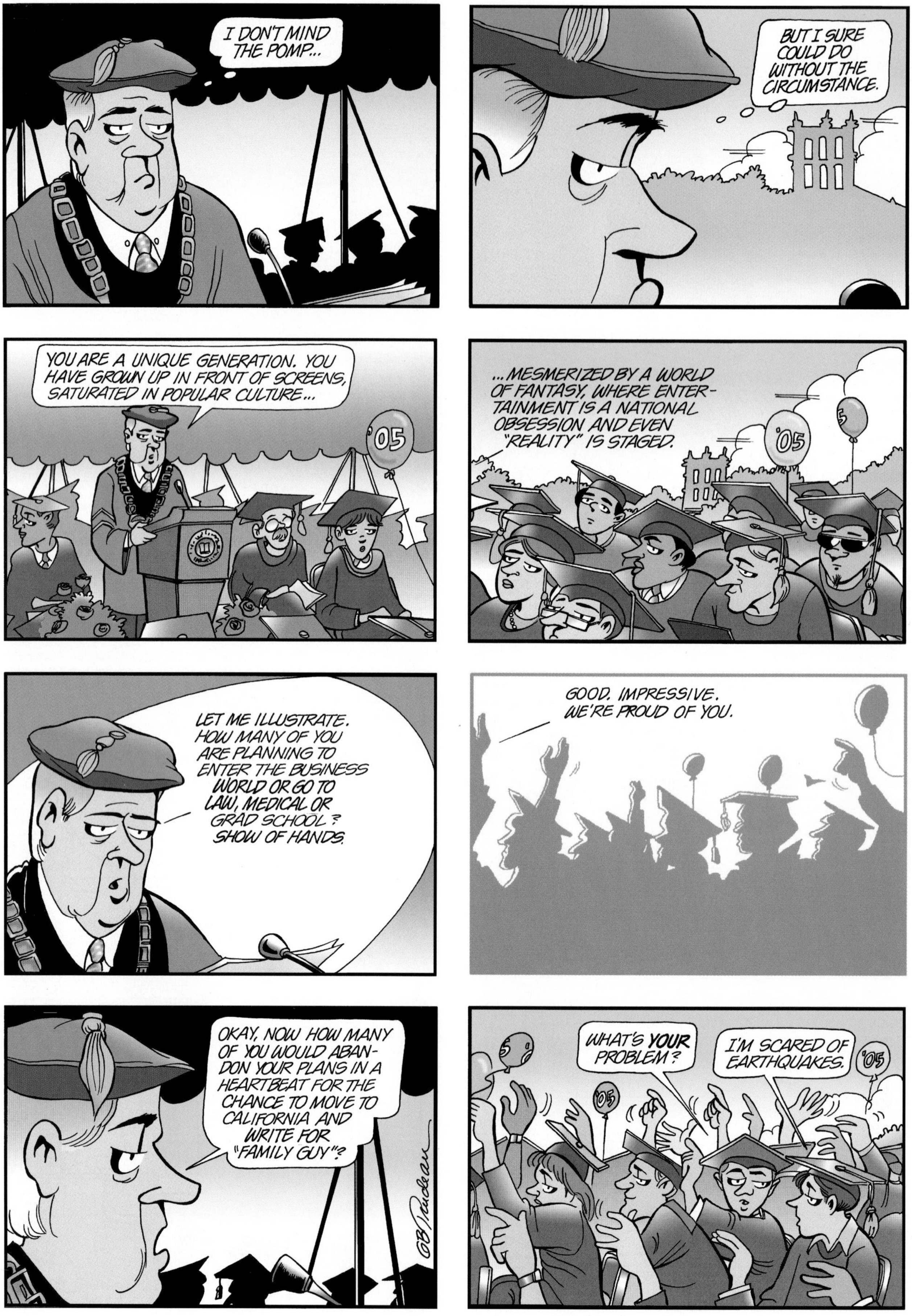
I DON'T MIND THE POMP...
BUT I SURE COULD DO WITHOUT THE CIRCUMSTANCE.
YOU ARE A UNIQUE GENERATION. YOU HAVE GROWN UP IN FRONT OF SCREENS, SATURATED IN POPULAR CULTURE...
'05
...MESMERIZED BY A WORLD OF FANTASY, WHERE ENTERTAINMENT IS A NATIONAL OBSESSION AND EVEN "REALITY" IS STAGED.
'05
LET ME ILLUSTRATE. HOW MANY OF YOU ARE PLANNING TO ENTER THE BUSINESS WORLD OR GO TO LAW, MEDICAL OR GRAD SCHOOL? SHOW OF HANDS.
GOOD. IMPRESSIVE. WE'RE PROUD OF YOU.
OKAY, NOW HOW MANY OF YOU WOULD ABANDON YOUR PLANS IN A HEARTBEAT FOR THE CHANCE TO MOVE TO CALIFORNIA AND WRITE FOR "FAMILY GUY"?
WHAT'S **YOUR** PROBLEM?
I'M SCARED OF EARTHQUAKES.
'05

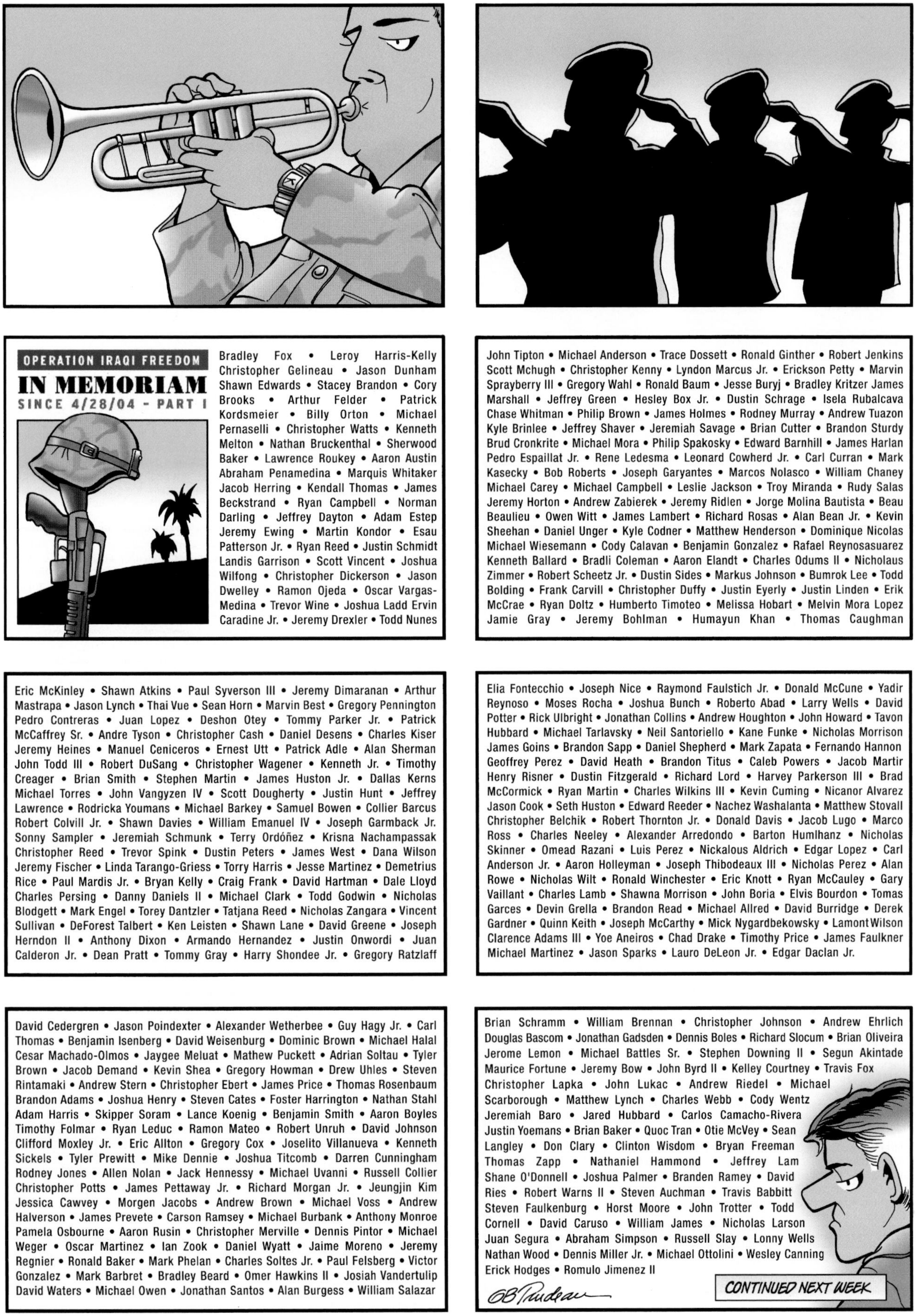
OPERATION IRAQI FREEDOM
IN MEMORIAM
SINCE 4/28/04 - PART I
Bradley Fox • Leroy Harris-Kelly Christopher Gelineau • Jason Dunham Shawn Edwards • Stacey Brandon • Cory Brooks • Arthur Felder • Patrick Kordsmeier • Billy Orton • Michael Pernaselli • Christopher Watts • Kenneth Melton • Nathan Bruckenthal • Sherwood Baker • Lawrence Roukey • Aaron Austin Abraham Penamedina • Marquis Whitaker Jacob Herring • Kendall Thomas • James Beckstrand • Ryan Campbell • Norman Darling • Jeffrey Dayton • Adam Estep Jeremy Ewing • Martin Kondor • Esau Patterson Jr. • Ryan Reed • Justin Schmidt Landis Garrison • Scott Vincent • Joshua Wilfong • Christopher Dickerson • Jason Dwelley • Ramon Ojeda • Oscar Vargas-Medina • Trevor Wine • Joshua Ladd Ervin Caradine Jr. • Jeremy Drexler • Todd Nunes
John Tipton • Michael Anderson • Trace Dossett • Ronald Ginther • Robert Jenkins Scott Mchugh • Christopher Kenny • Lyndon Marcus Jr. • Erickson Petty • Marvin Sprayberry III • Gregory Wahl • Ronald Baum • Jesse Buryj • Bradley Kritzer James Marshall • Jeffrey Green • Hesley Box Jr. • Dustin Schrage • Isela Rubalcava Chase Whitman • Philip Brown • James Holmes • Rodney Murray • Andrew Tuazon Kyle Brinlee • Jeffrey Shaver • Jeremiah Savage • Brian Cutter • Brandon Sturdy Brud Cronkrite • Michael Mora • Philip Spakosky • Edward Barnhill • James Harlan Pedro Espaillat Jr. • Rene Ledesma • Leonard Cowherd Jr. • Carl Curran • Mark Kasecky • Bob Roberts • Joseph Garyantes • Marcos Nolasco • William Chaney Michael Carey • Michael Campbell • Leslie Jackson • Troy Miranda • Rudy Salas Jeremy Horton • Andrew Zabierek • Jeremy Ridlen • Jorge Molina Bautista • Beau Beaulieu • Owen Witt • James Lambert • Richard Rosas • Alan Bean Jr. • Kevin Sheehan • Daniel Unger • Kyle Codner • Matthew Henderson • Dominique Nicolas Michael Wiesemann • Cody Calavan • Benjamin Gonzalez • Rafael Reynosasuarez Kenneth Ballard • Bradli Coleman • Aaron Elandt • Charles Odums II • Nicholaus Zimmer • Robert Scheetz Jr. • Dustin Sides • Markus Johnson • Bumrok Lee • Todd Bolding • Frank Carvill • Christopher Duffy • Justin Eyerly • Justin Linden • Erik McCrae • Ryan Doltz • Humberto Timoteo • Melissa Hobart • Melvin Mora Lopez Jamie Gray • Jeremy Bohlman • Humayun Khan • Thomas Caughman
Eric McKinley • Shawn Atkins • Paul Syverson III • Jeremy Dimaranan • Arthur Mastrapa • Jason Lynch • Thai Vue • Sean Horn • Marvin Best • Gregory Pennington Pedro Contreras • Juan Lopez • Deshon Otey • Tommy Parker Jr. • Patrick McCaffrey Sr. • Andre Tyson • Christopher Cash • Daniel Desens • Charles Kiser Jeremy Heines • Manuel Ceniceros • Ernest Utt • Patrick Adle • Alan Sherman John Todd III • Robert DuSang • Christopher Wagener • Kenneth Jr. • Timothy Creager • Brian Smith • Stephen Martin • James Huston Jr. • Dallas Kerns Michael Torres • John Vangyzen IV • Scott Dougherty • Justin Hunt • Jeffrey Lawrence • Rodricka Youmans • Michael Barkey • Samuel Bowen • Collier Barcus Robert Colvill Jr. • Shawn Davies • William Emanuel IV • Joseph Garmback Jr. Sonny Sampler • Jeremiah Schmunk • Terry Ordóñez • Krisna Nachampassak Christopher Reed • Trevor Spink • Dustin Peters • James West • Dana Wilson Jeremy Fischer • Linda Tarango-Griess • Torry Harris • Jesse Martinez • Demetrius Rice • Paul Mardis Jr. • Bryan Kelly • Craig Frank • David Hartman • Dale Lloyd Charles Persing • Danny Daniels II • Michael Clark • Todd Godwin • Nicholas Blodgett • Mark Engel • Torey Dantzler • Tatjana Reed • Nicholas Zangara • Vincent Sullivan • DeForest Talbert • Ken Leisten • Shawn Lane • David Greene • Joseph Herndon II • Anthony Dixon • Armando Hernandez • Justin Onwordi • Juan Calderon Jr. • Dean Pratt • Tommy Gray • Harry Shondee Jr. • Gregory Ratzlaff
Elia Fontecchio • Joseph Nice • Raymond Faulstich Jr. • Donald McCune • Yadir Reynoso • Moses Rocha • Joshua Bunch • Roberto Abad • Larry Wells • David Potter • Rick Ulbright • Jonathan Collins • Andrew Houghton • John Howard • Tavon Hubbard • Michael Tarlavsky • Neil Santoriello • Kane Funke • Nicholas Morrison James Goins • Brandon Sapp • Daniel Shepherd • Mark Zapata • Fernando Hannon Geoffrey Perez • David Heath • Brandon Titus • Caleb Powers • Jacob Martir Henry Risner • Dustin Fitzgerald • Richard Lord • Harvey Parkerson III • Brad McCormick • Ryan Martin • Charles Wilkins III • Kevin Cuming • Nicanor Alvarez Jason Cook • Seth Huston • Edward Reeder • Nachez Washalanta • Matthew Stovall Christopher Belchik • Robert Thornton Jr. • Donald Davis • Jacob Lugo • Marco Ross • Charles Neeley • Alexander Arredondo • Barton Humlhanz • Nicholas Skinner • Omead Razani • Luis Perez • Nickalous Aldrich • Edgar Lopez • Carl Anderson Jr. • Aaron Holleyman • Joseph Thibodeaux III • Nicholas Perez • Alan Rowe • Nicholas Wilt • Ronald Winchester • Eric Knott • Ryan McCauley • Gary Vaillant • Charles Lamb • Shawna Morrison • John Boria • Elvis Bourdon • Tomas Garces • Devin Grella • Brandon Read • Michael Allred • David Burridge • Derek Gardner • Quinn Keith • Joseph McCarthy • Mick Nygardbekowsky • LamontWilson Clarence Adams III • Yoe Aneiros • Chad Drake • Timothy Price • James Faulkner Michael Martinez • Jason Sparks • Lauro DeLeon Jr. • Edgar Daclan Jr.
David Cedergren • Jason Poindexter • Alexander Wetherbee • Guy Hagy Jr. • Carl Thomas • Benjamin Isenberg • David Weisenburg • Dominic Brown • Michael Halal Cesar Machado-Olmos • Jaygee Meluat • Mathew Puckett • Adrian Soltau • Tyler Brown • Jacob Demand • Kevin Shea • Gregory Howman • Drew Uhles • Steven Rintamaki • Andrew Stern • Christopher Ebert • James Price • Thomas Rosenbaum Brandon Adams • Joshua Henry • Steven Cates • Foster Harrington • Nathan Stahl Adam Harris • Skipper Soram • Lance Koenig • Benjamin Smith • Aaron Boyles Timothy Folmar • Ryan Leduc • Ramon Mateo • Robert Unruh • David Johnson Clifford Moxley Jr. • Eric Allton • Gregory Cox • Joselito Villanueva • Kenneth Sickels • Tyler Prewitt • Mike Dennie • Joshua Titcomb • Darren Cunningham Rodney Jones • Allen Nolan • Jack Hennessy • Michael Uvanni • Russell Collier Christopher Potts • James Pettaway Jr. • Richard Morgan Jr. • Jeungjin Kim Jessica Cawvey • Morgen Jacobs • Andrew Brown • Michael Voss • Andrew Halverson • James Prevete • Carson Ramsey • Michael Burbank • Anthony Monroe Pamela Osbourne • Aaron Rusin • Christopher Merville • Dennis Pintor • Michael Weger • Oscar Martinez • Ian Zook • Daniel Wyatt • Jaime Moreno • Jeremy Regnier • Ronald Baker • Mark Phelan • Charles Soltes Jr. • Paul Felsberg • Victor Gonzalez • Mark Barbret • Bradley Beard • Omer Hawkins II • Josiah Vandertulip David Waters • Michael Owen • Jonathan Santos • Alan Burgess • William Salazar
Brian Schramm • William Brennan • Christopher Johnson • Andrew Ehrlich Douglas Bascom • Jonathan Gadsden • Dennis Boles • Richard Slocum • Brian Oliveira Jerome Lemon • Michael Battles Sr. • Stephen Downing II • Segun Akintade Maurice Fortune • Jeremy Bow • John Byrd II • Kelley Courtney • Travis Fox Christopher Lapka • John Lukac • Andrew Riedel • Michael Scarborough • Matthew Lynch • Charles Webb • Cody Wentz Jeremiah Baro • Jared Hubbard • Carlos Camacho-Rivera Justin Yoemans • Brian Baker • Quoc Tran • Otie McVey • Sean Langley • Don Clary • Clinton Wisdom • Bryan Freeman Thomas Zapp • Nathaniel Hammond • Jeffrey Lam Shane O'Donnell • Joshua Palmer • Branden Ramey • David Ries • Robert Warns II • Steven Auchman • Travis Babbitt Steven Faulkenburg • Horst Moore • John Trotter • Todd Cornell • David Caruso • William James • Nicholas Larson Juan Segura • Abraham Simpson • Russell Slay • Lonny Wells Nathan Wood • Dennis Miller Jr. • Michael Ottolini • Wesley Canning Erick Hodges • Romulo Jimenez II
GBTrudeau
CONTINUED NEXT WEEK

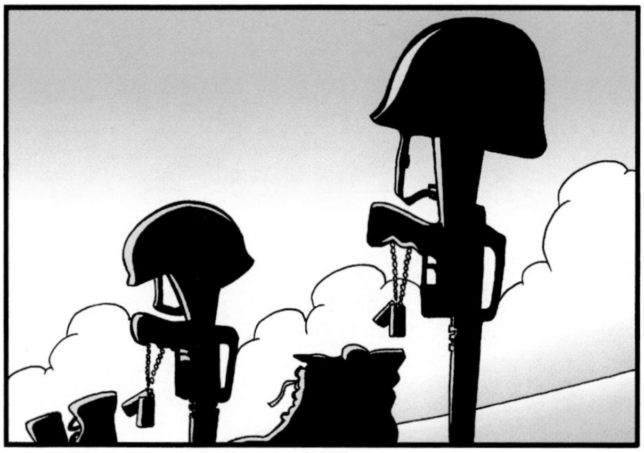

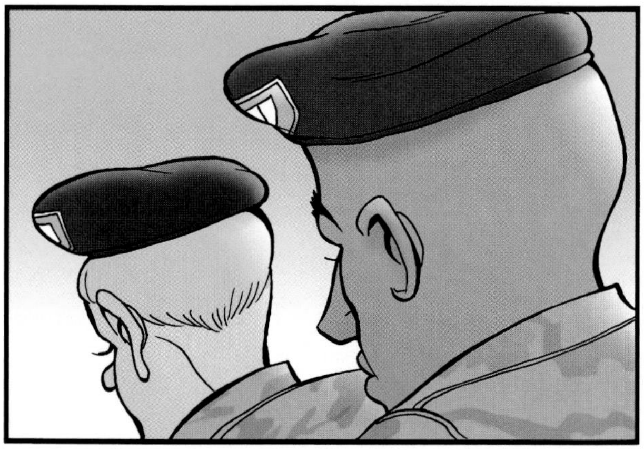

OPERATION IRAQI FREEDOM

IN MEMORIAM

SINCE 4/28/04 - PART II

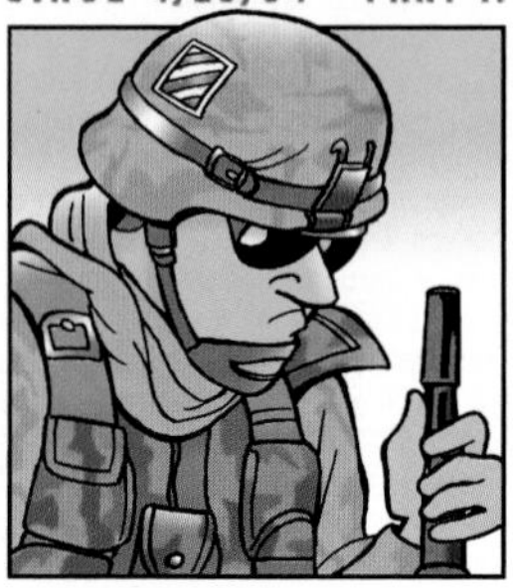

Dan Malcom Jr. • Aaron Pickering • Gene Ramirez • Julian Woods • Thomas Doerflinger • Sean Huey • James Blecksmith • Theodore Bowling • Kyle Burns • Theodore Holder II • Justin Reppuhn • Peter Giannopoulos • Edward Iwan • James Matteson • Jonathan Shields Raymond White • Nathan Anderson Nicholas Anderson • David Branning Jarrod Maher • Brian Medina • Morgan Strader • Brian Prening • Cole Larsen Sean Sims • Jose Velez • Catalin Dima Benjamin Bryan • Kevin Dempsey • Justin Ellsworth • Victor Lu • Justin McLeese Byron Norwood • Dale Burger Jr. • George Payton • Andres Perez • Nicholas Ziolkowski • Isaiah Hunt • Jeramy Ailes Travis Desiato • Shane Kielion • William Miller • Bradley Parker • Rafael Peralta Patrick Rapicault • Marc Ryan • Antoine

Smith • James Swain • Lance Thompson • Marshall Caddy • Jose Flores-Mejia Daniel McConnell • Luke Wullenwaber • Christopher Heflin • Louis Qualls • Michael Hanks • Joseph Nolan • Luis Figueroa • Demarkus Brown • Michael Downey Dimitrios Gavriel • Phillip West • Bradley Arms • Jack Jr. • David Roustum • Joseph Heredia • Joseph Welke • Blain Ebert • Michael Cohen • Benjamin Edinger • Sergio Varela • Nicholas Nolte • Jeffery Holmes • Gentian Marku • Ryan Cantafio • Brian Grant • Harrison Meyer • Bradley Faircloth • David Houck • Jordan Winkler Jeremy Christensen • Michael Smith • Kirk Bosselmann • Joshua Lucero • Stephen Benish • Carl Lee • Trinidad Martinezluis • Michael Shackelford • Adam Brooks Charles Hanson Jr. • Erik Hayes • Daryl Davis • Christian Engeldrum • Wilfredo Urbina • Blake Magaoay • Pablo Calderon • Jose Guereca Jr. • David Fisher • Javier Pena • Bryan Wilson • Zachary Kolda • George Harrison • David Mahlenbrock Henry Irizarry • Binh Le • Matthew Wyatt • Michael Boatright • Cari Gasiewicz David Mitts • Salamo Tuialuuluu • Joseph Behnke • Kyle Eggers • Edwin Roodhouse Marvin Trost III • Andrew Ward • Todd Gibbs • Mark Stubenhofer • In Kim • Arthur Williams IV • Patrick Leach • Andrew Shields • Christopher Adlesperger • Kyle Renehan • Robert Hoyt • Gregory Rund • Joshua Ramsey • Jeffery Blanton • Melvin Blazer • Jason Clairday • Joshua Dickinson • Jeffrey Kirk • Hilario Lopez • Ian Stewart • Tina Time • Brent Vroman • Richard Warner • Victor Martinez • Michael Anderson • Franklin Sweger • Donald Farmer • Barry Meza • Joel Baldwin • Lionel

Ayro • Jonathan Castro • Cory Hewitt • William Jacobsen Jr. • Robert Johnson Julian Melo • Robert ODell • Darren VanKomen • Thomas Dostie • Nicholas Mason Lynn Poulin Sr. • David Ruhren • Paul Karpowich • Neil Petsche • Christopher Barnett • Eric Hillenburg • James Phillips • Raleigh Smith • Jose Rivera-Serrano Todd Olson • Nathaniel Nyren • Jason Lehto • Pablito Briones Jr. • Oscar Sanchez Craig Nelson • Damien Ficek • Jason Smith • Jeff LeBrun • Brian Parrello • Thomas Houser • Cory Depew • Bennie Washington • Curtis Wooten III • Jimmy Buie Joshua Marcum • Jeremy McHalffey • Christopher Babin • Bradley Bergeron • Kurt Comeaux • Huey Fassbender • Armand Frickey • Warren Murphy • Kenneth Vonronn Julio Cisneros-Alvarez • Zachariah Davis • Daniel Guastaferro • Dwayne McFarlane Jr. • Joseph Fite • William Manuel • Robert Sweeney III • Michael Smith • Gunnar Becker • Brian Mack • Matthew Holloway • Juan Velasco • Paul Holter III Nathaniel Swindell • Jayton Patterson • Alain Kamolvathin • Jesus Fonseca George Geer • Thomas Vitagliano • Francis Obaji • Christopher Sullivan • Kyle Childress • Joe Lusk II • Nainoa Hoe • Jose Rangel • Michael Carlson • Jesus Leon-Perez • Javier Marin Jr. • Joseph Stevens • Brett Swank • Viktar Yolkin • Leonard Adams • John House • Taylor Burk • William Kinzer Jr. • Paul Alaniz • Brian Bland Jonathan Etterling • Michael Finke Jr. • Travis Fuller • Timothy Gibson • Richard Gilbert Jr. • Lyle Gordon • Kyle Grimes • Tony Hernandez • Brian Hopper • Saeed Jafarkhani-Torshizi Jr. • Stephen Johnson • Sean Kelly • Dexter Kimble • Allan

Klein • Timothy Knight • Fred Maciel • James Moore • Nathaniel Moore • Mourad Ragimov • Rhonald Rairdan • Hector Ramos • Gael Saintvil • Nathan Schubert Darrell Schumann • Dustin Shumney • Matthew Smith • Joseph Spence • Michael Starr Jr. • Jonathan Bowling • Karl Linn • Jesse Strong • Christopher Weaver Kevin Luna • Jonathan Beatty • Orlando Bonilla • Stephen Castellano • Charles Jones • Joseph Rodriguez • Mickey Zaun • Michael Evans II • Christopher Ramsey Jonathan Reed • Lyle Rymer II • Andrew Farrar Jr. • Edward Jack • Lindsey James Barbara Heald • Keith Taylor • James Miller IV • Nazario Serrano • Mark Warren Jason Redifer • Harry Swain IV • Christopher Zimny • Robert Hendrickson • Sean Brock • Sean Maher • Stephen Sherman • Sean Cooley • Richard Clifton • Steven Bayow • Daniel Torres • Travis Wichlacz • Jeremy Allmon • Zachary Wobler Jeffrey Henthorn • Jessica Housby • William Robbins • Richard Perez Jr. Kristopher Shepherd • Robert McNail • Ray Rangel • David Brangman • Dakotah Gooding • Rene Knox Jr. • Chad Lake • David Salie • Michael Arciola • Katrina Bell-Johnson • Justin Carter • Jason Hendrix • Adam Plumondore • Christopher Pusateri Timothy Osbey • Joseph Rahaim • Frank Hernandez • Carlos Gil • Clinton Gertson Adam Malson • Seth Trahan • Kevin Clarke • David Day • Jesse Lhotka • Jason Timmerman • John Olson • Trevor Aston • Eric Steffeney • Nicholas Olivier Alexander Crackel • Michael Deem • Daniel Gresham • Jacob Palmatier • Adam Brewer • Colby Farnan • Chassan Henry • Jason Moski • Min-su Choi • Landon

Giles • Andrew Nowacki • Danny Anderson • Richard Gienau • Julio Negron Lizbeth Robles • Azhar Ali • Wai Lwin • Robert Pugh • Michael Jones • Donald Eacho • Sean Grimes • Stephen McGowan • Adriana Salem • Juan Solorio • Wade Twyman • Seth Garceau • Andrew Bossert • Michael Franklin • Matthew Koch Donald Griffith Jr. • Nicholas Wilson • Joshua Torrence • Paul Heltzel • Ricky Kieffer Rocky Payne • Lee Lewis Jr. • Jonathan Hughes • Francisco Martinez • Paul Thomason III • Kevin Smith • Travis Bruce • Bryan Richardson • Lee Godbolt • Isiah Sinclair • Samuel Lee • Kelly Morris • Kenneth Ridgley • Eric Toth • Charles Wells Jr. • Robbie McNary • Garrywesley Rimes • Ioasa Tavae Jr. • Tenzin Dengkhim William Richardson • James Sherrill • Stephen Kennedy • Christopher Dill Jeremiah Kinchen • Javier Garcia • Glenn Watkins • Juan Venegas • Kevin Davis Casey LaWare • Tyler Dickens • Manuel Lopez III • John Miller • Michael Lindemuth James Edge • Aleina Ramirezgonzalez • Aaron Hudson • Angelo Lozada Jr. • Randy Stevens • Tromaine Toy Sr. • Joseph Knott • Steven Sirko • Sam Huff • Steven Thornton • Jacob Pfister • Kevin Wessel • Kelly Cannan • Marty Mortenson • Gavin Colburn

OPERATION ENDURING FREEDOM (AFGHANISTAN) SINCE 4/28/04

Patrick Tillman • Phillip Witkowski • Brandon Wadman • Ronald Payne Jr. • Bruce Price • Joseph Jeffries • Robert Mogensen • Daniel Eggers • Brian Ouellette

David Fraise • Russell White • Juston Thacker • Daniel McClenney • Robert McGee Julie Hickey • Juan Torres • Bobby Beasley • Craig Cherry • Daniel Galvan • Wesley Wells • Tony Olaes • Robert Goodwin • Alan Rogers • Kyle Fernandez • Brian Hobbs William Amundson Jr. • Jesse Samek • Billy Gomez • James Kearney III Michael O'Neill • Jacob Fleischer • Dale Fracker Jr. • Harley Miller Travis Grogan • Michael McMahon • Isaac Diaz • Pedro Munoz Jeremy Wright • Richard Crane • Alec Mazur • Shane Koele Norman Snyder • Brett Hershey • Michael Hiester • Michael Fiscus • Sascha Struble • Daniel Freeman • Romanes Woodard • Edward Murphy • Pendelton Sykes II • Michael Spivey • Charles Sanders Jr. • David Ayala • Clint Prather Stephen High • Chrystal Stout • David Connolly • James Lee Edwin Matoscolon • Barbaralien Banks

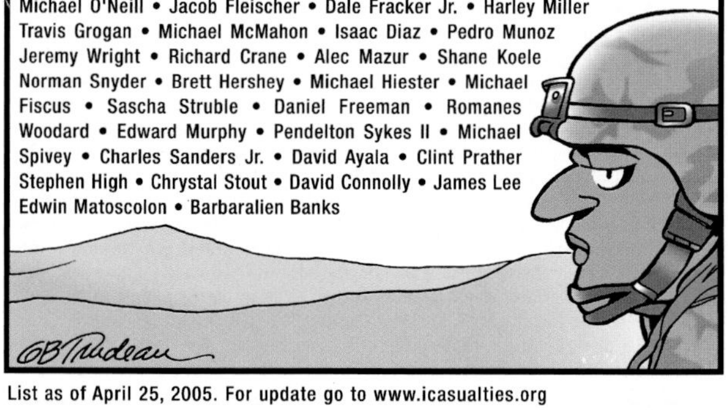
GBTrudeau

List as of April 25, 2005. For update go to www.icasualties.org

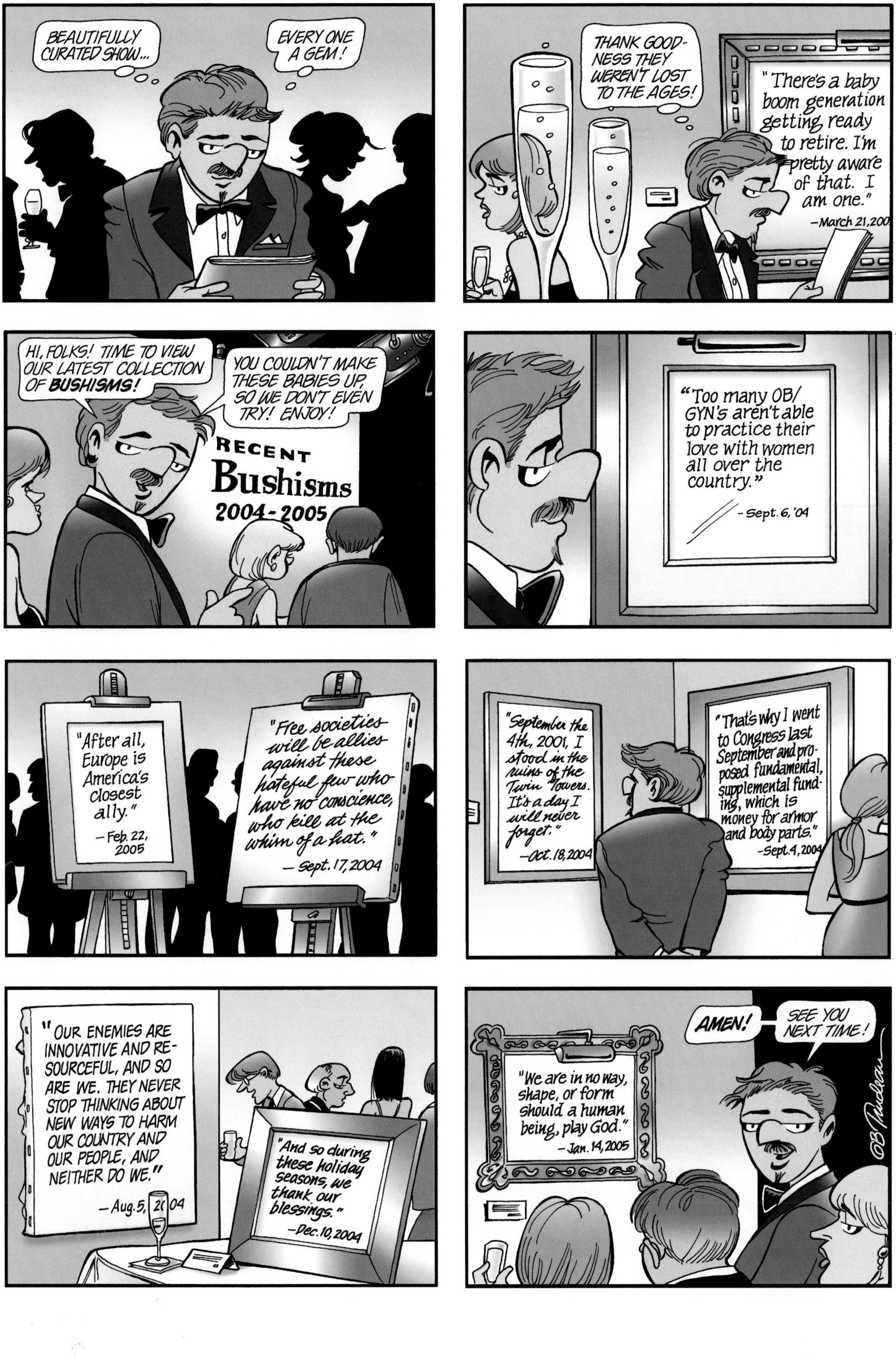
BEAUTIFULLY CURATED SHOW...
EVERY ONE A GEM!
THANK GOODNESS THEY WEREN'T LOST TO THE AGES!
"There's a baby boom generation getting ready to retire. I'm pretty aware of that. I am one."
–March 21,200
HI, FOLKS! TIME TO VIEW OUR LATEST COLLECTION OF BUSHISMS!
YOU COULDN'T MAKE THESE BABIES UP, SO WE DON'T EVEN TRY! ENJOY!
RECENT Bushisms 2004-2005
"Too many OB/GYN's aren't able to practice their love with women all over the country."
– Sept. 6, '04
"After all, Europe is America's closest ally."
– Feb. 22, 2005
"Free societies will be allies against these hateful few who have no conscience, who kill at the whim of a hat."
– Sept. 17, 2004
"September the 4th, 2001, I stood in the ruins of the Twin Towers. It's a day I will never forget."
–Oct. 18, 2004
"That's why I went to Congress last September and proposed fundamental, supplemental funding, which is money for armor and body parts."
–Sept. 4, 2004
"OUR ENEMIES ARE INNOVATIVE AND RESOURCEFUL, AND SO ARE WE. THEY NEVER STOP THINKING ABOUT NEW WAYS TO HARM OUR COUNTRY AND OUR PEOPLE, AND NEITHER DO WE."
– Aug. 5, 2004
"And so during these holiday seasons, we thank our blessings."
–Dec. 10, 2004
"We are in no way, shape, or form should a human being, play God."
– Jan. 14, 2005
AMEN!
SEE YOU NEXT TIME!

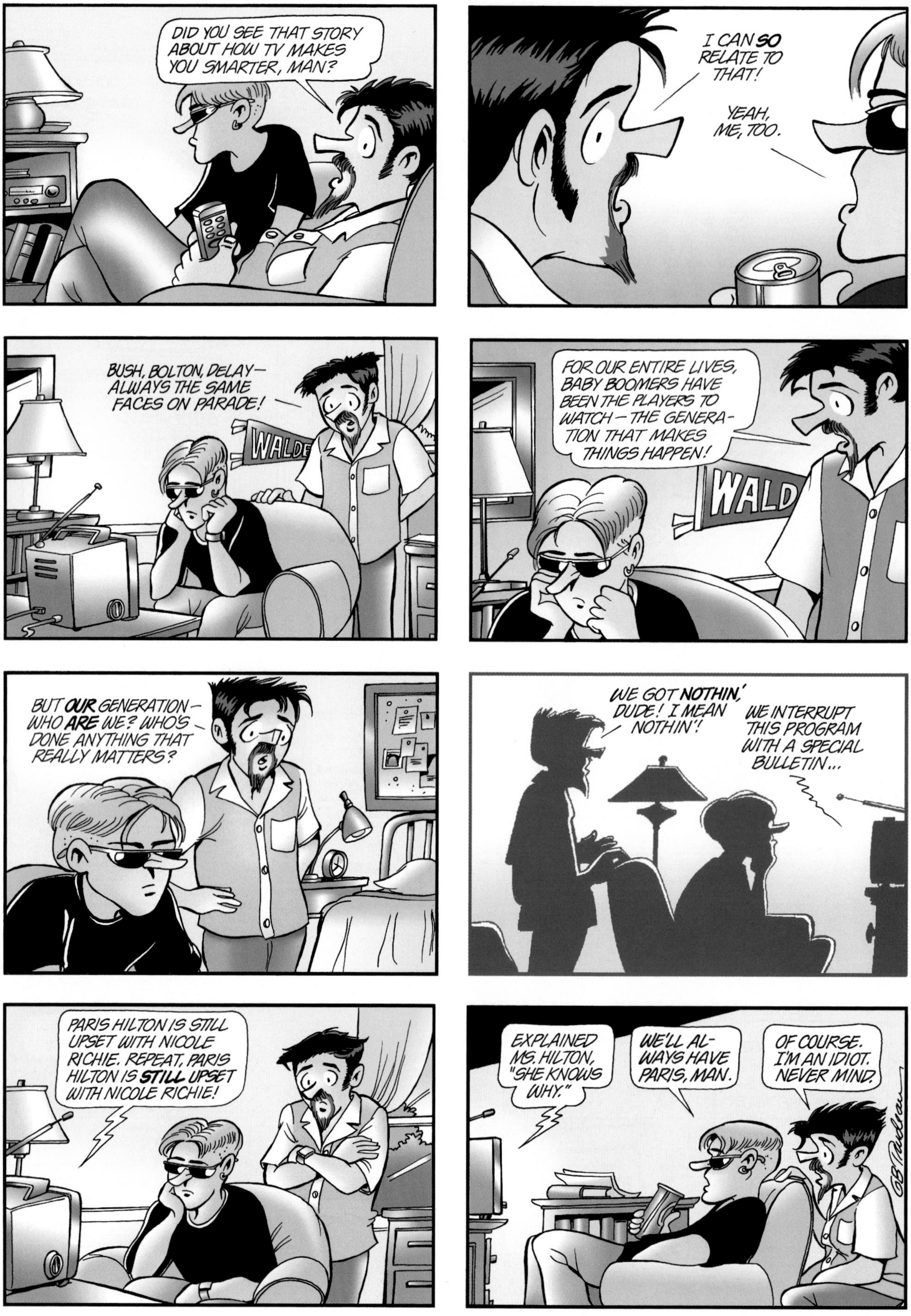
DID YOU SEE THAT STORY ABOUT HOW TV MAKES YOU SMARTER, MAN?
I CAN **SO** RELATE TO THAT!
YEAH, ME, TOO.
BUSH, BOLTON, DELAY— ALWAYS THE SAME FACES ON PARADE!
WALDE
FOR OUR ENTIRE LIVES, BABY BOOMERS HAVE BEEN THE PLAYERS TO WATCH—THE GENERATION THAT MAKES THINGS HAPPEN!
WALD
BUT **OUR** GENERATION— WHO **ARE** WE? WHO'S DONE ANYTHING THAT REALLY MATTERS?
WE GOT **NOTHIN',** DUDE! I MEAN NOTHIN'!
WE INTERRUPT THIS PROGRAM WITH A SPECIAL BULLETIN...
PARIS HILTON IS STILL UPSET WITH NICOLE RICHIE. REPEAT, PARIS HILTON IS **STILL** UPSET WITH NICOLE RICHIE!
EXPLAINED MS. HILTON, "SHE KNOWS WHY."
WE'LL ALWAYS HAVE PARIS, MAN.
OF COURSE. I'M AN IDIOT. NEVER MIND.
GBTrudeau

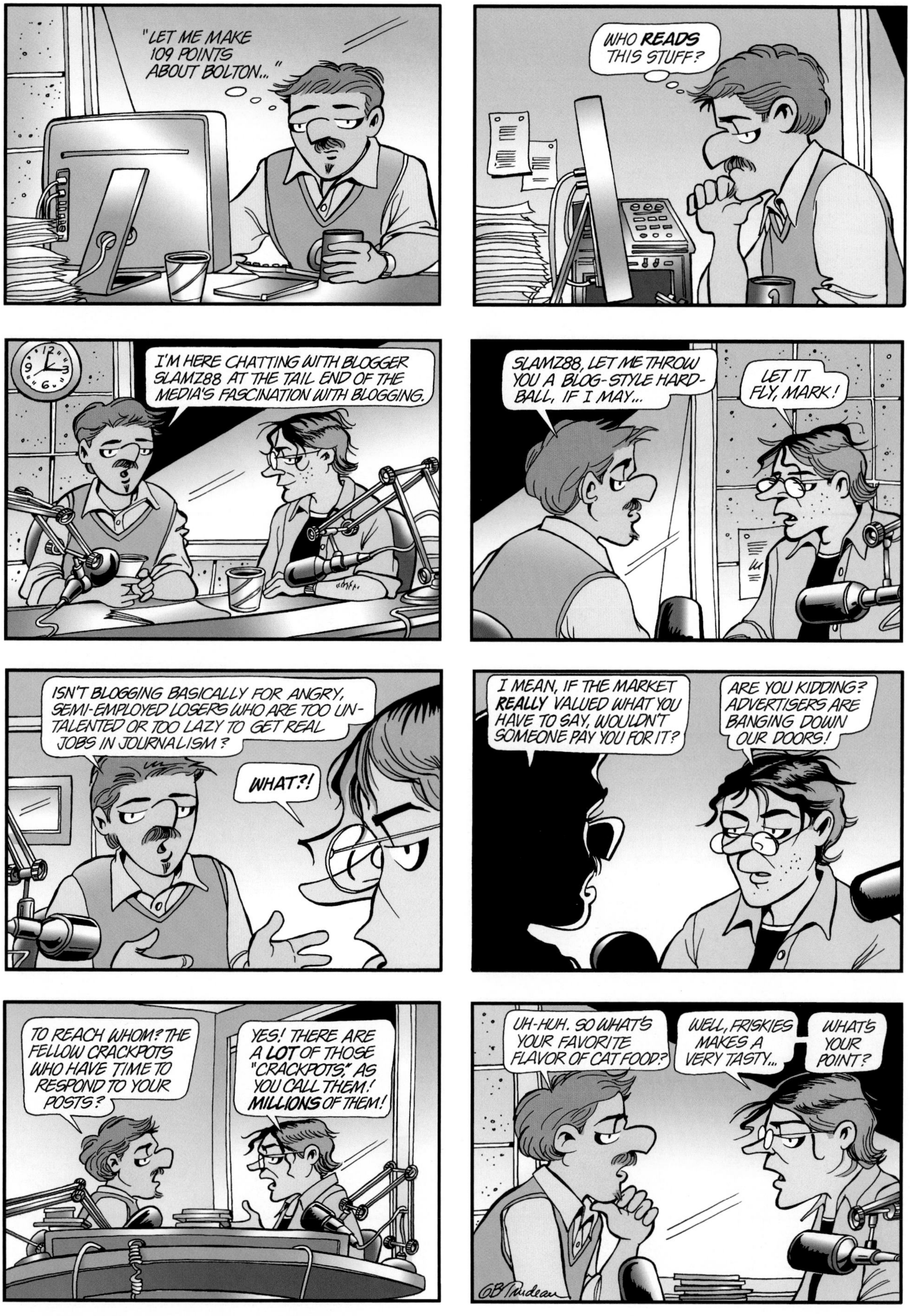
"LET ME MAKE 109 POINTS ABOUT BOLTON..."
WHO READS THIS STUFF?
I'M HERE CHATTING WITH BLOGGER SLAMZ88 AT THE TAIL END OF THE MEDIA'S FASCINATION WITH BLOGGING.
SLAMZ88, LET ME THROW YOU A BLOG-STYLE HARDBALL, IF I MAY...
LET IT FLY, MARK!
ISN'T BLOGGING BASICALLY FOR ANGRY, SEMI-EMPLOYED LOSERS WHO ARE TOO UNTALENTED OR TOO LAZY TO GET REAL JOBS IN JOURNALISM?
WHAT?!
I MEAN, IF THE MARKET REALLY VALUED WHAT YOU HAVE TO SAY, WOULDN'T SOMEONE PAY YOU FOR IT?
ARE YOU KIDDING? ADVERTISERS ARE BANGING DOWN OUR DOORS!
TO REACH WHOM? THE FELLOW CRACKPOTS WHO HAVE TIME TO RESPOND TO YOUR POSTS?
YES! THERE ARE A LOT OF THOSE "CRACKPOTS," AS YOU CALL THEM! MILLIONS OF THEM!
UH-HUH. SO WHAT'S YOUR FAVORITE FLAVOR OF CAT FOOD?
WELL, FRISKIES MAKES A VERY TASTY...
WHAT'S YOUR POINT?
©B Trudeau

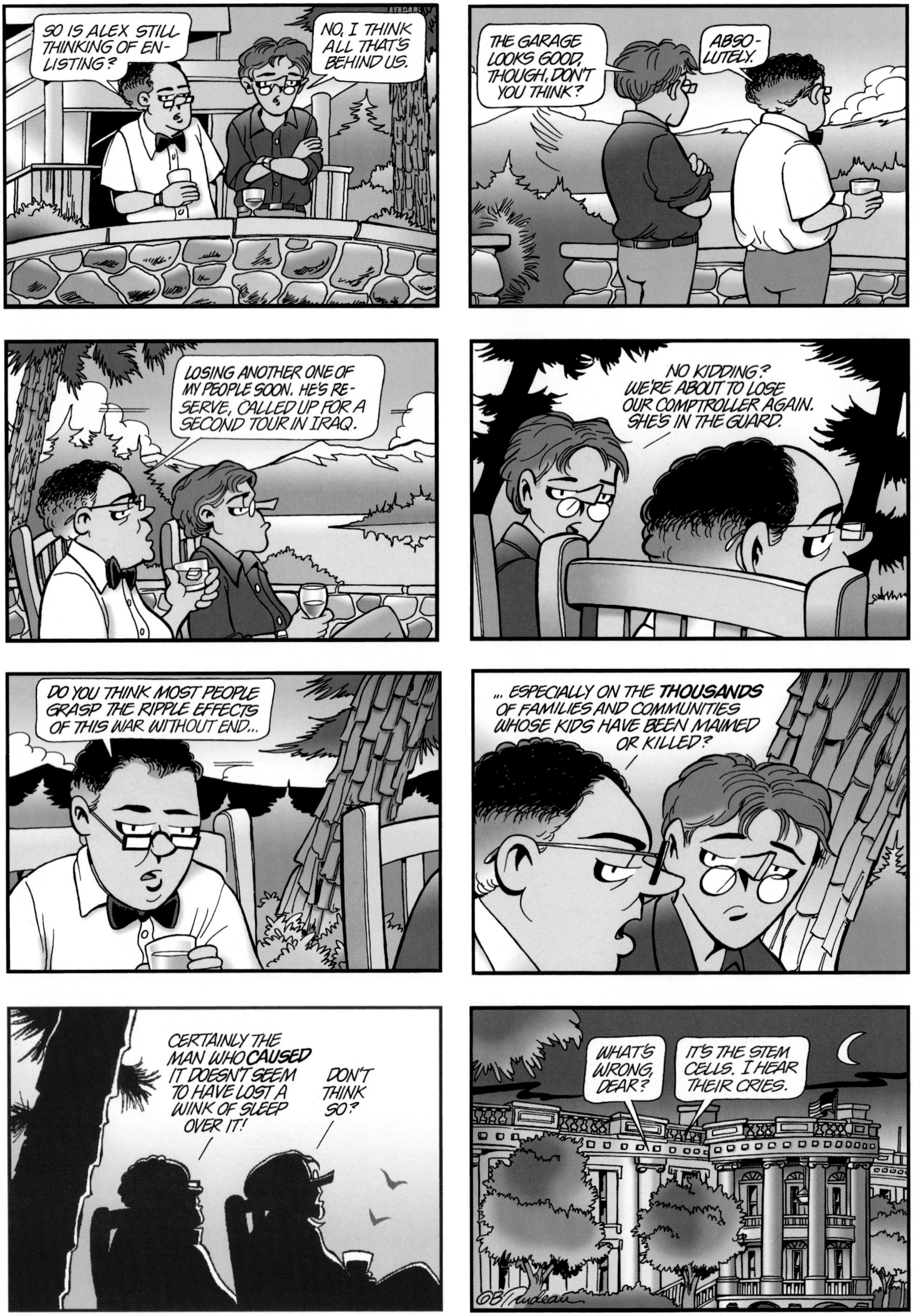
SO IS ALEX STILL THINKING OF EN-LISTING?
NO, I THINK ALL THAT'S BEHIND US.
THE GARAGE LOOKS GOOD, THOUGH, DON'T YOU THINK?
ABSO-LUTELY.
LOSING ANOTHER ONE OF MY PEOPLE SOON. HE'S RE-SERVE, CALLED UP FOR A SECOND TOUR IN IRAQ.
NO KIDDING? WE'RE ABOUT TO LOSE OUR COMPTROLLER AGAIN. SHE'S IN THE GUARD.
DO YOU THINK MOST PEOPLE GRASP THE RIPPLE EFFECTS OF THIS WAR WITHOUT END...
... ESPECIALLY ON THE **THOUSANDS** OF FAMILIES AND COMMUNITIES WHOSE KIDS HAVE BEEN MAIMED OR KILLED?
CERTAINLY THE MAN WHO **CAUSED** IT DOESN'T SEEM TO HAVE LOST A WINK OF SLEEP OVER IT!
DON'T THINK SO?
WHAT'S WRONG, DEAR?
IT'S THE STEM CELLS. I HEAR THEIR CRIES.
©B Trudeau

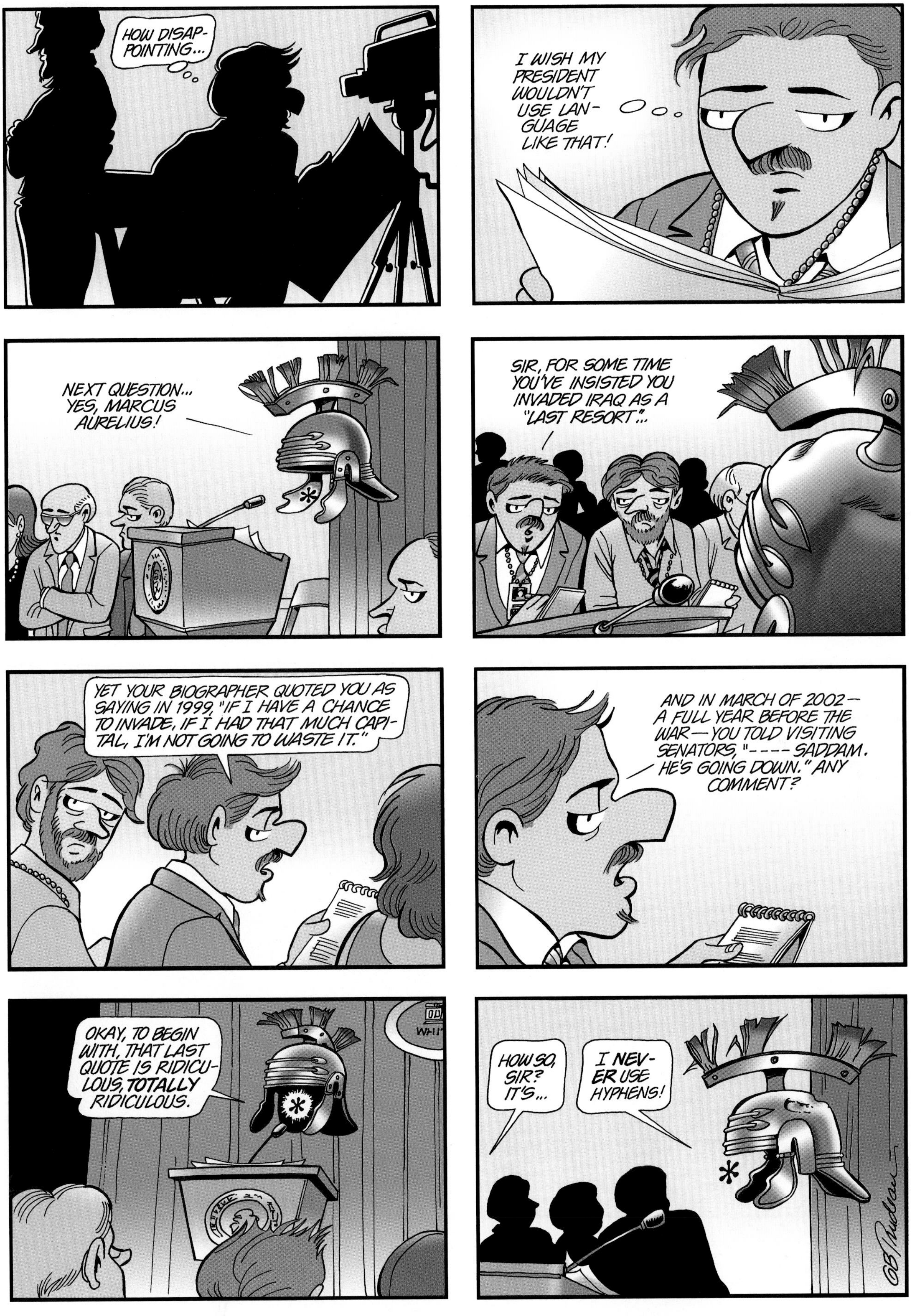
HOW DISAP-
POINTING...
I WISH MY PRESIDENT WOULDN'T USE LAN-GUAGE LIKE THAT!
NEXT QUESTION... YES, MARCUS AURELIUS!
SIR, FOR SOME TIME YOU'VE INSISTED YOU INVADED IRAQ AS A "LAST RESORT"...
YET YOUR BIOGRAPHER QUOTED YOU AS SAYING IN 1999, "IF I HAVE A CHANCE TO INVADE, IF I HAD THAT MUCH CAPI-TAL, I'M NOT GOING TO WASTE IT."
AND IN MARCH OF 2002— A FULL YEAR BEFORE THE WAR—YOU TOLD VISITING SENATORS, "---- SADDAM. HE'S GOING DOWN." ANY COMMENT?
OKAY, TO BEGIN WITH, THAT LAST QUOTE IS RIDICU-LOUS, TOTALLY RIDICULOUS.
HOW SO, SIR? IT'S...
I NEV-ER USE HYPHENS!

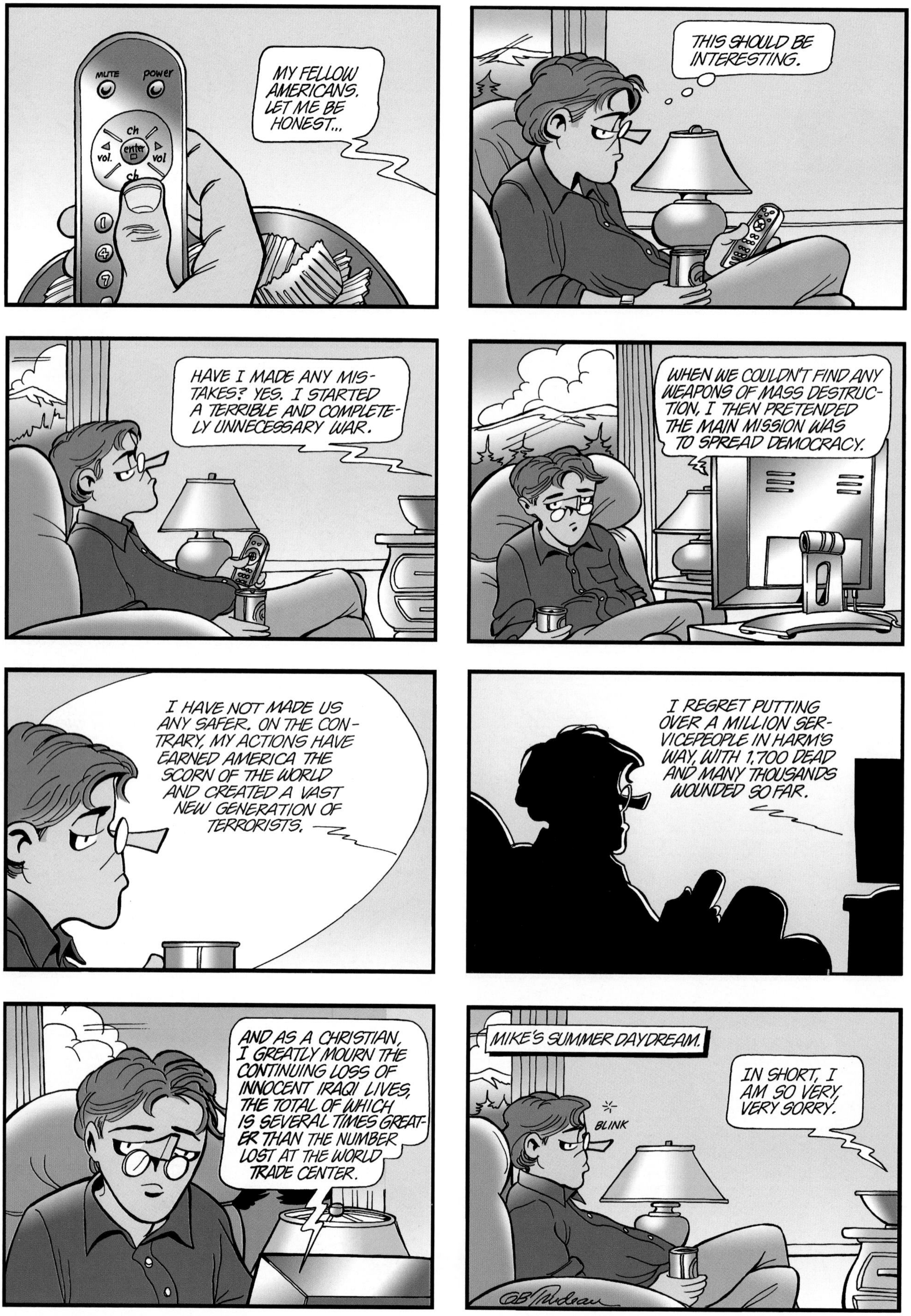
MUTE
power
ch
enter
vol.
vol
ch
MY FELLOW AMERICANS. LET ME BE HONEST...
THIS SHOULD BE INTERESTING.
HAVE I MADE ANY MISTAKES? YES. I STARTED A TERRIBLE AND COMPLETELY UNNECESSARY WAR.
WHEN WE COULDN'T FIND ANY WEAPONS OF MASS DESTRUCTION, I THEN PRETENDED THE MAIN MISSION WAS TO SPREAD DEMOCRACY.
I HAVE NOT MADE US ANY SAFER. ON THE CONTRARY, MY ACTIONS HAVE EARNED AMERICA THE SCORN OF THE WORLD AND CREATED A VAST NEW GENERATION OF TERRORISTS.
I REGRET PUTTING OVER A MILLION SERVICEPEOPLE IN HARM'S WAY, WITH 1,700 DEAD AND MANY THOUSANDS WOUNDED SO FAR.
AND AS A CHRISTIAN, I GREATLY MOURN THE CONTINUING LOSS OF INNOCENT IRAQI LIVES, THE TOTAL OF WHICH IS SEVERAL TIMES GREATER THAN THE NUMBER LOST AT THE WORLD TRADE CENTER.
MIKE'S SUMMER DAYDREAM.
BLINK
IN SHORT, I AM SO VERY, VERY SORRY.
GB Trudeau

THE NIGHTMARE IS OVER...

ADIOS, LAWSUIT!

HI, FOLKS! MR. BUTTS HERE, AND BOY, AM *I* RELIEVED!

CHECK OUT THE SMILE IF YOU DON'T BELIEVE ME, OKAY?

WHY THE HAPPY FACE? WELL, FOR FIVE YEARS BIG TOBACCO HAS LOOKED ON WITH ENVY AS THE ADMINISTRATION HAS GOTTEN INTO BED WITH BIG OIL, BIG STEEL, BIG SUGAR AND OTHERS!

HEY, WHAT ABOUT *US*, WE WONDERED!

WE SHOULDN'T HAVE! LAST MONTH, OUR GOOD FRIENDS AT THE JUSTICE DEPARTMENT OVERRULED THEIR OWN LAWYERS...

...REDUCING A POTENTIAL $130 BILLION INDUSTRY SETTLEMENT TO A *VERY* AFFORDABLE $14 BILLION!

$130 BILLION

$14

AND HERE'S THE BEAUTY PART— WE DIDN'T EVEN HAVE TO NEGOTIATE!

HOW CAN WE *EVER* REPAY THE ADMINISTRATION FOR ITS INTERFERENCE? WE CAN'T, REALLY...

SO, THEY'LL JUST HAVE TO SETTLE FOR A BIG, WET ONE FROM ALL OF US AT BIG TOBACCO!

MAAH!

SMACK!

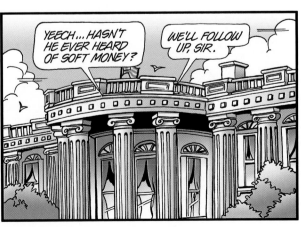

YEECH...HASN'T HE EVER HEARD OF SOFT MONEY?

WE'LL FOLLOW UP, SIR.

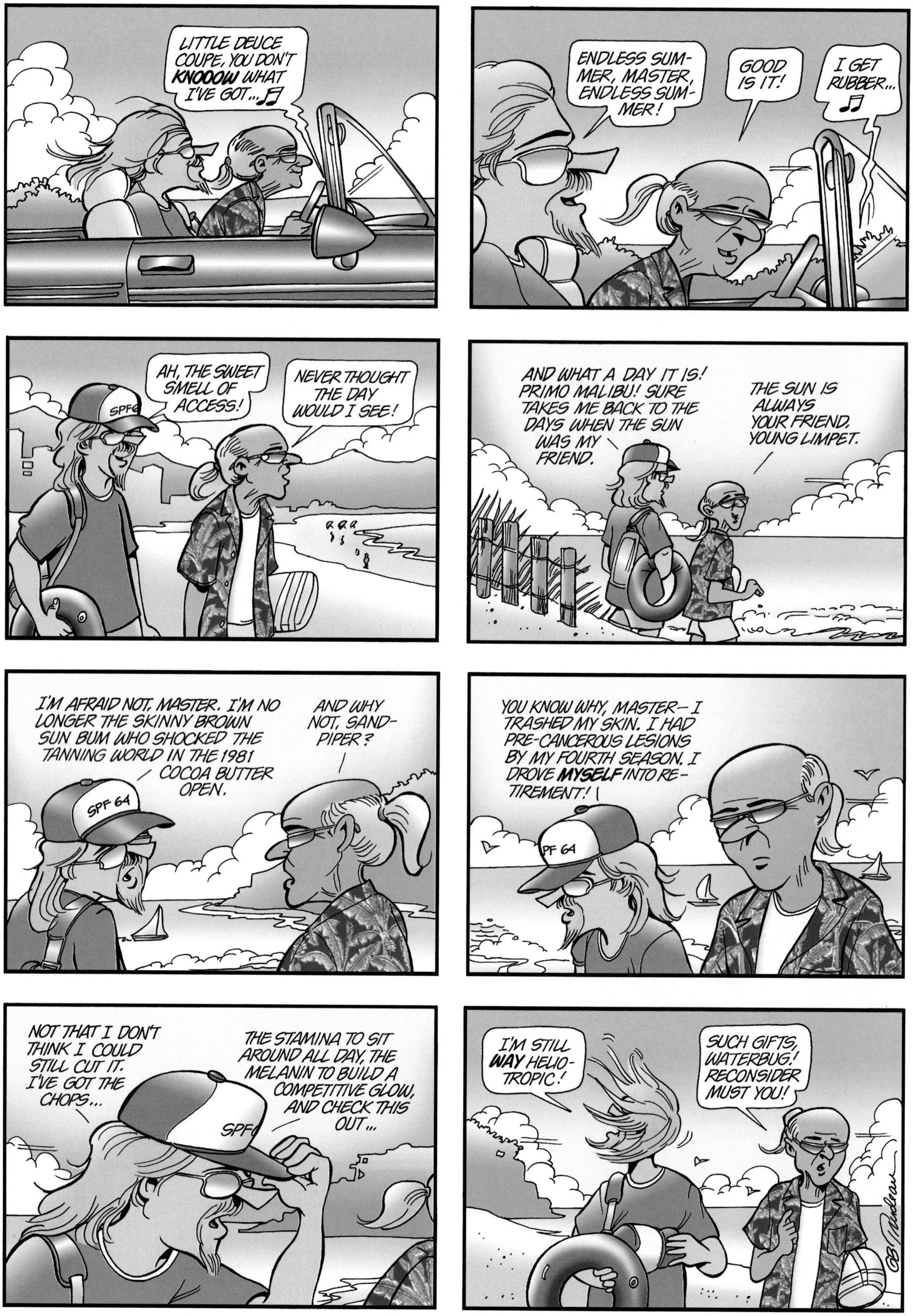
LITTLE DEUCE COUPE, YOU DON'T KNOOOW WHAT I'VE GOT...
ENDLESS SUMMER, MASTER, ENDLESS SUMMER!
GOOD IS IT!
I GET RUBBER...
AH, THE SWEET SMELL OF ACCESS!
NEVER THOUGHT THE DAY WOULD I SEE!
AND WHAT A DAY IT IS! PRIMO MALIBU! SURE TAKES ME BACK TO THE DAYS WHEN THE SUN WAS MY FRIEND.
THE SUN IS ALWAYS YOUR FRIEND, YOUNG LIMPET.
AND WHY NOT, SANDPIPER?
I'M AFRAID NOT, MASTER. I'M NO LONGER THE SKINNY BROWN SUN BUM WHO SHOCKED THE TANNING WORLD IN THE 1981 COCOA BUTTER OPEN.
YOU KNOW WHY, MASTER— I TRASHED MY SKIN. I HAD PRE-CANCEROUS LESIONS BY MY FOURTH SEASON. I DROVE MYSELF INTO RETIREMENT!
NOT THAT I DON'T THINK I COULD STILL CUT IT. I'VE GOT THE CHOPS...
THE STAMINA TO SIT AROUND ALL DAY, THE MELANIN TO BUILD A COMPETITIVE GLOW, AND CHECK THIS OUT...
I'M STILL WAY HELIOTROPIC!
SUCH GIFTS, WATERBUG! RECONSIDER MUST YOU!

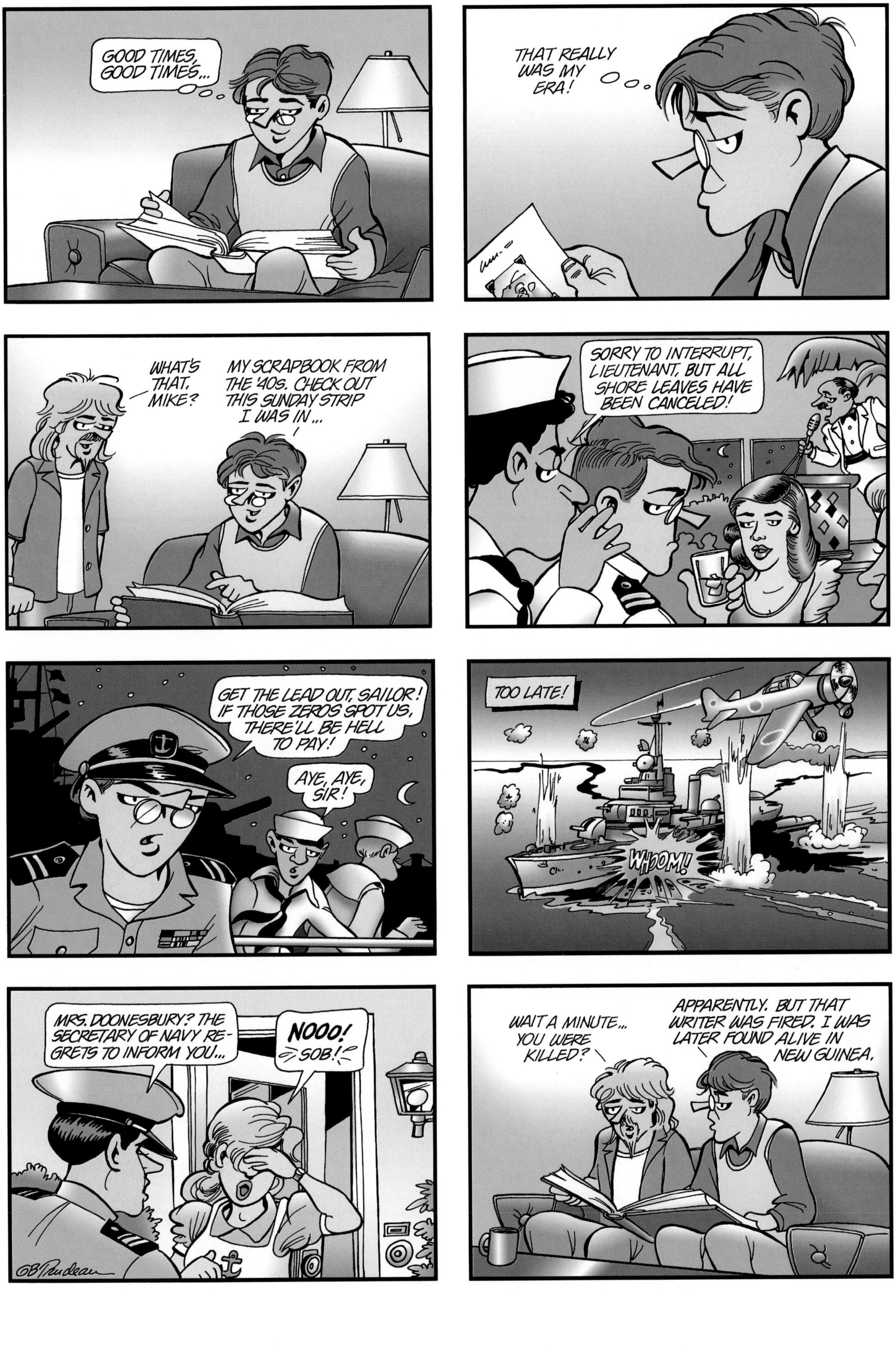
GOOD TIMES, GOOD TIMES...
THAT REALLY WAS MY ERA!
WHAT'S THAT, MIKE?
MY SCRAPBOOK FROM THE '40S. CHECK OUT THIS SUNDAY STRIP I WAS IN...
SORRY TO INTERRUPT, LIEUTENANT, BUT ALL SHORE LEAVES HAVE BEEN CANCELED!
GET THE LEAD OUT, SAILOR! IF THOSE ZEROS SPOT US, THERE'LL BE HELL TO PAY!
AYE, AYE, SIR!
TOO LATE!
WHOOM!
MRS. DOONESBURY? THE SECRETARY OF NAVY REGRETS TO INFORM YOU...
NOOO!
SOB!
GB Trudeau
WAIT A MINUTE... YOU WERE KILLED?
APPARENTLY. BUT THAT WRITER WAS FIRED. I WAS LATER FOUND ALIVE IN NEW GUINEA.

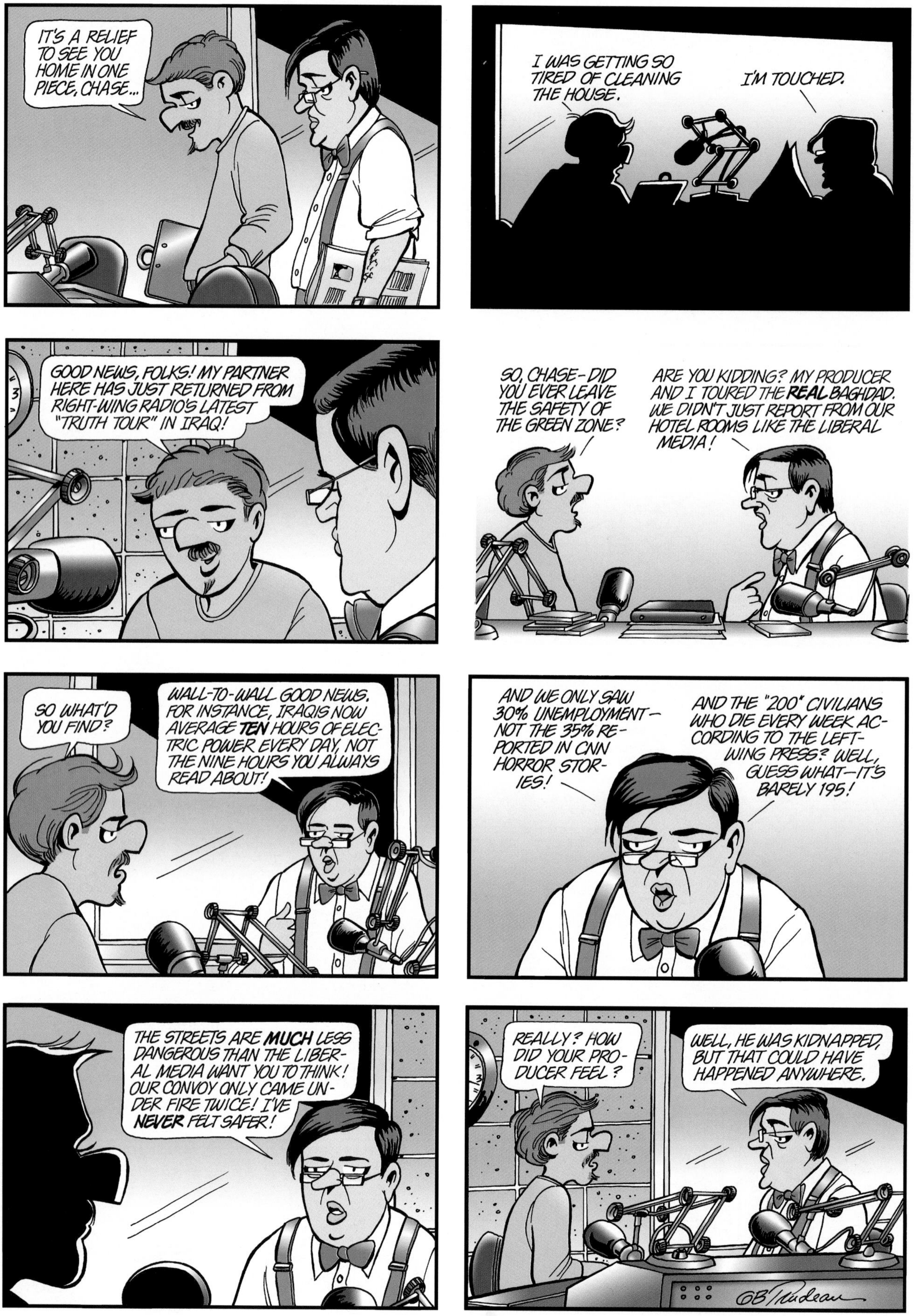
IT'S A RELIEF TO SEE YOU HOME IN ONE PIECE, CHASE...
I WAS GETTING SO TIRED OF CLEANING THE HOUSE.
I'M TOUCHED.
GOOD NEWS, FOLKS! MY PARTNER HERE HAS JUST RETURNED FROM RIGHT-WING RADIO'S LATEST "TRUTH TOUR" IN IRAQ!
SO, CHASE-DID YOU EVER LEAVE THE SAFETY OF THE GREEN ZONE?
ARE YOU KIDDING? MY PRODUCER AND I TOURED THE **REAL** BAGHDAD. WE DIDN'T JUST REPORT FROM OUR HOTEL ROOMS LIKE THE LIBERAL MEDIA!
SO WHAT'D YOU FIND?
WALL-TO-WALL GOOD NEWS. FOR INSTANCE, IRAQIS NOW AVERAGE **TEN** HOURS OF ELECTRIC POWER EVERY DAY, NOT THE NINE HOURS YOU ALWAYS READ ABOUT!
AND WE ONLY SAW 30% UNEMPLOYMENT—NOT THE 35% REPORTED IN CNN HORROR STORIES!
AND THE "200" CIVILIANS WHO DIE EVERY WEEK ACCORDING TO THE LEFT-WING PRESS? WELL, GUESS WHAT—IT'S BARELY 195!
THE STREETS ARE **MUCH** LESS DANGEROUS THAN THE LIBERAL MEDIA WANT YOU TO THINK! OUR CONVOY ONLY CAME UNDER FIRE TWICE! I'VE **NEVER** FELT SAFER!
REALLY? HOW DID YOUR PRODUCER FEEL?
WELL, HE WAS KIDNAPPED, BUT THAT COULD HAVE HAPPENED ANYWHERE.

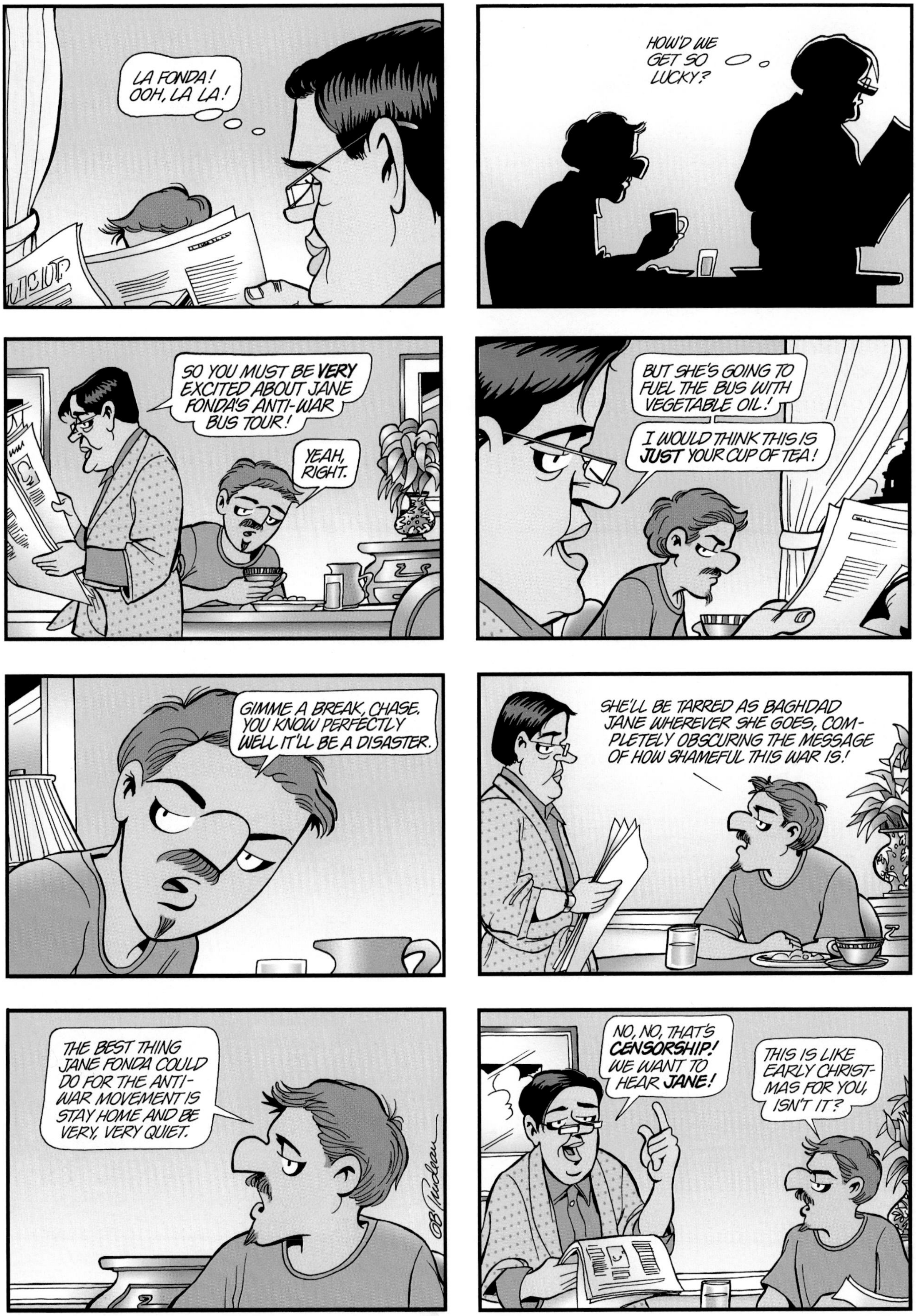
LA FONDA! OOH, LA LA!
HOW'D WE GET SO LUCKY?
SO YOU MUST BE **VERY** EXCITED ABOUT JANE FONDA'S ANTI-WAR BUS TOUR!
YEAH, RIGHT.
BUT SHE'S GOING TO FUEL THE BUS WITH VEGETABLE OIL!
I WOULD THINK THIS IS **JUST** YOUR CUP OF TEA!
GIMME A BREAK, CHASE. YOU KNOW PERFECTLY WELL IT'LL BE A DISASTER.
SHE'LL BE TARRED AS BAGHDAD JANE WHEREVER SHE GOES, COMPLETELY OBSCURING THE MESSAGE OF HOW SHAMEFUL THIS WAR IS!
THE BEST THING JANE FONDA COULD DO FOR THE ANTI-WAR MOVEMENT IS STAY HOME AND BE VERY, VERY QUIET.
NO, NO, THAT'S **CENSORSHIP!** WE WANT TO HEAR **JANE!**
THIS IS LIKE EARLY CHRISTMAS FOR YOU, ISN'T IT?

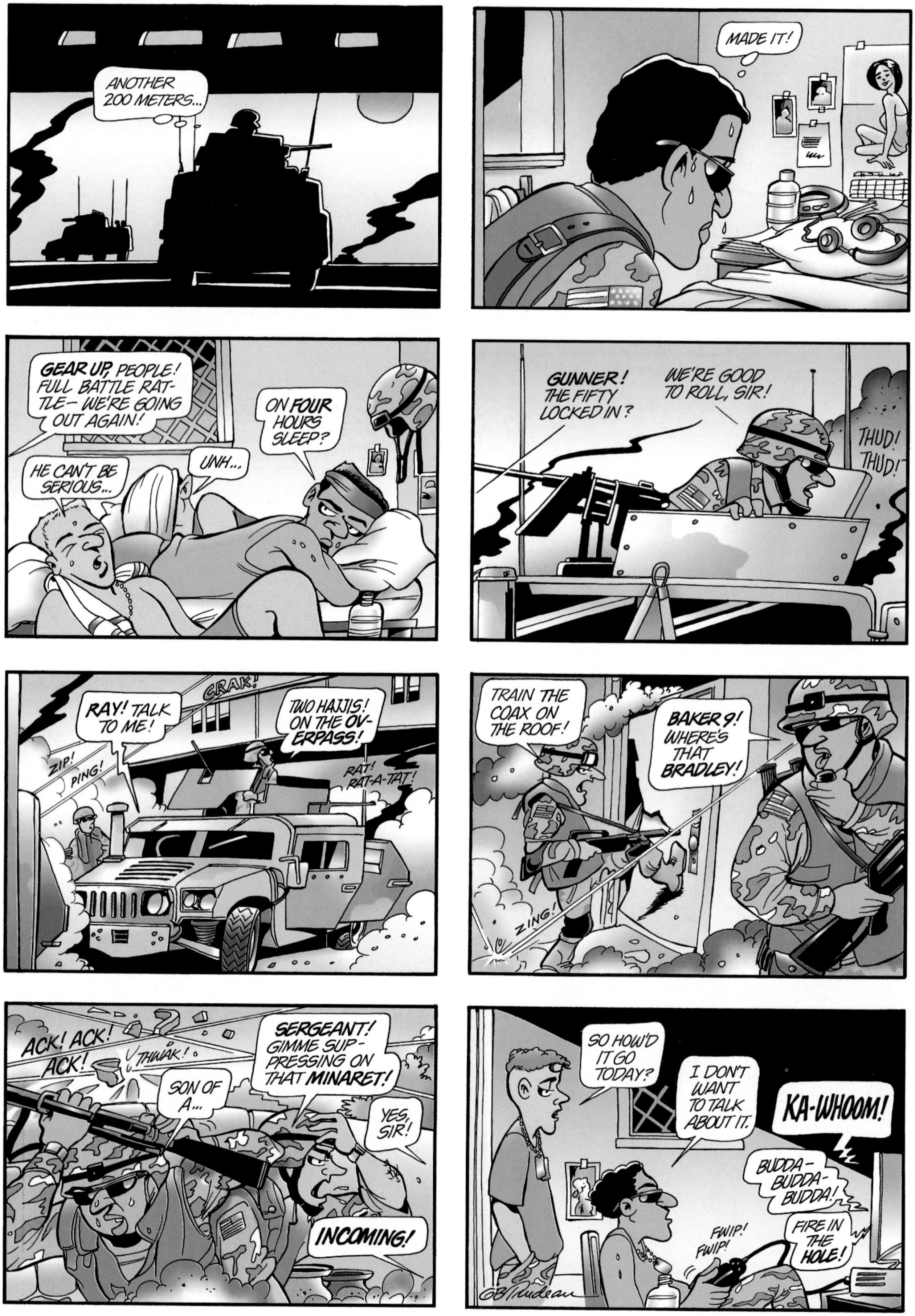
ANOTHER 200 METERS...
MADE IT!
GEAR UP, PEOPLE! FULL BATTLE RAT-TLE— WE'RE GOING OUT AGAIN!
HE CAN'T BE SERIOUS...
UNH...
ON FOUR HOURS SLEEP?
GUNNER! THE FIFTY LOCKED IN?
WE'RE GOOD TO ROLL, SIR!
THUD! THUD!
CRAK!
RAY! TALK TO ME!
TWO HAJJIS! ON THE OV-ERPASS!
ZIP!
PING!
RAT! RAT-A-TAT!
TRAIN THE COAX ON THE ROOF!
BAKER 9! WHERE'S THAT BRADLEY!
ZING!
ACK! ACK! ACK!
THWAK!
SERGEANT! GIMME SUP-PRESSING ON THAT MINARET!
SON OF A...
YES, SIR!
INCOMING!
SO HOW'D IT GO TODAY?
I DON'T WANT TO TALK ABOUT IT.
KA-WHOOM!
BUDDA-BUDDA-BUDDA!
FWIP! FWIP!
FIRE IN THE HOLE!
GBTrudeau

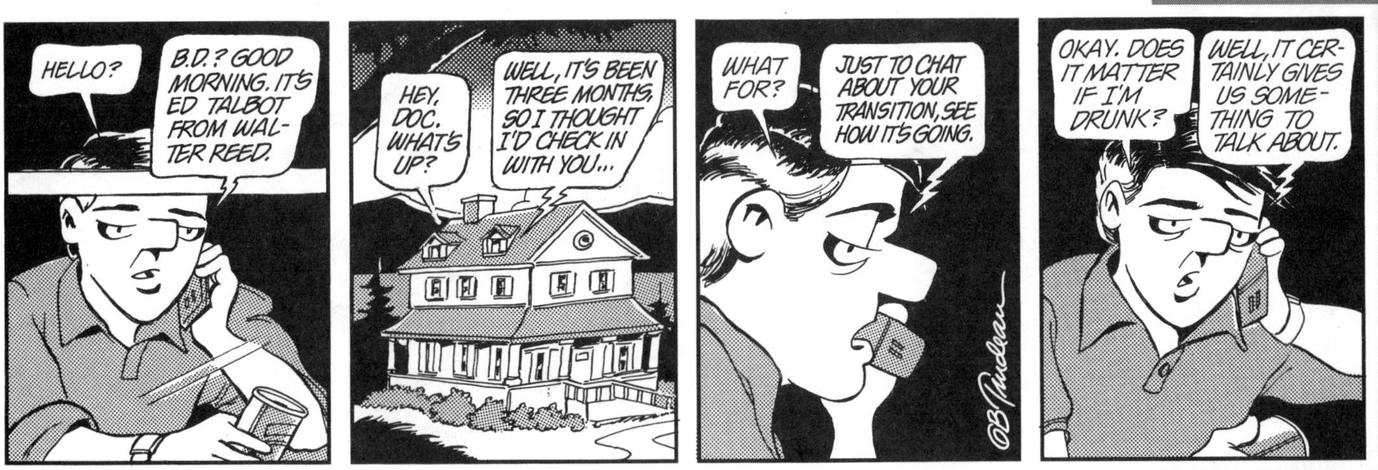
HELLO?
B.D.? GOOD MORNING. IT'S ED TALBOT FROM WALTER REED.
HEY, DOC. WHAT'S UP?
WELL, IT'S BEEN THREE MONTHS, SO I THOUGHT I'D CHECK IN WITH YOU...
WHAT FOR?
JUST TO CHAT ABOUT YOUR TRANSITION, SEE HOW IT'S GOING.
OKAY. DOES IT MATTER IF I'M DRUNK?
WELL, IT CERTAINLY GIVES US SOMETHING TO TALK ABOUT.

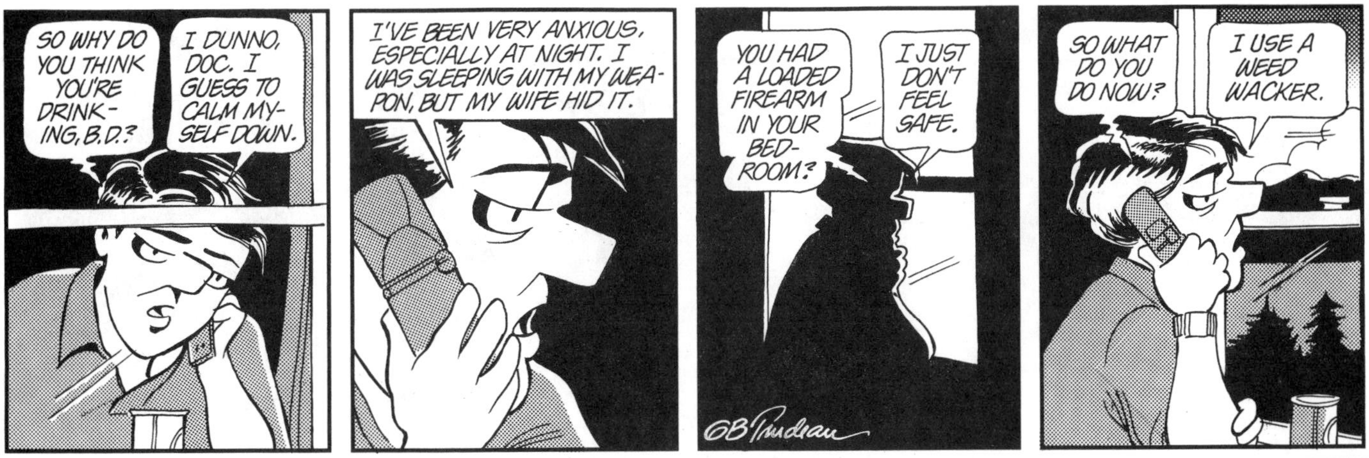
SO WHY DO YOU THINK YOU'RE DRINKING, B.D.?
I DUNNO, DOC. I GUESS TO CALM MYSELF DOWN.
I'VE BEEN VERY ANXIOUS, ESPECIALLY AT NIGHT. I WAS SLEEPING WITH MY WEAPON, BUT MY WIFE HID IT.
YOU HAD A LOADED FIREARM IN YOUR BEDROOM?
I JUST DON'T FEEL SAFE.
SO WHAT DO YOU DO NOW?
I USE A WEED WACKER.

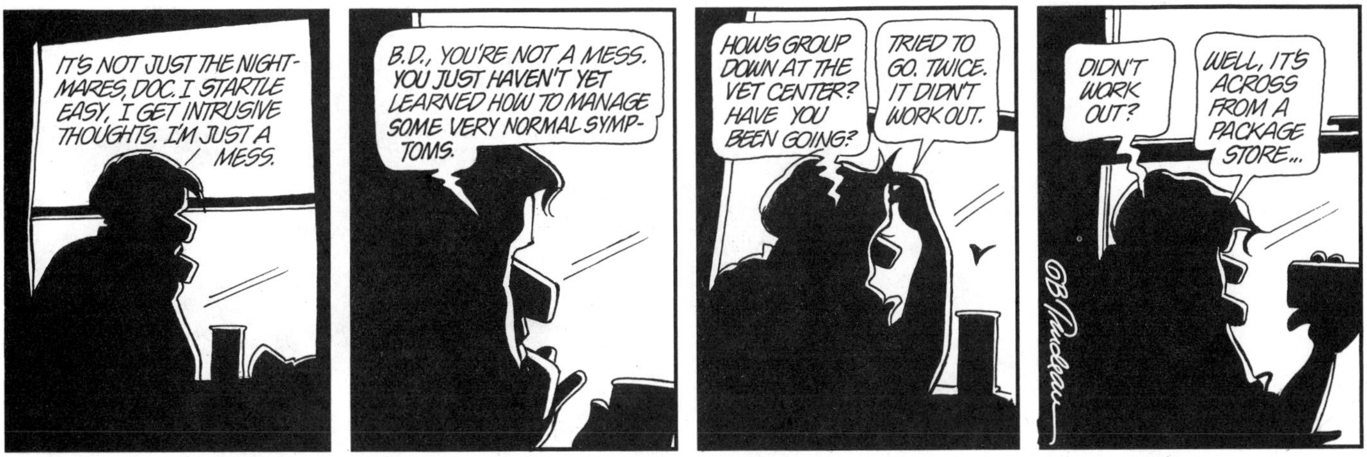
IT'S NOT JUST THE NIGHTMARES, DOC. I STARTLE EASY, I GET INTRUSIVE THOUGHTS. I'M JUST A MESS.
B.D., YOU'RE NOT A MESS. YOU JUST HAVEN'T YET LEARNED HOW TO MANAGE SOME VERY NORMAL SYMPTOMS.
HOW'S GROUP DOWN AT THE VET CENTER? HAVE YOU BEEN GOING?
TRIED TO GO. TWICE. IT DIDN'T WORK OUT.
DIDN'T WORK OUT?
WELL, IT'S ACROSS FROM A PACKAGE STORE...

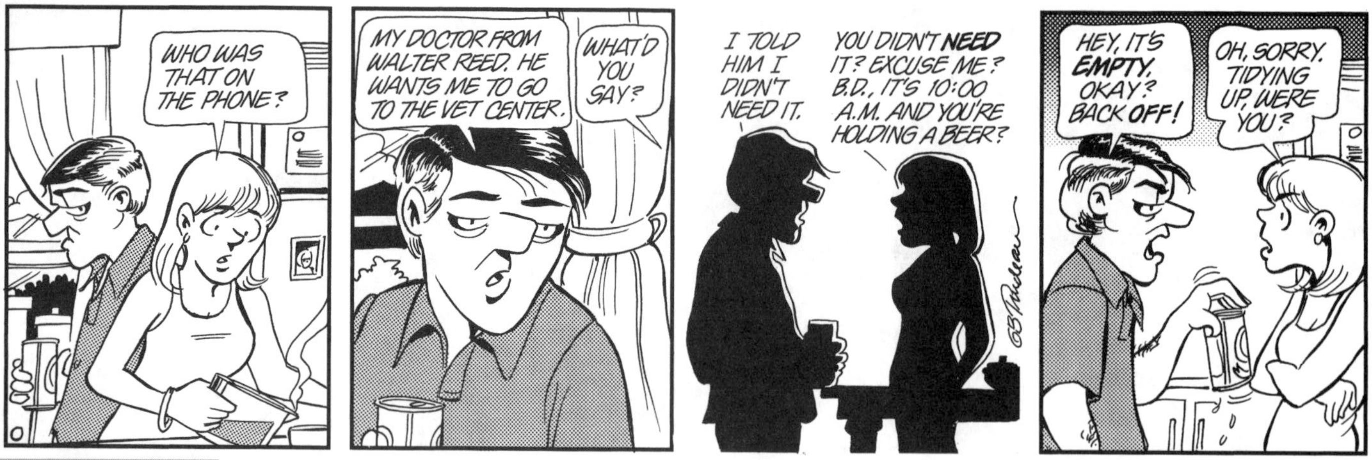
WHO WAS THAT ON THE PHONE?
MY DOCTOR FROM WALTER REED. HE WANTS ME TO GO TO THE VET CENTER.
WHAT'D YOU SAY?
I TOLD HIM I DIDN'T NEED IT.
YOU DIDN'T **NEED** IT? EXCUSE ME? B.D., IT'S 10:00 A.M. AND YOU'RE HOLDING A BEER?
HEY, IT'S **EMPTY**, OKAY? BACK **OFF!**
OH, SORRY. TIDYING UP, WERE YOU?

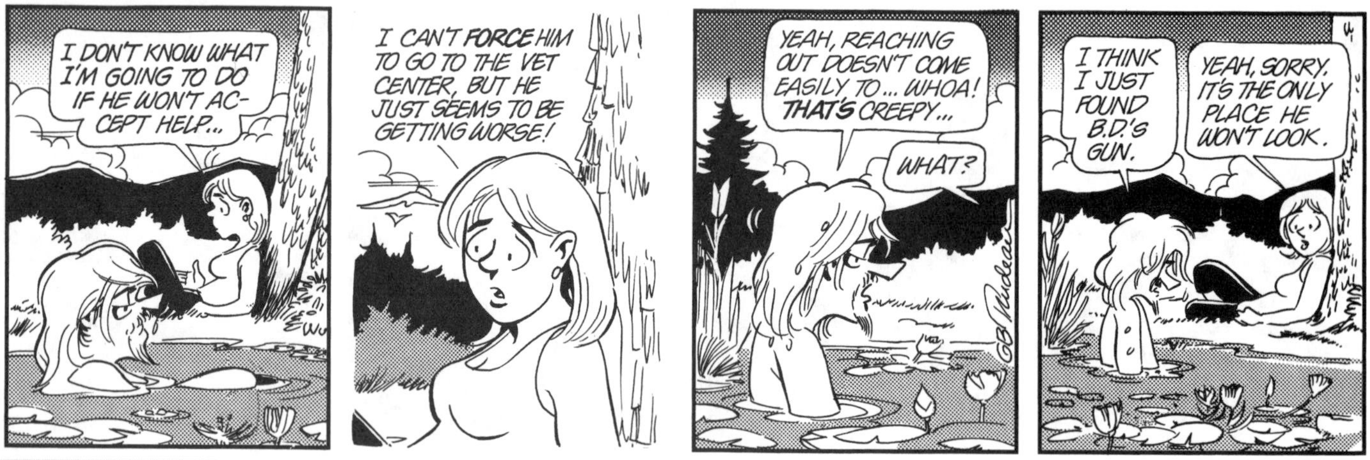
I DON'T KNOW WHAT I'M GOING TO DO IF HE WON'T ACCEPT HELP...
I CAN'T **FORCE** HIM TO GO TO THE VET CENTER, BUT HE JUST SEEMS TO BE GETTING WORSE!
YEAH, REACHING OUT DOESN'T COME EASILY TO ... WHOA! **THAT'S** CREEPY...
WHAT?
I THINK I JUST FOUND B.D.'S GUN.
YEAH, SORRY. IT'S THE ONLY PLACE HE WON'T LOOK.

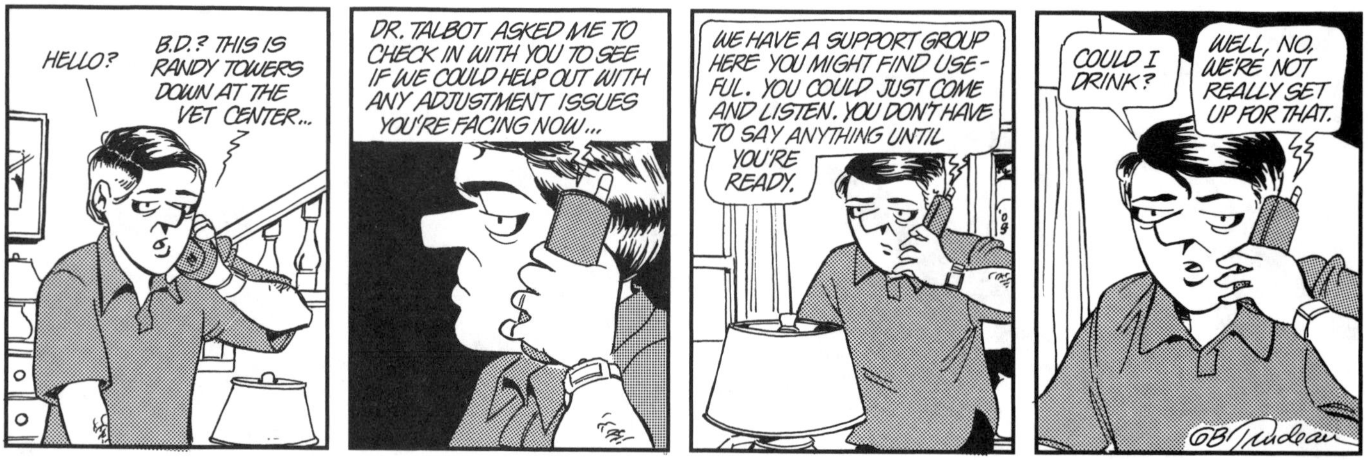
HELLO?
B.D.? THIS IS RANDY TOWERS DOWN AT THE VET CENTER...
DR. TALBOT ASKED ME TO CHECK IN WITH YOU TO SEE IF WE COULD HELP OUT WITH ANY ADJUSTMENT ISSUES YOU'RE FACING NOW...
WE HAVE A SUPPORT GROUP HERE YOU MIGHT FIND USEFUL. YOU COULD JUST COME AND LISTEN. YOU DON'T HAVE TO SAY ANYTHING UNTIL YOU'RE READY.
COULD I DRINK?
WELL, NO. WE'RE NOT REALLY SET UP FOR THAT.

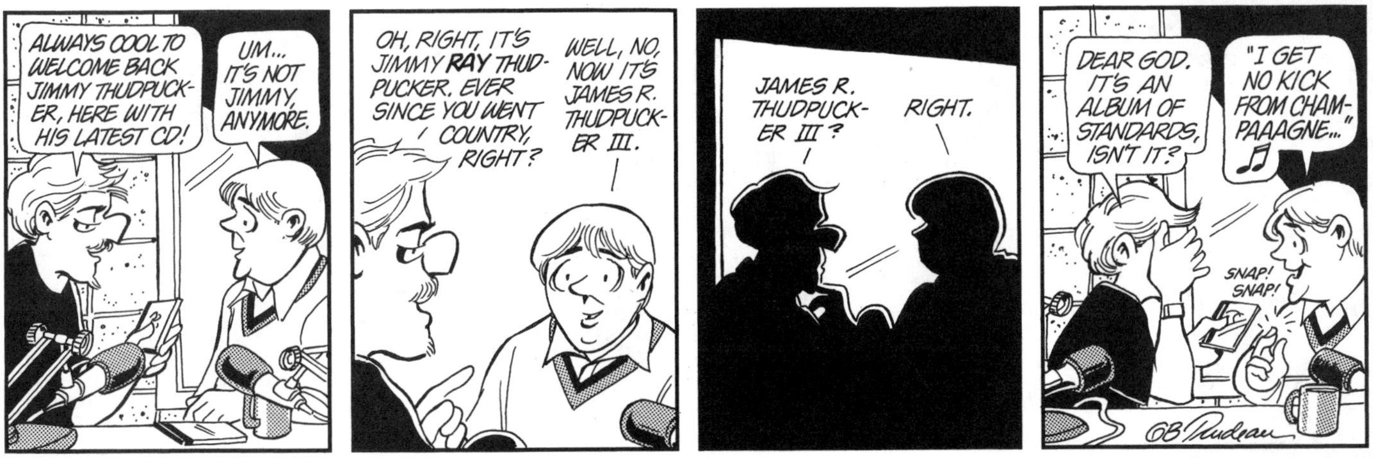
ALWAYS COOL TO WELCOME BACK JIMMY THUDPUCKER, HERE WITH HIS LATEST CD!
UM... IT'S NOT JIMMY, ANYMORE.
OH, RIGHT, IT'S JIMMY RAY THUDPUCKER. EVER SINCE YOU WENT COUNTRY, RIGHT?
WELL, NO, NOW IT'S JAMES R. THUDPUCKER III.
JAMES R. THUDPUCKER III?
RIGHT.
DEAR GOD. IT'S AN ALBUM OF STANDARDS, ISN'T IT?
"I GET NO KICK FROM CHAMPAAAGNE..."
SNAP! SNAP!

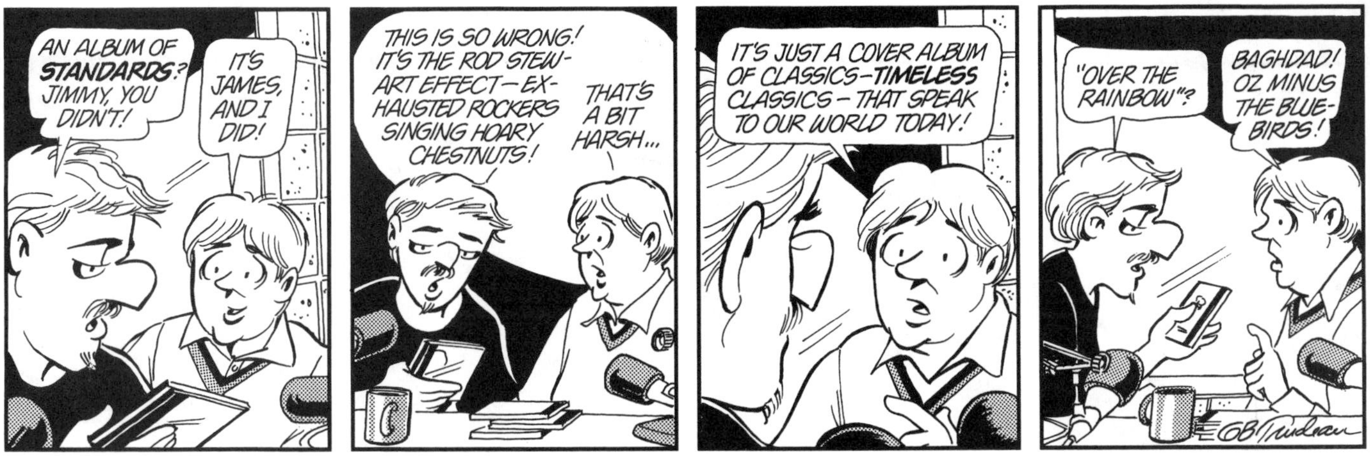
AN ALBUM OF STANDARDS? JIMMY, YOU DIDN'T!
IT'S JAMES, AND I DID!
THIS IS SO WRONG! IT'S THE ROD STEWART EFFECT—EXHAUSTED ROCKERS SINGING HOARY CHESTNUTS!
THAT'S A BIT HARSH...
IT'S JUST A COVER ALBUM OF CLASSICS—TIMELESS CLASSICS—THAT SPEAK TO OUR WORLD TODAY!
"OVER THE RAINBOW"?
BAGHDAD! OZ MINUS THE BLUEBIRDS!

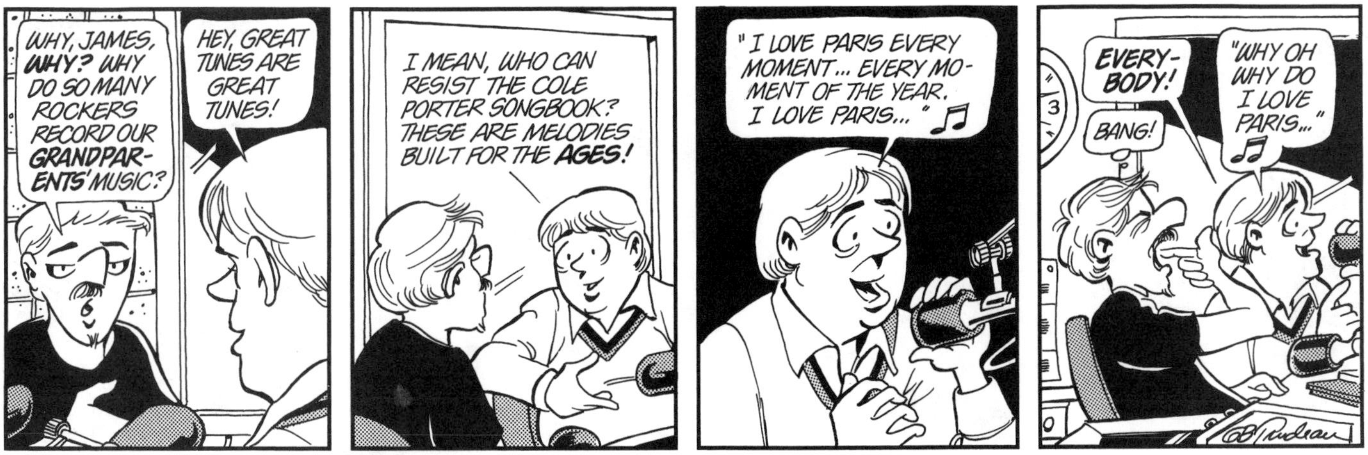
WHY, JAMES, WHY? WHY DO SO MANY ROCKERS RECORD OUR GRANDPARENTS' MUSIC?
HEY, GREAT TUNES ARE GREAT TUNES!
I MEAN, WHO CAN RESIST THE COLE PORTER SONGBOOK? THESE ARE MELODIES BUILT FOR THE AGES!
"I LOVE PARIS EVERY MOMENT... EVERY MOMENT OF THE YEAR. I LOVE PARIS..."
EVERYBODY!
BANG!
"WHY OH WHY DO I LOVE PARIS..."

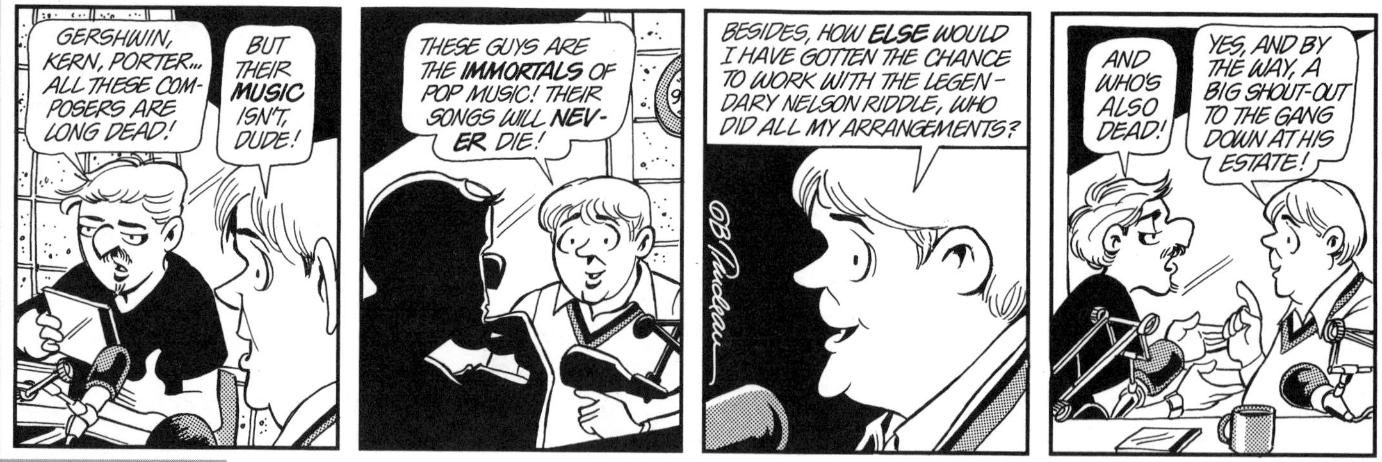
GERSHWIN, KERN, PORTER... ALL THESE COMPOSERS ARE LONG DEAD!
BUT THEIR MUSIC ISN'T, DUDE!
THESE GUYS ARE THE IMMORTALS OF POP MUSIC! THEIR SONGS WILL NEVER DIE!
BESIDES, HOW ELSE WOULD I HAVE GOTTEN THE CHANCE TO WORK WITH THE LEGENDARY NELSON RIDDLE, WHO DID ALL MY ARRANGEMENTS?
AND WHO'S ALSO DEAD!
YES, AND BY THE WAY, A BIG SHOUT-OUT TO THE GANG DOWN AT HIS ESTATE!

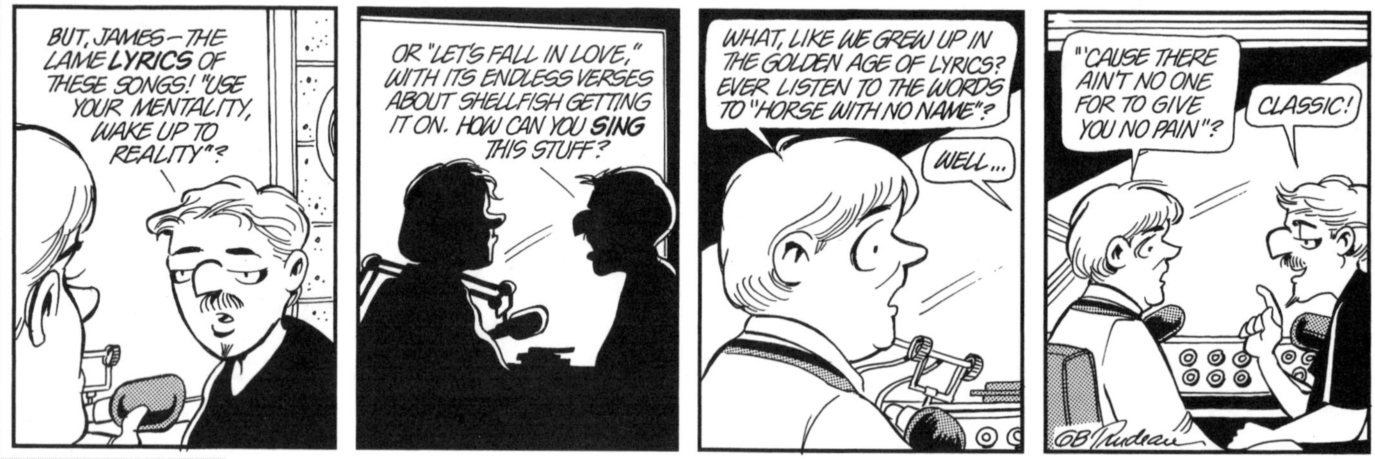
BUT, JAMES—THE LAME LYRICS OF THESE SONGS! "USE YOUR MENTALITY, WAKE UP TO REALITY"?
OR "LET'S FALL IN LOVE," WITH ITS ENDLESS VERSES ABOUT SHELLFISH GETTING IT ON. HOW CAN YOU SING THIS STUFF?
WHAT, LIKE WE GREW UP IN THE GOLDEN AGE OF LYRICS? EVER LISTEN TO THE WORDS TO "HORSE WITH NO NAME"?
WELL...
"'CAUSE THERE AIN'T NO ONE FOR TO GIVE YOU NO PAIN"?
CLASSIC!

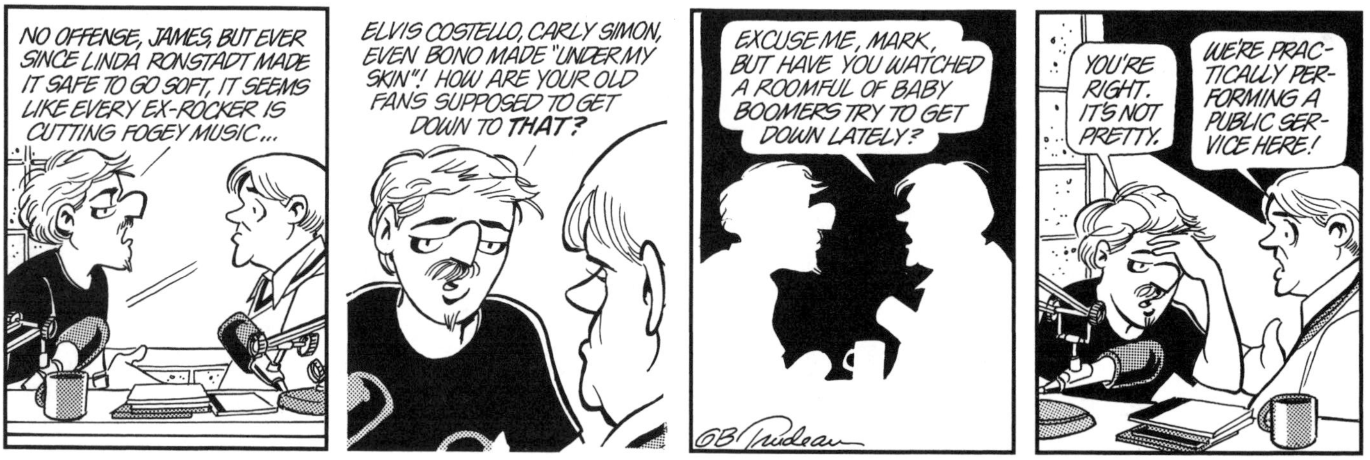
NO OFFENSE, JAMES, BUT EVER SINCE LINDA RONSTADT MADE IT SAFE TO GO SOFT, IT SEEMS LIKE EVERY EX-ROCKER IS CUTTING FOGEY MUSIC...
ELVIS COSTELLO, CARLY SIMON, EVEN BONO MADE "UNDER MY SKIN"! HOW ARE YOUR OLD FANS SUPPOSED TO GET DOWN TO THAT?
EXCUSE ME, MARK, BUT HAVE YOU WATCHED A ROOMFUL OF BABY BOOMERS TRY TO GET DOWN LATELY?
YOU'RE RIGHT. IT'S NOT PRETTY.
WE'RE PRACTICALLY PERFORMING A PUBLIC SERVICE HERE!

'SUP, JONESY?
YO, ZIPPY McNO-SHOW! IT'S FRIDAY NIGHT, RE-MEMBER?
SORRY, MAN. I'M ON DEAD-LINE FOR MY BLOG.
WHAT COULD BE THAT IMPOR-TANT, DAWG?
PROMISE YOU WON'T RIP OFF THE IDEA FOR YOUR BLOG?
YEAH, OKAY.
I'M REVIEWING KRISPY KREME'S DONUT OF THE MONTH.
DUDE. I'M SO STEALING THAT.

"POSTED 1630 EST. KRISPY KREME HAS INTRODUCED ITS NEW DONUT OF THE MONTH. IMHO, IT'S A WINNER!"
NOW HERE'S GREAT TV.
TAP! TAP!
WHAT NOW?
CNN IS ACTUALLY BROADCASTING SCREEN SHOTS OF RANDOM OPINION BLOGS!
WHAT A CONCEPT— TAKE THE UNREAD-ABLE AND MAKE IT ILLEGIBLE!
OH... YEAH, THAT'S PRETTY LAME...
LOOK AT **THIS** ONE! IT'S ABOUT DONUTS!

MY DONUT REVIEW IS ON **CNN?**
IT WAS. THEY'RE ON TO CINDY SHEEHAN NOW.
NOW, **THERE'S** A BLOG-GER'S DELIGHT. LOVE HER OR HATE HER, THE LADY REPRESENTS A TRUE TURNING POINT!
AGAINST ALL LOGIC AND ODDS, SHE'S SINGLE-HANDEDLY KICKED THE ANTI-WAR MOVEMENT INTO GEAR!
WE'RE WATCHIN' **HISTORY,** MAN, HISTORY!
DO YOU THINK MY DONUT RE-VIEW IS IN ROTATION?

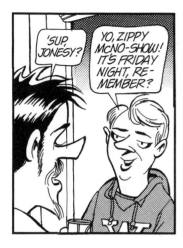

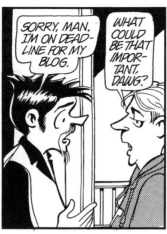

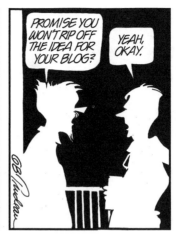

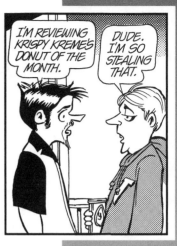

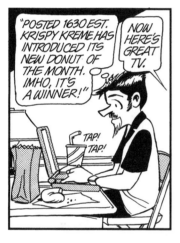

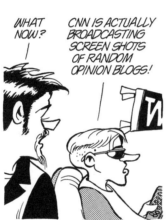

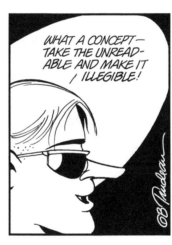

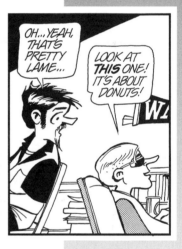

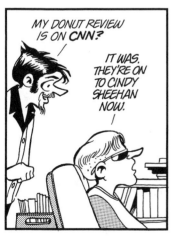

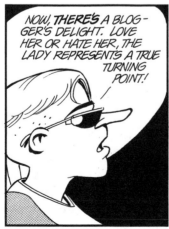

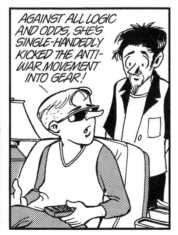

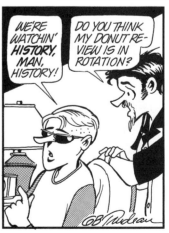

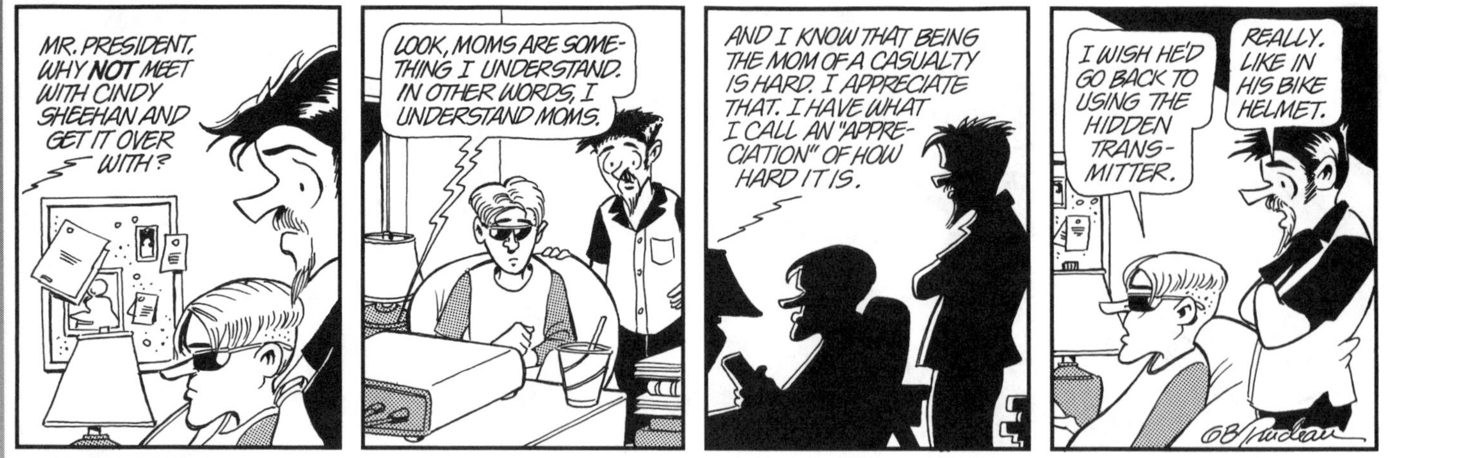
MR. PRESIDENT, WHY NOT MEET WITH CINDY SHEEHAN AND GET IT OVER WITH?
LOOK, MOMS ARE SOMETHING I UNDERSTAND. IN OTHER WORDS, I UNDERSTAND MOMS.
AND I KNOW THAT BEING THE MOM OF A CASUALTY IS HARD. I APPRECIATE THAT. I HAVE WHAT I CALL AN "APPRECIATION" OF HOW HARD IT IS.
I WISH HE'D GO BACK TO USING THE HIDDEN TRANSMITTER.
REALLY. LIKE IN HIS BIKE HELMET.

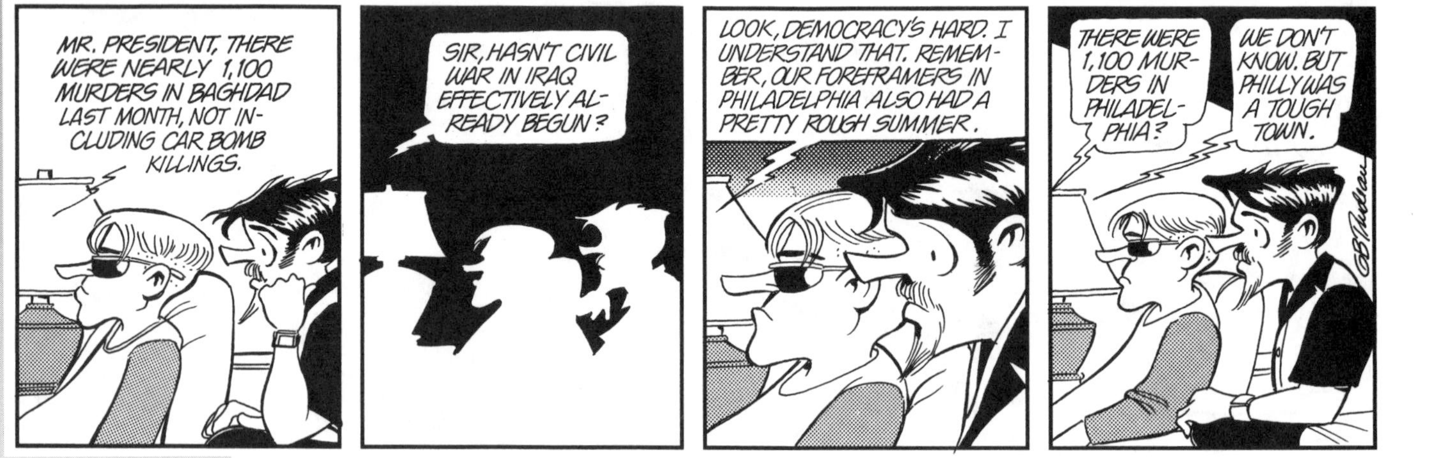
MR. PRESIDENT, THERE WERE NEARLY 1,100 MURDERS IN BAGHDAD LAST MONTH, NOT INCLUDING CAR BOMB KILLINGS.
SIR, HASN'T CIVIL WAR IN IRAQ EFFECTIVELY ALREADY BEGUN?
LOOK, DEMOCRACY'S HARD. I UNDERSTAND THAT. REMEMBER, OUR FOREFRAMERS IN PHILADELPHIA ALSO HAD A PRETTY ROUGH SUMMER.
THERE WERE 1,100 MURDERS IN PHILADELPHIA?
WE DON'T KNOW. BUT PHILLY WAS A TOUGH TOWN.

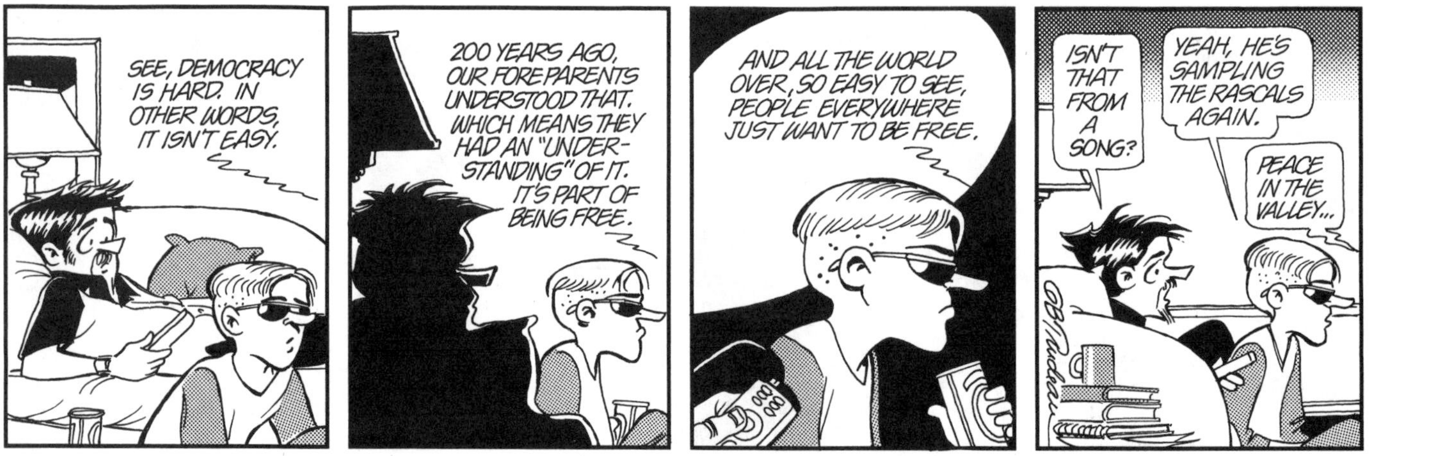
SEE, DEMOCRACY IS HARD. IN OTHER WORDS, IT ISN'T EASY.
200 YEARS AGO, OUR FOREPARENTS UNDERSTOOD THAT. WHICH MEANS THEY HAD AN "UNDERSTANDING" OF IT. IT'S PART OF BEING FREE.
AND ALL THE WORLD OVER, SO EASY TO SEE, PEOPLE EVERYWHERE JUST WANT TO BE FREE.
ISN'T THAT FROM A SONG?
YEAH, HE'S SAMPLING THE RASCALS AGAIN.
PEACE IN THE VALLEY...

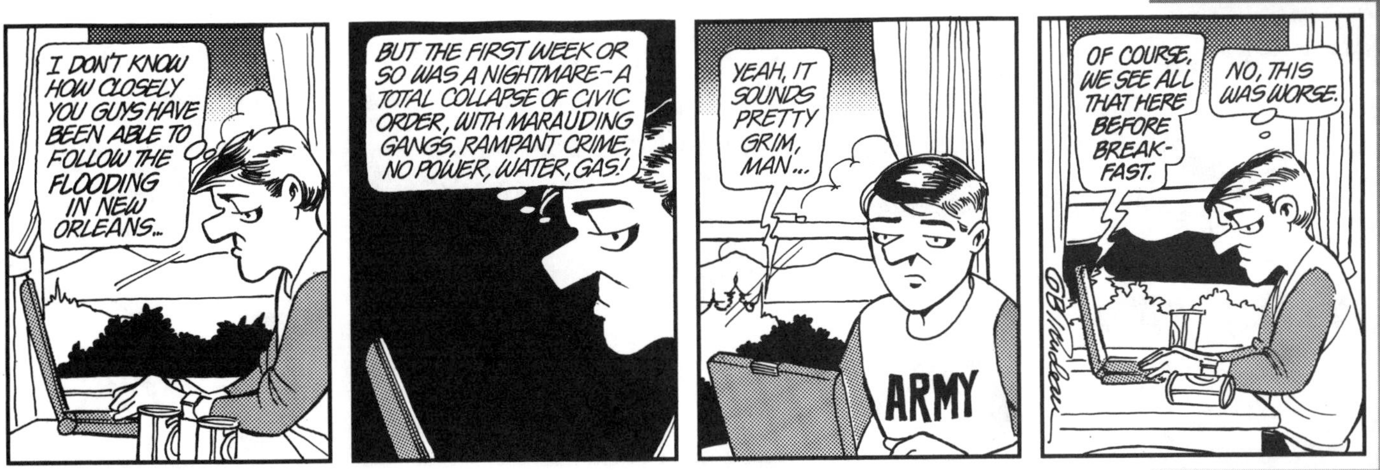
I DON'T KNOW HOW CLOSELY YOU GUYS HAVE BEEN ABLE TO FOLLOW THE FLOODING IN NEW ORLEANS...
BUT THE FIRST WEEK OR SO WAS A NIGHTMARE—A TOTAL COLLAPSE OF CIVIC ORDER, WITH MARAUDING GANGS, RAMPANT CRIME, NO POWER, WATER, GAS!
YEAH, IT SOUNDS PRETTY GRIM, MAN...
ARMY
OF COURSE, WE SEE ALL THAT HERE BEFORE BREAKFAST.
NO, THIS WAS WORSE.
GB Trudeau

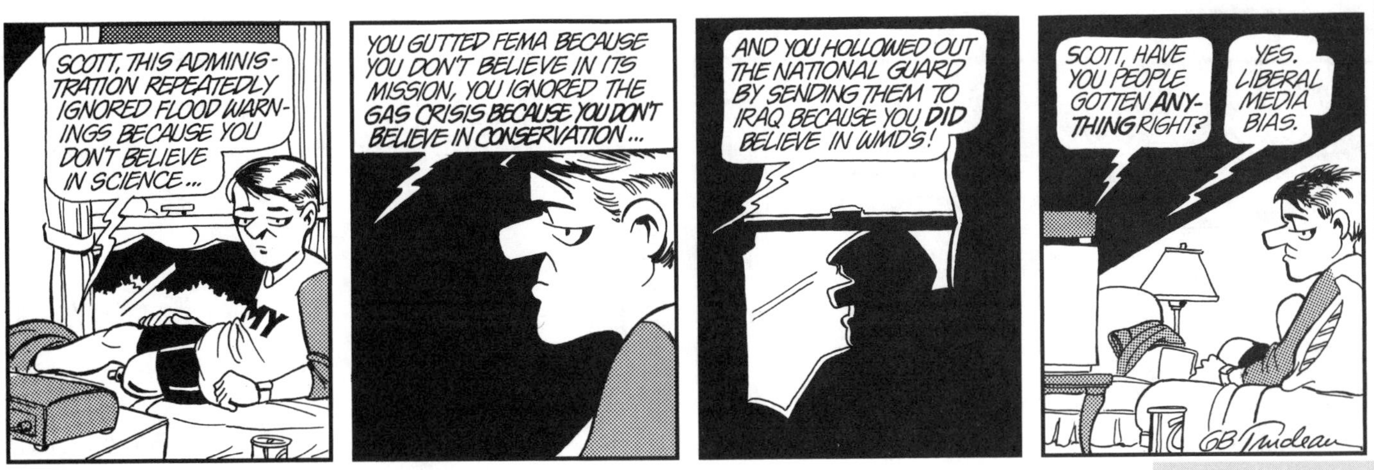
SCOTT, THIS ADMINISTRATION REPEATEDLY IGNORED FLOOD WARNINGS BECAUSE YOU DON'T BELIEVE IN SCIENCE...
YOU GUTTED FEMA BECAUSE YOU DON'T BELIEVE IN ITS MISSION, YOU IGNORED THE GAS CRISIS BECAUSE YOU DON'T BELIEVE IN CONSERVATION...
AND YOU HOLLOWED OUT THE NATIONAL GUARD BY SENDING THEM TO IRAQ BECAUSE YOU DID BELIEVE IN WMD'S!
SCOTT, HAVE YOU PEOPLE GOTTEN ANYTHING RIGHT?
YES. LIBERAL MEDIA BIAS.
GB Trudeau

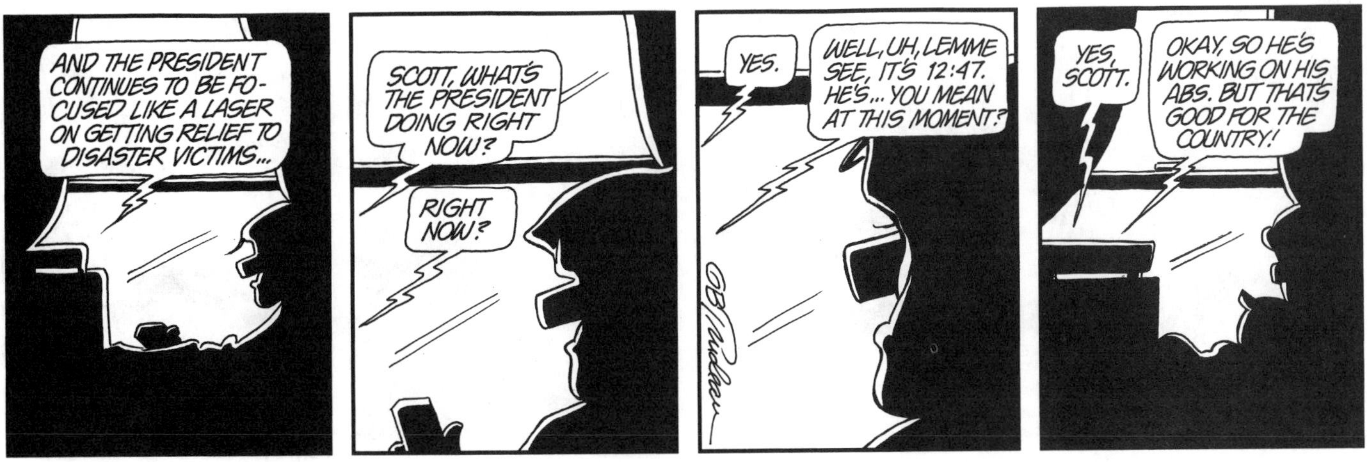
AND THE PRESIDENT CONTINUES TO BE FOCUSED LIKE A LASER ON GETTING RELIEF TO DISASTER VICTIMS...
SCOTT, WHAT'S THE PRESIDENT DOING RIGHT NOW?
RIGHT NOW?
YES.
WELL, UH, LEMME SEE, IT'S 12:47. HE'S... YOU MEAN AT THIS MOMENT?
GB Trudeau
YES, SCOTT.
OKAY, SO HE'S WORKING ON HIS ABS. BUT THAT'S GOOD FOR THE COUNTRY!

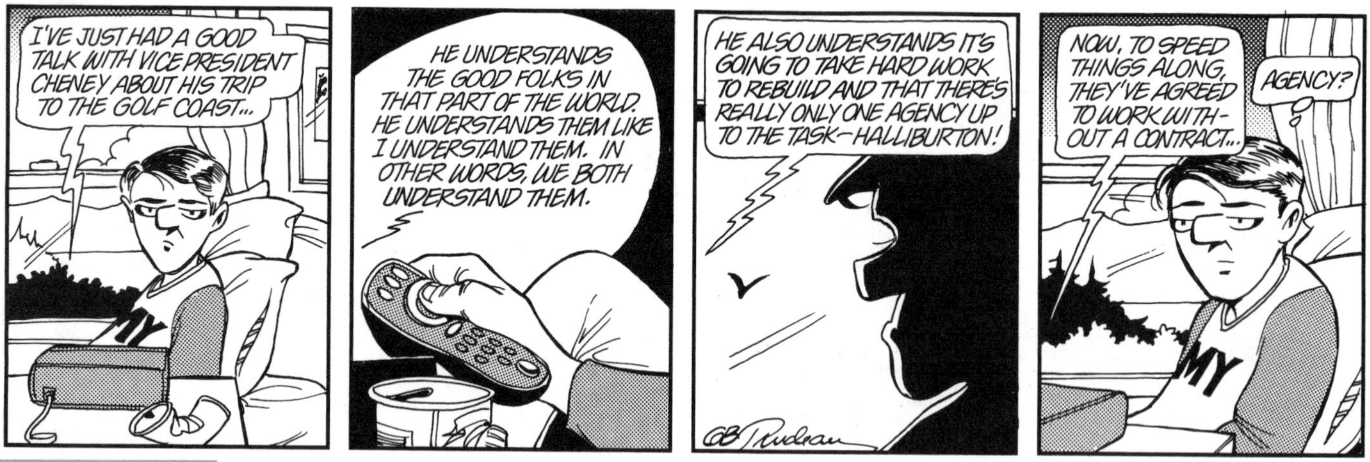
I'VE JUST HAD A GOOD TALK WITH VICE PRESIDENT CHENEY ABOUT HIS TRIP TO THE GOLF COAST...
HE UNDERSTANDS THE GOOD FOLKS IN THAT PART OF THE WORLD. HE UNDERSTANDS THEM LIKE I UNDERSTAND THEM. IN OTHER WORDS, WE BOTH UNDERSTAND THEM.
HE ALSO UNDERSTANDS IT'S GOING TO TAKE HARD WORK TO REBUILD AND THAT THERE'S REALLY ONLY ONE AGENCY UP TO THE TASK—HALLIBURTON!
NOW, TO SPEED THINGS ALONG, THEY'VE AGREED TO WORK WITHOUT A CONTRACT...
AGENCY?

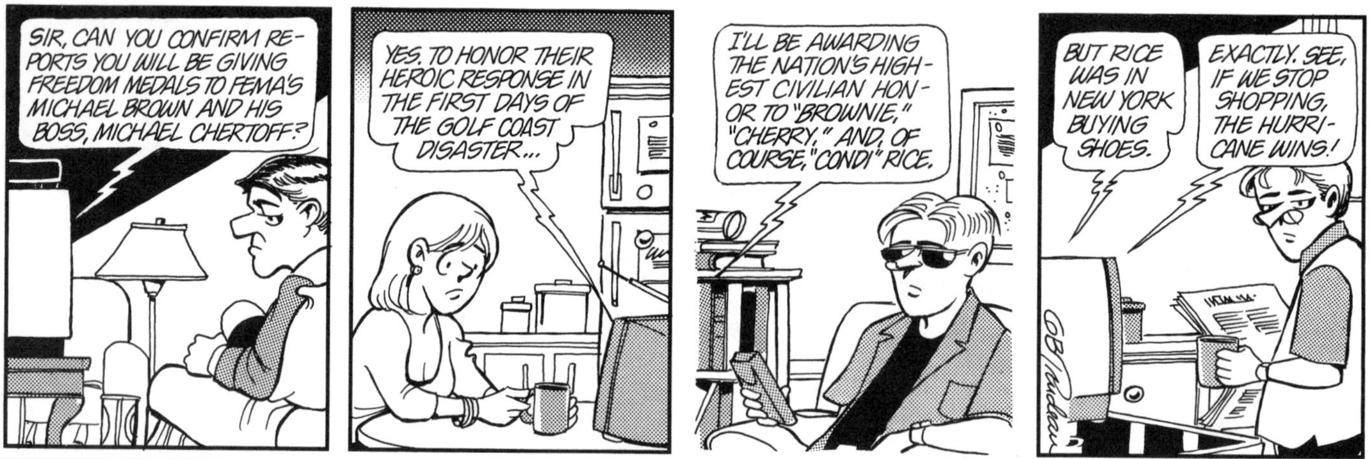
SIR, CAN YOU CONFIRM REPORTS YOU WILL BE GIVING FREEDOM MEDALS TO FEMA'S MICHAEL BROWN AND HIS BOSS, MICHAEL CHERTOFF?
YES. TO HONOR THEIR HEROIC RESPONSE IN THE FIRST DAYS OF THE GOLF COAST DISASTER...
I'LL BE AWARDING THE NATION'S HIGHEST CIVILIAN HONOR TO "BROWNIE," "CHERRY," AND, OF COURSE, "CONDI" RICE.
BUT RICE WAS IN NEW YORK BUYING SHOES.
EXACTLY. SEE, IF WE STOP SHOPPING, THE HURRICANE WINS!

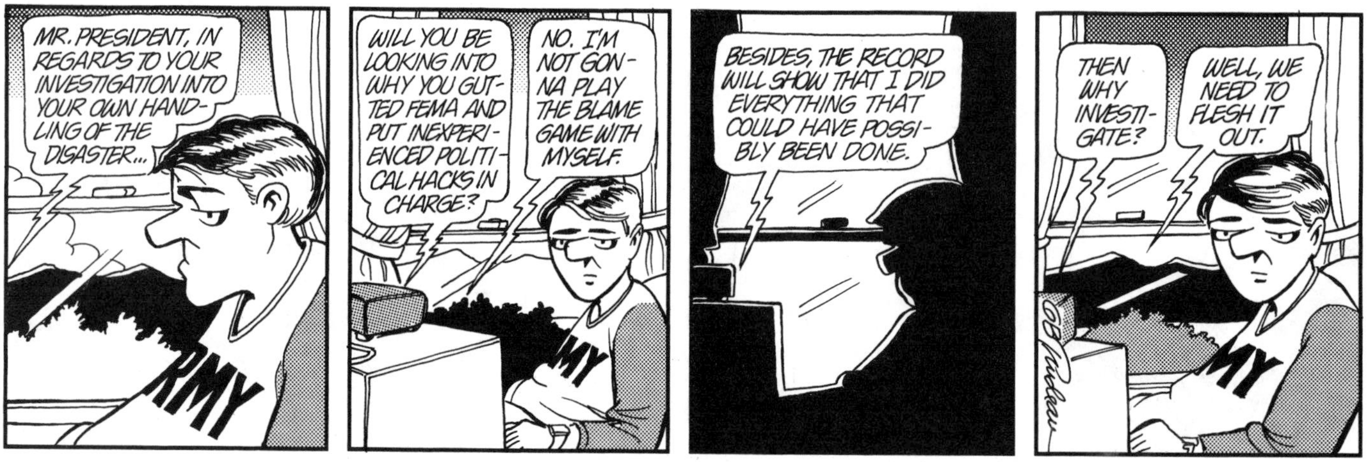
MR. PRESIDENT, IN REGARDS TO YOUR INVESTIGATION INTO YOUR OWN HANDLING OF THE DISASTER...
WILL YOU BE LOOKING INTO WHY YOU GUTTED FEMA AND PUT INEXPERIENCED POLITICAL HACKS IN CHARGE?
NO. I'M NOT GONNA PLAY THE BLAME GAME WITH MYSELF.
BESIDES, THE RECORD WILL SHOW THAT I DID EVERYTHING THAT COULD HAVE POSSIBLY BEEN DONE.
THEN WHY INVESTIGATE?
WELL, WE NEED TO FLESH IT OUT.

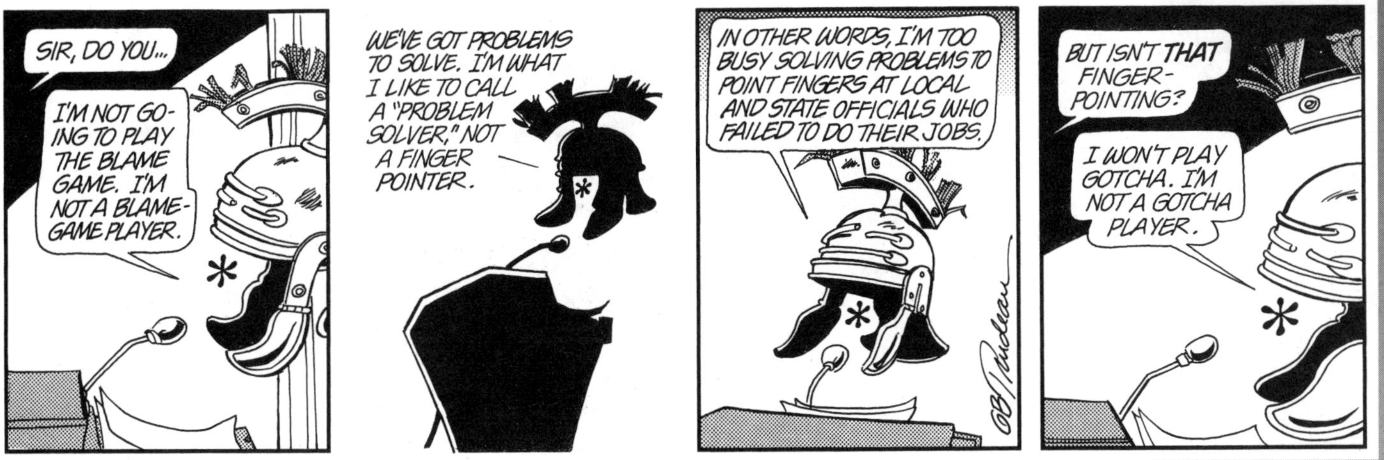
SIR, DO YOU...
I'M NOT GOING TO PLAY THE BLAME GAME. I'M NOT A BLAME-GAME PLAYER.
WE'VE GOT PROBLEMS TO SOLVE. I'M WHAT I LIKE TO CALL A "PROBLEM SOLVER," NOT A FINGER POINTER.
IN OTHER WORDS, I'M TOO BUSY SOLVING PROBLEMS TO POINT FINGERS AT LOCAL AND STATE OFFICIALS WHO FAILED TO DO THEIR JOBS.
BUT ISN'T **THAT** FINGER-POINTING?
I WON'T PLAY GOTCHA. I'M NOT A GOTCHA PLAYER.

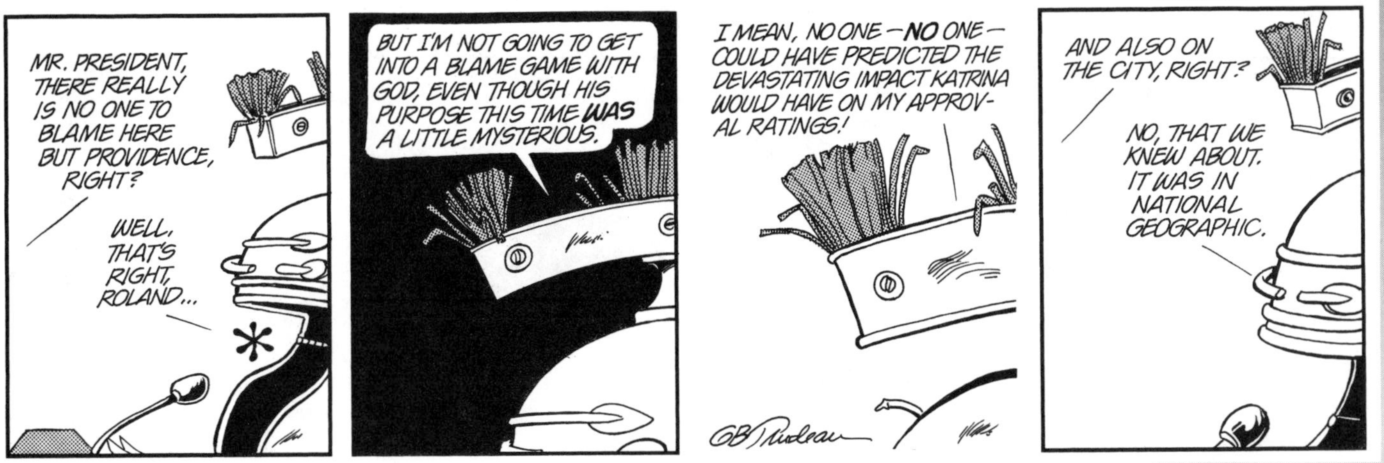
MR. PRESIDENT, THERE REALLY IS NO ONE TO BLAME HERE BUT PROVIDENCE, RIGHT?
WELL, THAT'S RIGHT, ROLAND...
BUT I'M NOT GOING TO GET INTO A BLAME GAME WITH GOD, EVEN THOUGH HIS PURPOSE THIS TIME **WAS** A LITTLE MYSTERIOUS.
I MEAN, NO ONE — **NO** ONE — COULD HAVE PREDICTED THE DEVASTATING IMPACT KATRINA WOULD HAVE ON MY APPROVAL RATINGS!
AND ALSO ON THE CITY, RIGHT?
NO, THAT WE KNEW ABOUT. IT WAS IN NATIONAL GEOGRAPHIC.

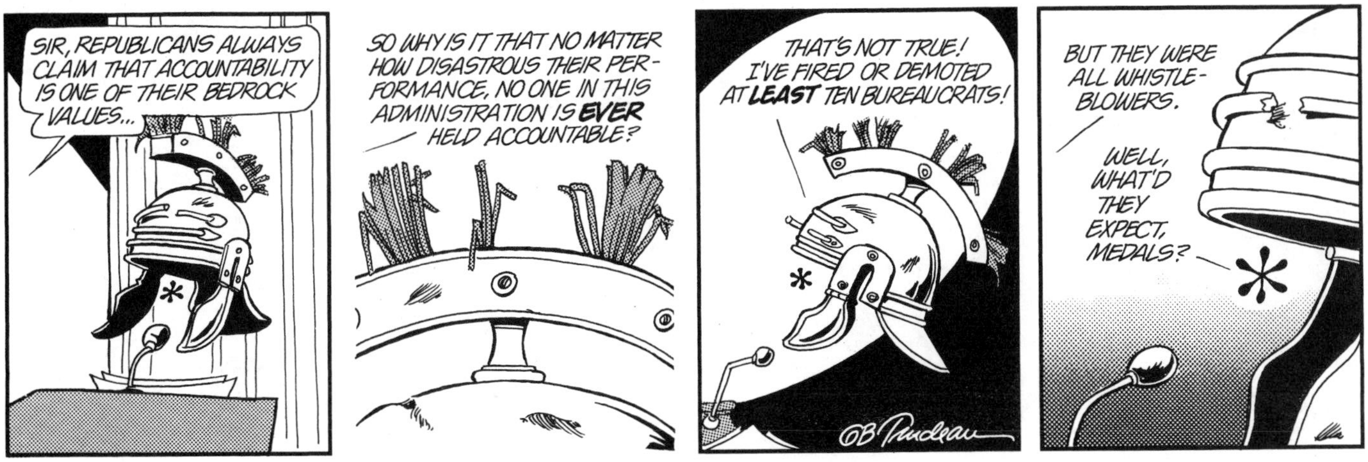
SIR, REPUBLICANS ALWAYS CLAIM THAT ACCOUNTABILITY IS ONE OF THEIR BEDROCK VALUES...
SO WHY IS IT THAT NO MATTER HOW DISASTROUS THEIR PERFORMANCE, NO ONE IN THIS ADMINISTRATION IS **EVER** HELD ACCOUNTABLE?
THAT'S NOT TRUE! I'VE FIRED OR DEMOTED AT **LEAST** TEN BUREAUCRATS!
BUT THEY WERE ALL WHISTLE-BLOWERS.
WELL, WHAT'D THEY EXPECT, MEDALS?

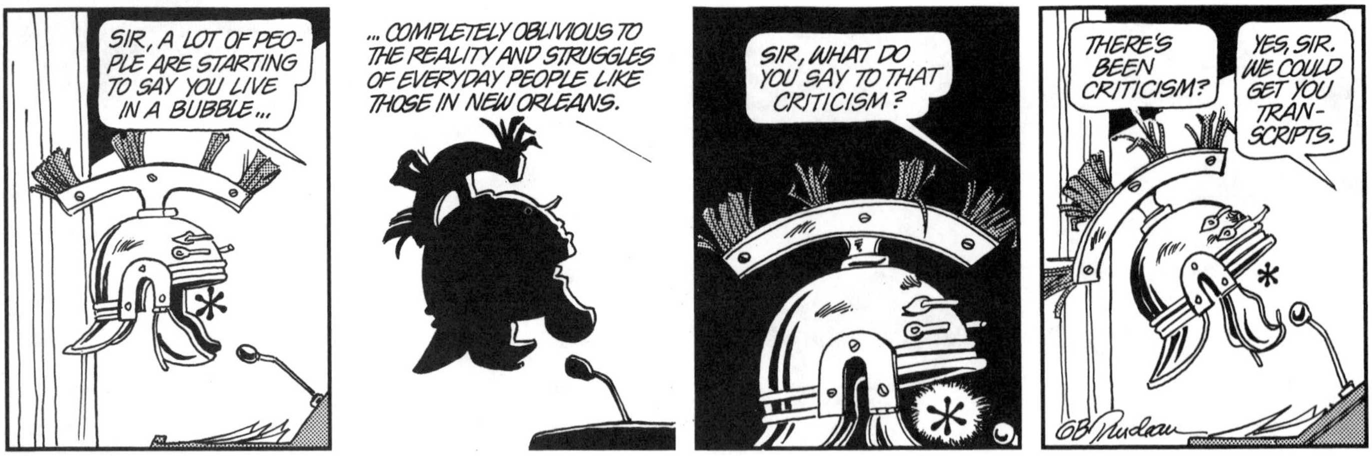
SIR, A LOT OF PEOPLE ARE STARTING TO SAY YOU LIVE IN A BUBBLE...
...COMPLETELY OBLIVIOUS TO THE REALITY AND STRUGGLES OF EVERYDAY PEOPLE LIKE THOSE IN NEW ORLEANS.
SIR, WHAT DO YOU SAY TO THAT CRITICISM?
THERE'S BEEN CRITICISM?
YES, SIR. WE COULD GET YOU TRANSCRIPTS.
GB Trudeau

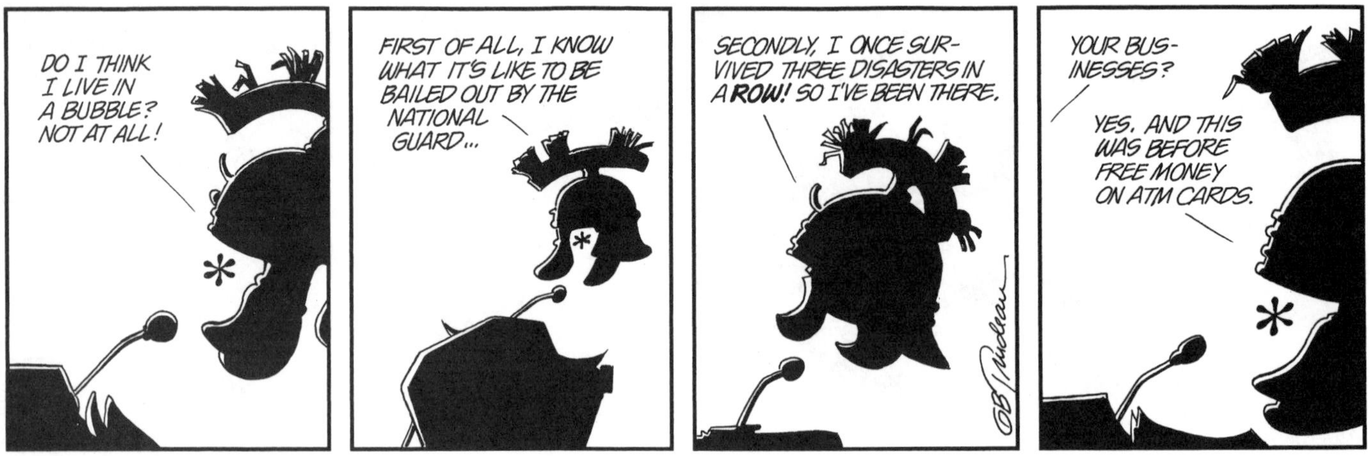
DO I THINK I LIVE IN A BUBBLE? NOT AT ALL!
FIRST OF ALL, I KNOW WHAT IT'S LIKE TO BE BAILED OUT BY THE NATIONAL GUARD...
SECONDLY, I ONCE SURVIVED THREE DISASTERS IN A **ROW!** SO I'VE BEEN THERE.
GB Trudeau
YOUR BUSINESSES?
YES. AND THIS WAS BEFORE FREE MONEY ON ATM CARDS.

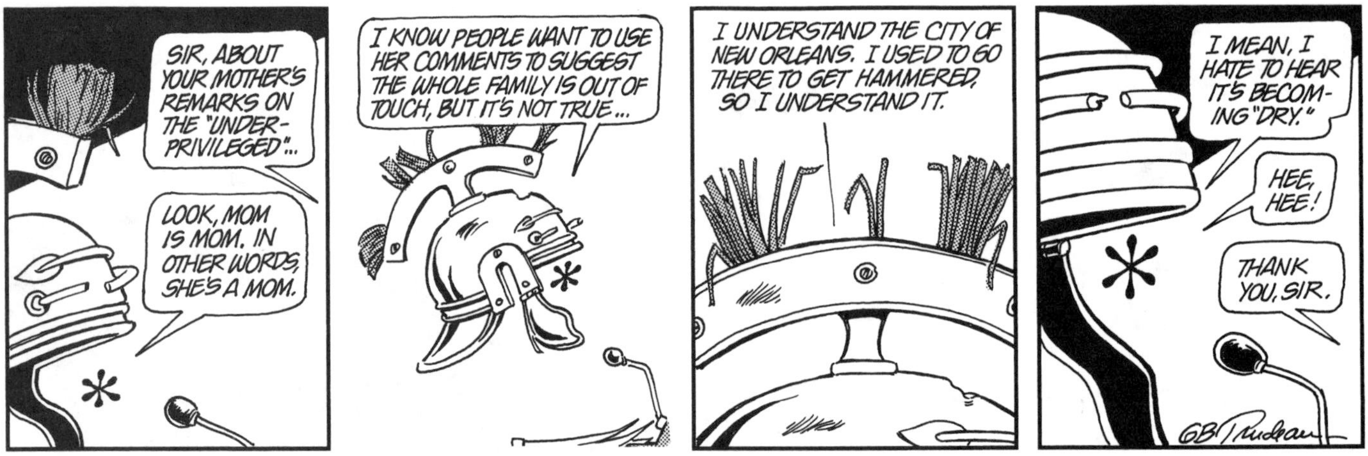
SIR, ABOUT YOUR MOTHER'S REMARKS ON THE "UNDERPRIVILEGED"...
LOOK, MOM IS MOM. IN OTHER WORDS, SHE'S A MOM.
I KNOW PEOPLE WANT TO USE HER COMMENTS TO SUGGEST THE WHOLE FAMILY IS OUT OF TOUCH, BUT IT'S NOT TRUE...
I UNDERSTAND THE CITY OF NEW ORLEANS. I USED TO GO THERE TO GET HAMMERED, SO I UNDERSTAND IT.
I MEAN, I HATE TO HEAR IT'S BECOMING "DRY."
HEE, HEE!
THANK YOU, SIR.
GB Trudeau

OVER THERE, SIR— SEE THAT CLOUD OF DUST? IT'S SOME SORT OF MILITARY CONVOY...
THAT'S NOT MILITARY, HONEY— THAT'S THE HALLIBURTON GANG, PULLING UP STAKES!
I DON'T GET IT. WHY THE HELL WOULD CHENEY'S BOYS BE LEAVING THE... THE...
NEW ORLEANS.
GO PACK, HONEY.

PACK FOR NEW ORLEANS? ARE YOU SERIOUS, SIR?
DO IT, HONEY!
BUT WHY, SIR?
THE RECOVERY EFFORT, OF COURSE. I NEED TO BE PART OF IT!
WHICH PART EXACTLY?
THINK, HONEY! WHAT DO I HAVE VAST EXPERTISE IN NOW?
LOOTING. GRAFT. PROFITEERING.
EXACTLY. IT'S ALL ABOUT THE SKILL SET, HONEY!

YOU SURE YOU WANT TO DECAMP TO NEW ORLEANS, SIR?
ARE YOU KIDDING? LISTEN TO THIS...
"SAID WASHINGTON LOBBYIST JAMES ALBERTINE EXCITEDLY, 'THEY ARE THROWING MONEY OUT— THEY ARE SHOVELING IT OUT THE DOOR!'"
NOW, THAT'S MY KIND OF ENTREPRENEURIAL ENVIRONMENT! YOU KNOW WHAT THEY SAY AT HALLIBURTON, HONEY...
WHAT'S THAT?
THERE'S NO BIDNESS LIKE NO-BIDNESS!
IT DOES SEEM LIKE A GREAT FIT FOR YOU, SIR.

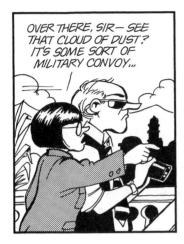

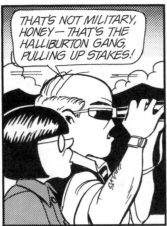

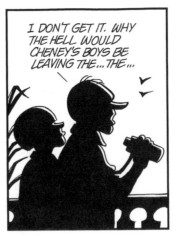

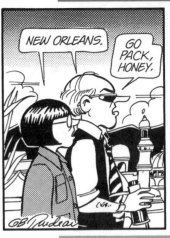

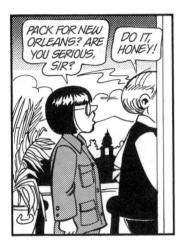

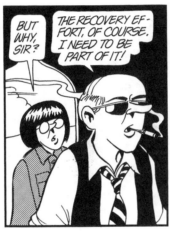

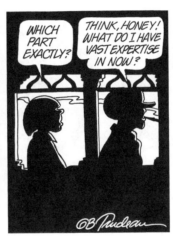

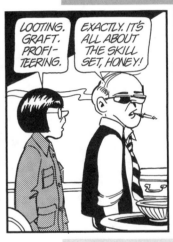

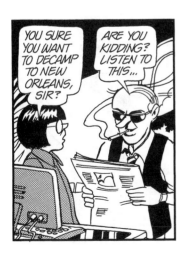

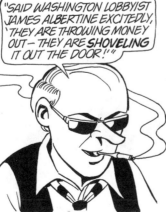

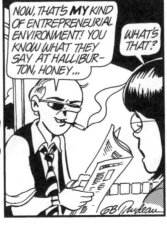

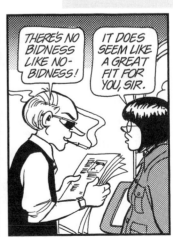

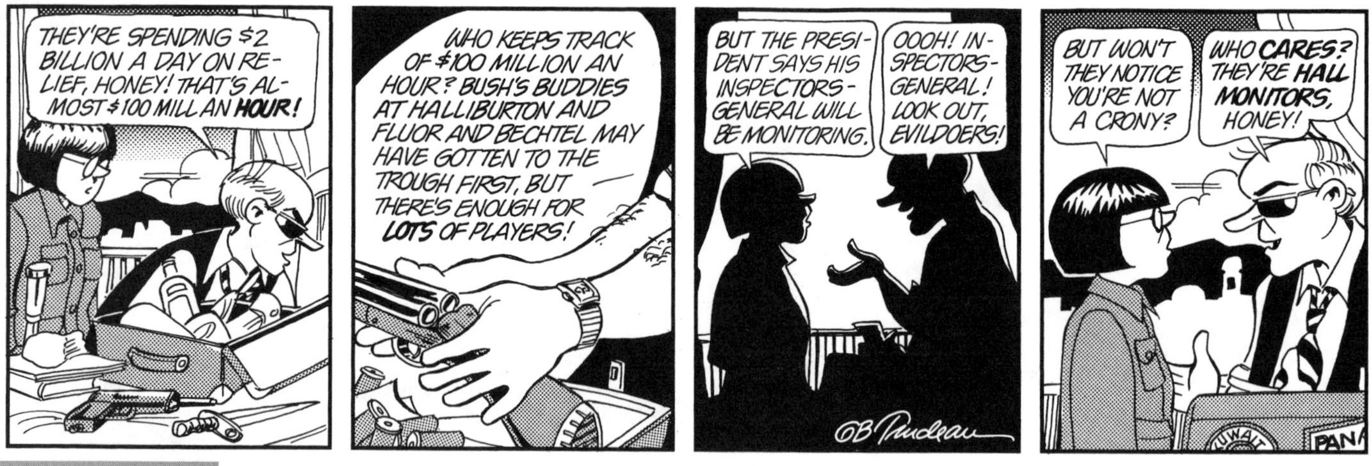
THEY'RE SPENDING $2 BILLION A DAY ON RELIEF, HONEY! THAT'S ALMOST $100 MILL AN HOUR!
WHO KEEPS TRACK OF $100 MILLION AN HOUR? BUSH'S BUDDIES AT HALLIBURTON AND FLUOR AND BECHTEL MAY HAVE GOTTEN TO THE TROUGH FIRST, BUT THERE'S ENOUGH FOR LOTS OF PLAYERS!
BUT THE PRESIDENT SAYS HIS INSPECTORS-GENERAL WILL BE MONITORING.
OOOH! INSPECTORS-GENERAL! LOOK OUT, EVILDOERS!
GB Trudeau
BUT WON'T THEY NOTICE YOU'RE NOT A CRONY?
WHO CARES? THEY'RE HALL MONITORS, HONEY!

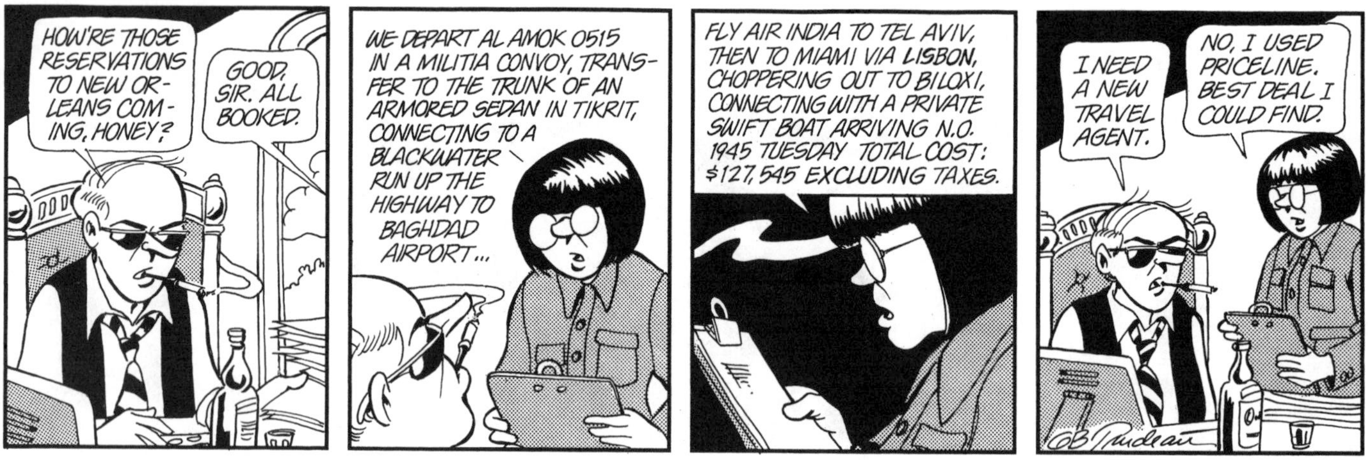
HOW'RE THOSE RESERVATIONS TO NEW ORLEANS COMING, HONEY?
GOOD, SIR. ALL BOOKED.
WE DEPART AL AMOK 0515 IN A MILITIA CONVOY, TRANSFER TO THE TRUNK OF AN ARMORED SEDAN IN TIKRIT, CONNECTING TO A BLACKWATER RUN UP THE HIGHWAY TO BAGHDAD AIRPORT...
FLY AIR INDIA TO TEL AVIV, THEN TO MIAMI VIA LISBON, CHOPPERING OUT TO BILOXI, CONNECTING WITH A PRIVATE SWIFT BOAT ARRIVING N.O. 1945 TUESDAY TOTAL COST: $127,545 EXCLUDING TAXES.
I NEED A NEW TRAVEL AGENT.
NO, I USED PRICELINE. BEST DEAL I COULD FIND.
GB Trudeau

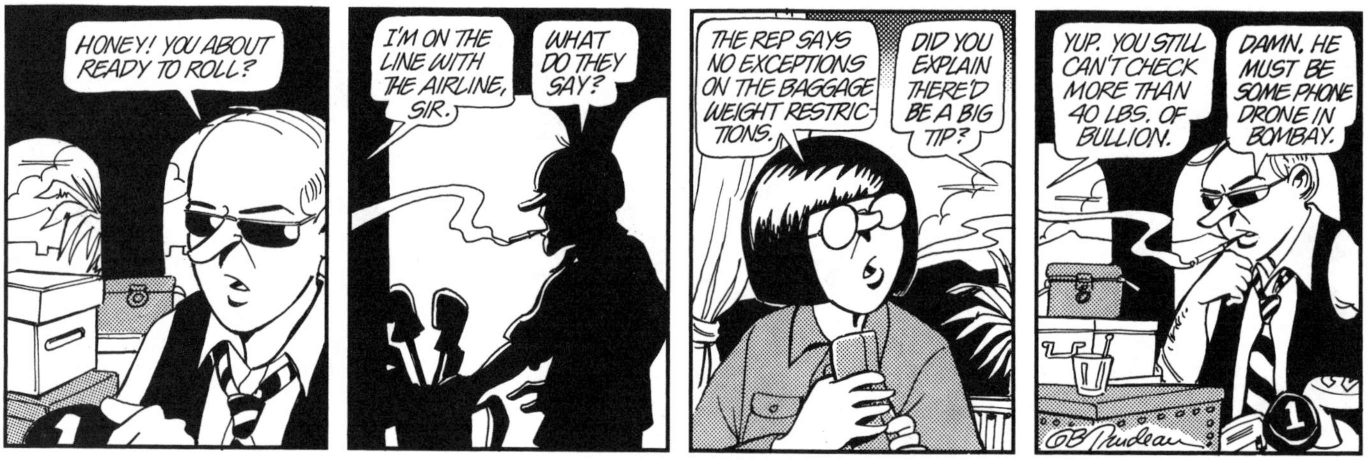
HONEY! YOU ABOUT READY TO ROLL?
I'M ON THE LINE WITH THE AIRLINE, SIR.
WHAT DO THEY SAY?
THE REP SAYS NO EXCEPTIONS ON THE BAGGAGE WEIGHT RESTRICTIONS.
DID YOU EXPLAIN THERE'D BE A BIG TIP?
YUP. YOU STILL CAN'T CHECK MORE THAN 40 LBS. OF BULLION.
DAMN. HE MUST BE SOME PHONE DRONE IN BOMBAY.
GB Trudeau

I'M JUST A GROCER! I'M GOING TO VISIT MY MOTHER IN BAGHDAD! I SWEAR IT!
DON'T LIE, OLD MAN! GOD MAY FORGIVE YOU, BUT I WON'T!
HE'S ONLY CARRYING MELONS, BROTHER. LET HIM PASS.
OKAY, ON YOUR WAY, OLD MAN!
WAIT A MINUTE... DID YOU CHECK THE TRUNK?
THE TRUNK? NO...
BETTER PUT A FEW ROUNDS INTO IT.
DAMMIT, HONEY!
SORRY, SIR.

HE'S STOPPING, SIR! WE STILL MIGHT MAKE OUR PLANE!
WHO CARES? THEY GOT EVERYTHING! EVERYTHING!
WHAT ARE YOU DOING OUT HERE IN THE DESERT, WOMAN? ARE YOU MAD?
WE'VE BEEN ROBBED, SIR! AND WE NEED TO GET TO BAGHDAD!
ROBBED? MEANING YOU HAVE NO MONEY?
NO, SIR. BUT I DO HAVE THE TAG NUMBER OF A CAR HEADING NORTH FILLED WITH BULLION.
WHA...?
SWEET. HOP IN.
NO... NO! IDIOT!

DUKE PARTY OF TWO— FOR THE BAGHDAD AIRPORT.
HEY! WE WERE WONDERING IF YOU FOLKS WOULD SHOW!
BAGHDAD AIRPORT
HERE, JUST SIGN THIS AND WE'LL GET YOU ON YOUR WAY! EVER BEEN ON THE AIRPORT HIGHWAY BEFORE?
NO.
WELL, AFTER 2½ YEARS, IT'S STILL NOT SECURE, SO IT'S QUITE A THRILL! THE MOST CHALLENGING SEVEN MILES IN IRAQ!
THIS IS A WILL.
JUST TO HAVE ON FILE. AS SOON AS YOU ARRIVE, WE TEAR IT UP.

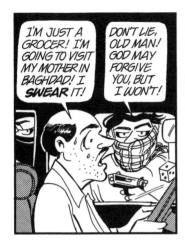

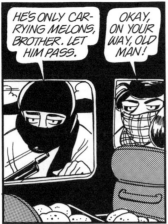

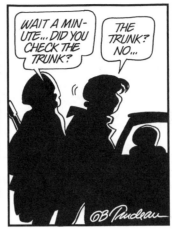

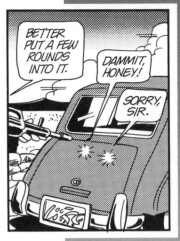

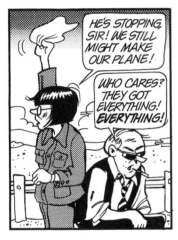

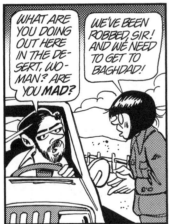

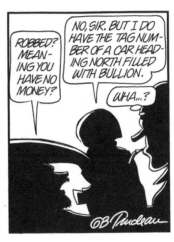

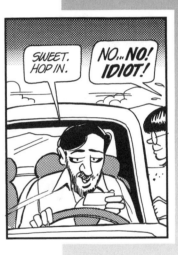

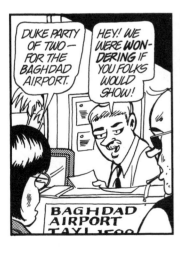

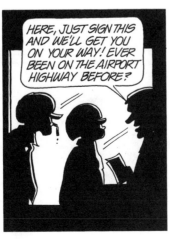

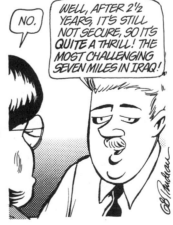

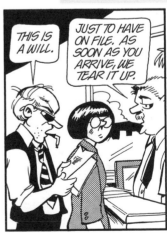

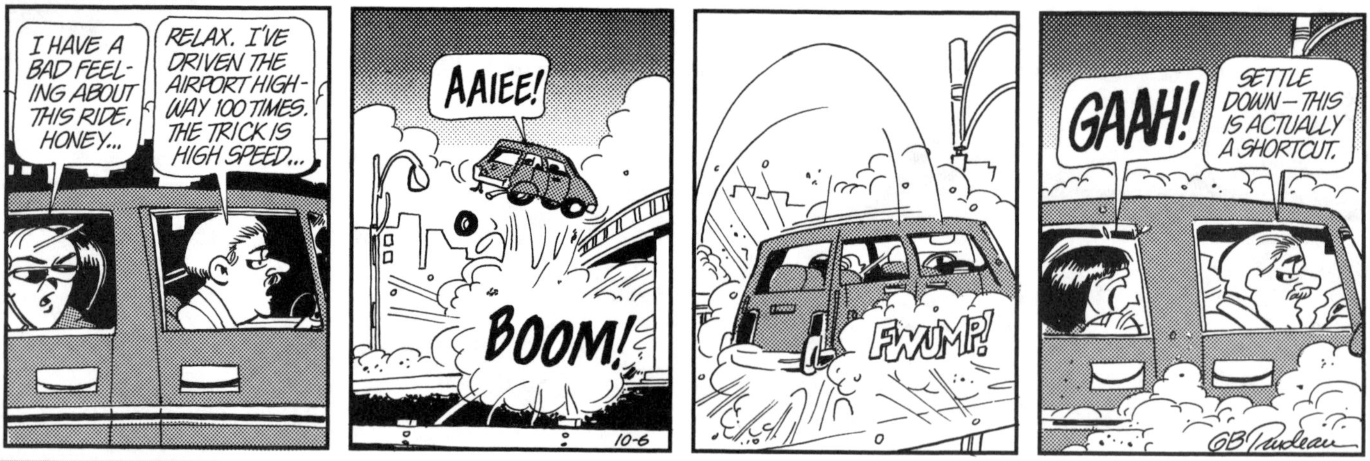
I HAVE A BAD FEELING ABOUT THIS RIDE, HONEY...
RELAX. I'VE DRIVEN THE AIRPORT HIGHWAY 100 TIMES. THE TRICK IS HIGH SPEED...
AAIEE!
BOOM!
10-6
FWUMP!
GAAH!
SETTLE DOWN—THIS IS ACTUALLY A SHORTCUT.
©B Trudeau

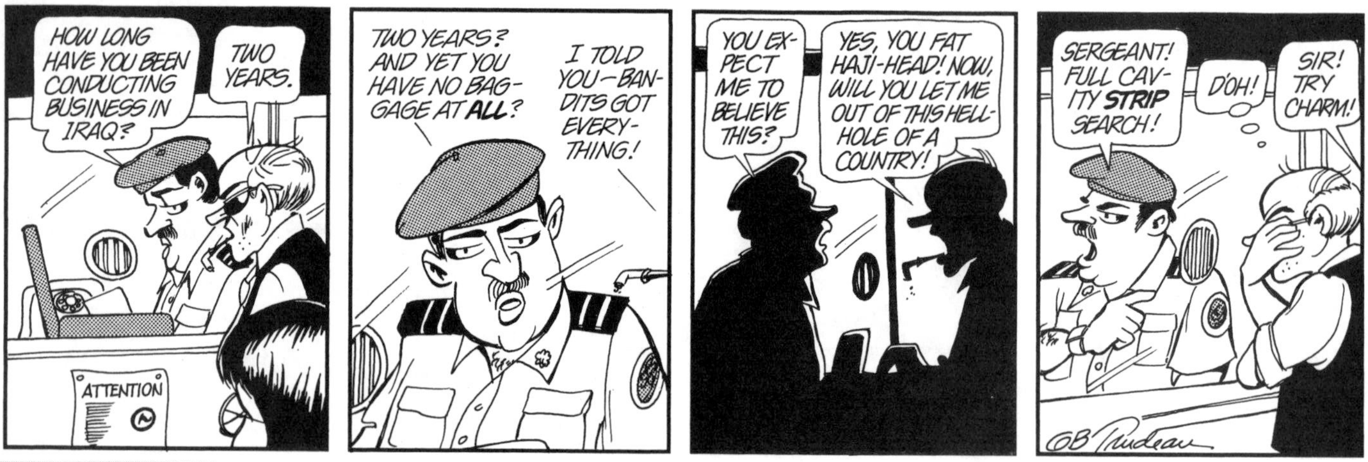
HOW LONG HAVE YOU BEEN CONDUCTING BUSINESS IN IRAQ?
TWO YEARS.
ATTENTION
TWO YEARS? AND YET YOU HAVE NO BAGGAGE AT **ALL**?
I TOLD YOU—BANDITS GOT EVERYTHING!
YOU EXPECT ME TO BELIEVE THIS?
YES, YOU FAT HAJI-HEAD! NOW, WILL YOU LET ME OUT OF THIS HELL-HOLE OF A COUNTRY!
SERGEANT! FULL CAVITY **STRIP** SEARCH!
D'OH!
SIR! TRY CHARM!
©B Trudeau

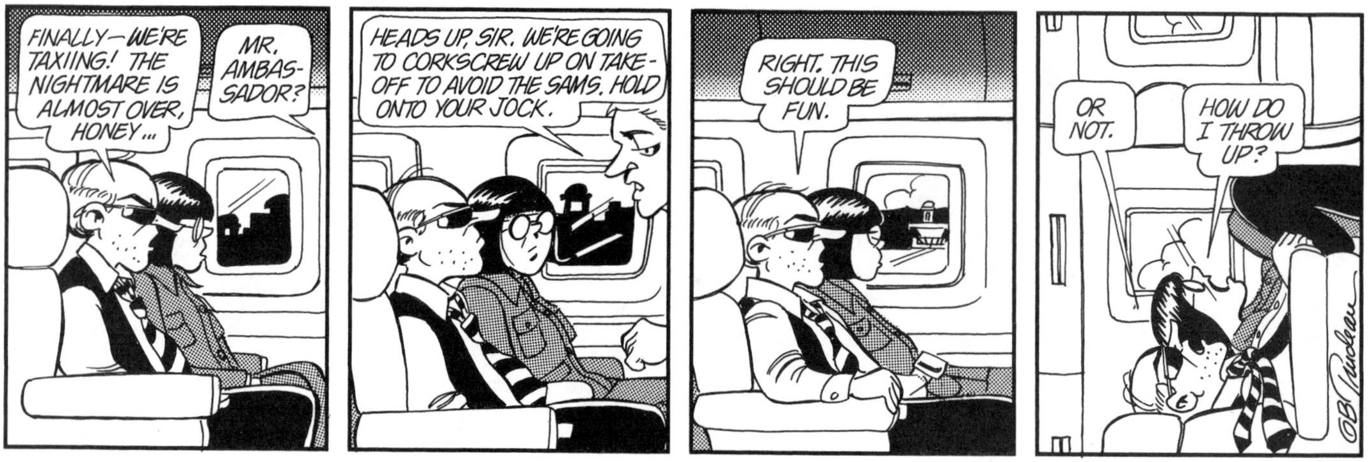
FINALLY—**WE'RE** TAXIING! THE NIGHTMARE IS ALMOST OVER, HONEY...
MR. AMBASSADOR?
HEADS UP, SIR. WE'RE GOING TO CORKSCREW UP ON TAKE-OFF TO AVOID THE SAMS. HOLD ONTO YOUR JOCK.
RIGHT. THIS SHOULD BE FUN.
OR NOT.
HOW DO I THROW UP?
©B Trudeau

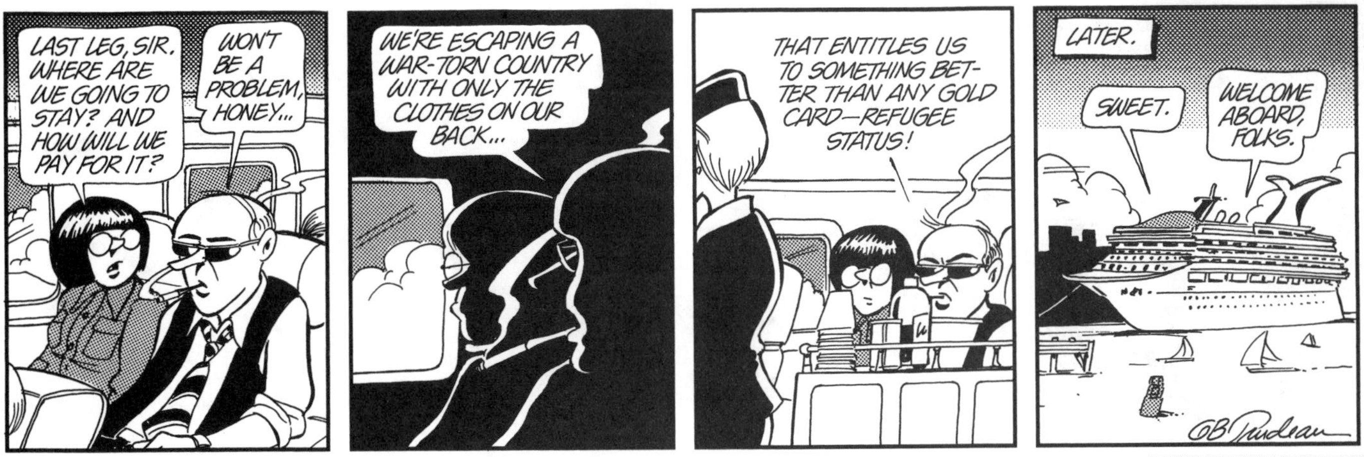
LAST LEG, SIR. WHERE ARE WE GOING TO STAY? AND HOW WILL WE PAY FOR IT?
WON'T BE A PROBLEM, HONEY...
WE'RE ESCAPING A WAR-TORN COUNTRY WITH ONLY THE CLOTHES ON OUR BACK...
THAT ENTITLES US TO SOMETHING BETTER THAN ANY GOLD CARD—REFUGEE STATUS!
LATER.
SWEET.
WELCOME ABOARD, FOLKS.

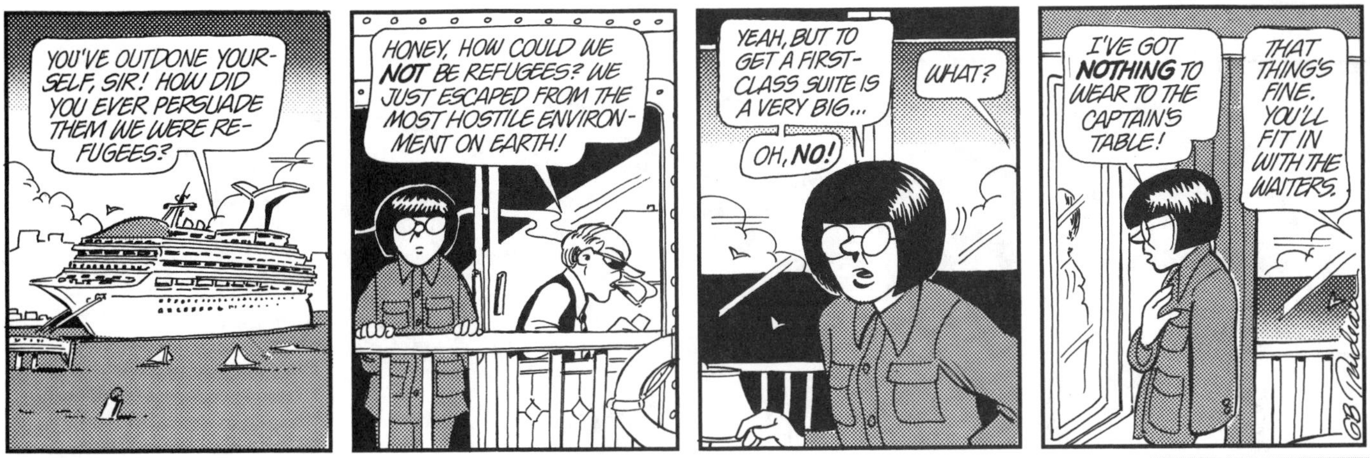
YOU'VE OUTDONE YOURSELF, SIR! HOW DID YOU EVER PERSUADE THEM WE WERE REFUGEES?
HONEY, HOW COULD WE **NOT** BE REFUGEES? WE JUST ESCAPED FROM THE MOST HOSTILE ENVIRONMENT ON EARTH!
YEAH, BUT TO GET A FIRST-CLASS SUITE IS A VERY BIG...
WHAT?
OH, **NO!**
I'VE GOT **NOTHING** TO WEAR TO THE CAPTAIN'S TABLE!
THAT THING'S FINE. YOU'LL FIT IN WITH THE WAITERS.

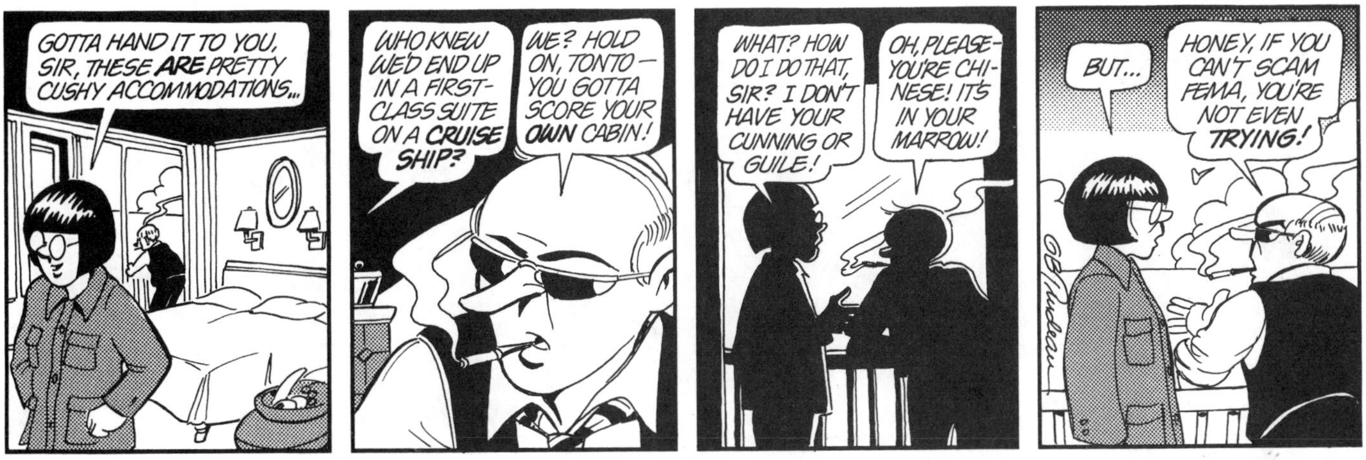
GOTTA HAND IT TO YOU, SIR, THESE **ARE** PRETTY CUSHY ACCOMMODATIONS...
WHO KNEW WE'D END UP IN A FIRST-CLASS SUITE ON A **CRUISE SHIP?**
WE? HOLD ON, TONTO— YOU GOTTA SCORE YOUR **OWN** CABIN!
WHAT? HOW DO I DO THAT, SIR? I DON'T HAVE YOUR CUNNING OR GUILE!
OH, PLEASE— YOU'RE CHINESE! IT'S IN YOUR MARROW!
BUT...
HONEY, IF YOU CAN'T SCAM FEMA, YOU'RE NOT EVEN **TRYING!**

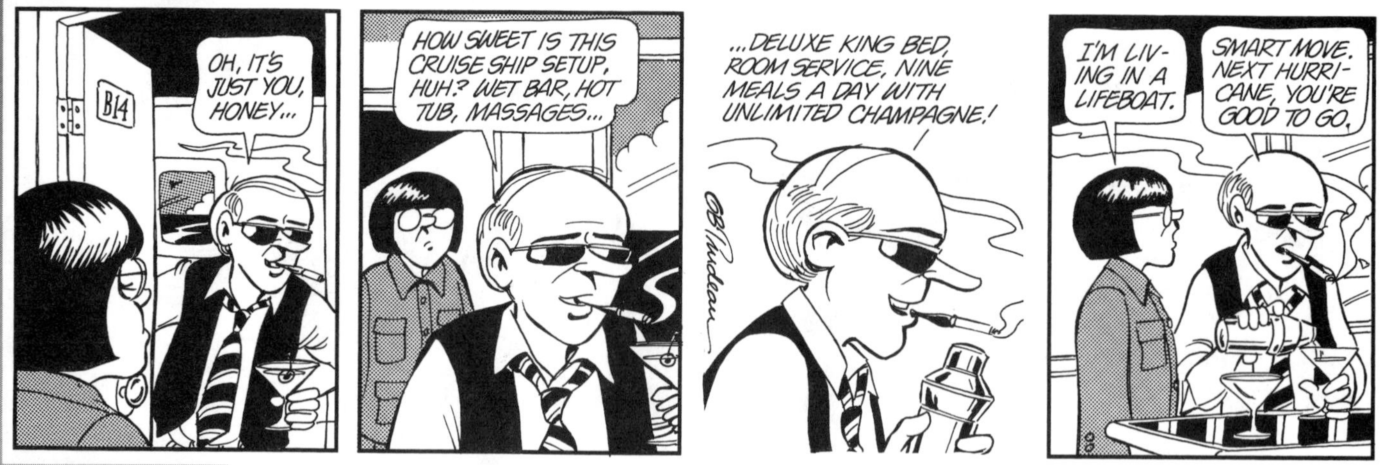
OH, IT'S JUST YOU, HONEY...
B14
HOW SWEET IS THIS CRUISE SHIP SETUP, HUH? WET BAR, HOT TUB, MASSAGES...
...DELUXE KING BED, ROOM SERVICE, NINE MEALS A DAY WITH UNLIMITED CHAMPAGNE!
GB Trudeau
I'M LIVING IN A LIFEBOAT.
SMART MOVE. NEXT HURRICANE, YOU'RE GOOD TO GO.

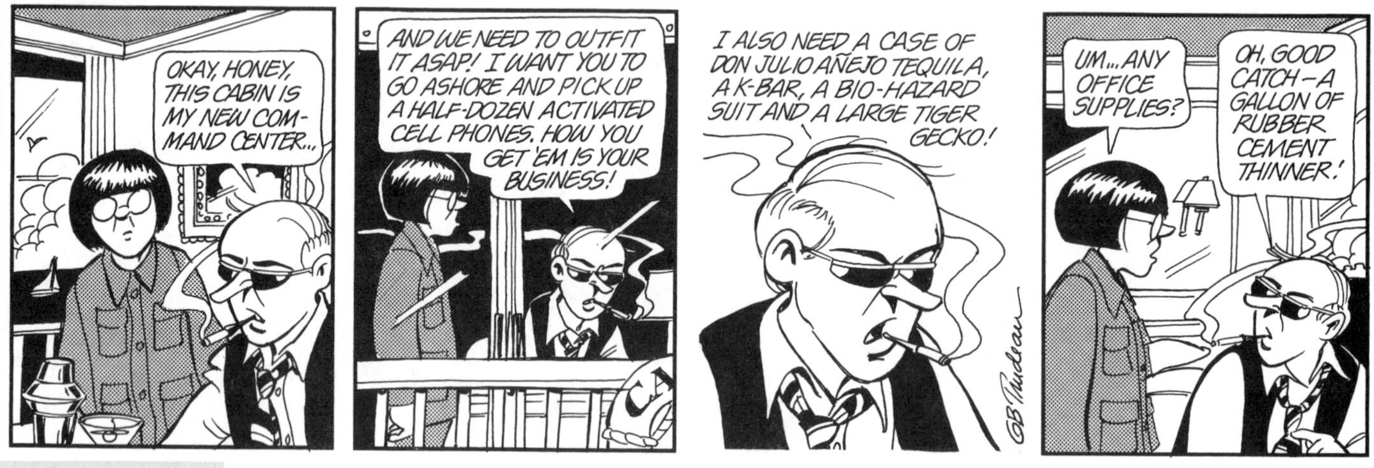
OKAY, HONEY, THIS CABIN IS MY NEW COMMAND CENTER...
AND WE NEED TO OUTFIT IT ASAP! I WANT YOU TO GO ASHORE AND PICK UP A HALF-DOZEN ACTIVATED CELL PHONES. HOW YOU GET 'EM IS YOUR BUSINESS!
I ALSO NEED A CASE OF DON JULIO AÑEJO TEQUILA, A K-BAR, A BIO-HAZARD SUIT AND A LARGE TIGER GECKO!
GB Trudeau
UM... ANY OFFICE SUPPLIES?
OH, GOOD CATCH—A GALLON OF RUBBER CEMENT THINNER!

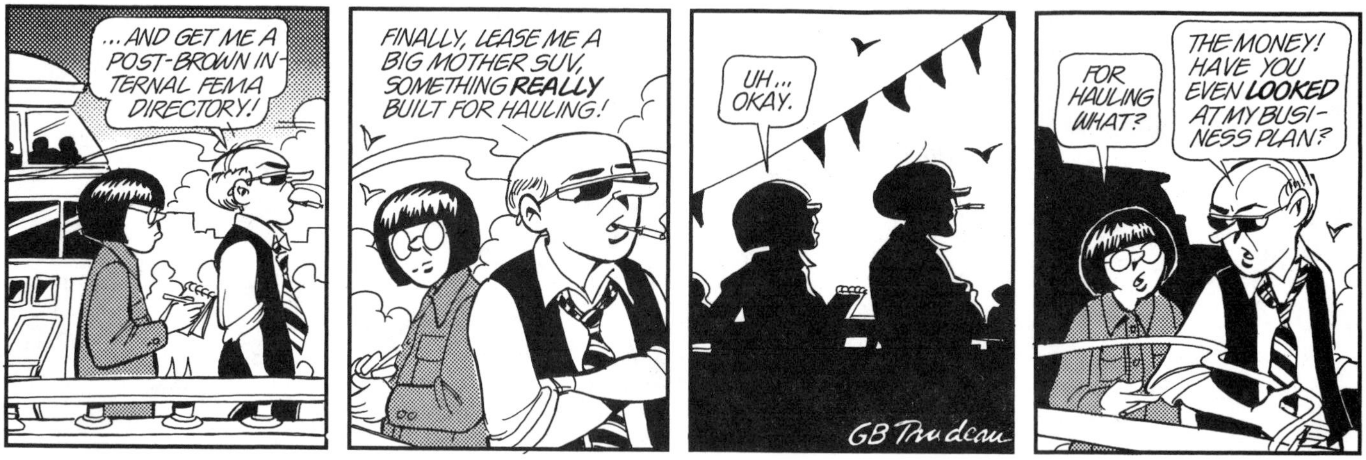
...AND GET ME A POST-BROWN INTERNAL FEMA DIRECTORY!
FINALLY, LEASE ME A BIG MOTHER SUV, SOMETHING **REALLY** BUILT FOR HAULING!
UH... OKAY.
GB Trudeau
FOR HAULING WHAT?
THE MONEY! HAVE YOU EVEN **LOOKED** AT MY BUSINESS PLAN?

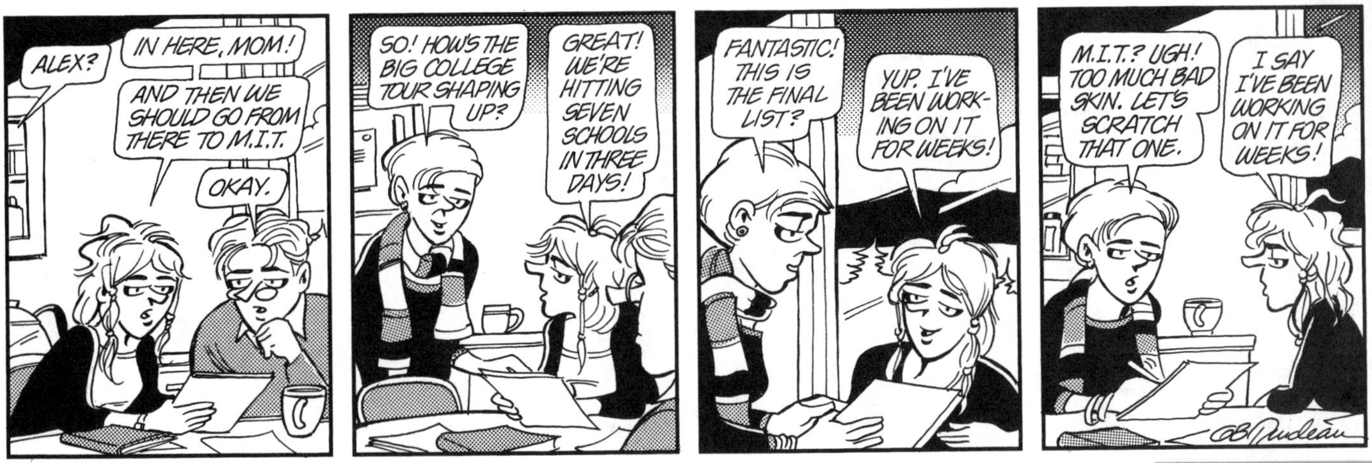
ALEX?
IN HERE, MOM!
AND THEN WE SHOULD GO FROM THERE TO M.I.T.
OKAY.
SO! HOW'S THE BIG COLLEGE TOUR SHAPING UP?
GREAT! WE'RE HITTING SEVEN SCHOOLS IN THREE DAYS!
FANTASTIC! THIS IS THE FINAL LIST?
YUP. I'VE BEEN WORKING ON IT FOR WEEKS!
M.I.T.? UGH! TOO MUCH BAD SKIN. LET'S SCRATCH THAT ONE.
I SAY I'VE BEEN WORKING ON IT FOR WEEKS!

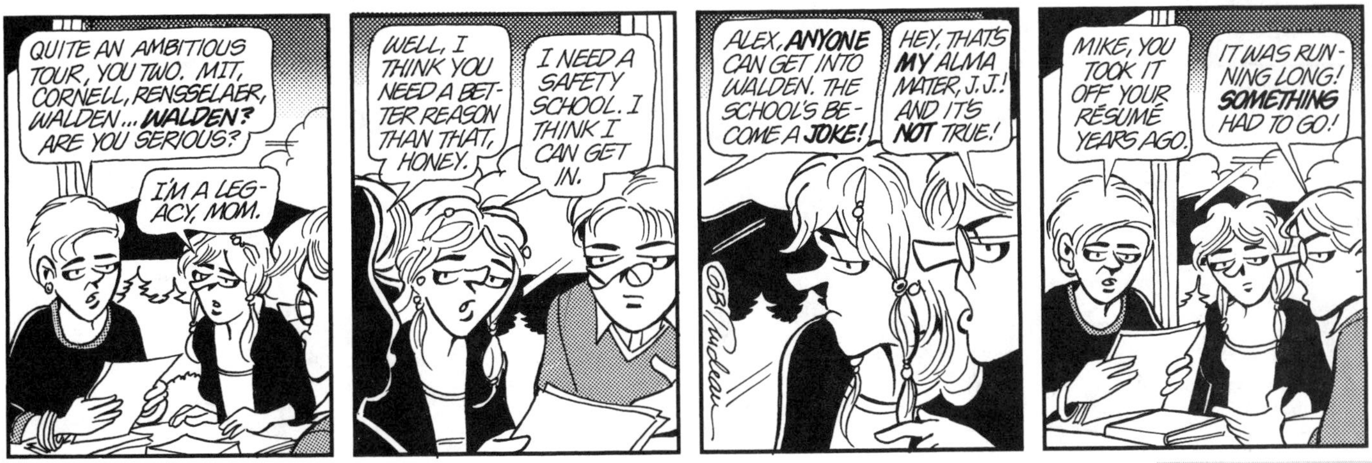
QUITE AN AMBITIOUS TOUR, YOU TWO. MIT, CORNELL, RENSSELAER, WALDEN... **WALDEN?** ARE YOU SERIOUS?
I'M A LEGACY, MOM.
WELL, I THINK YOU NEED A BETTER REASON THAN THAT, HONEY.
I NEED A SAFETY SCHOOL. I THINK I CAN GET IN.
ALEX, **ANYONE** CAN GET INTO WALDEN. THE SCHOOL'S BECOME A **JOKE**!
HEY, THAT'S **MY** ALMA MATER, J.J.! AND IT'S **NOT** TRUE!
MIKE, YOU TOOK IT OFF YOUR RÉSUMÉ YEARS AGO.
IT WAS RUNNING LONG! **SOMETHING** HAD TO GO!

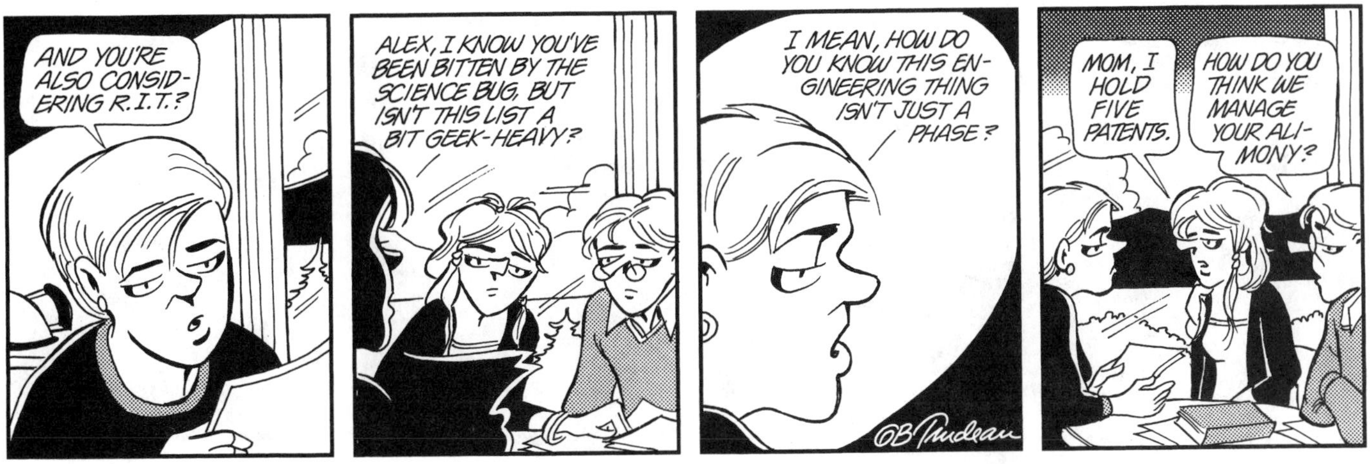
AND YOU'RE ALSO CONSIDERING R.I.T.?
ALEX, I KNOW YOU'VE BEEN BITTEN BY THE SCIENCE BUG, BUT ISN'T THIS LIST A BIT GEEK-HEAVY?
I MEAN, HOW DO YOU KNOW THIS ENGINEERING THING ISN'T JUST A PHASE?
MOM, I HOLD FIVE PATENTS.
HOW DO YOU THINK WE MANAGE YOUR ALIMONY?

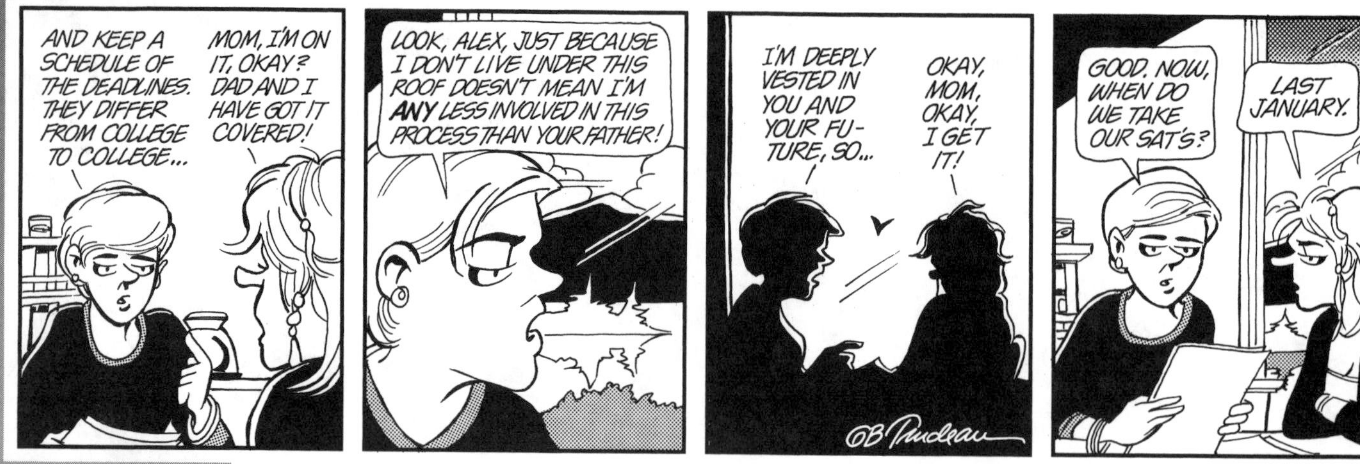
AND KEEP A SCHEDULE OF THE DEADLINES. THEY DIFFER FROM COLLEGE TO COLLEGE...
MOM, I'M ON IT, OKAY? DAD AND I HAVE GOT IT COVERED!
LOOK, ALEX, JUST BECAUSE I DON'T LIVE UNDER THIS ROOF DOESN'T MEAN I'M ANY LESS INVOLVED IN THIS PROCESS THAN YOUR FATHER!
I'M DEEPLY VESTED IN YOU AND YOUR FU-TURE, SO...
OKAY, MOM, OKAY, I GET IT!
GOOD. NOW, WHEN DO WE TAKE OUR SAT'S?
LAST JANUARY.

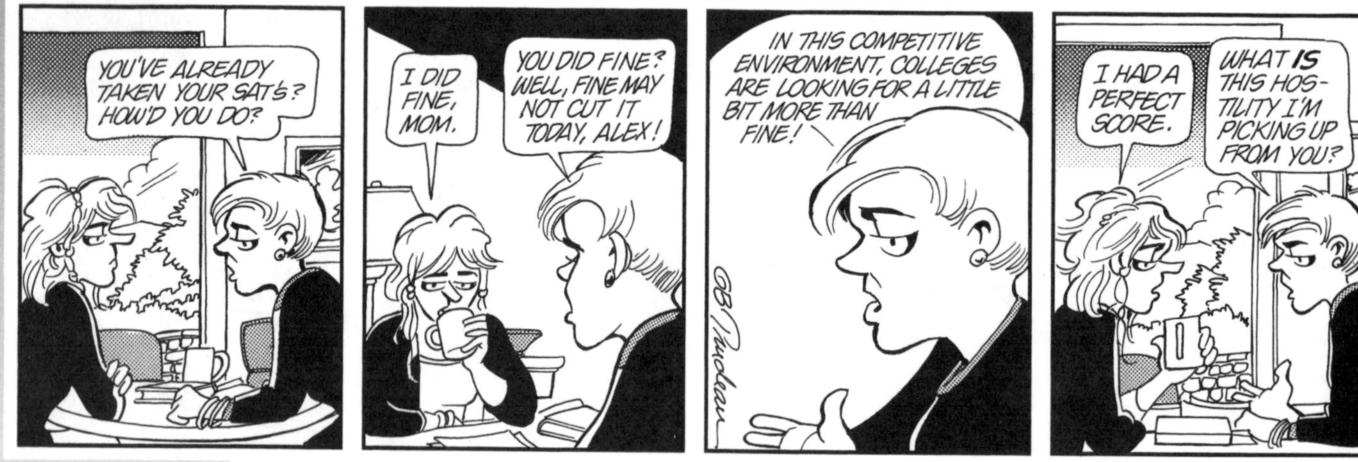
YOU'VE ALREADY TAKEN YOUR SAT'S? HOW'D YOU DO?
I DID FINE, MOM.
YOU DID FINE? WELL, FINE MAY NOT CUT IT TODAY, ALEX!
IN THIS COMPETITIVE ENVIRONMENT, COLLEGES ARE LOOKING FOR A LITTLE BIT MORE THAN FINE!
I HAD A PERFECT SCORE.
WHAT IS THIS HOS-TILITY I'M PICKING UP FROM YOU?

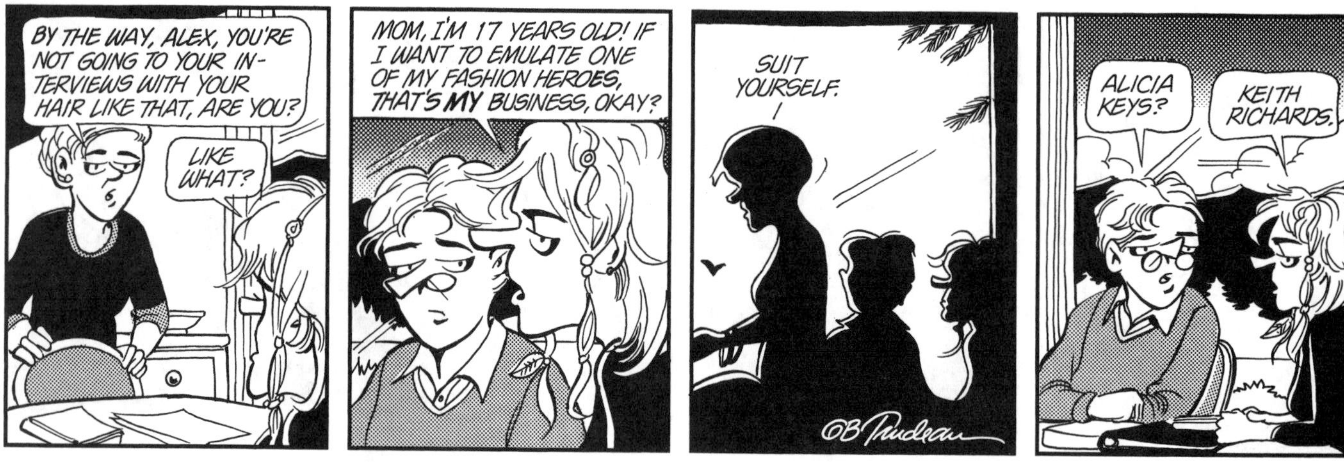
BY THE WAY, ALEX, YOU'RE NOT GOING TO YOUR IN-TERVIEWS WITH YOUR HAIR LIKE THAT, ARE YOU?
LIKE WHAT?
MOM, I'M 17 YEARS OLD! IF I WANT TO EMULATE ONE OF MY FASHION HEROES, THAT'S MY BUSINESS, OKAY?
SUIT YOURSELF.
ALICIA KEYS?
KEITH RICHARDS.

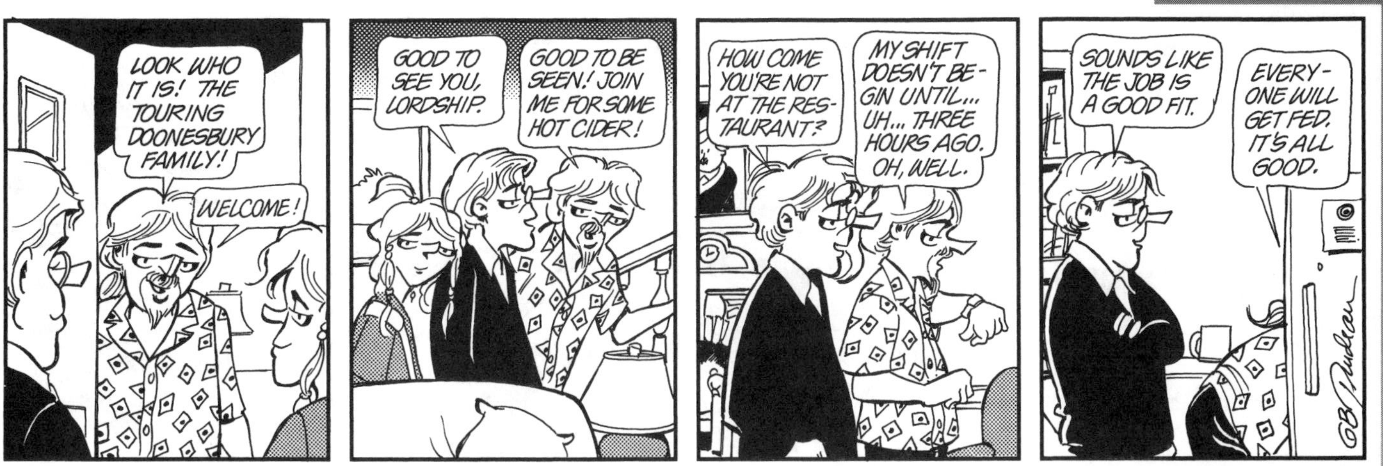
LOOK WHO IT IS! THE TOURING DOONESBURY FAMILY!
WELCOME!
GOOD TO SEE YOU, LORDSHIP.
GOOD TO BE SEEN! JOIN ME FOR SOME HOT CIDER!
HOW COME YOU'RE NOT AT THE RESTAURANT?
MY SHIFT DOESN'T BEGIN UNTIL... UH... THREE HOURS AGO. OH, WELL.
SOUNDS LIKE THE JOB IS A GOOD FIT.
EVERYONE WILL GET FED. IT'S ALL GOOD.
©B. Trudeau

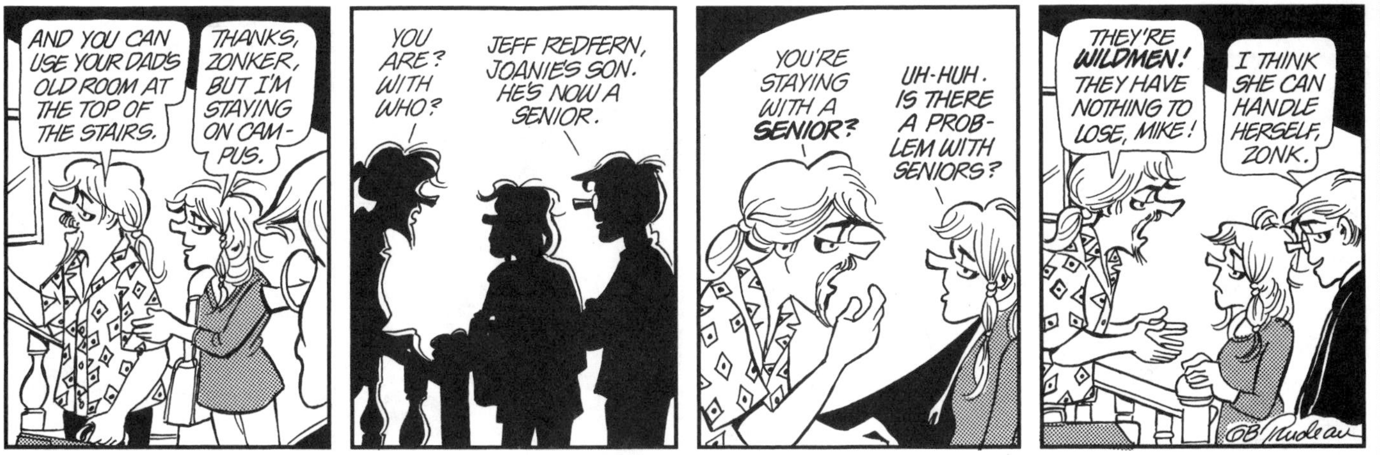
AND YOU CAN USE YOUR DAD'S OLD ROOM AT THE TOP OF THE STAIRS.
THANKS, ZONKER, BUT I'M STAYING ON CAMPUS.
YOU ARE? WITH WHO?
JEFF REDFERN, JOANIE'S SON. HE'S NOW A SENIOR.
YOU'RE STAYING WITH A SENIOR?
UH-HUH. IS THERE A PROBLEM WITH SENIORS?
THEY'RE WILDMEN! THEY HAVE NOTHING TO LOSE, MIKE!
I THINK SHE CAN HANDLE HERSELF, ZONK.
©B. Trudeau

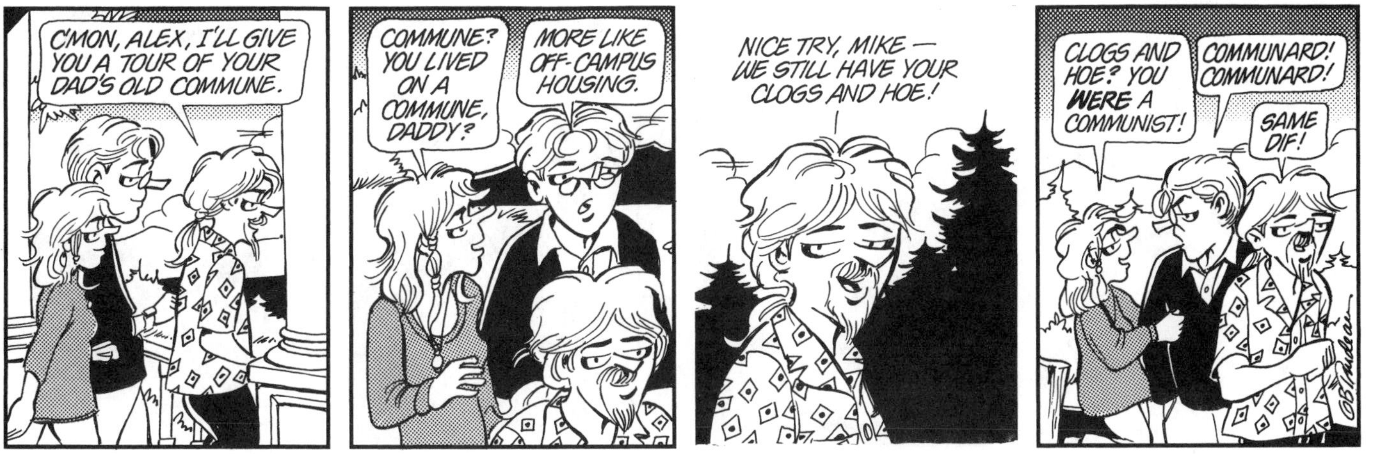
C'MON, ALEX, I'LL GIVE YOU A TOUR OF YOUR DAD'S OLD COMMUNE.
COMMUNE? YOU LIVED ON A COMMUNE, DADDY?
MORE LIKE OFF-CAMPUS HOUSING.
NICE TRY, MIKE — WE STILL HAVE YOUR CLOGS AND HOE!
CLOGS AND HOE? YOU WERE A COMMUNIST!
COMMUNARD! COMMUNARD!
SAME DIF!
©B. Trudeau

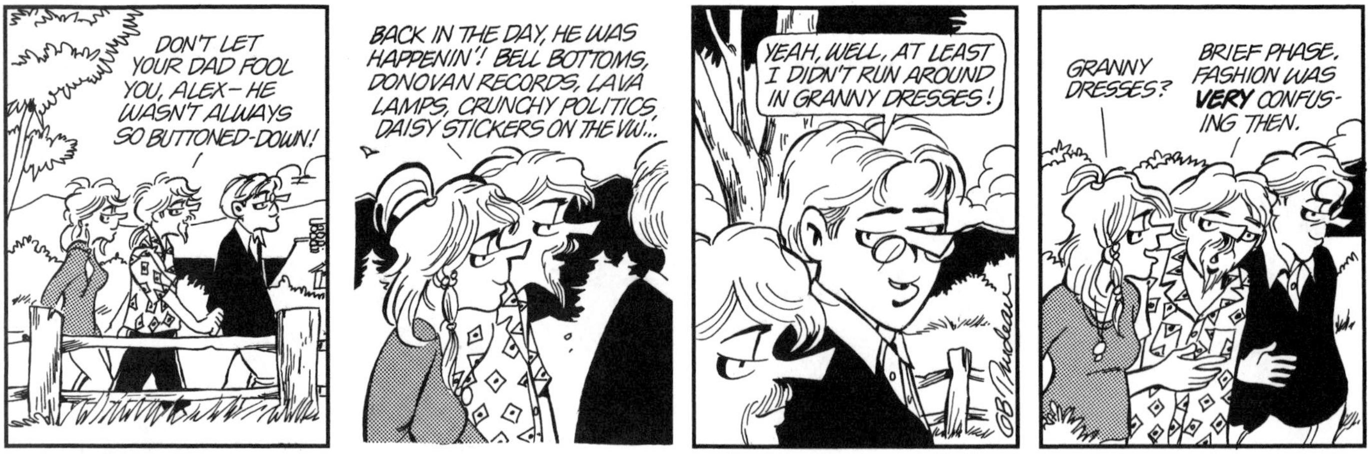
DON'T LET YOUR DAD FOOL YOU, ALEX– HE WASN'T ALWAYS SO BUTTONED-DOWN!
BACK IN THE DAY, HE WAS HAPPENIN'! BELL BOTTOMS, DONOVAN RECORDS, LAVA LAMPS, CRUNCHY POLITICS, DAISY STICKERS ON THE VW...
YEAH, WELL, AT LEAST I DIDN'T RUN AROUND IN GRANNY DRESSES!
GRANNY DRESSES?
BRIEF PHASE. FASHION WAS VERY CONFUSING THEN.

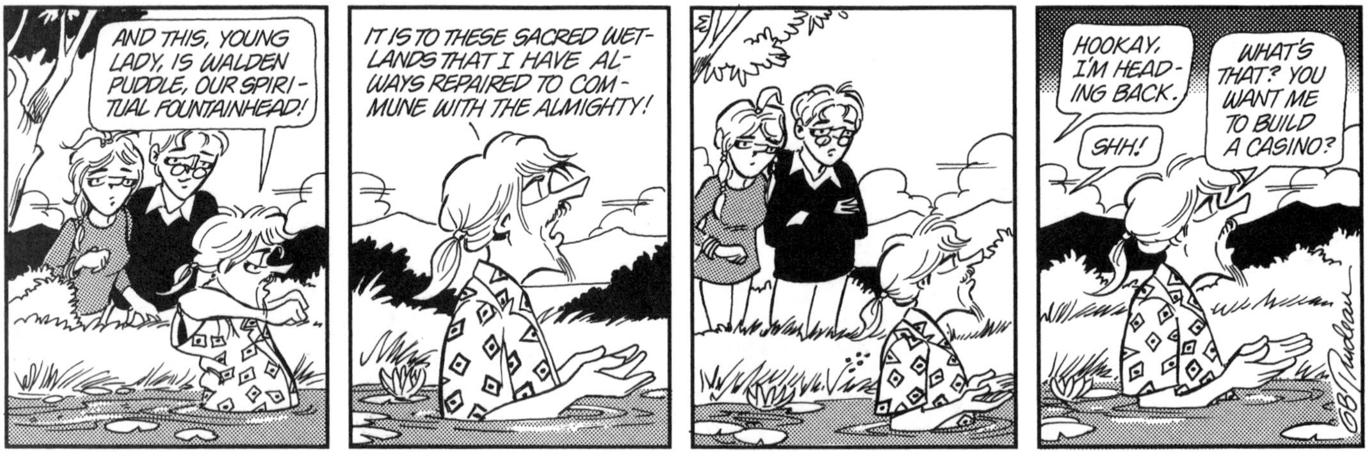
AND THIS, YOUNG LADY, IS WALDEN PUDDLE, OUR SPIRITUAL FOUNTAINHEAD!
IT IS TO THESE SACRED WETLANDS THAT I HAVE ALWAYS REPAIRED TO COMMUNE WITH THE ALMIGHTY!
HOOKAY. I'M HEADING BACK.
SHH!
WHAT'S THAT? YOU WANT ME TO BUILD A CASINO?

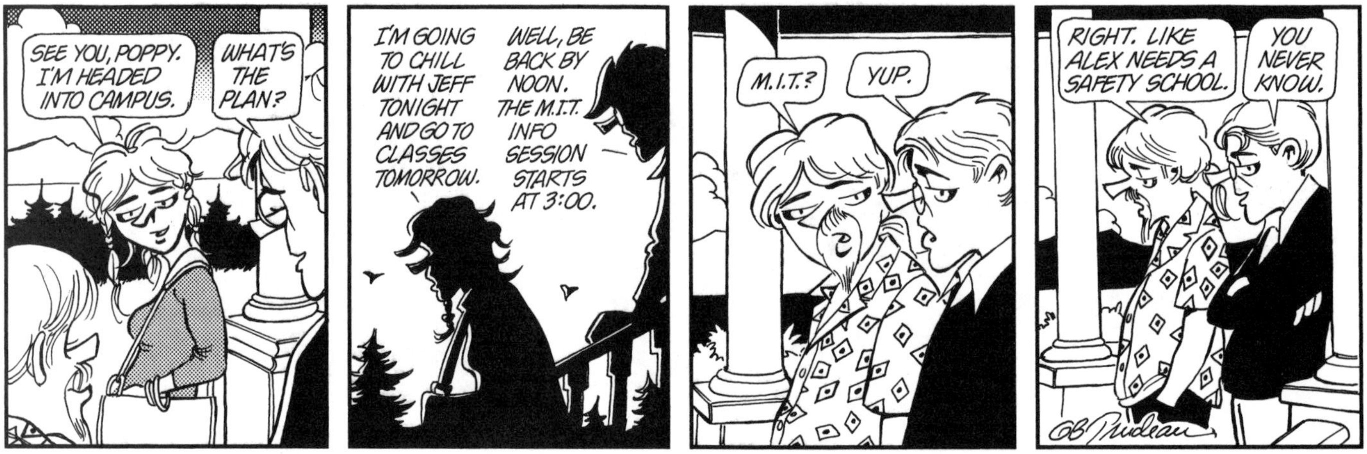
SEE YOU, POPPY. I'M HEADED INTO CAMPUS.
WHAT'S THE PLAN?
I'M GOING TO CHILL WITH JEFF TONIGHT AND GO TO CLASSES TOMORROW.
WELL, BE BACK BY NOON. THE M.I.T. INFO SESSION STARTS AT 3:00.
M.I.T.?
YUP.
RIGHT. LIKE ALEX NEEDS A SAFETY SCHOOL.
YOU NEVER KNOW.

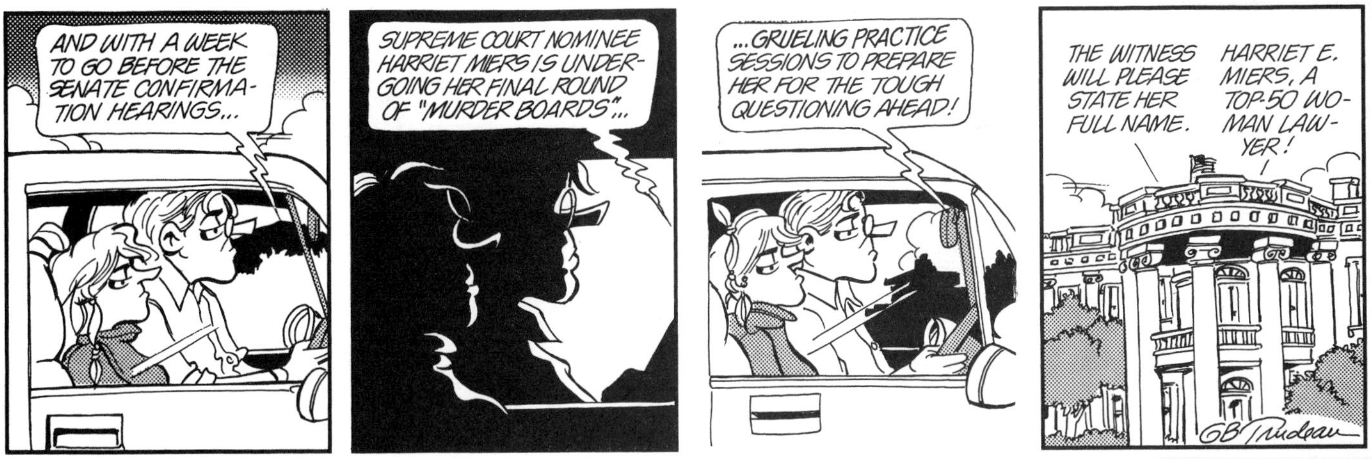
AND WITH A WEEK TO GO BEFORE THE SENATE CONFIRMATION HEARINGS...
SUPREME COURT NOMINEE HARRIET MIERS IS UNDERGOING HER FINAL ROUND OF "MURDER BOARDS"...
...GRUELING PRACTICE SESSIONS TO PREPARE HER FOR THE TOUGH QUESTIONING AHEAD!
THE WITNESS WILL PLEASE STATE HER FULL NAME.
HARRIET E. MIERS, A TOP-50 WOMAN LAWYER!

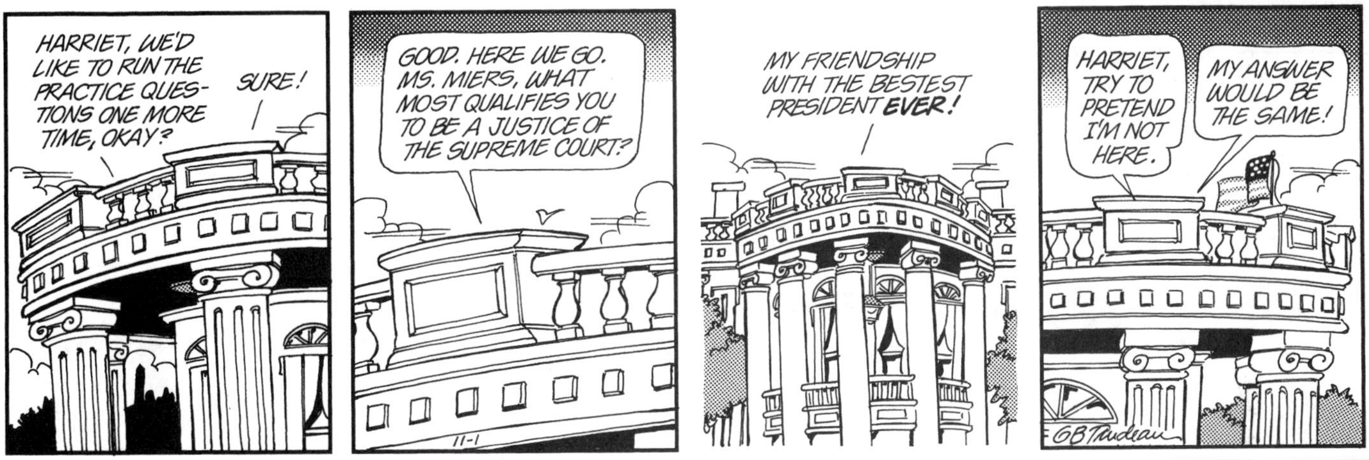
HARRIET, WE'D LIKE TO RUN THE PRACTICE QUESTIONS ONE MORE TIME, OKAY?
SURE!
GOOD. HERE WE GO. MS. MIERS, WHAT MOST QUALIFIES YOU TO BE A JUSTICE OF THE SUPREME COURT?
11-1
MY FRIENDSHIP WITH THE BESTEST PRESIDENT **EVER**!
HARRIET, TRY TO PRETEND I'M NOT HERE.
MY ANSWER WOULD BE THE SAME!

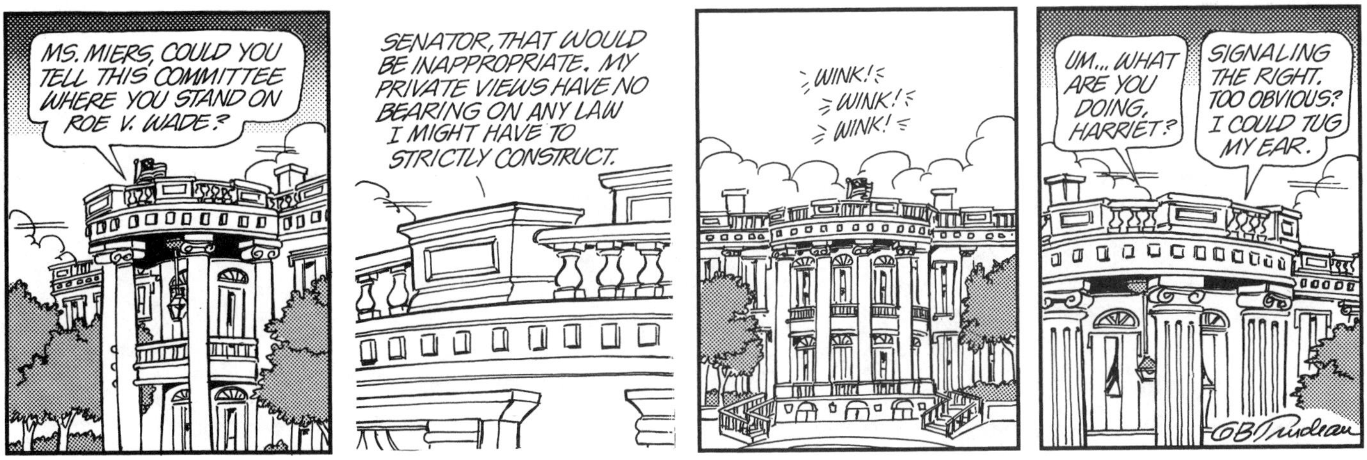
MS. MIERS, COULD YOU TELL THIS COMMITTEE WHERE YOU STAND ON ROE V. WADE?
SENATOR, THAT WOULD BE INAPPROPRIATE. MY PRIVATE VIEWS HAVE NO BEARING ON ANY LAW I MIGHT HAVE TO STRICTLY CONSTRUCT.
WINK! WINK! WINK!
UM... WHAT ARE YOU DOING, HARRIET?
SIGNALING THE RIGHT, TOO OBVIOUS? I COULD TUG MY EAR.

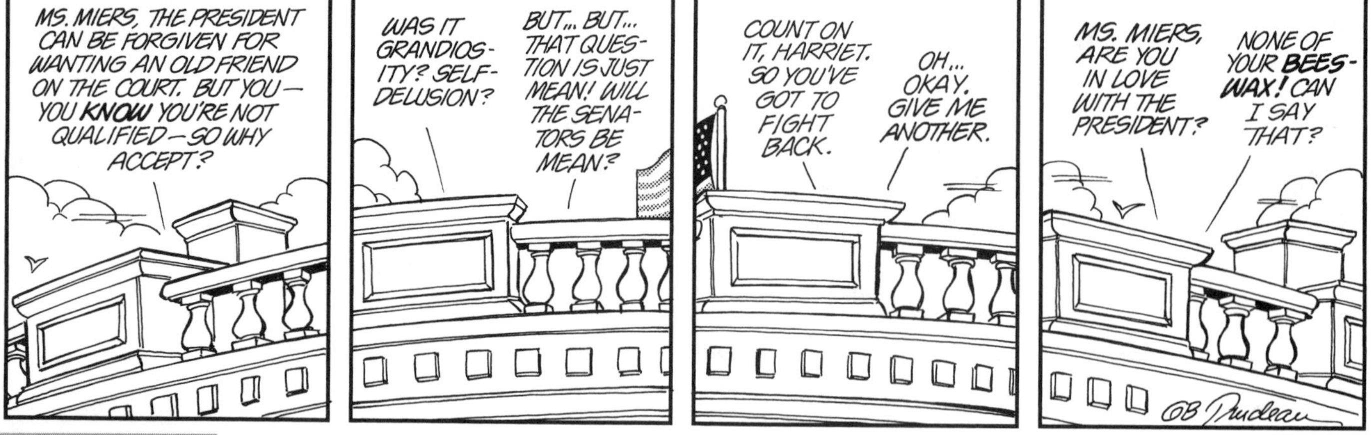
MS. MIERS, THE PRESIDENT CAN BE FORGIVEN FOR WANTING AN OLD FRIEND ON THE COURT. BUT YOU— YOU **KNOW** YOU'RE NOT QUALIFIED—SO WHY ACCEPT?
WAS IT GRANDIOS-ITY? SELF-DELUSION?
BUT... BUT... THAT QUES-TION IS JUST MEAN! WILL THE SENA-TORS BE MEAN?
COUNT ON IT, HARRIET. SO YOU'VE GOT TO FIGHT BACK.
OH... OKAY. GIVE ME ANOTHER.
MS. MIERS, ARE YOU IN LOVE WITH THE PRESIDENT?
NONE OF YOUR **BEES-WAX!** CAN I SAY THAT?

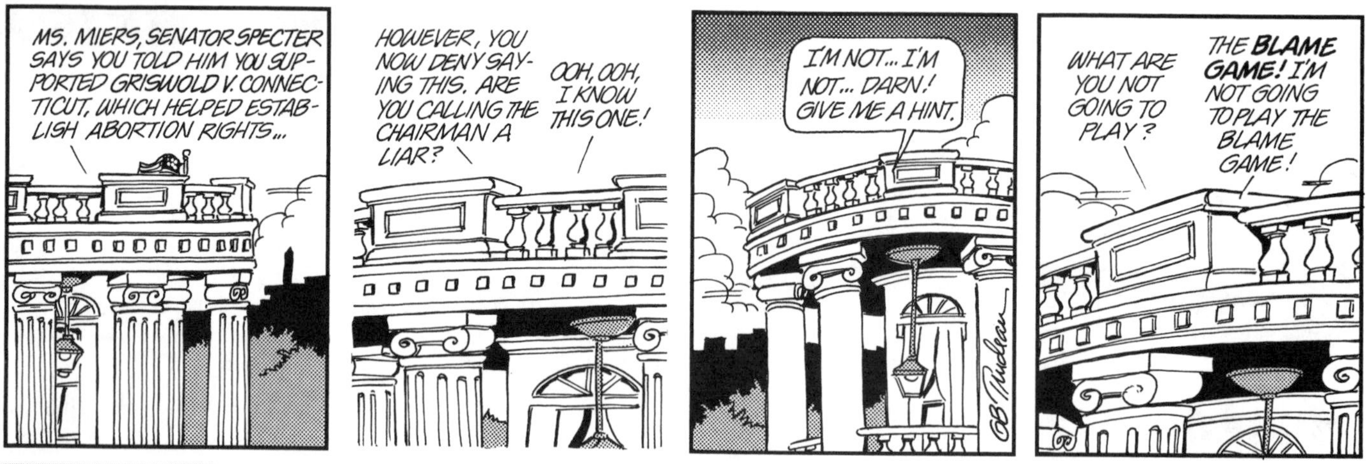
MS. MIERS, SENATOR SPECTER SAYS YOU TOLD HIM YOU SUP-PORTED GRISWOLD V. CONNEC-TICUT, WHICH HELPED ESTAB-LISH ABORTION RIGHTS...
HOWEVER, YOU NOW DENY SAY-ING THIS. ARE YOU CALLING THE CHAIRMAN A LIAR?
OOH, OOH, I KNOW THIS ONE!
I'M NOT... I'M NOT... DARN! GIVE ME A HINT.
WHAT ARE YOU NOT GOING TO PLAY?
THE **BLAME GAME!** I'M NOT GOING TO PLAY THE BLAME GAME!

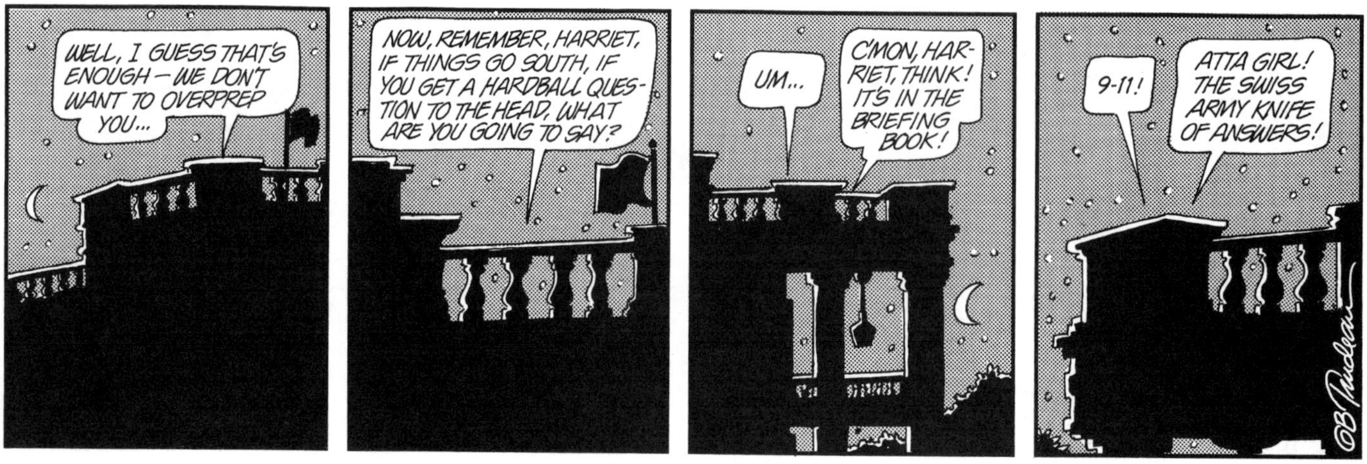
WELL, I GUESS THAT'S ENOUGH—WE DON'T WANT TO OVERPREP YOU...
NOW, REMEMBER, HARRIET, IF THINGS GO SOUTH, IF YOU GET A HARDBALL QUES-TION TO THE HEAD, WHAT ARE YOU GOING TO SAY?
UM...
C'MON, HAR-RIET, THINK! IT'S IN THE BRIEFING BOOK!
9-11!
ATTA GIRL! THE SWISS ARMY KNIFE OF ANSWERS!

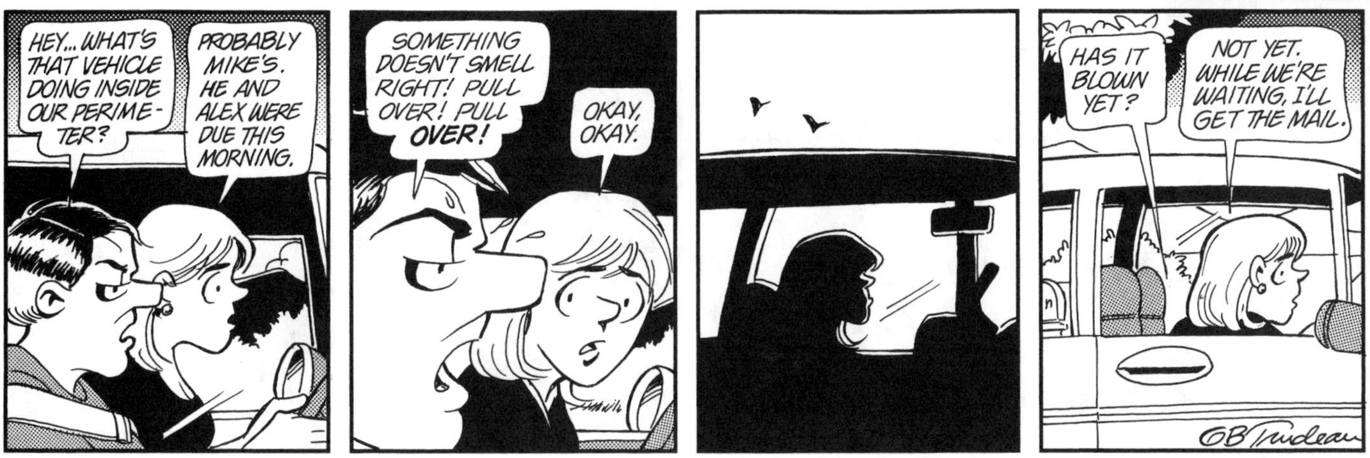
HEY... WHAT'S THAT VEHICLE DOING INSIDE OUR PERIME-TER?
PROBABLY MIKE'S. HE AND ALEX WERE DUE THIS MORNING.
SOMETHING DOESN'T SMELL RIGHT! PULL OVER! PULL **OVER!**
OKAY, OKAY.
HAS IT BLOWN YET?
NOT YET. WHILE WE'RE WAITING, I'LL GET THE MAIL.
GB Trudeau

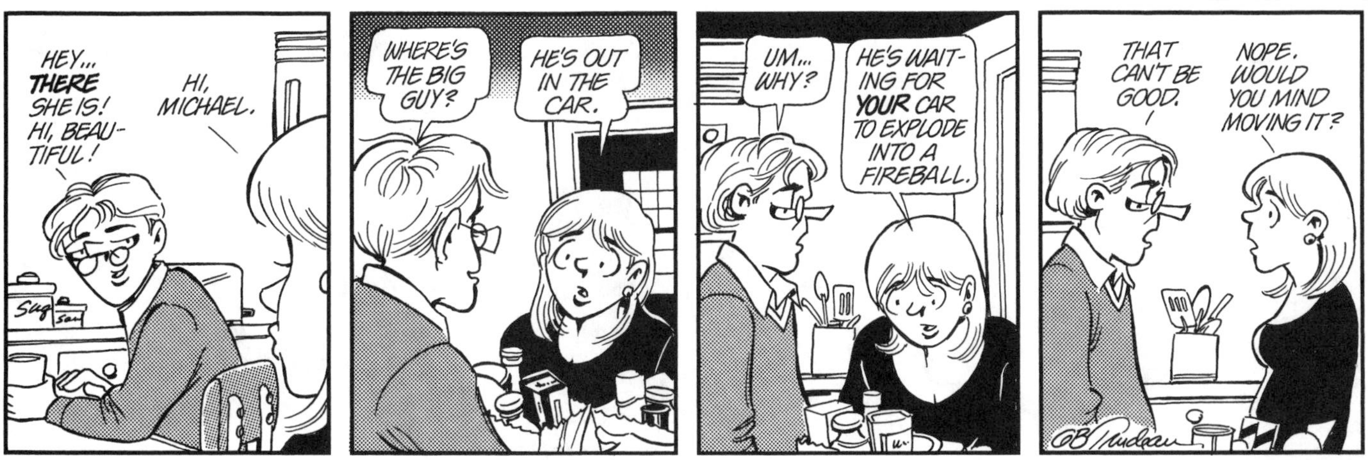
HEY... **THERE** SHE IS! HI, BEAU-TIFUL!
HI, MICHAEL.
WHERE'S THE BIG GUY?
HE'S OUT IN THE CAR.
UM... WHY?
HE'S WAIT-ING FOR **YOUR** CAR TO EXPLODE INTO A FIREBALL.
THAT CAN'T BE GOOD.
NOPE. WOULD YOU MIND MOVING IT?
GB Trudeau

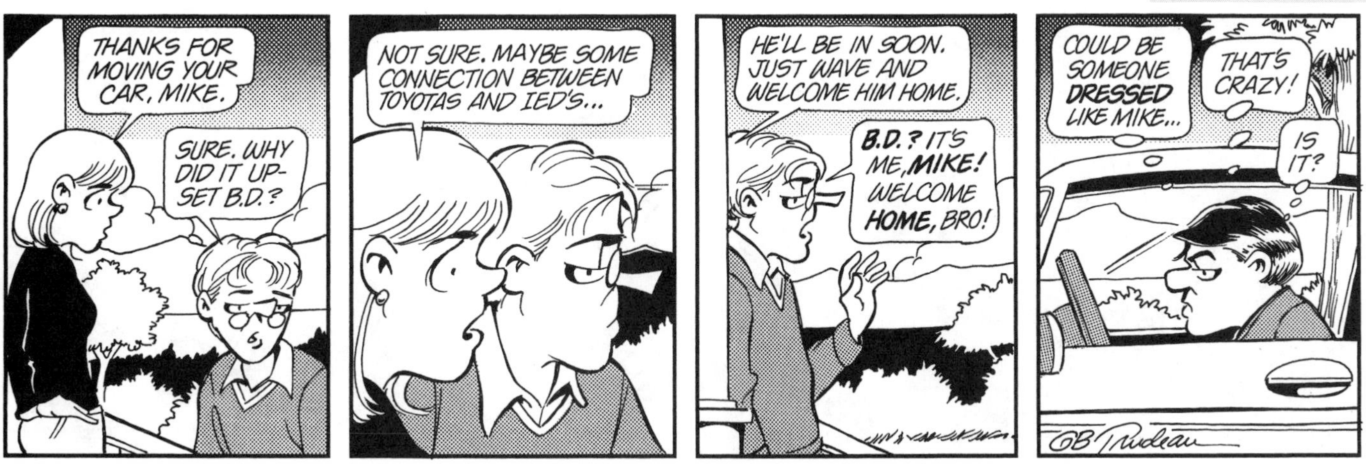
THANKS FOR MOVING YOUR CAR, MIKE.
SURE. WHY DID IT UP-SET B.D.?
NOT SURE. MAYBE SOME CONNECTION BETWEEN TOYOTAS AND IED'S...
HE'LL BE IN SOON. JUST WAVE AND WELCOME HIM HOME.
B.D.? IT'S ME, **MIKE!** WELCOME **HOME,** BRO!
COULD BE SOMEONE **DRESSED** LIKE MIKE...
THAT'S CRAZY!
IS IT?
GB Trudeau

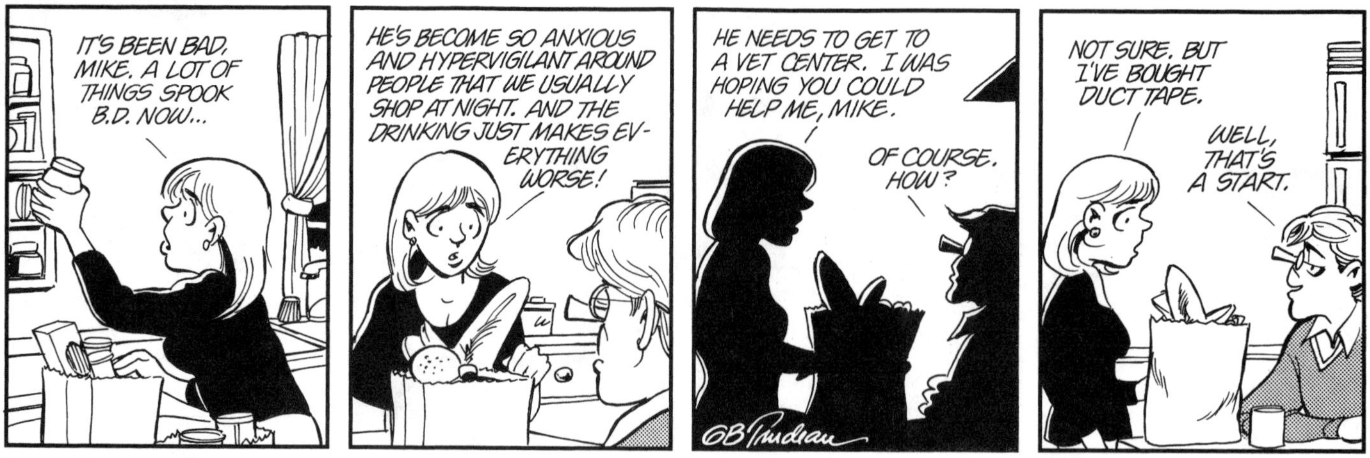
IT'S BEEN BAD, MIKE. A LOT OF THINGS SPOOK B.D. NOW...
HE'S BECOME SO ANXIOUS AND HYPERVIGILANT AROUND PEOPLE THAT WE USUALLY SHOP AT NIGHT. AND THE DRINKING JUST MAKES EVERYTHING WORSE!
HE NEEDS TO GET TO A VET CENTER. I WAS HOPING YOU COULD HELP ME, MIKE.
OF COURSE. HOW?
NOT SURE. BUT I'VE BOUGHT DUCT TAPE.
WELL, THAT'S A START.
©B Trudeau

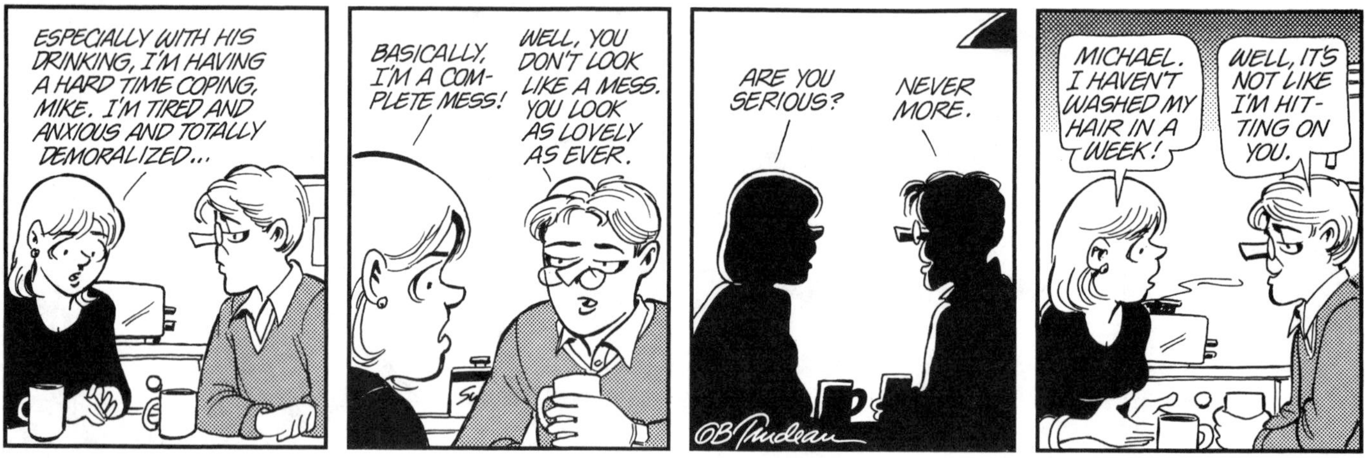
ESPECIALLY WITH HIS DRINKING, I'M HAVING A HARD TIME COPING, MIKE. I'M TIRED AND ANXIOUS AND TOTALLY DEMORALIZED...
BASICALLY, I'M A COMPLETE MESS!
WELL, YOU DON'T LOOK LIKE A MESS. YOU LOOK AS LOVELY AS EVER.
ARE YOU SERIOUS?
NEVER MORE.
MICHAEL. I HAVEN'T WASHED MY HAIR IN A WEEK!
WELL, IT'S NOT LIKE I'M HITTING ON YOU.
©B Trudeau

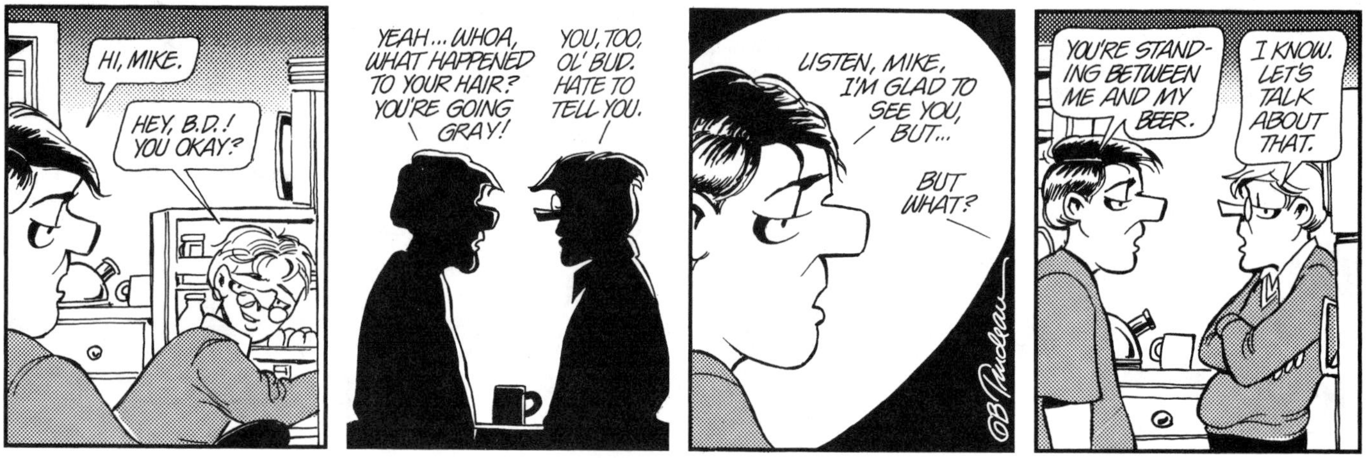
HI, MIKE.
HEY, B.D.! YOU OKAY?
YEAH... WHOA, WHAT HAPPENED TO YOUR HAIR? YOU'RE GOING GRAY!
YOU, TOO, OL' BUD. HATE TO TELL YOU.
LISTEN, MIKE, I'M GLAD TO SEE YOU, BUT...
BUT WHAT?
YOU'RE STANDING BETWEEN ME AND MY BEER.
I KNOW. LET'S TALK ABOUT THAT.
©B Trudeau

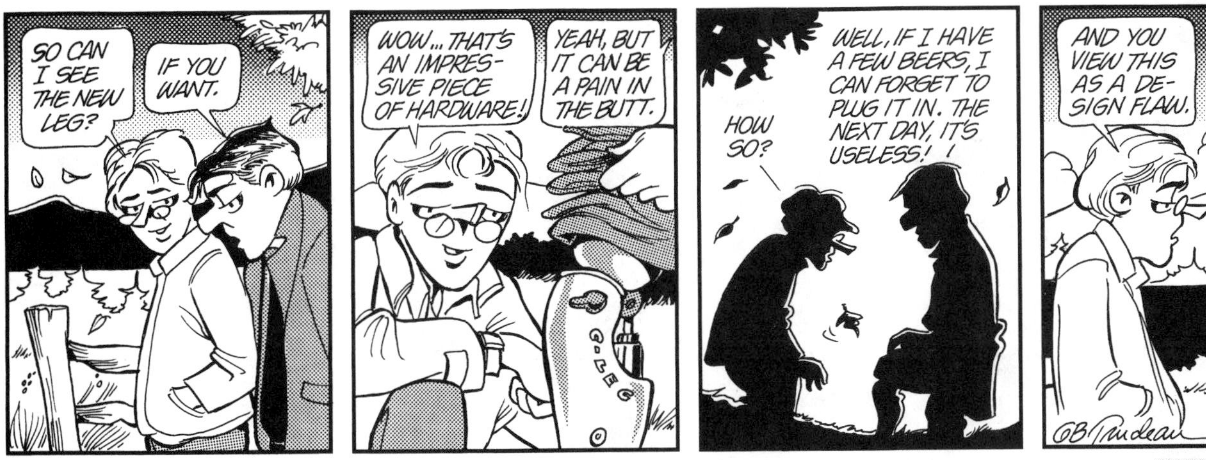
SO CAN I SEE THE NEW LEG?
IF YOU WANT.
WOW... THAT'S AN IMPRESSIVE PIECE OF HARDWARE!
YEAH, BUT IT CAN BE A PAIN IN THE BUTT.
HOW SO?
WELL, IF I HAVE A FEW BEERS, I CAN FORGET TO PLUG IT IN. THE NEXT DAY, IT'S USELESS!
AND YOU VIEW THIS AS A DESIGN FLAW.
DAMN STRAIGHT. I WROTE THE COMPANY.

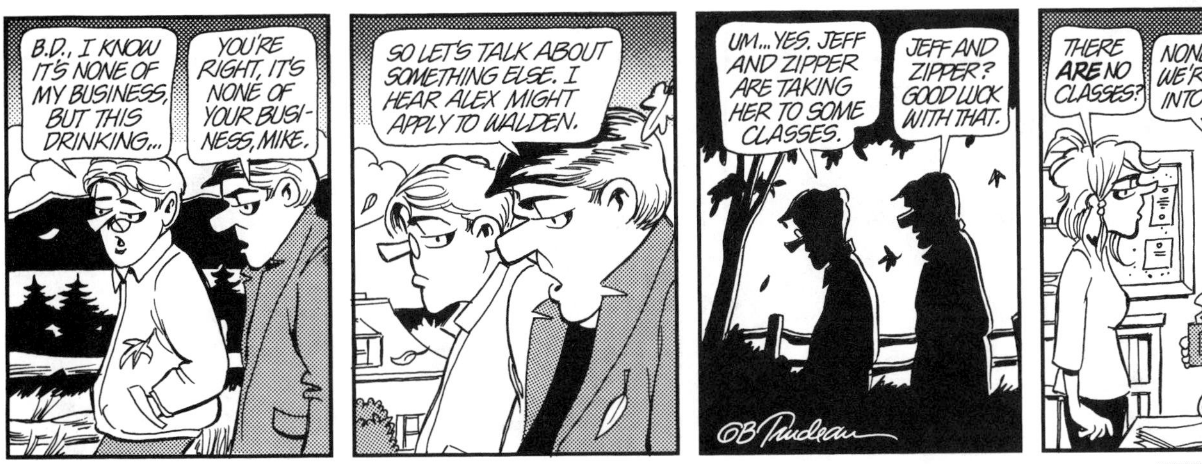
B.D., I KNOW IT'S NONE OF MY BUSINESS, BUT THIS DRINKING...
YOU'RE RIGHT, IT'S NONE OF YOUR BUSINESS, MIKE.
SO LET'S TALK ABOUT SOMETHING ELSE. I HEAR ALEX MIGHT APPLY TO WALDEN.
UM... YES. JEFF AND ZIPPER ARE TAKING HER TO SOME CLASSES.
JEFF AND ZIPPER? GOOD LUCK WITH THAT.
THERE ARE NO CLASSES?
NONE WE'RE INTO.
AT LEAST NOT THIS TIME OF DAY.

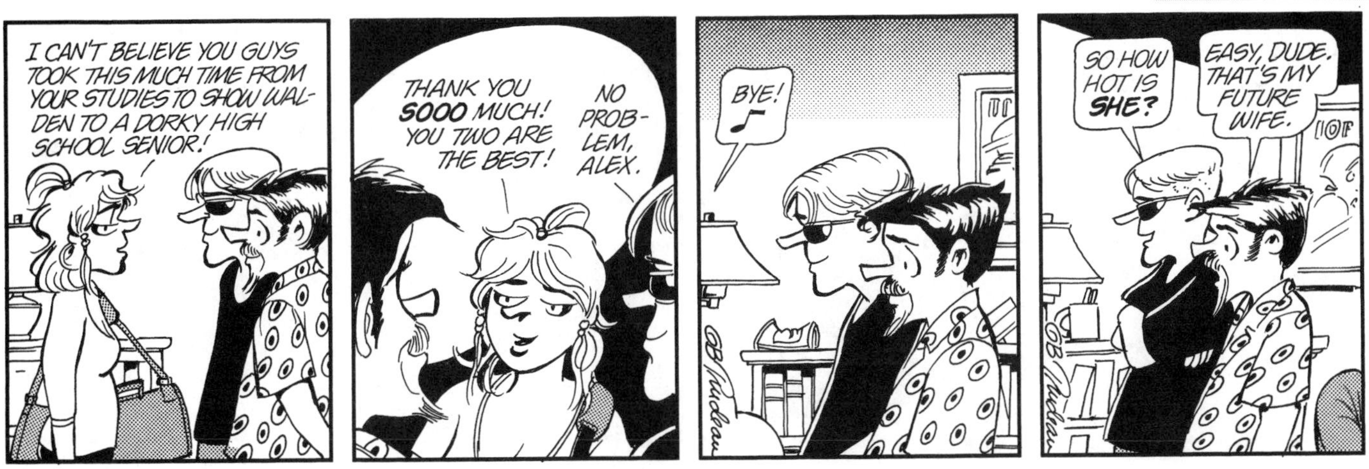
I CAN'T BELIEVE YOU GUYS TOOK THIS MUCH TIME FROM YOUR STUDIES TO SHOW WALDEN TO A DORKY HIGH SCHOOL SENIOR!
THANK YOU SOOO MUCH! YOU TWO ARE THE BEST!
NO PROBLEM, ALEX.
BYE!
SO HOW HOT IS SHE?
EASY, DUDE. THAT'S MY FUTURE WIFE.

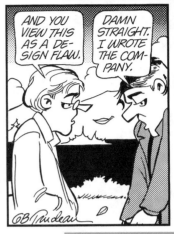

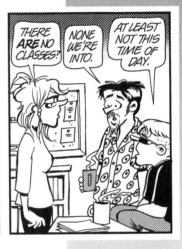

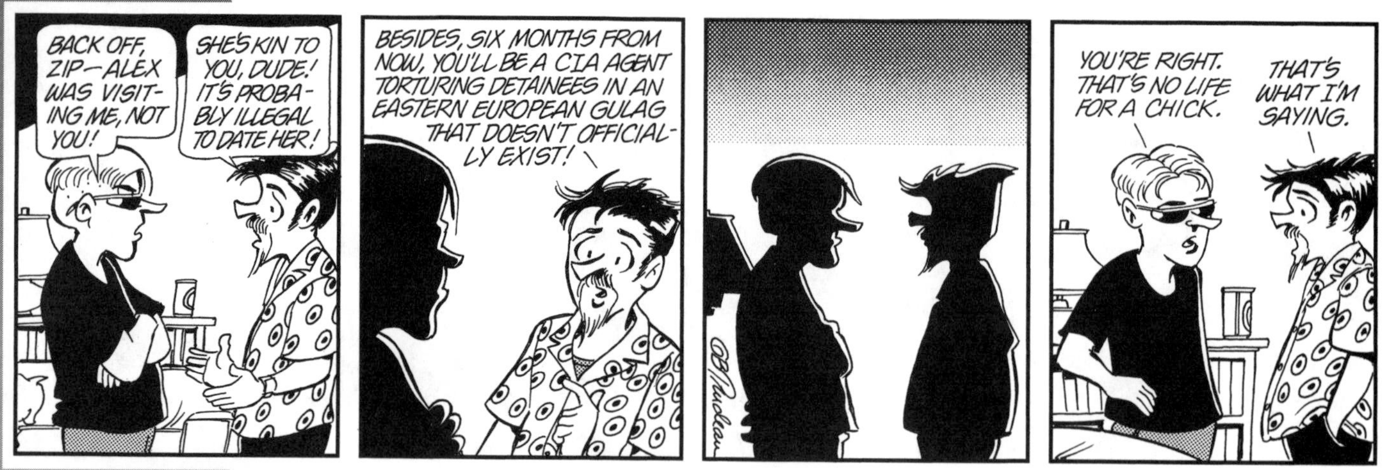
BACK OFF, ZIP—ALEX WAS VISITING ME, NOT YOU!
SHE'S KIN TO YOU, DUDE! IT'S PROBABLY ILLEGAL TO DATE HER!
BESIDES, SIX MONTHS FROM NOW, YOU'LL BE A CIA AGENT TORTURING DETAINEES IN AN EASTERN EUROPEAN GULAG THAT DOESN'T OFFICIALLY EXIST!
YOU'RE RIGHT. THAT'S NO LIFE FOR A CHICK.
THAT'S WHAT I'M SAYING.

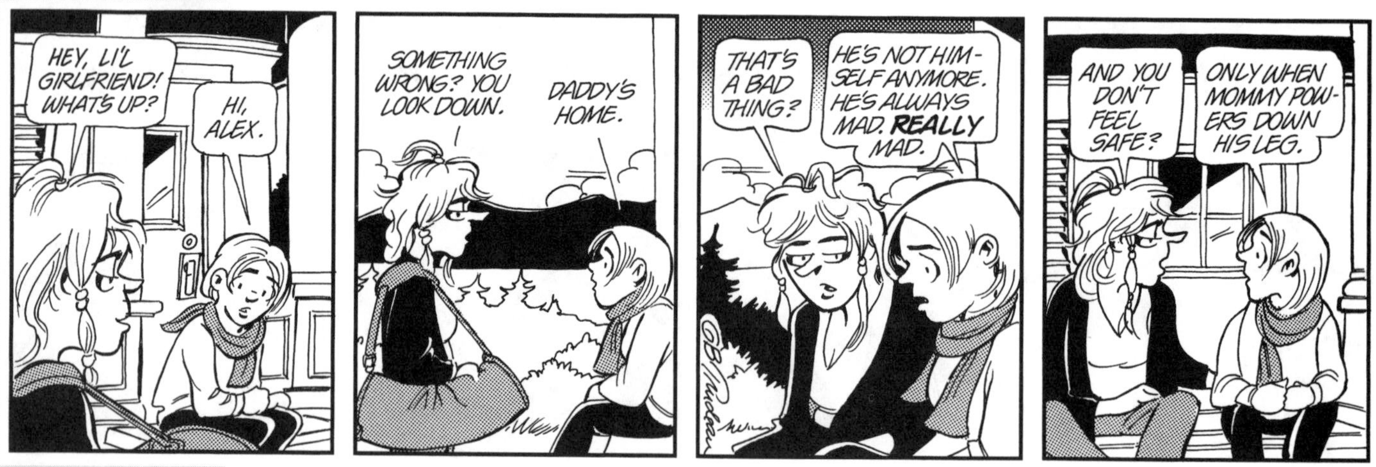
HEY, LI'L GIRLFRIEND! WHAT'S UP?
HI, ALEX.
SOMETHING WRONG? YOU LOOK DOWN.
DADDY'S HOME.
THAT'S A BAD THING?
HE'S NOT HIMSELF ANYMORE. HE'S ALWAYS MAD. REALLY MAD.
AND YOU DON'T FEEL SAFE?
ONLY WHEN MOMMY POWERS DOWN HIS LEG.

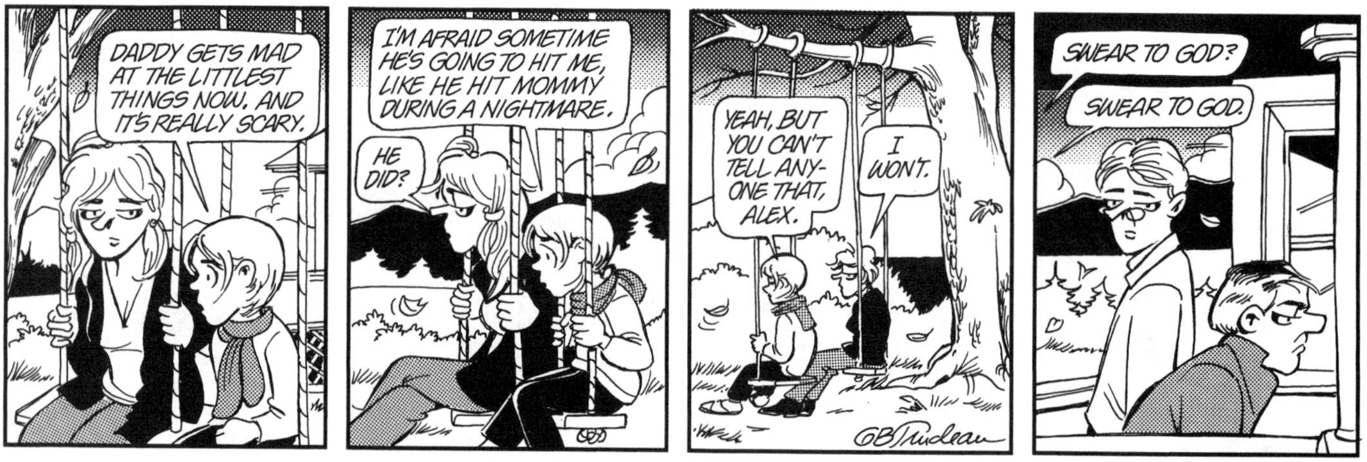
DADDY GETS MAD AT THE LITTLEST THINGS NOW, AND IT'S REALLY SCARY.
I'M AFRAID SOMETIME HE'S GOING TO HIT ME, LIKE HE HIT MOMMY DURING A NIGHTMARE.
HE DID?
YEAH, BUT YOU CAN'T TELL ANYONE THAT, ALEX.
I WON'T.
SWEAR TO GOD?
SWEAR TO GOD.

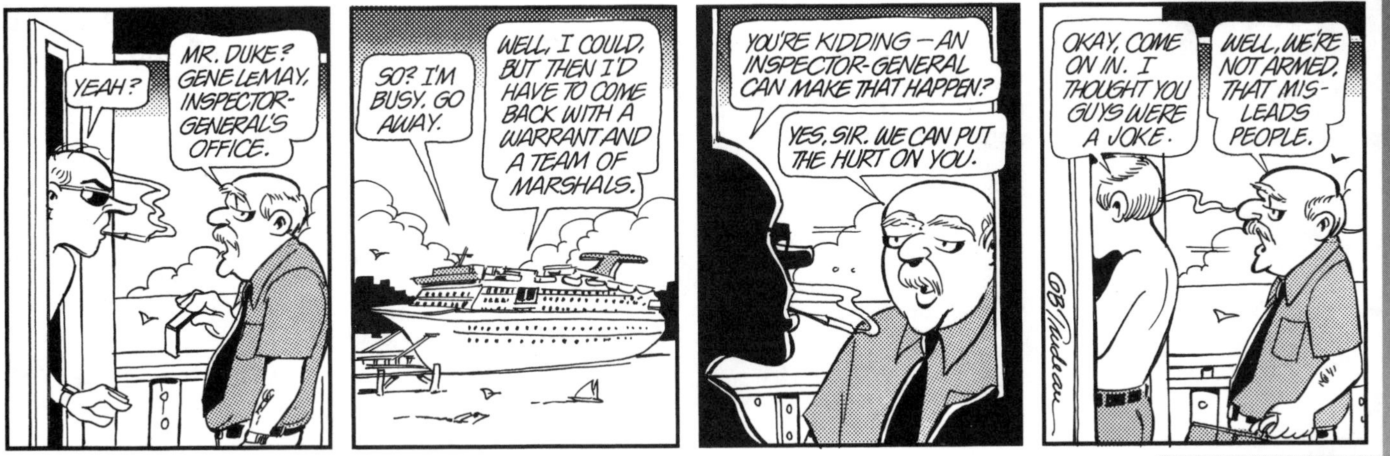
YEAH?
MR. DUKE? GENE LEMAY, INSPECTOR-GENERAL'S OFFICE.
SO? I'M BUSY. GO AWAY.
WELL, I COULD, BUT THEN I'D HAVE TO COME BACK WITH A WARRANT AND A TEAM OF MARSHALS.
YOU'RE KIDDING — AN INSPECTOR-GENERAL CAN MAKE THAT HAPPEN?
YES, SIR. WE CAN PUT THE HURT ON YOU.
OKAY, COME ON IN. I THOUGHT YOU GUYS WERE A JOKE.
WELL, WE'RE NOT ARMED. THAT MISLEADS PEOPLE.

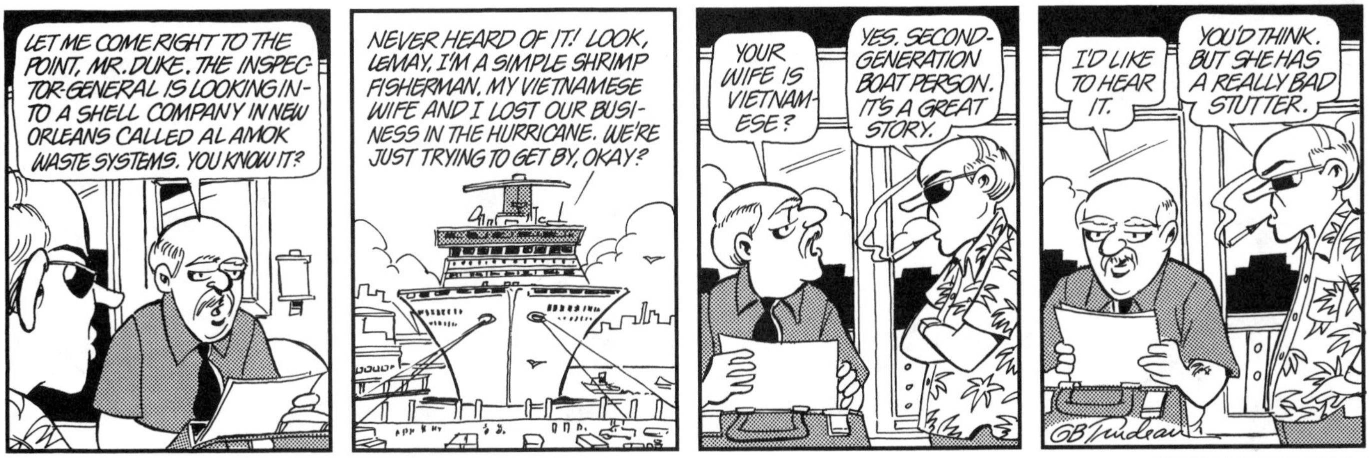
LET ME COME RIGHT TO THE POINT, MR. DUKE. THE INSPECTOR-GENERAL IS LOOKING INTO A SHELL COMPANY IN NEW ORLEANS CALLED AL AMOK WASTE SYSTEMS. YOU KNOW IT?
NEVER HEARD OF IT! LOOK, LEMAY, I'M A SIMPLE SHRIMP FISHERMAN. MY VIETNAMESE WIFE AND I LOST OUR BUSINESS IN THE HURRICANE. WE'RE JUST TRYING TO GET BY, OKAY?
YOUR WIFE IS VIETNAMESE?
YES. SECOND-GENERATION BOAT PERSON. IT'S A GREAT STORY.
I'D LIKE TO HEAR IT.
YOU'D THINK. BUT SHE HAS A REALLY BAD STUTTER.

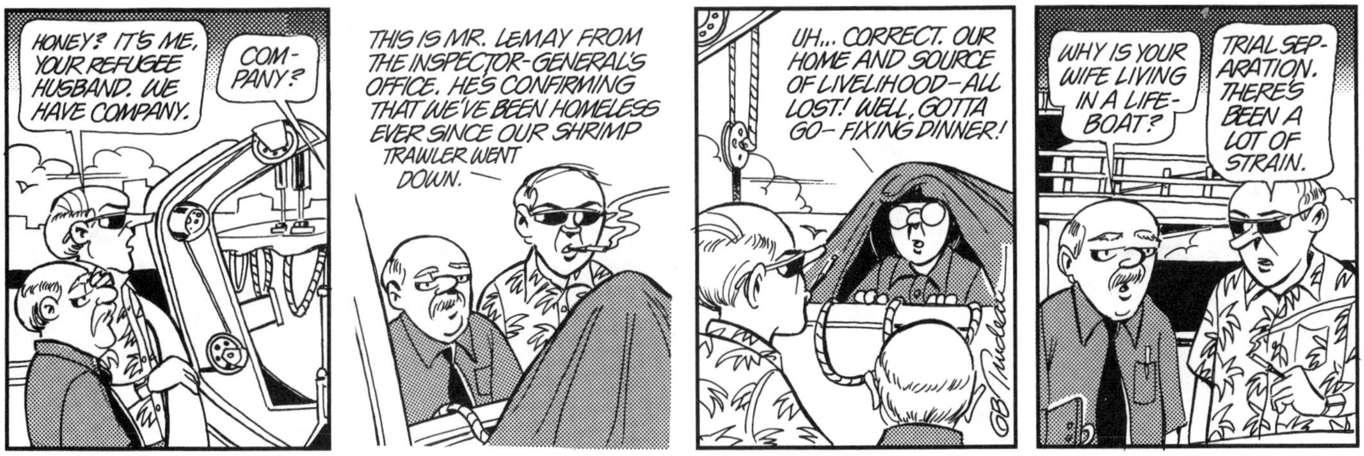
HONEY? IT'S ME, YOUR REFUGEE HUSBAND. WE HAVE COMPANY.
COMPANY?
THIS IS MR. LEMAY FROM THE INSPECTOR-GENERAL'S OFFICE. HE'S CONFIRMING THAT WE'VE BEEN HOMELESS EVER SINCE OUR SHRIMP TRAWLER WENT DOWN.
UH... CORRECT. OUR HOME AND SOURCE OF LIVELIHOOD—ALL LOST! WELL, GOTTA GO—FIXING DINNER!
WHY IS YOUR WIFE LIVING IN A LIFEBOAT?
TRIAL SEPARATION. THERE'S BEEN A LOT OF STRAIN.

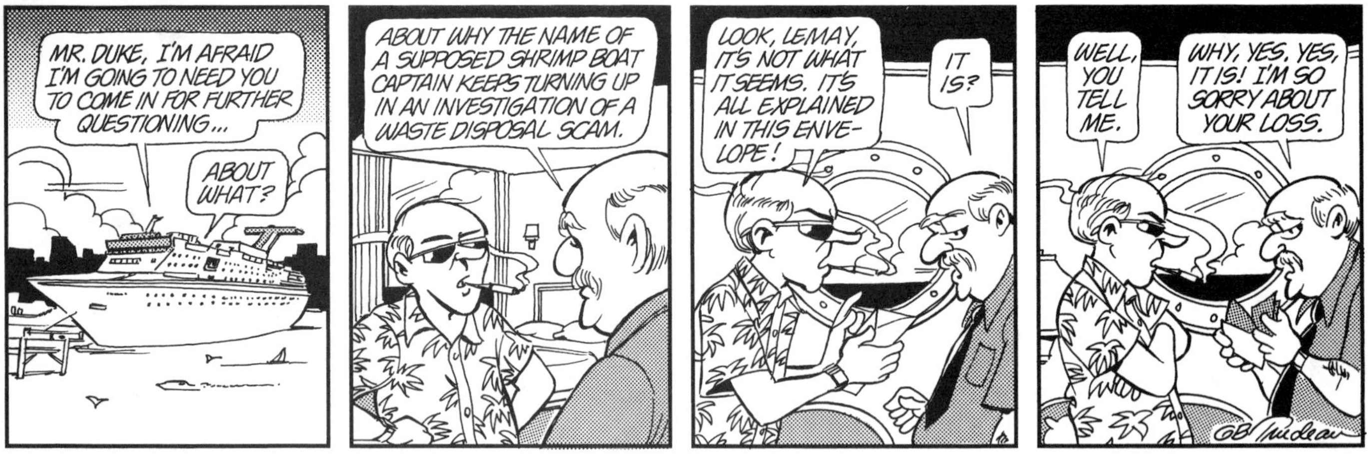
MR. DUKE, I'M AFRAID I'M GOING TO NEED YOU TO COME IN FOR FURTHER QUESTIONING...
ABOUT WHAT?
ABOUT WHY THE NAME OF A SUPPOSED SHRIMP BOAT CAPTAIN KEEPS TURNING UP IN AN INVESTIGATION OF A WASTE DISPOSAL SCAM.
LOOK, LEMAY, IT'S NOT WHAT IT SEEMS. IT'S ALL EXPLAINED IN THIS ENVELOPE!
IT IS?
WELL, YOU TELL ME.
WHY, YES, YES, IT IS! I'M SO SORRY ABOUT YOUR LOSS.

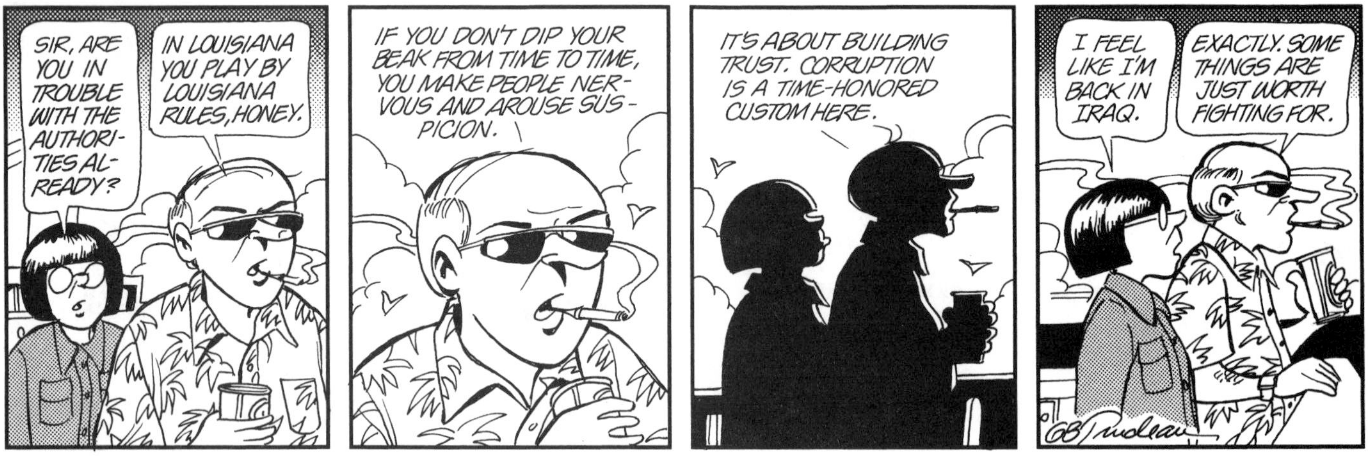
SIR, ARE YOU IN TROUBLE WITH THE AUTHORITIES ALREADY?
IN LOUISIANA YOU PLAY BY LOUISIANA RULES, HONEY.
IF YOU DON'T DIP YOUR BEAK FROM TIME TO TIME, YOU MAKE PEOPLE NERVOUS AND AROUSE SUSPICION.
IT'S ABOUT BUILDING TRUST. CORRUPTION IS A TIME-HONORED CUSTOM HERE.
I FEEL LIKE I'M BACK IN IRAQ.
EXACTLY. SOME THINGS ARE JUST WORTH FIGHTING FOR.

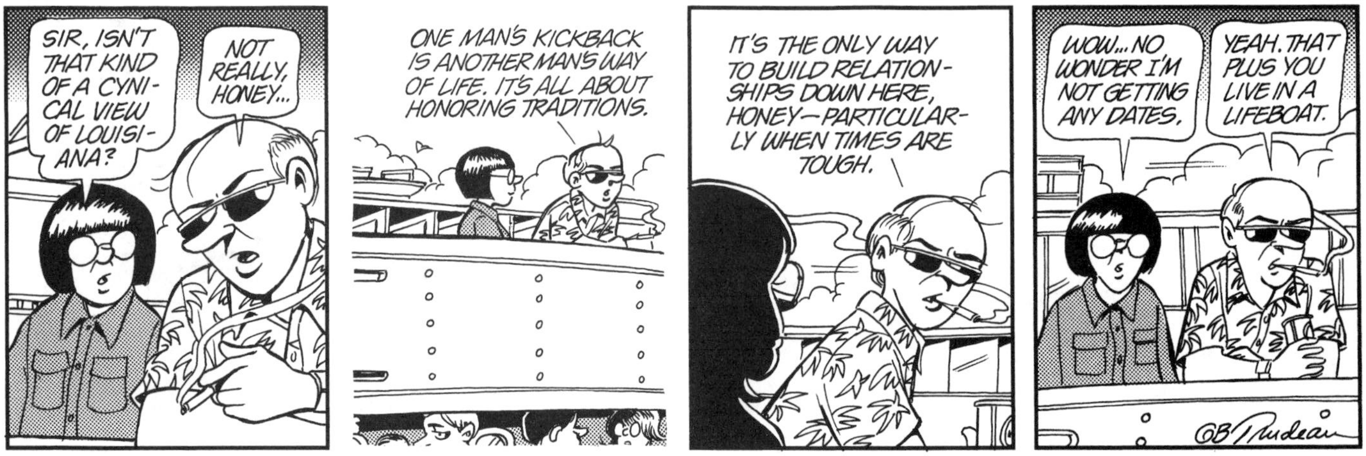
SIR, ISN'T THAT KIND OF A CYNICAL VIEW OF LOUISIANA?
NOT REALLY, HONEY...
ONE MAN'S KICKBACK IS ANOTHER MAN'S WAY OF LIFE. IT'S ALL ABOUT HONORING TRADITIONS.
IT'S THE ONLY WAY TO BUILD RELATIONSHIPS DOWN HERE, HONEY—PARTICULARLY WHEN TIMES ARE TOUGH.
WOW... NO WONDER I'M NOT GETTING ANY DATES.
YEAH. THAT PLUS YOU LIVE IN A LIFEBOAT.

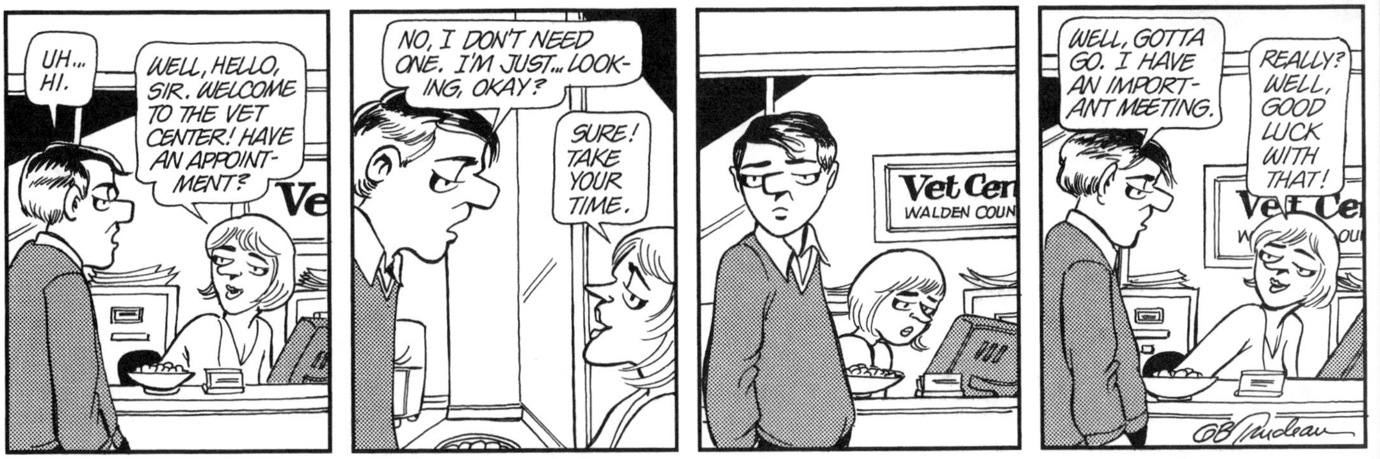
UH... HI.
WELL, HELLO, SIR. WELCOME TO THE VET CENTER! HAVE AN APPOINT-MENT?
NO, I DON'T NEED ONE. I'M JUST... LOOK-ING, OKAY?
SURE! TAKE YOUR TIME.
WELL, GOTTA GO. I HAVE AN IMPORT-ANT MEETING.
REALLY? WELL, GOOD LUCK WITH THAT!

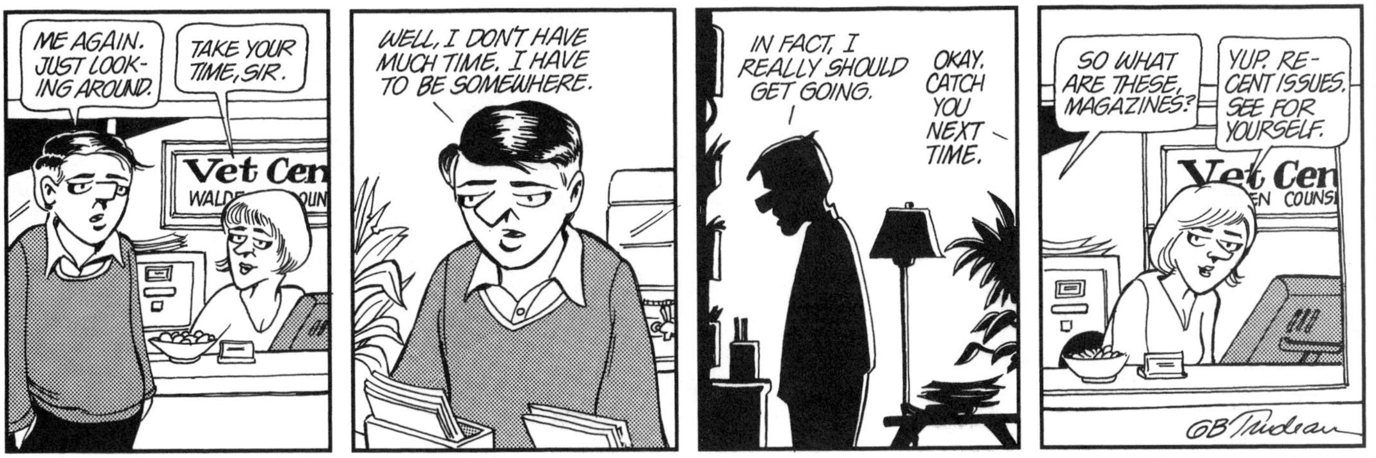
ME AGAIN. JUST LOOK-ING AROUND.
TAKE YOUR TIME, SIR.
WELL, I DON'T HAVE MUCH TIME. I HAVE TO BE SOMEWHERE.
IN FACT, I REALLY SHOULD GET GOING.
OKAY. CATCH YOU NEXT TIME.
SO WHAT ARE THESE, MAGAZINES?
YUP. RE-CENT ISSUES. SEE FOR YOURSELF.

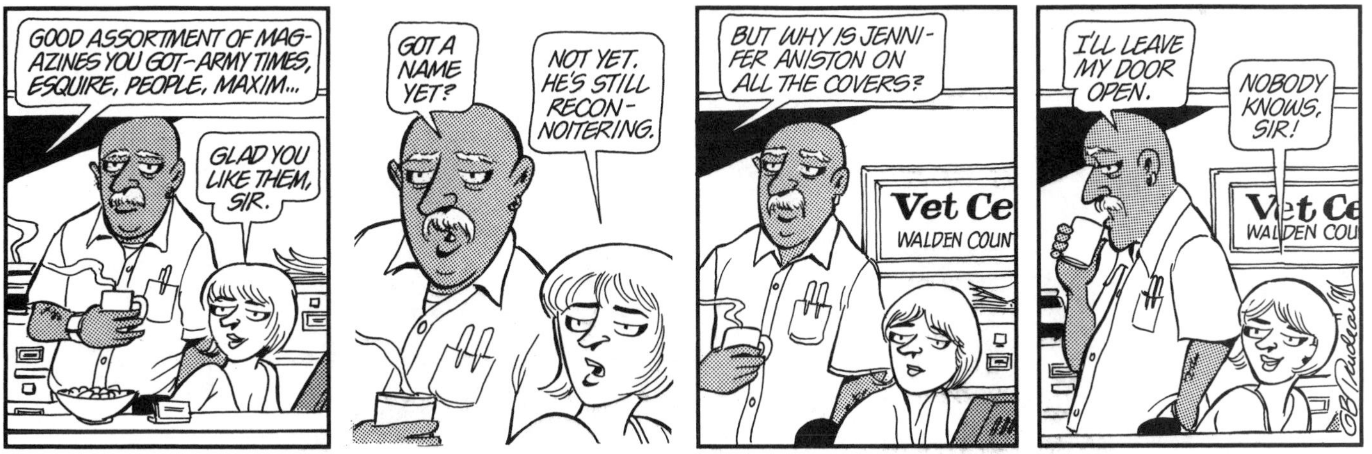
GOOD ASSORTMENT OF MAG-AZINES YOU GOT–ARMY TIMES, ESQUIRE, PEOPLE, MAXIM...
GLAD YOU LIKE THEM, SIR.
GOT A NAME YET?
NOT YET. HE'S STILL RECON-NOITERING.
BUT WHY IS JENNI-FER ANISTON ON ALL THE COVERS?
I'LL LEAVE MY DOOR OPEN.
NOBODY KNOWS, SIR!

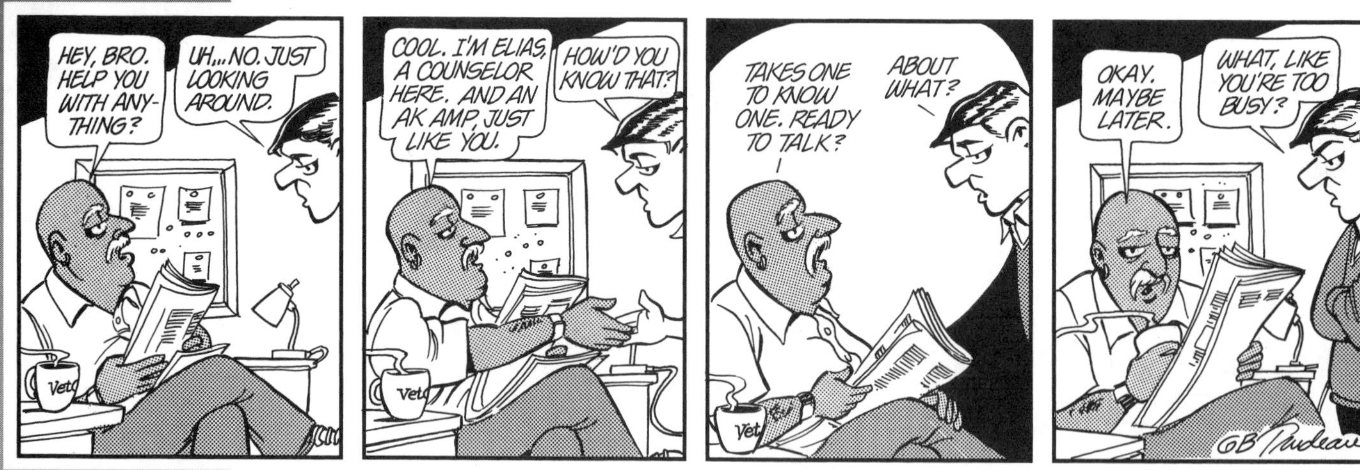
HEY, BRO. HELP YOU WITH ANYTHING?
UH... NO. JUST LOOKING AROUND.
COOL. I'M ELIAS, A COUNSELOR HERE. AND AN AK AMP, JUST LIKE YOU.
HOW'D YOU KNOW THAT?
TAKES ONE TO KNOW ONE. READY TO TALK?
ABOUT WHAT?
OKAY. MAYBE LATER.
WHAT, LIKE YOU'RE TOO BUSY?
GB Trudeau

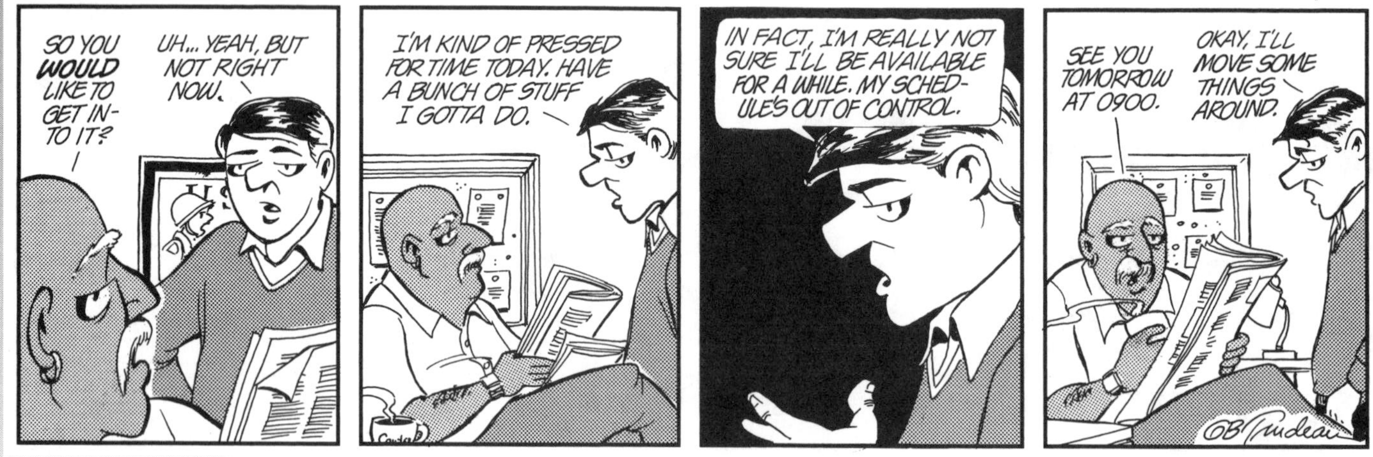
SO YOU **WOULD** LIKE TO GET INTO IT?
UH... YEAH, BUT NOT RIGHT NOW.
I'M KIND OF PRESSED FOR TIME TODAY. HAVE A BUNCH OF STUFF I GOTTA DO.
IN FACT, I'M REALLY NOT SURE I'LL BE AVAILABLE FOR A WHILE. MY SCHEDULE'S OUT OF CONTROL.
SEE YOU TOMORROW AT 0900.
OKAY, I'LL MOVE SOME THINGS AROUND.
GB Trudeau

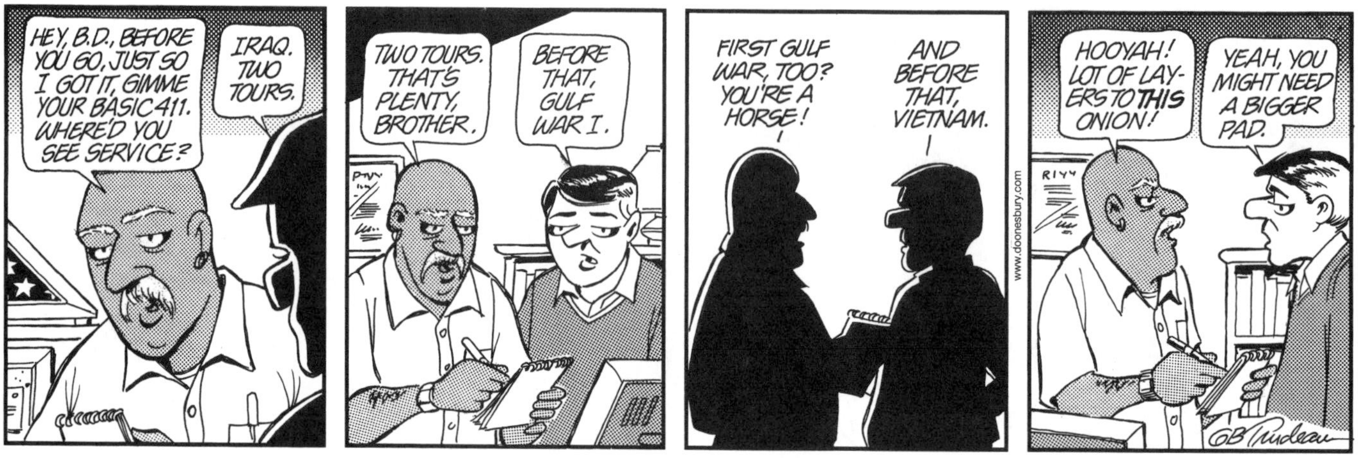
HEY, B.D., BEFORE YOU GO, JUST SO I GOT IT, GIMME YOUR BASIC 411. WHERE'D YOU SEE SERVICE?
IRAQ. TWO TOURS.
TWO TOURS. THAT'S PLENTY, BROTHER.
BEFORE THAT, GULF WAR I.
FIRST GULF WAR, TOO? YOU'RE A HORSE!
AND BEFORE THAT, VIETNAM.
www.doonesbury.com
HOOYAH! LOT OF LAYERS TO **THIS** ONION!
YEAH, YOU MIGHT NEED A BIGGER PAD.
GB Trudeau

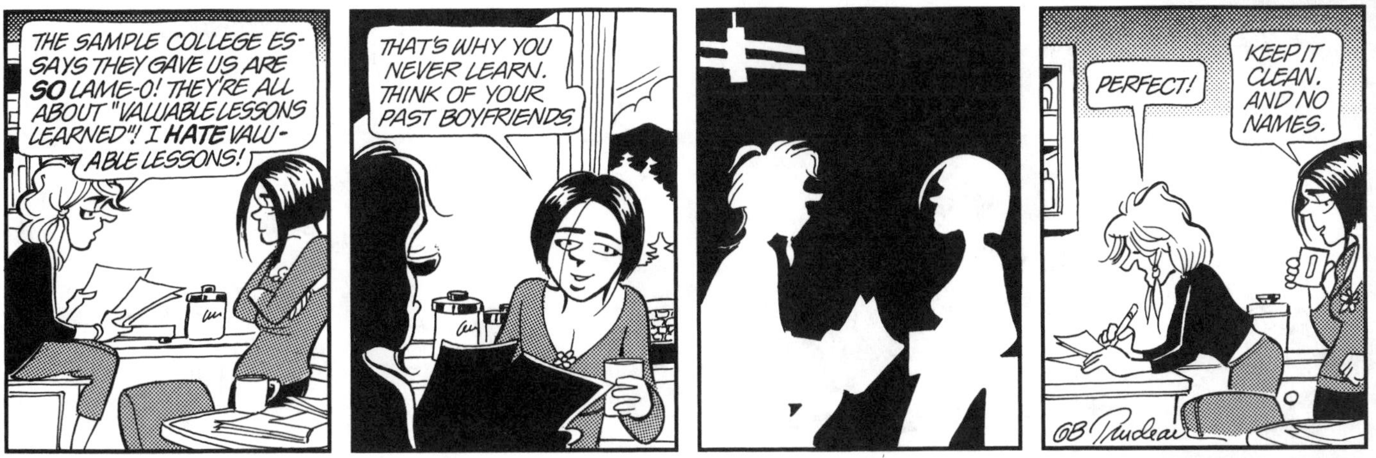
THE SAMPLE COLLEGE ES-SAYS THEY GAVE US ARE **SO** LAME-O! THEY'RE ALL ABOUT "VALUABLE LESSONS LEARNED"! I **HATE** VALU-ABLE LESSONS!
THAT'S WHY YOU NEVER LEARN. THINK OF YOUR PAST BOYFRIENDS.
PERFECT!
KEEP IT CLEAN. AND NO NAMES.

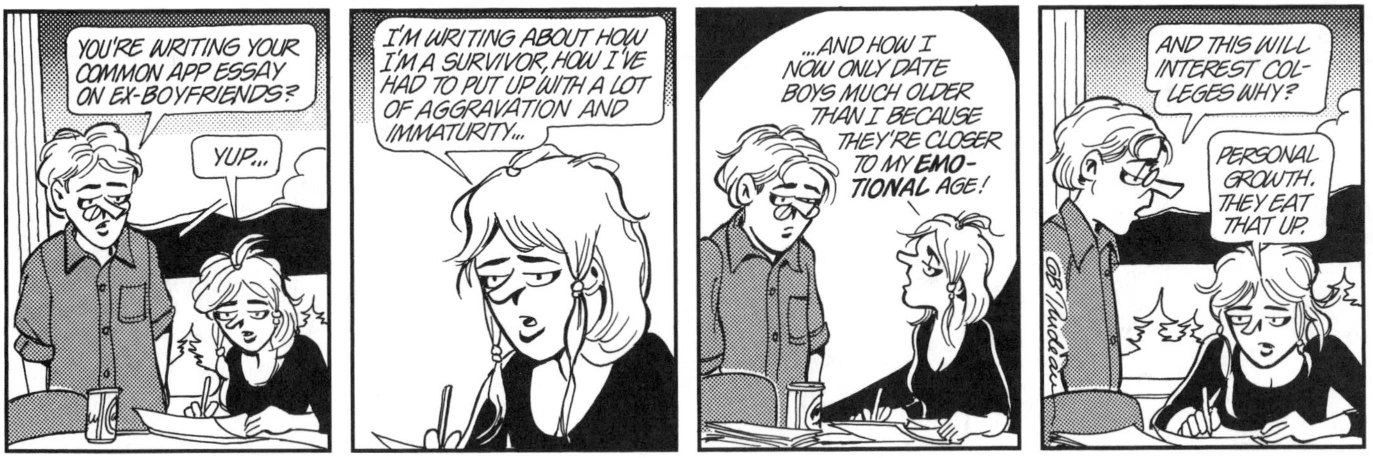
YOU'RE WRITING YOUR COMMON APP ESSAY ON EX-BOYFRIENDS?
YUP...
I'M WRITING ABOUT HOW I'M A SURVIVOR, HOW I'VE HAD TO PUT UP WITH A LOT OF AGGRAVATION AND IMMATURITY...
...AND HOW I NOW ONLY DATE BOYS MUCH OLDER THAN I BECAUSE THEY'RE CLOSER TO MY **EMO-TIONAL** AGE!
AND THIS WILL INTEREST COL-LEGES WHY?
PERSONAL GROWTH. THEY EAT THAT UP.

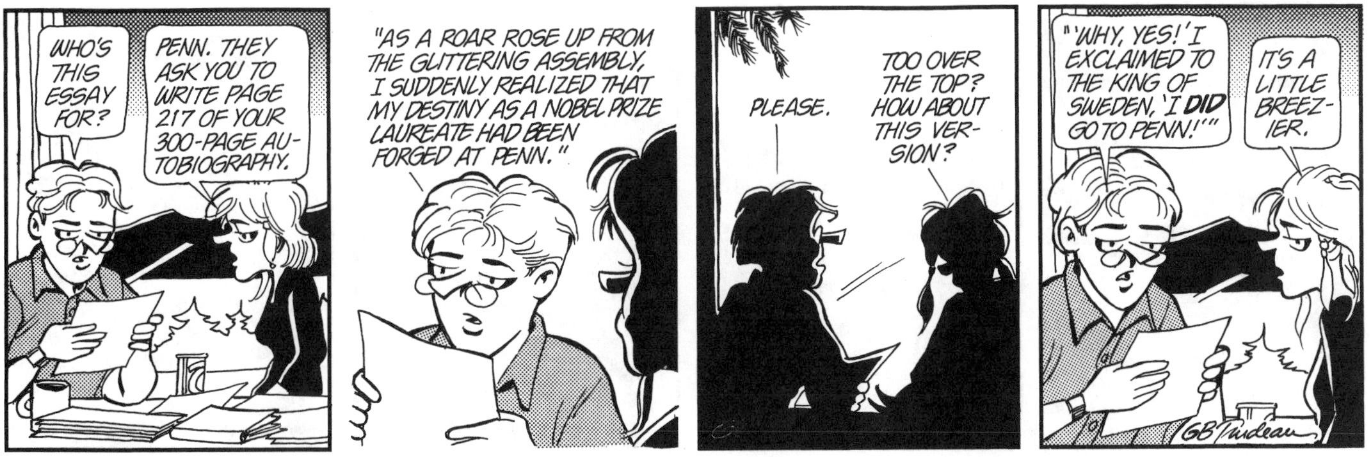
WHO'S THIS ESSAY FOR?
PENN. THEY ASK YOU TO WRITE PAGE 217 OF YOUR 300-PAGE AU-TOBIOGRAPHY.
"AS A ROAR ROSE UP FROM THE GLITTERING ASSEMBLY, I SUDDENLY REALIZED THAT MY DESTINY AS A NOBEL PRIZE LAUREATE HAD BEEN FORGED AT PENN."
PLEASE.
TOO OVER THE TOP? HOW ABOUT THIS VER-SION?
"'WHY, YES!' I EXCLAIMED TO THE KING OF SWEDEN, 'I **DID** GO TO PENN!'"
IT'S A LITTLE BREEZ-IER.

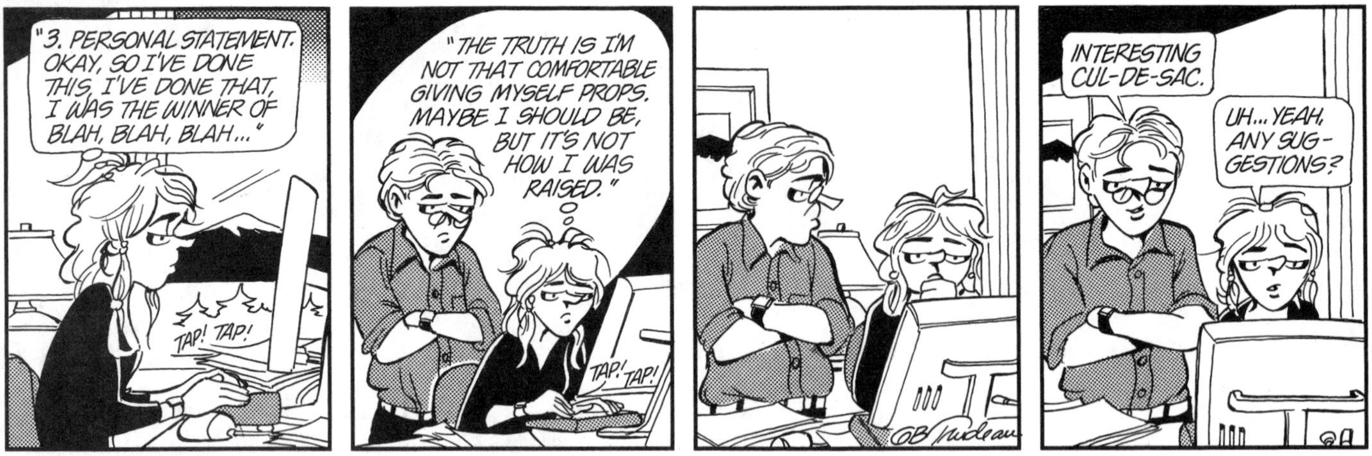
"3. PERSONAL STATEMENT. OKAY, SO I'VE DONE THIS, I'VE DONE THAT, I WAS THE WINNER OF BLAH, BLAH, BLAH..."
TAP! TAP!
"THE TRUTH IS I'M NOT THAT COMFORTABLE GIVING MYSELF PROPS. MAYBE I SHOULD BE, BUT IT'S NOT HOW I WAS RAISED."
TAP! TAP!
INTERESTING CUL-DE-SAC.
UH... YEAH, ANY SUGGESTIONS?

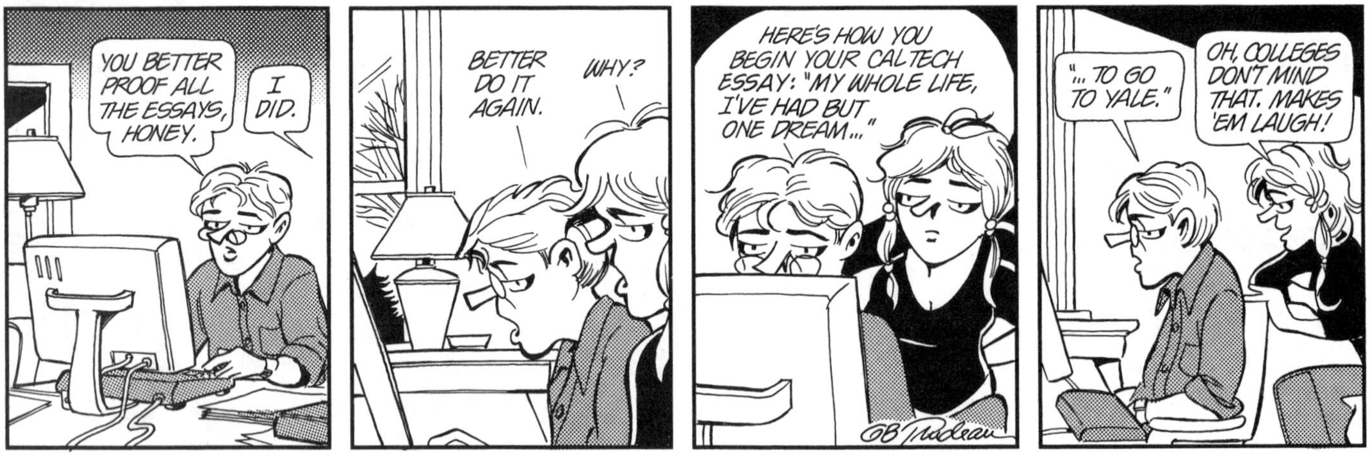
YOU BETTER PROOF ALL THE ESSAYS, HONEY.
I DID.
BETTER DO IT AGAIN.
WHY?
HERE'S HOW YOU BEGIN YOUR CALTECH ESSAY: "MY WHOLE LIFE, I'VE HAD BUT ONE DREAM..."
"...TO GO TO YALE."
OH, COLLEGES DON'T MIND THAT. MAKES 'EM LAUGH!

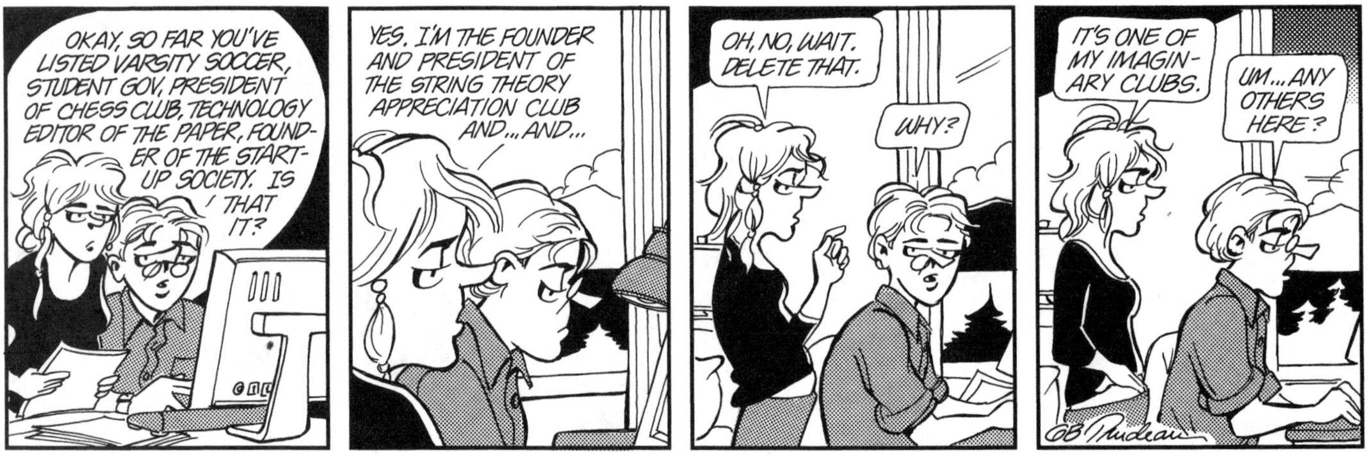
OKAY, SO FAR YOU'VE LISTED VARSITY SOCCER, STUDENT GOV, PRESIDENT OF CHESS CLUB, TECHNOLOGY EDITOR OF THE PAPER, FOUNDER OF THE START-UP SOCIETY. IS THAT IT?
YES. I'M THE FOUNDER AND PRESIDENT OF THE STRING THEORY APPRECIATION CLUB AND... AND...
OH, NO, WAIT. DELETE THAT.
WHY?
IT'S ONE OF MY IMAGINARY CLUBS.
UM... ANY OTHERS HERE?

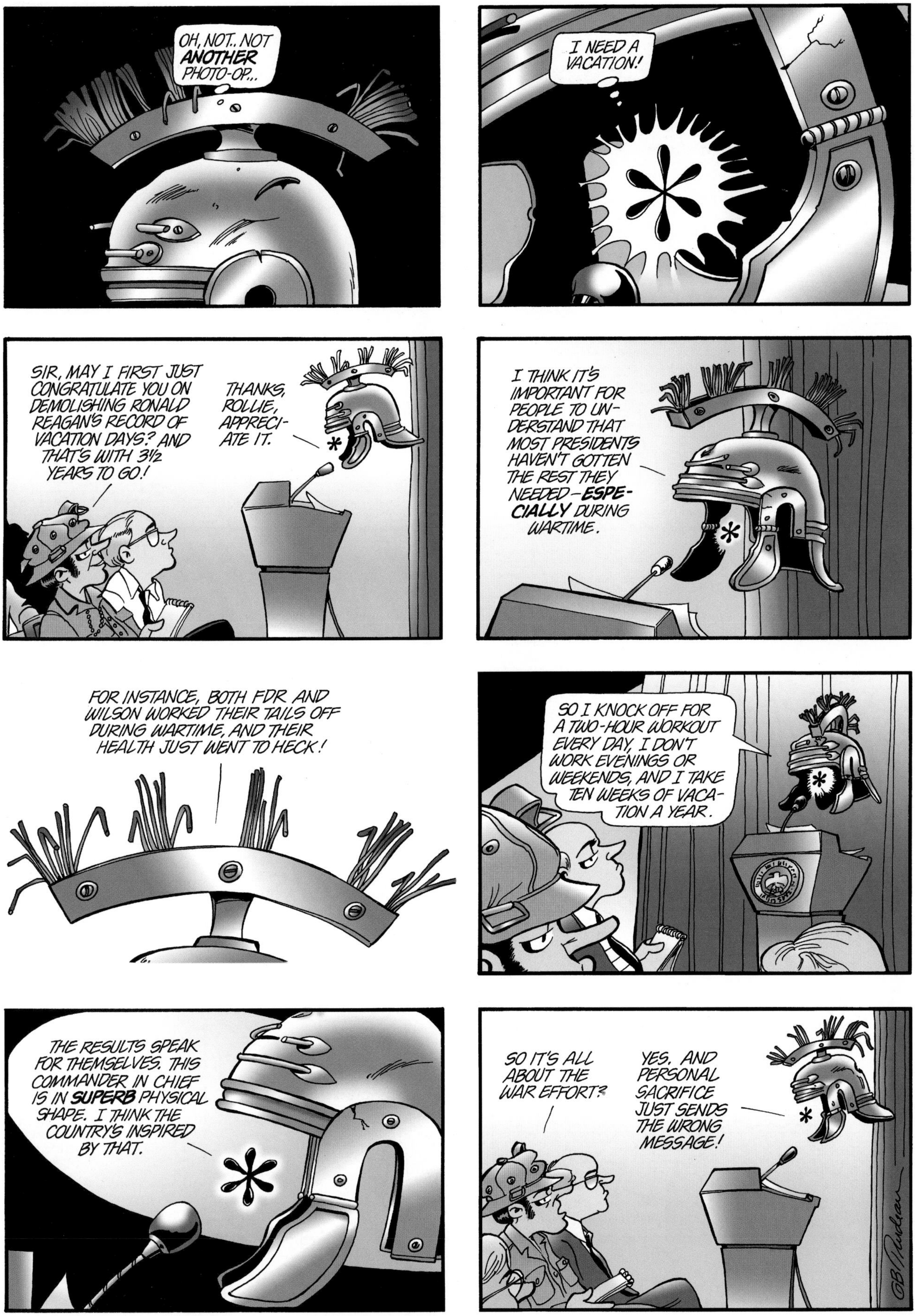
OH, NOT.. NOT ANOTHER PHOTO-OP...
I NEED A VACATION!
SIR, MAY I FIRST JUST CONGRATULATE YOU ON DEMOLISHING RONALD REAGAN'S RECORD OF VACATION DAYS? AND THAT'S WITH 3½ YEARS TO GO!
THANKS, ROLLIE, APPRECIATE IT.
I THINK IT'S IMPORTANT FOR PEOPLE TO UNDERSTAND THAT MOST PRESIDENTS HAVEN'T GOTTEN THE REST THEY NEEDED—ESPECIALLY DURING WARTIME.
FOR INSTANCE, BOTH FDR AND WILSON WORKED THEIR TAILS OFF DURING WARTIME, AND THEIR HEALTH JUST WENT TO HECK!
SO I KNOCK OFF FOR A TWO-HOUR WORKOUT EVERY DAY, I DON'T WORK EVENINGS OR WEEKENDS, AND I TAKE TEN WEEKS OF VACATION A YEAR.
THE RESULTS SPEAK FOR THEMSELVES. THIS COMMANDER IN CHIEF IS IN SUPERB PHYSICAL SHAPE. I THINK THE COUNTRY'S INSPIRED BY THAT.
SO IT'S ALL ABOUT THE WAR EFFORT?
YES. AND PERSONAL SACRIFICE JUST SENDS THE WRONG MESSAGE!

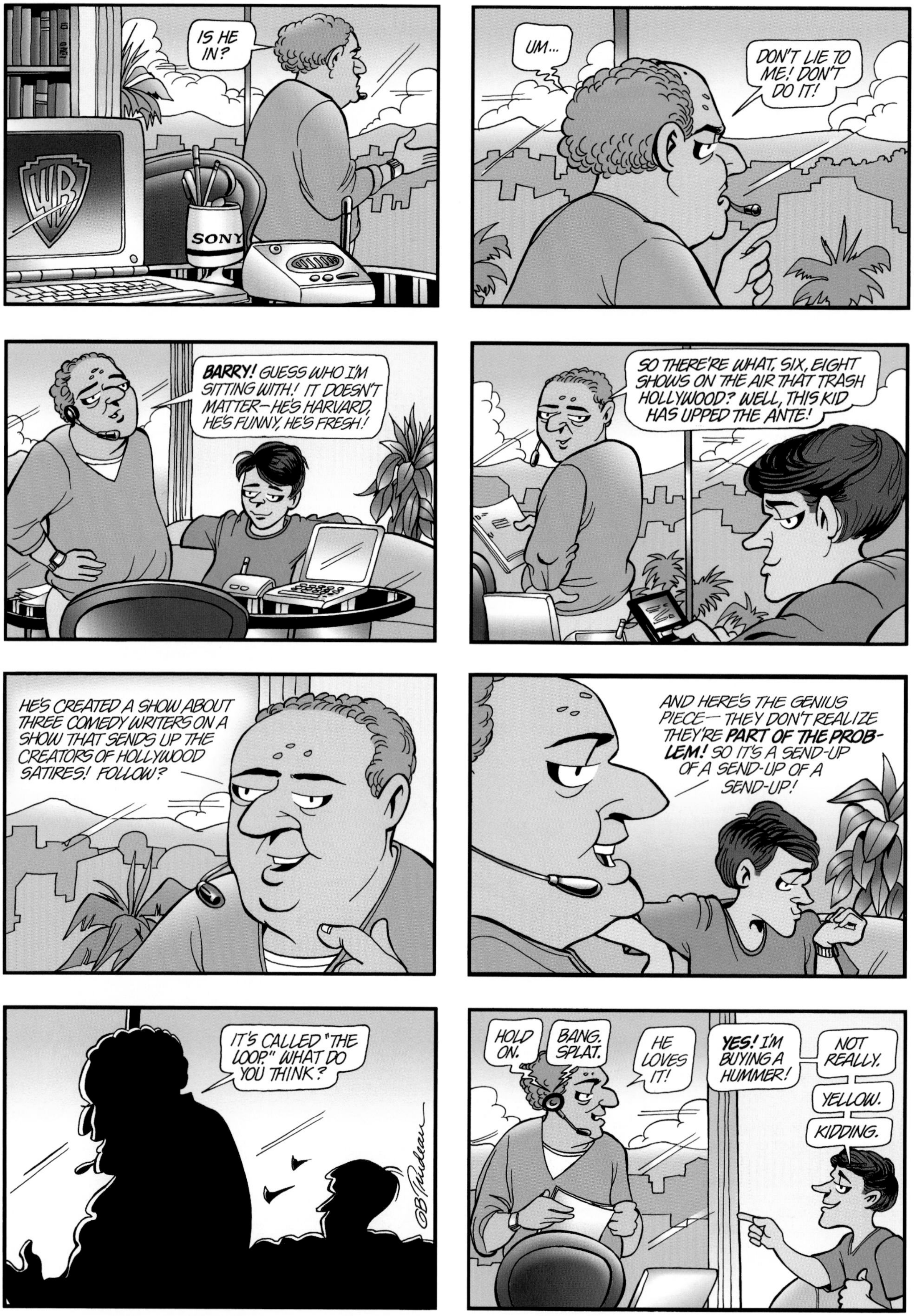
IS HE IN?
SONY
UM...
DON'T LIE TO ME! DON'T DO IT!
BARRY! GUESS WHO I'M SITTING WITH! IT DOESN'T MATTER—HE'S HARVARD, HE'S FUNNY, HE'S FRESH!
SO THERE'RE WHAT, SIX, EIGHT SHOWS ON THE AIR THAT TRASH HOLLYWOOD? WELL, THIS KID HAS UPPED THE ANTE!
HE'S CREATED A SHOW ABOUT THREE COMEDY WRITERS ON A SHOW THAT SENDS UP THE CREATORS OF HOLLYWOOD SATIRES! FOLLOW?
AND HERE'S THE GENIUS PIECE— THEY DON'T REALIZE THEY'RE PART OF THE PROBLEM! SO IT'S A SEND-UP OF A SEND-UP OF A SEND-UP!
IT'S CALLED "THE LOOP." WHAT DO YOU THINK?
HOLD ON.
BANG. SPLAT.
HE LOVES IT!
YES! I'M BUYING A HUMMER!
NOT REALLY.
YELLOW.
KIDDING.

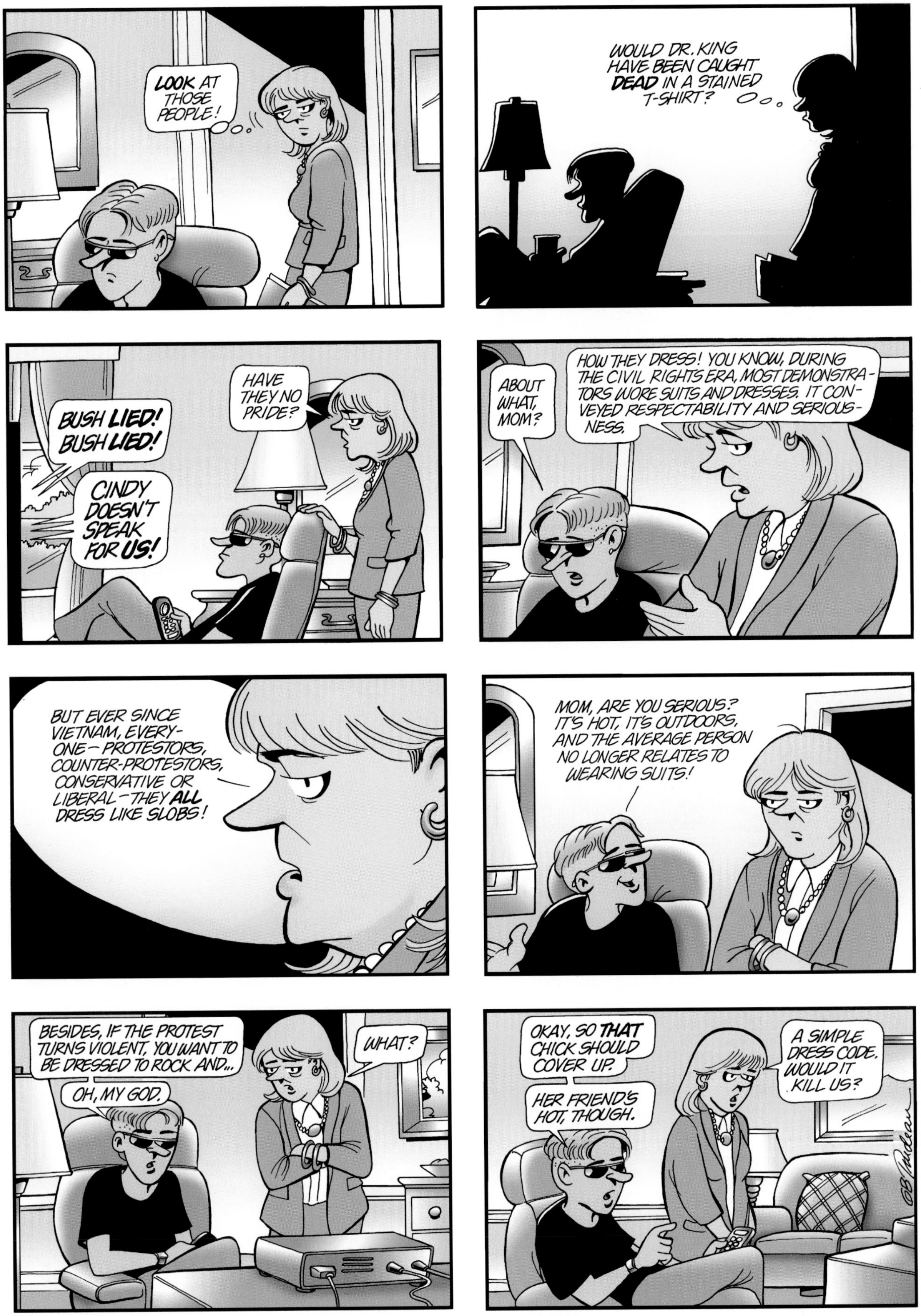
LOOK AT THOSE PEOPLE!
WOULD DR. KING HAVE BEEN CAUGHT DEAD IN A STAINED T-SHIRT?
BUSH LIED! BUSH LIED!
CINDY DOESN'T SPEAK FOR US!
HAVE THEY NO PRIDE?
ABOUT WHAT, MOM?
HOW THEY DRESS! YOU KNOW, DURING THE CIVIL RIGHTS ERA, MOST DEMONSTRATORS WORE SUITS AND DRESSES. IT CONVEYED RESPECTABILITY AND SERIOUSNESS.
BUT EVER SINCE VIETNAM, EVERYONE – PROTESTORS, COUNTER-PROTESTORS, CONSERVATIVE OR LIBERAL – THEY ALL DRESS LIKE SLOBS!
MOM, ARE YOU SERIOUS? IT'S HOT, IT'S OUTDOORS, AND THE AVERAGE PERSON NO LONGER RELATES TO WEARING SUITS!
BESIDES, IF THE PROTEST TURNS VIOLENT, YOU WANT TO BE DRESSED TO ROCK AND...
WHAT?
OH, MY GOD.
OKAY, SO THAT CHICK SHOULD COVER UP.
HER FRIEND'S HOT, THOUGH.
A SIMPLE DRESS CODE. WOULD IT KILL US?
GB Trudeau

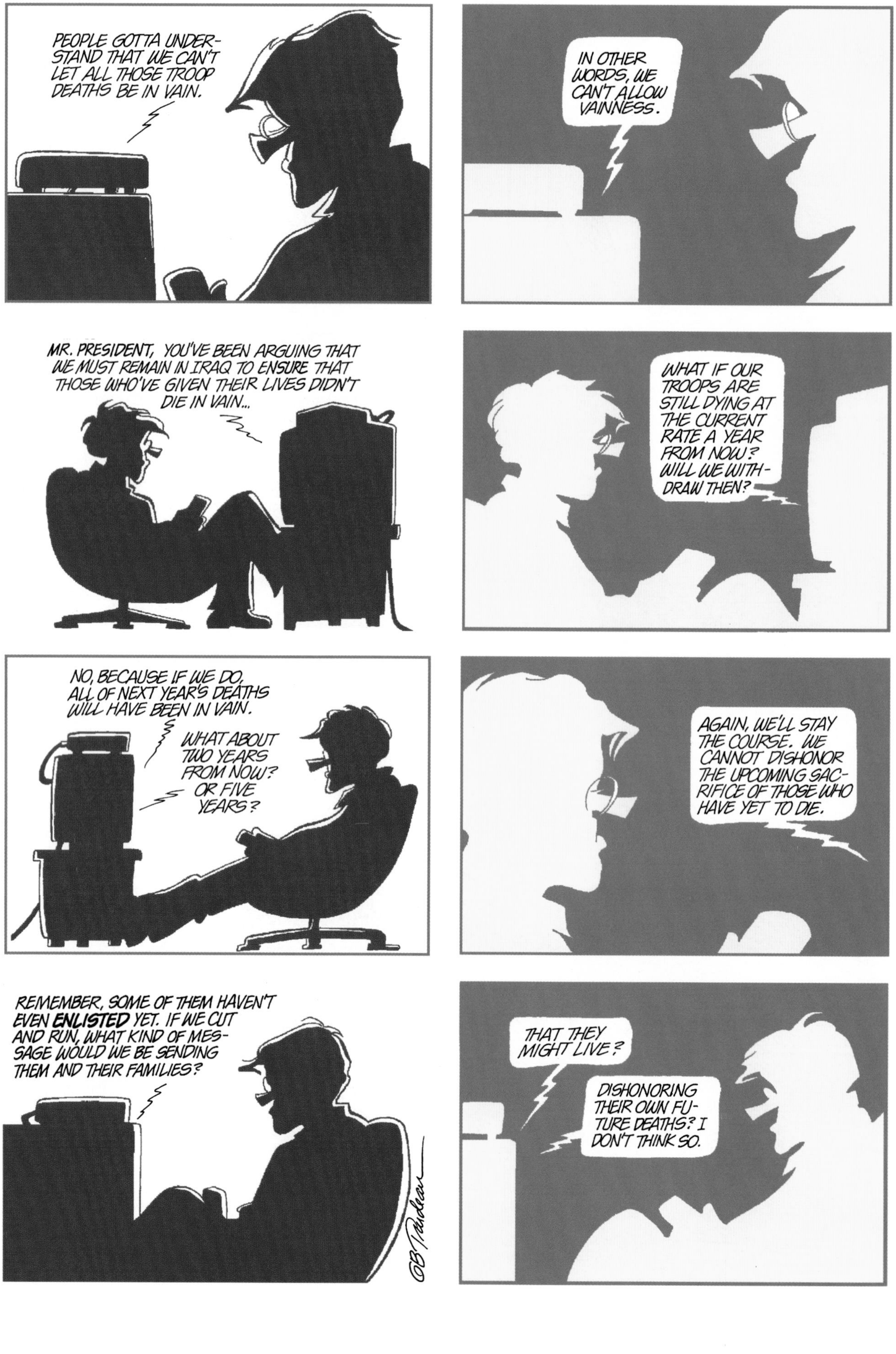
PEOPLE GOTTA UNDERSTAND THAT WE CAN'T LET ALL THOSE TROOP DEATHS BE IN VAIN.
IN OTHER WORDS, WE CAN'T ALLOW VAINNESS.
MR. PRESIDENT, YOU'VE BEEN ARGUING THAT WE MUST REMAIN IN IRAQ TO ENSURE THAT THOSE WHO'VE GIVEN THEIR LIVES DIDN'T DIE IN VAIN...
WHAT IF OUR TROOPS ARE STILL DYING AT THE CURRENT RATE A YEAR FROM NOW? WILL WE WITHDRAW THEN?
NO, BECAUSE IF WE DO, ALL OF NEXT YEAR'S DEATHS WILL HAVE BEEN IN VAIN.
WHAT ABOUT TWO YEARS FROM NOW? OR FIVE YEARS?
AGAIN, WE'LL STAY THE COURSE. WE CANNOT DISHONOR THE UPCOMING SACRIFICE OF THOSE WHO HAVE YET TO DIE.
REMEMBER, SOME OF THEM HAVEN'T EVEN **ENLISTED** YET. IF WE CUT AND RUN, WHAT KIND OF MESSAGE WOULD WE BE SENDING THEM AND THEIR FAMILIES?
THAT THEY MIGHT LIVE?
DISHONORING THEIR OWN FUTURE DEATHS? I DON'T THINK SO.
GBTrudeau

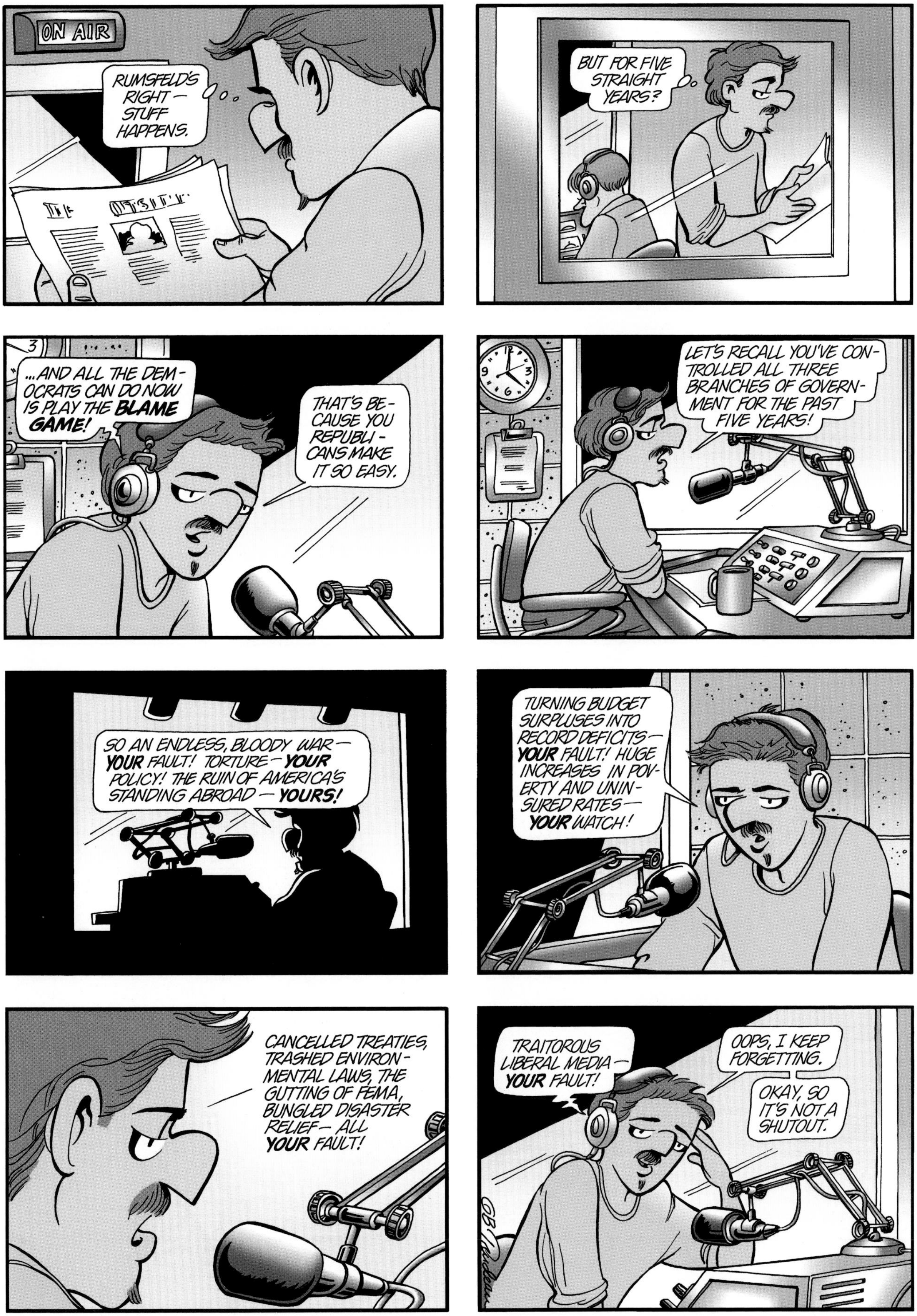
ON AIR
RUMSFELD'S RIGHT— STUFF HAPPENS.
BUT FOR FIVE STRAIGHT YEARS?
...AND ALL THE DEMOCRATS CAN DO NOW IS PLAY THE BLAME GAME!
THAT'S BECAUSE YOU REPUBLICANS MAKE IT SO EASY.
LET'S RECALL YOU'VE CONTROLLED ALL THREE BRANCHES OF GOVERNMENT FOR THE PAST FIVE YEARS!
SO AN ENDLESS, BLOODY WAR— YOUR FAULT! TORTURE— YOUR POLICY! THE RUIN OF AMERICA'S STANDING ABROAD— YOURS!
TURNING BUDGET SURPLUSES INTO RECORD DEFICITS— YOUR FAULT! HUGE INCREASES IN POVERTY AND UNINSURED RATES— YOUR WATCH!
CANCELLED TREATIES, TRASHED ENVIRONMENTAL LAWS, THE GUTTING OF FEMA, BUNGLED DISASTER RELIEF— ALL YOUR FAULT!
TRAITOROUS LIBERAL MEDIA— YOUR FAULT!
OOPS, I KEEP FORGETTING.
OKAY, SO IT'S NOT A SHUTOUT.

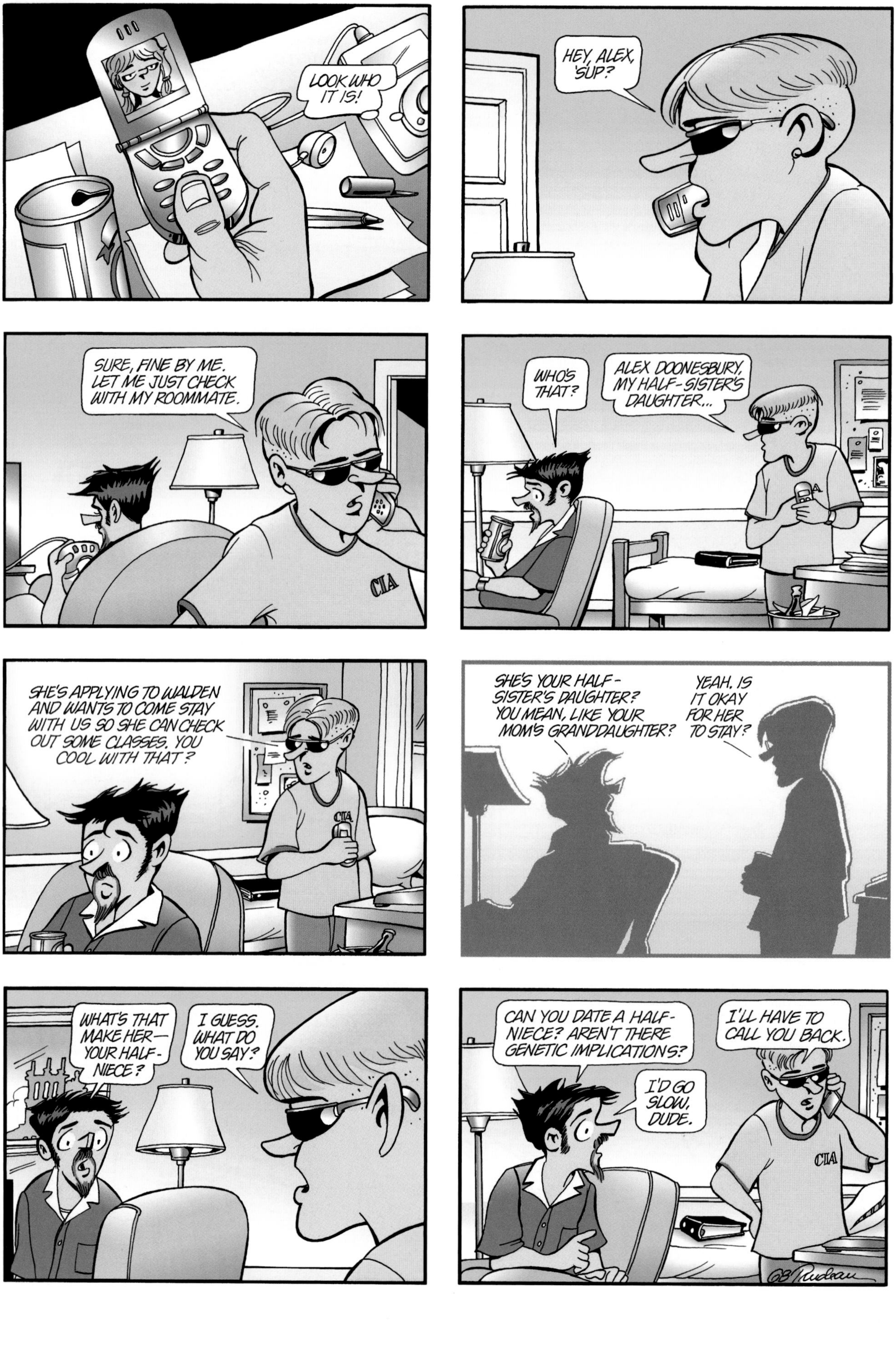
LOOK WHO IT IS!
HEY, ALEX, 'SUP?
SURE, FINE BY ME. LET ME JUST CHECK WITH MY ROOMMATE.
CIA
WHO'S THAT?
ALEX DOONESBURY, MY HALF-SISTER'S DAUGHTER...
SHE'S APPLYING TO WALDEN AND WANTS TO COME STAY WITH US SO SHE CAN CHECK OUT SOME CLASSES. YOU COOL WITH THAT?
CIA
SHE'S YOUR HALF-SISTER'S DAUGHTER? YOU MEAN, LIKE YOUR MOM'S GRANDDAUGHTER?
YEAH. IS IT OKAY FOR HER TO STAY?
WHAT'S THAT MAKE HER— YOUR HALF-NIECE?
I GUESS. WHAT DO YOU SAY?
CAN YOU DATE A HALF-NIECE? AREN'T THERE GENETIC IMPLICATIONS?
I'LL HAVE TO CALL YOU BACK.
I'D GO SLOW, DUDE.
CIA

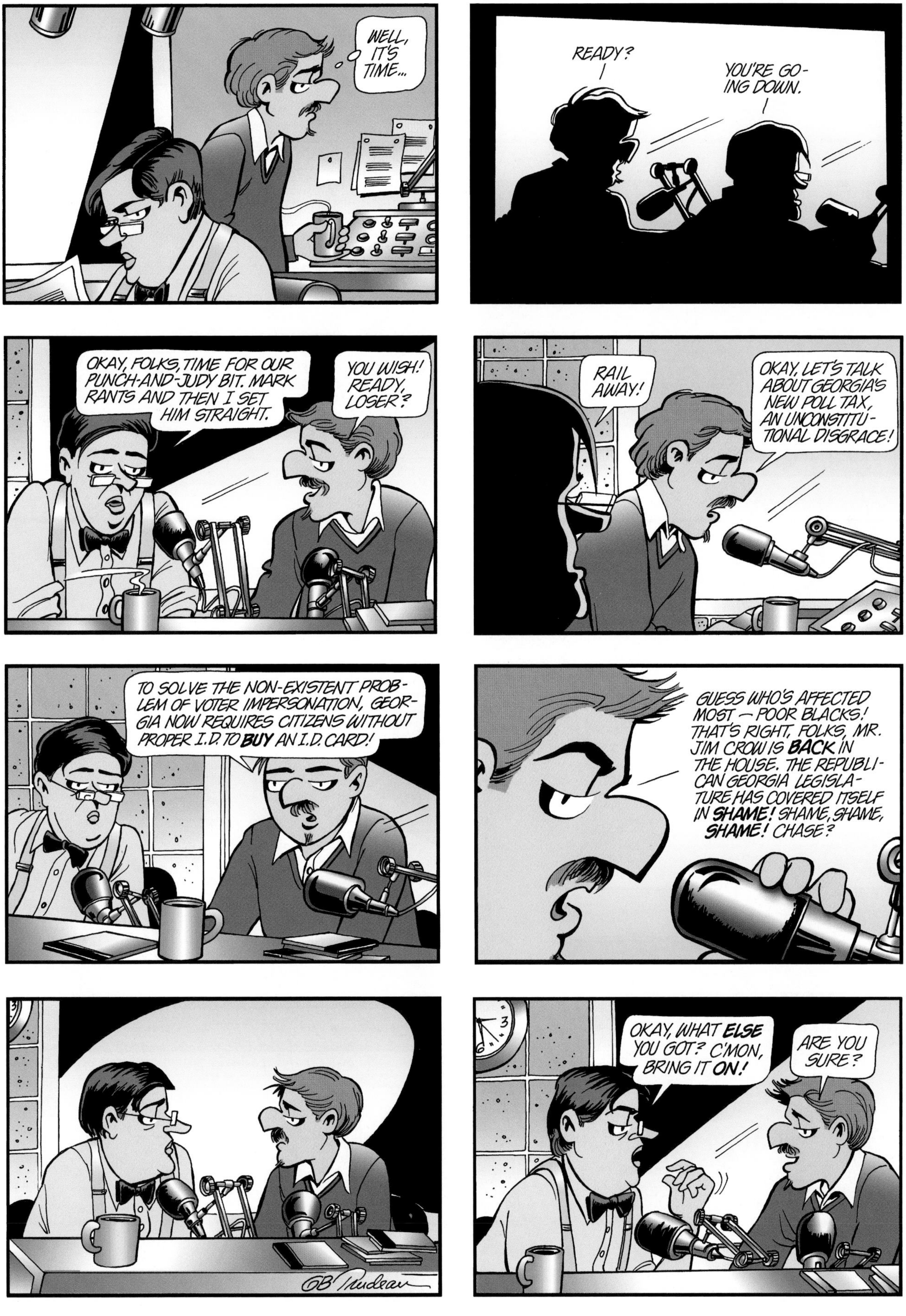
WELL, IT'S TIME...
READY?
YOU'RE GOING DOWN.
OKAY, FOLKS, TIME FOR OUR PUNCH-AND-JUDY BIT. MARK RANTS AND THEN I SET HIM STRAIGHT.
YOU WISH! READY, LOSER?
RAIL AWAY!
OKAY, LET'S TALK ABOUT GEORGIA'S NEW POLL TAX, AN UNCONSTITUTIONAL DISGRACE!
TO SOLVE THE NON-EXISTENT PROBLEM OF VOTER IMPERSONATION, GEORGIA NOW REQUIRES CITIZENS WITHOUT PROPER I.D. TO BUY AN I.D. CARD!
GUESS WHO'S AFFECTED MOST — POOR BLACKS! THAT'S RIGHT, FOLKS, MR. JIM CROW IS BACK IN THE HOUSE. THE REPUBLICAN GEORGIA LEGISLATURE HAS COVERED ITSELF IN SHAME! SHAME, SHAME, SHAME! CHASE?
GB Trudeau
OKAY, WHAT ELSE YOU GOT? C'MON, BRING IT ON!
ARE YOU SURE?

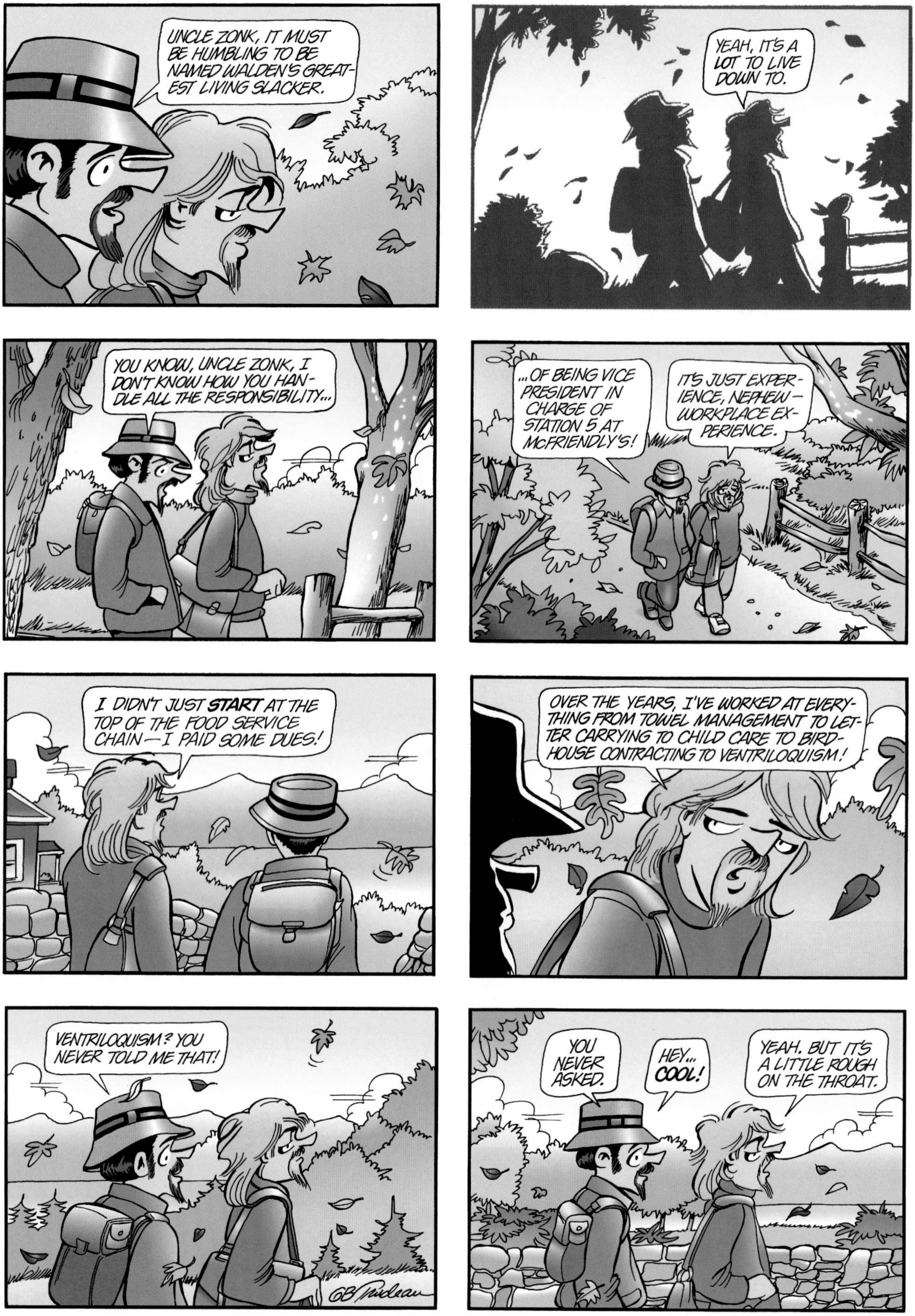
UNCLE ZONK, IT MUST BE HUMBLING TO BE NAMED WALDEN'S GREATEST LIVING SLACKER.
YEAH, IT'S A LOT TO LIVE DOWN TO.
YOU KNOW, UNCLE ZONK, I DON'T KNOW HOW YOU HANDLE ALL THE RESPONSIBILITY...
...OF BEING VICE PRESIDENT IN CHARGE OF STATION 5 AT McFRIENDLY'S!
IT'S JUST EXPERIENCE, NEPHEW — WORKPLACE EXPERIENCE.
I DIDN'T JUST START AT THE TOP OF THE FOOD SERVICE CHAIN — I PAID SOME DUES!
OVER THE YEARS, I'VE WORKED AT EVERYTHING FROM TOWEL MANAGEMENT TO LETTER CARRYING TO CHILD CARE TO BIRDHOUSE CONTRACTING TO VENTRILOQUISM!
VENTRILOQUISM? YOU NEVER TOLD ME THAT!
GB Trudeau
YOU NEVER ASKED.
HEY... COOL!
YEAH. BUT IT'S A LITTLE ROUGH ON THE THROAT.

AGAINST TORTURE?
THAT'S NUTS!
WHAT'S WRONG WITH McCAIN?
GOOD EVENING AND WELCOME TO ANOTHER EDITION OF "DEFINING MOMENTS IN TORTURE"!
BUSH OPPOSES ANTI-TORTURE AMENDMENT
Prez favors degrading treatment
SO HOW CAN AN AMERICAN PRESIDENT ACTUALLY FAVOR "CRUEL, INHUMANE AND DEGRADING" TREATMENT OF PRISONERS?
THE ANSWER MAY LIE IN A LONG-FORGOTTEN INCIDENT ON THIS IVY LEAGUE CAMPUS...
FALL, 1967. YALE STUDENTS REPORT HEARING SCREAMS COMING FROM DKE HOUSE.
DKE
AAIIEE!
Y
THE STUDENT PAPER BREAKS THE STORY: DKE HAS BEEN BRANDING THEIR PLEDGES ON THEIR BACKSIDES WITH RED-HOT COAT HANGERS.
BRANDED!
Dekes
DKE PRESIDENT GEORGE W. BUSH DEFENDS THE BRANDING RITUAL IN STATEMENTS TO THE PRESS.
"INSIGNIFICANT! THERE'S NO SCARRING MARK PHYSICALLY OR MENTALLY!"
THE REST IS HISTORY.
THIS HAS BEEN "DEFINING MOMENTS IN TORTURE"!
HUMAN PYRAMIDS? HELL, I DID THOSE AS A CHEERLEADER!
GB Trudeau

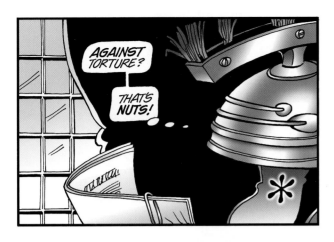

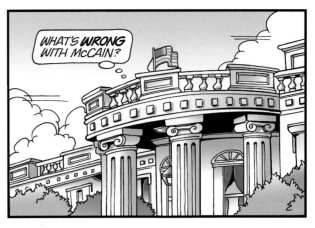

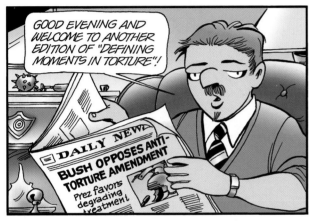

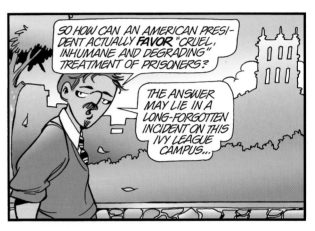

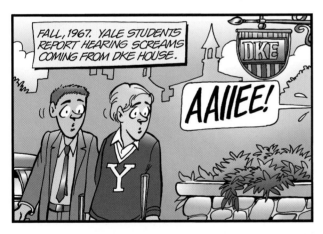

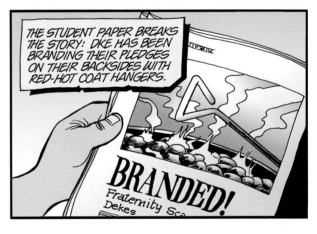

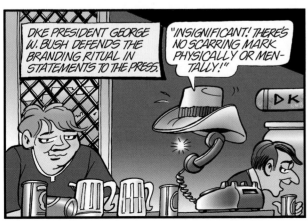

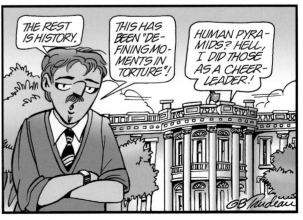

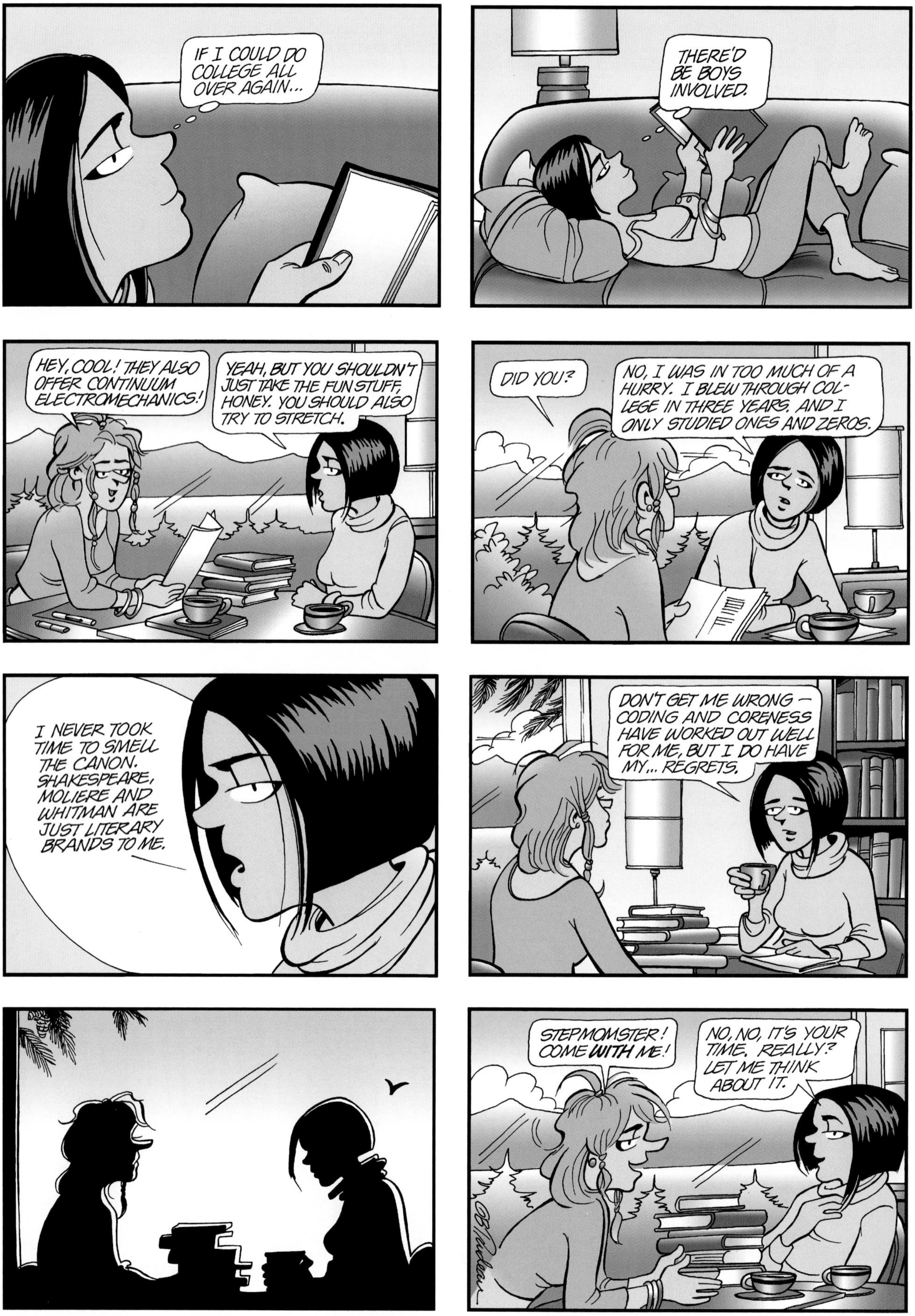
IF I COULD DO COLLEGE ALL OVER AGAIN...
THERE'D BE BOYS INVOLVED.
HEY, COOL! THEY ALSO OFFER CONTINUUM ELECTROMECHANICS!
YEAH, BUT YOU SHOULDN'T JUST TAKE THE FUN STUFF, HONEY. YOU SHOULD ALSO TRY TO STRETCH.
DID YOU?
NO, I WAS IN TOO MUCH OF A HURRY. I BLEW THROUGH COL-LEGE IN THREE YEARS, AND I ONLY STUDIED ONES AND ZEROS.
I NEVER TOOK TIME TO SMELL THE CANON. SHAKESPEARE, MOLIERE AND WHITMAN ARE JUST LITERARY BRANDS TO ME.
DON'T GET ME WRONG — CODING AND CORENESS HAVE WORKED OUT WELL FOR ME, BUT I DO HAVE MY... REGRETS.
STEPMOMSTER! COME WITH ME!
NO, NO, IT'S YOUR TIME. REALLY? LET ME THINK ABOUT IT.

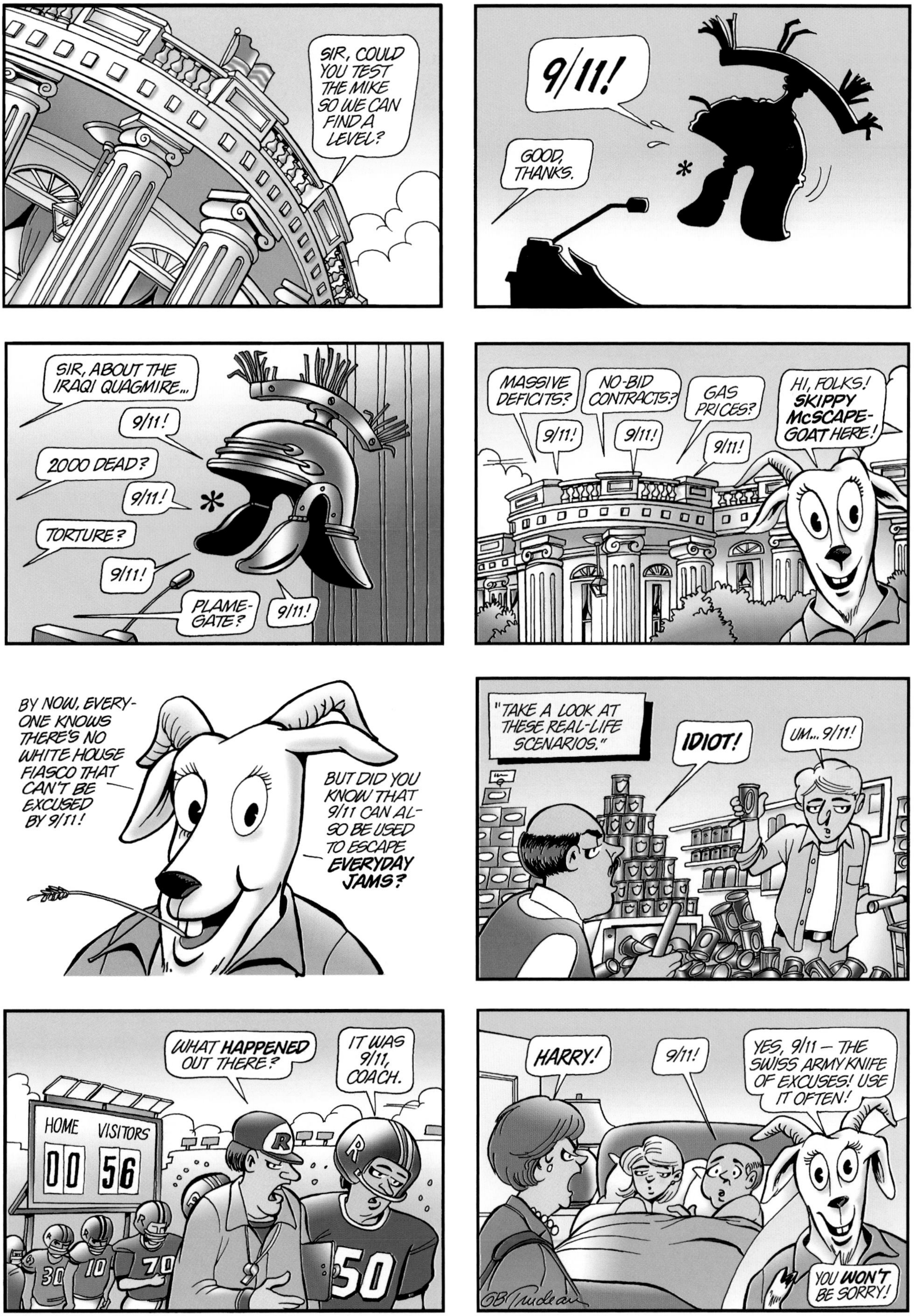

SIR, COULD YOU TEST THE MIKE SO WE CAN FIND A LEVEL?
9/11!
GOOD, THANKS.
SIR, ABOUT THE IRAQI QUAGMIRE...
9/11!
2000 DEAD?
9/11!
TORTURE?
9/11!
PLAME-GATE?
9/11!
MASSIVE DEFICITS?
9/11!
NO-BID CONTRACTS?
9/11!
GAS PRICES?
9/11!
HI, FOLKS! SKIPPY McSCAPE-GOAT HERE!
BY NOW, EVERY-ONE KNOWS THERE'S NO WHITE HOUSE FIASCO THAT CAN'T BE EXCUSED BY 9/11!
BUT DID YOU KNOW THAT 9/11 CAN AL-SO BE USED TO ESCAPE EVERYDAY JAMS?
"TAKE A LOOK AT THESE REAL-LIFE SCENARIOS."
IDIOT!
UM... 9/11!
WHAT HAPPENED OUT THERE?
IT WAS 9/11, COACH.
HOME VISITORS
00 56
HARRY!
9/11!
YES, 9/11 — THE SWISS ARMY KNIFE OF EXCUSES! USE IT OFTEN!
YOU WON'T BE SORRY!
GBTrudeau

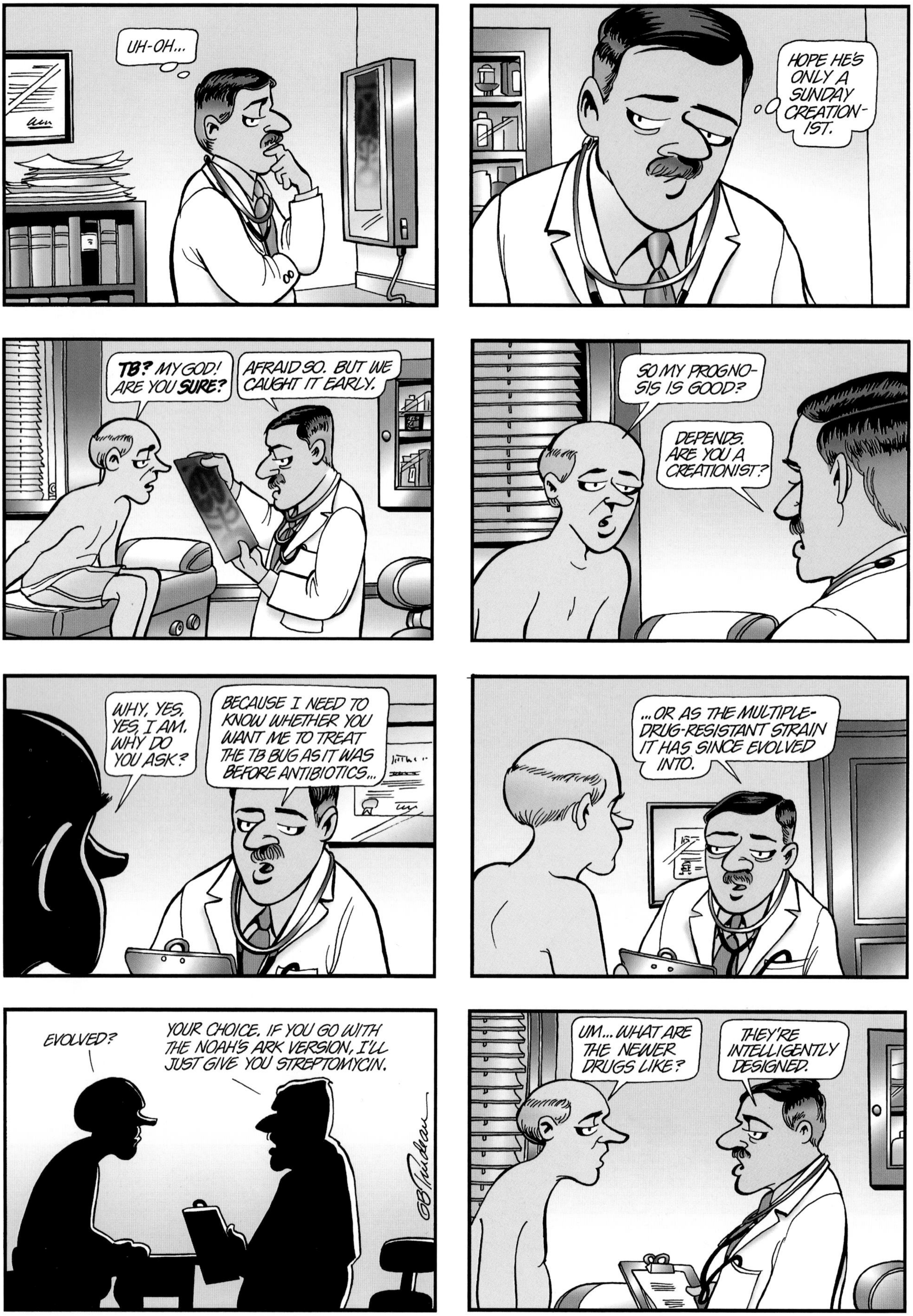
UH-OH...
HOPE HE'S ONLY A SUNDAY CREATIONIST.
TB? MY GOD! ARE YOU SURE?
AFRAID SO. BUT WE CAUGHT IT EARLY.
SO MY PROGNOSIS IS GOOD?
DEPENDS. ARE YOU A CREATIONIST?
WHY, YES, YES, I AM. WHY DO YOU ASK?
BECAUSE I NEED TO KNOW WHETHER YOU WANT ME TO TREAT THE TB BUG AS IT WAS BEFORE ANTIBIOTICS...
...OR AS THE MULTIPLE-DRUG-RESISTANT STRAIN IT HAS SINCE EVOLVED INTO.
EVOLVED?
YOUR CHOICE. IF YOU GO WITH THE NOAH'S ARK VERSION, I'LL JUST GIVE YOU STREPTOMYCIN.
UM... WHAT ARE THE NEWER DRUGS LIKE?
THEY'RE INTELLIGENTLY DESIGNED.

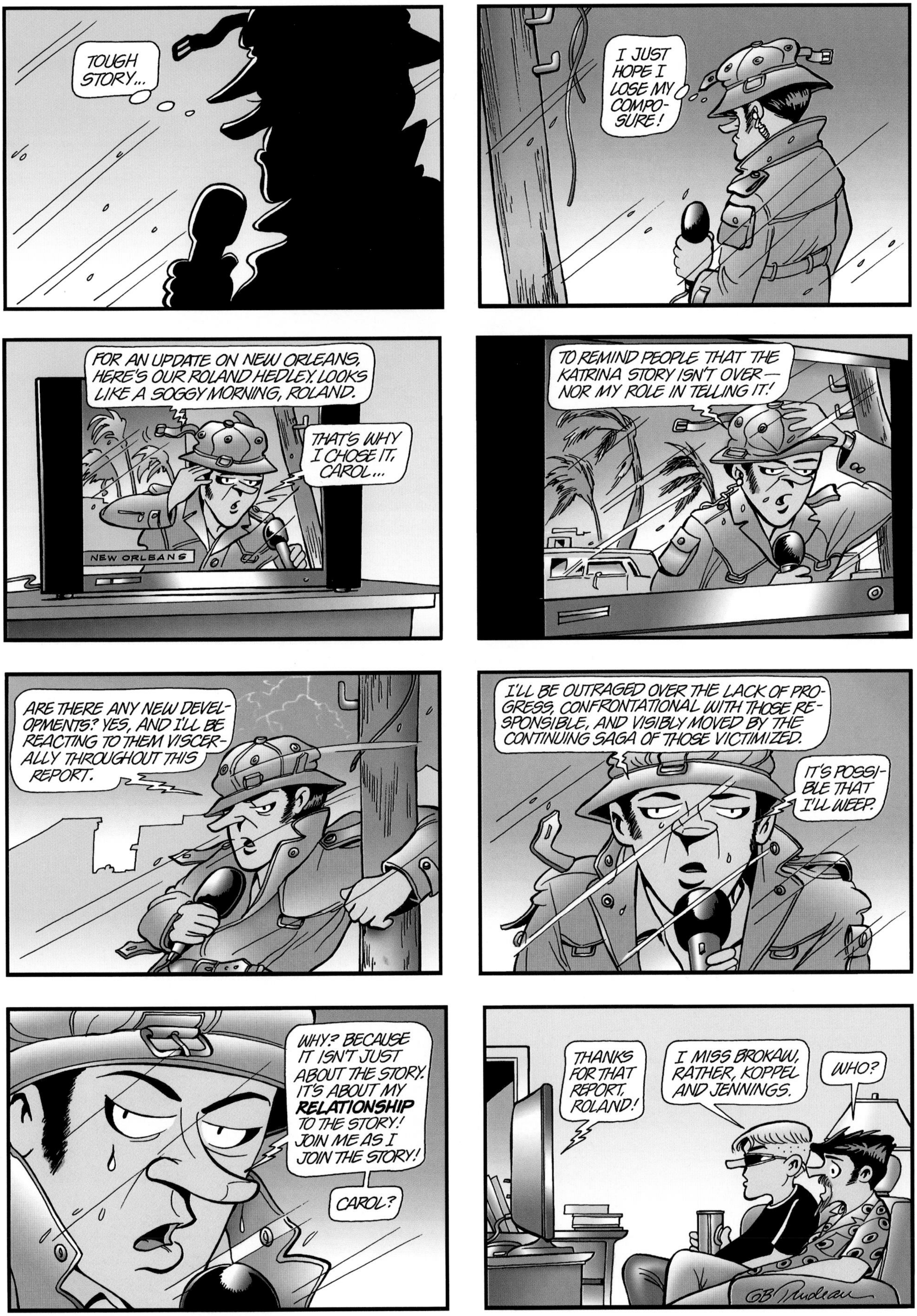
TOUGH STORY...
I JUST HOPE I LOSE MY COMPO-SURE!
FOR AN UPDATE ON NEW ORLEANS, HERE'S OUR ROLAND HEDLEY. LOOKS LIKE A SOGGY MORNING, ROLAND.
NEW ORLEANS
THAT'S WHY I CHOSE IT, CAROL...
TO REMIND PEOPLE THAT THE KATRINA STORY ISN'T OVER— NOR MY ROLE IN TELLING IT!
ARE THERE ANY NEW DEVEL-OPMENTS? YES, AND I'LL BE REACTING TO THEM VISCER-ALLY THROUGHOUT THIS REPORT.
I'LL BE OUTRAGED OVER THE LACK OF PRO-GRESS, CONFRONTATIONAL WITH THOSE RE-SPONSIBLE, AND VISIBLY MOVED BY THE CONTINUING SAGA OF THOSE VICTIMIZED.
IT'S POSSI-BLE THAT I'LL WEEP.
WHY? BECAUSE IT ISN'T JUST ABOUT THE STORY. IT'S ABOUT MY **RELATIONSHIP** TO THE STORY! JOIN ME AS I JOIN THE STORY!
CAROL?
THANKS FOR THAT REPORT, ROLAND!
I MISS BROKAW, RATHER, KOPPEL AND JENNINGS.
WHO?
GB Trudeau

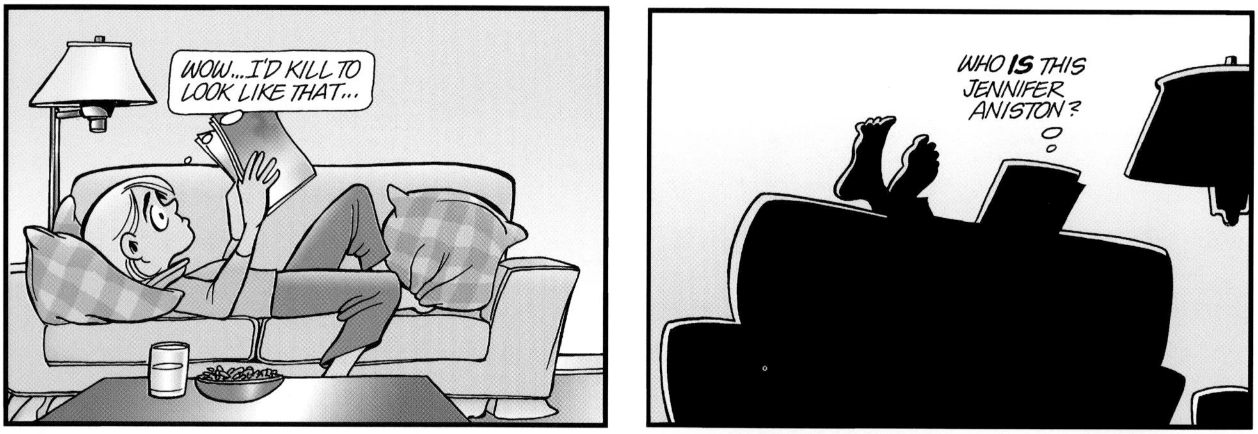
WOW...I'D KILL TO LOOK LIKE THAT...
WHO IS THIS JENNIFER ANISTON?

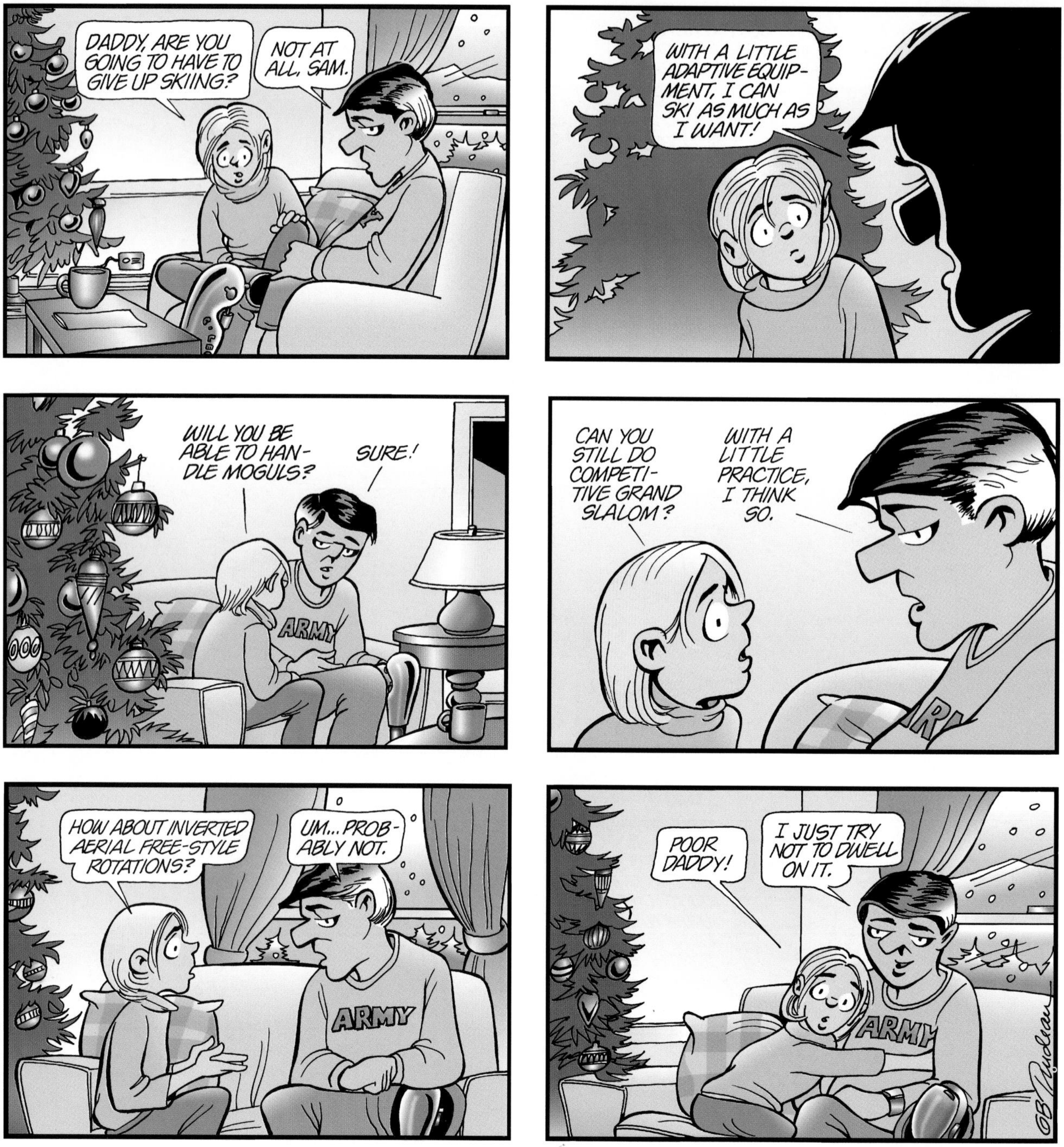
DADDY, ARE YOU GOING TO HAVE TO GIVE UP SKIING?
NOT AT ALL, SAM.
WITH A LITTLE ADAPTIVE EQUIPMENT, I CAN SKI AS MUCH AS I WANT!
WILL YOU BE ABLE TO HANDLE MOGULS?
SURE!
ARMY
CAN YOU STILL DO COMPETITIVE GRAND SLALOM?
WITH A LITTLE PRACTICE, I THINK SO.
HOW ABOUT INVERTED AERIAL FREE-STYLE ROTATIONS?
UM...PROBABLY NOT.
ARMY
POOR DADDY!
I JUST TRY NOT TO DWELL ON IT.
ARMY

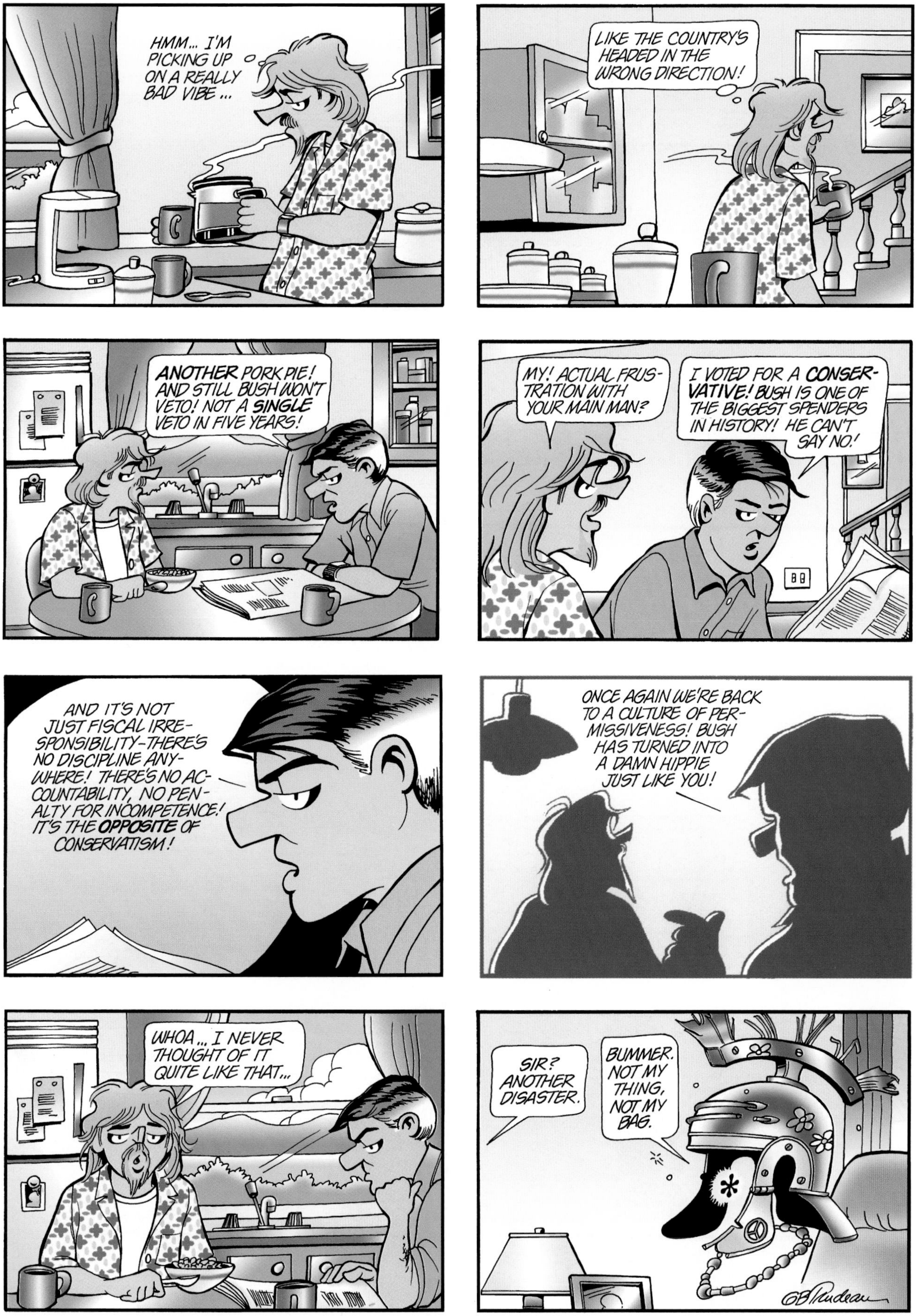

HMM... I'M PICKING UP ON A REALLY BAD VIBE...
LIKE THE COUNTRY'S HEADED IN THE WRONG DIRECTION!
ANOTHER PORK PIE! AND STILL BUSH WON'T VETO! NOT A SINGLE VETO IN FIVE YEARS!
MY! ACTUAL FRUS-TRATION WITH YOUR MAIN MAN?
I VOTED FOR A CONSER-VATIVE! BUSH IS ONE OF THE BIGGEST SPENDERS IN HISTORY! HE CAN'T SAY NO!
AND IT'S NOT JUST FISCAL IRRE-SPONSIBILITY–THERE'S NO DISCIPLINE ANY-WHERE! THERE'S NO AC-COUNTABILITY, NO PEN-ALTY FOR INCOMPETENCE! IT'S THE OPPOSITE OF CONSERVATISM!
ONCE AGAIN WE'RE BACK TO A CULTURE OF PER-MISSIVENESS! BUSH HAS TURNED INTO A DAMN HIPPIE JUST LIKE YOU!
WHOA... I NEVER THOUGHT OF IT QUITE LIKE THAT...
SIR? ANOTHER DISASTER.
BUMMER. NOT MY THING, NOT MY BAG.
GBTrudeau

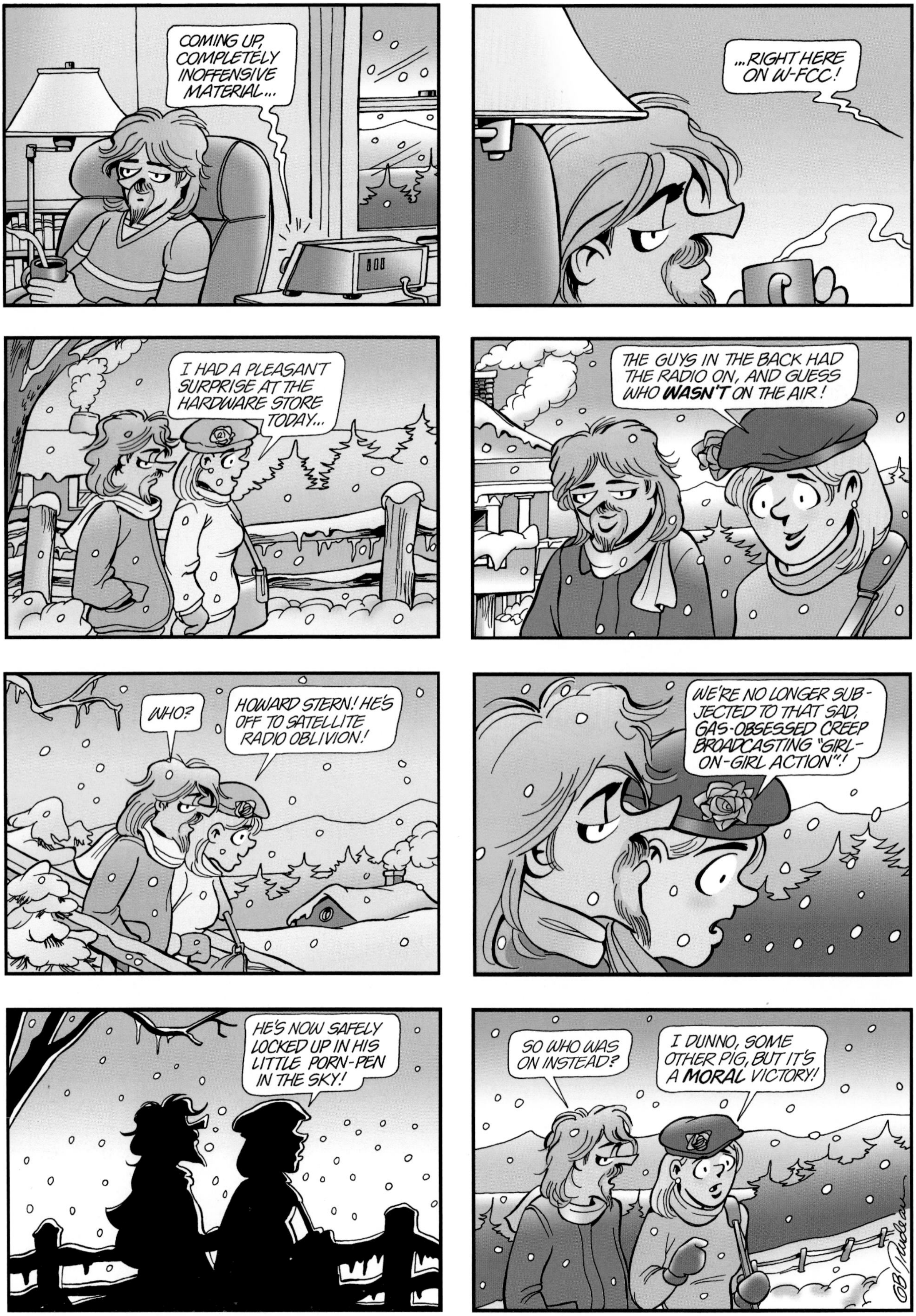
COMING UP, COMPLETELY INOFFENSIVE MATERIAL...
...RIGHT HERE ON W-FCC!
I HAD A PLEASANT SURPRISE AT THE HARDWARE STORE TODAY...
THE GUYS IN THE BACK HAD THE RADIO ON, AND GUESS WHO WASN'T ON THE AIR!
WHO?
HOWARD STERN! HE'S OFF TO SATELLITE RADIO OBLIVION!
WE'RE NO LONGER SUB-JECTED TO THAT SAD, GAS-OBSESSED CREEP BROADCASTING "GIRL-ON-GIRL ACTION"!
HE'S NOW SAFELY LOCKED UP IN HIS LITTLE PORN-PEN IN THE SKY!
SO WHO WAS ON INSTEAD?
I DUNNO, SOME OTHER PIG, BUT IT'S A MORAL VICTORY!

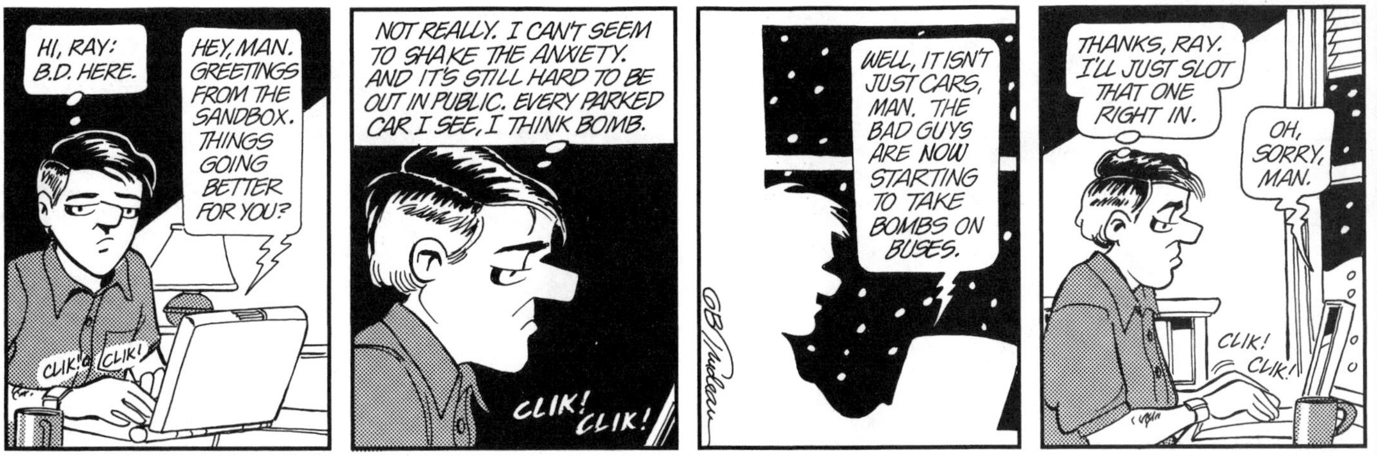
HI, RAY: B.D. HERE.
HEY, MAN. GREETINGS FROM THE SANDBOX. THINGS GOING BETTER FOR YOU?
CLIK! CLIK!
NOT REALLY. I CAN'T SEEM TO SHAKE THE ANXIETY. AND IT'S STILL HARD TO BE OUT IN PUBLIC. EVERY PARKED CAR I SEE, I THINK BOMB.
CLIK! CLIK!
WELL, IT ISN'T JUST CARS, MAN. THE BAD GUYS ARE NOW STARTING TO TAKE BOMBS ON BUSES.
THANKS, RAY. I'LL JUST SLOT THAT ONE RIGHT IN.
OH, SORRY, MAN.
CLIK! CLIK!

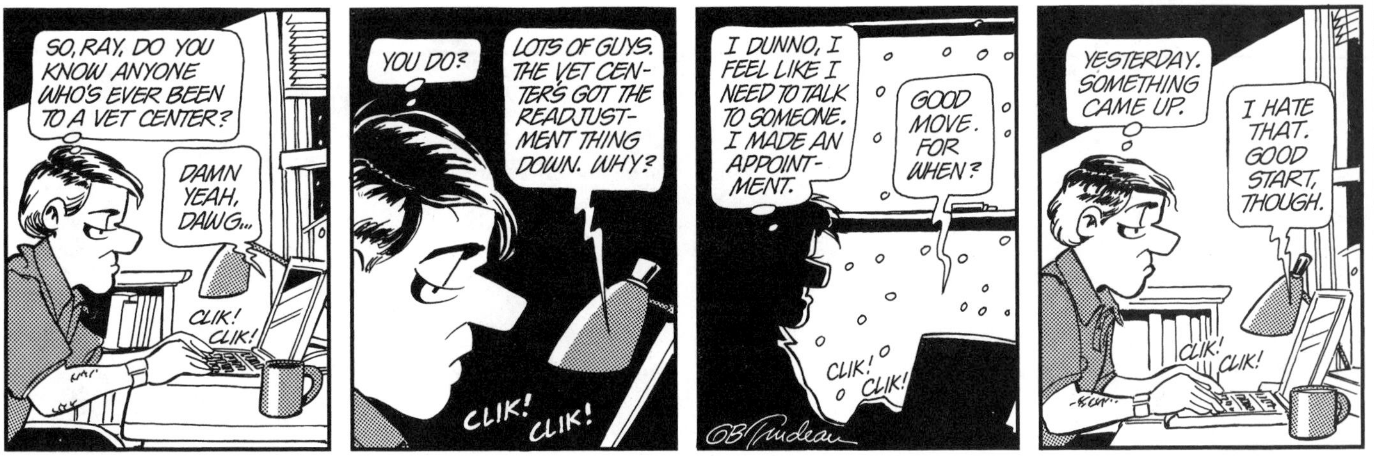
SO, RAY, DO YOU KNOW ANYONE WHO'S EVER BEEN TO A VET CENTER?
DAMN YEAH, DAWG...
CLIK! CLIK!
YOU DO?
LOTS OF GUYS. THE VET CENTER'S GOT THE READJUSTMENT THING DOWN. WHY?
CLIK! CLIK!
I DUNNO, I FEEL LIKE I NEED TO TALK TO SOMEONE. I MADE AN APPOINTMENT.
GOOD MOVE. FOR WHEN?
CLIK! CLIK!
YESTERDAY. SOMETHING CAME UP.
I HATE THAT. GOOD START, THOUGH.
CLIK! CLIK!

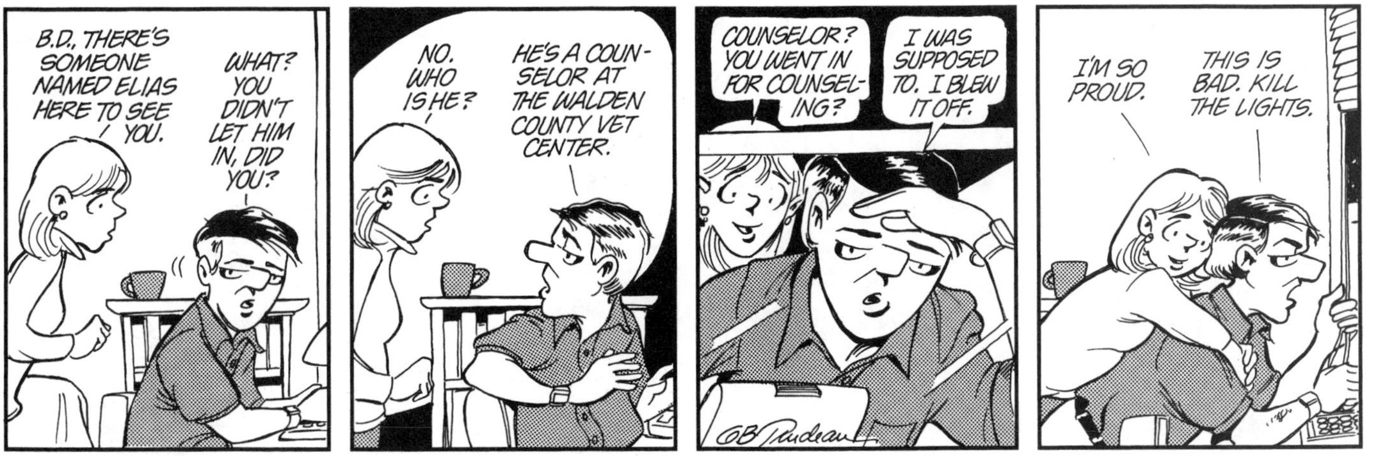
B.D., THERE'S SOMEONE NAMED ELIAS HERE TO SEE YOU.
WHAT? YOU DIDN'T LET HIM IN, DID YOU?
NO. WHO IS HE?
HE'S A COUNSELOR AT THE WALDEN COUNTY VET CENTER.
COUNSELOR? YOU WENT IN FOR COUNSELING?
I WAS SUPPOSED TO. I BLEW IT OFF.
I'M SO PROUD.
THIS IS BAD. KILL THE LIGHTS.

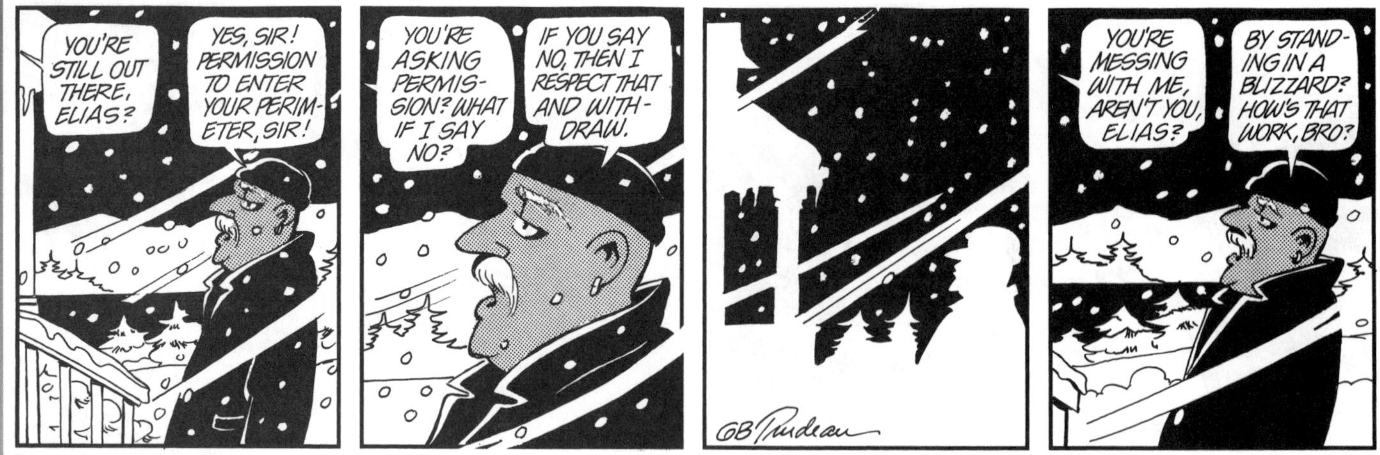
YOU'RE STILL OUT THERE, ELIAS?
YES, SIR! PERMISSION TO ENTER YOUR PERIMETER, SIR!
YOU'RE ASKING PERMISSION? WHAT IF I SAY NO?
IF YOU SAY NO, THEN I RESPECT THAT AND WITHDRAW.
GB Trudeau
YOU'RE MESSING WITH ME, AREN'T YOU, ELIAS?
BY STANDING IN A BLIZZARD? HOW'S THAT WORK, BRO?

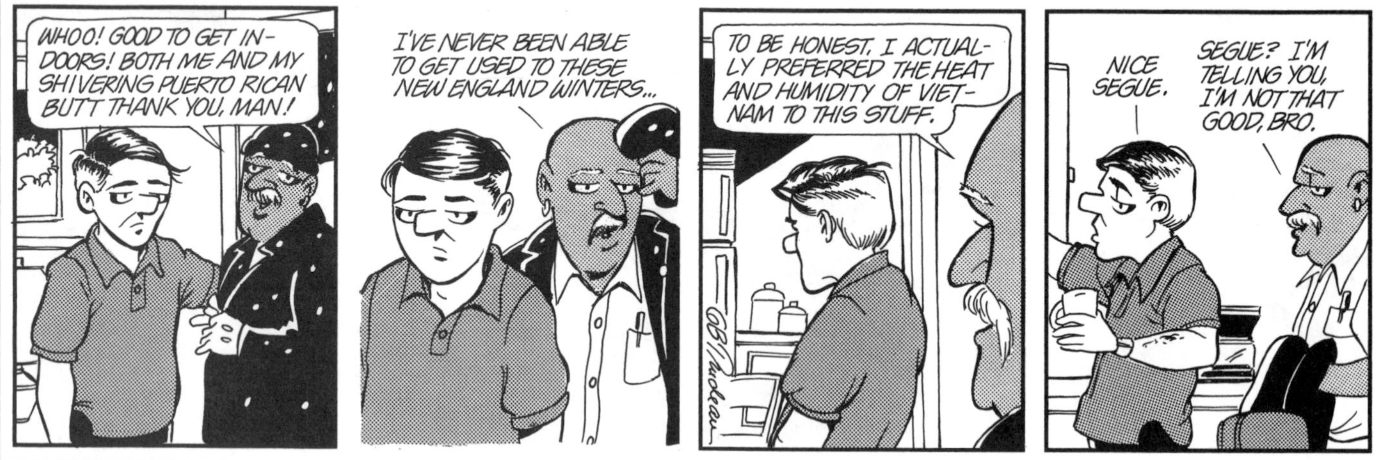
WHOO! GOOD TO GET INDOORS! BOTH ME AND MY SHIVERING PUERTO RICAN BUTT THANK YOU, MAN!
I'VE NEVER BEEN ABLE TO GET USED TO THESE NEW ENGLAND WINTERS...
TO BE HONEST, I ACTUALLY PREFERRED THE HEAT AND HUMIDITY OF VIETNAM TO THIS STUFF.
GB Trudeau
NICE SEGUE.
SEGUE? I'M TELLING YOU, I'M NOT THAT GOOD, BRO.

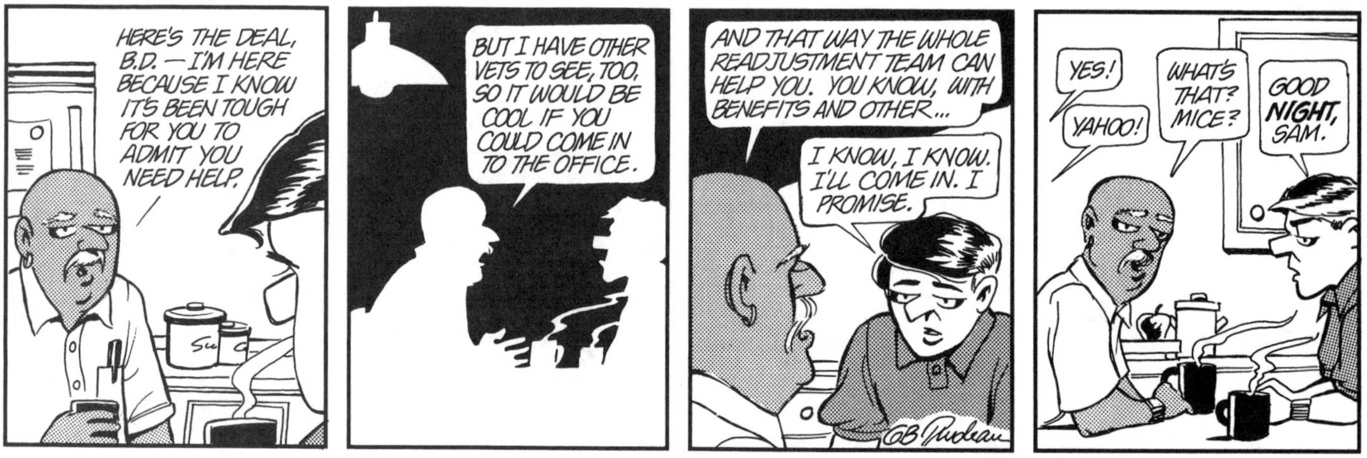
HERE'S THE DEAL, B.D. — I'M HERE BECAUSE I KNOW IT'S BEEN TOUGH FOR YOU TO ADMIT YOU NEED HELP.
BUT I HAVE OTHER VETS TO SEE, TOO, SO IT WOULD BE COOL IF YOU COULD COME IN TO THE OFFICE.
AND THAT WAY THE WHOLE READJUSTMENT TEAM CAN HELP YOU. YOU KNOW, WITH BENEFITS AND OTHER...
I KNOW, I KNOW. I'LL COME IN. I PROMISE.
GB Trudeau
YES!
YAHOO!
WHAT'S THAT? MICE?
GOOD NIGHT, SAM.

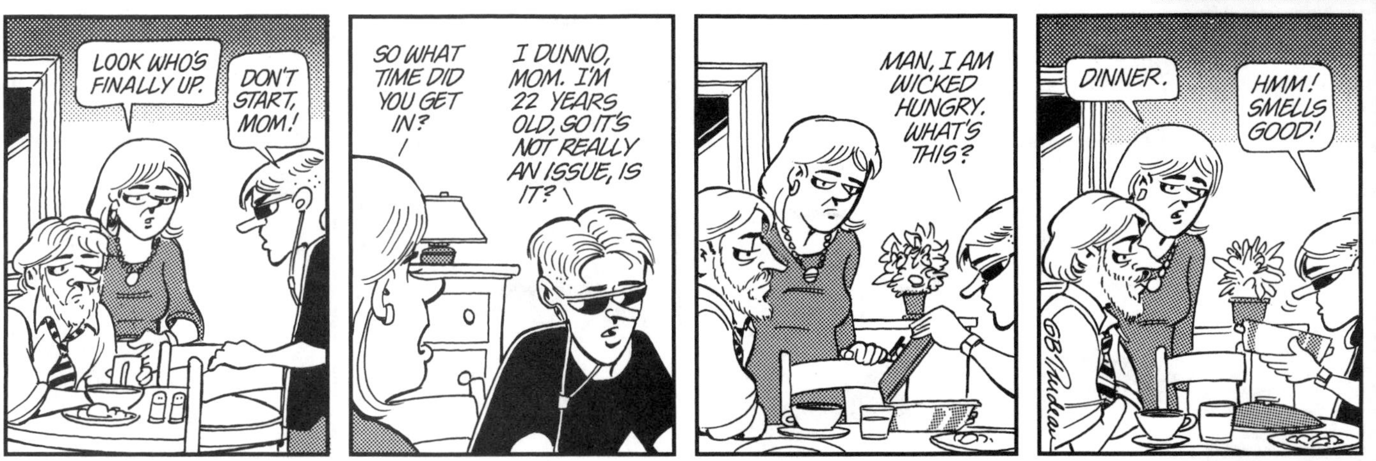
LOOK WHO'S FINALLY UP.
DON'T START, MOM!
SO WHAT TIME DID YOU GET IN?
I DUNNO, MOM. I'M 22 YEARS OLD, SO IT'S NOT REALLY AN ISSUE, IS IT?
MAN, I AM WICKED HUNGRY. WHAT'S THIS?
DINNER.
HMM! SMELLS GOOD!
GB Trudeau

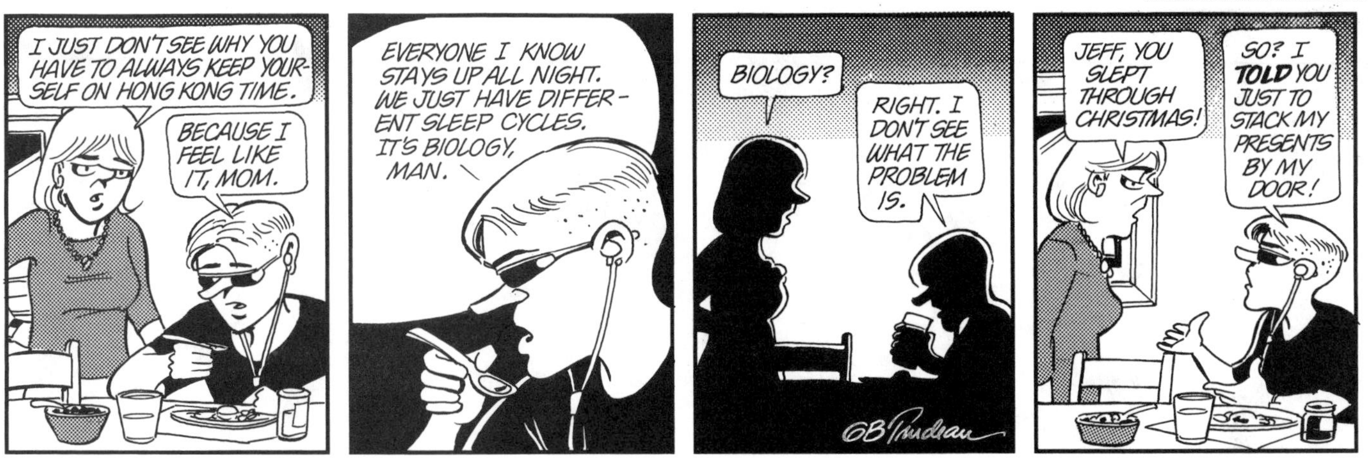
I JUST DON'T SEE WHY YOU HAVE TO ALWAYS KEEP YOURSELF ON HONG KONG TIME.
BECAUSE I FEEL LIKE IT, MOM.
EVERYONE I KNOW STAYS UP ALL NIGHT. WE JUST HAVE DIFFERENT SLEEP CYCLES. IT'S BIOLOGY, MAN.
BIOLOGY?
RIGHT. I DON'T SEE WHAT THE PROBLEM IS.
GB Trudeau
JEFF, YOU SLEPT THROUGH CHRISTMAS!
SO? I **TOLD** YOU JUST TO STACK MY PRESENTS BY MY DOOR!

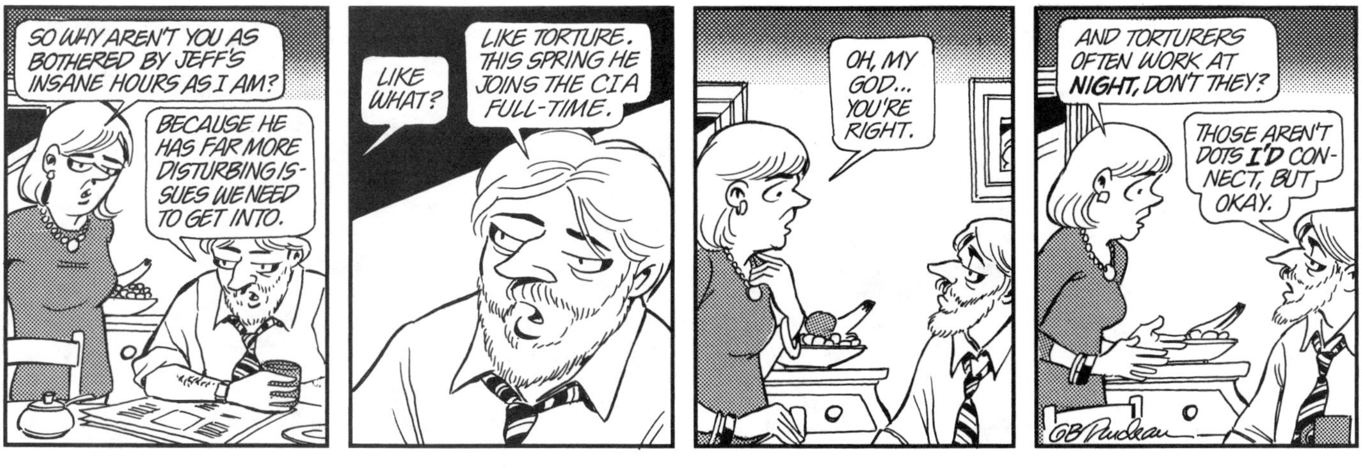
SO WHY AREN'T YOU AS BOTHERED BY JEFF'S INSANE HOURS AS I AM?
BECAUSE HE HAS FAR MORE DISTURBING ISSUES WE NEED TO GET INTO.
LIKE WHAT?
LIKE TORTURE. THIS SPRING HE JOINS THE CIA FULL-TIME.
OH, MY GOD... YOU'RE RIGHT.
AND TORTURERS OFTEN WORK AT **NIGHT**, DON'T THEY?
THOSE AREN'T DOTS **I'D** CONNECT, BUT OKAY.
GB Trudeau

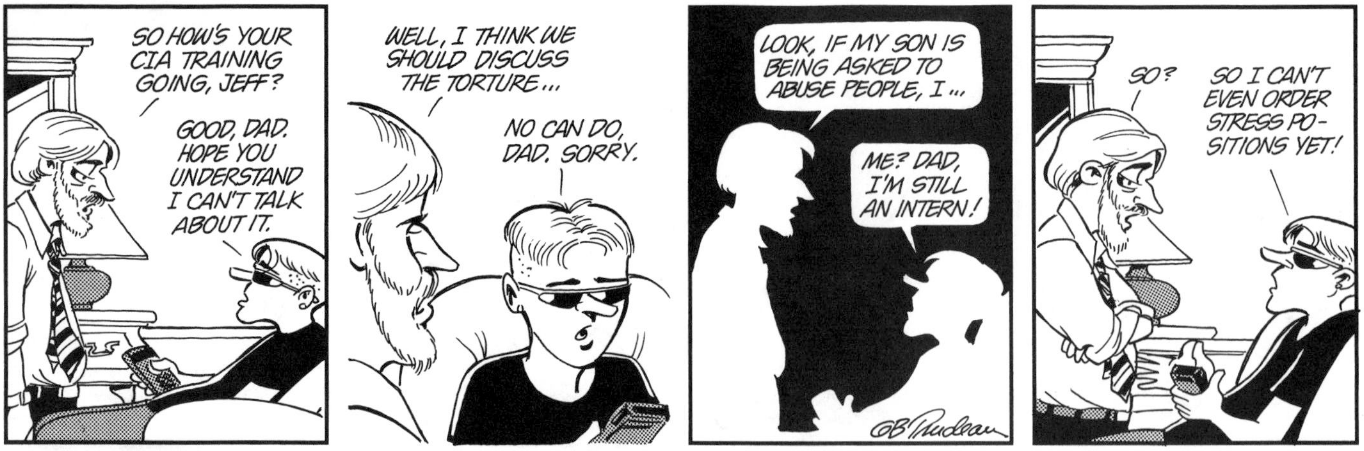
SO HOW'S YOUR CIA TRAINING GOING, JEFF?
GOOD, DAD. HOPE YOU UNDERSTAND I CAN'T TALK ABOUT IT.
WELL, I THINK WE SHOULD DISCUSS THE TORTURE...
NO CAN DO, DAD. SORRY.
LOOK, IF MY SON IS BEING ASKED TO ABUSE PEOPLE, I...
ME? DAD, I'M STILL AN INTERN!
SO?
SO I CAN'T EVEN ORDER STRESS POSITIONS YET!

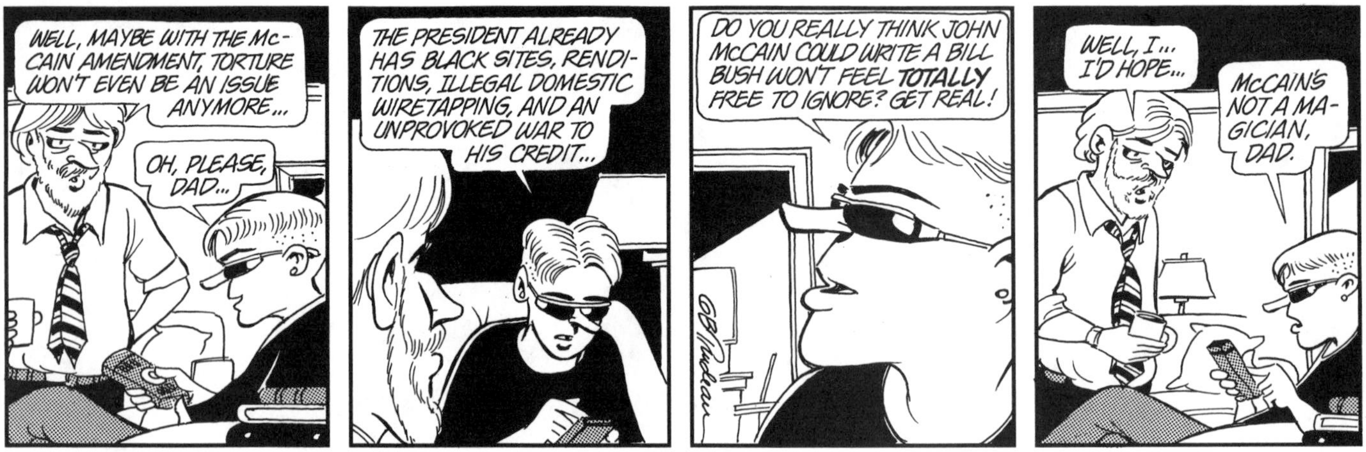
WELL, MAYBE WITH THE McCAIN AMENDMENT, TORTURE WON'T EVEN BE AN ISSUE ANYMORE...
OH, PLEASE, DAD...
THE PRESIDENT ALREADY HAS BLACK SITES, RENDITIONS, ILLEGAL DOMESTIC WIRETAPPING, AND AN UNPROVOKED WAR TO HIS CREDIT...
DO YOU REALLY THINK JOHN McCAIN COULD WRITE A BILL BUSH WON'T FEEL **TOTALLY** FREE TO IGNORE? GET REAL!
WELL, I... I'D HOPE...
McCAIN'S NOT A MAGICIAN, DAD.

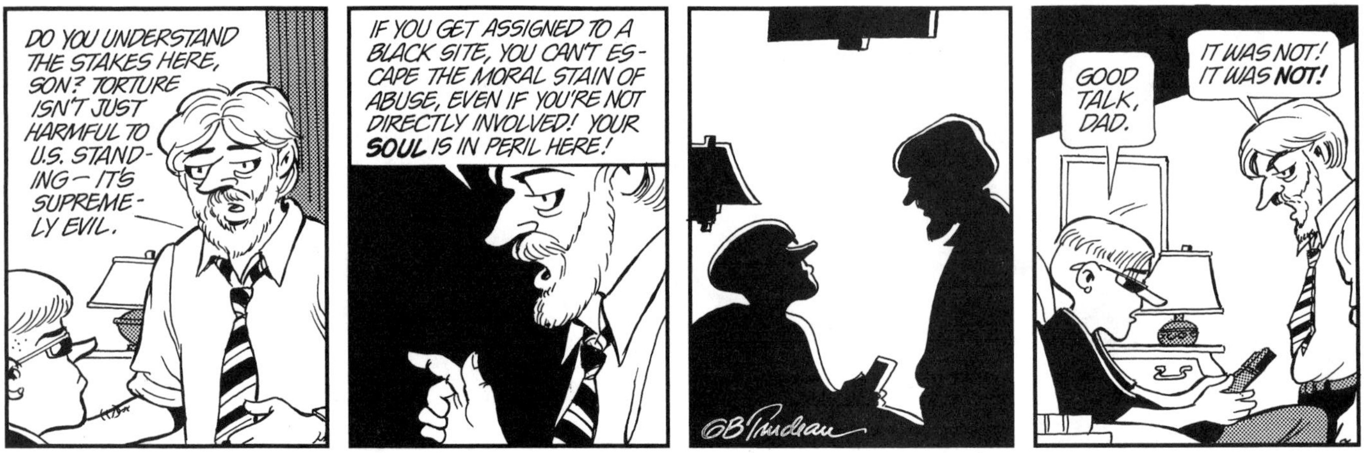
DO YOU UNDERSTAND THE STAKES HERE, SON? TORTURE ISN'T JUST HARMFUL TO U.S. STANDING — IT'S SUPREMELY EVIL.
IF YOU GET ASSIGNED TO A BLACK SITE, YOU CAN'T ESCAPE THE MORAL STAIN OF ABUSE, EVEN IF YOU'RE NOT DIRECTLY INVOLVED! YOUR **SOUL** IS IN PERIL HERE!
GOOD TALK, DAD.
IT WAS NOT! IT WAS **NOT!**

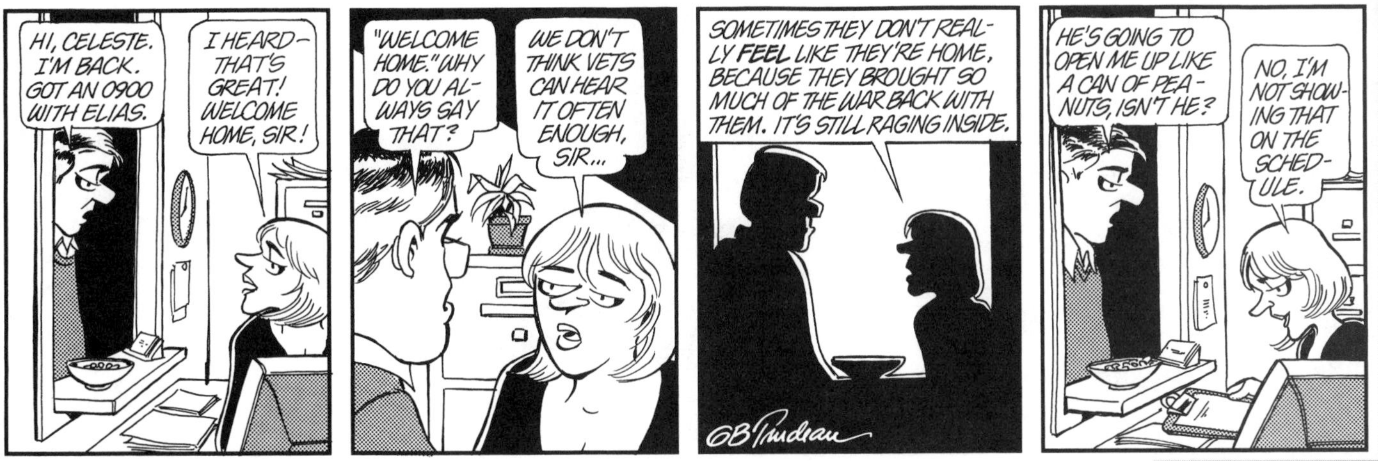
HI, CELESTE. I'M BACK. GOT AN 0900 WITH ELIAS.
I HEARD— THAT'S GREAT! WELCOME HOME, SIR!
"WELCOME HOME." WHY DO YOU ALWAYS SAY THAT?
WE DON'T THINK VETS CAN HEAR IT OFTEN ENOUGH, SIR...
SOMETIMES THEY DON'T REALLY FEEL LIKE THEY'RE HOME, BECAUSE THEY BROUGHT SO MUCH OF THE WAR BACK WITH THEM. IT'S STILL RAGING INSIDE.
GB Trudeau
HE'S GOING TO OPEN ME UP LIKE A CAN OF PEANUTS, ISN'T HE?
NO, I'M NOT SHOWING THAT ON THE SCHEDULE.

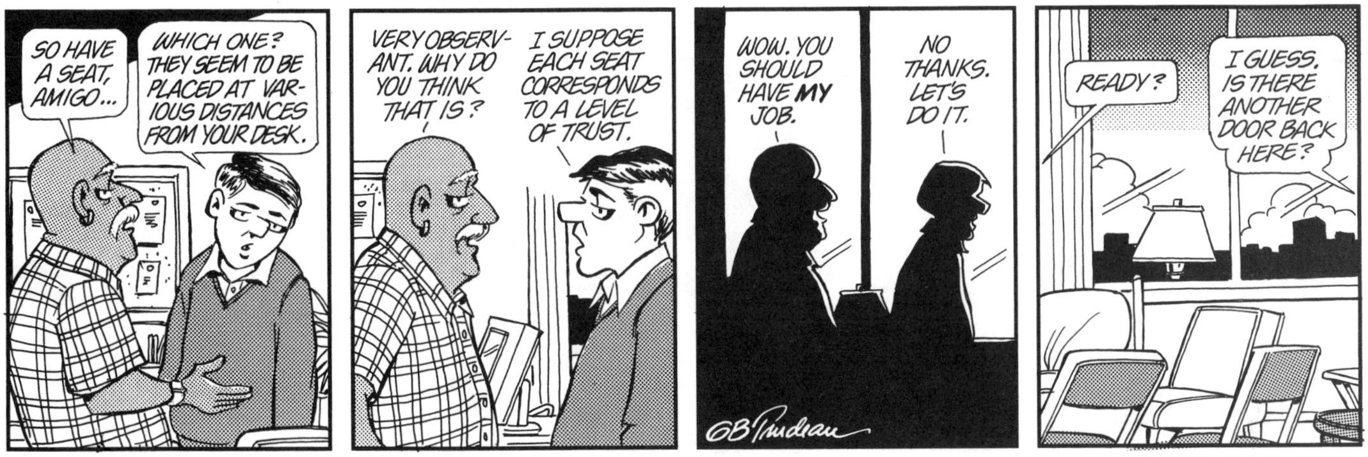
SO HAVE A SEAT, AMIGO...
WHICH ONE? THEY SEEM TO BE PLACED AT VARIOUS DISTANCES FROM YOUR DESK.
VERY OBSERVANT. WHY DO YOU THINK THAT IS?
I SUPPOSE EACH SEAT CORRESPONDS TO A LEVEL OF TRUST.
WOW. YOU SHOULD HAVE MY JOB.
NO THANKS. LET'S DO IT.
GB Trudeau
READY?
I GUESS. IS THERE ANOTHER DOOR BACK HERE?

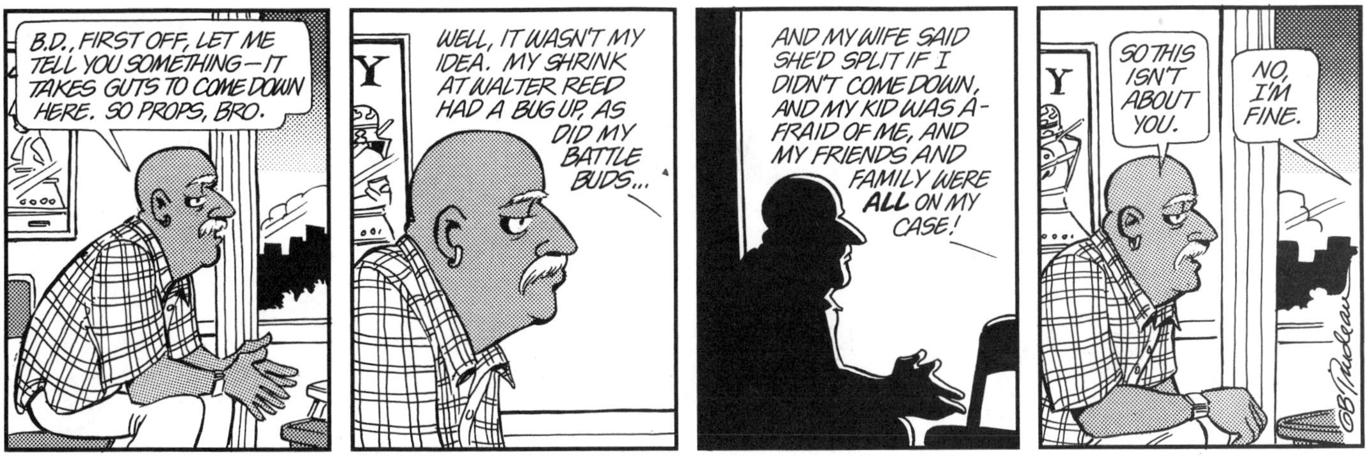
B.D., FIRST OFF, LET ME TELL YOU SOMETHING—IT TAKES GUTS TO COME DOWN HERE. SO PROPS, BRO.
WELL, IT WASN'T MY IDEA. MY SHRINK AT WALTER REED HAD A BUG UP, AS DID MY BATTLE BUDS...
AND MY WIFE SAID SHE'D SPLIT IF I DIDN'T COME DOWN, AND MY KID WAS AFRAID OF ME, AND MY FRIENDS AND FAMILY WERE ALL ON MY CASE!
SO THIS ISN'T ABOUT YOU.
NO, I'M FINE.
GB Trudeau

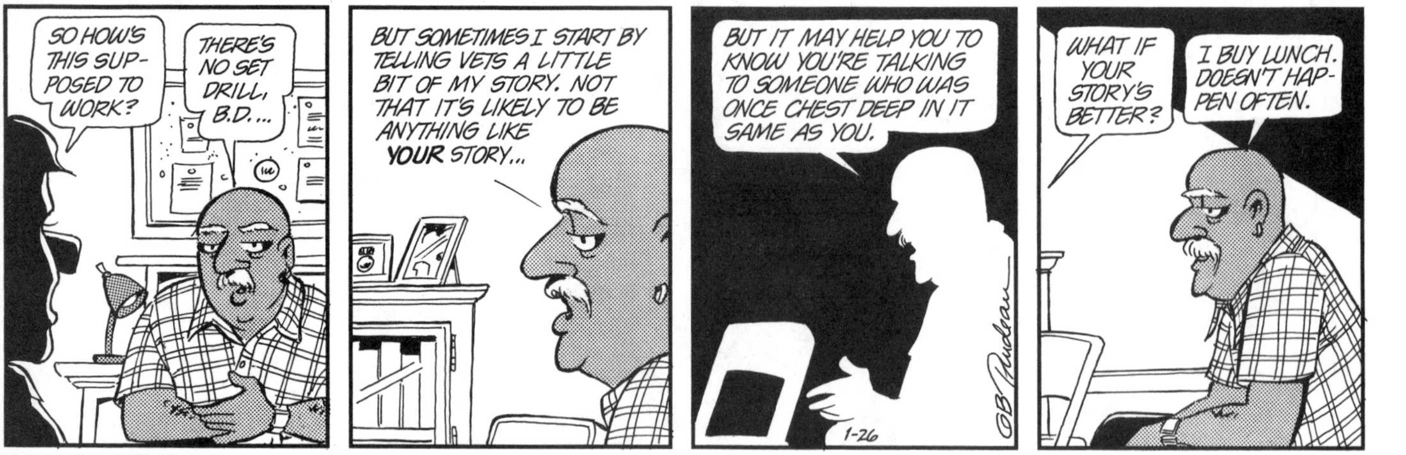
SO HOW'S THIS SUPPOSED TO WORK?
THERE'S NO SET DRILL, B.D. ...
BUT SOMETIMES I START BY TELLING VETS A LITTLE BIT OF MY STORY. NOT THAT IT'S LIKELY TO BE ANYTHING LIKE **YOUR** STORY...
BUT IT MAY HELP YOU TO KNOW YOU'RE TALKING TO SOMEONE WHO WAS ONCE CHEST DEEP IN IT SAME AS YOU.
WHAT IF YOUR STORY'S BETTER?
I BUY LUNCH. DOESN'T HAPPEN OFTEN.
1-26

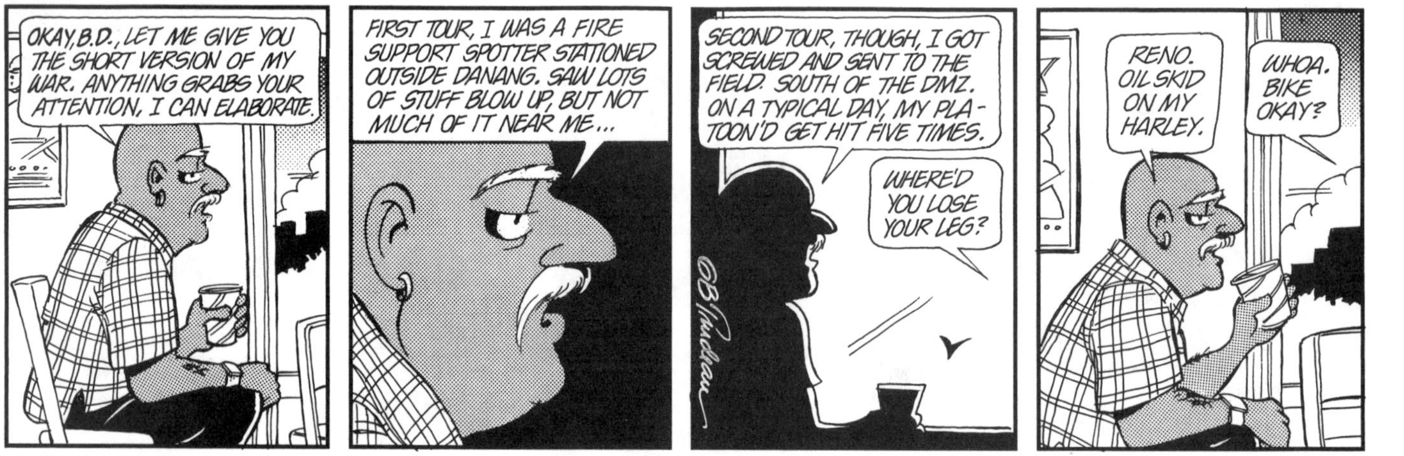
OKAY, B.D., LET ME GIVE YOU THE SHORT VERSION OF MY WAR. ANYTHING GRABS YOUR ATTENTION, I CAN ELABORATE.
FIRST TOUR, I WAS A FIRE SUPPORT SPOTTER STATIONED OUTSIDE DANANG. SAW LOTS OF STUFF BLOW UP, BUT NOT MUCH OF IT NEAR ME...
SECOND TOUR, THOUGH, I GOT SCREWED AND SENT TO THE FIELD. SOUTH OF THE DMZ. ON A TYPICAL DAY, MY PLATOON'D GET HIT FIVE TIMES.
WHERE'D YOU LOSE YOUR LEG?
RENO. OIL SKID ON MY HARLEY.
WHOA. BIKE OKAY?

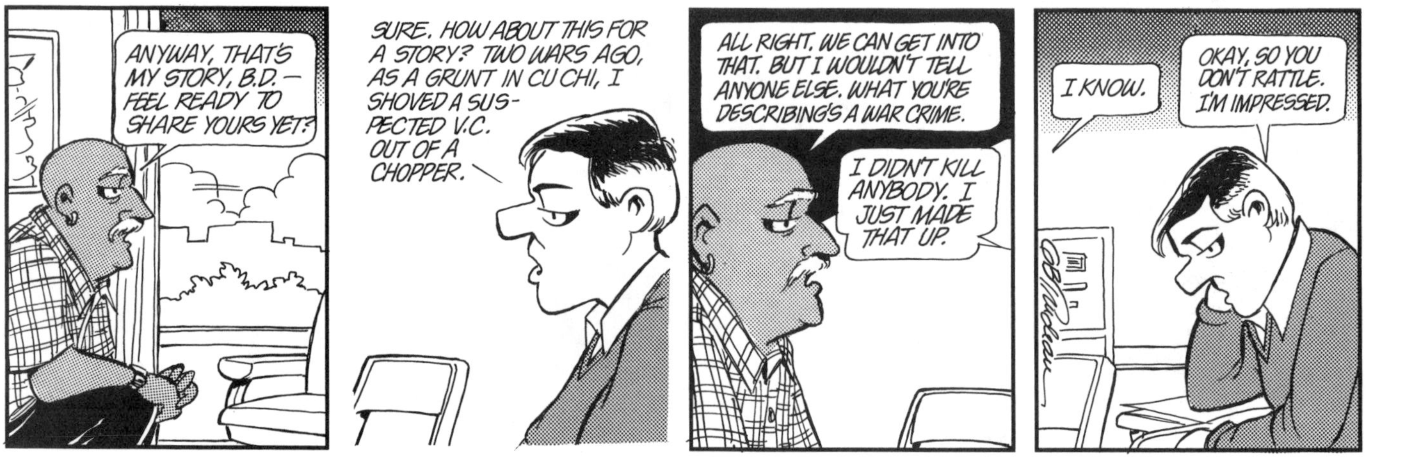
ANYWAY, THAT'S MY STORY, B.D.— FEEL READY TO SHARE YOURS YET?
SURE. HOW ABOUT THIS FOR A STORY? TWO WARS AGO, AS A GRUNT IN CU CHI, I SHOVED A SUSPECTED V.C. OUT OF A CHOPPER.
ALL RIGHT, WE CAN GET INTO THAT. BUT I WOULDN'T TELL ANYONE ELSE. WHAT YOU'RE DESCRIBING'S A WAR CRIME.
I DIDN'T KILL ANYBODY. I JUST MADE THAT UP.
I KNOW.
OKAY, SO YOU DON'T RATTLE. I'M IMPRESSED.

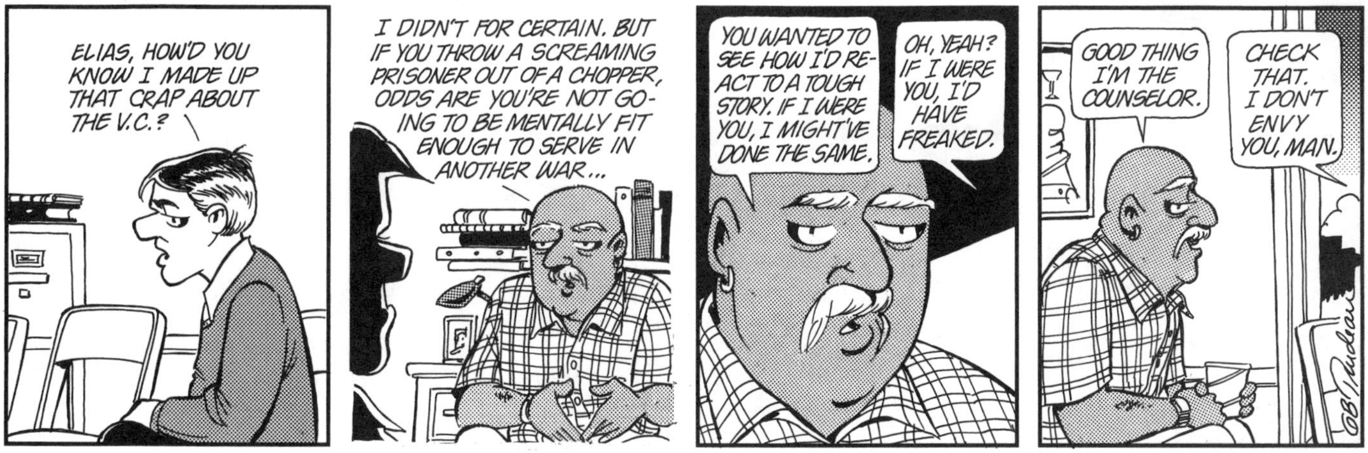
ELIAS, HOW'D YOU KNOW I MADE UP THAT CRAP ABOUT THE V.C.?
I DIDN'T FOR CERTAIN. BUT IF YOU THROW A SCREAMING PRISONER OUT OF A CHOPPER, ODDS ARE YOU'RE NOT GOING TO BE MENTALLY FIT ENOUGH TO SERVE IN ANOTHER WAR...
YOU WANTED TO SEE HOW I'D REACT TO A TOUGH STORY. IF I WERE YOU, I MIGHT'VE DONE THE SAME.
OH, YEAH? IF I WERE YOU, I'D HAVE FREAKED.
GOOD THING I'M THE COUNSELOR.
CHECK THAT. I DON'T ENVY YOU, MAN.

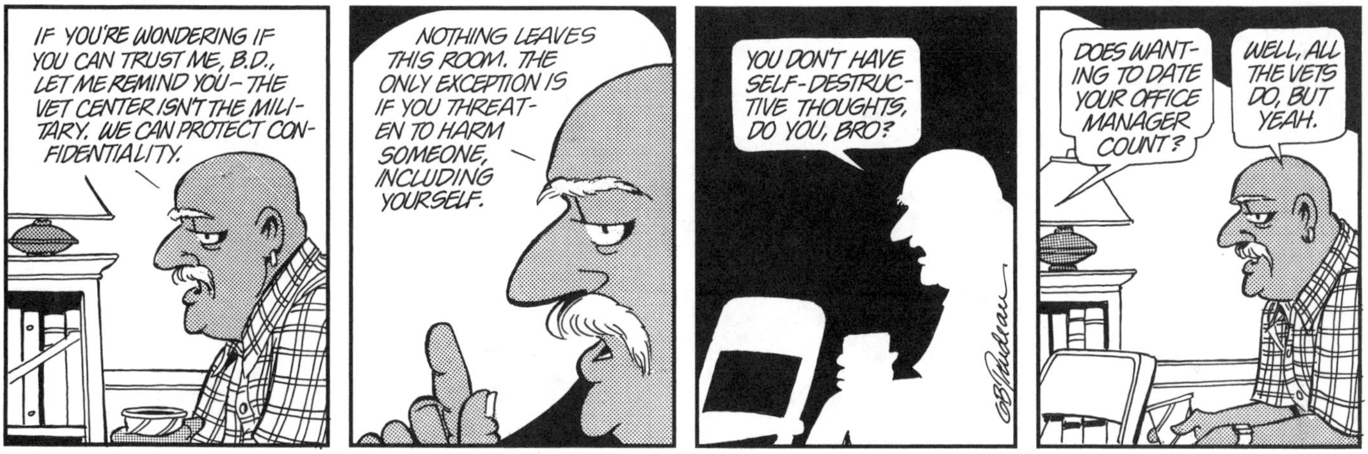
IF YOU'RE WONDERING IF YOU CAN TRUST ME, B.D., LET ME REMIND YOU – THE VET CENTER ISN'T THE MILITARY. WE CAN PROTECT CONFIDENTIALITY.
NOTHING LEAVES THIS ROOM. THE ONLY EXCEPTION IS IF YOU THREATEN TO HARM SOMEONE, INCLUDING YOURSELF.
YOU DON'T HAVE SELF-DESTRUCTIVE THOUGHTS, DO YOU, BRO?
DOES WANTING TO DATE YOUR OFFICE MANAGER COUNT?
WELL, ALL THE VETS DO, BUT YEAH.

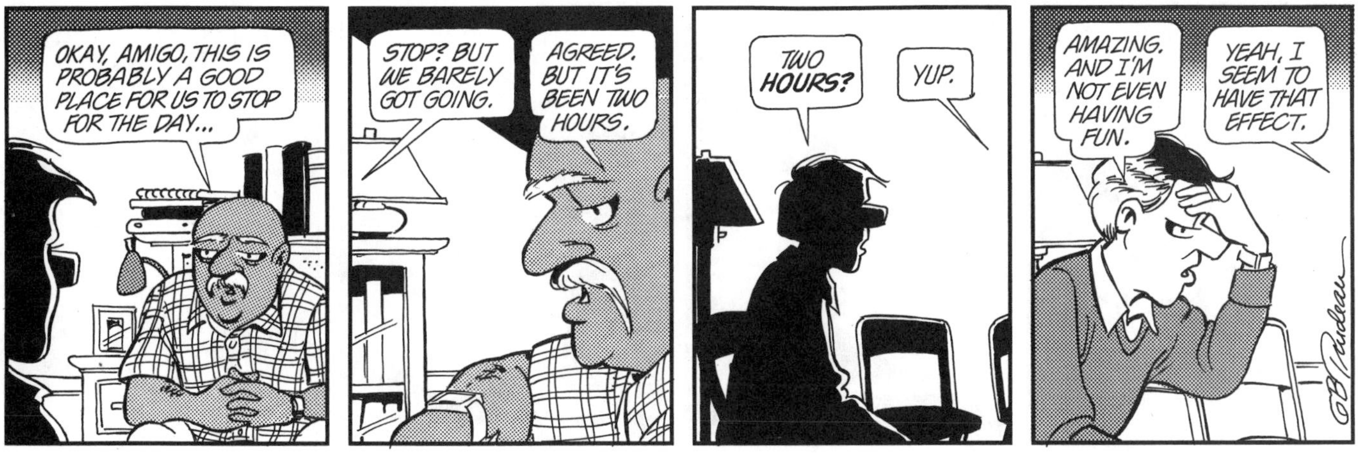
OKAY, AMIGO, THIS IS PROBABLY A GOOD PLACE FOR US TO STOP FOR THE DAY...
STOP? BUT WE BARELY GOT GOING.
AGREED. BUT IT'S BEEN TWO HOURS.
TWO HOURS?
YUP.
AMAZING. AND I'M NOT EVEN HAVING FUN.
YEAH, I SEEM TO HAVE THAT EFFECT.

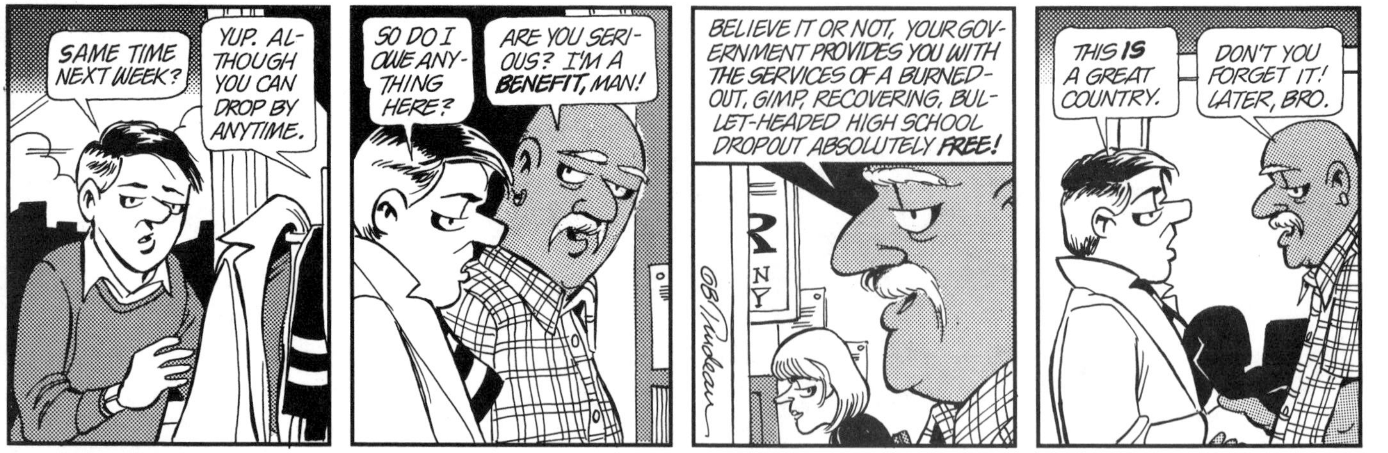
SAME TIME NEXT WEEK?
YUP. ALTHOUGH YOU CAN DROP BY ANYTIME.
SO DO I OWE ANYTHING HERE?
ARE YOU SERIOUS? I'M A BENEFIT, MAN!
BELIEVE IT OR NOT, YOUR GOVERNMENT PROVIDES YOU WITH THE SERVICES OF A BURNED-OUT, GIMP, RECOVERING, BULLET-HEADED HIGH SCHOOL DROPOUT ABSOLUTELY FREE!
THIS IS A GREAT COUNTRY.
DON'T YOU FORGET IT! LATER, BRO.

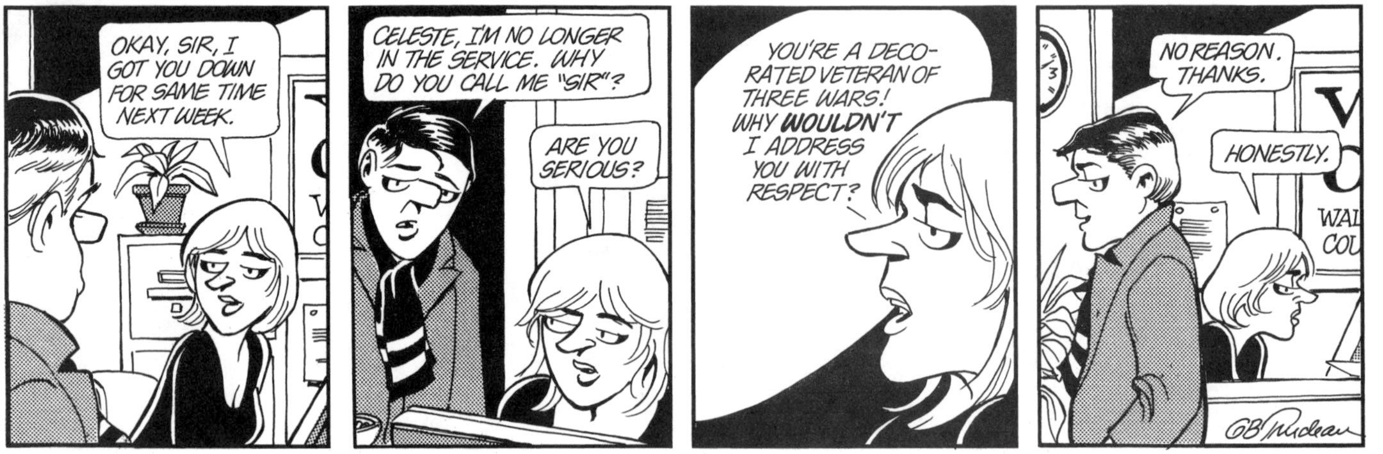
OKAY, SIR, I GOT YOU DOWN FOR SAME TIME NEXT WEEK.
CELESTE, I'M NO LONGER IN THE SERVICE. WHY DO YOU CALL ME "SIR"?
ARE YOU SERIOUS?
YOU'RE A DECORATED VETERAN OF THREE WARS! WHY WOULDN'T I ADDRESS YOU WITH RESPECT?
NO REASON. THANKS.
HONESTLY.

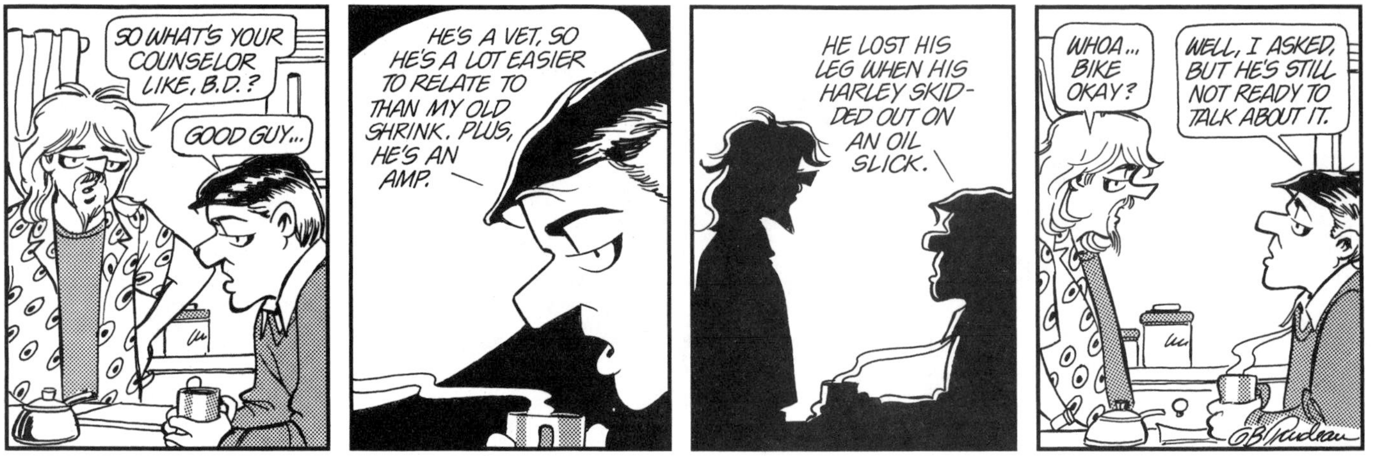
SO WHAT'S YOUR COUNSELOR LIKE, B.D.?
GOOD GUY...
HE'S A VET, SO HE'S A LOT EASIER TO RELATE TO THAN MY OLD SHRINK. PLUS, HE'S AN AMP.
HE LOST HIS LEG WHEN HIS HARLEY SKIDDED OUT ON AN OIL SLICK.
WHOA... BIKE OKAY?
WELL, I ASKED, BUT HE'S STILL NOT READY TO TALK ABOUT IT.

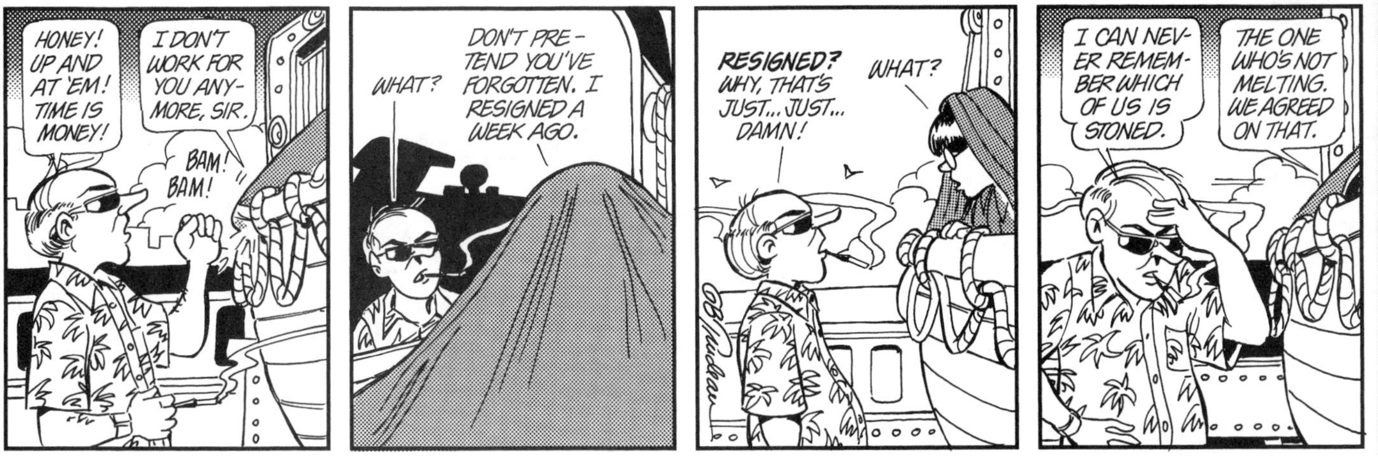
HONEY! UP AND AT 'EM! TIME IS MONEY!
I DON'T WORK FOR YOU ANYMORE, SIR.
BAM! BAM!
WHAT?
DON'T PRETEND YOU'VE FORGOTTEN. I RESIGNED A WEEK AGO.
RESIGNED? WHY, THAT'S JUST... JUST... DAMN!
WHAT?
I CAN NEVER REMEMBER WHICH OF US IS STONED.
THE ONE WHO'S NOT MELTING. WE AGREED ON THAT.

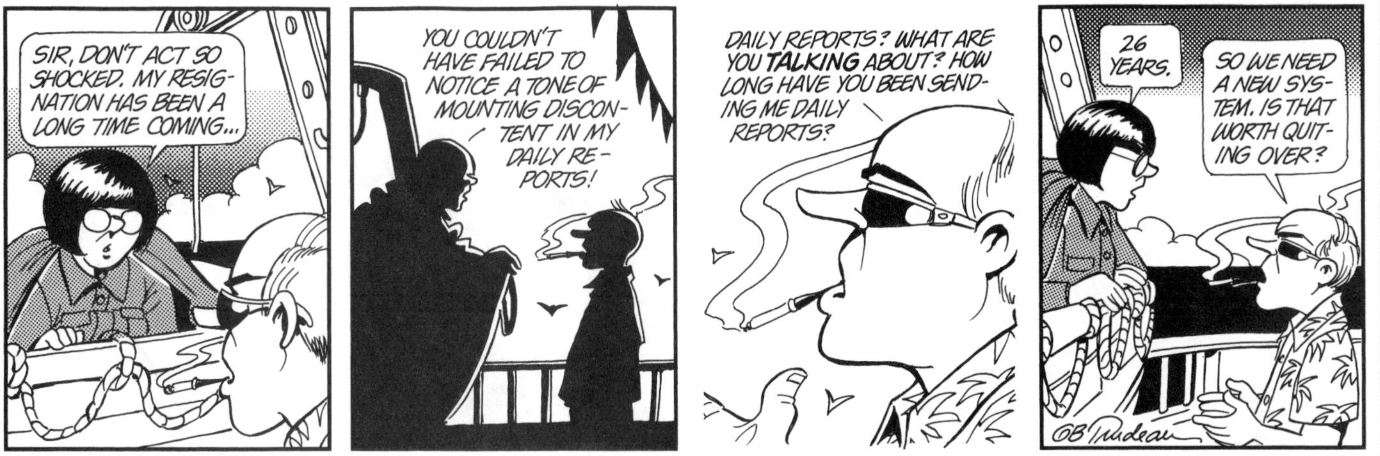
SIR, DON'T ACT SO SHOCKED. MY RESIGNATION HAS BEEN A LONG TIME COMING...
YOU COULDN'T HAVE FAILED TO NOTICE A TONE OF MOUNTING DISCONTENT IN MY DAILY REPORTS!
DAILY REPORTS? WHAT ARE YOU TALKING ABOUT? HOW LONG HAVE YOU BEEN SENDING ME DAILY REPORTS?
26 YEARS.
SO WE NEED A NEW SYSTEM. IS THAT WORTH QUITTING OVER?

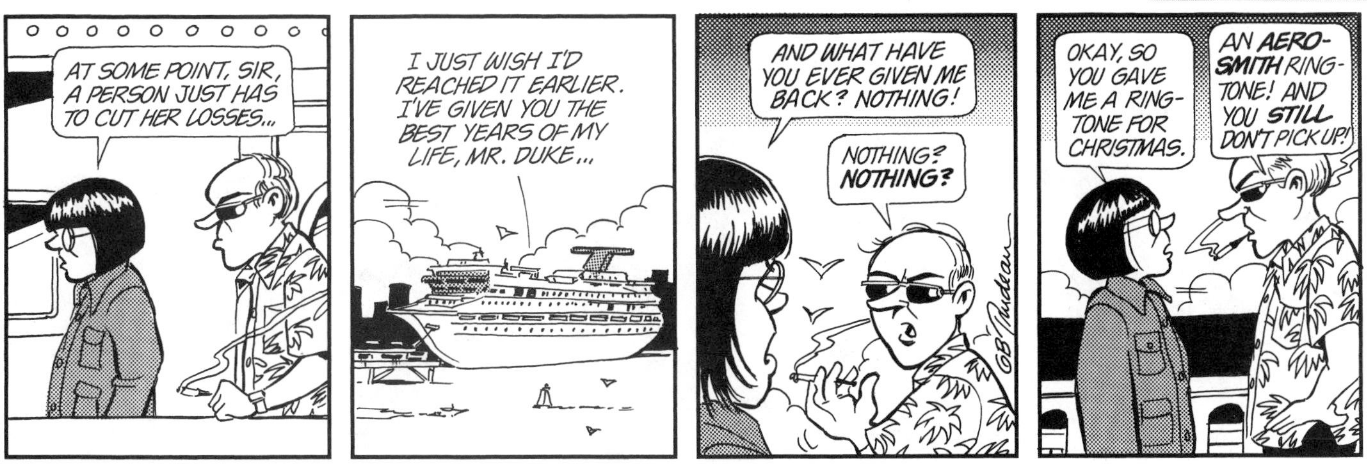
AT SOME POINT, SIR, A PERSON JUST HAS TO CUT HER LOSSES...
I JUST WISH I'D REACHED IT EARLIER. I'VE GIVEN YOU THE BEST YEARS OF MY LIFE, MR. DUKE...
AND WHAT HAVE YOU EVER GIVEN ME BACK? NOTHING!
NOTHING? NOTHING?
OKAY, SO YOU GAVE ME A RINGTONE FOR CHRISTMAS.
AN AEROSMITH RINGTONE! AND YOU STILL DON'T PICK UP!

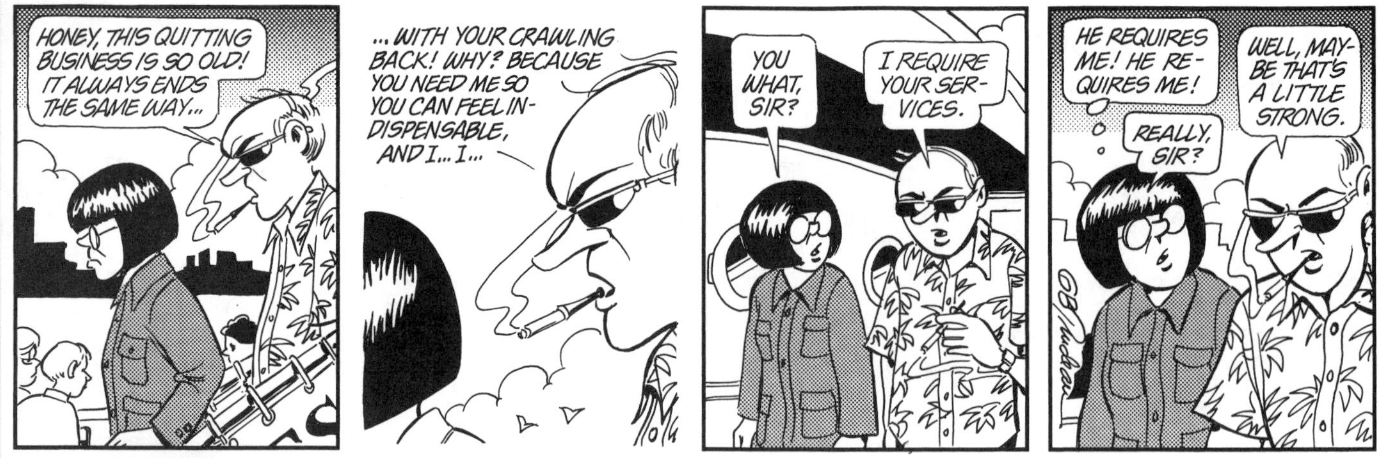
HONEY, THIS QUITTING BUSINESS IS SO OLD! IT ALWAYS ENDS THE SAME WAY...
...WITH YOUR CRAWLING BACK! WHY? BECAUSE YOU NEED ME SO YOU CAN FEEL INDISPENSABLE, AND I... I...
YOU WHAT, SIR?
I REQUIRE YOUR SERVICES.
HE REQUIRES ME! HE REQUIRES ME!
REALLY, SIR?
WELL, MAYBE THAT'S A LITTLE STRONG.

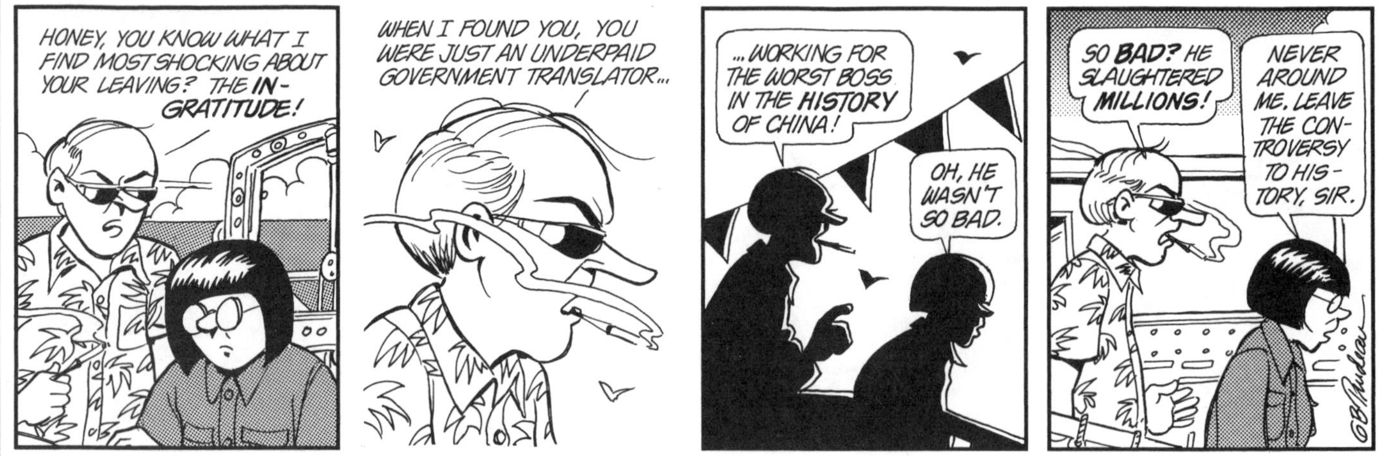
HONEY, YOU KNOW WHAT I FIND MOST SHOCKING ABOUT YOUR LEAVING? THE INGRATITUDE!
WHEN I FOUND YOU, YOU WERE JUST AN UNDERPAID GOVERNMENT TRANSLATOR...
...WORKING FOR THE WORST BOSS IN THE HISTORY OF CHINA!
OH, HE WASN'T SO BAD.
SO BAD? HE SLAUGHTERED MILLIONS!
NEVER AROUND ME. LEAVE THE CONTROVERSY TO HISTORY, SIR.

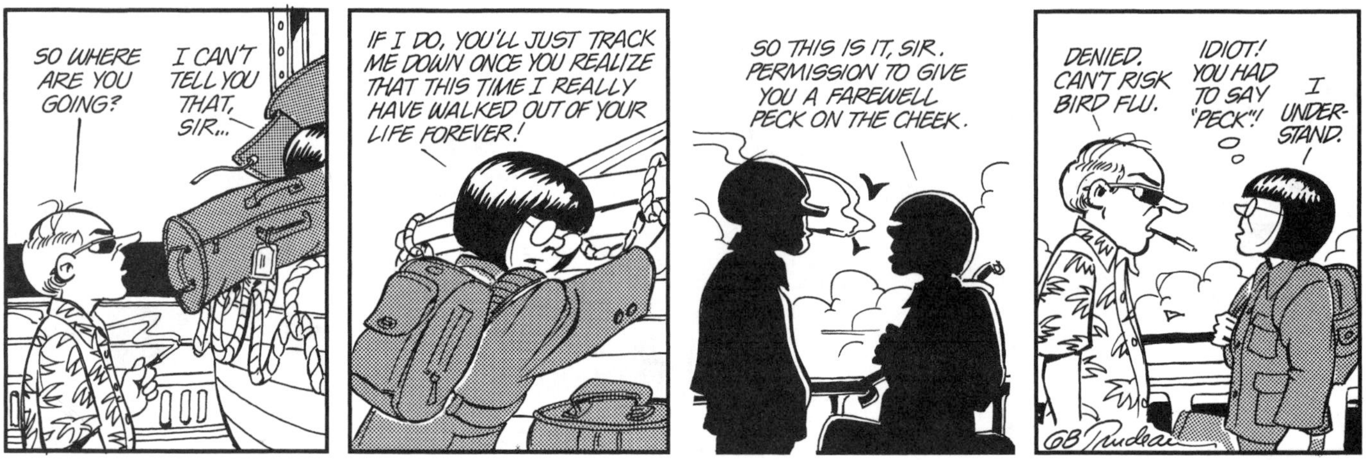
SO WHERE ARE YOU GOING?
I CAN'T TELL YOU THAT, SIR...
IF I DO, YOU'LL JUST TRACK ME DOWN ONCE YOU REALIZE THAT THIS TIME I REALLY HAVE WALKED OUT OF YOUR LIFE FOREVER!
SO THIS IS IT, SIR. PERMISSION TO GIVE YOU A FAREWELL PECK ON THE CHEEK.
DENIED. CAN'T RISK BIRD FLU.
IDIOT! YOU HAD TO SAY "PECK"!
I UNDERSTAND.

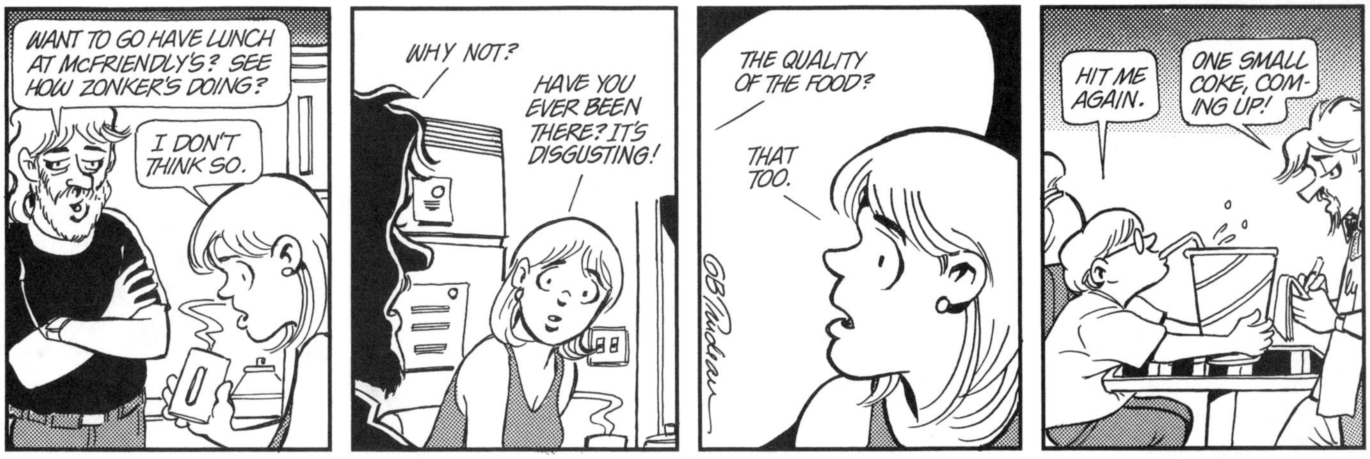
WANT TO GO HAVE LUNCH AT McFRIENDLY'S? SEE HOW ZONKER'S DOING?
I DON'T THINK SO.
WHY NOT?
HAVE YOU EVER BEEN THERE? IT'S DISGUSTING!
THE QUALITY OF THE FOOD?
THAT TOO.
HIT ME AGAIN.
ONE SMALL COKE, COMING UP!

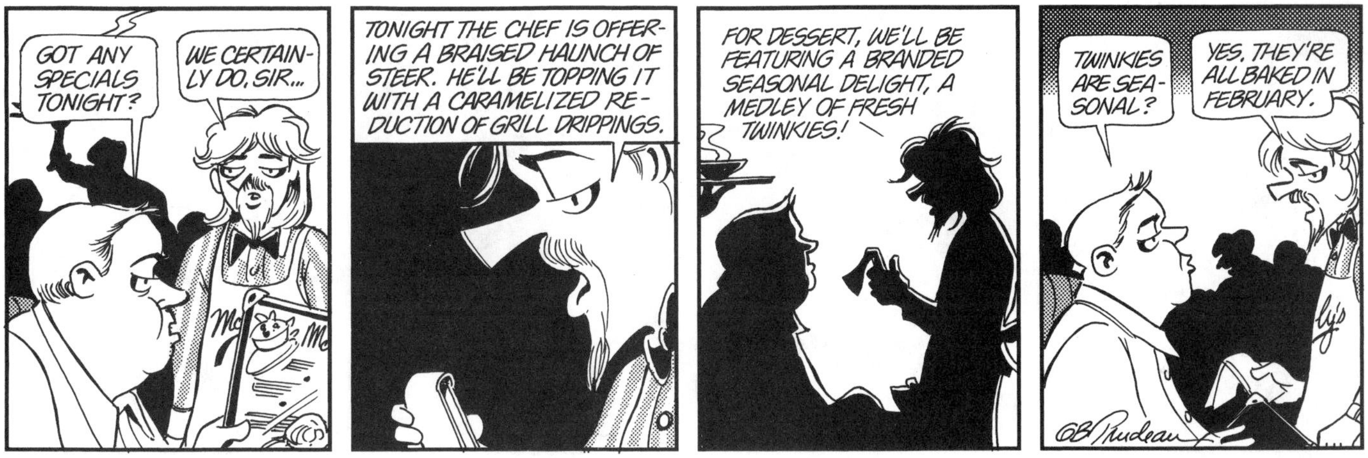
GOT ANY SPECIALS TONIGHT?
WE CERTAINLY DO, SIR...
TONIGHT THE CHEF IS OFFERING A BRAISED HAUNCH OF STEER. HE'LL BE TOPPING IT WITH A CARAMELIZED REDUCTION OF GRILL DRIPPINGS.
FOR DESSERT, WE'LL BE FEATURING A BRANDED SEASONAL DELIGHT, A MEDLEY OF FRESH TWINKIES!
TWINKIES ARE SEASONAL?
YES, THEY'RE ALL BAKED IN FEBRUARY.

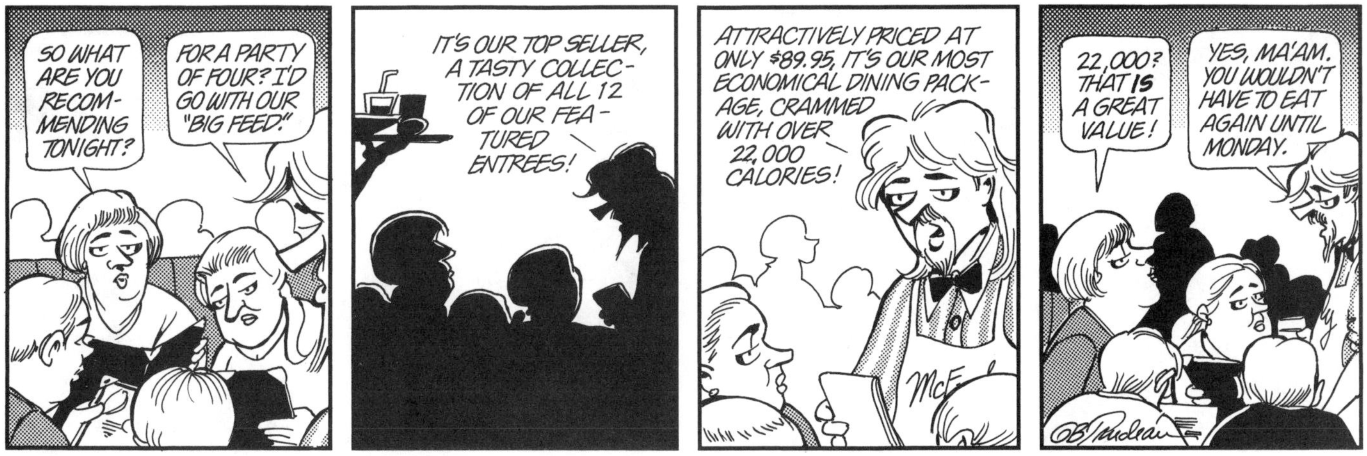
SO WHAT ARE YOU RECOMMENDING TONIGHT?
FOR A PARTY OF FOUR? I'D GO WITH OUR "BIG FEED."
IT'S OUR TOP SELLER, A TASTY COLLECTION OF ALL 12 OF OUR FEATURED ENTREES!
ATTRACTIVELY PRICED AT ONLY $89.95, IT'S OUR MOST ECONOMICAL DINING PACKAGE, CRAMMED WITH OVER 22,000 CALORIES!
22,000? THAT **IS** A GREAT VALUE!
YES, MA'AM. YOU WOULDN'T HAVE TO EAT AGAIN UNTIL MONDAY.

YO, WAITER, I'D LIKE A PITCHER OF SCOTCH.
YOU GOT IT, SIR!
WILL YOU BE HAVING ANYTHING TO EAT WITH YOUR BEVERAGE?
YEAH, GIMME A 128-OZ. SIR-LOIN, RARE.
128-OZ.? I DON'T KNOW IF WE CAN HANDLE THAT, SIR.
YEAH, YOU CAN. I HAVE A PRIVATE MEAT LOCKER.
VERY GOOD, SIR. MAY I HAVE YOUR PIN NUMBER?

HAVE A GOOD SHIFT, MAN?
YEAH. I THINK I'M CLOSING IN ON ONE OF THE COMPANY PERFOR-MANCE AWARDS.
WHICH ONE?
THE FREE TRIP TO THE ROCK 'N' ROLL HALL OF FAME.
COOL. HOW'D YOU DO TO-NIGHT?
I MOVED... 115,650 CALORIES.
DUDE. YOU'RE SO GOING TO CLEVELAND.

HEY, NEWT, WHY DO YOU SUPPOSE THEY CHANGED ALL THE PHRASES IN OUR MANUAL TO THE FUTURE TENSE?
LIKE, "THIS WILL BE YOUR TABLE," AND "WE'LL BE OFFERING THREE KINDS OF BREAD" AND "THE CHEF WILL BE PREPARING IT ON A BED OF PEANUT SHELLS."
WELL, THEY USE THE FUTURE TENSE IN ALL THE HIGH-END RESTAURANTS NOW. IT'S SUP-POSED TO MAKE US SOUND CLASSY.
OH.
IT'S ALSO HANDY IF THE FOOD'S LATE.
GOOD POINT! IT GIVES THE CUSTOMER HOPE!

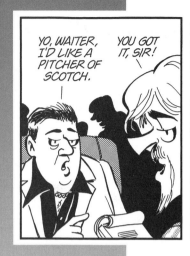

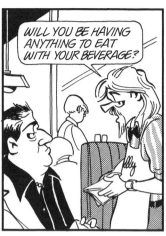

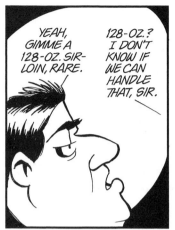

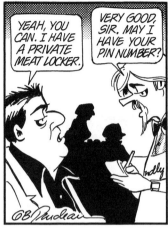

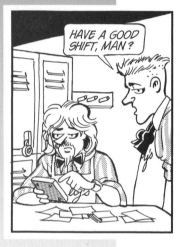

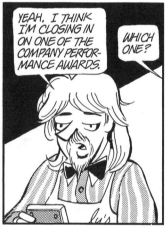

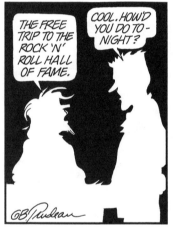

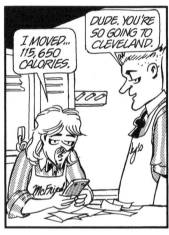

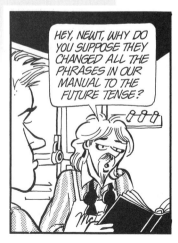

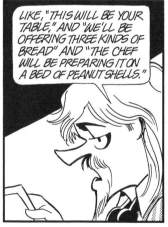

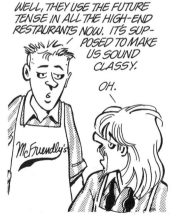

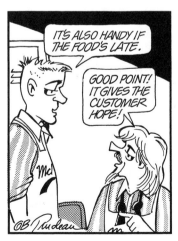

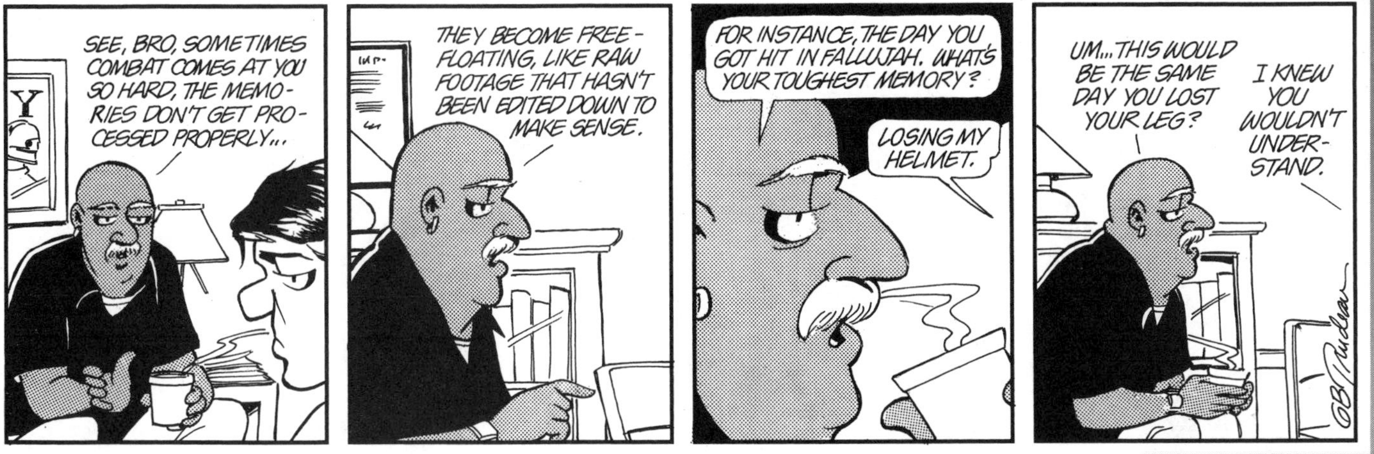
SEE, BRO, SOMETIMES COMBAT COMES AT YOU SO HARD, THE MEMORIES DON'T GET PROCESSED PROPERLY...
THEY BECOME FREE-FLOATING, LIKE RAW FOOTAGE THAT HASN'T BEEN EDITED DOWN TO MAKE SENSE.
FOR INSTANCE, THE DAY YOU GOT HIT IN FALLUJAH. WHAT'S YOUR TOUGHEST MEMORY?
LOSING MY HELMET.
UM... THIS WOULD BE THE SAME DAY YOU LOST YOUR LEG?
I KNEW YOU WOULDN'T UNDERSTAND.

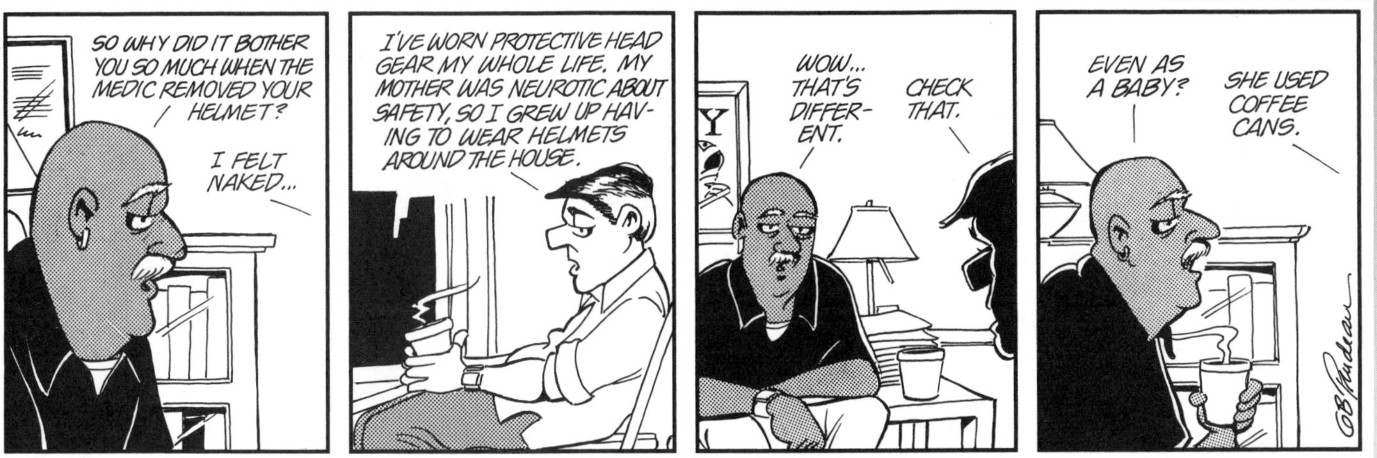
SO WHY DID IT BOTHER YOU SO MUCH WHEN THE MEDIC REMOVED YOUR HELMET?
I FELT NAKED...
I'VE WORN PROTECTIVE HEAD GEAR MY WHOLE LIFE. MY MOTHER WAS NEUROTIC ABOUT SAFETY, SO I GREW UP HAVING TO WEAR HELMETS AROUND THE HOUSE.
WOW... THAT'S DIFFERENT.
CHECK THAT.
EVEN AS A BABY?
SHE USED COFFEE CANS.

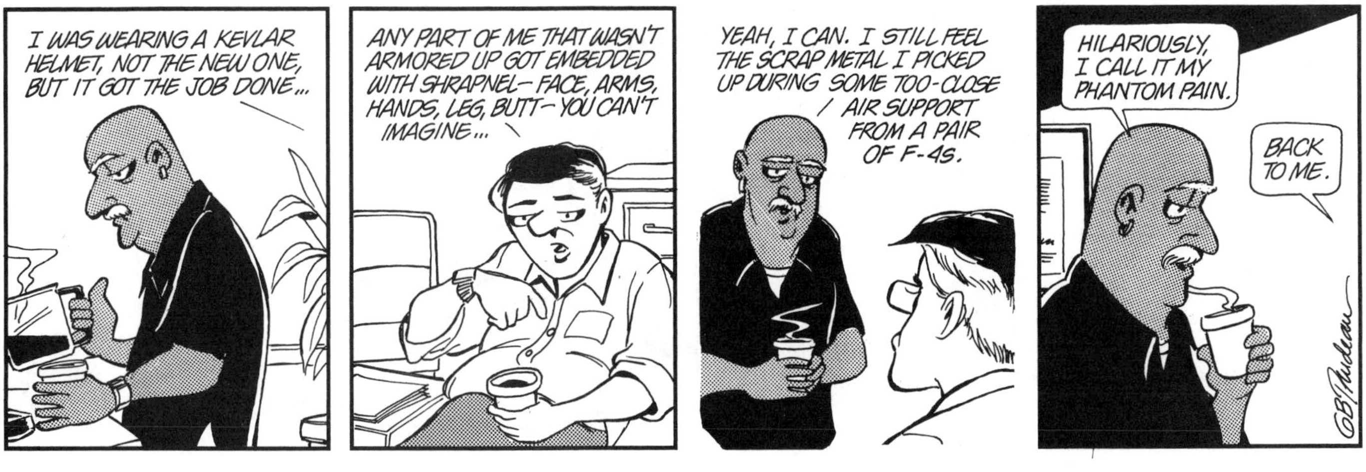
I WAS WEARING A KEVLAR HELMET, NOT THE NEW ONE, BUT IT GOT THE JOB DONE...
ANY PART OF ME THAT WASN'T ARMORED UP GOT EMBEDDED WITH SHRAPNEL— FACE, ARMS, HANDS, LEG, BUTT— YOU CAN'T IMAGINE...
YEAH, I CAN. I STILL FEEL THE SCRAP METAL I PICKED UP DURING SOME TOO-CLOSE AIR SUPPORT FROM A PAIR OF F-4S.
HILARIOUSLY, I CALL IT MY PHANTOM PAIN.
BACK TO ME.

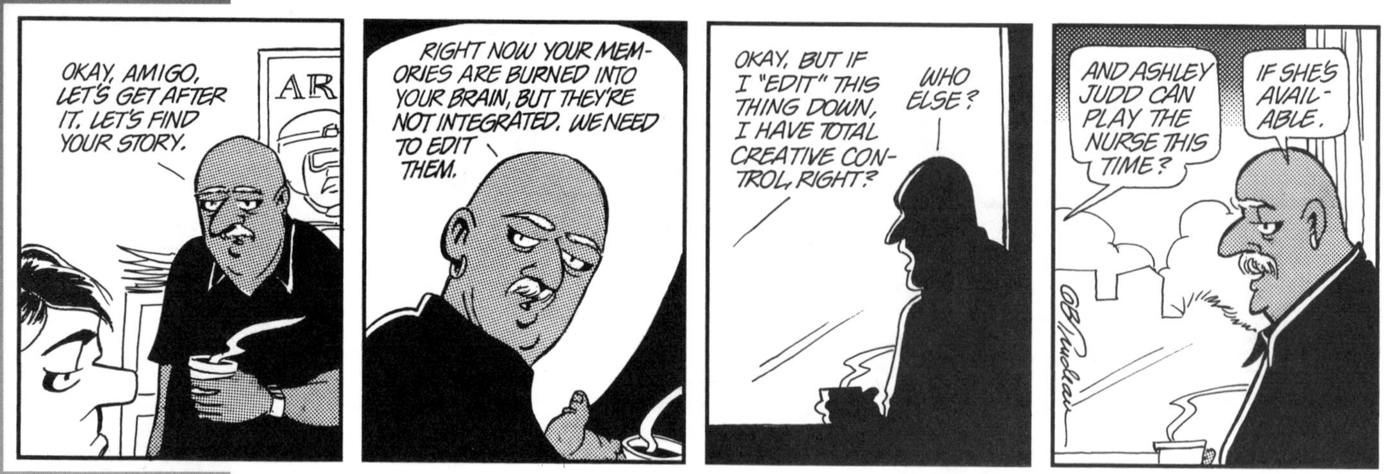
OKAY, AMIGO, LET'S GET AFTER IT. LET'S FIND YOUR STORY.
RIGHT NOW YOUR MEMORIES ARE BURNED INTO YOUR BRAIN, BUT THEY'RE NOT INTEGRATED. WE NEED TO EDIT THEM.
OKAY, BUT IF I "EDIT" THIS THING DOWN, I HAVE TOTAL CREATIVE CONTROL, RIGHT?
WHO ELSE?
AND ASHLEY JUDD CAN PLAY THE NURSE THIS TIME?
IF SHE'S AVAILABLE.

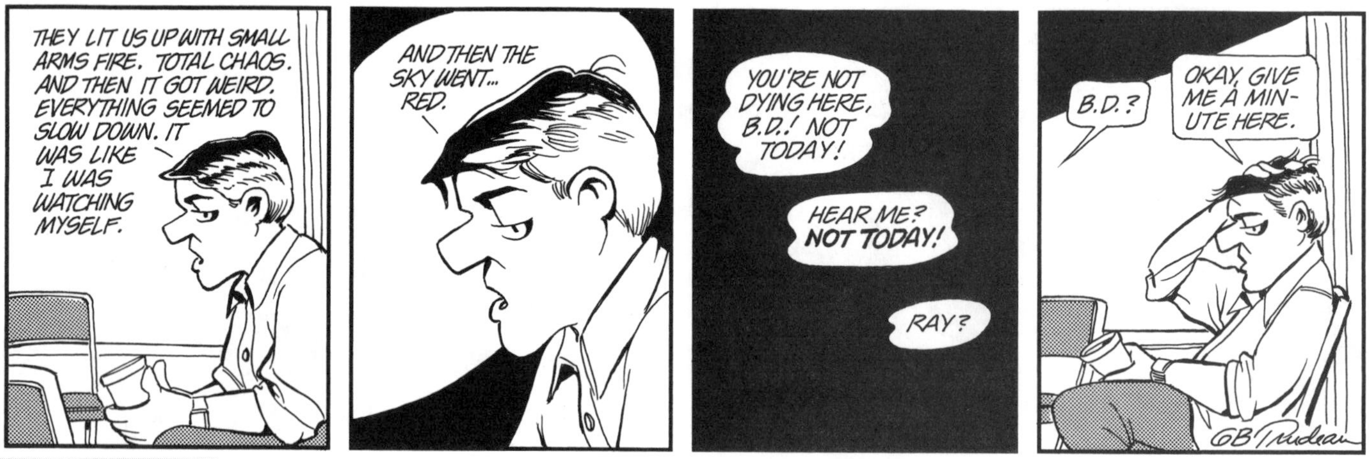
THEY LIT US UP WITH SMALL ARMS FIRE. TOTAL CHAOS. AND THEN IT GOT WEIRD. EVERYTHING SEEMED TO SLOW DOWN. IT WAS LIKE I WAS WATCHING MYSELF.
AND THEN THE SKY WENT... RED.
YOU'RE NOT DYING HERE, B.D.! NOT TODAY!
HEAR ME? NOT TODAY!
RAY?
B.D.?
OKAY, GIVE ME A MINUTE HERE.

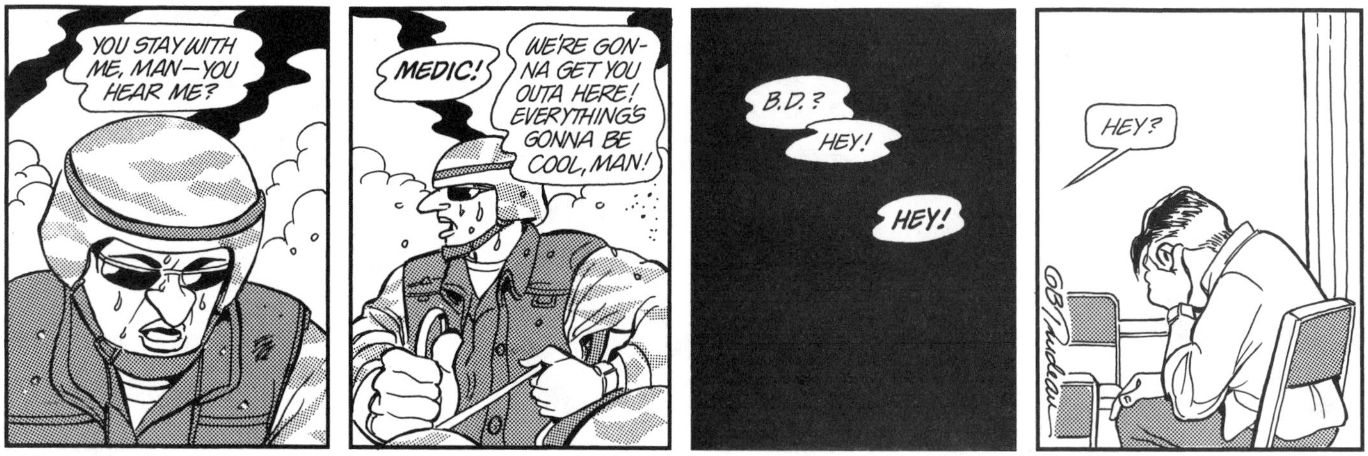
YOU STAY WITH ME, MAN—YOU HEAR ME?
MEDIC!
WE'RE GONNA GET YOU OUTA HERE! EVERYTHING'S GONNA BE COOL, MAN!
B.D.?
HEY!
HEY!
HEY?

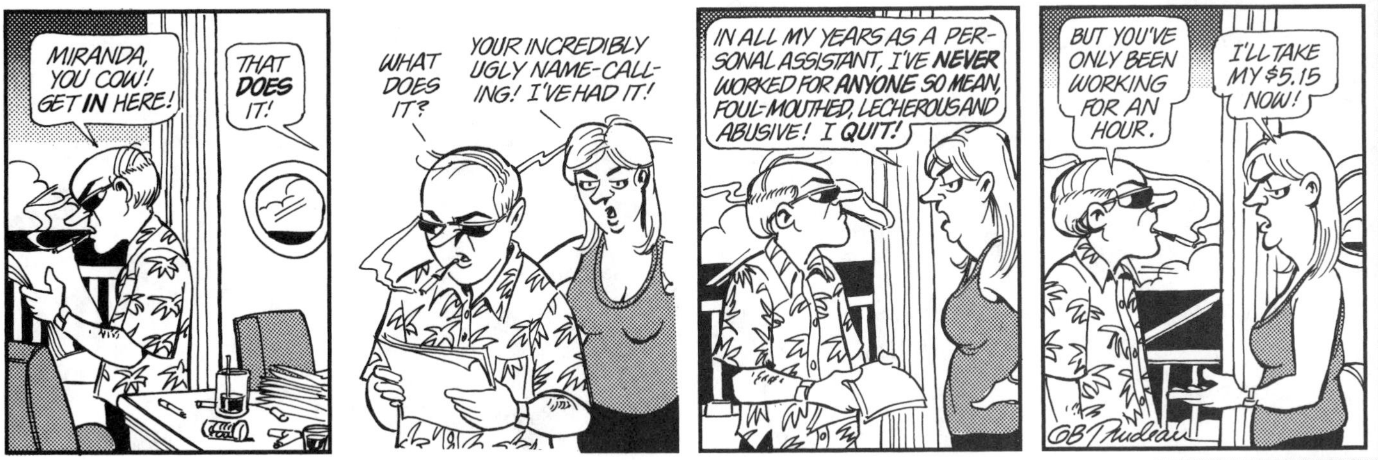
MIRANDA, YOU COW! GET **IN** HERE!
THAT **DOES** IT!
WHAT DOES IT?
YOUR INCREDIBLY UGLY NAME-CALLING! I'VE HAD IT!
IN ALL MY YEARS AS A PERSONAL ASSISTANT, I'VE **NEVER** WORKED FOR **ANYONE** SO MEAN, FOUL-MOUTHED, LECHEROUS AND ABUSIVE! I **QUIT!**
BUT YOU'VE ONLY BEEN WORKING FOR AN HOUR.
I'LL TAKE MY $5.15 NOW!

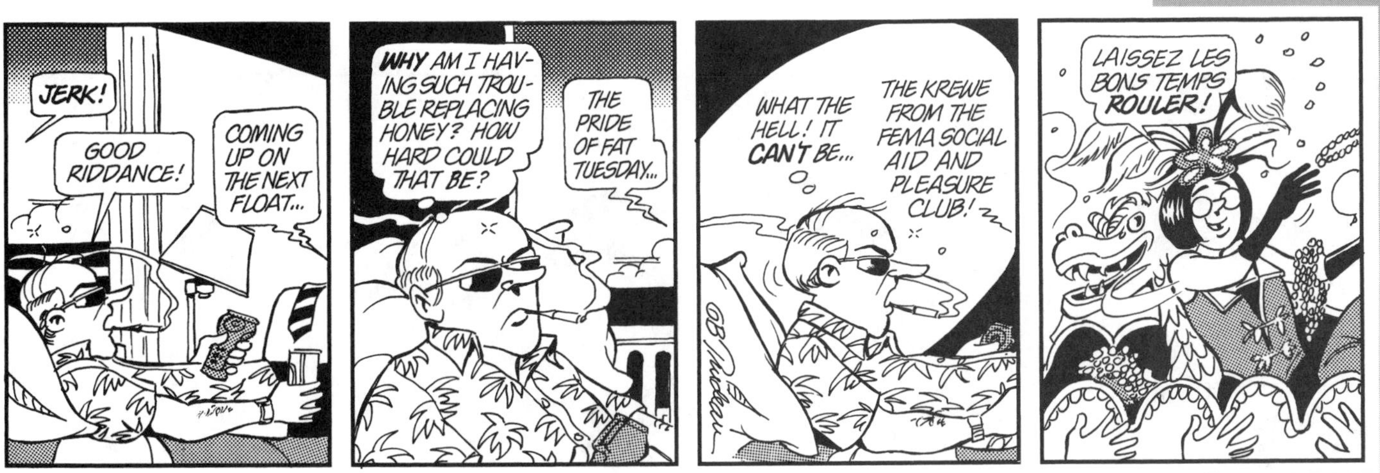
JERK!
GOOD RIDDANCE!
COMING UP ON THE NEXT FLOAT...
WHY AM I HAVING SUCH TROUBLE REPLACING HONEY? HOW HARD COULD THAT **BE**?
THE PRIDE OF FAT TUESDAY...
WHAT THE HELL! IT **CAN'T** BE...
THE KREWE FROM THE FEMA SOCIAL AID AND PLEASURE CLUB!
LAISSEZ LES BONS TEMPS **ROULER!**

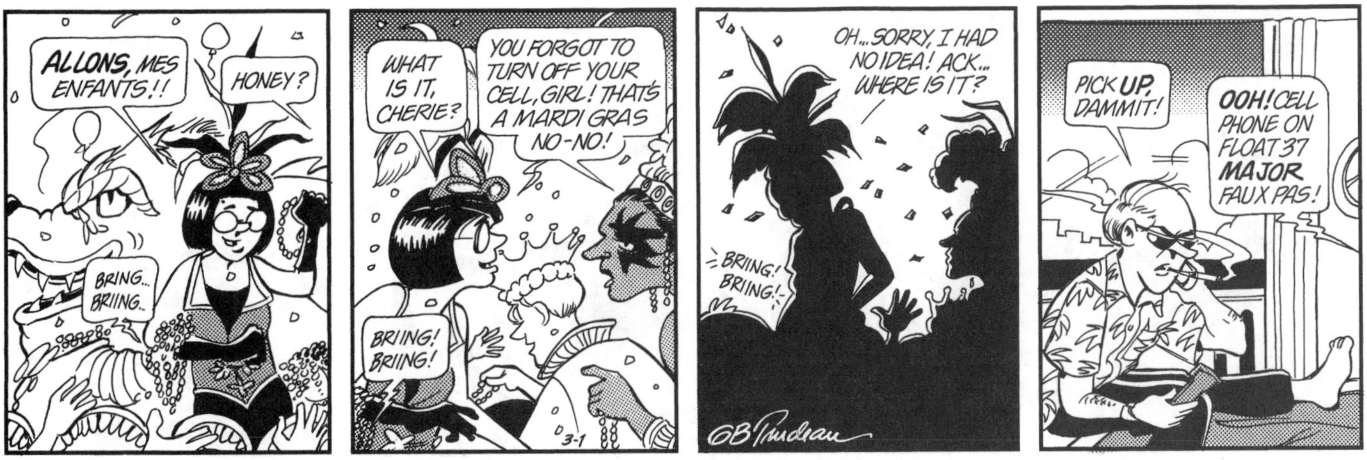
ALLONS, MES ENFANTS!!
HONEY?
BRING... BRIING...
WHAT IS IT, CHERIE?
YOU FORGOT TO TURN OFF YOUR CELL, GIRL! THAT'S A MARDI GRAS NO-NO!
BRIING! BRIING!
OH... SORRY, I HAD NO IDEA! ACK... WHERE IS IT?
BRIING! BRIING!
PICK **UP,** DAMMIT!
OOH! CELL PHONE ON FLOAT 37 **MAJOR** FAUX PAS!

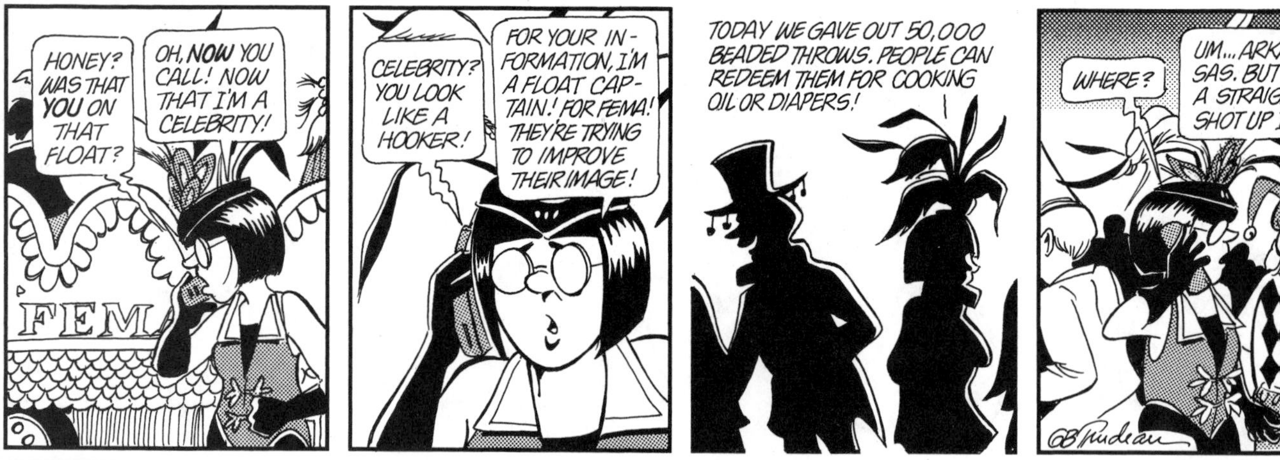
HONEY? WAS THAT YOU ON THAT FLOAT?
OH, NOW YOU CALL! NOW THAT I'M A CELEBRITY!
FEM
CELEBRITY? YOU LOOK LIKE A HOOKER!
FOR YOUR INFORMATION, I'M A FLOAT CAPTAIN! FOR FEMA! THEY'RE TRYING TO IMPROVE THEIR IMAGE!
TODAY WE GAVE OUT 50,000 BEADED THROWS. PEOPLE CAN REDEEM THEM FOR COOKING OIL OR DIAPERS!
WHERE?
UM... ARKANSAS. BUT IT'S A STRAIGHT SHOT UP I-55.

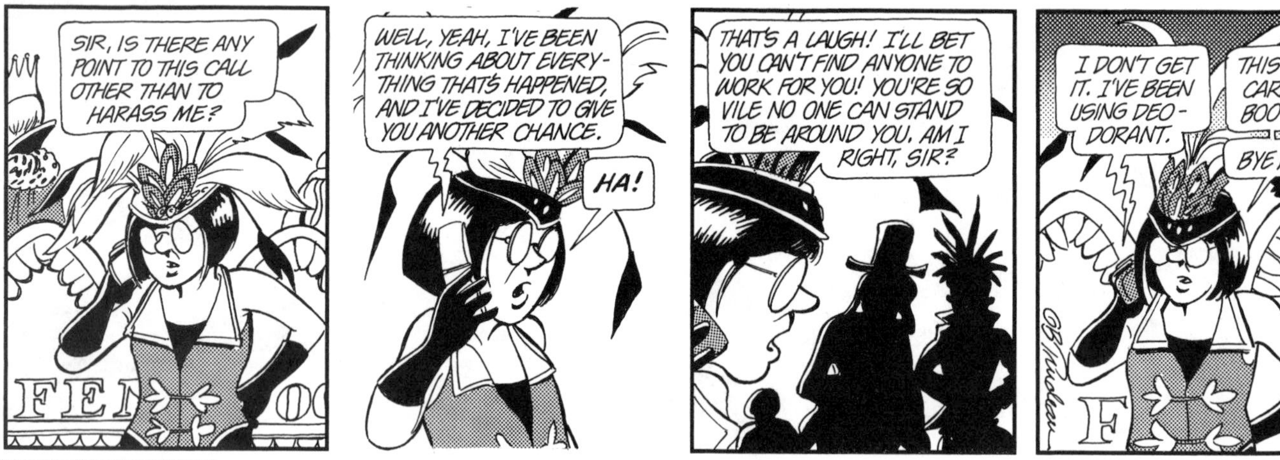
SIR, IS THERE ANY POINT TO THIS CALL OTHER THAN TO HARASS ME?
FEM
WELL, YEAH, I'VE BEEN THINKING ABOUT EVERYTHING THAT'S HAPPENED, AND I'VE DECIDED TO GIVE YOU ANOTHER CHANCE.
HA!
THAT'S A LAUGH! I'LL BET YOU CAN'T FIND ANYONE TO WORK FOR YOU! YOU'RE SO VILE NO ONE CAN STAND TO BE AROUND YOU. AM I RIGHT, SIR?
I DON'T GET IT. I'VE BEEN USING DEODORANT.
THIS IS ME CARING: BOO-HOO!
BYE NOW!

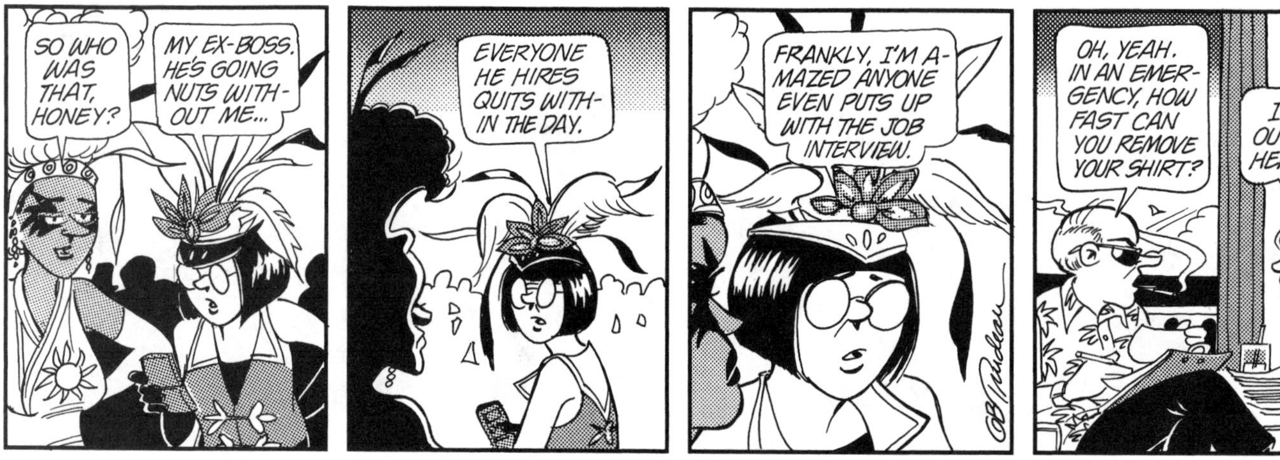
SO WHO WAS THAT, HONEY?
MY EX-BOSS. HE'S GOING NUTS WITHOUT ME...
EVERYONE HE HIRES QUITS WITHIN THE DAY.
FRANKLY, I'M AMAZED ANYONE EVEN PUTS UP WITH THE JOB INTERVIEW.
OH, YEAH. IN AN EMERGENCY, HOW FAST CAN YOU REMOVE YOUR SHIRT?
I'M OUTA HERE.

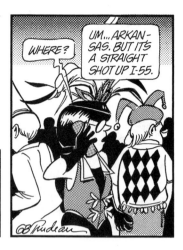

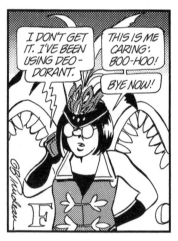

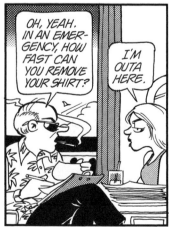

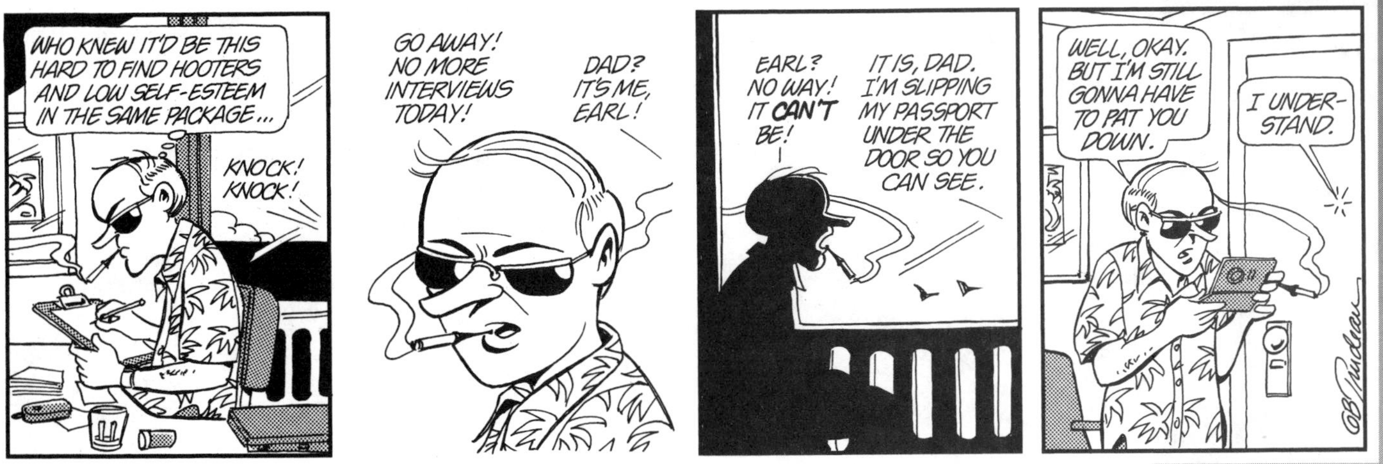
WHO KNEW IT'D BE THIS HARD TO FIND HOOTERS AND LOW SELF-ESTEEM IN THE SAME PACKAGE...
KNOCK! KNOCK!
GO AWAY! NO MORE INTERVIEWS TODAY!
DAD? IT'S ME, EARL!
EARL? NO WAY! IT **CAN'T** BE!
IT IS, DAD. I'M SLIPPING MY PASSPORT UNDER THE DOOR SO YOU CAN SEE.
WELL, OKAY. BUT I'M STILL GONNA HAVE TO PAT YOU DOWN.
I UNDER-STAND.

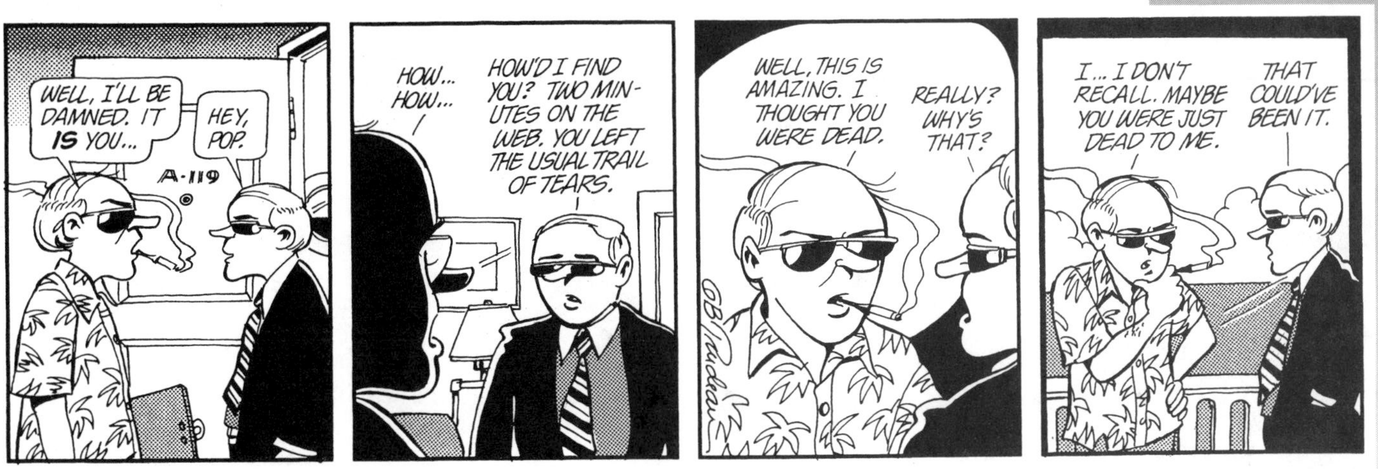
WELL, I'LL BE DAMNED. IT **IS** YOU...
HEY, POP.
A-119
HOW... HOW...
HOW'D I FIND YOU? TWO MIN-UTES ON THE WEB. YOU LEFT THE USUAL TRAIL OF TEARS.
WELL, THIS IS AMAZING. I THOUGHT YOU WERE DEAD.
REALLY? WHY'S THAT?
I... I DON'T RECALL. MAYBE YOU WERE JUST DEAD TO ME.
THAT COULD'VE BEEN IT.

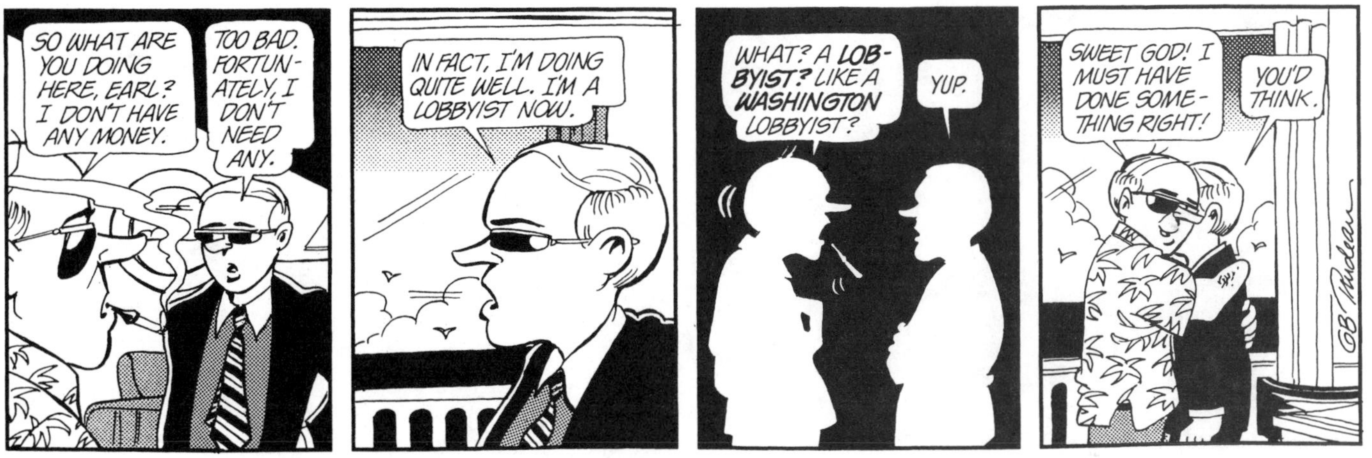
SO WHAT ARE YOU DOING HERE, EARL? I DON'T HAVE ANY MONEY.
TOO BAD. FORTUN-ATELY, I DON'T NEED ANY.
IN FACT, I'M DOING QUITE WELL. I'M A LOBBYIST NOW.
WHAT? A **LOB-BYIST?** LIKE A **WASHINGTON** LOBBYIST?
YUP.
SWEET GOD! I MUST HAVE DONE SOME-THING RIGHT!
YOU'D THINK.

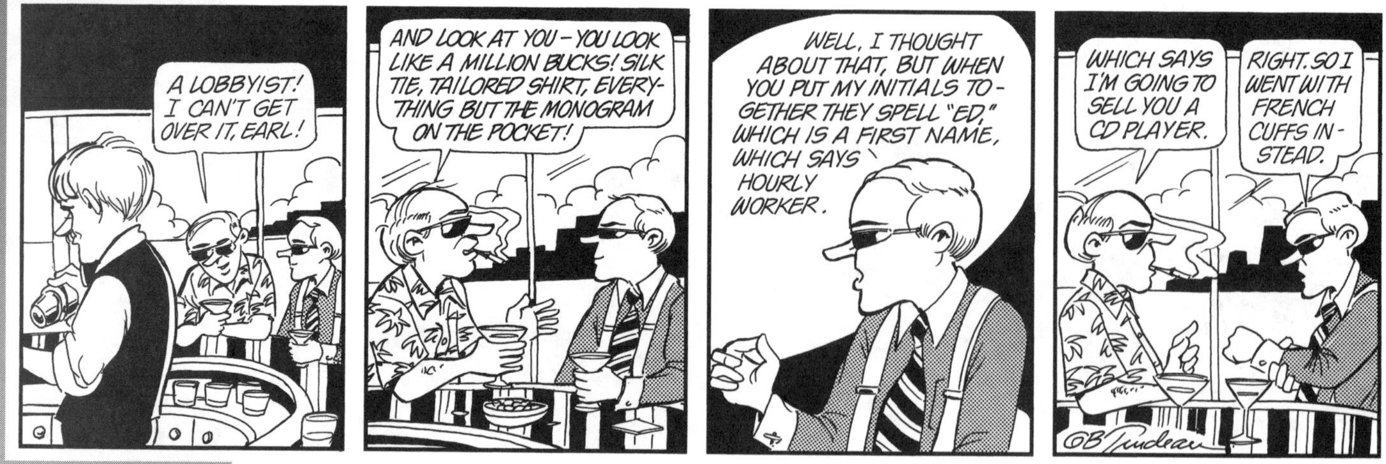
A LOBBYIST! I CAN'T GET OVER IT, EARL!
AND LOOK AT YOU – YOU LOOK LIKE A MILLION BUCKS! SILK TIE, TAILORED SHIRT, EVERYTHING BUT THE MONOGRAM ON THE POCKET!
WELL, I THOUGHT ABOUT THAT, BUT WHEN YOU PUT MY INITIALS TOGETHER THEY SPELL "ED," WHICH IS A FIRST NAME, WHICH SAYS HOURLY WORKER.
WHICH SAYS I'M GOING TO SELL YOU A CD PLAYER.
RIGHT. SO I WENT WITH FRENCH CUFFS INSTEAD.
GB Trudeau

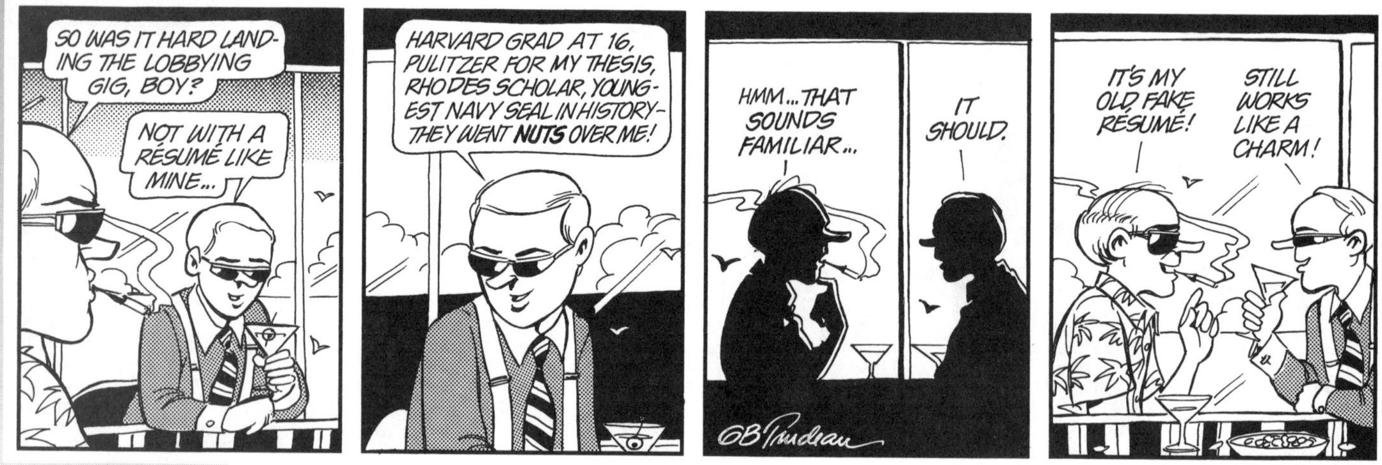
SO WAS IT HARD LANDING THE LOBBYING GIG, BOY?
NOT WITH A RÉSUMÉ LIKE MINE...
HARVARD GRAD AT 16, PULITZER FOR MY THESIS, RHODES SCHOLAR, YOUNGEST NAVY SEAL IN HISTORY – THEY WENT **NUTS** OVER ME!
HMM... THAT SOUNDS FAMILIAR...
IT SHOULD.
GB Trudeau
IT'S MY OLD FAKE RÉSUMÉ!
STILL WORKS LIKE A CHARM!

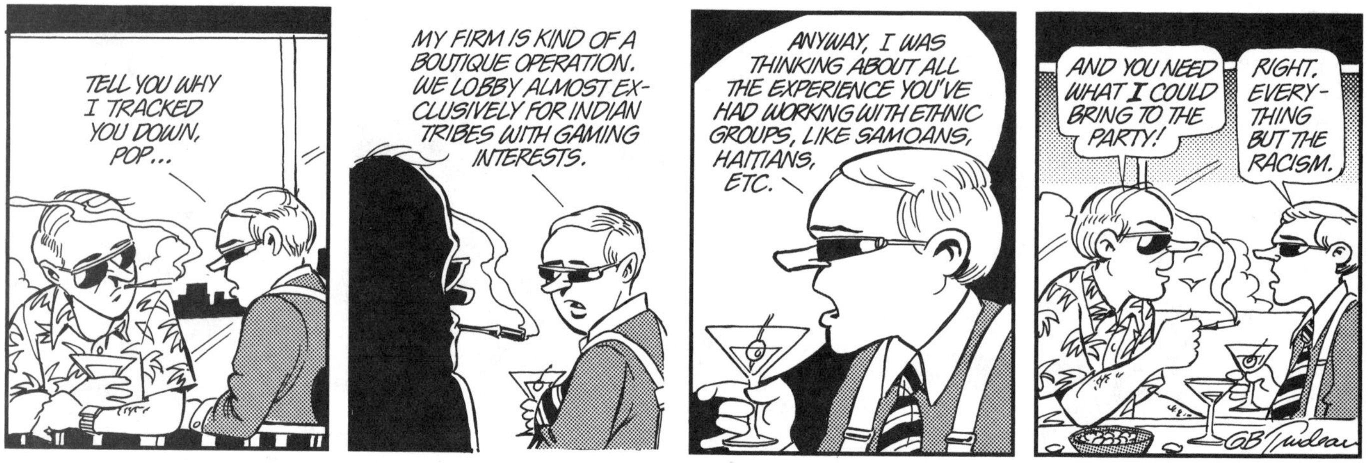
TELL YOU WHY I TRACKED YOU DOWN, POP...
MY FIRM IS KIND OF A BOUTIQUE OPERATION. WE LOBBY ALMOST EXCLUSIVELY FOR INDIAN TRIBES WITH GAMING INTERESTS.
ANYWAY, I WAS THINKING ABOUT ALL THE EXPERIENCE YOU'VE HAD WORKING WITH ETHNIC GROUPS, LIKE SAMOANS, HAITIANS, ETC.
AND YOU NEED WHAT **I** COULD BRING TO THE PARTY!
RIGHT. EVERYTHING BUT THE RACISM.
GB Trudeau

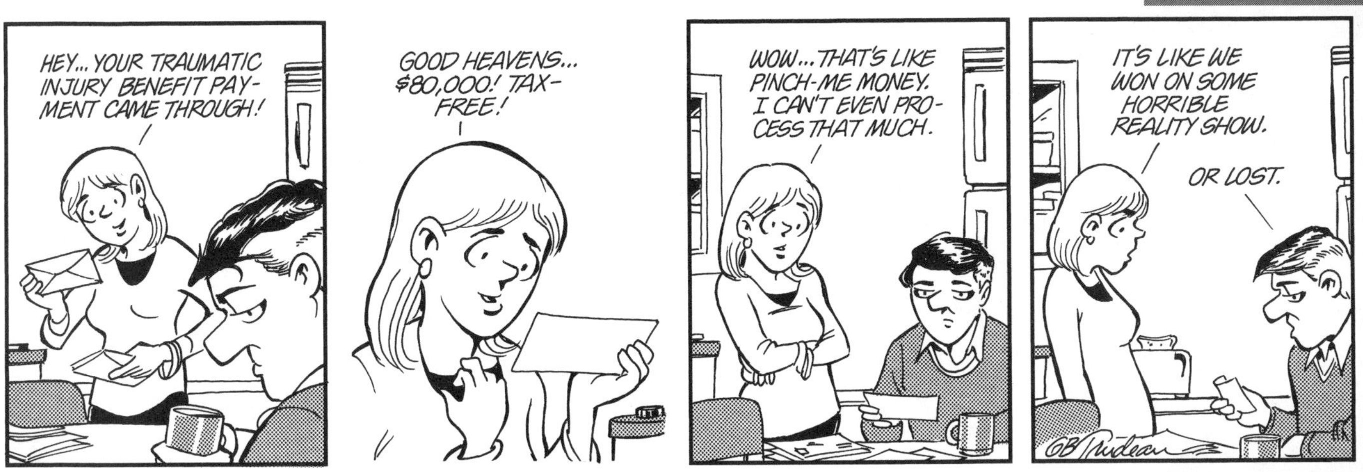
HEY... YOUR TRAUMATIC INJURY BENEFIT PAYMENT CAME THROUGH!
GOOD HEAVENS... $80,000! TAX-FREE!
WOW... THAT'S LIKE PINCH-ME MONEY. I CAN'T EVEN PROCESS THAT MUCH.
IT'S LIKE WE WON ON SOME HORRIBLE REALITY SHOW.
OR LOST.

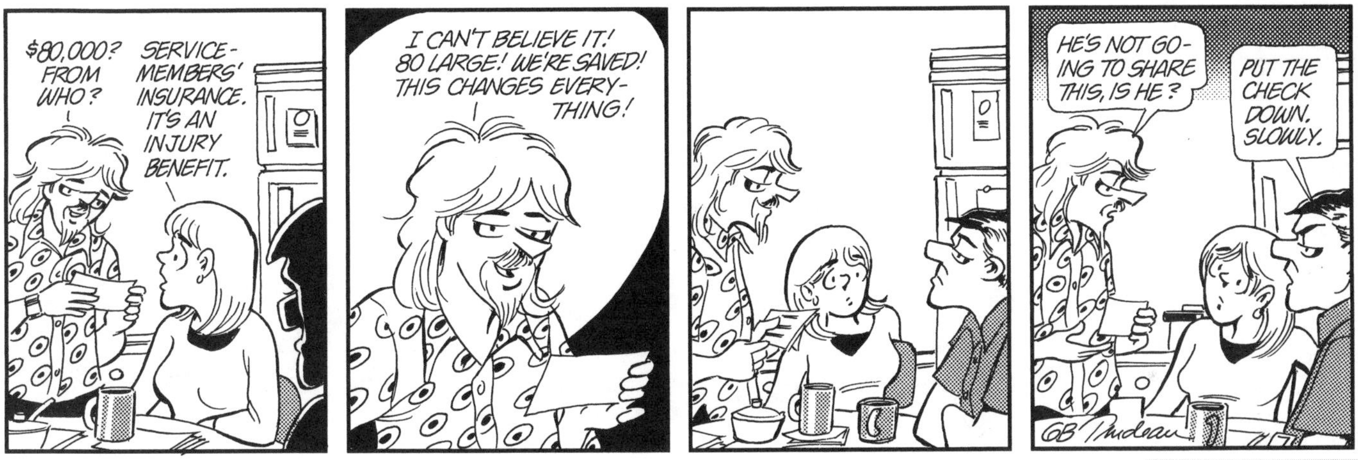
$80,000? FROM WHO?
SERVICE-MEMBERS' INSURANCE. IT'S AN INJURY BENEFIT.
I CAN'T BELIEVE IT! 80 LARGE! WE'RE SAVED! THIS CHANGES EVERYTHING!
HE'S NOT GOING TO SHARE THIS, IS HE?
PUT THE CHECK DOWN. SLOWLY.

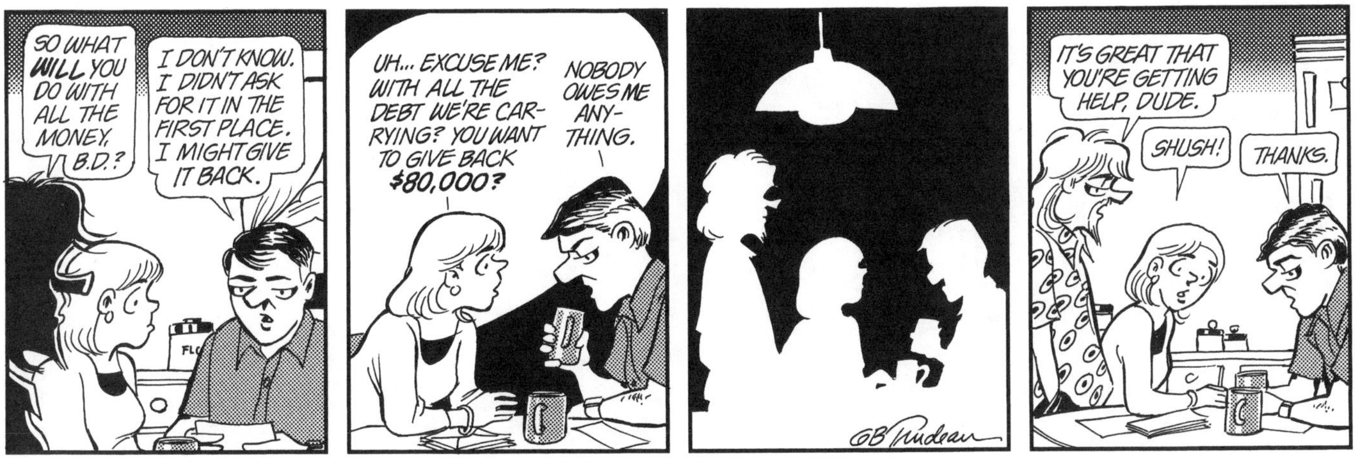
SO WHAT WILL YOU DO WITH ALL THE MONEY, B.D.?
I DON'T KNOW. I DIDN'T ASK FOR IT IN THE FIRST PLACE. I MIGHT GIVE IT BACK.
UH... EXCUSE ME? WITH ALL THE DEBT WE'RE CARRYING? YOU WANT TO GIVE BACK $80,000?
NOBODY OWES ME ANYTHING.
IT'S GREAT THAT YOU'RE GETTING HELP, DUDE.
SHUSH!
THANKS.

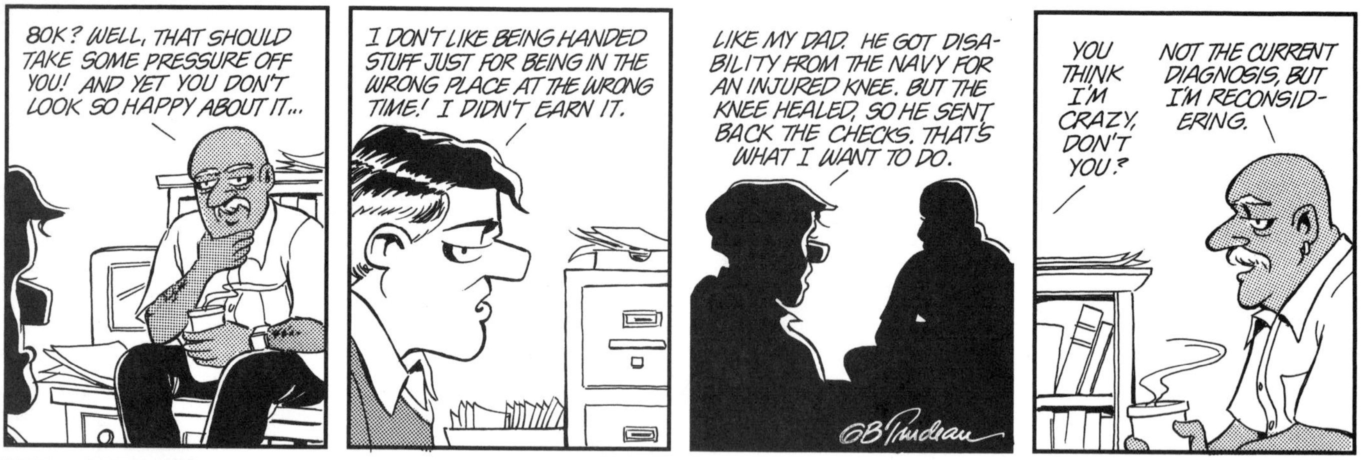
80K? WELL, THAT SHOULD TAKE SOME PRESSURE OFF YOU! AND YET YOU DON'T LOOK SO HAPPY ABOUT IT...
I DON'T LIKE BEING HANDED STUFF JUST FOR BEING IN THE WRONG PLACE AT THE WRONG TIME! I DIDN'T EARN IT.
LIKE MY DAD. HE GOT DISA-BILITY FROM THE NAVY FOR AN INJURED KNEE. BUT THE KNEE HEALED, SO HE SENT BACK THE CHECKS. THAT'S WHAT I WANT TO DO.
YOU THINK I'M CRAZY, DON'T YOU?
NOT THE CURRENT DIAGNOSIS, BUT I'M RECONSID-ERING.

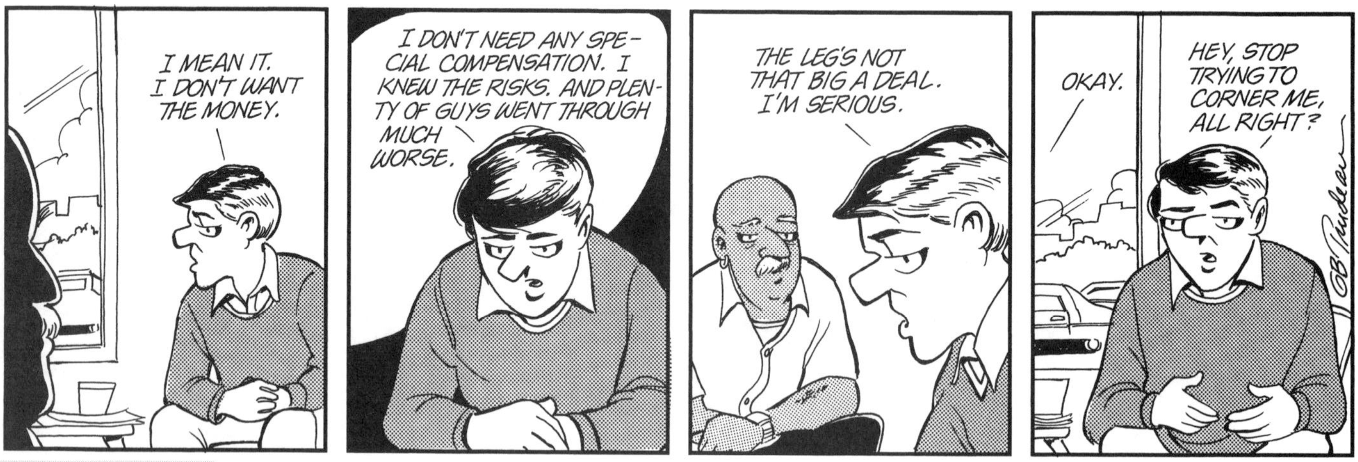
I MEAN IT. I DON'T WANT THE MONEY.
I DON'T NEED ANY SPE-CIAL COMPENSATION. I KNEW THE RISKS. AND PLEN-TY OF GUYS WENT THROUGH MUCH WORSE.
THE LEG'S NOT THAT BIG A DEAL. I'M SERIOUS.
OKAY.
HEY, STOP TRYING TO CORNER ME, ALL RIGHT?

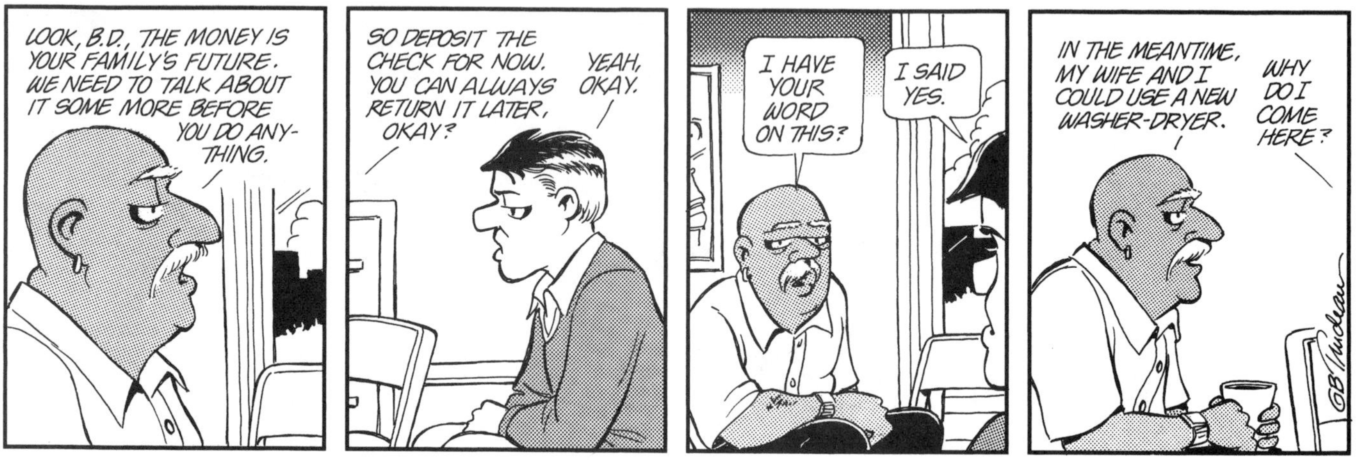
LOOK, B.D., THE MONEY IS YOUR FAMILY'S FUTURE. WE NEED TO TALK ABOUT IT SOME MORE BEFORE YOU DO ANY-THING.
SO DEPOSIT THE CHECK FOR NOW. YOU CAN ALWAYS RETURN IT LATER, OKAY?
YEAH, OKAY.
I HAVE YOUR WORD ON THIS?
I SAID YES.
IN THE MEANTIME, MY WIFE AND I COULD USE A NEW WASHER-DRYER.
WHY DO I COME HERE?

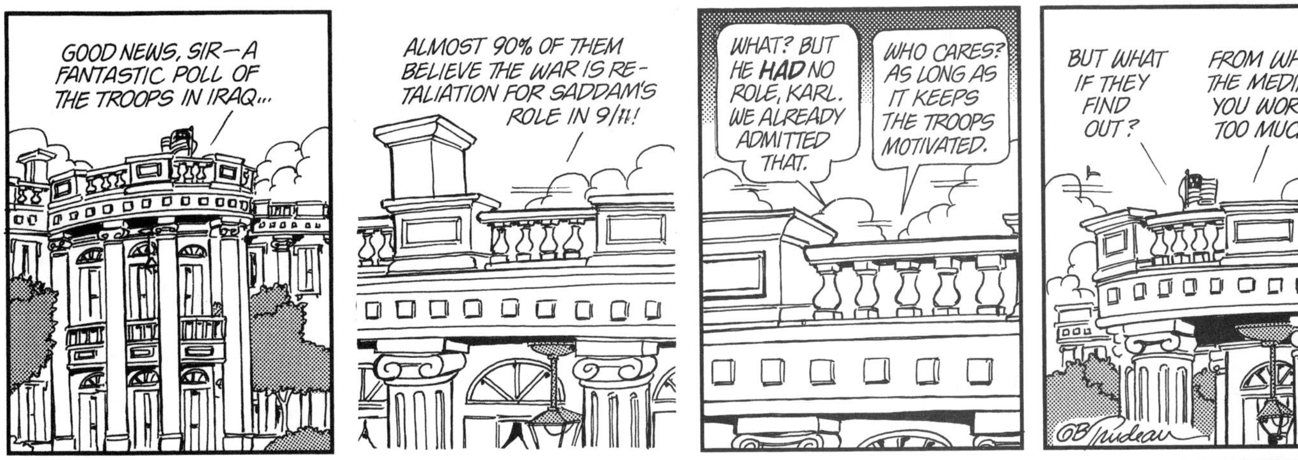
GOOD NEWS, SIR—A FANTASTIC POLL OF THE TROOPS IN IRAQ...
ALMOST 90% OF THEM BELIEVE THE WAR IS RETALIATION FOR SADDAM'S ROLE IN 9/11!
WHAT? BUT HE HAD NO ROLE, KARL. WE ALREADY ADMITTED THAT.
WHO CARES? AS LONG AS IT KEEPS THE TROOPS MOTIVATED.
BUT WHAT IF THEY FIND OUT?
FROM WHO—THE MEDIA? YOU WORRY TOO MUCH.
GBTrudeau

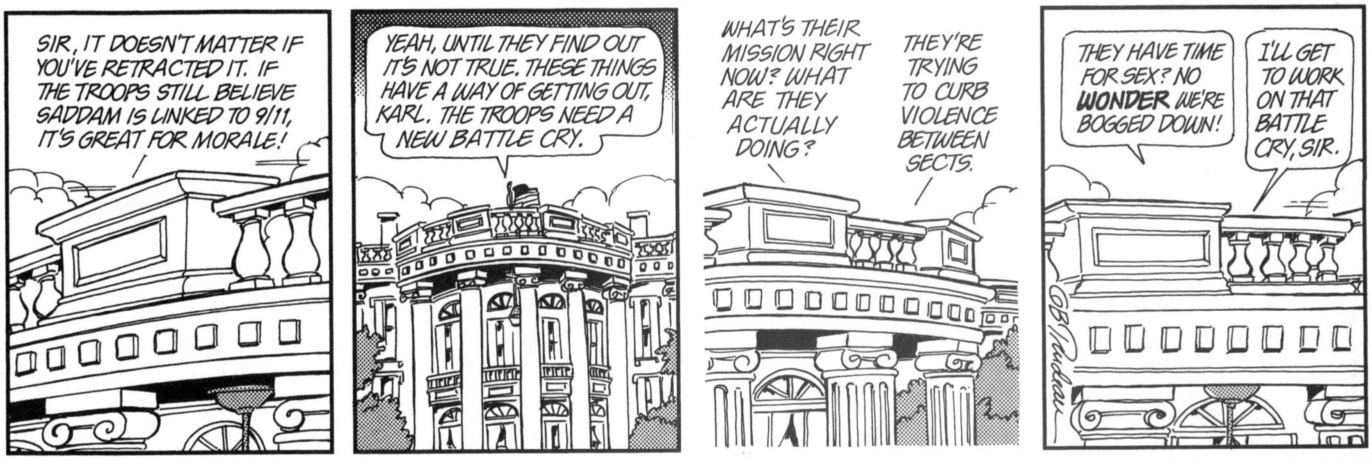
SIR, IT DOESN'T MATTER IF YOU'VE RETRACTED IT. IF THE TROOPS STILL BELIEVE SADDAM IS LINKED TO 9/11, IT'S GREAT FOR MORALE!
YEAH, UNTIL THEY FIND OUT IT'S NOT TRUE. THESE THINGS HAVE A WAY OF GETTING OUT, KARL. THE TROOPS NEED A NEW BATTLE CRY.
WHAT'S THEIR MISSION RIGHT NOW? WHAT ARE THEY ACTUALLY DOING?
THEY'RE TRYING TO CURB VIOLENCE BETWEEN SECTS.
THEY HAVE TIME FOR SEX? NO WONDER WE'RE BOGGED DOWN!
I'LL GET TO WORK ON THAT BATTLE CRY, SIR.
GBTrudeau

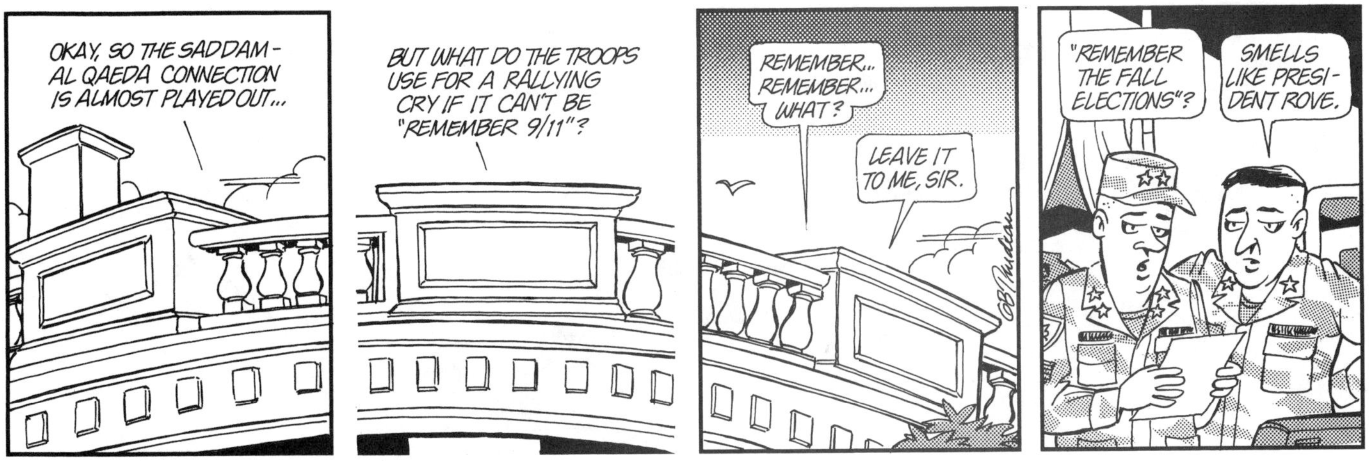
OKAY, SO THE SADDAM-AL QAEDA CONNECTION IS ALMOST PLAYED OUT...
BUT WHAT DO THE TROOPS USE FOR A RALLYING CRY IF IT CAN'T BE "REMEMBER 9/11"?
REMEMBER... REMEMBER... WHAT?
LEAVE IT TO ME, SIR.
GBTrudeau
"REMEMBER THE FALL ELECTIONS"?
SMELLS LIKE PRESIDENT ROVE.

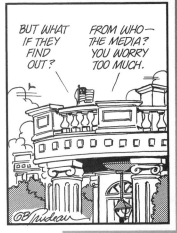

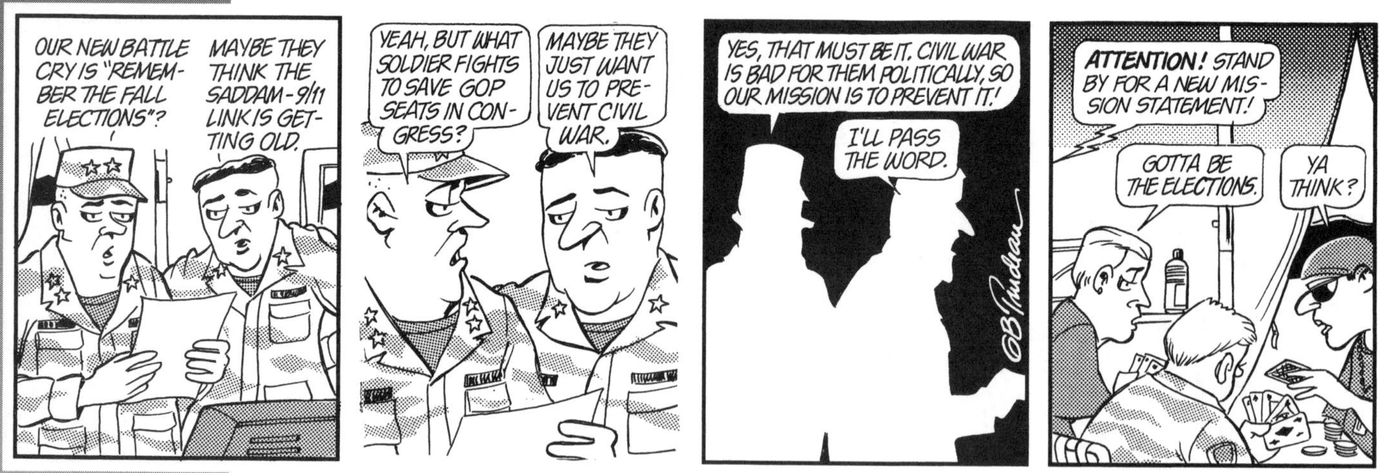
OUR NEW BATTLE CRY IS "REMEMBER THE FALL ELECTIONS"?
MAYBE THEY THINK THE SADDAM-9/11 LINK IS GETTING OLD.
YEAH, BUT WHAT SOLDIER FIGHTS TO SAVE GOP SEATS IN CONGRESS?
MAYBE THEY JUST WANT US TO PREVENT CIVIL WAR.
YES, THAT MUST BE IT. CIVIL WAR IS BAD FOR THEM POLITICALLY, SO OUR MISSION IS TO PREVENT IT!
I'LL PASS THE WORD.
ATTENTION! STAND BY FOR A NEW MISSION STATEMENT!
GOTTA BE THE ELECTIONS.
YA THINK?

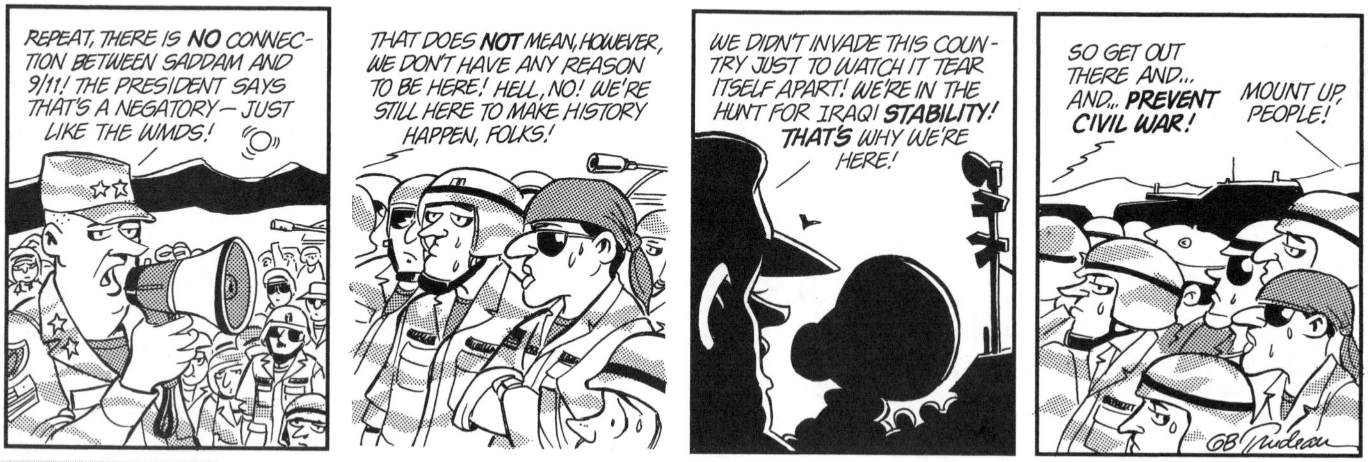
REPEAT, THERE IS NO CONNECTION BETWEEN SADDAM AND 9/11! THE PRESIDENT SAYS THAT'S A NEGATORY — JUST LIKE THE WMDS!
THAT DOES NOT MEAN, HOWEVER, WE DON'T HAVE ANY REASON TO BE HERE! HELL, NO! WE'RE STILL HERE TO MAKE HISTORY HAPPEN, FOLKS!
WE DIDN'T INVADE THIS COUNTRY JUST TO WATCH IT TEAR ITSELF APART! WE'RE IN THE HUNT FOR IRAQI STABILITY! THAT'S WHY WE'RE HERE!
SO GET OUT THERE AND... AND... PREVENT CIVIL WAR!
MOUNT UP, PEOPLE!

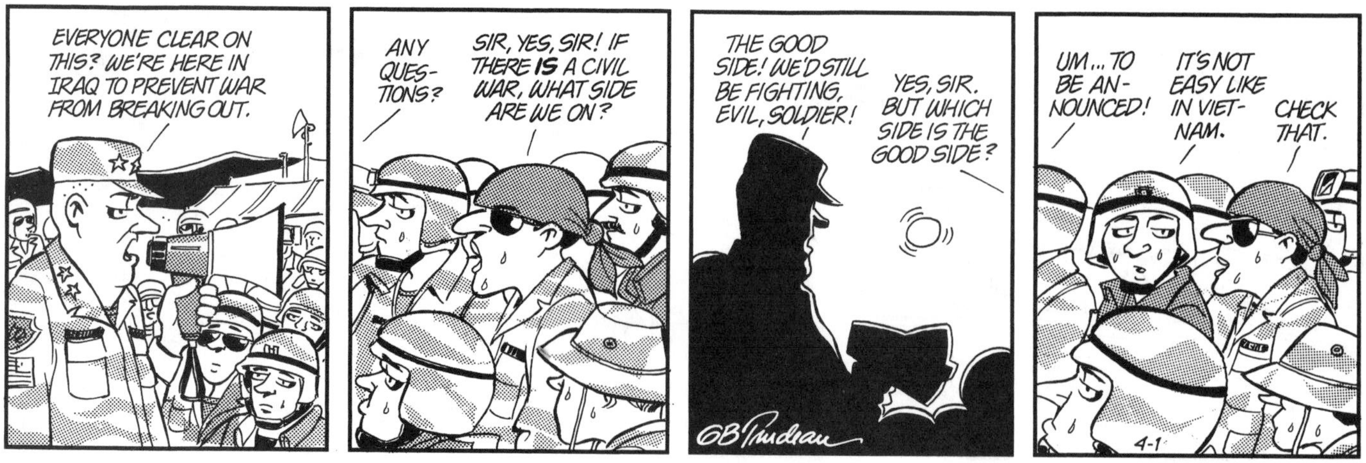
EVERYONE CLEAR ON THIS? WE'RE HERE IN IRAQ TO PREVENT WAR FROM BREAKING OUT.
ANY QUESTIONS?
SIR, YES, SIR! IF THERE IS A CIVIL WAR, WHAT SIDE ARE WE ON?
THE GOOD SIDE! WE'D STILL BE FIGHTING EVIL, SOLDIER!
YES, SIR. BUT WHICH SIDE IS THE GOOD SIDE?
UM... TO BE ANNOUNCED!
IT'S NOT EASY LIKE IN VIETNAM.
CHECK THAT.

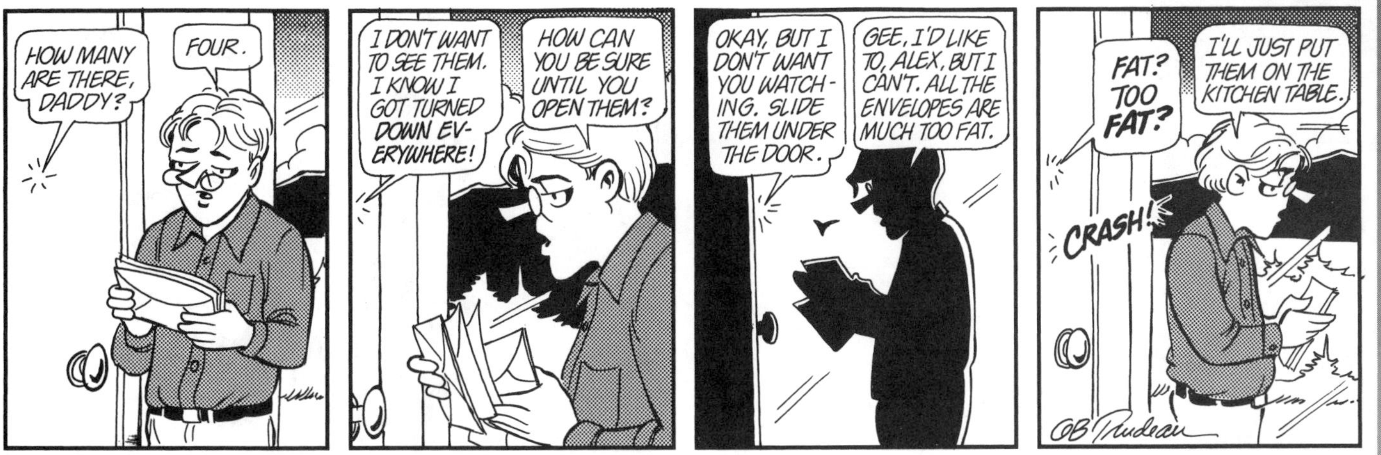
HOW MANY ARE THERE, DADDY?
FOUR.
I DON'T WANT TO SEE THEM. I KNOW I GOT TURNED **DOWN EVERYWHERE**!
HOW CAN YOU BE SURE UNTIL YOU OPEN THEM?
OKAY, BUT I DON'T WANT YOU WATCHING. SLIDE THEM UNDER THE DOOR.
GEE, I'D LIKE TO, ALEX, BUT I CAN'T. ALL THE ENVELOPES ARE MUCH TOO FAT.
FAT? TOO FAT?
I'LL JUST PUT THEM ON THE KITCHEN TABLE.
CRASH!
GB Trudeau

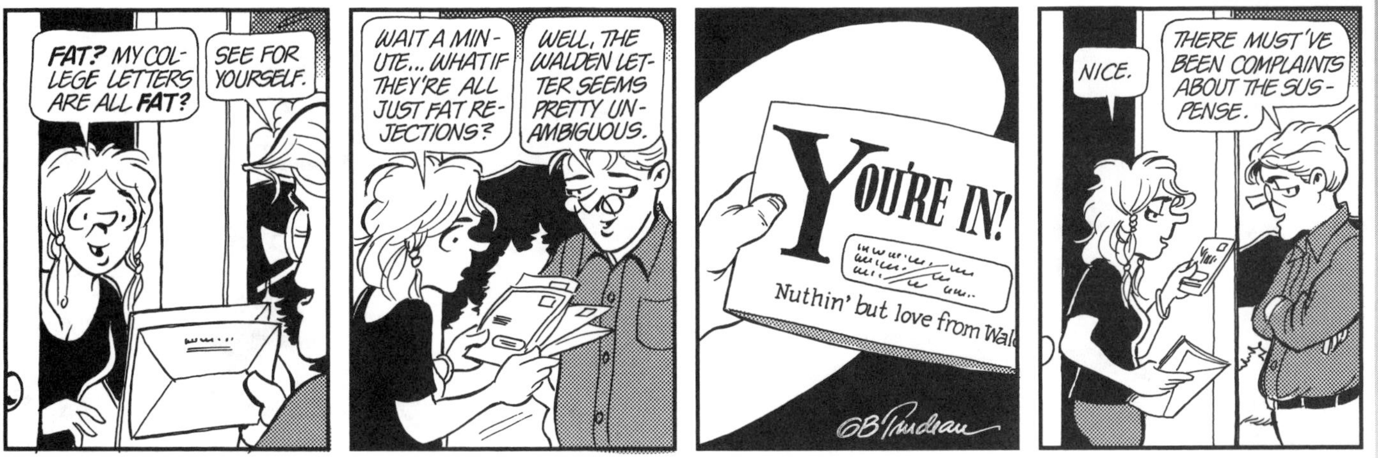
FAT? MY COLLEGE LETTERS ARE ALL **FAT**?
SEE FOR YOURSELF.
WAIT A MINUTE... WHAT IF THEY'RE ALL JUST FAT REJECTIONS?
WELL, THE WALDEN LETTER SEEMS PRETTY UNAMBIGUOUS.
YOU'RE IN!
Nuthin' but love from Wald
GB Trudeau
NICE.
THERE MUST'VE BEEN COMPLAINTS ABOUT THE SUSPENSE.

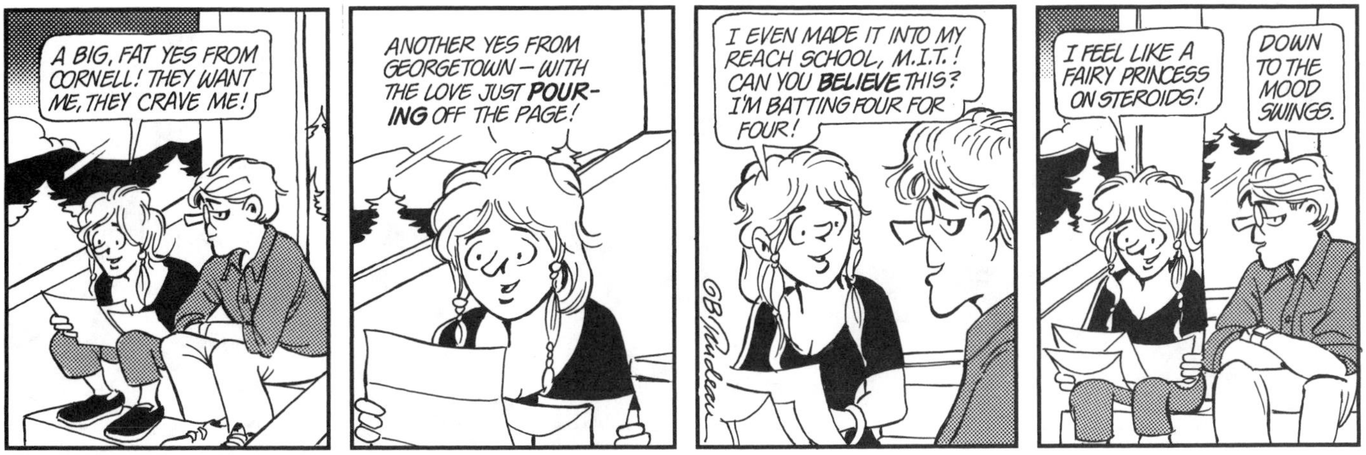
A BIG, FAT YES FROM CORNELL! THEY WANT ME, THEY CRAVE ME!
ANOTHER YES FROM GEORGETOWN – WITH THE LOVE JUST **POURING** OFF THE PAGE!
GB Trudeau
I EVEN MADE IT INTO MY REACH SCHOOL, M.I.T.! CAN YOU **BELIEVE** THIS? I'M BATTING FOUR FOR FOUR!
I FEEL LIKE A FAIRY PRINCESS ON STEROIDS!
DOWN TO THE MOOD SWINGS.

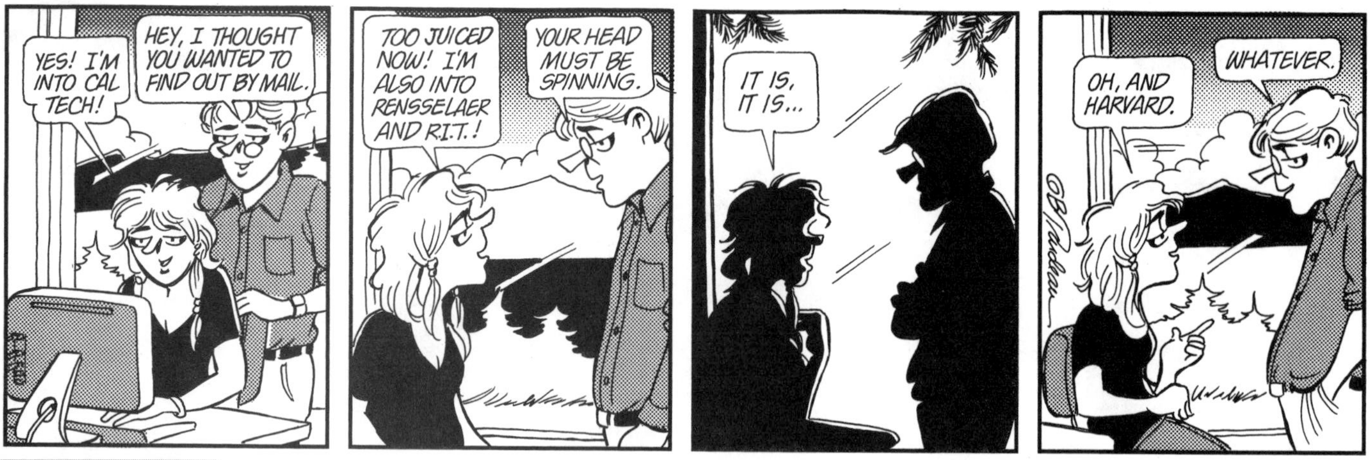
YES! I'M INTO CAL TECH!
HEY, I THOUGHT YOU WANTED TO FIND OUT BY MAIL.
TOO JUICED NOW! I'M ALSO INTO RENSSELAER AND R.I.T.!
YOUR HEAD MUST BE SPINNING.
IT IS, IT IS...
OH, AND HARVARD.
WHATEVER.

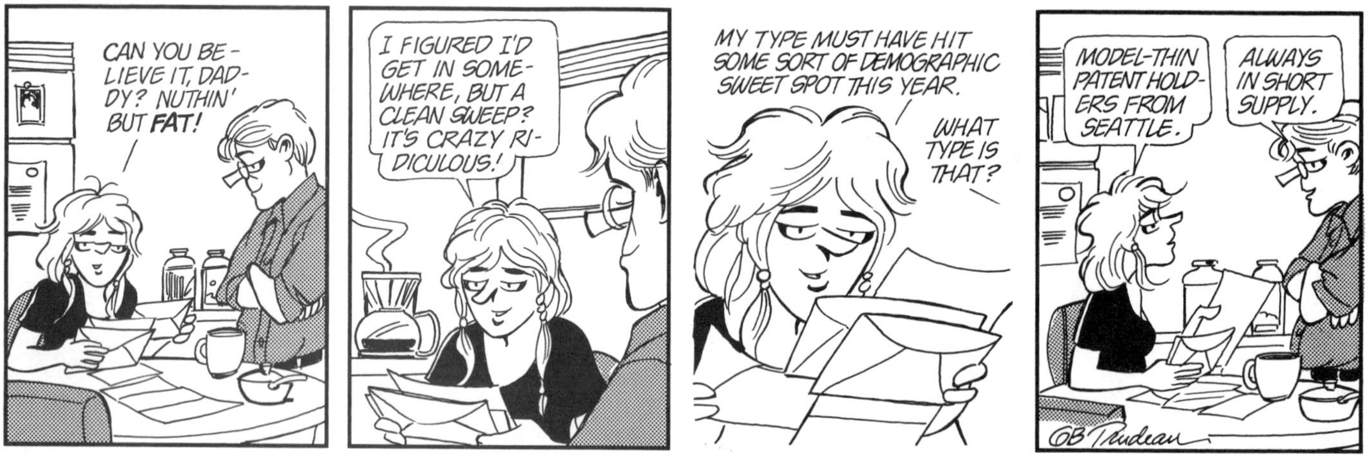
CAN YOU BE-LIEVE IT, DAD-DY? NUTHIN' BUT FAT!
I FIGURED I'D GET IN SOME-WHERE, BUT A CLEAN SWEEP? IT'S CRAZY RI-DICULOUS!
MY TYPE MUST HAVE HIT SOME SORT OF DEMOGRAPHIC SWEET SPOT THIS YEAR.
WHAT TYPE IS THAT?
MODEL-THIN PATENT HOLD-ERS FROM SEATTLE.
ALWAYS IN SHORT SUPPLY.

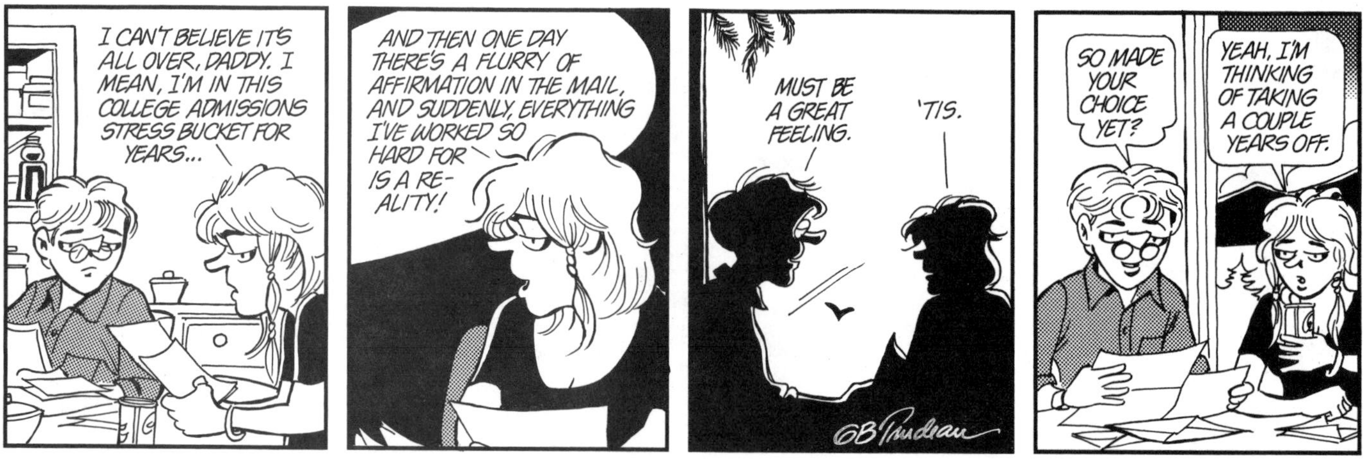
I CAN'T BELIEVE IT'S ALL OVER, DADDY. I MEAN, I'M IN THIS COLLEGE ADMISSIONS STRESS BUCKET FOR YEARS...
AND THEN ONE DAY THERE'S A FLURRY OF AFFIRMATION IN THE MAIL, AND SUDDENLY, EVERYTHING I'VE WORKED SO HARD FOR IS A RE-ALITY!
MUST BE A GREAT FEELING.
'TIS.
SO MADE YOUR CHOICE YET?
YEAH, I'M THINKING OF TAKING A COUPLE YEARS OFF.

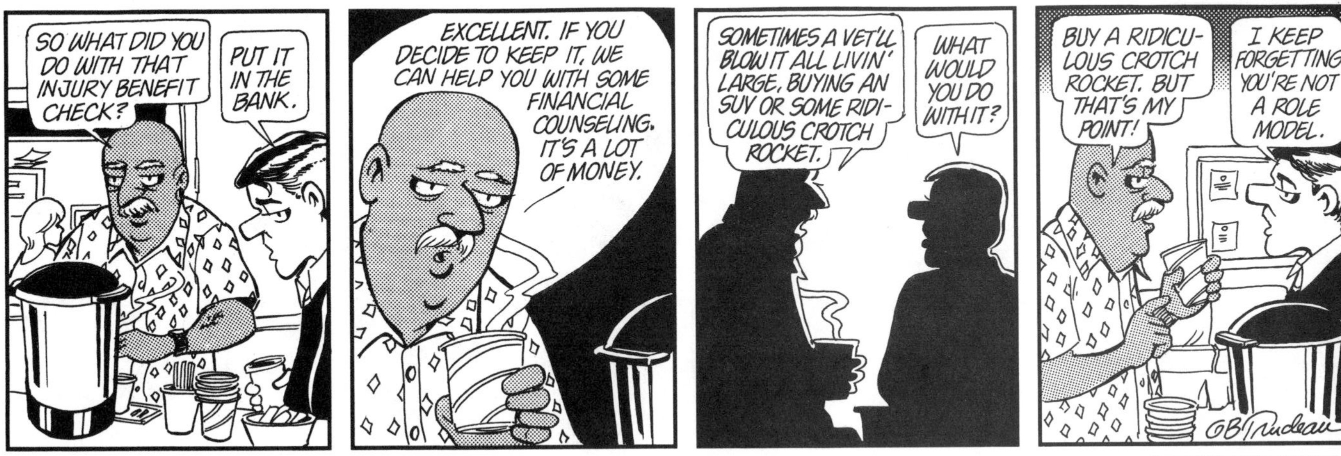
SO WHAT DID YOU DO WITH THAT INJURY BENEFIT CHECK?
PUT IT IN THE BANK.
EXCELLENT. IF YOU DECIDE TO KEEP IT, WE CAN HELP YOU WITH SOME FINANCIAL COUNSELING. IT'S A LOT OF MONEY.
SOMETIMES A VET'LL BLOW IT ALL LIVIN' LARGE, BUYING AN SUV OR SOME RIDICULOUS CROTCH ROCKET.
WHAT WOULD YOU DO WITH IT?
BUY A RIDICULOUS CROTCH ROCKET. BUT THAT'S MY POINT!
I KEEP FORGETTING YOU'RE NOT A ROLE MODEL.
GBTrudeau

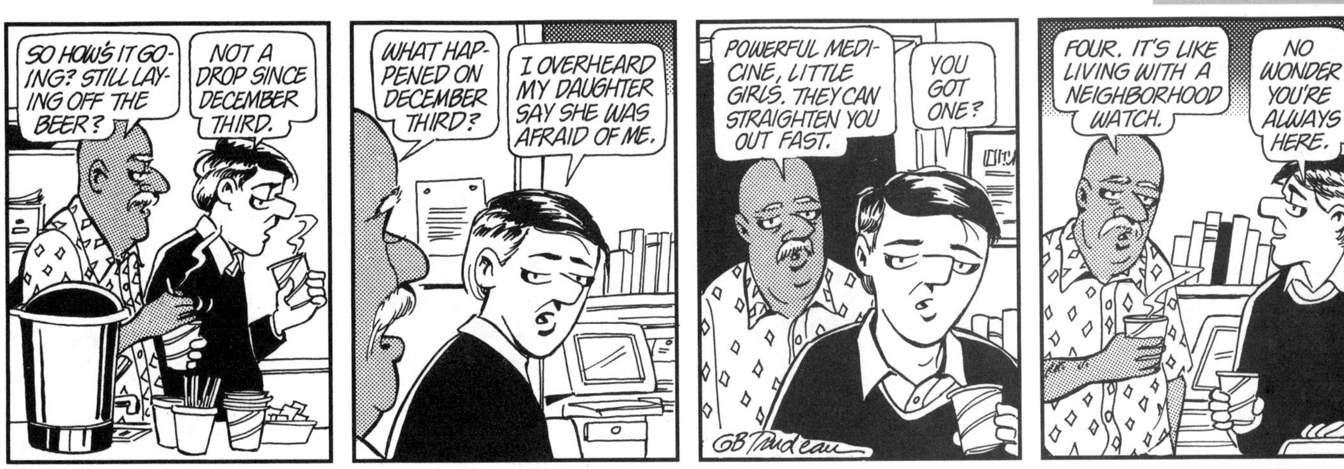
SO HOW'S IT GOING? STILL LAYING OFF THE BEER?
NOT A DROP SINCE DECEMBER THIRD.
WHAT HAPPENED ON DECEMBER THIRD?
I OVERHEARD MY DAUGHTER SAY SHE WAS AFRAID OF ME.
POWERFUL MEDICINE, LITTLE GIRLS. THEY CAN STRAIGHTEN YOU OUT FAST.
YOU GOT ONE?
GBTrudeau
FOUR. IT'S LIKE LIVING WITH A NEIGHBORHOOD WATCH.
NO WONDER YOU'RE ALWAYS HERE.

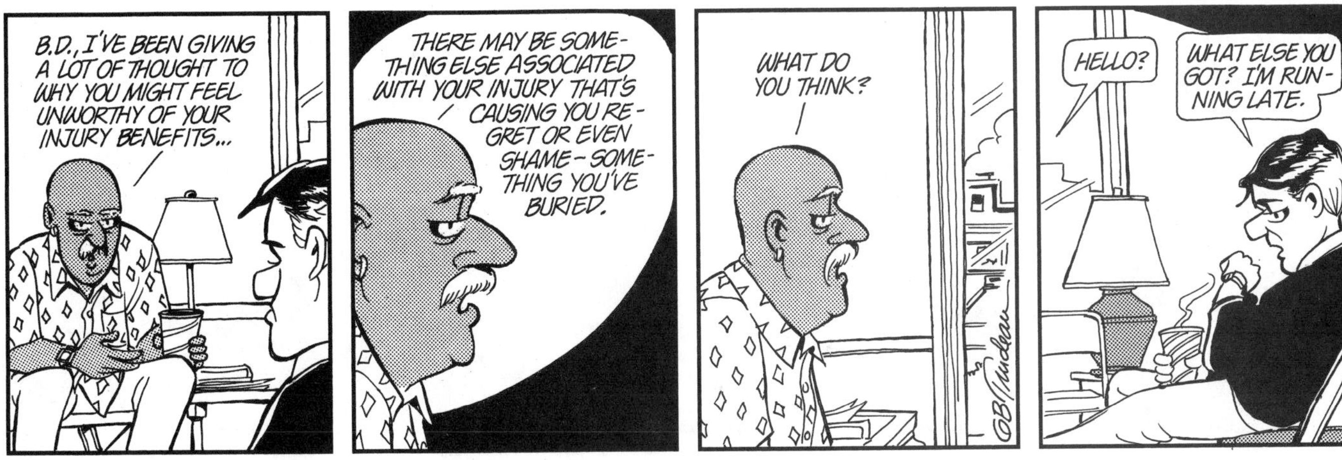
B.D., I'VE BEEN GIVING A LOT OF THOUGHT TO WHY YOU MIGHT FEEL UNWORTHY OF YOUR INJURY BENEFITS...
THERE MAY BE SOMETHING ELSE ASSOCIATED WITH YOUR INJURY THAT'S CAUSING YOU REGRET OR EVEN SHAME – SOMETHING YOU'VE BURIED.
WHAT DO YOU THINK?
GBTrudeau
HELLO?
WHAT ELSE YOU GOT? I'M RUNNING LATE.

B.D., BEFORE WE CAN PUT THE PUZZLE TOGETHER, WE HAVE TO FIND ALL THE PIECES...
MAYBE SOMETHING ELSE HAPPENED THAT DAY, SOMETHING BAD YOU CAN'T MAKE RIGHT. WHICH IS WHY YOU HAVE THIS FEELING OF UNWORTHINESS.
YOU GONNA HELP ME OUT HERE?
WARMER, WARMER, COLDER. CAN I GO NOW?
©B Trudeau

I DON'T WANT TO TALK ABOUT THIS ANYMORE!
THIS IS KEY, B.D.—I MEAN, YOU LEFT A LEG ON THE BATTLEFIELD...
YEAH, WELL, THAT'S NOT THE ONLY THING I LEFT ON THE BATTLEFIELD!
OKAY, THAT PROBABLY MEANS SOMETHING, DOESN'T IT?
YOU THINK?
©B Trudeau

"THAT'S NOT ALL I LEFT ON THE BATTLEFIELD"? BRO, THAT'S WHAT'S KNOWN IN THE TRADE AS A DOORKNOB MOMENT.
WHAT'S THAT?
IT'S WHEN YOU SAY SOMETHING INSANELY LOADED JUST AS YOU'RE LEAVING, WHEN THE SESSION'S OVER.
WELL, GUESS WHAT, MY FRIEND—THE SESSION ISN'T OVER! I GOT ALL DAY, SO LET'S GET AFTER IT!
©B Trudeau
BUT I NEED TO GO HOME.
NO, B.D., YOU NEED TO COME HOME! SO PARK IT!

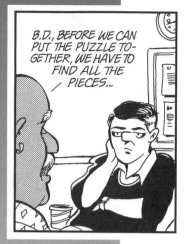

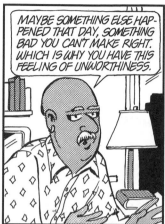

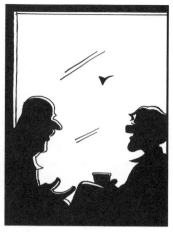

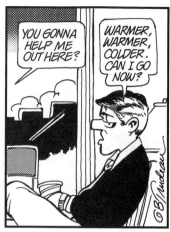

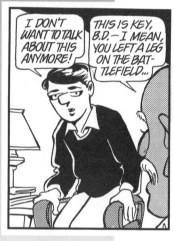

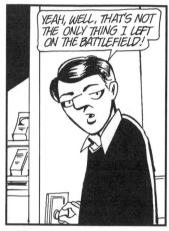

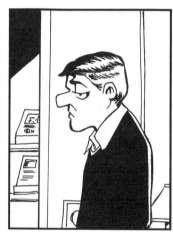

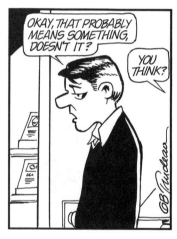

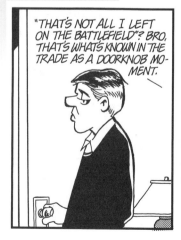

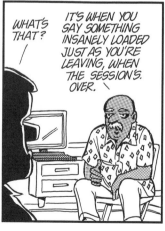

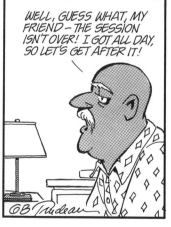

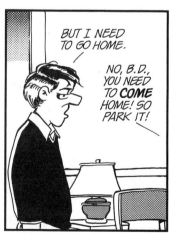

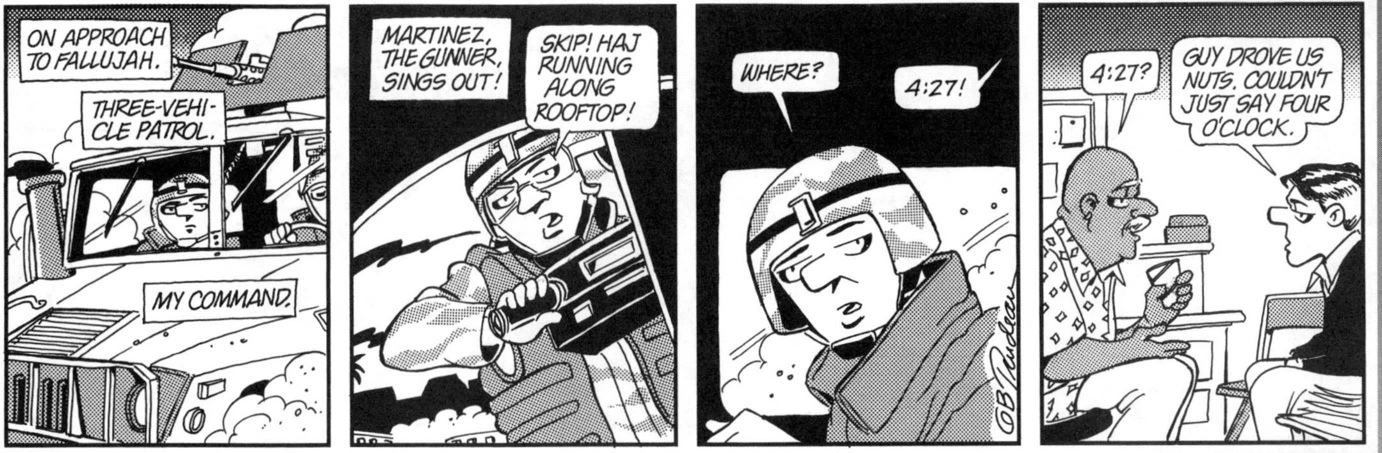

ON APPROACH TO FALLUJAH.
THREE-VEHICLE PATROL.
MY COMMAND.
MARTINEZ, THE GUNNER, SINGS OUT!
SKIP! HAJ RUNNING ALONG ROOFTOP!
WHERE?
4:27!
4:27?
GUY DROVE US NUTS. COULDN'T JUST SAY FOUR O'CLOCK.

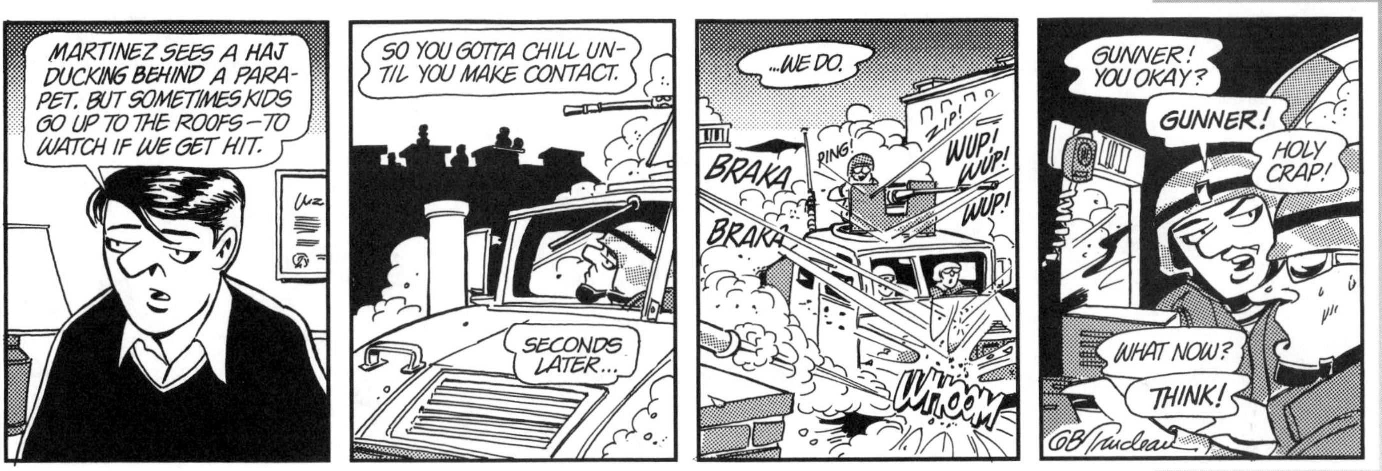

MARTINEZ SEES A HAJ DUCKING BEHIND A PARAPET. BUT SOMETIMES KIDS GO UP TO THE ROOFS—TO WATCH IF WE GET HIT.
SO YOU GOTTA CHILL UNTIL YOU MAKE CONTACT.
SECONDS LATER...
...WE DO.
PING!
ZIP!
WUP!
WUP!
WUP!
BRAKA
BRAKA
WHOOM
GUNNER! YOU OKAY?
GUNNER!
HOLY CRAP!
WHAT NOW?
THINK!

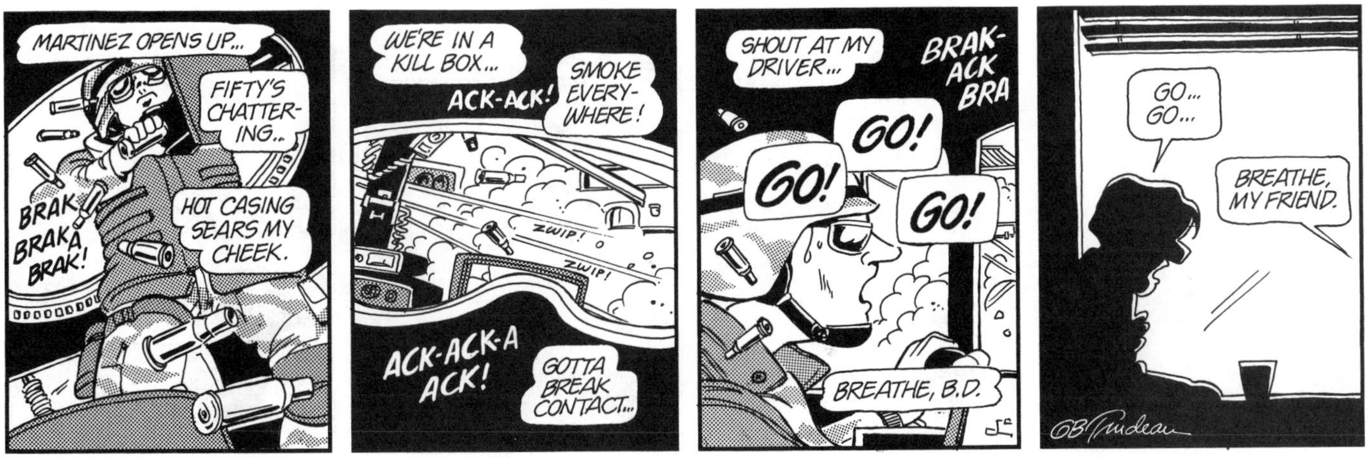

MARTINEZ OPENS UP...
FIFTY'S CHATTERING...
BRAK BRAKA BRAK!
HOT CASING SEARS MY CHEEK.
WE'RE IN A KILL BOX...
SMOKE EVERYWHERE!
ACK-ACK!
ZWIP!
ZWIP!
ACK-ACK-A ACK!
GOTTA BREAK CONTACT...
SHOUT AT MY DRIVER...
BRAK-ACK BRA
GO!
GO!
GO!
BREATHE, B.D.
GO... GO...
BREATHE, MY FRIEND.

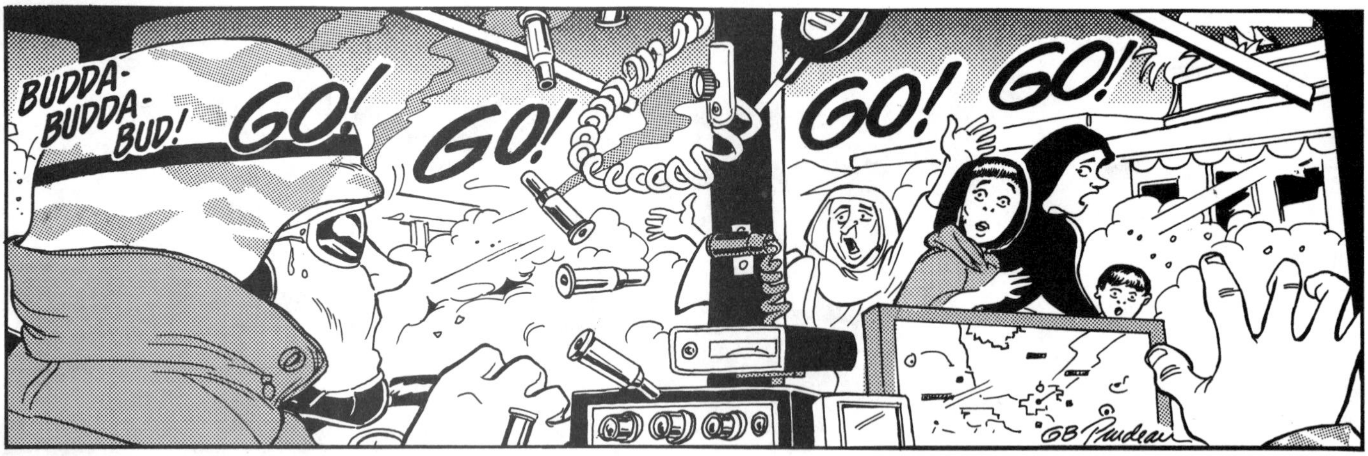
BUDDA-BUDDA-BUD!
GO! GO!
GO! GO!

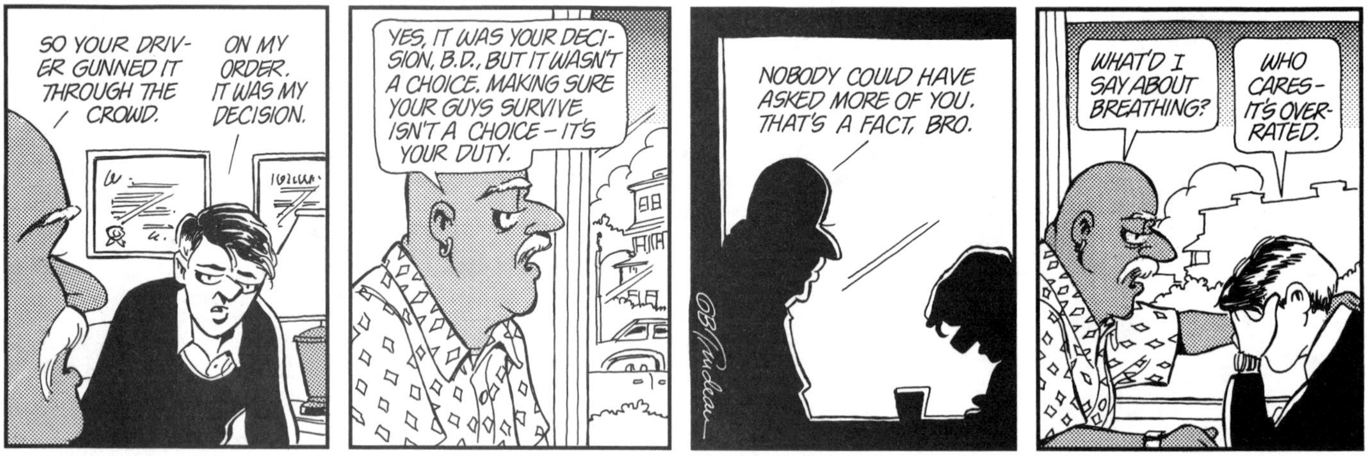
SO YOUR DRIVER GUNNED IT THROUGH THE CROWD.
ON MY ORDER. IT WAS MY DECISION.
YES, IT WAS YOUR DECISION, B.D., BUT IT WASN'T A CHOICE. MAKING SURE YOUR GUYS SURVIVE ISN'T A CHOICE – IT'S YOUR DUTY.
NOBODY COULD HAVE ASKED MORE OF YOU. THAT'S A FACT, BRO.
WHAT'D I SAY ABOUT BREATHING?
WHO CARES – IT'S OVERRATED.

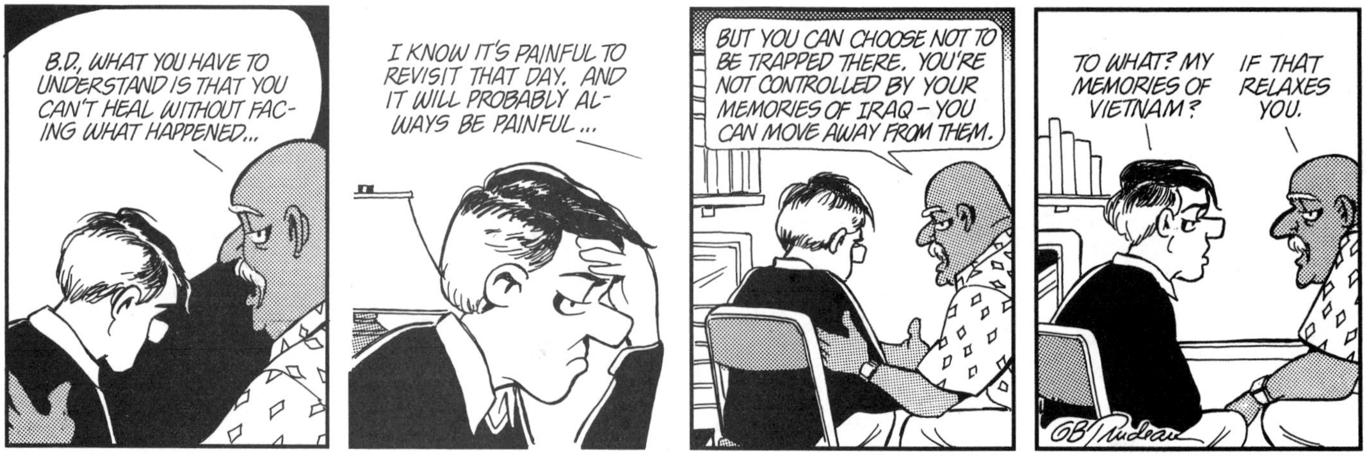
B.D, WHAT YOU HAVE TO UNDERSTAND IS THAT YOU CAN'T HEAL WITHOUT FACING WHAT HAPPENED...
I KNOW IT'S PAINFUL TO REVISIT THAT DAY. AND IT WILL PROBABLY ALWAYS BE PAINFUL ...
BUT YOU CAN CHOOSE NOT TO BE TRAPPED THERE. YOU'RE NOT CONTROLLED BY YOUR MEMORIES OF IRAQ – YOU CAN MOVE AWAY FROM THEM.
TO WHAT? MY MEMORIES OF VIETNAM?
IF THAT RELAXES YOU.

HI, IS ALEX HOME?
SORRY, SHE'S STILL BACK EAST LOOKING AT COLLEGES. TAKE A MESSAGE?
YES, THIS IS GREG FROM ADMISSIONS AT WALDEN COLLEGE. WE'RE HOPING SHE CAN MAKE IT TO AN OPEN HOUSE.
UH-HUH.
AND TELL HER WE OFFER MAJOR SWAG TO KIDS WHO VISIT.
DON'T ALL THE COLLEGES DO THAT NOW?
WE GIVE OUT LAPTOPS.
WOW. THAT SHOULD HELP YOUR YIELD.
HOW FAST?

'MORNING, GRAMMY!
GOOD MORNING, SWEETHEART. HOW'D THE OVERNIGHT AT GEORGETOWN GO?
IT WAS PRETTY LAME. THE KIDS JUST SAT AROUND WATCHING VIRAL VIDEOS AND EATING PINEAPPLE PIZZA.
WHAT'S WRONG WITH THAT, DEAR? SOUNDS LIKE FUN...
GRAMMY, WHO PUTS PINEAPPLE ON PIZZA?
OH. SO IT'S ALL IN THE DETAILS?

SO WHAT OTHER OPEN HOUSES HAVE YOU BEEN TO, ALEX?
LET'S SEE, R.I.T....
...AND RENSSELAER. THEY WERE FINE, BUT A LITTLE OUT OF THE WAY. IDEALLY, I'D PREFER TO BE NEAR A BIG CITY.
WHAT ABOUT HARVARD?
GREAT LOCATION, OF COURSE. BUT HARVARD SEEMED TO HAVE A SELF-ESTEEM PROBLEM.
TOO LITTLE?
TOO MUCH. WHO WANTS TO START EVERY DAY GETTING OVER YOURSELF?

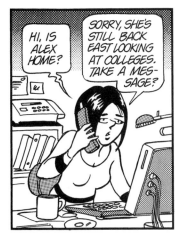

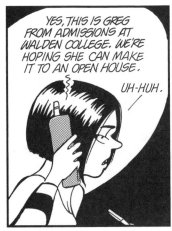

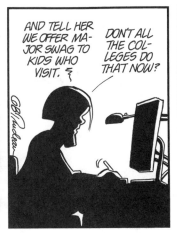

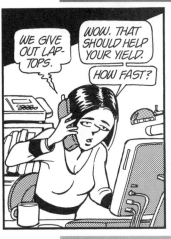

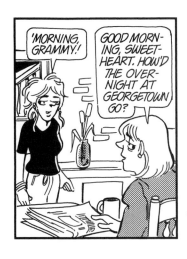

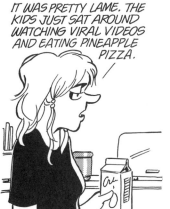

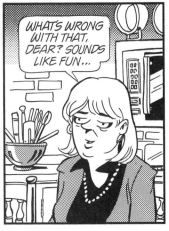

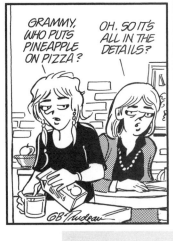

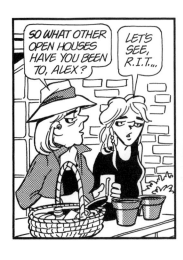

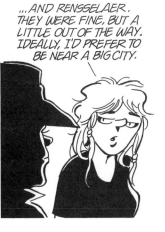

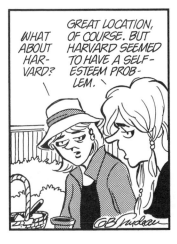

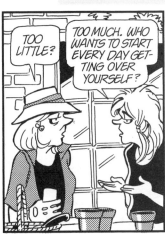

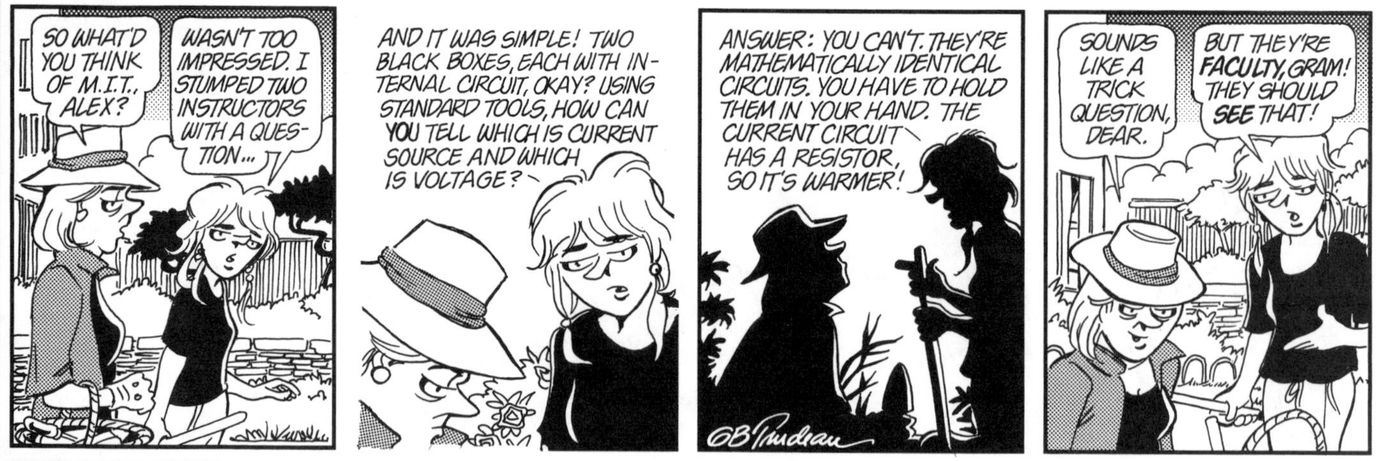
SO WHAT'D YOU THINK OF M.I.T., ALEX?
WASN'T TOO IMPRESSED. I STUMPED TWO INSTRUCTORS WITH A QUESTION...
AND IT WAS SIMPLE! TWO BLACK BOXES, EACH WITH INTERNAL CIRCUIT, OKAY? USING STANDARD TOOLS, HOW CAN YOU TELL WHICH IS CURRENT SOURCE AND WHICH IS VOLTAGE?
ANSWER: YOU CAN'T. THEY'RE MATHEMATICALLY IDENTICAL CIRCUITS. YOU HAVE TO HOLD THEM IN YOUR HAND. THE CURRENT CIRCUIT HAS A RESISTOR, SO IT'S WARMER!
GB Trudeau
SOUNDS LIKE A TRICK QUESTION, DEAR.
BUT THEY'RE FACULTY, GRAM! THEY SHOULD SEE THAT!

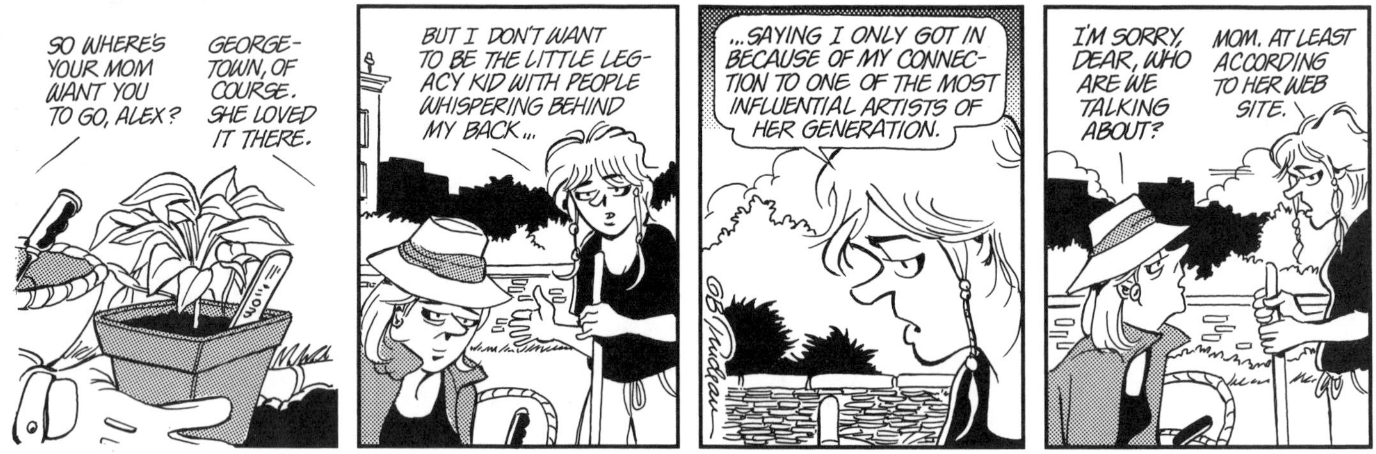
SO WHERE'S YOUR MOM WANT YOU TO GO, ALEX?
GEORGETOWN, OF COURSE. SHE LOVED IT THERE.
BUT I DON'T WANT TO BE THE LITTLE LEGACY KID WITH PEOPLE WHISPERING BEHIND MY BACK...
...SAYING I ONLY GOT IN BECAUSE OF MY CONNECTION TO ONE OF THE MOST INFLUENTIAL ARTISTS OF HER GENERATION.
GB Trudeau
I'M SORRY, DEAR, WHO ARE WE TALKING ABOUT?
MOM. AT LEAST ACCORDING TO HER WEB SITE.

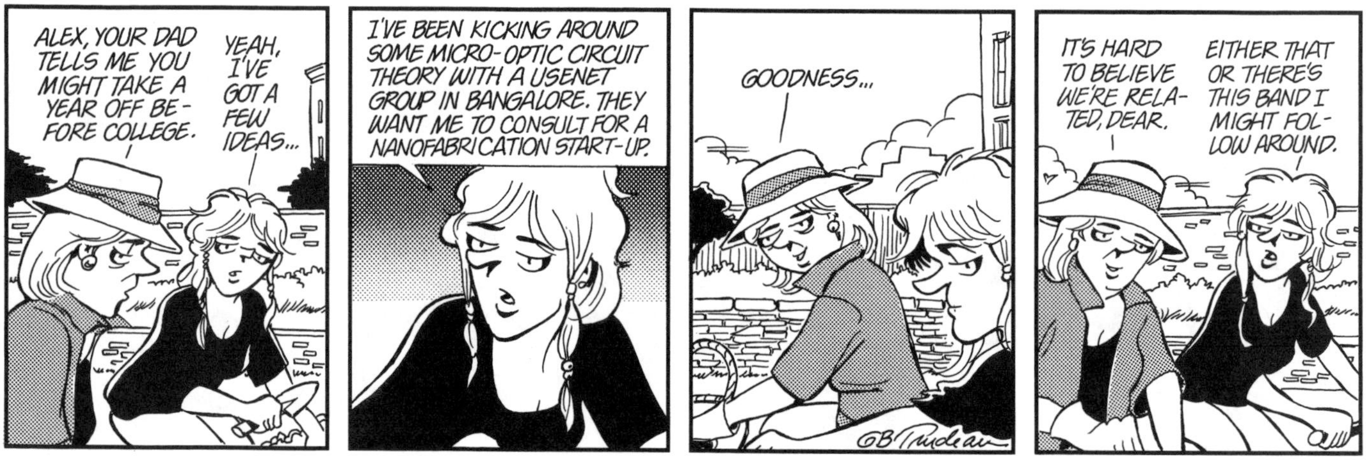
ALEX, YOUR DAD TELLS ME YOU MIGHT TAKE A YEAR OFF BEFORE COLLEGE.
YEAH, I'VE GOT A FEW IDEAS...
I'VE BEEN KICKING AROUND SOME MICRO-OPTIC CIRCUIT THEORY WITH A USENET GROUP IN BANGALORE. THEY WANT ME TO CONSULT FOR A NANOFABRICATION START-UP.
GOODNESS...
GB Trudeau
IT'S HARD TO BELIEVE WE'RE RELATED, DEAR.
EITHER THAT OR THERE'S THIS BAND I MIGHT FOLLOW AROUND.

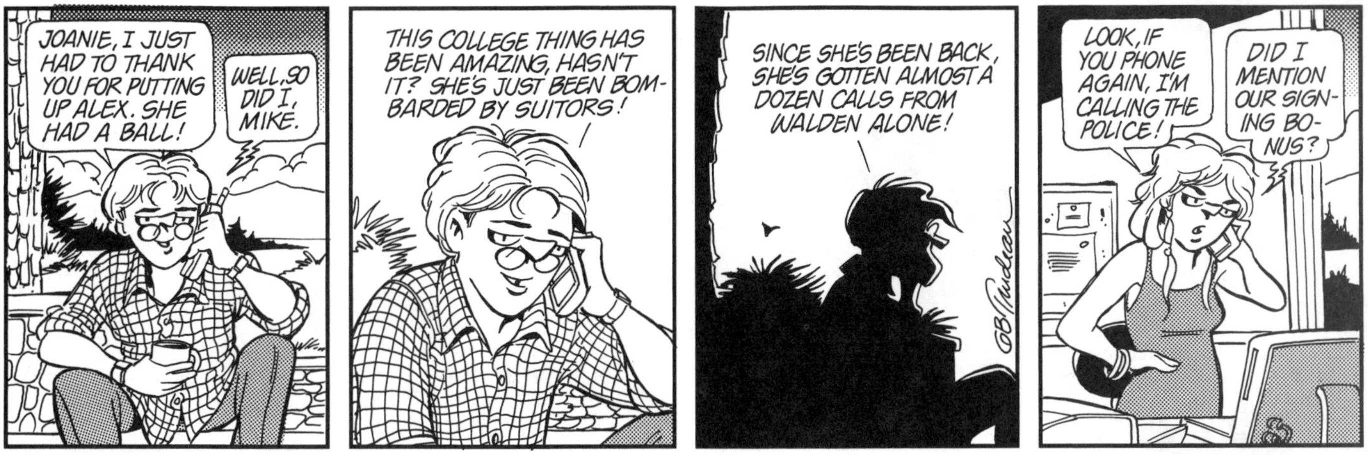
JOANIE, I JUST HAD TO THANK YOU FOR PUTTING UP ALEX. SHE HAD A BALL!
WELL, SO DID I, MIKE.
THIS COLLEGE THING HAS BEEN AMAZING, HASN'T IT? SHE'S JUST BEEN BOMBARDED BY SUITORS!
SINCE SHE'S BEEN BACK, SHE'S GOTTEN ALMOST A DOZEN CALLS FROM WALDEN ALONE!
LOOK, IF YOU PHONE AGAIN, I'M CALLING THE POLICE!
DID I MENTION OUR SIGNING BONUS?

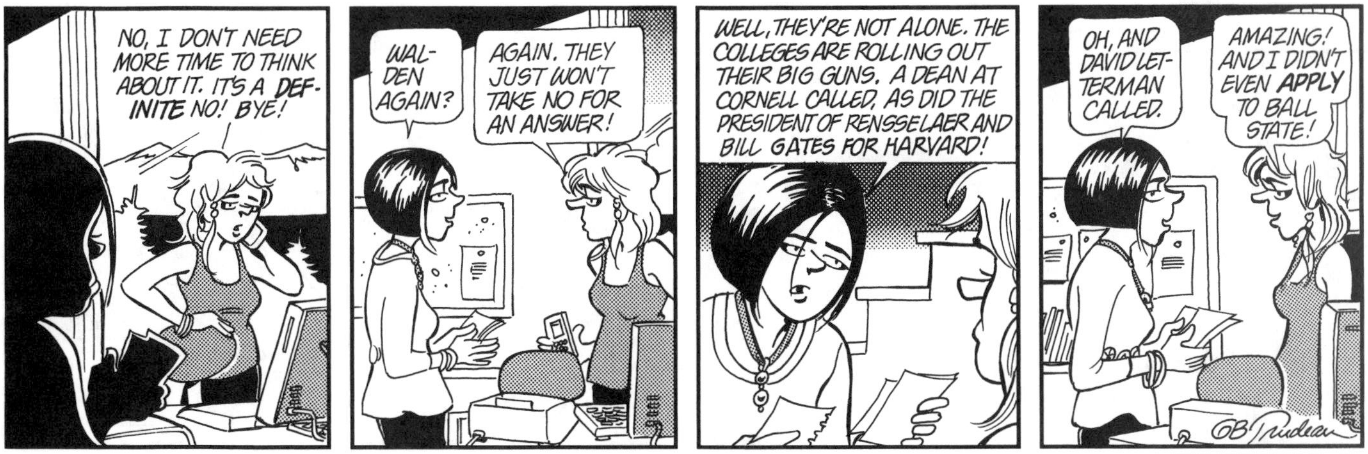
NO, I DON'T NEED MORE TIME TO THINK ABOUT IT. IT'S A **DEFINITE** NO! BYE!
WALDEN AGAIN?
AGAIN. THEY JUST WON'T TAKE NO FOR AN ANSWER!
WELL, THEY'RE NOT ALONE. THE COLLEGES ARE ROLLING OUT THEIR BIG GUNS. A DEAN AT CORNELL CALLED, AS DID THE PRESIDENT OF RENSSELAER AND BILL GATES FOR HARVARD!
OH, AND DAVID LETTERMAN CALLED.
AMAZING! AND I DIDN'T EVEN **APPLY** TO BALL STATE!

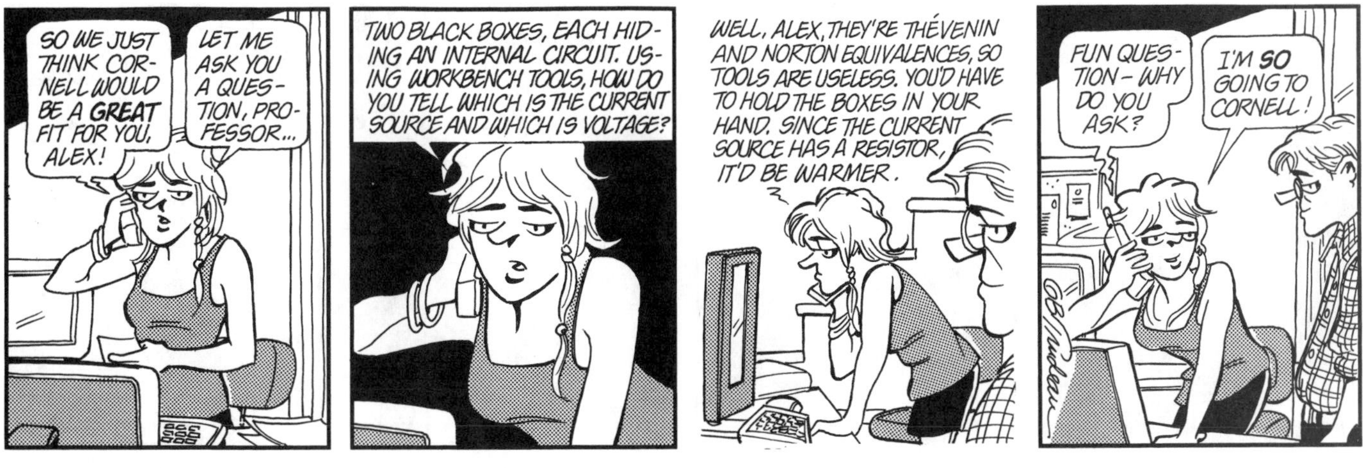
SO WE JUST THINK CORNELL WOULD BE A **GREAT** FIT FOR YOU, ALEX!
LET ME ASK YOU A QUESTION, PROFESSOR...
TWO BLACK BOXES, EACH HIDING AN INTERNAL CIRCUIT. USING WORKBENCH TOOLS, HOW DO YOU TELL WHICH IS THE CURRENT SOURCE AND WHICH IS VOLTAGE?
WELL, ALEX, THEY'RE THÉVENIN AND NORTON EQUIVALENCES, SO TOOLS ARE USELESS. YOU'D HAVE TO HOLD THE BOXES IN YOUR HAND. SINCE THE CURRENT SOURCE HAS A RESISTOR, IT'D BE WARMER.
FUN QUESTION - WHY DO YOU ASK?
I'M **SO** GOING TO CORNELL!

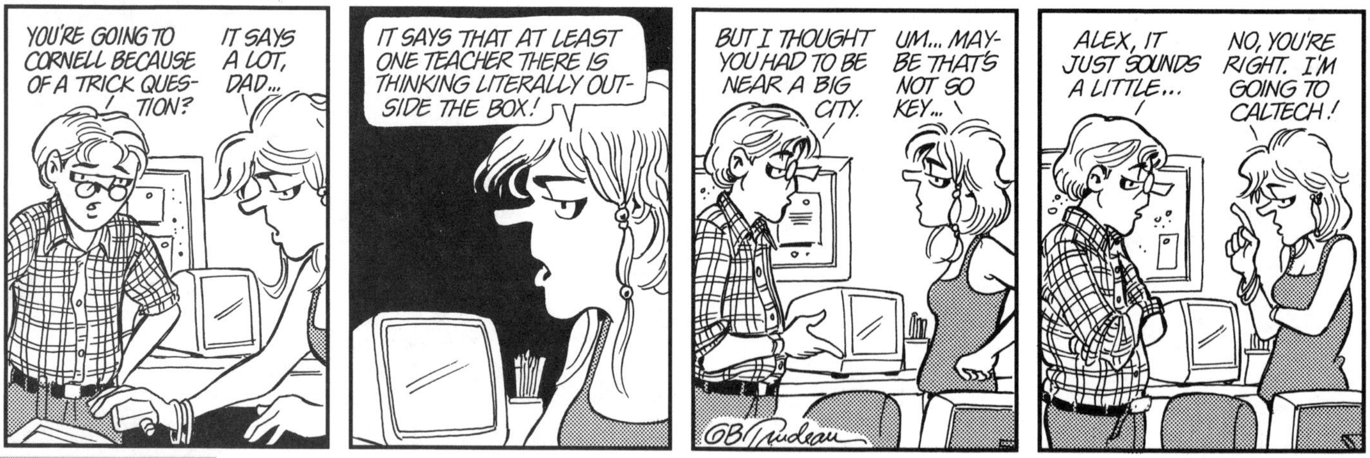
YOU'RE GOING TO CORNELL BECAUSE OF A TRICK QUESTION?
IT SAYS A LOT, DAD...
IT SAYS THAT AT LEAST ONE TEACHER THERE IS THINKING LITERALLY OUTSIDE THE BOX!
BUT I THOUGHT YOU HAD TO BE NEAR A BIG CITY.
UM... MAYBE THAT'S NOT SO KEY...
ALEX, IT JUST SOUNDS A LITTLE...
NO, YOU'RE RIGHT. I'M GOING TO CALTECH!
GB Trudeau

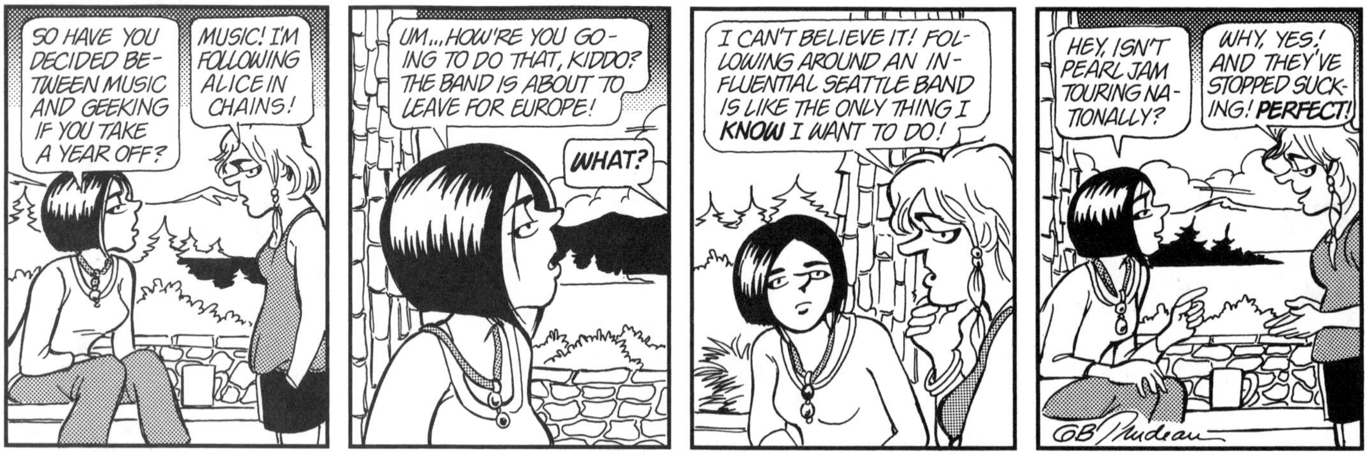
SO HAVE YOU DECIDED BETWEEN MUSIC AND GEEKING IF YOU TAKE A YEAR OFF?
MUSIC! I'M FOLLOWING ALICE IN CHAINS!
UM..., HOW'RE YOU GOING TO DO THAT, KIDDO? THE BAND IS ABOUT TO LEAVE FOR EUROPE!
WHAT?
I CAN'T BELIEVE IT! FOLLOWING AROUND AN INFLUENTIAL SEATTLE BAND IS LIKE THE ONLY THING I **KNOW** I WANT TO DO!
HEY, ISN'T PEARL JAM TOURING NATIONALLY?
WHY, YES! AND THEY'VE STOPPED SUCKING! **PERFECT!**
GB Trudeau

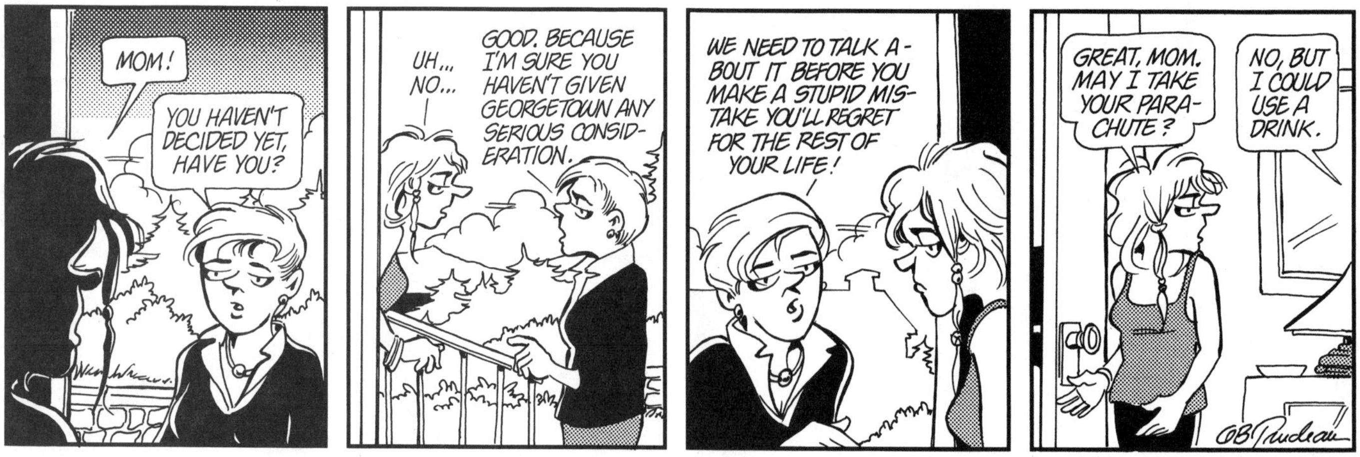
MOM!
YOU HAVEN'T DECIDED YET, HAVE YOU?
UH... NO...
GOOD. BECAUSE I'M SURE YOU HAVEN'T GIVEN GEORGETOWN ANY SERIOUS CONSIDERATION.
WE NEED TO TALK ABOUT IT BEFORE YOU MAKE A STUPID MISTAKE YOU'LL REGRET FOR THE REST OF YOUR LIFE!
GREAT, MOM. MAY I TAKE YOUR PARACHUTE?
NO, BUT I COULD USE A DRINK.
GB Trudeau

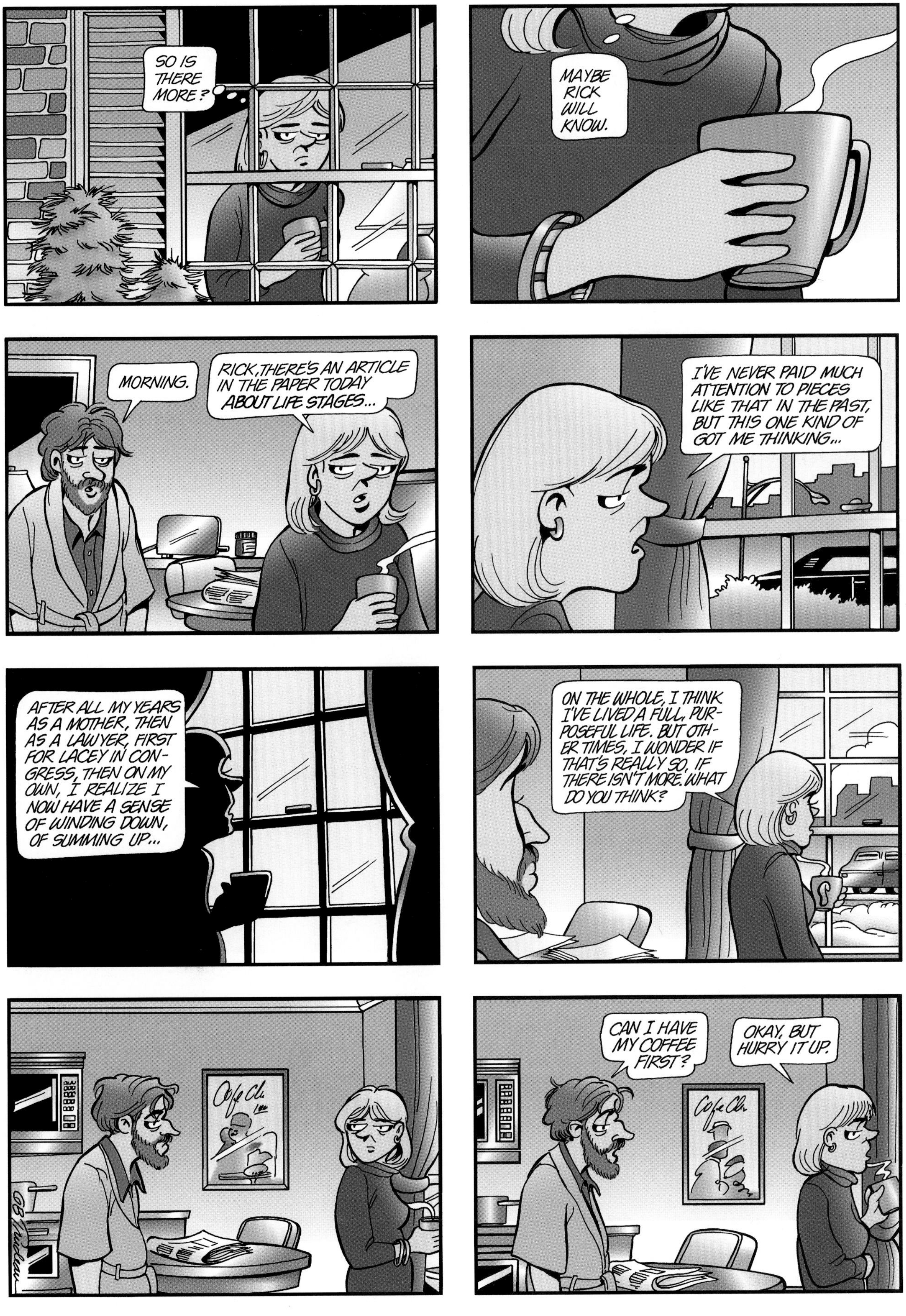
SO IS THERE MORE?
MAYBE RICK WILL KNOW.
MORNING.
RICK, THERE'S AN ARTICLE IN THE PAPER TODAY ABOUT LIFE STAGES...
I'VE NEVER PAID MUCH ATTENTION TO PIECES LIKE THAT IN THE PAST, BUT THIS ONE KIND OF GOT ME THINKING...
AFTER ALL MY YEARS AS A MOTHER, THEN AS A LAWYER, FIRST FOR LACEY IN CONGRESS, THEN ON MY OWN, I REALIZE I NOW HAVE A SENSE OF WINDING DOWN, OF SUMMING UP...
ON THE WHOLE, I THINK I'VE LIVED A FULL, PURPOSEFUL LIFE. BUT OTHER TIMES, I WONDER IF THAT'S REALLY SO, IF THERE ISN'T MORE. WHAT DO YOU THINK?
CAN I HAVE MY COFFEE FIRST?
OKAY, BUT HURRY IT UP.

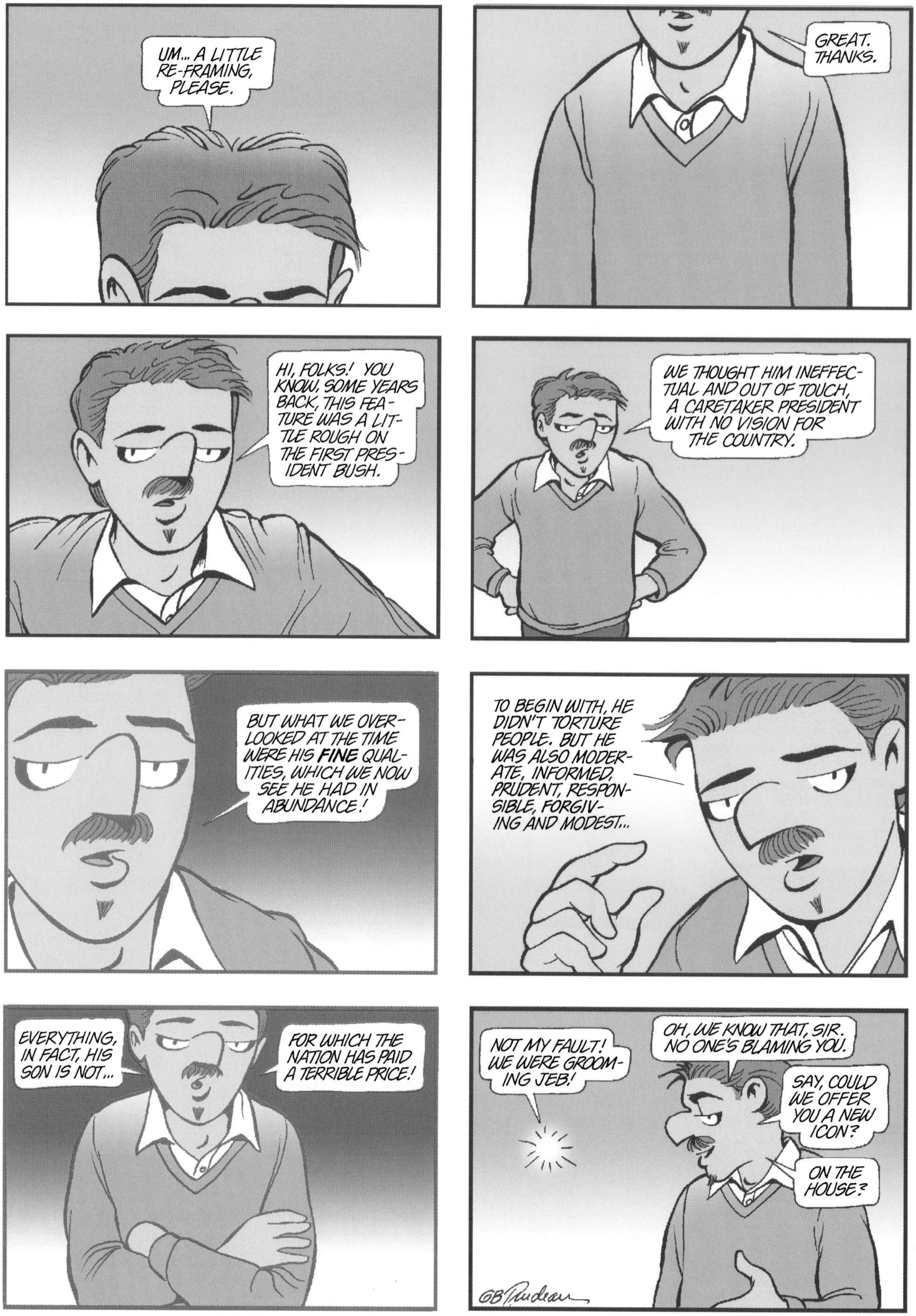
UM... A LITTLE RE-FRAMING, PLEASE.
GREAT. THANKS.
HI, FOLKS! YOU KNOW, SOME YEARS BACK, THIS FEATURE WAS A LITTLE ROUGH ON THE FIRST PRESIDENT BUSH.
WE THOUGHT HIM INEFFECTUAL AND OUT OF TOUCH, A CARETAKER PRESIDENT WITH NO VISION FOR THE COUNTRY.
BUT WHAT WE OVERLOOKED AT THE TIME WERE HIS **FINE** QUALITIES, WHICH WE NOW SEE HE HAD IN ABUNDANCE!
TO BEGIN WITH, HE DIDN'T TORTURE PEOPLE. BUT HE WAS ALSO MODERATE, INFORMED, PRUDENT, RESPONSIBLE, FORGIVING AND MODEST...
EVERYTHING, IN FACT, HIS SON IS NOT...
FOR WHICH THE NATION HAS PAID A TERRIBLE PRICE!
NOT MY FAULT! WE WERE GROOMING JEB!
OH, WE KNOW THAT, SIR. NO ONE'S BLAMING YOU.
SAY, COULD WE OFFER YOU A NEW ICON?
ON THE HOUSE?
GBTrudeau

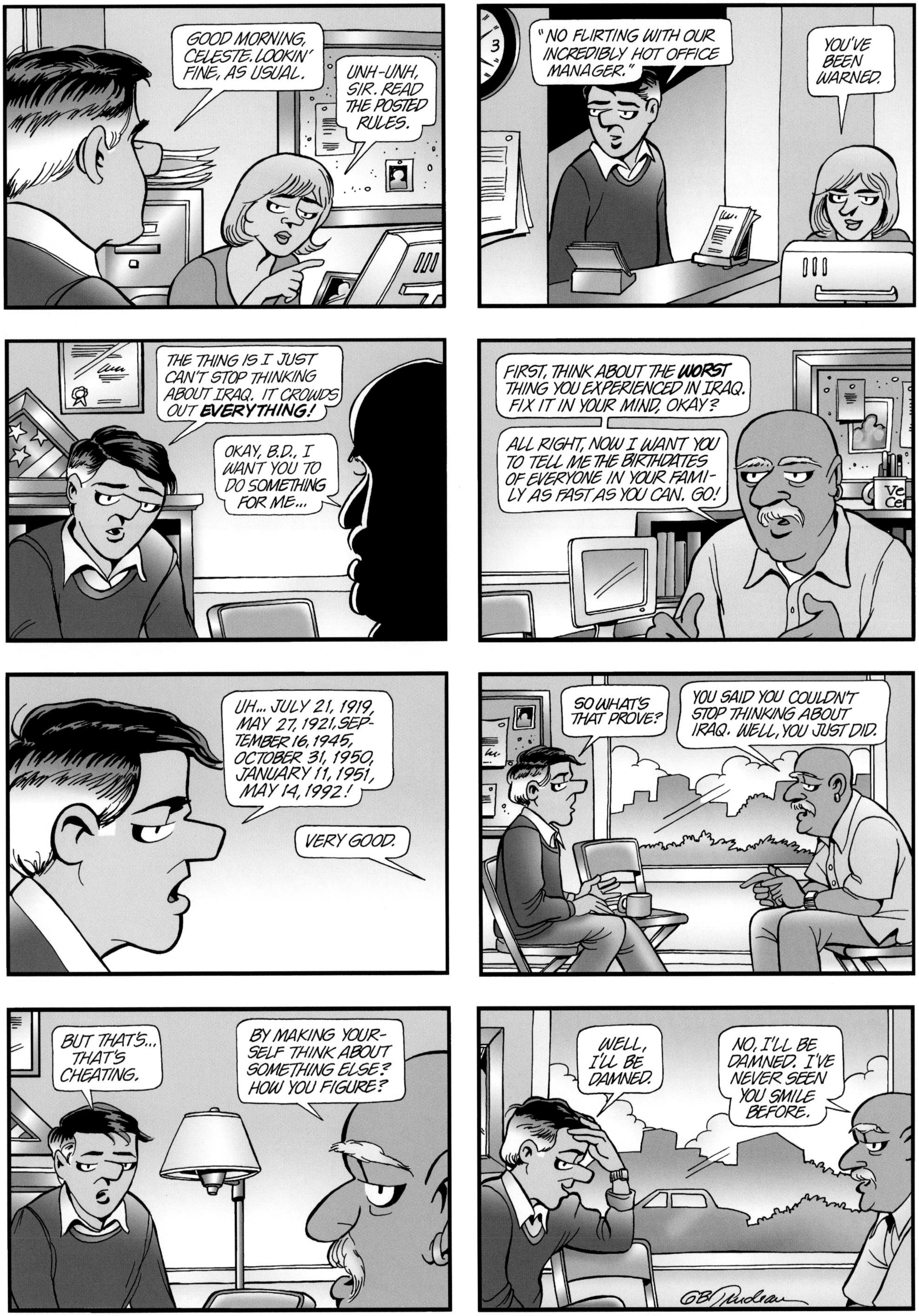
GOOD MORNING, CELESTE. LOOKIN' FINE, AS USUAL.
UNH-UNH, SIR. READ THE POSTED RULES.
"NO FLIRTING WITH OUR INCREDIBLY HOT OFFICE MANAGER."
YOU'VE BEEN WARNED.
THE THING IS I JUST CAN'T STOP THINKING ABOUT IRAQ. IT CROWDS OUT EVERYTHING!
OKAY, B.D., I WANT YOU TO DO SOMETHING FOR ME...
FIRST, THINK ABOUT THE WORST THING YOU EXPERIENCED IN IRAQ. FIX IT IN YOUR MIND, OKAY?
ALL RIGHT, NOW I WANT YOU TO TELL ME THE BIRTHDATES OF EVERYONE IN YOUR FAMILY AS FAST AS YOU CAN. GO!
UH... JULY 21, 1919, MAY 27, 1921, SEPTEMBER 16, 1945, OCTOBER 31, 1950, JANUARY 11, 1951, MAY 14, 1992!
VERY GOOD.
SO WHAT'S THAT PROVE?
YOU SAID YOU COULDN'T STOP THINKING ABOUT IRAQ. WELL, YOU JUST DID.
BUT THAT'S... THAT'S CHEATING.
BY MAKING YOURSELF THINK ABOUT SOMETHING ELSE? HOW YOU FIGURE?
WELL, I'LL BE DAMNED.
NO, I'LL BE DAMNED. I'VE NEVER SEEN YOU SMILE BEFORE.

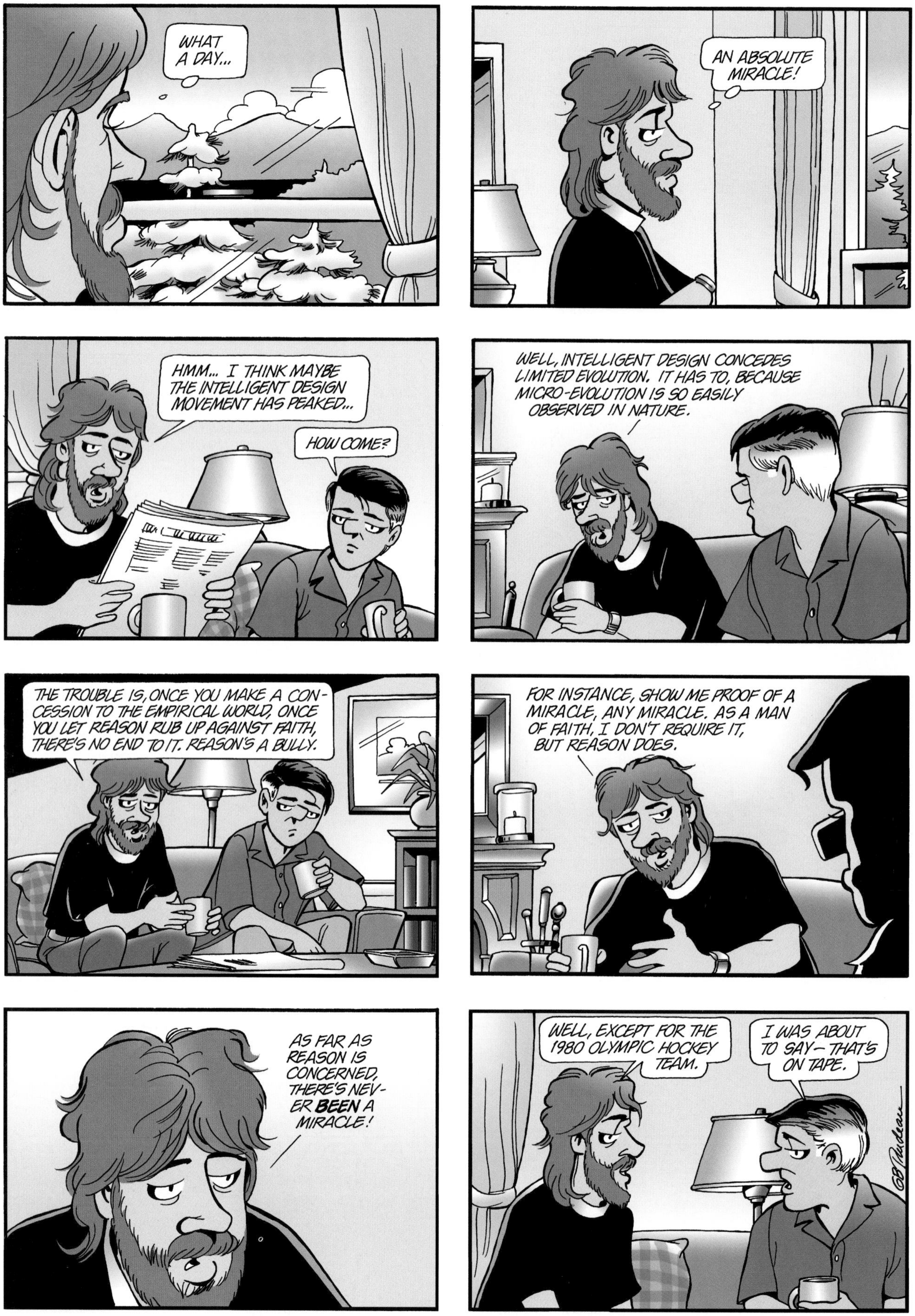
WHAT A DAY...
AN ABSOLUTE MIRACLE!
HMM... I THINK MAYBE THE INTELLIGENT DESIGN MOVEMENT HAS PEAKED...
HOW COME?
WELL, INTELLIGENT DESIGN CONCEDES LIMITED EVOLUTION. IT HAS TO, BECAUSE MICRO-EVOLUTION IS SO EASILY OBSERVED IN NATURE.
THE TROUBLE IS, ONCE YOU MAKE A CONCESSION TO THE EMPIRICAL WORLD, ONCE YOU LET REASON RUB UP AGAINST FAITH, THERE'S NO END TO IT. REASON'S A BULLY.
FOR INSTANCE, SHOW ME PROOF OF A MIRACLE, ANY MIRACLE. AS A MAN OF FAITH, I DON'T REQUIRE IT, BUT REASON DOES.
AS FAR AS REASON IS CONCERNED, THERE'S NEVER **BEEN** A MIRACLE!
WELL, EXCEPT FOR THE 1980 OLYMPIC HOCKEY TEAM.
I WAS ABOUT TO SAY— THAT'S ON TAPE.

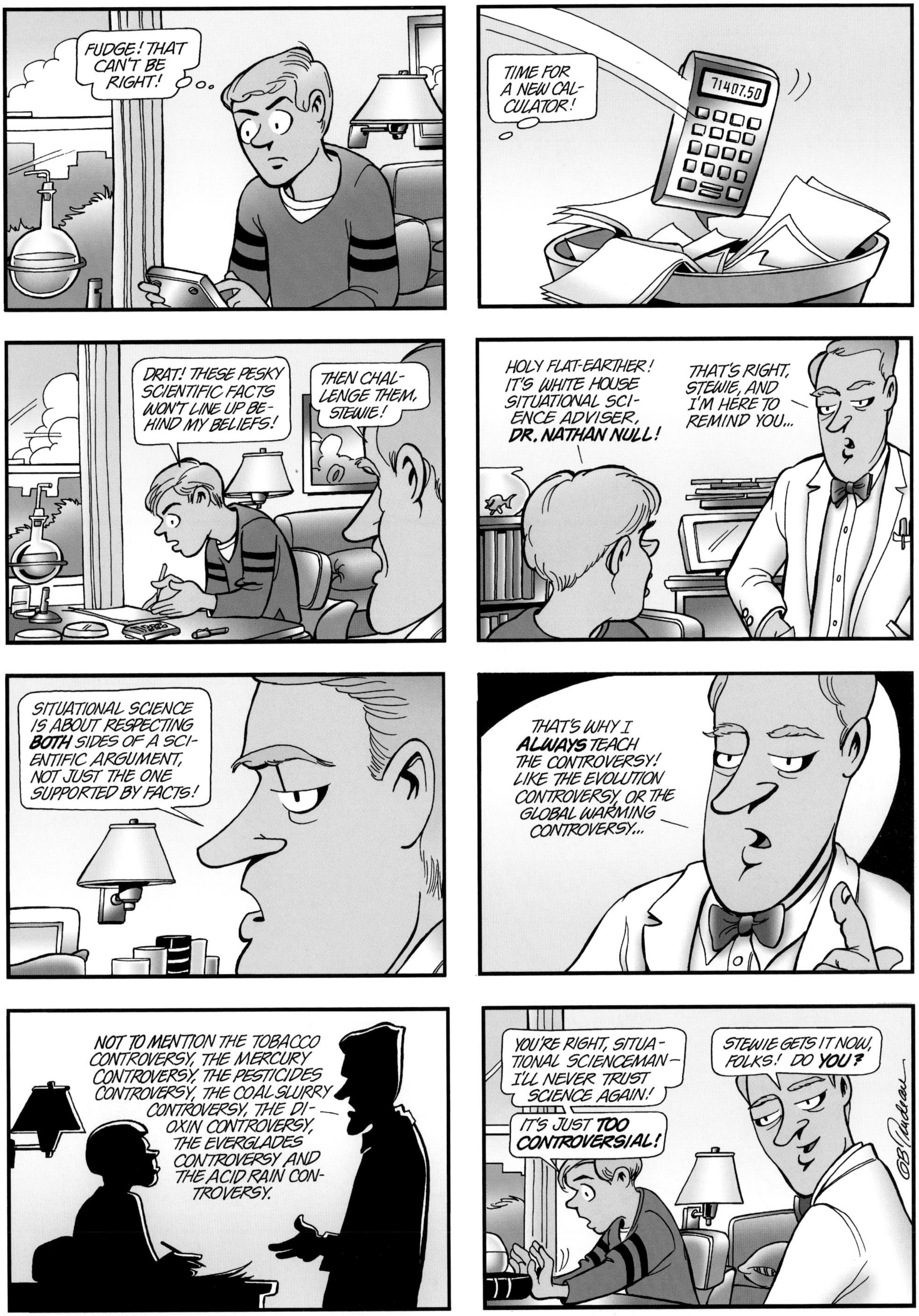
FUDGE! THAT CAN'T BE RIGHT!
TIME FOR A NEW CALCULATOR!
71407.50
DRAT! THESE PESKY SCIENTIFIC FACTS WON'T LINE UP BEHIND MY BELIEFS!
THEN CHALLENGE THEM, STEWIE!
HOLY FLAT-EARTHER! IT'S WHITE HOUSE SITUATIONAL SCIENCE ADVISER, DR. NATHAN NULL!
THAT'S RIGHT, STEWIE, AND I'M HERE TO REMIND YOU...
SITUATIONAL SCIENCE IS ABOUT RESPECTING BOTH SIDES OF A SCIENTIFIC ARGUMENT, NOT JUST THE ONE SUPPORTED BY FACTS!
THAT'S WHY I ALWAYS TEACH THE CONTROVERSY! LIKE THE EVOLUTION CONTROVERSY, OR THE GLOBAL WARMING CONTROVERSY...
NOT TO MENTION THE TOBACCO CONTROVERSY, THE MERCURY CONTROVERSY, THE PESTICIDES CONTROVERSY, THE COAL SLURRY CONTROVERSY, THE DIOXIN CONTROVERSY, THE EVERGLADES CONTROVERSY AND THE ACID RAIN CONTROVERSY.
YOU'RE RIGHT, SITUATIONAL SCIENCEMAN– I'LL NEVER TRUST SCIENCE AGAIN!
IT'S JUST TOO CONTROVERSIAL!
STEWIE GETS IT NOW, FOLKS! DO YOU?

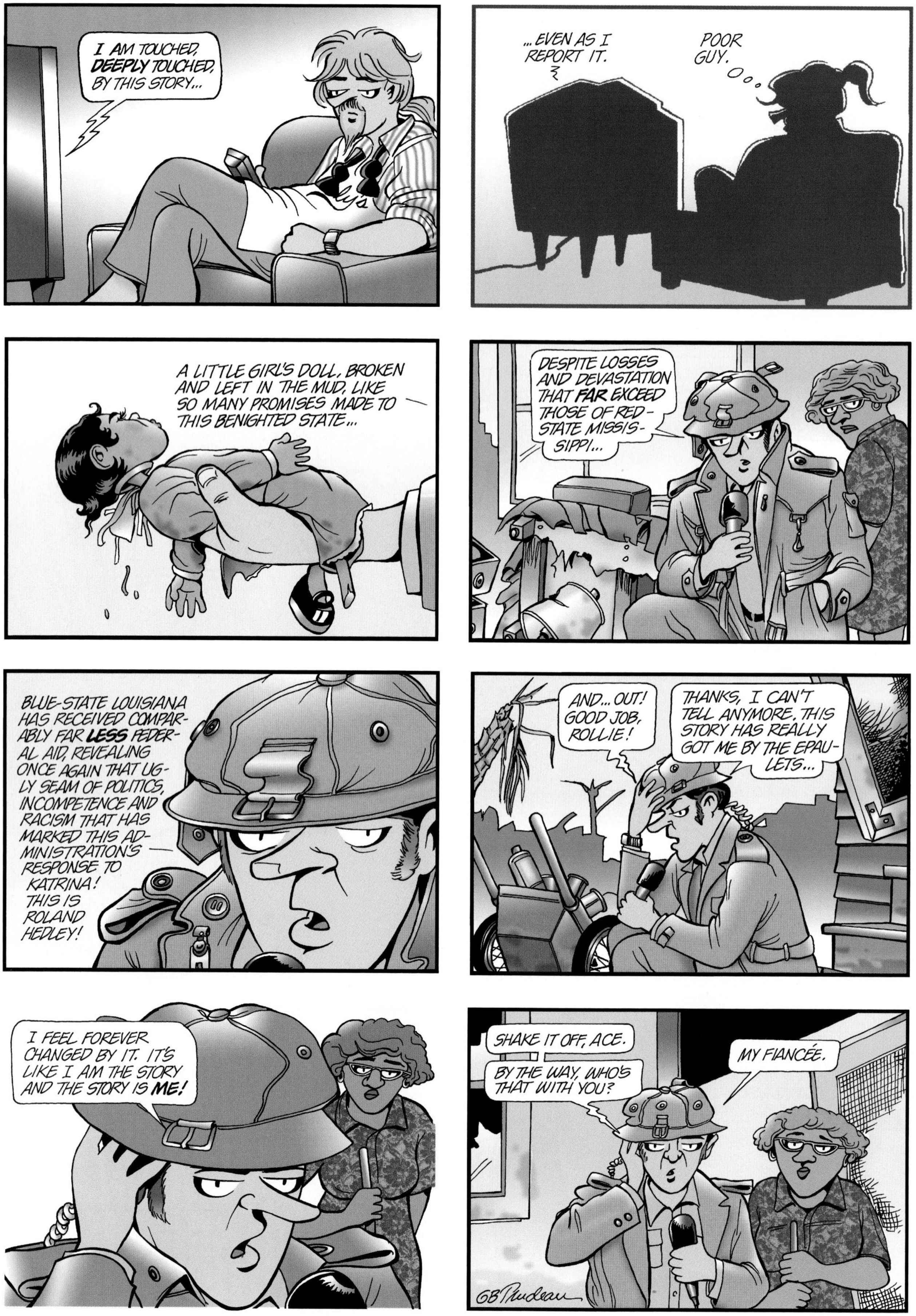
I AM TOUCHED, DEEPLY TOUCHED, BY THIS STORY...
...EVEN AS I REPORT IT.
POOR GUY.
A LITTLE GIRL'S DOLL, BROKEN AND LEFT IN THE MUD, LIKE SO MANY PROMISES MADE TO THIS BENIGHTED STATE...
DESPITE LOSSES AND DEVASTATION THAT FAR EXCEED THOSE OF RED-STATE MISSISSIPPI...
BLUE-STATE LOUISIANA HAS RECEIVED COMPARABLY FAR LESS FEDERAL AID, REVEALING ONCE AGAIN THAT UGLY SEAM OF POLITICS, INCOMPETENCE AND RACISM THAT HAS MARKED THIS ADMINISTRATION'S RESPONSE TO KATRINA! THIS IS ROLAND HEDLEY!
AND... OUT! GOOD JOB, ROLLIE!
THANKS, I CAN'T TELL ANYMORE. THIS STORY HAS REALLY GOT ME BY THE EPAULETS...
I FEEL FOREVER CHANGED BY IT. IT'S LIKE I AM THE STORY AND THE STORY IS ME!
SHAKE IT OFF, ACE.
BY THE WAY, WHO'S THAT WITH YOU?
MY FIANCÉE.
GBTrudeau

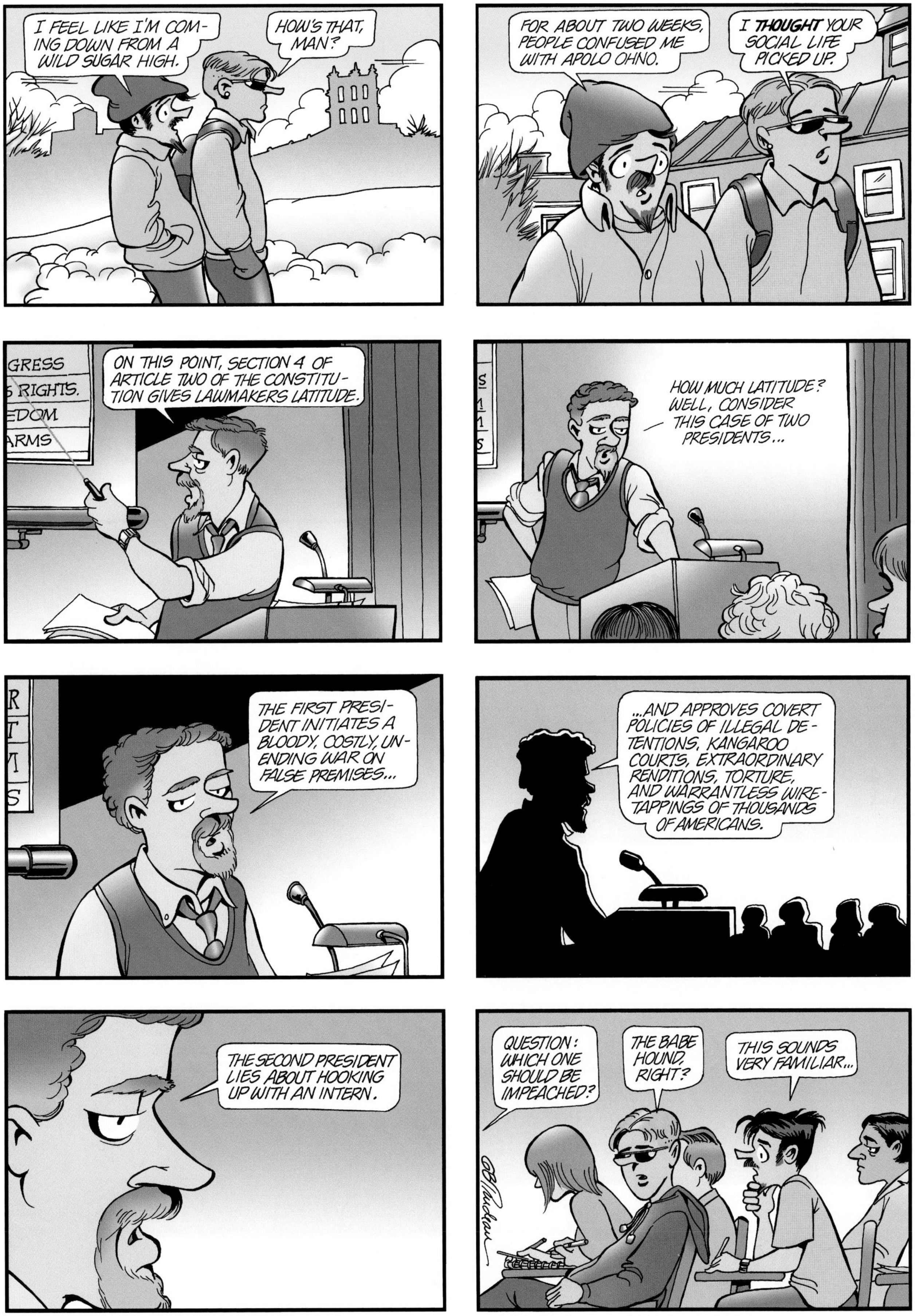
I FEEL LIKE I'M COMING DOWN FROM A WILD SUGAR HIGH.
HOW'S THAT, MAN?
FOR ABOUT TWO WEEKS, PEOPLE CONFUSED ME WITH APOLO OHNO.
I **THOUGHT** YOUR SOCIAL LIFE PICKED UP.
ON THIS POINT, SECTION 4 OF ARTICLE TWO OF THE CONSTITUTION GIVES LAWMAKERS LATITUDE.
HOW MUCH LATITUDE? WELL, CONSIDER THIS CASE OF TWO PRESIDENTS...
THE FIRST PRESIDENT INITIATES A BLOODY, COSTLY, UNENDING WAR ON FALSE PREMISES...
...AND APPROVES COVERT POLICIES OF ILLEGAL DETENTIONS, KANGAROO COURTS, EXTRAORDINARY RENDITIONS, TORTURE, AND WARRANTLESS WIRETAPPINGS OF THOUSANDS OF AMERICANS.
THE SECOND PRESIDENT LIES ABOUT HOOKING UP WITH AN INTERN.
QUESTION: WHICH ONE SHOULD BE IMPEACHED?
THE BABE HOUND, RIGHT?
THIS SOUNDS VERY FAMILIAR...

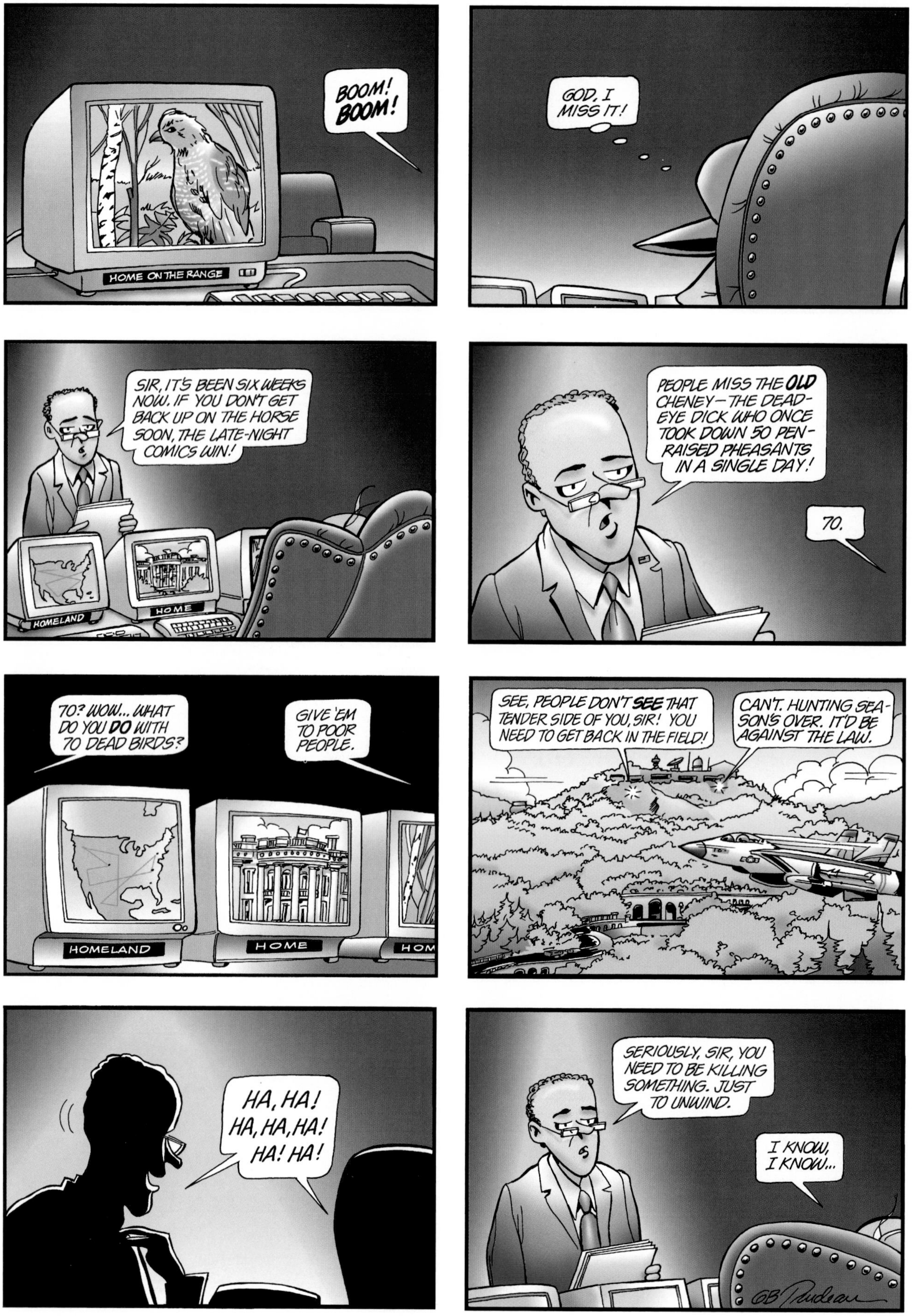
HOME ON THE RANGE
BOOM! BOOM!
GOD, I MISS IT!
SIR, IT'S BEEN SIX WEEKS NOW. IF YOU DON'T GET BACK UP ON THE HORSE SOON, THE LATE-NIGHT COMICS WIN!
HOMELAND
HOME
PEOPLE MISS THE OLD CHENEY—THE DEAD-EYE DICK WHO ONCE TOOK DOWN 50 PEN-RAISED PHEASANTS IN A SINGLE DAY!
70.
70? WOW... WHAT DO YOU DO WITH 70 DEAD BIRDS?
GIVE 'EM TO POOR PEOPLE.
HOMELAND
HOME
HOM
SEE, PEOPLE DON'T SEE THAT TENDER SIDE OF YOU, SIR! YOU NEED TO GET BACK IN THE FIELD!
CAN'T. HUNTING SEASON'S OVER. IT'D BE AGAINST THE LAW.
HA, HA! HA, HA, HA! HA! HA!
SERIOUSLY, SIR, YOU NEED TO BE KILLING SOMETHING. JUST TO UNWIND.
I KNOW, I KNOW...
GB Trudeau

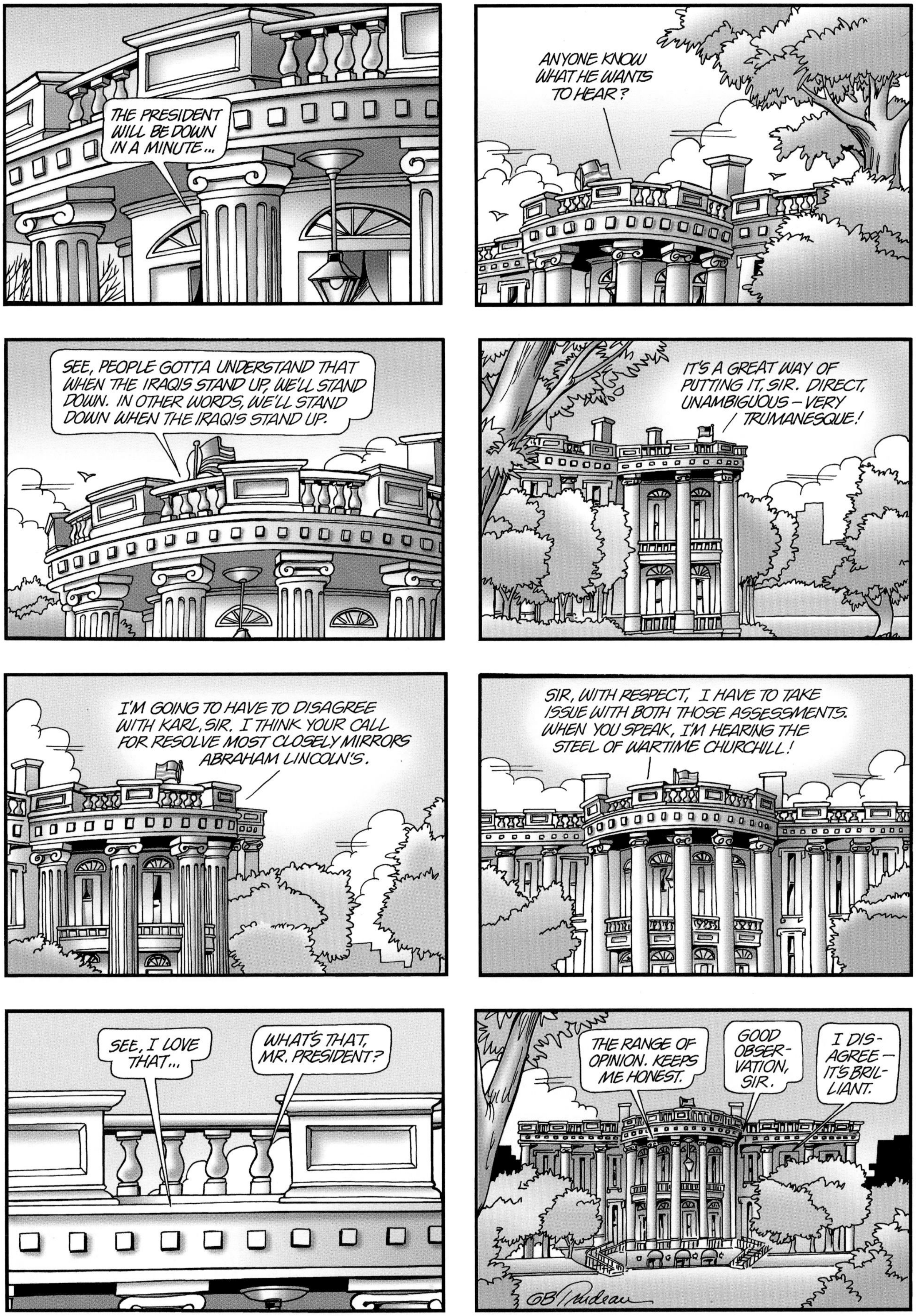
THE PRESIDENT WILL BE DOWN IN A MINUTE...
ANYONE KNOW WHAT HE WANTS TO HEAR?
SEE, PEOPLE GOTTA UNDERSTAND THAT WHEN THE IRAQIS STAND UP, WE'LL STAND DOWN. IN OTHER WORDS, WE'LL STAND DOWN WHEN THE IRAQIS STAND UP.
IT'S A GREAT WAY OF PUTTING IT, SIR. DIRECT, UNAMBIGUOUS – VERY TRUMANESQUE!
I'M GOING TO HAVE TO DISAGREE WITH KARL, SIR. I THINK YOUR CALL FOR RESOLVE MOST CLOSELY MIRRORS ABRAHAM LINCOLN'S.
SIR, WITH RESPECT, I HAVE TO TAKE ISSUE WITH BOTH THOSE ASSESSMENTS. WHEN YOU SPEAK, I'M HEARING THE STEEL OF WARTIME CHURCHILL!
SEE, I LOVE THAT...
WHAT'S THAT, MR. PRESIDENT?
THE RANGE OF OPINION. KEEPS ME HONEST.
GOOD OBSERVATION, SIR.
I DISAGREE – IT'S BRILLIANT.
GB Trudeau

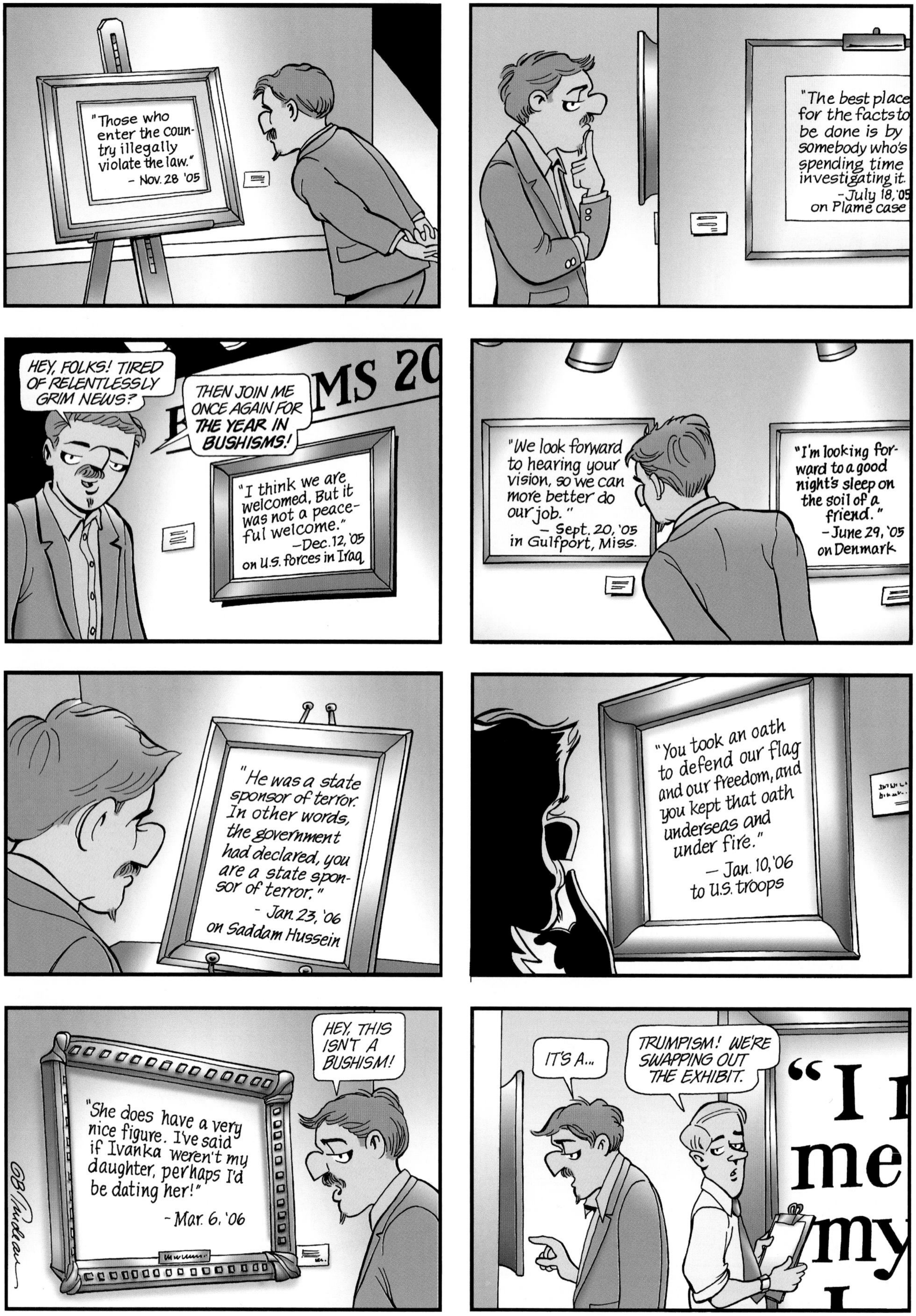
"Those who enter the country illegally violate the law." - Nov. 28 '05
"The best place for the facts to be done is by somebody who's spending time investigating it. - July 18, '05 on Plame case
HEY, FOLKS! TIRED OF RELENTLESSLY GRIM NEWS?
THEN JOIN ME ONCE AGAIN FOR THE YEAR IN BUSHISMS!
"I think we are welcomed. But it was not a peaceful welcome." —Dec. 12, '05 on U.S. forces in Iraq
"We look forward to hearing your vision, so we can more better do our job." — Sept. 20, '05 in Gulfport, Miss.
"I'm looking forward to a good night's sleep on the soil of a friend." - June 29, '05 on Denmark
"He was a state sponsor of terror. In other words, the government had declared, you are a state sponsor of terror." - Jan. 23, '06 on Saddam Hussein
"You took an oath to defend our flag and our freedom, and you kept that oath underseas and under fire." — Jan. 10, '06 to U.S. troops
"She does have a very nice figure. I've said if Ivanka weren't my daughter, perhaps I'd be dating her!" - Mar. 6, '06
HEY, THIS ISN'T A BUSHISM!
IT'S A...
TRUMPISM! WE'RE SWAPPING OUT THE EXHIBIT.

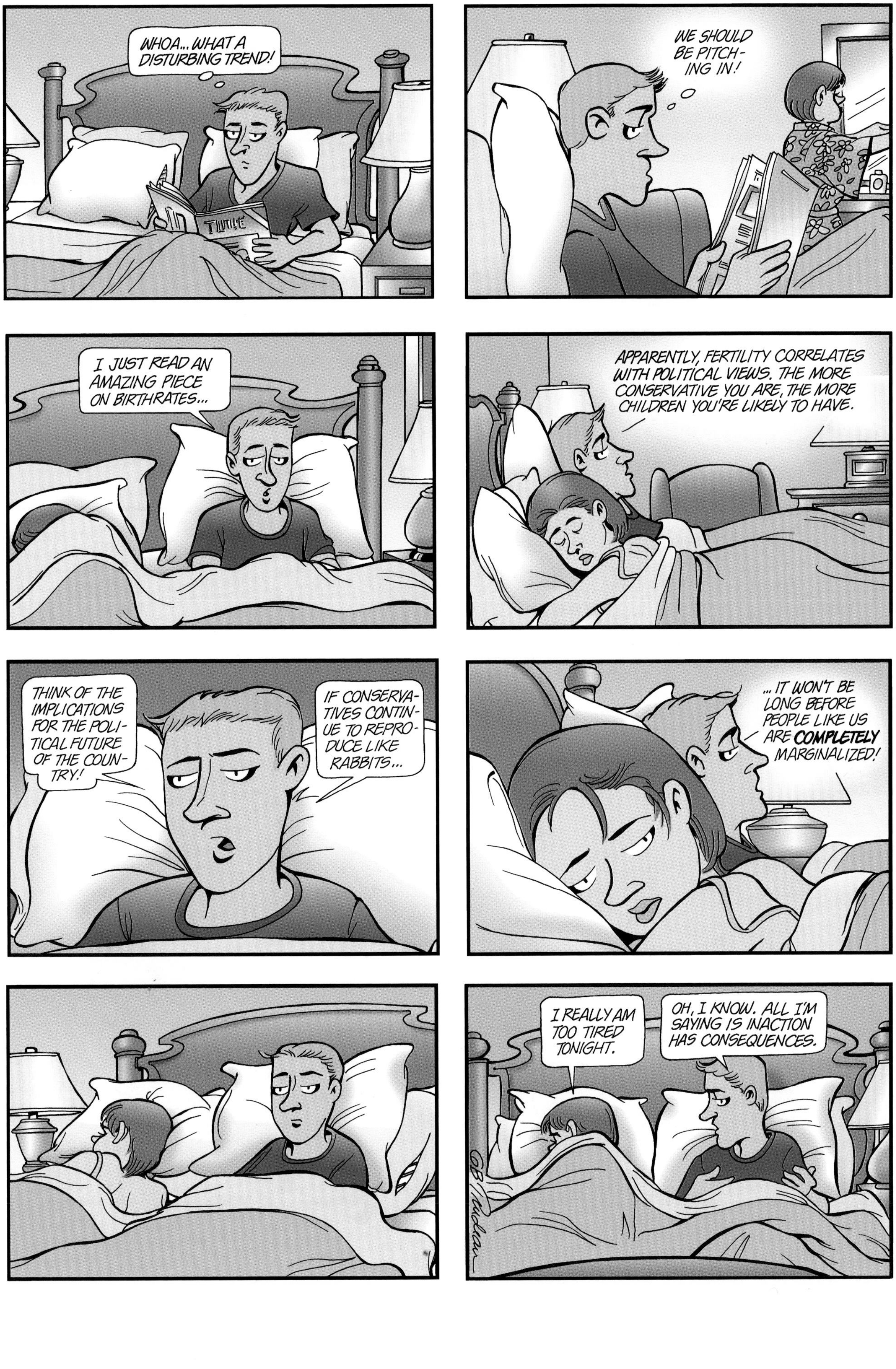
WHOA... WHAT A DISTURBING TREND!
WE SHOULD BE PITCHING IN!
I JUST READ AN AMAZING PIECE ON BIRTHRATES...
APPARENTLY, FERTILITY CORRELATES WITH POLITICAL VIEWS. THE MORE CONSERVATIVE YOU ARE, THE MORE CHILDREN YOU'RE LIKELY TO HAVE.
THINK OF THE IMPLICATIONS FOR THE POLITICAL FUTURE OF THE COUNTRY!
IF CONSERVATIVES CONTINUE TO REPRODUCE LIKE RABBITS...
...IT WON'T BE LONG BEFORE PEOPLE LIKE US ARE **COMPLETELY** MARGINALIZED!
I REALLY AM TOO TIRED TONIGHT.
OH, I KNOW. ALL I'M SAYING IS INACTION HAS CONSEQUENCES.

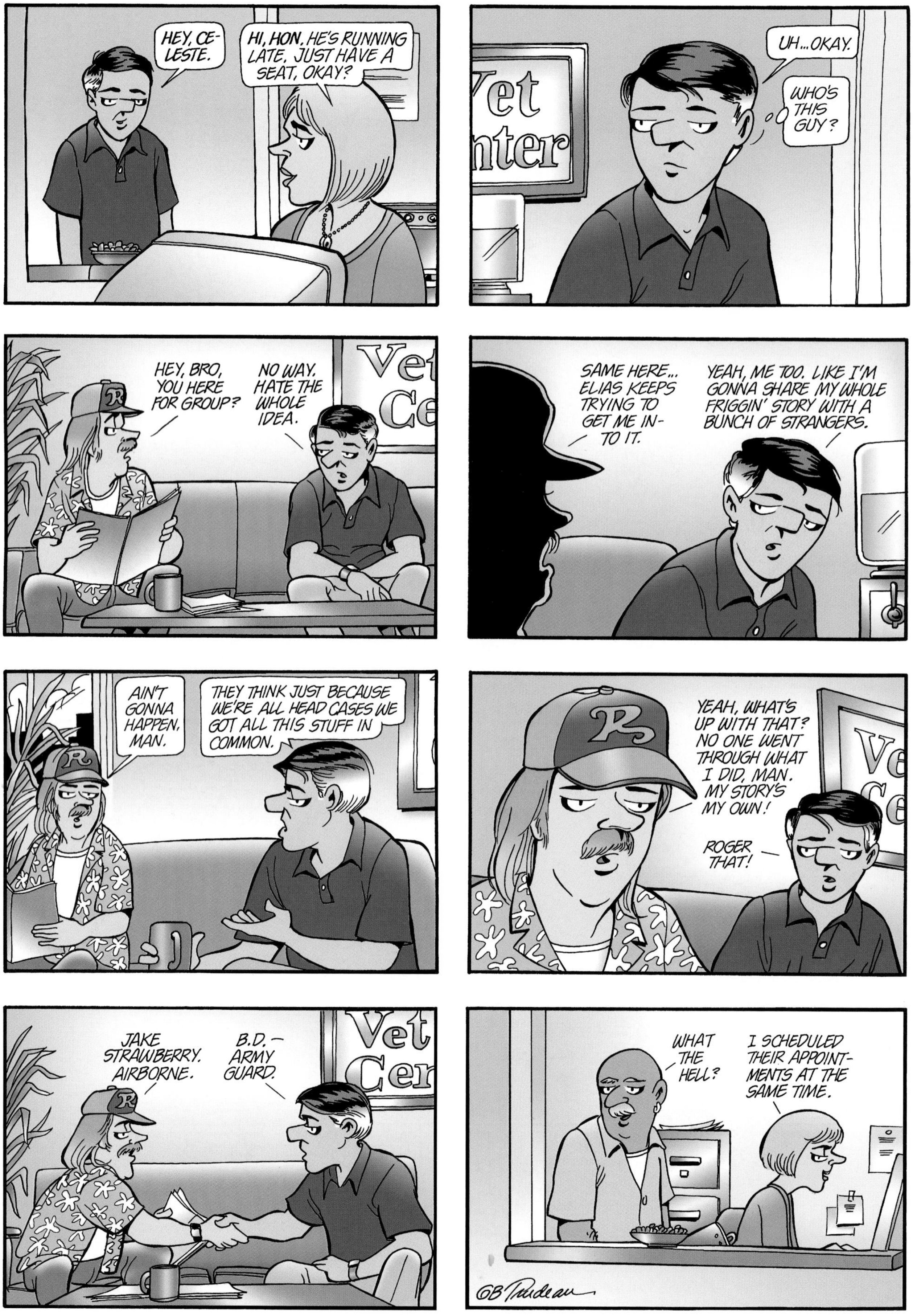
HEY, CE-LESTE.
HI, HON. HE'S RUNNING LATE. JUST HAVE A SEAT, OKAY?
UH... OKAY.
WHO'S THIS GUY?
Vet Center
HEY, BRO, YOU HERE FOR GROUP?
NO WAY. HATE THE WHOLE IDEA.
SAME HERE... ELIAS KEEPS TRYING TO GET ME IN-TO IT.
YEAH, ME TOO. LIKE I'M GONNA SHARE MY WHOLE FRIGGIN' STORY WITH A BUNCH OF STRANGERS.
AIN'T GONNA HAPPEN, MAN.
THEY THINK JUST BECAUSE WE'RE ALL HEAD CASES WE GOT ALL THIS STUFF IN COMMON.
YEAH, WHAT'S UP WITH THAT? NO ONE WENT THROUGH WHAT I DID, MAN. MY STORY'S MY OWN!
ROGER THAT!
JAKE STRAWBERRY. AIRBORNE.
B.D.— ARMY GUARD.
WHAT THE HELL?
I SCHEDULED THEIR APPOINT-MENTS AT THE SAME TIME.
GB Trudeau

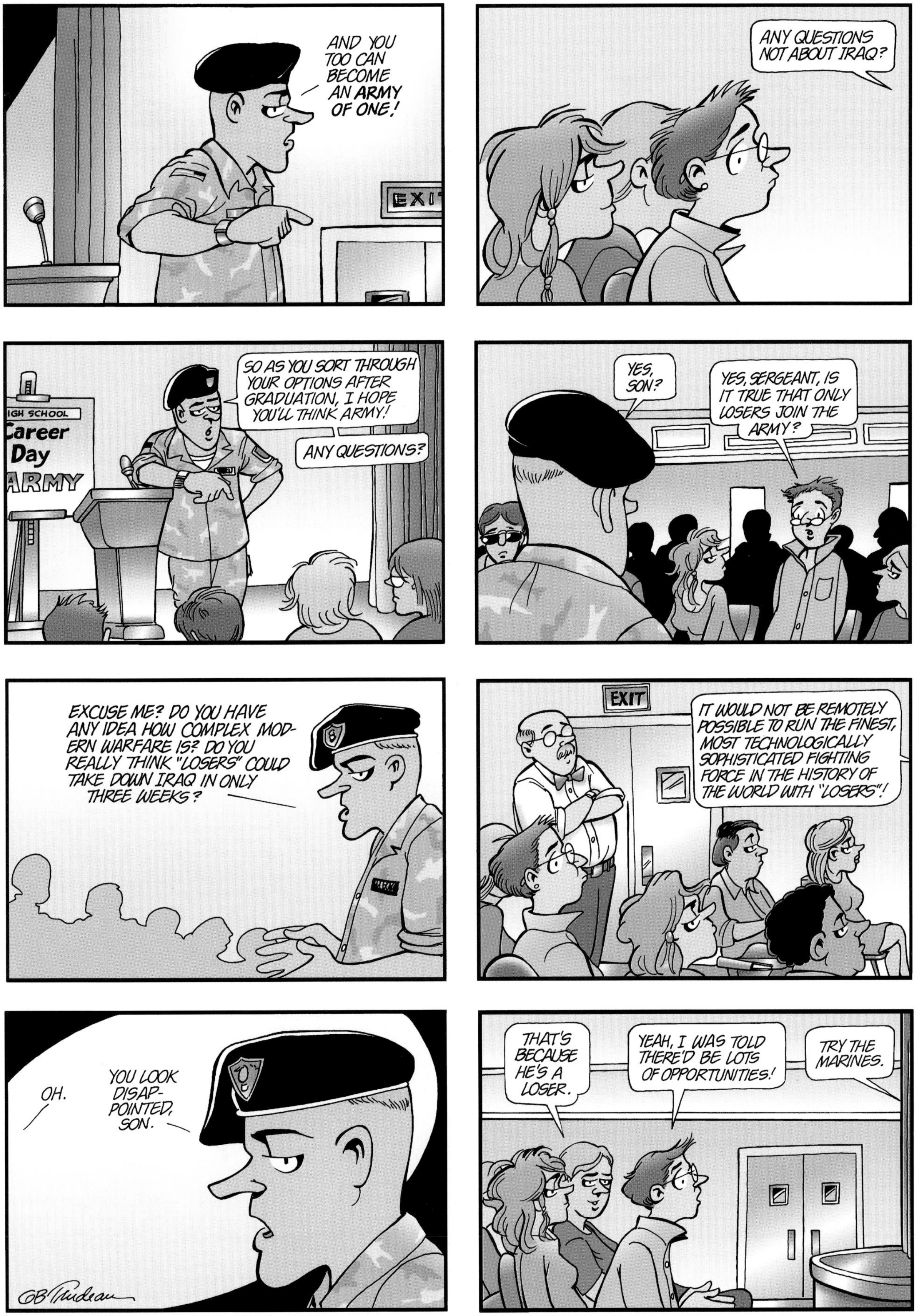
AND YOU TOO CAN BECOME AN ARMY OF ONE!
EXIT
ANY QUESTIONS NOT ABOUT IRAQ?
Career Day
SO AS YOU SORT THROUGH YOUR OPTIONS AFTER GRADUATION, I HOPE YOU'LL THINK ARMY!
ANY QUESTIONS?
YES, SON?
YES, SERGEANT, IS IT TRUE THAT ONLY LOSERS JOIN THE ARMY?
EXCUSE ME? DO YOU HAVE ANY IDEA HOW COMPLEX MODERN WARFARE IS? DO YOU REALLY THINK "LOSERS" COULD TAKE DOWN IRAQ IN ONLY THREE WEEKS?
EXIT
IT WOULD NOT BE REMOTELY POSSIBLE TO RUN THE FINEST, MOST TECHNOLOGICALLY SOPHISTICATED FIGHTING FORCE IN THE HISTORY OF THE WORLD WITH "LOSERS"!
YOU LOOK DISAP-POINTED, SON.
OH.
GBTrudeau
THAT'S BECAUSE HE'S A LOSER.
YEAH, I WAS TOLD THERE'D BE LOTS OF OPPORTUNITIES!
TRY THE MARINES.

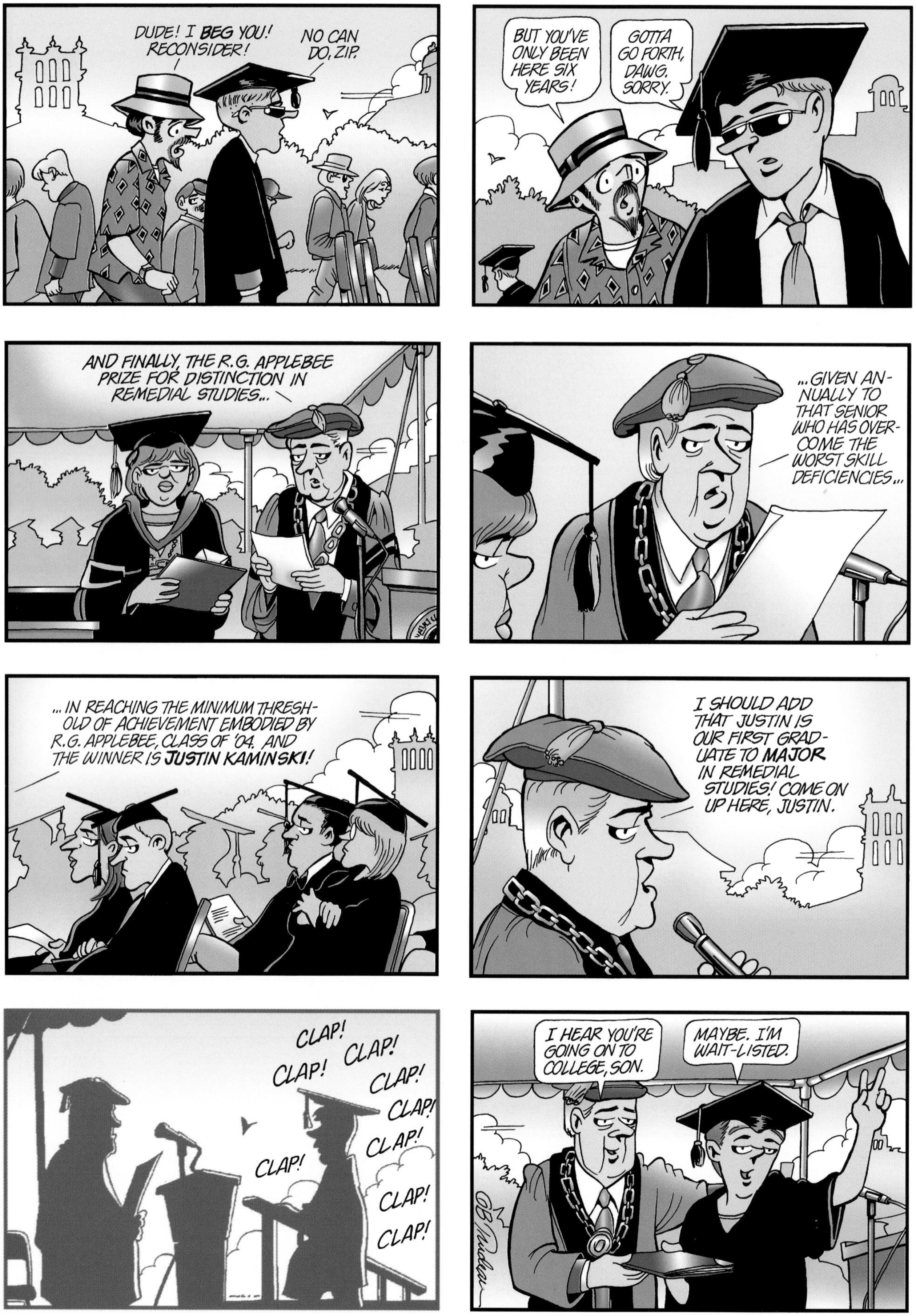
DUDE! I BEG YOU! RECONSIDER!
NO CAN DO, ZIP.
BUT YOU'VE ONLY BEEN HERE SIX YEARS!
GOTTA GO FORTH, DAWG. SORRY.
AND FINALLY, THE R.G. APPLEBEE PRIZE FOR DISTINCTION IN REMEDIAL STUDIES...
...GIVEN ANNUALLY TO THAT SENIOR WHO HAS OVERCOME THE WORST SKILL DEFICIENCIES...
...IN REACHING THE MINIMUM THRESHOLD OF ACHIEVEMENT EMBODIED BY R.G. APPLEBEE, CLASS OF '04. AND THE WINNER IS JUSTIN KAMINSKI!
I SHOULD ADD THAT JUSTIN IS OUR FIRST GRADUATE TO MAJOR IN REMEDIAL STUDIES! COME ON UP HERE, JUSTIN.
CLAP! CLAP! CLAP! CLAP! CLAP! CLAP! CLAP! CLAP! CLAP!
I HEAR YOU'RE GOING ON TO COLLEGE, SON.
MAYBE. I'M WAIT-LISTED.

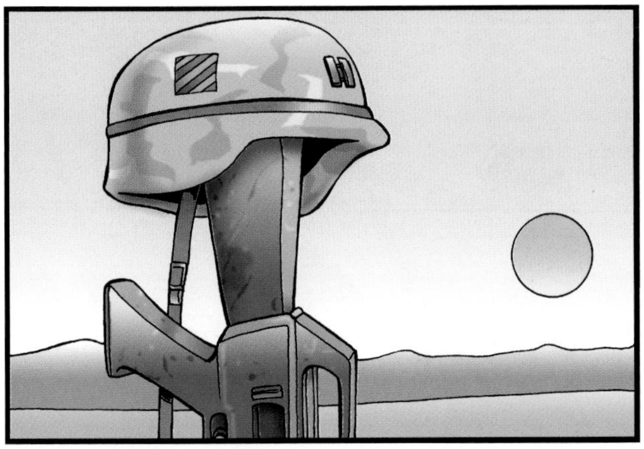

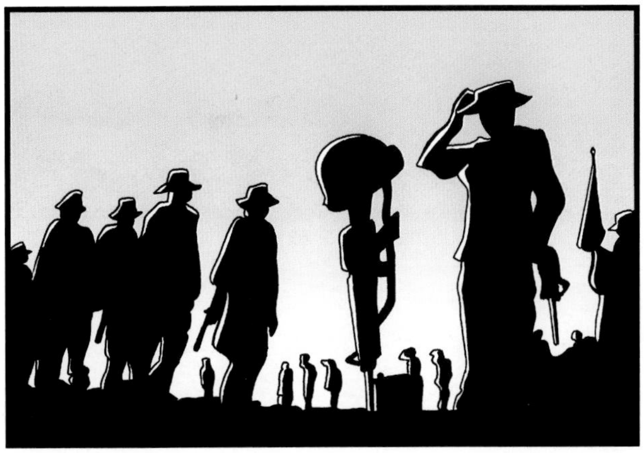

OPERATION IRAQI FREEDOM

IN MEMORIAM

SINCE 4/23/05 - PART I

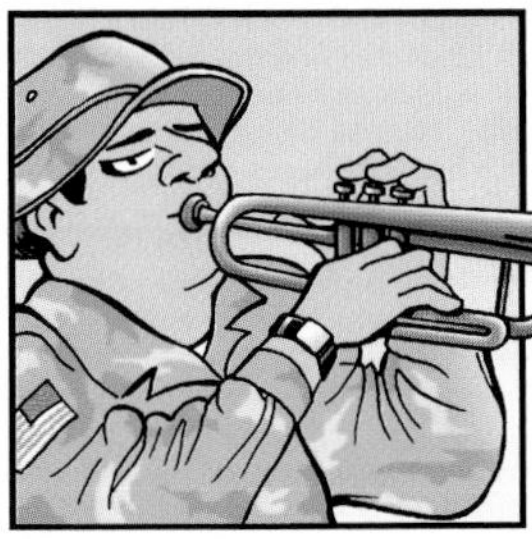

Robert Guy • Anthony Davis Jr. • Kevin Prince • Aaron Kent • Gary Walters Jr. Timmy Millsap • David Rice • Joseph Tremblay • William Edens • Eric Morris Robert Murray Jr. • Ricky Rockholt Jr. Timothy Kiser • Charles Cooper Jr. • Darren Deblanc • Stephen Frank • Clifford Gadsden Ralph Harting III • Juan Garcia-Arana Kenya Parker • Derrick Lutters • Tommy Little • John McGee • Kelly Hinz • John Spahr • William Brooks • Stephen Saxton • Michael Postal • Aaron Cepeda Sr. • Lance Graham Michael Marzano • Jeffery Wiener Steven Givens • Thor Ingraham Nicolas Messmer • Gary Eckert Jr. Lawrence Philippon • Dustin Derga Stephen Baldwyn • Anthony Goodwin Marcus Mahdee • Taylor Prazynski • Michael Bordelon • Samuel Castle • Kendall Ivy II

John Schmidt III • Wesley Davids • Christopher Dixon • Nicholas Erdy • Jonathan Grant • Jourdan Grez • Andrew Jodon • John Smith • Kenneth Zeigler II • Travis Anderson • Charles Gillican III • Jacob Simpson • Wesley Riggs • Antwan Walker Wyatt Eisenhauer • Robin Fell • Bernard Sembly • Kurt Schamberg • Brad Wentz Tyler Creamean • Benjamin Morton • Kenneth Schall • Aaron Seesan • Charles Wilkerson • Carl Morgain • John Ogburn III • Joshua Brazee • Russell Verdugo • Bryan Barron • Audrey Lunsford • Saburant Parker • Daniel Varnado • Christopher Perez Randy Collins • Charles Drier • Dustin Fisher • Jeffrey Wallace • Peter Hahn • Alfred Siler • David Wimberg • Ricardo Crocker • Matthew Lourey • Mark Maida • Joshua Scott • Phillip Sayles • Albert Smart • Michael Barnhill • Victor Cortes III • Derek Argel Casey Crate • William Downs • Jeremy Fresques • Jeffrey Starr • Steven Langmack Miguel Ramos • Phillip Edmundson • Louis Niedermeier • Virgil Case • Linda Villar Antonio Mendoza • Eric Poelman • Brian Ulbrich • Justin Vasquez • Theodore Westhusing • Carrie French • Brian Romines • Robert Mininger • Jonathan Smith Eric Burri • Terrence Crowe • Roberto Arizola Jr. • Michael Fasnacht • Douglas Kashmer • Louis Allen • Phillip Esposito • Marc Tucker • Mark Edwards • David Murray Daniel Chavez • Dustin Birch • Thomas Keeling • Devon Seymour • Brad Squires Mario Castillo • Andrew Kilpela • Stanley Lapinski • Neil Prince • Larry Arnold Sr. Casey Byers • Terrance Lee • Anthony Kinslow • Larry Kuhns Jr. • John Mattek Jr. Anthony Jones • Michael Hayes • Nathan Clemons • Joshua Klinger • Jonathan Flores

Jesse Jaime • Chad Maynard • Tyler Trovillion • Dion Whitley • Cesar Baez • Anthony Cometa • Erik Heldt • John Maloney • Robert Horrigan • Michael McNulty • Noah Harris • William Long • Adam Crumpler • Christopher Kilpatrick • Christopher Hoskins Nicholas Idalski • James Stewart • Brian Vaughn • Arnold Duplantier II • Christopher Phelps • Joseph Tackett • Holly Charette • Veashna Muy • Chad Powell • Ramona Valdez • Regina Clark • Carlos Pineda • Charles Kaufman • Matthew Coutu • Keith Mariotti • Steven Shepard • Rafael Carrillo Jr. • Manny Hornedo • Robert Hall Jr. Chad Mercer • Jeremy Brown • Ryan Montgomery • Scottie Bright • Lyle Cambridge Christopher Dickison • Anthony Mazzarella • Deyson Cariaga • Hoby Bradfield Jr. Eric Woods • Joseph Goodrich • Ryan Kovacicek • Timothy Sutton • Benyahmin Yahudah • Timothy Hines Jr. • Tricia Jameson • Clifton Mounce • Christopher Winchester • Jared Hartley • Jorge Pena-Romero • Travis Cooper • Ronald Wood Ronnie Williams • Frank Tiai • Efrain Sanchez Jr. • Lavena Johnson • Arthur McGill Jefferey Farrow • Steven Gill • Travis Youngblood • Bryan Opskar • Ernest Dallas Jr. Jason Montefering • Milton Monzon Jr. • Christopher Taylor • Ramon Villatoro Jr. Jacques Brunson • Carl Fuller • James Kinlow • John Thomas • Adam Harting • Adrian Butler • Edward Myers • John Tollefson • Benjamin Jansky • Christopher Lyons Andre Williams • Ernesto Guerra • Jason Scheuerman • Robert Swaney • Victor Anderson • Jonathon Haggin • David Jones Sr. • Ronnie Shelley Sr. • James Carroll Jeffrey Boskovitch • Roger Castleberry Jr. • David Coullard • Daniel Deyarmin Jr.

James Graham III • Brian Montgomery • Nathaniel Rock • James McNaughton Thomas Hull • Jerry Ganey Jr. • Mathew Gibbs • Charles Warren • Adam Strain Timothy Bell • Eric Bernholtz • Nicholas Bloem • Michael Cifuentes • Christopher Dyer Grant Fraser • Bradley Harper • Justin Hoffman • David Kreuter • Aaron Reed Edward Schroeder II • David Stewart • Kevin Waruinge • William Wightman • Nils Thompson • Chad Simon • Brett Walden • Robert Derenda • Terry Ball Jr. • Brahim Jeffcoat • Kurt Krout • Chase Comley • Seferino Reyna • Anthony Kalladeen Hernando Rios • Ramon Cordova • Miguel Carrasquillo • Nathaniel Detample • John Kulick • Ryan Ostrom • Gennaro Pellegrini Jr. • Francis Straub Jr. • Michael Benson Evenor Herrera • Rusty Bell • David Giaimo • Brian Derks • Toccara Green • Asbury Hawn II • Gary Reese Jr. • Shannon Taylor • Jose Ruiz • Joshua Dingler • Paul Saylor Thomas Strickland • Michael Stokely • Nathan Bouchard • Jeremy Doyle • Ray Fuhrmann II • Timothy Seamans • Willard Partridge • Elden Arcand • Brian Morris Joseph Nurre • James Cathey • Hatim Kathiria • Joseph Hunt • Victoir Lieurance Ramon Romero • Carlos Diaz • Chris Chapin • Trevor Diesing • Ivica Jerak • Timothy Shea • Joseph Martinez • Obediah Kolath • Dennis Hay • Charles Rubado • Gregory Fester • Jason Ames • Monta Ruth • Lowell Miller II • George Draughn Jr. • Robert Hollar Jr. • Lonnie Parson • Matthew Bohling • Jeffrey Williams • Luke Williams • Jude Jonaus • Franklin Vilorio • Robert Martens • Christopher Everett • Kurtis Arcala Jeremy Campbell • Robert Macrum • Alfredo Silva • Shane Swanberg

Matthew Deckard • David Ford IV • Alan Gifford • Regilio Nelom • Mark Dooley Michael Egan • William Evans • William Fernandez • Lawrence Morrison • William Allers III • Pierre Raymond • Travis Arndt • Kevin Jones • Scott McLaughlin • Mike Sonoda Jr. • Andrew Derrick • Paul Neubauer • Daniel Schelle • Brian Dunlap • Shawn Graham • Casey Howe • Tulsa Tuliau • Howard Allen • Andrew Wallace • Michael Wendling • Elijah Ortega • Jason Benford • Elizabeth Jacobson • Daniel Arnold Oliver Brown • Steve Morin Jr. • George Pugliese • Eric Slebodnik • Lee Wiegand Joshua Kynoch • Jens Schelbert • Marshall Westbrook • Timothy Roark • Roberto Baez • Bryan Large • Jacob Vanderbosch • Sean Berry • Larry Pankey Jr. • John Stalvey • Andrew Bedard • Brian Joplin • Jeremiah Robinson • Shayne Cabino Nicholas Cherava • Jason Frye • Patrick Kenny • Daniel McVicker • Carl Raines II Eric Fifer • Nicholas Greer • Sergio Escobar • Gary Harper Jr. • Leon James II • Leon Johnson • Brandon Sneed • Jerry Bonifacio Jr. • Jeremy Hodge • Matthew Kimmell Donald Furman • Lorenzo Ruiz • James Grijalva • Kenneth Hunt Jr. • Robert Tucker Howard Babcock IV • Samuel Boswell • Bernard Ceo • Brian Conner • Thomas Byrd Jeffrey Corban • Richard Hardy • Vincent Summers • Timothy Watkins • Mark Adams Paul Pillen • Daniel Bubb • Chad Hildebrandt • Christopher Poston • Lucas Frantz Daniel Bartels • Arthur Mora Jr. • Russell Nahvi • Jose Rosario • Tommy Folks Jr. Kendall Frederick • Norman Anderson III • Jacob Dones • Dennis Merck • Richard Pummill • Andrew Russoli • Steven Szwydek • Kenneth Butler • Benny Cockerham III

Tyler Swisher • Seamus Davey • Christopher Thompson • George Alexander Jr. Jonathan Spears • Michael Robertson • Benjamin Hoeffner • Christopher Monroe • Ramon Acevedoaponte • Lewis Gentry • Thomas Wallsmith Evan Parker • James Witkowski • Michael Mackinnon • William Wood Daniel Lightner Jr. • Robert Eckfield Jr. • Jared Kremm • Dillon Jutras Debra Banaszak • Kenny Rojas • Shaker Guy • Raymond Hill II Joel Dameron • Michael Hodshire • William Byler • Adam Johnson David Martin • Jonathan Tessar • Robert Oneto-Sikorski • Derence Jack • Matthew Kading • Wilgene Lieto • Daniel Tsue • Allan Espiritu • Dennis Ferderer Jr. • Tyler MacKenzie • Joshua Munger • Benjamin Smith • Mark Procopio Gerald Bloomfield II • Michael Martino Darren Howe

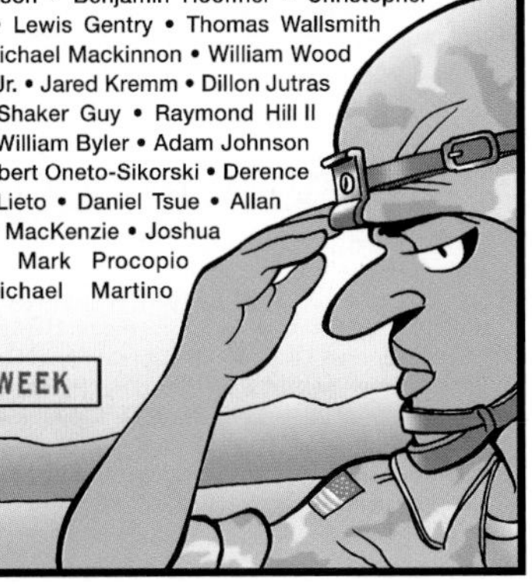

CONTINUED NEXT WEEK

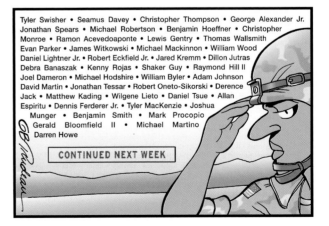

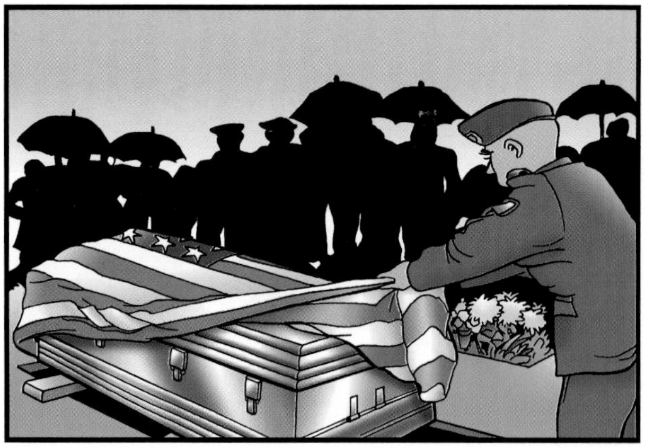

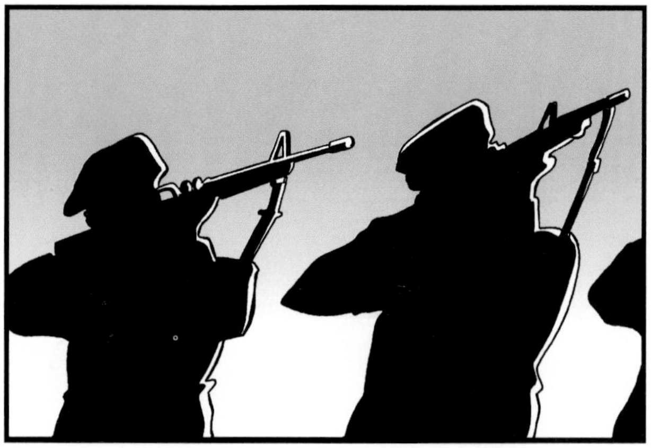

OPERATION IRAQI FREEDOM

IN MEMORIAM

SINCE 4/23/05 - PART II

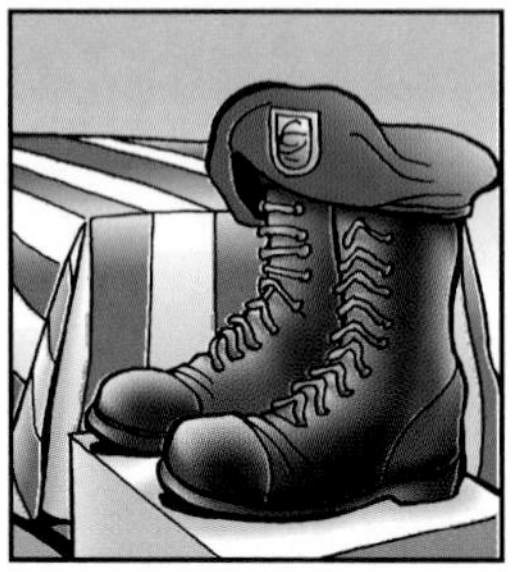

Jeffrey Toczylowski • Daniel Pratt • Kyle Wehrly • Jason Fegler • James Gurbisz Dustin Yancey • Timothy Brown • Darrell Boatman • Thomas Wren • Joel Cahill James Hayes • Ryan Sorensen • Brian Freeman • Robert Pope II • Mario Reyes Justin Smith • Alwyn Cashe • Jeremy Tamburello • Michael Parrott • Joshua Terando • Daniel Swaim • Tyrone Chisholm • Donald Fisher II • Antonio Sanchez • Stephen Sutherland • David Ruiz • Scott Zubowski • John Longoria Christopher McCrackin • Ramon Mendoza Jr. • James Estep • Travis Grigg • Matthew Holley • Nickolas Schiavoni • Dylan Paytas Alexis Roman-Cruz • Roger Deeds John Lucente • Donald McGlothin Jeremy Murray • Jeffry Rogers • Joshua Ware • Ivan Alarcon • Vernon Widner Anthony Gaunky • Luis Reyes

Christopher Alcozer • Jonathan Blair• Dominic Hinton • Michael Idanan Edward Karolasz • Anthony Yost • Dennis Zilinski • Miguel Terrazas • Tyler Troyer Dominic Sacco • John Dearing • Denis Gallardo • Aram Bass • Allen Knop William Meeuwsen • Ryan Christensen • Marc Delgado • Eric Pearrow • Steven Reynolds • Javier Villanueva • Gregory Tull • Brett Angus • Donald Hasse • Jerry Mills Jr. • Grzegorz Jakoniuk • William Richardson • Joshua Snyder • William Taylor • Brent Adams • Daniel Clay • John Holmason • David Huhn • Adam Kaiser Robert Martinez • Anthony McElveen • Scott Modeen • Andrew Patten • Andy Stevens • Craig Watson • Philip Dodson Jr. • Marcus Futrell • Philip Travis Jimmy Shelton • Daniel Cuka • Richard Schild • Thomas Siekert • Brian Wright Michael Taylor • Joseph Bier • Kevin Smith • Spencer Akers • Milton Rivera-Vargas • Adrian Orosco • Julia Atkins • Kenith Casica • Clarence Floyd Jr. • Travis Nelson • James Moudy • Keith Bennett • Jared Kubasak • Curtis Mitchell • Lex Nelson • Brian Karim • James Kesinger • Peter Navarro • Michael Zyla • Kenneth Pospisil • Michael Presley • Timothy Boyce • Joseph Lucas • Adam Fales Samuel Tapia • Johnnie Mason • Michael Cleary • Richard Naputi • Benjamin Britt William Lopez-Feliciano • Regina Reali • Cheyenne Willey • Joseph Andres Jr. Myla Maravillosa • Anthony Cardinal • Sergio Gudino • Dominic Coles • Richard Salter • Isaias Santos • Dane Carver • Joshua Morberg • Lance Sage • Aaron Forbes • George Lutz II • Prince Teewia • Shawn Dostie • Jonathan Pfender

Ayman Taha • Marcelino Corniel • Jason Bishop • Christopher Vanderhorn William Hecker III • Jason Lopezreyes • Robbie Mariano • Johnny Peralez Jr. Christopher Petty • Ryan Walker • Stephen White • Michael McLaughlin • Adam Cann • Albert Gettings • Ryan McCurdy • Radhames Camilomatos • Joseph deMoors • Douglas LaBouff • Michael Martinez • Clinton Upchurch • Jaime Campbell • Michael Edwards • Jacob Melson • Chester Troxel • Stuart Anderson Nathan Field • Robert Johnson • Darren Braswell • Kyle Brown • Jeriad Jacobs Jason Little • Brett Lundstrom • Raul Mercado • Michael McMullen • Mitchell Carver Jr. • Kyle Jackson • Jonathan Price • Michael Jordan • Justin Watts Kasper Dudkiewicz • Dustin Kendall • Ruel Garcia • Rex Kenyon • Adam Shepherd • Dennis Flanagan • Matthew Frantz • Rickey Scott • Clifton Yazzie Carlos Pandura • Brandon Dewey • Brian McElroy • Jason Norton • Lance Chase Matthew Hunter • Peter Wagler • Lewis Calapini • Joshua Scott • Sean Miles Jerry Durbin Jr. • Joshua Johnson • Hugo Lopez • David Herrera • Brian Schoff Felipe Barbosa • Garrison Avery • Marlon Bustamante • Anthony Owens Caesar Viglienzone • Sean Cardelli • Simon Cox Jr. • Walter Howard II • Scott Messer • Lance Cornett • Jesse Zamora • Roberto Salazar • Jeremiah Boehmer William Hayes III • Sergio Saez • Christopher Morningstar • Patrick Herried Orville Gerena • David Parr • Brandon Schuck • Jacob Spann • Allen Kokesh Jr. Steven Phillips • Javier Chavez Jr. • Ross Smith • Felipe Villareal

Andrew Kemple • Nicholas Wilson • Matthew Barnes • Michael Probst • Rusty Washam • Anthony Garcia • Amos Edwards Jr. • Charles Matheny IV • Matthew Conley • Jessie Davila • Daniel Kuhlmeier • Jay Collado • Almar Fitzgerald Gregson Gourley • Curtis Howard II • Rickey Jones • Christopher Marion Gordon Misner II • Allan Morr • Thomas Wilwerth • Dimitri Muscat • Joshua Powers • Benjamin Schuster • John Thornton • Adam VanAlstine • Clay Farr Joshua Humble • Joshua Pearce • Christopher Schornak • Dwayne Lewis • Tina Priest • Christopher Merchant • Joshua Youmans • Matthew Snyder • Kevin Jessen • Adam Zanutto • Ricky Salas Jr. • Justin Martone • John Fry • Bunny Long • Amy Duerksen • Kristen Marino • Corey Dan • Bryan Lewis • Marco Silva Angelo Zawaydeh • Carlos Gonzalez • Amanda Pinson • Nyle Yates III • Ricardo Barraza • Dale Brehm • Antoine McKinzie • Brock Beery • Randy McCaulley Frederick Carlson • Michael Rowe • Sean Tharp • Robert Hernandez • Walter Moss Jr. • Joseph Duenas • Jacob Beisel • Darrell Clay • Israel Garcia • Michael Hartwick • Timothy Moshier • Jeremy Ehle • Andres Aguilar Jr. • David Bass Patrick Gallagher • Kun Kim • Eric McIntosh • Eric Palmisano • Scott Procopio Felipe Sandoval-Flores • Brian St. Germain • Abraham Twitchell • Marcques Nettles • Geovani Aleman • Ty Johnson • Dustin Harris • Daniel Sesker • Chase Edwards • Bryan Taylor • Richard Waller • Shawn Creighton • Jody Missildine Philip Martini • Juana Navarro Arellano • David Collins • Joseph Love-Fowler

List as of April 25, 2006. For update go to www.icasualties.org

Gregory Rogers • James Gardner • Randall Lamberson • Joseph Blanco • James Costello III • Kenneth Hess • George Roehl Jr. • Scott Bandhold • Roland Calderon-Ascencio • Marcus Glimpse • Andrew Waits • Salem Bachar • Stephen Perez • Darin Settle • Mark Melcher • Derrick Cothran • Pablo Mayorga • Justin Sims • Ryan Winslow • Clinton Cubert • Ian Weikel • Robert Settle • Patrick Tinnell • Jason Ramseyer • Travis Zimmerman • Eric Lueken • Jason Daniel

OPERATION ENDURING FREEDOM (AFGHANISTAN) SINCE 4/23/05

Clayton Adamkavicius • John Stone • Christopher Robinson • Nicholas Anderson Joshua Hill • Anton Hiett • Kevin Akins • Joseph Ray • Emigdio Elizarraras • Luis Sanchez • Alecia Good • Bryan Willard • Nicholas Sovie • Jonathan McColley Matthieu Marcellus • Donnie Levens • Samuel Large Jr. • James Fordyce Brandon Dronet • Alberto Montrond • Chad Gonsalves • Clinton Newman • Edwin Dazachacon • Matthew Bertolino • John Fralish • Billy Brixey Jr. • Tobias Meister Jason Hasenauer • John Morton • Matthew Steyart • Emory Turpin • James Ochsner • Travis Nixon • Joseph Cruz • Fabricio Moreno • Scott Mullen • Troy Ezernack • Benny Franklin • Moses Armstead • James Stoddard Jr. • John Doles Steven Valdez • Robert White • Kenneth Ross • Tane Baum • Adrian Stump Patrick Stewart • John Flynn • Ryan Nass • Derek Hines • Damion Campbell

Christopher L. Palmer • Michael R. Lehmiller • Joshua Hyland • Blake Hall Phillip George • Robert Davis • Laura Walker • Jeremy Chandler • Edward Heselton • Christopher Katzenberger • Christopher Falkel • John M. Henderson Jr. • Damian Garza • Theodore Clark Jr. • Michael Schafer Jason Palmerton • Matthew Axelson • Michael Murphy • Danny Dietz Jeffrey Taylor • James Suh • Eric Shane Patton • Michael McGreevy Jr. • Jeffery Lucas • Erik Kristensen • Daniel Healy Jacques Fontan • Chris Scherkenbach • Michael L. Russell Stephen Reich • James Ponder III • Marcus Muralles • Kip Jacoby Corey Goodnature • Shamus Goare • Kevin Joyce • Duane W. Dively Christopher Piper • Victor Cervantes • Emmanuel Hernandez Michael Kelley • Charles Robinson Leroy Alexander • Kyle Hemauer Steven Tucker • Nicholas Kirven Richard Schoener • Allen Johnson Robert Defazio • Robert White III

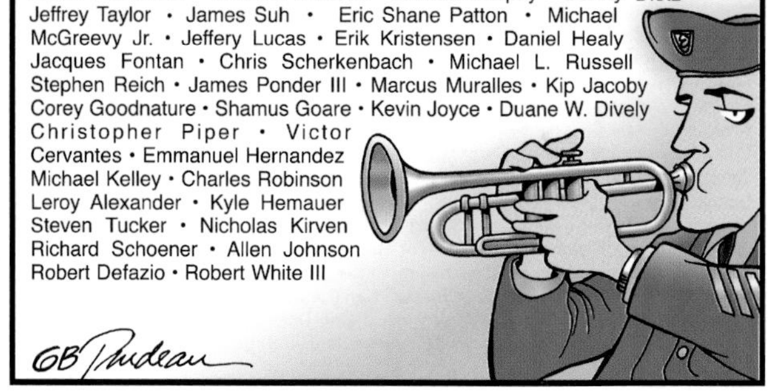
GB Trudeau

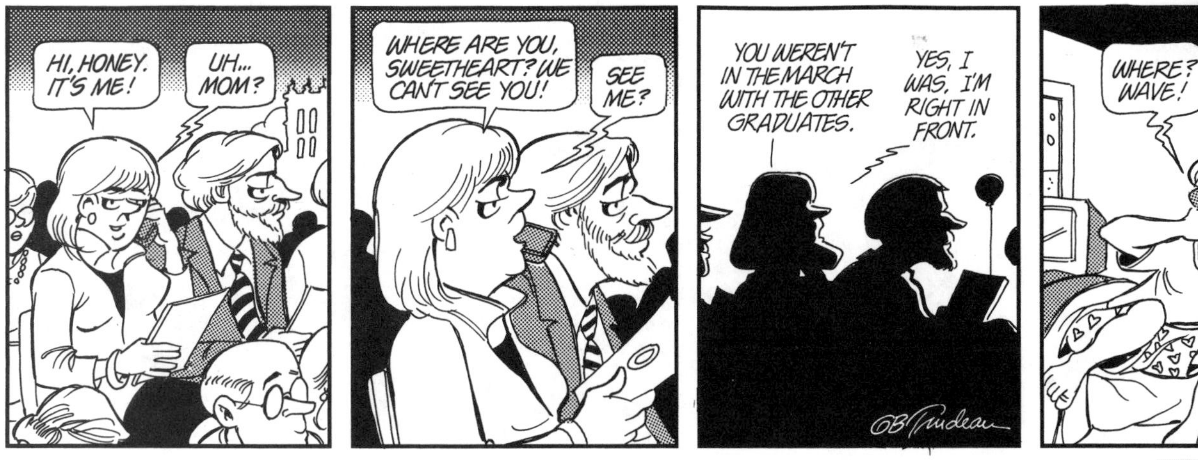
HI, HONEY. IT'S ME!
UH... MOM?
WHERE ARE YOU, SWEETHEART? WE CAN'T SEE YOU!
SEE ME?
YOU WEREN'T IN THE MARCH WITH THE OTHER GRADUATES.
YES, I WAS, I'M RIGHT IN FRONT.
GB Trudeau
WHERE? WAVE!
MOM, NO, THAT'S EMBARRASSING!

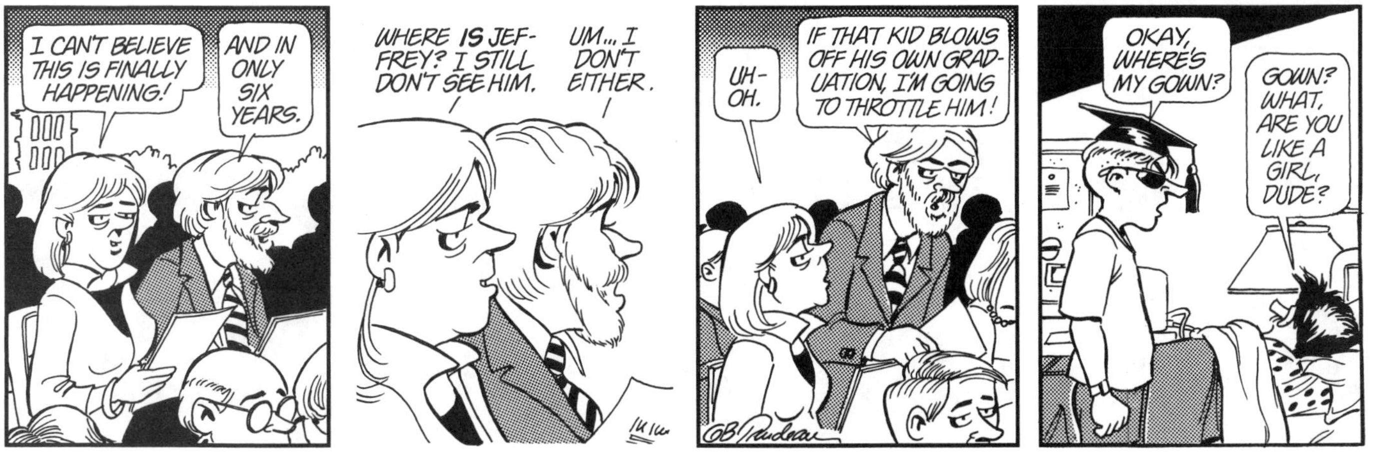
I CAN'T BELIEVE THIS IS FINALLY HAPPENING!
AND IN ONLY SIX YEARS.
WHERE IS JEFFREY? I STILL DON'T SEE HIM.
UM... I DON'T EITHER.
UH-OH.
IF THAT KID BLOWS OFF HIS OWN GRADUATION, I'M GOING TO THROTTLE HIM!
GB Trudeau
OKAY, WHERE'S MY GOWN?
GOWN? WHAT, ARE YOU LIKE A GIRL, DUDE?

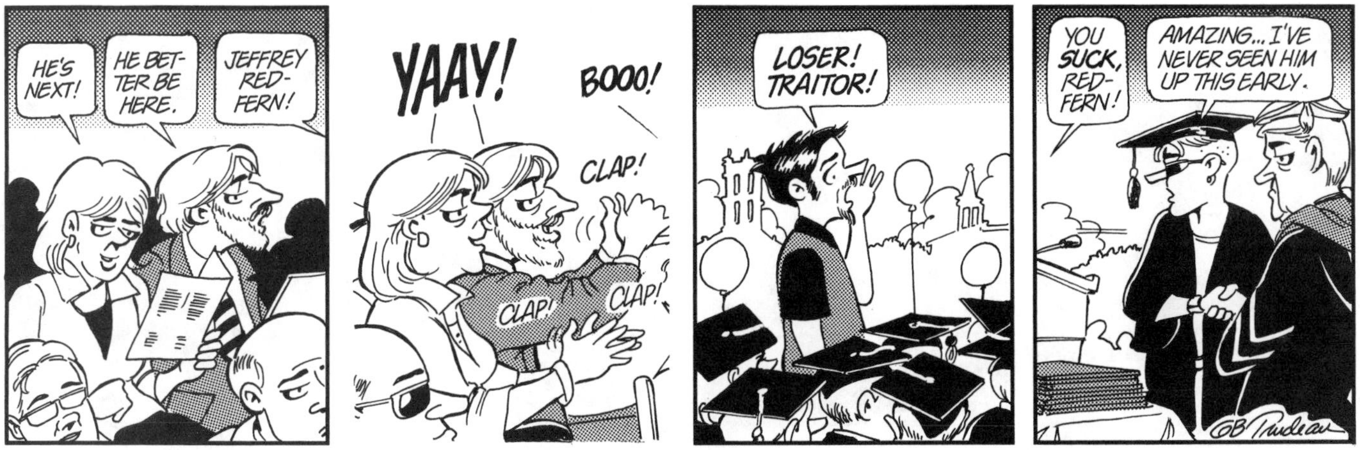
HE'S NEXT!
HE BETTER BE HERE.
JEFFREY REDFERN!
YAAY!
BOOO!
CLAP!
CLAP!
CLAP!
LOSER! TRAITOR!
YOU SUCK, REDFERN!
AMAZING... I'VE NEVER SEEN HIM UP THIS EARLY.
GB Trudeau

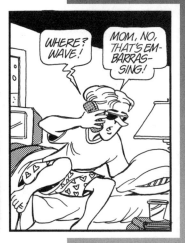

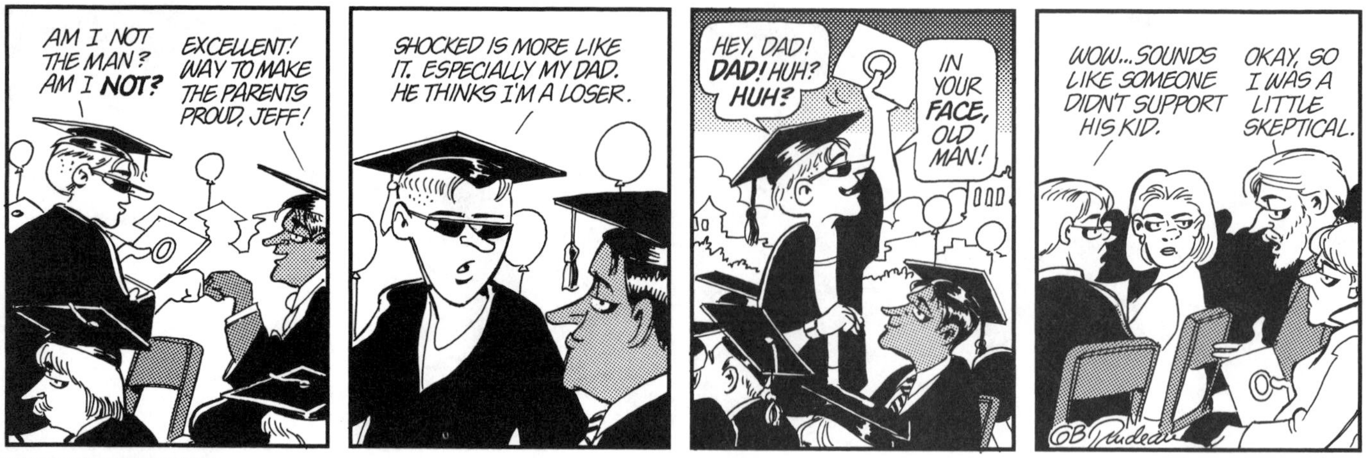
AM I NOT THE MAN? AM I **NOT?**
EXCELLENT! WAY TO MAKE THE PARENTS PROUD, JEFF!
SHOCKED IS MORE LIKE IT. ESPECIALLY MY DAD. HE THINKS I'M A LOSER.
HEY, DAD! **DAD!** HUH? **HUH?**
IN YOUR **FACE,** OLD MAN!
WOW... SOUNDS LIKE SOMEONE DIDN'T SUPPORT HIS KID.
OKAY, SO I WAS A LITTLE SKEPTICAL.
GB Trudeau

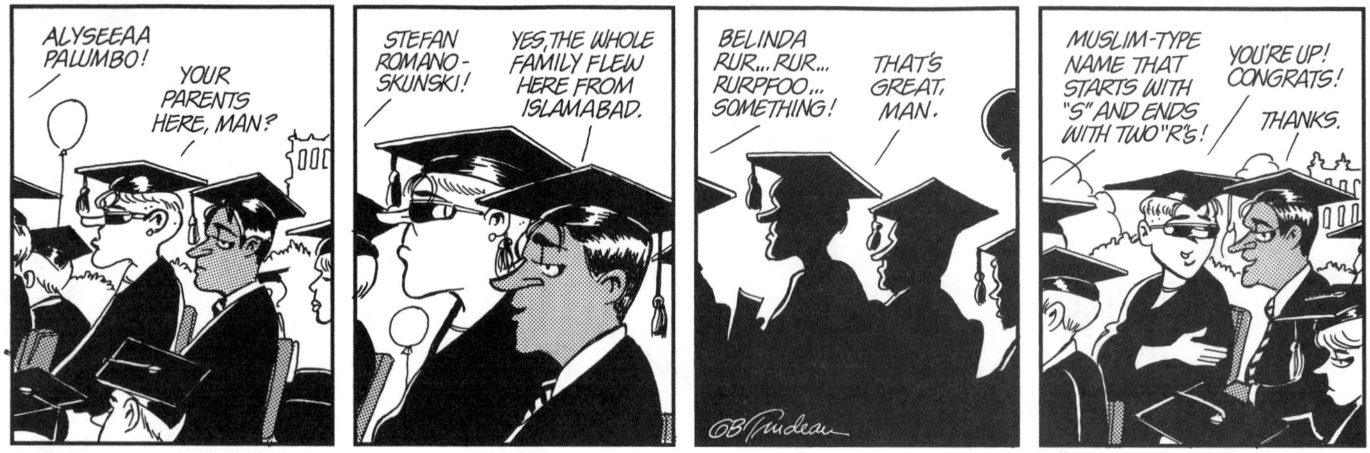
ALYSEEAA PALUMBO!
YOUR PARENTS HERE, MAN?
STEFAN ROMANO-SKUNSKI!
YES, THE WHOLE FAMILY FLEW HERE FROM ISLAMABAD.
BELINDA RUR... RUR... RURPFOO... SOMETHING!
THAT'S GREAT, MAN.
GB Trudeau
MUSLIM-TYPE NAME THAT STARTS WITH "S" AND ENDS WITH TWO "R"S!
YOU'RE UP! CONGRATS!
THANKS.

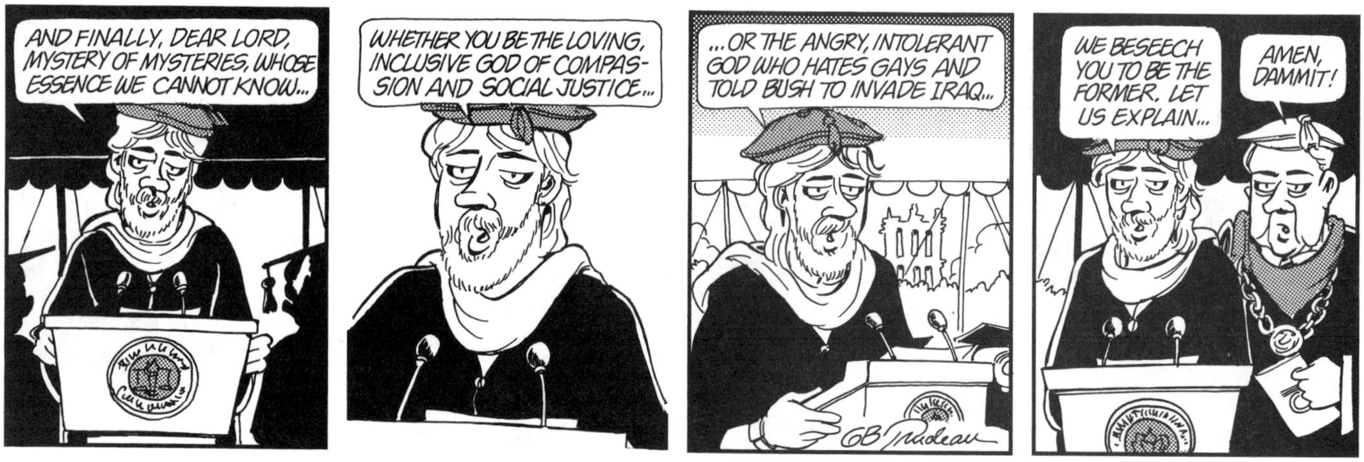
AND FINALLY, DEAR LORD, MYSTERY OF MYSTERIES, WHOSE ESSENCE WE CANNOT KNOW...
WHETHER YOU BE THE LOVING, INCLUSIVE GOD OF COMPASSION AND SOCIAL JUSTICE...
...OR THE ANGRY, INTOLERANT GOD WHO HATES GAYS AND TOLD BUSH TO INVADE IRAQ...
GB Trudeau
WE BESEECH YOU TO BE THE FORMER. LET US EXPLAIN...
AMEN, DAMMIT!

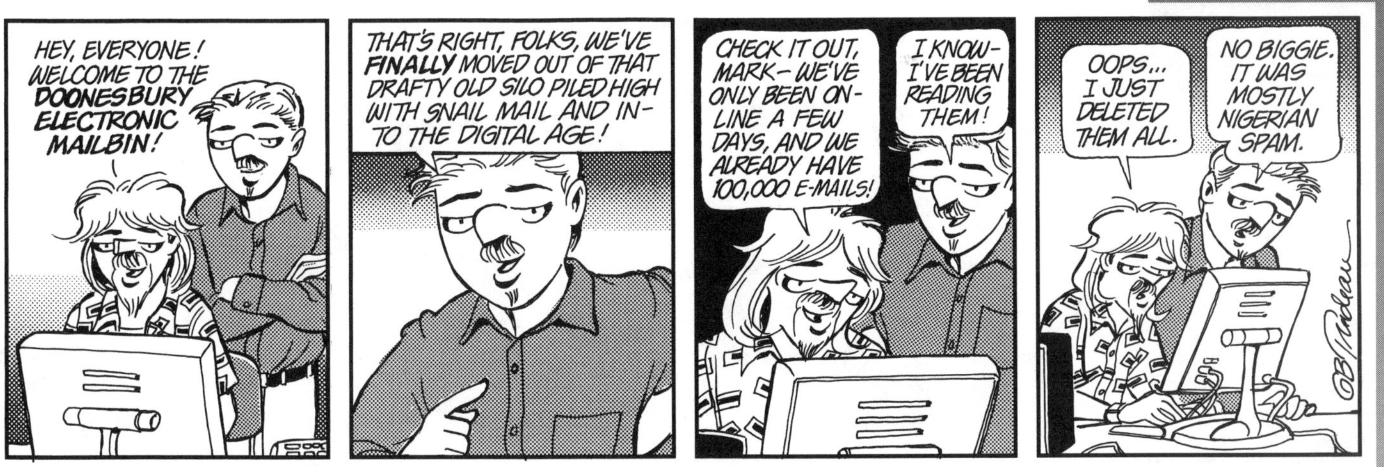
HEY, EVERYONE! WELCOME TO THE **DOONESBURY ELECTRONIC MAILBIN**!
THAT'S RIGHT, FOLKS, WE'VE **FINALLY** MOVED OUT OF THAT DRAFTY OLD SILO PILED HIGH WITH SNAIL MAIL AND INTO THE DIGITAL AGE!
CHECK IT OUT, MARK – WE'VE ONLY BEEN ON-LINE A FEW DAYS, AND WE ALREADY HAVE 100,000 E-MAILS!
I KNOW – I'VE BEEN READING THEM!
OOPS... I JUST DELETED THEM ALL.
NO BIGGIE. IT WAS MOSTLY NIGERIAN SPAM.
GBTrudeau

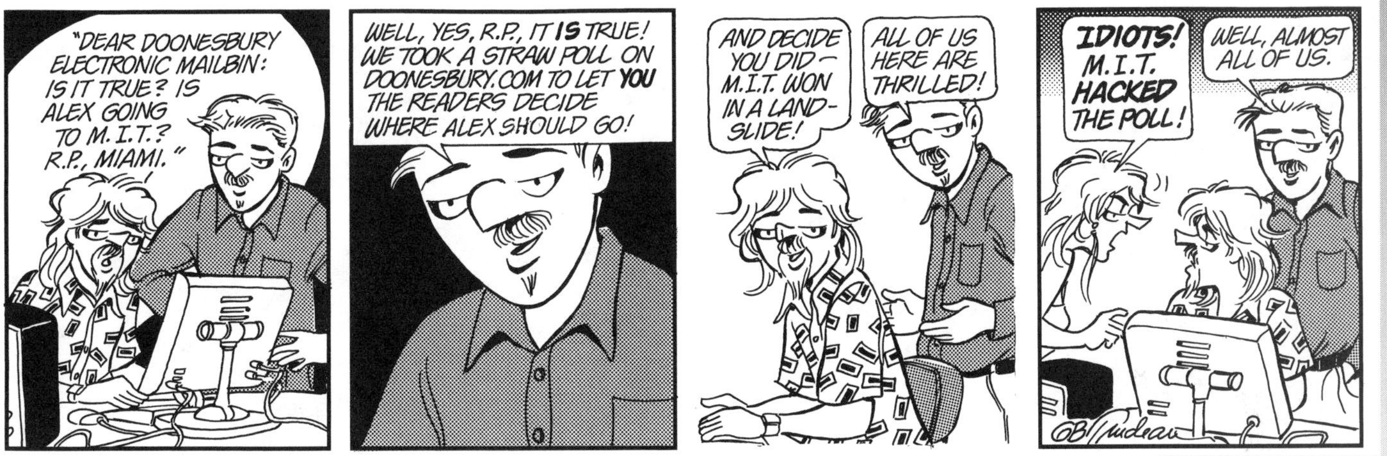
"DEAR DOONESBURY ELECTRONIC MAILBIN: IS IT TRUE? IS ALEX GOING TO M.I.T.? R.P., MIAMI."
WELL, YES, R.P., IT **IS** TRUE! WE TOOK A STRAW POLL ON DOONESBURY.COM TO LET **YOU** THE READERS DECIDE WHERE ALEX SHOULD GO!
AND DECIDE YOU DID – M.I.T. WON IN A LANDSLIDE!
ALL OF US HERE ARE THRILLED!
IDIOTS! M.I.T. **HACKED** THE POLL!
WELL, ALMOST ALL OF US.
GBTrudeau

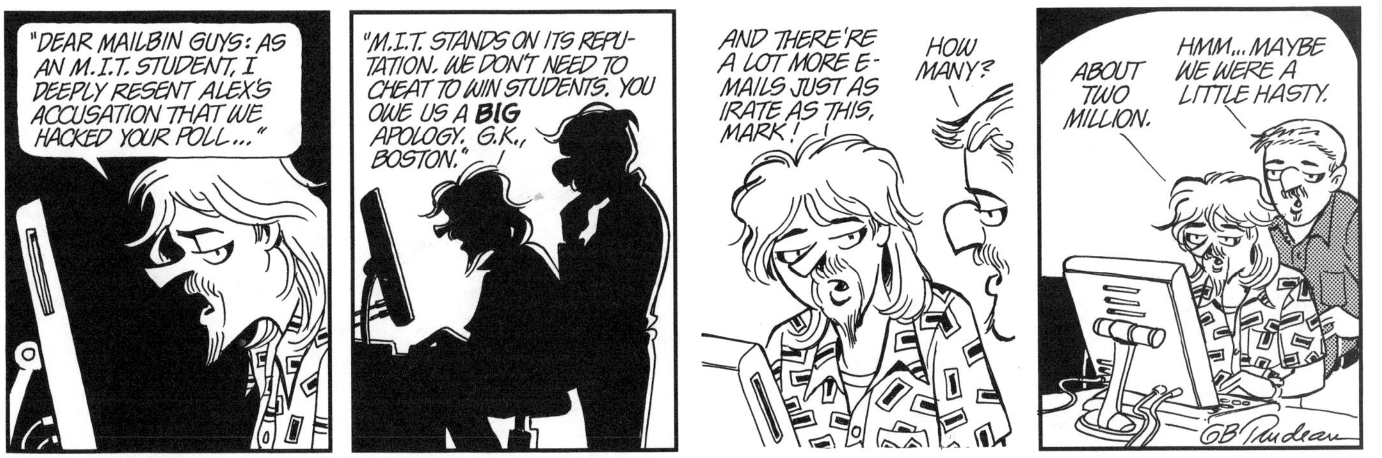
"DEAR MAILBIN GUYS: AS AN M.I.T. STUDENT, I DEEPLY RESENT ALEX'S ACCUSATION THAT WE HACKED YOUR POLL..."
"M.I.T. STANDS ON ITS REPUTATION. WE DON'T NEED TO CHEAT TO WIN STUDENTS. YOU OWE US A **BIG** APOLOGY. G.K., BOSTON."
AND THERE'RE A LOT MORE E-MAILS JUST AS IRATE AS THIS, MARK!
HOW MANY?
ABOUT TWO MILLION.
HMM... MAYBE WE WERE A LITTLE HASTY.
GBTrudeau

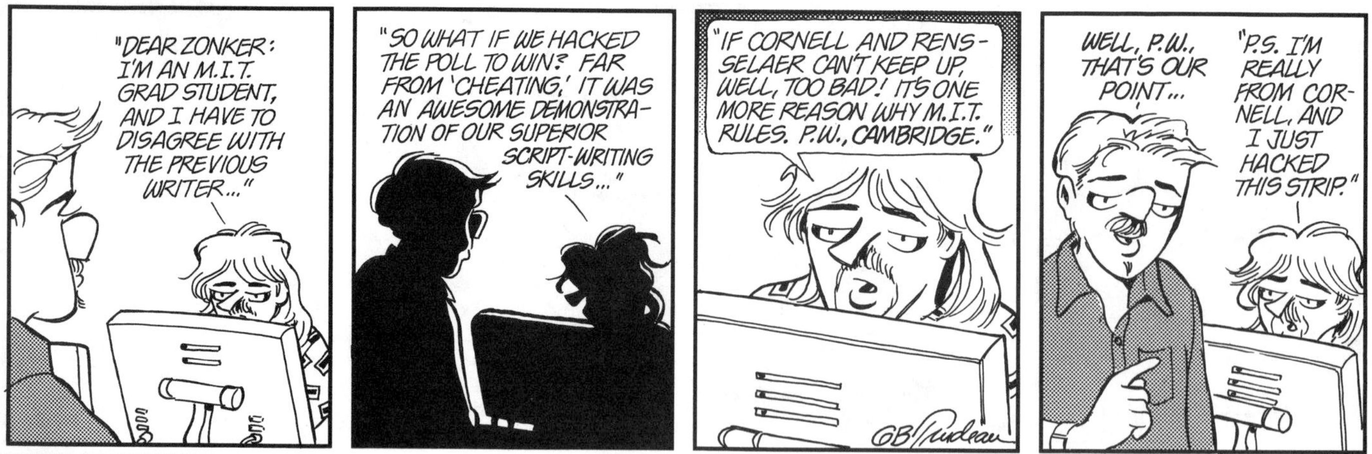
"DEAR ZONKER: I'M AN M.I.T. GRAD STUDENT, AND I HAVE TO DISAGREE WITH THE PREVIOUS WRITER..."
"SO WHAT IF WE HACKED THE POLL TO WIN? FAR FROM 'CHEATING,' IT WAS AN AWESOME DEMONSTRATION OF OUR SUPERIOR SCRIPT-WRITING SKILLS..."
"IF CORNELL AND RENSSELAER CAN'T KEEP UP, WELL, TOO BAD! IT'S ONE MORE REASON WHY M.I.T. RULES. P.W., CAMBRIDGE."
GB Trudeau
WELL, P.W., THAT'S OUR POINT...
"P.S. I'M REALLY FROM CORNELL, AND I JUST HACKED THIS STRIP."

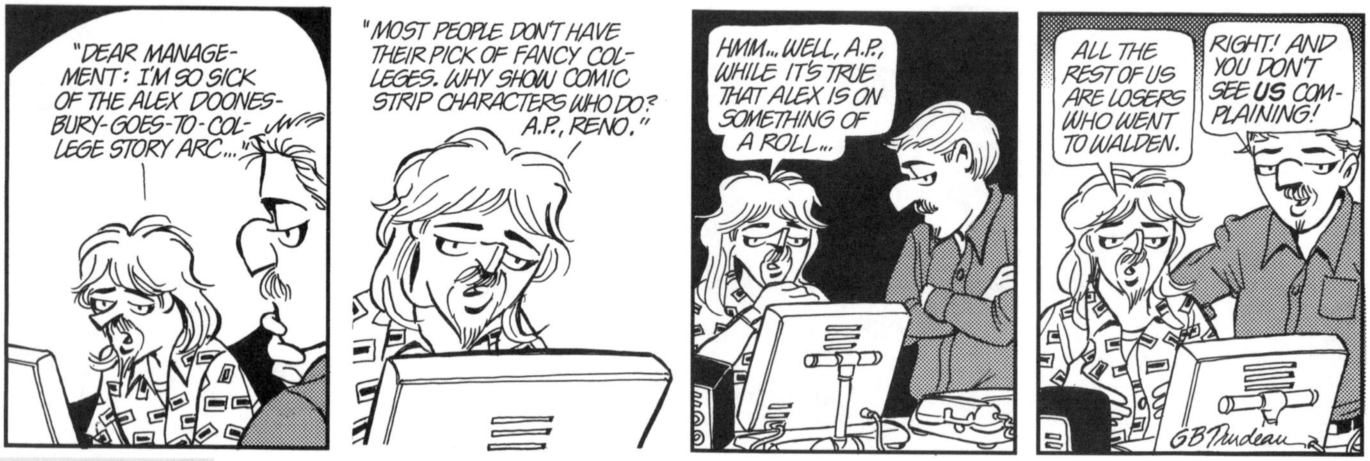
"DEAR MANAGEMENT: I'M SO SICK OF THE ALEX DOONESBURY-GOES-TO-COLLEGE STORY ARC..."
"MOST PEOPLE DON'T HAVE THEIR PICK OF FANCY COLLEGES. WHY SHOW COMIC STRIP CHARACTERS WHO DO? A.P., RENO."
HMM... WELL, A.P., WHILE IT'S TRUE THAT ALEX IS ON SOMETHING OF A ROLL...
ALL THE REST OF US ARE LOSERS WHO WENT TO WALDEN.
RIGHT! AND YOU DON'T SEE **US** COMPLAINING!
GB Trudeau

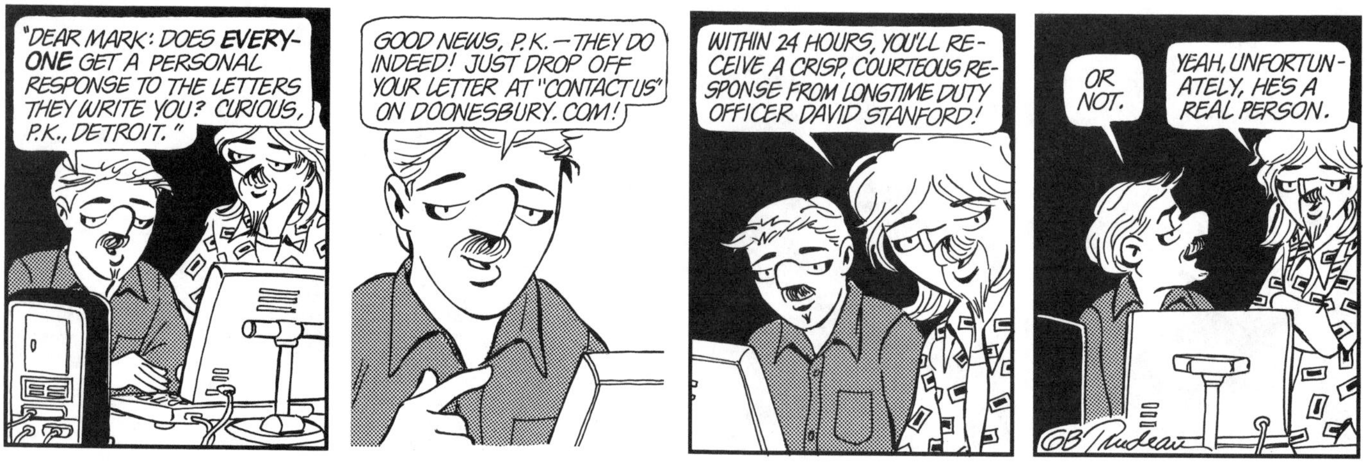
"DEAR MARK: DOES **EVERYONE** GET A PERSONAL RESPONSE TO THE LETTERS THEY WRITE YOU? CURIOUS, P.K., DETROIT."
GOOD NEWS, P.K.—THEY DO INDEED! JUST DROP OFF YOUR LETTER AT "CONTACT US" ON DOONESBURY.COM!
WITHIN 24 HOURS, YOU'LL RECEIVE A CRISP, COURTEOUS RESPONSE FROM LONGTIME DUTY OFFICER DAVID STANFORD!
OR NOT.
YEAH, UNFORTUNATELY, HE'S A REAL PERSON.
GB Trudeau

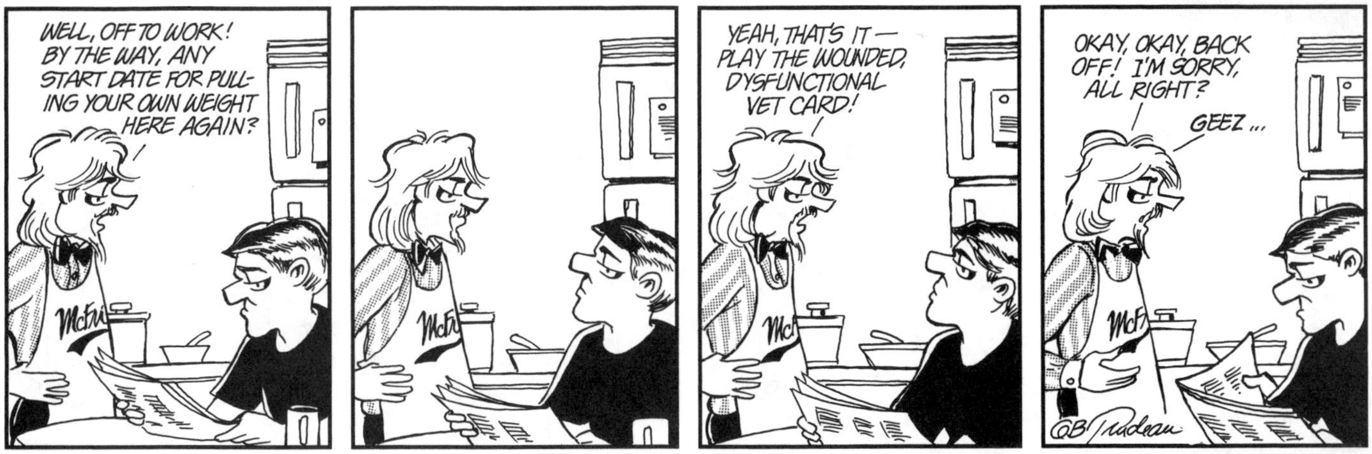
WELL, OFF TO WORK! BY THE WAY, ANY START DATE FOR PULLING YOUR OWN WEIGHT HERE AGAIN?
YEAH, THAT'S IT — PLAY THE WOUNDED, DYSFUNCTIONAL VET CARD!
OKAY, OKAY, BACK OFF! I'M SORRY, ALL RIGHT?
GEEZ ...

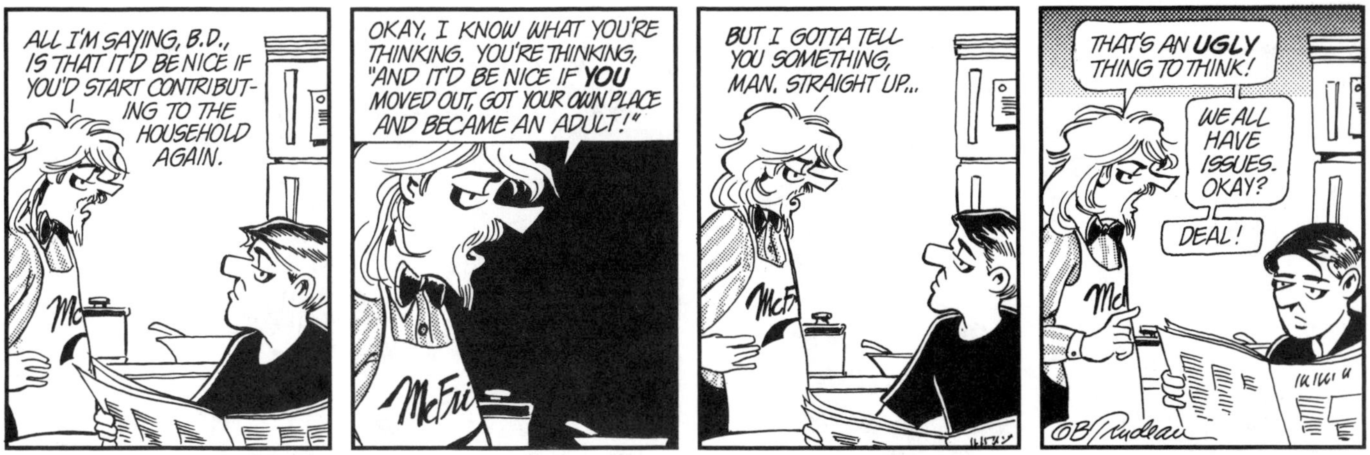
ALL I'M SAYING, B.D., IS THAT IT'D BE NICE IF YOU'D START CONTRIBUTING TO THE HOUSEHOLD AGAIN.
OKAY, I KNOW WHAT YOU'RE THINKING. YOU'RE THINKING, "AND IT'D BE NICE IF YOU MOVED OUT, GOT YOUR OWN PLACE AND BECAME AN ADULT!"
BUT I GOTTA TELL YOU SOMETHING, MAN. STRAIGHT UP...
THAT'S AN UGLY THING TO THINK!
WE ALL HAVE ISSUES. OKAY?
DEAL!

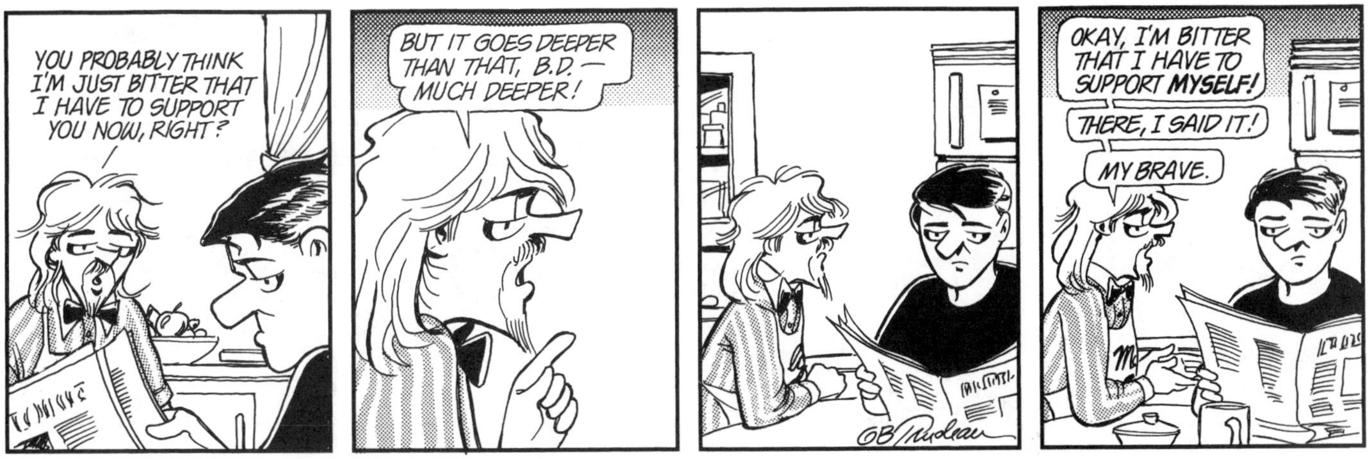
YOU PROBABLY THINK I'M JUST BITTER THAT I HAVE TO SUPPORT YOU NOW, RIGHT?
BUT IT GOES DEEPER THAN THAT, B.D. — MUCH DEEPER!
OKAY, I'M BITTER THAT I HAVE TO SUPPORT MYSELF!
THERE, I SAID IT!
MY BRAVE.

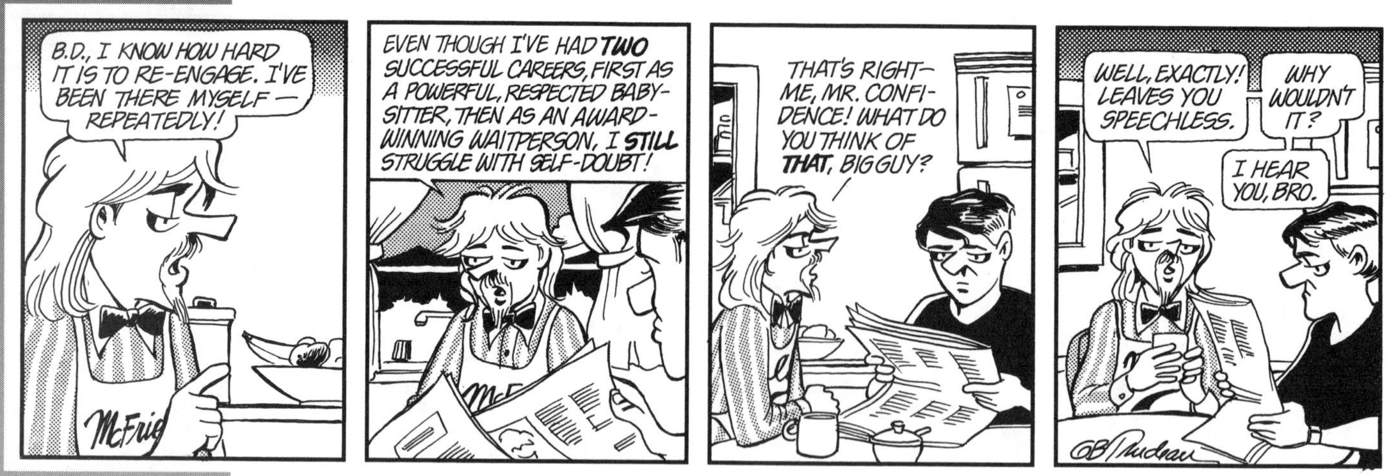
B.D., I KNOW HOW HARD IT IS TO RE-ENGAGE. I'VE BEEN THERE MYSELF — REPEATEDLY!
EVEN THOUGH I'VE HAD **TWO** SUCCESSFUL CAREERS, FIRST AS A POWERFUL, RESPECTED BABY-SITTER, THEN AS AN AWARD-WINNING WAITPERSON, I **STILL** STRUGGLE WITH SELF-DOUBT!
THAT'S RIGHT— ME, MR. CONFI-DENCE! WHAT DO YOU THINK OF **THAT**, BIG GUY?
WELL, EXACTLY! LEAVES YOU SPEECHLESS.
WHY WOULDN'T IT?
I HEAR YOU, BRO.

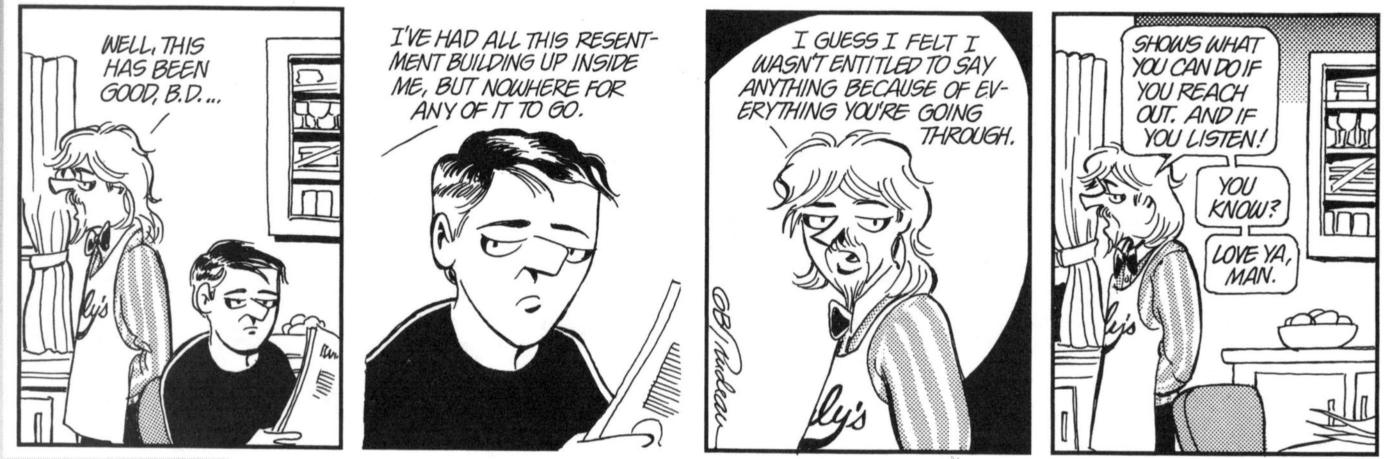
WELL, THIS HAS BEEN GOOD, B.D....
I'VE HAD ALL THIS RESENT-MENT BUILDING UP INSIDE ME, BUT NOWHERE FOR ANY OF IT TO GO.
I GUESS I FELT I WASN'T ENTITLED TO SAY ANYTHING BECAUSE OF EV-ERYTHING YOU'RE GOING THROUGH.
SHOWS WHAT YOU CAN DO IF YOU REACH OUT. AND IF YOU LISTEN!
YOU KNOW?
LOVE YA, MAN.

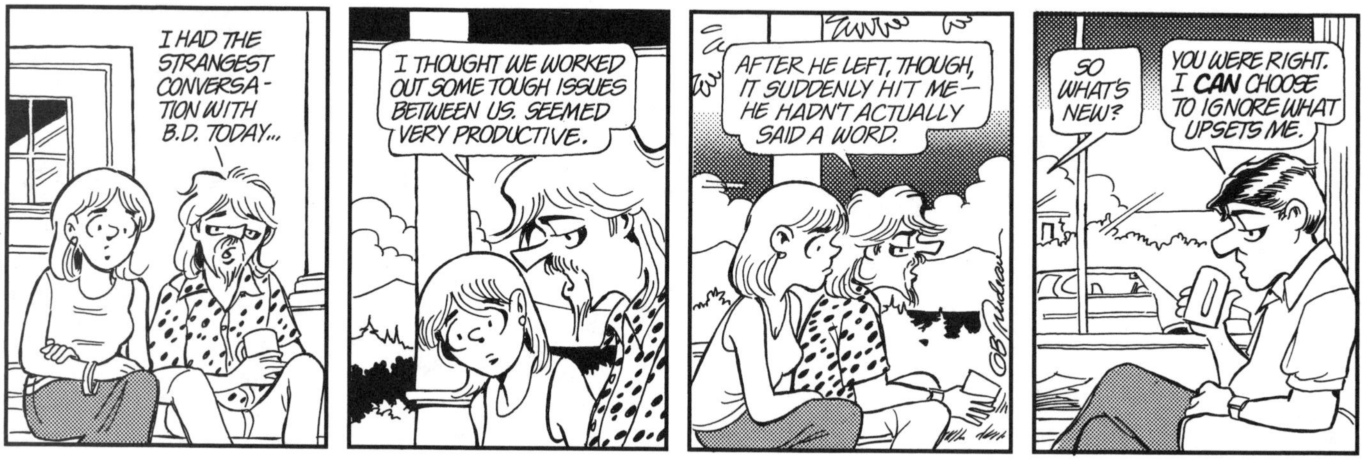
I HAD THE STRANGEST CONVERSA-TION WITH B.D. TODAY...
I THOUGHT WE WORKED OUT SOME TOUGH ISSUES BETWEEN US. SEEMED VERY PRODUCTIVE.
AFTER HE LEFT, THOUGH, IT SUDDENLY HIT ME— HE HADN'T ACTUALLY SAID A WORD.
SO WHAT'S NEW?
YOU WERE RIGHT. I **CAN** CHOOSE TO IGNORE WHAT UPSETS ME.

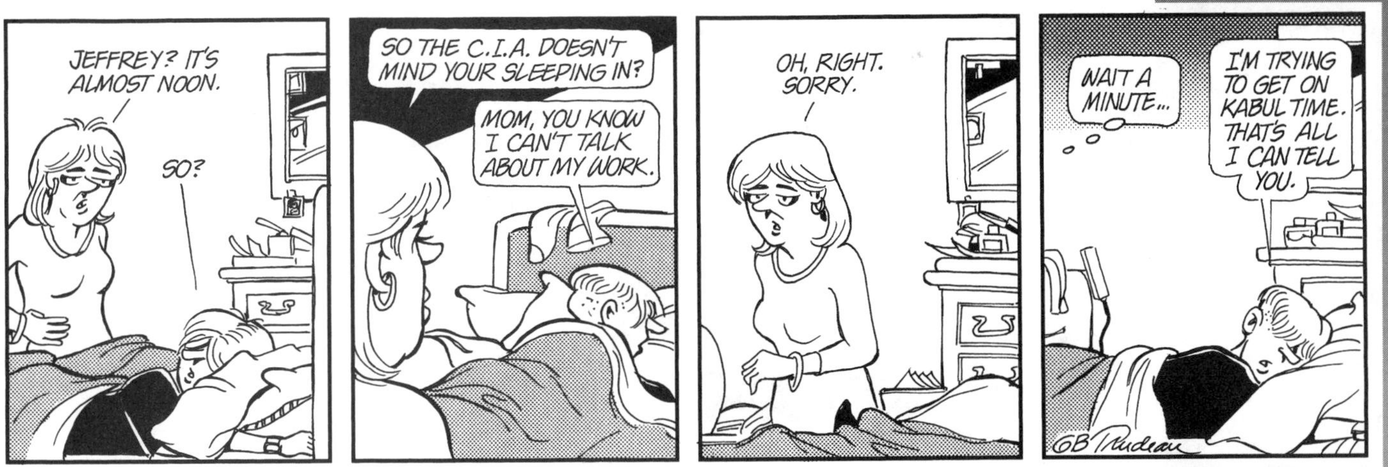
JEFFREY? IT'S ALMOST NOON.
SO?
SO THE C.I.A. DOESN'T MIND YOUR SLEEPING IN?
MOM, YOU KNOW I CAN'T TALK ABOUT MY WORK.
OH, RIGHT. SORRY.
WAIT A MINUTE...
I'M TRYING TO GET ON KABUL TIME. THAT'S ALL I CAN TELL YOU.
GB Trudeau

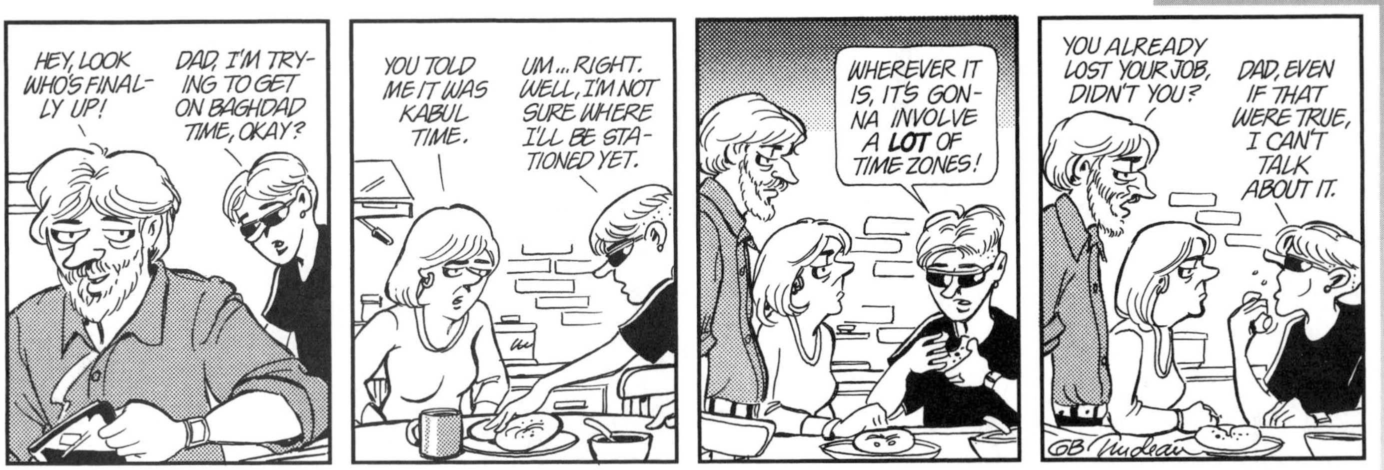
HEY, LOOK WHO'S FINALLY UP!
DAD, I'M TRYING TO GET ON BAGHDAD TIME, OKAY?
YOU TOLD ME IT WAS KABUL TIME.
UM... RIGHT. WELL, I'M NOT SURE WHERE I'LL BE STATIONED YET.
WHEREVER IT IS, IT'S GONNA INVOLVE A LOT OF TIME ZONES!
YOU ALREADY LOST YOUR JOB, DIDN'T YOU?
DAD, EVEN IF THAT WERE TRUE, I CAN'T TALK ABOUT IT.
GB Trudeau

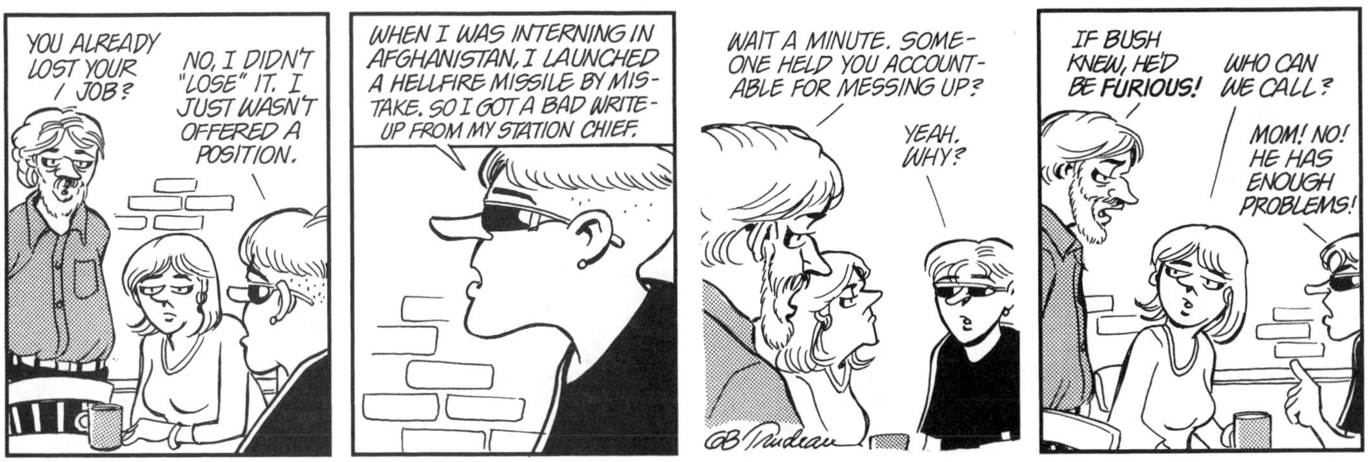
YOU ALREADY LOST YOUR JOB?
NO, I DIDN'T "LOSE" IT. I JUST WASN'T OFFERED A POSITION.
WHEN I WAS INTERNING IN AFGHANISTAN, I LAUNCHED A HELLFIRE MISSILE BY MISTAKE. SO I GOT A BAD WRITE-UP FROM MY STATION CHIEF.
WAIT A MINUTE. SOMEONE HELD YOU ACCOUNTABLE FOR MESSING UP?
YEAH. WHY?
GB Trudeau
IF BUSH KNEW, HE'D BE FURIOUS!
WHO CAN WE CALL?
MOM! NO! HE HAS ENOUGH PROBLEMS!

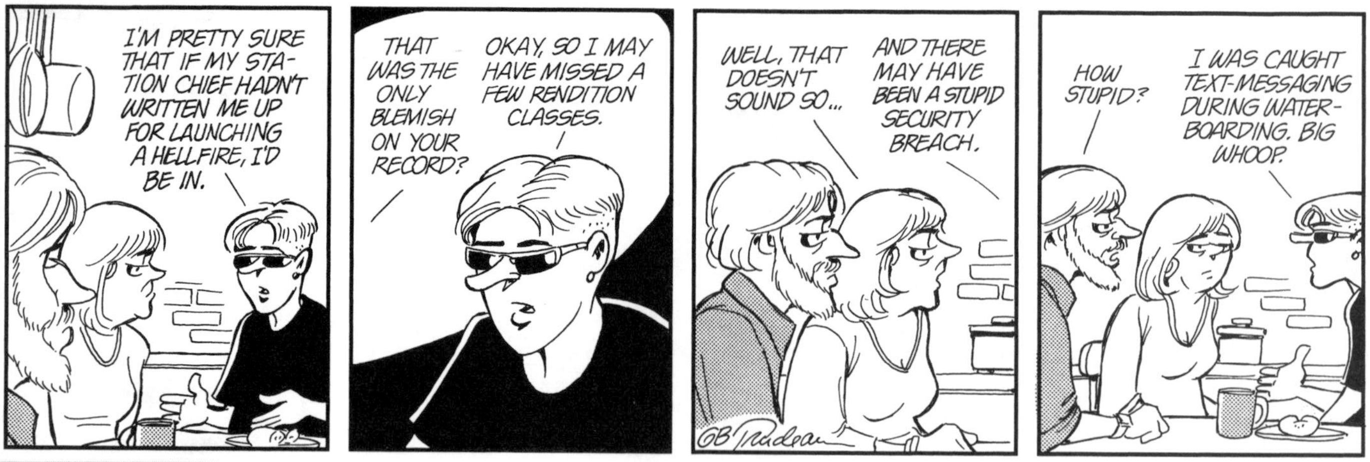
I'M PRETTY SURE THAT IF MY STATION CHIEF HADN'T WRITTEN ME UP FOR LAUNCHING A HELLFIRE, I'D BE IN.
THAT WAS THE ONLY BLEMISH ON YOUR RECORD?
OKAY, SO I MAY HAVE MISSED A FEW RENDITION CLASSES.
WELL, THAT DOESN'T SOUND SO...
AND THERE MAY HAVE BEEN A STUPID SECURITY BREACH.
HOW STUPID?
I WAS CAUGHT TEXT-MESSAGING DURING WATER-BOARDING. BIG WHOOP.

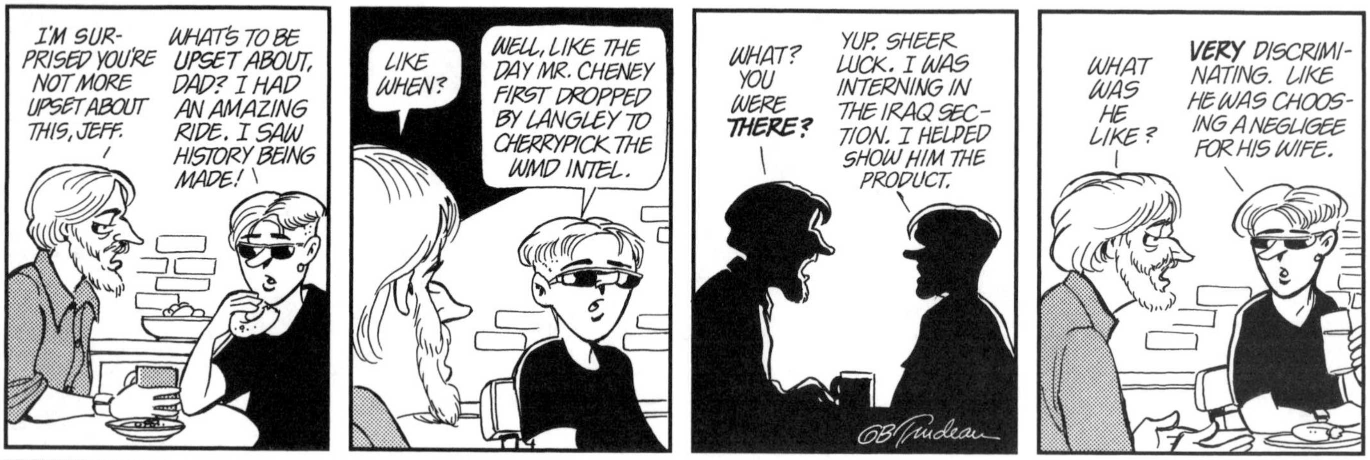
I'M SURPRISED YOU'RE NOT MORE UPSET ABOUT THIS, JEFF.
WHAT'S TO BE UPSET ABOUT, DAD? I HAD AN AMAZING RIDE. I SAW HISTORY BEING MADE!
LIKE WHEN?
WELL, LIKE THE DAY MR. CHENEY FIRST DROPPED BY LANGLEY TO CHERRYPICK THE WMD INTEL.
WHAT? YOU WERE THERE?
YUP. SHEER LUCK. I WAS INTERNING IN THE IRAQ SECTION. I HELPED SHOW HIM THE PRODUCT.
WHAT WAS HE LIKE?
VERY DISCRIMINATING. LIKE HE WAS CHOOSING A NEGLIGEE FOR HIS WIFE.

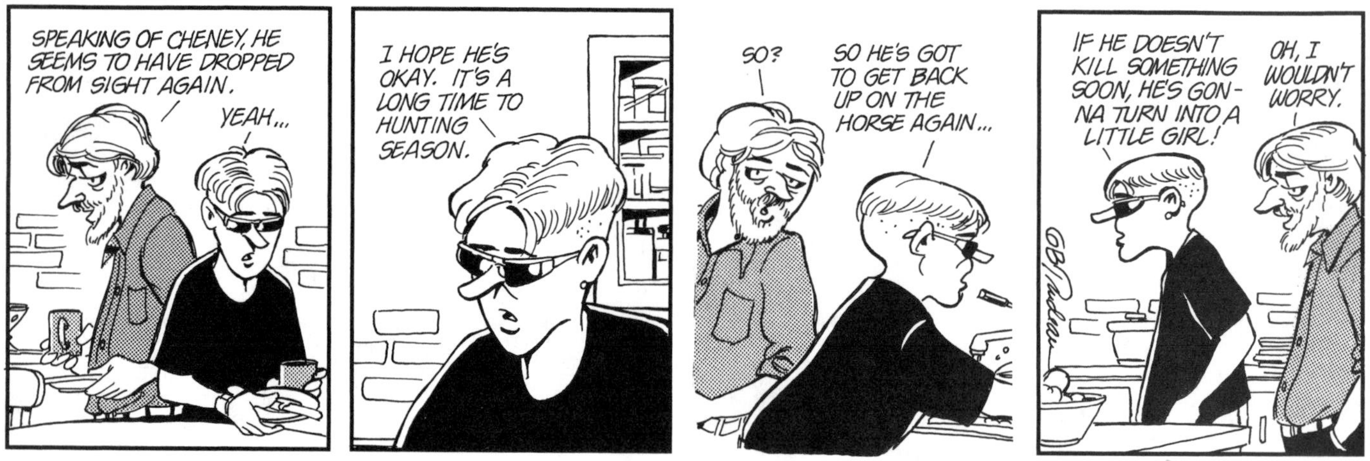
SPEAKING OF CHENEY, HE SEEMS TO HAVE DROPPED FROM SIGHT AGAIN.
YEAH...
I HOPE HE'S OKAY. IT'S A LONG TIME TO HUNTING SEASON.
SO?
SO HE'S GOT TO GET BACK UP ON THE HORSE AGAIN...
IF HE DOESN'T KILL SOMETHING SOON, HE'S GONNA TURN INTO A LITTLE GIRL!
OH, I WOULDN'T WORRY.

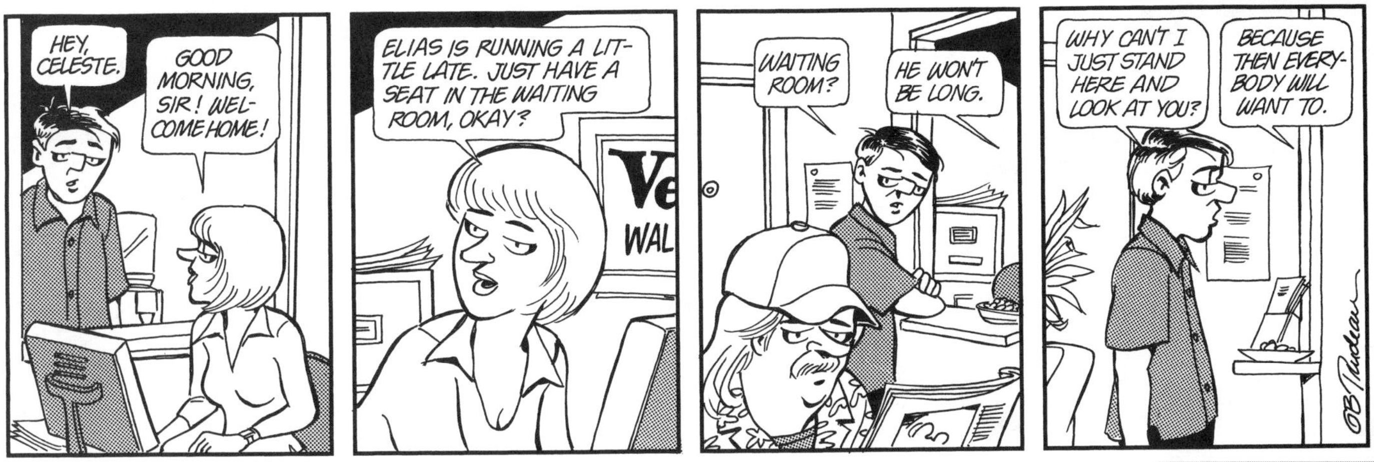
HEY, CELESTE.
GOOD MORNING, SIR! WEL-COME HOME!
ELIAS IS RUNNING A LIT-TLE LATE. JUST HAVE A SEAT IN THE WAITING ROOM, OKAY?
WAITING ROOM?
HE WON'T BE LONG.
WHY CAN'T I JUST STAND HERE AND LOOK AT YOU?
BECAUSE THEN EVERY-BODY WILL WANT TO.
GB Trudeau

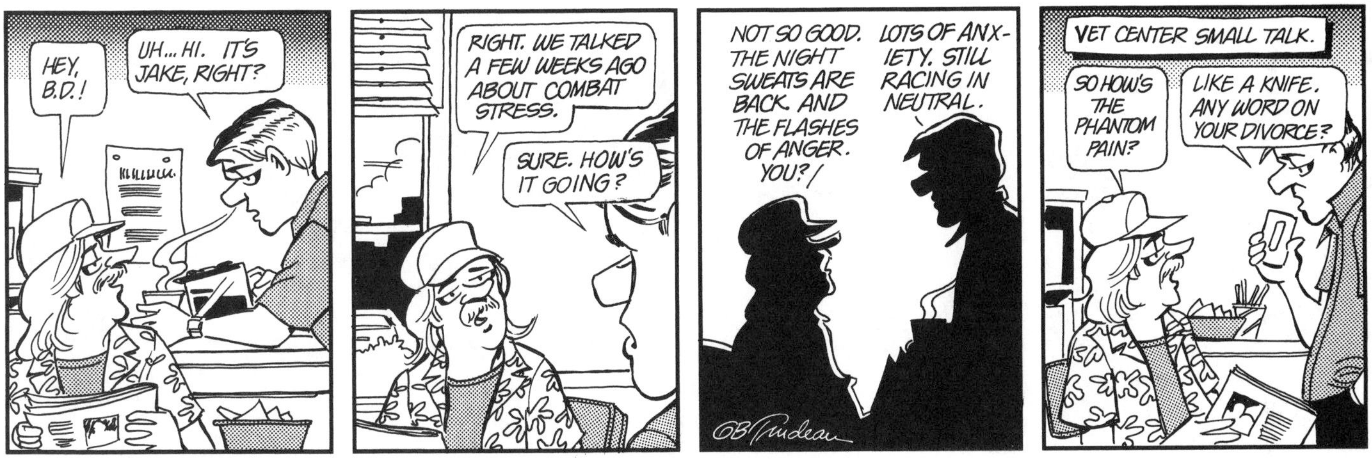
HEY, B.D.!
UH... HI. IT'S JAKE, RIGHT?
RIGHT. WE TALKED A FEW WEEKS AGO ABOUT COMBAT STRESS.
SURE. HOW'S IT GOING?
NOT SO GOOD. THE NIGHT SWEATS ARE BACK. AND THE FLASHES OF ANGER. YOU?
LOTS OF ANX-IETY. STILL RACING IN NEUTRAL.
GB Trudeau
VET CENTER SMALL TALK.
SO HOW'S THE PHANTOM PAIN?
LIKE A KNIFE. ANY WORD ON YOUR DIVORCE?

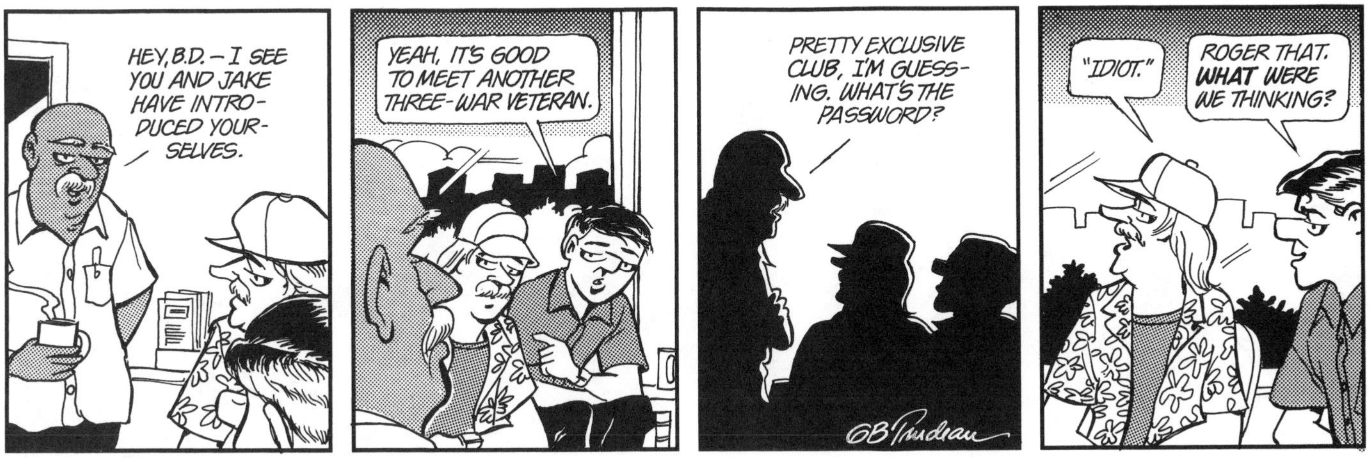
HEY, B.D. – I SEE YOU AND JAKE HAVE INTRO-DUCED YOUR-SELVES.
YEAH, IT'S GOOD TO MEET ANOTHER THREE-WAR VETERAN.
PRETTY EXCLUSIVE CLUB, I'M GUESS-ING. WHAT'S THE PASSWORD?
GB Trudeau
"IDIOT."
ROGER THAT. WHAT WERE WE THINKING?

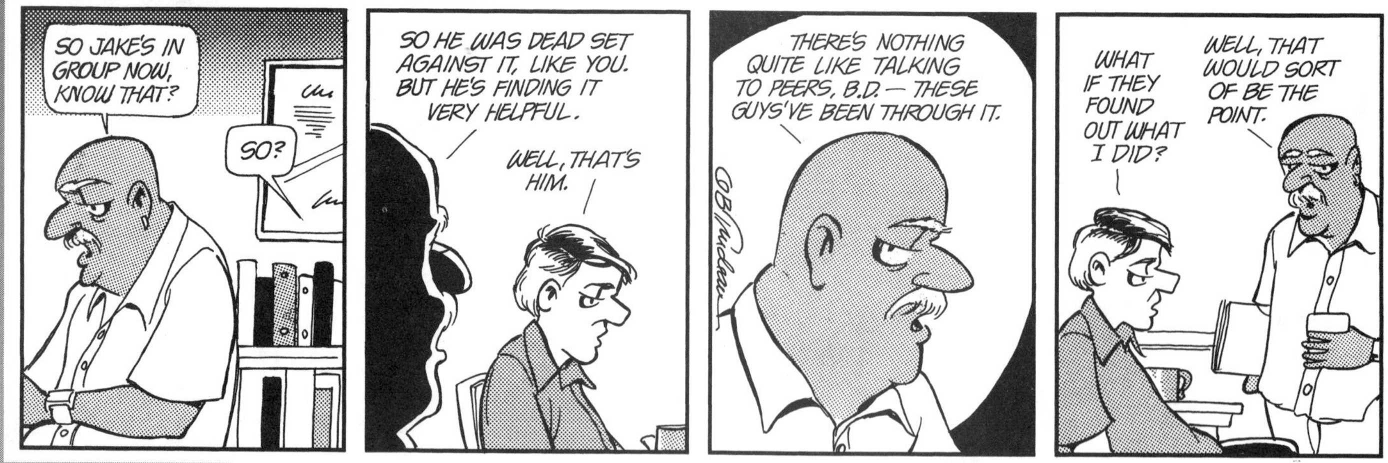
SO JAKE'S IN GROUP NOW, KNOW THAT?
SO?
SO HE WAS DEAD SET AGAINST IT, LIKE YOU. BUT HE'S FINDING IT VERY HELPFUL.
WELL, THAT'S HIM.
THERE'S NOTHING QUITE LIKE TALKING TO PEERS, B.D. — THESE GUYS'VE BEEN THROUGH IT.
WHAT IF THEY FOUND OUT WHAT I DID?
WELL, THAT WOULD SORT OF BE THE POINT.

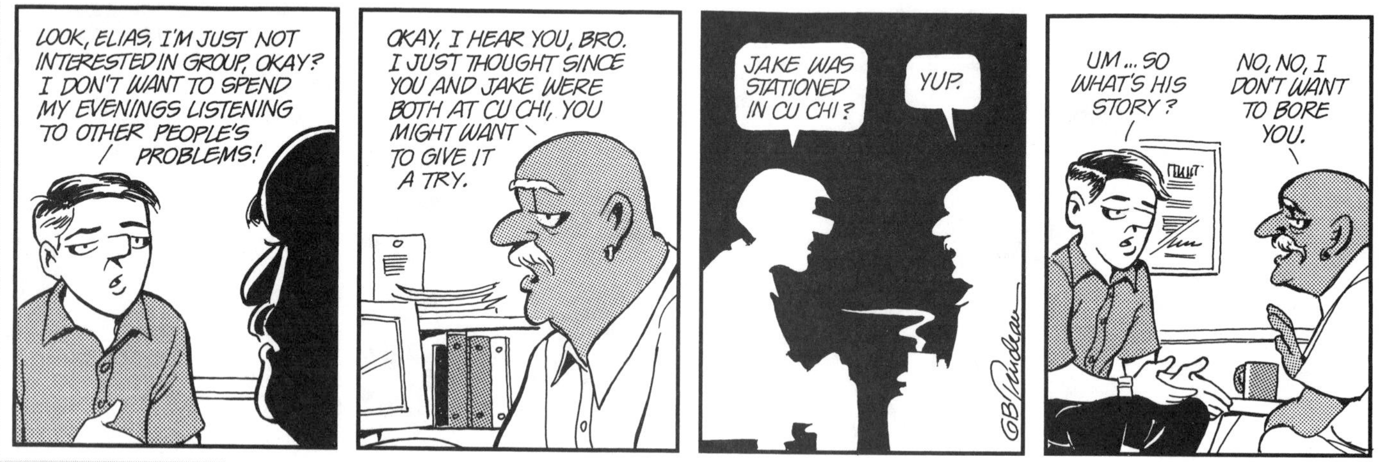
LOOK, ELIAS, I'M JUST NOT INTERESTED IN GROUP, OKAY? I DON'T WANT TO SPEND MY EVENINGS LISTENING TO OTHER PEOPLE'S PROBLEMS!
OKAY, I HEAR YOU, BRO. I JUST THOUGHT SINCE YOU AND JAKE WERE BOTH AT CU CHI, YOU MIGHT WANT TO GIVE IT A TRY.
JAKE WAS STATIONED IN CU CHI?
YUP.
UM... SO WHAT'S HIS STORY?
NO, NO, I DON'T WANT TO BORE YOU.

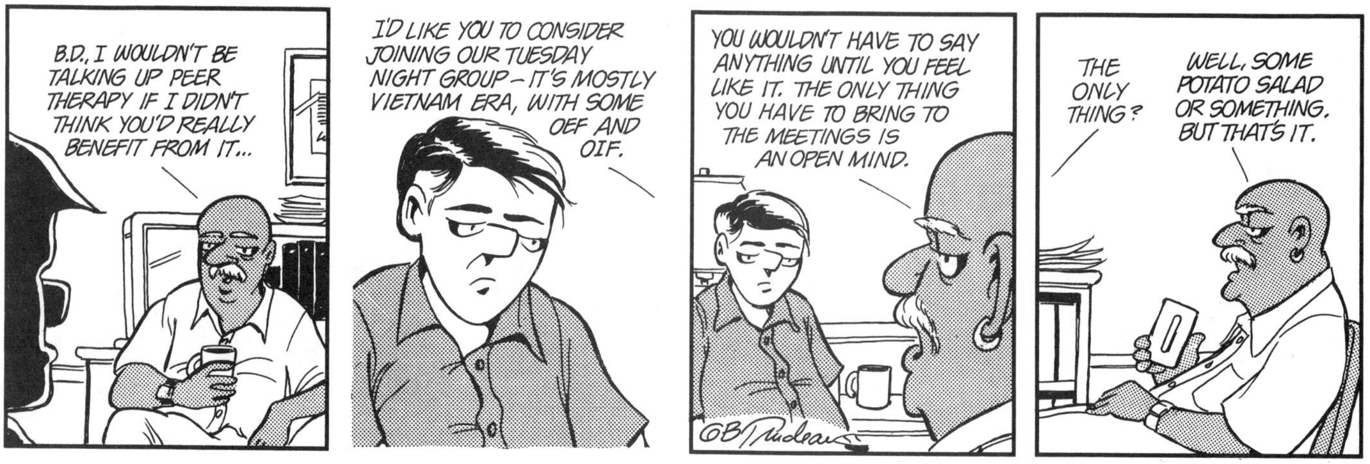
B.D., I WOULDN'T BE TALKING UP PEER THERAPY IF I DIDN'T THINK YOU'D REALLY BENEFIT FROM IT...
I'D LIKE YOU TO CONSIDER JOINING OUR TUESDAY NIGHT GROUP – IT'S MOSTLY VIETNAM ERA, WITH SOME OEF AND OIF.
YOU WOULDN'T HAVE TO SAY ANYTHING UNTIL YOU FEEL LIKE IT. THE ONLY THING YOU HAVE TO BRING TO THE MEETINGS IS AN OPEN MIND.
THE ONLY THING?
WELL, SOME POTATO SALAD OR SOMETHING. BUT THAT'S IT.

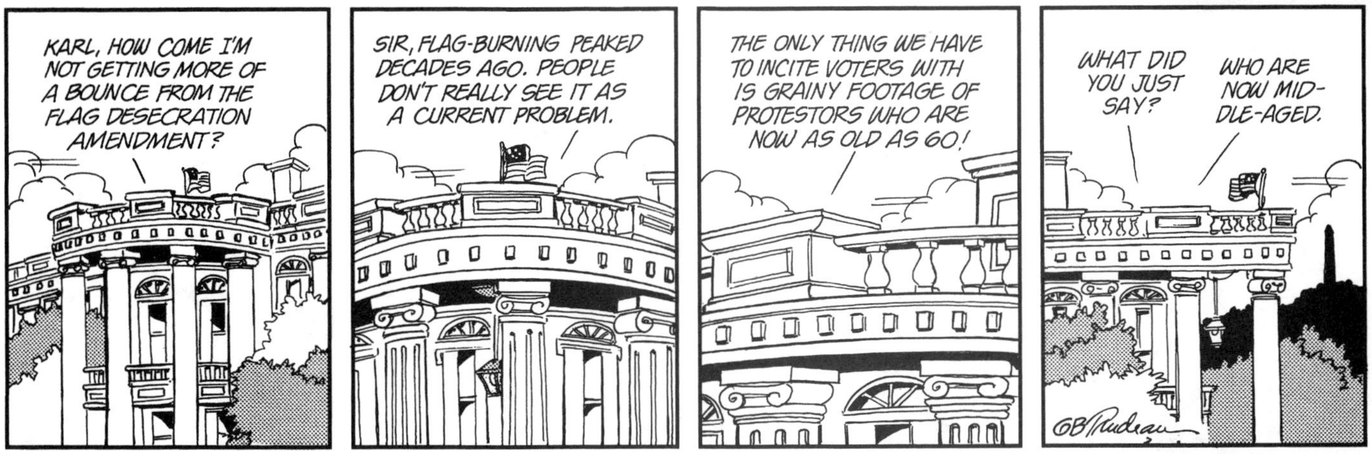
KARL, HOW COME I'M NOT GETTING MORE OF A BOUNCE FROM THE FLAG DESECRATION AMENDMENT?
SIR, FLAG-BURNING PEAKED DECADES AGO. PEOPLE DON'T REALLY SEE IT AS A CURRENT PROBLEM.
THE ONLY THING WE HAVE TO INCITE VOTERS WITH IS GRAINY FOOTAGE OF PROTESTORS WHO ARE NOW AS OLD AS 60!
WHAT DID YOU JUST SAY?
WHO ARE NOW MID-DLE-AGED.
GB Trudeau

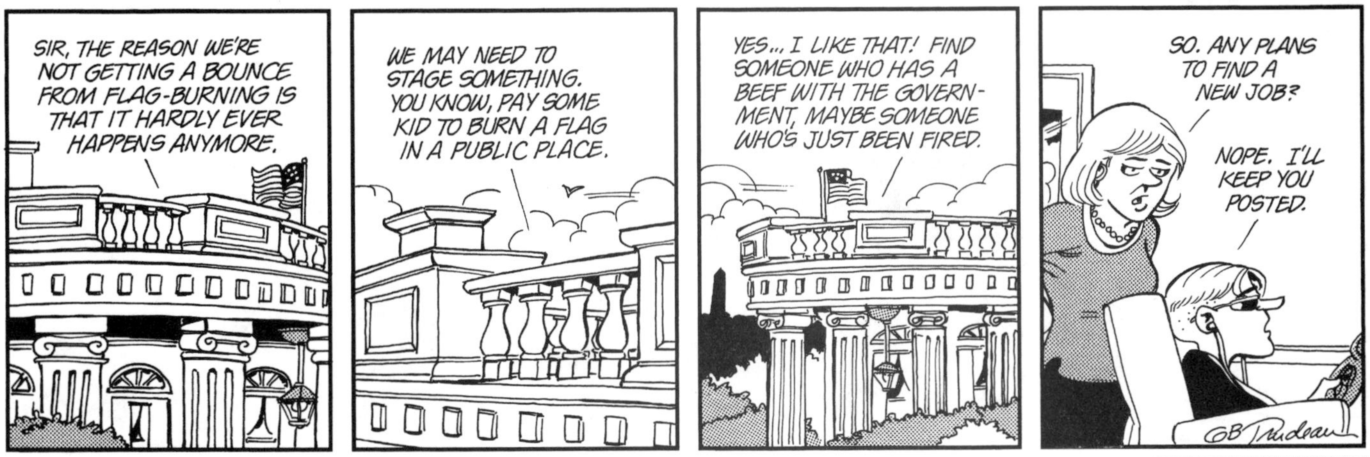
SIR, THE REASON WE'RE NOT GETTING A BOUNCE FROM FLAG-BURNING IS THAT IT HARDLY EVER HAPPENS ANYMORE.
WE MAY NEED TO STAGE SOMETHING. YOU KNOW, PAY SOME KID TO BURN A FLAG IN A PUBLIC PLACE.
YES... I LIKE THAT! FIND SOMEONE WHO HAS A BEEF WITH THE GOVERN-MENT, MAYBE SOMEONE WHO'S JUST BEEN FIRED.
SO. ANY PLANS TO FIND A NEW JOB?
NOPE. I'LL KEEP YOU POSTED.
GB Trudeau

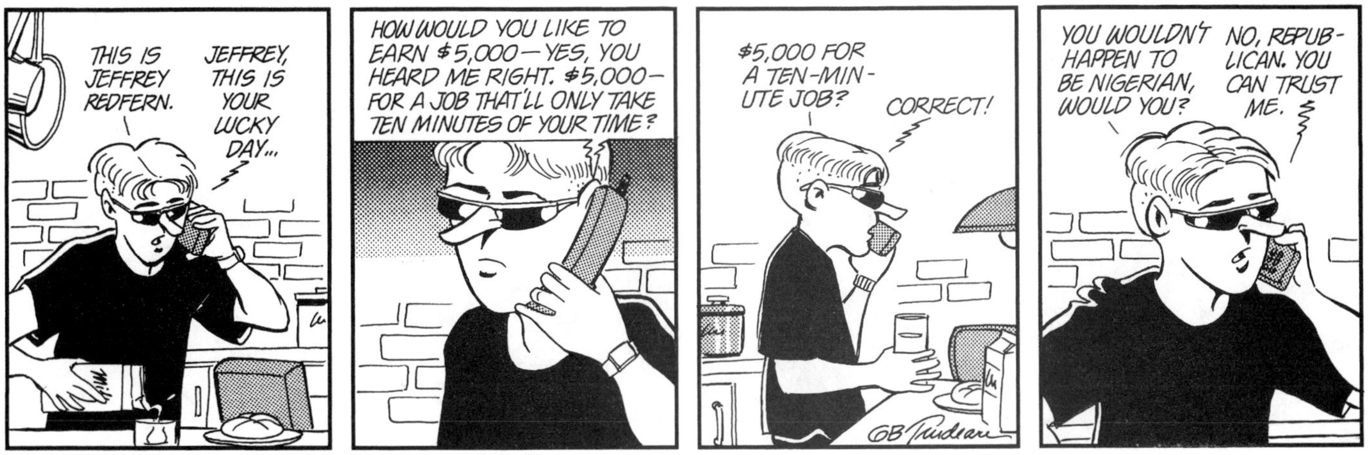
THIS IS JEFFREY REDFERN.
JEFFREY, THIS IS YOUR LUCKY DAY...
HOW WOULD YOU LIKE TO EARN $5,000—YES, YOU HEARD ME RIGHT. $5,000—FOR A JOB THAT'LL ONLY TAKE TEN MINUTES OF YOUR TIME?
$5,000 FOR A TEN-MIN-UTE JOB?
CORRECT!
YOU WOULDN'T HAPPEN TO BE NIGERIAN, WOULD YOU?
NO, REPUB-LICAN. YOU CAN TRUST ME.
GB Trudeau

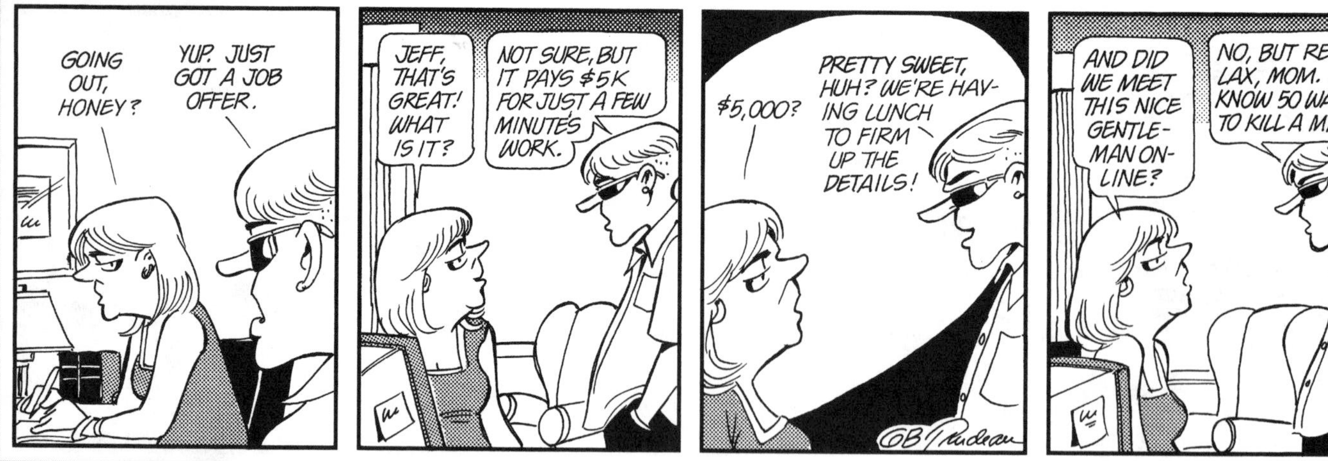
GOING OUT, HONEY?
YUP. JUST GOT A JOB OFFER.
JEFF, THAT'S GREAT! WHAT IS IT?
NOT SURE, BUT IT PAYS $5K FOR JUST A FEW MINUTES WORK.
$5,000?
PRETTY SWEET, HUH? WE'RE HAVING LUNCH TO FIRM UP THE DETAILS!
AND DID WE MEET THIS NICE GENTLEMAN ONLINE?
NO, BUT RELAX, MOM. I KNOW 50 WAYS TO KILL A MAN.

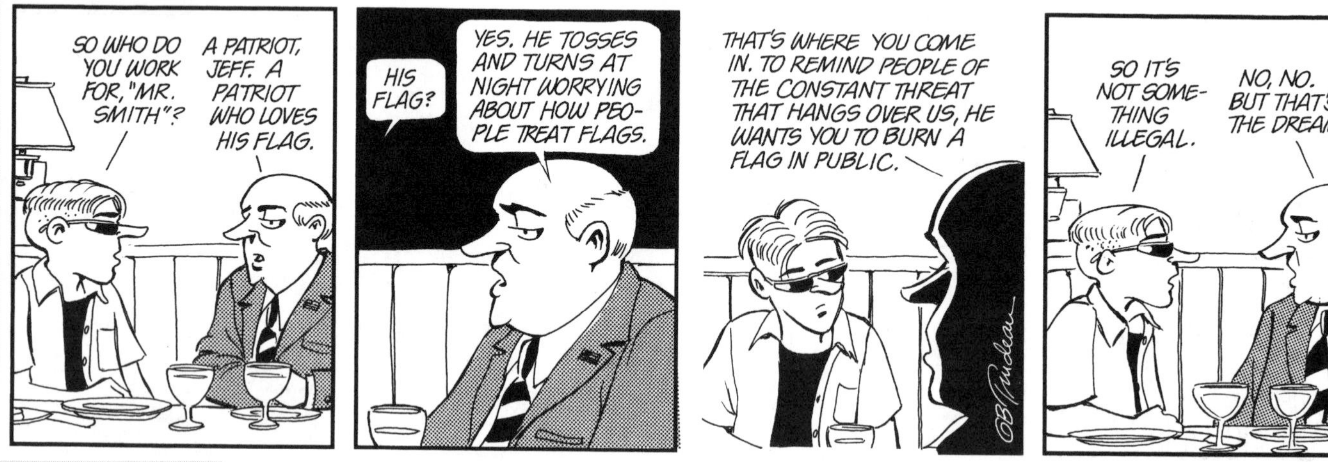
SO WHO DO YOU WORK FOR, "MR. SMITH"?
A PATRIOT, JEFF. A PATRIOT WHO LOVES HIS FLAG.
HIS FLAG?
YES. HE TOSSES AND TURNS AT NIGHT WORRYING ABOUT HOW PEOPLE TREAT FLAGS.
THAT'S WHERE YOU COME IN. TO REMIND PEOPLE OF THE CONSTANT THREAT THAT HANGS OVER US, HE WANTS YOU TO BURN A FLAG IN PUBLIC.
SO IT'S NOT SOMETHING ILLEGAL.
NO, NO. BUT THAT'S THE DREAM.

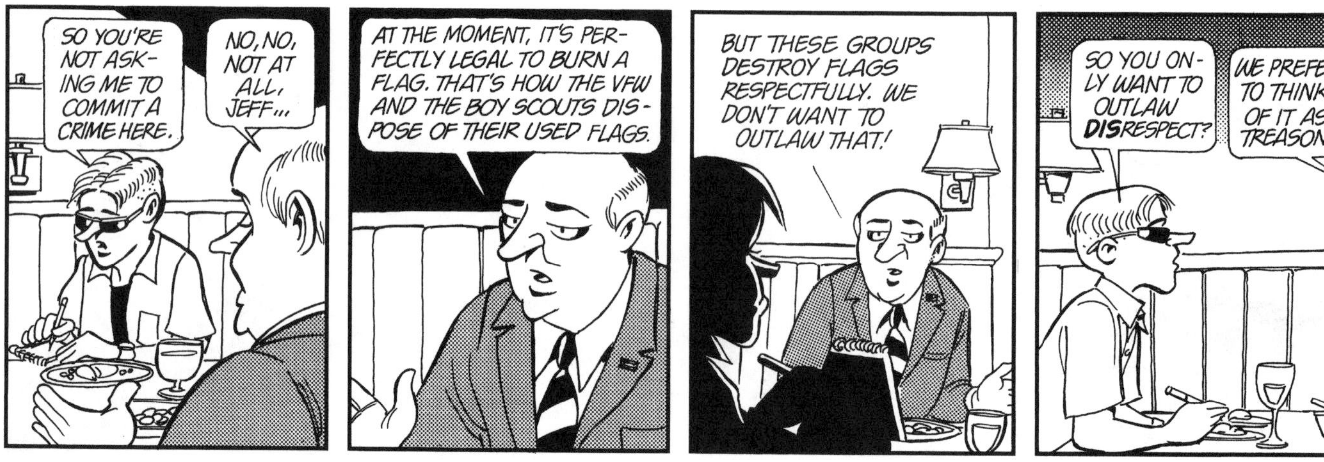
SO YOU'RE NOT ASKING ME TO COMMIT A CRIME HERE.
NO, NO, NOT AT ALL, JEFF...
AT THE MOMENT, IT'S PERFECTLY LEGAL TO BURN A FLAG. THAT'S HOW THE VFW AND THE BOY SCOUTS DISPOSE OF THEIR USED FLAGS.
BUT THESE GROUPS DESTROY FLAGS RESPECTFULLY. WE DON'T WANT TO OUTLAW THAT!
SO YOU ONLY WANT TO OUTLAW **DIS**RESPECT?
WE PREFER TO THINK OF IT AS TREASON.

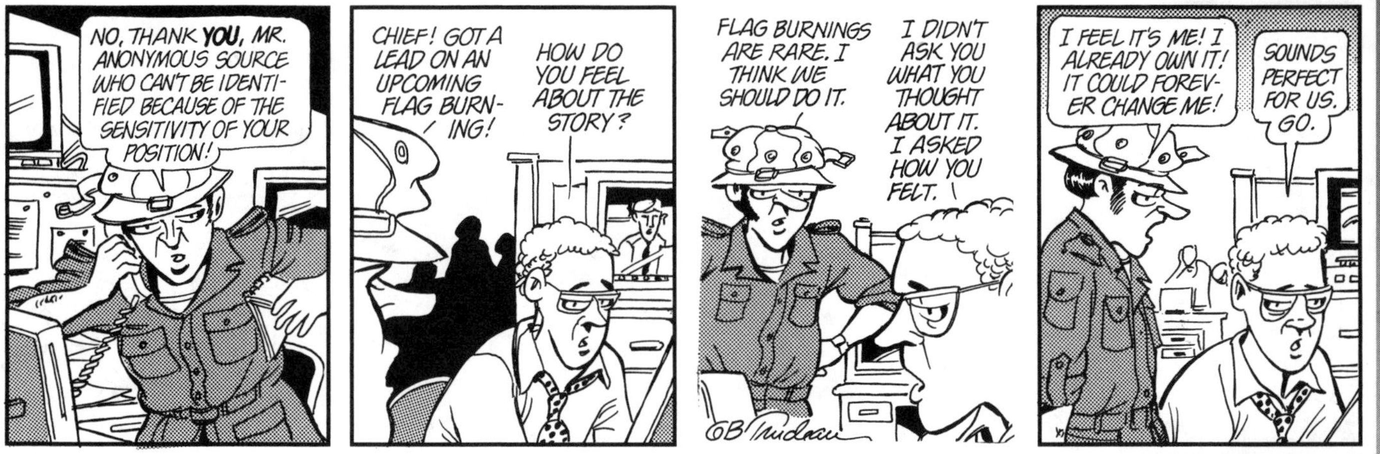
NO, THANK **YOU**, MR. ANONYMOUS SOURCE WHO CAN'T BE IDENTIFIED BECAUSE OF THE SENSITIVITY OF YOUR POSITION!
CHIEF! GOT A LEAD ON AN UPCOMING FLAG BURNING!
HOW DO YOU FEEL ABOUT THE STORY?
FLAG BURNINGS ARE RARE. I THINK WE SHOULD DO IT.
I DIDN'T ASK YOU WHAT YOU THOUGHT ABOUT IT. I ASKED HOW YOU FELT.
I FEEL IT'S ME! I ALREADY OWN IT! IT COULD FOREVER CHANGE ME!
SOUNDS PERFECT FOR US. GO.

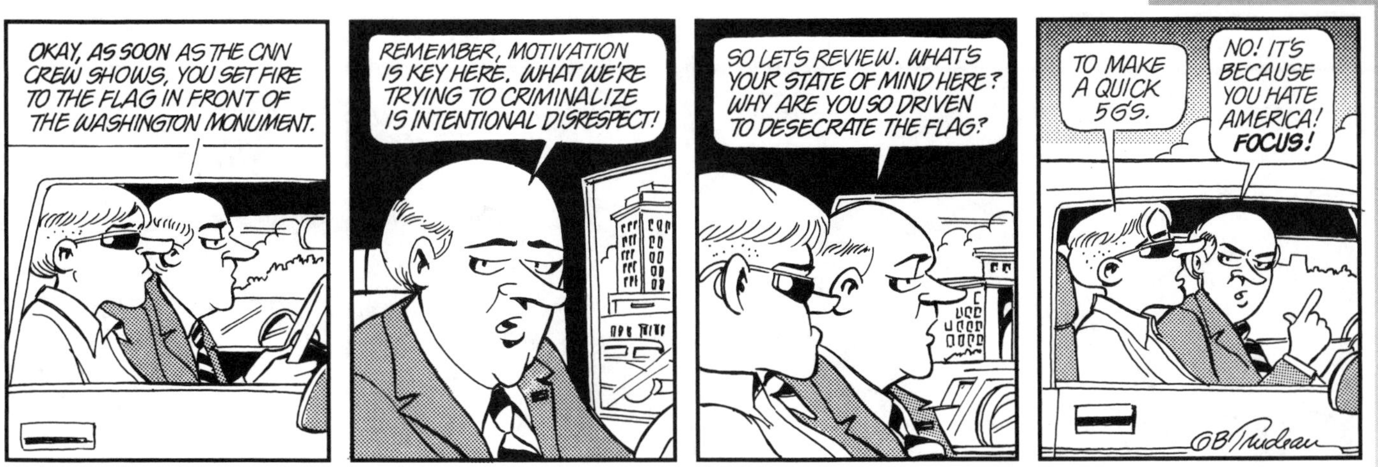
OKAY, AS SOON AS THE CNN CREW SHOWS, YOU SET FIRE TO THE FLAG IN FRONT OF THE WASHINGTON MONUMENT.
REMEMBER, MOTIVATION IS KEY HERE. WHAT WE'RE TRYING TO CRIMINALIZE IS INTENTIONAL DISRESPECT!
SO LET'S REVIEW. WHAT'S YOUR STATE OF MIND HERE? WHY ARE YOU SO DRIVEN TO DESECRATE THE FLAG?
TO MAKE A QUICK 5G'S.
NO! IT'S BECAUSE YOU HATE AMERICA! **FOCUS!**

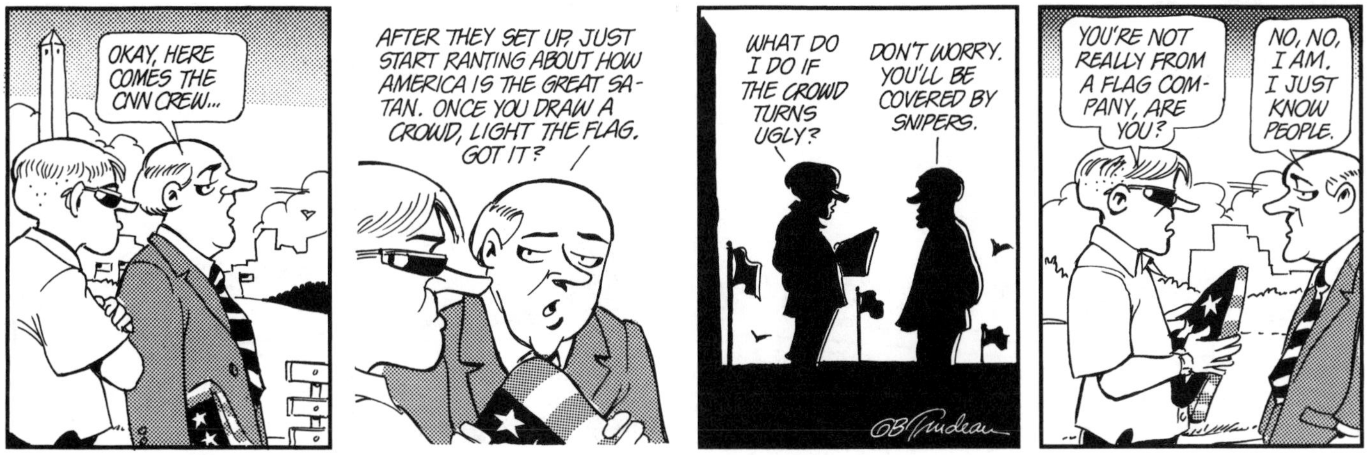
OKAY, HERE COMES THE CNN CREW...
AFTER THEY SET UP, JUST START RANTING ABOUT HOW AMERICA IS THE GREAT SATAN. ONCE YOU DRAW A CROWD, LIGHT THE FLAG. GOT IT?
WHAT DO I DO IF THE CROWD TURNS UGLY?
DON'T WORRY. YOU'LL BE COVERED BY SNIPERS.
YOU'RE NOT REALLY FROM A FLAG COMPANY, ARE YOU?
NO, NO, I AM. I JUST KNOW PEOPLE.

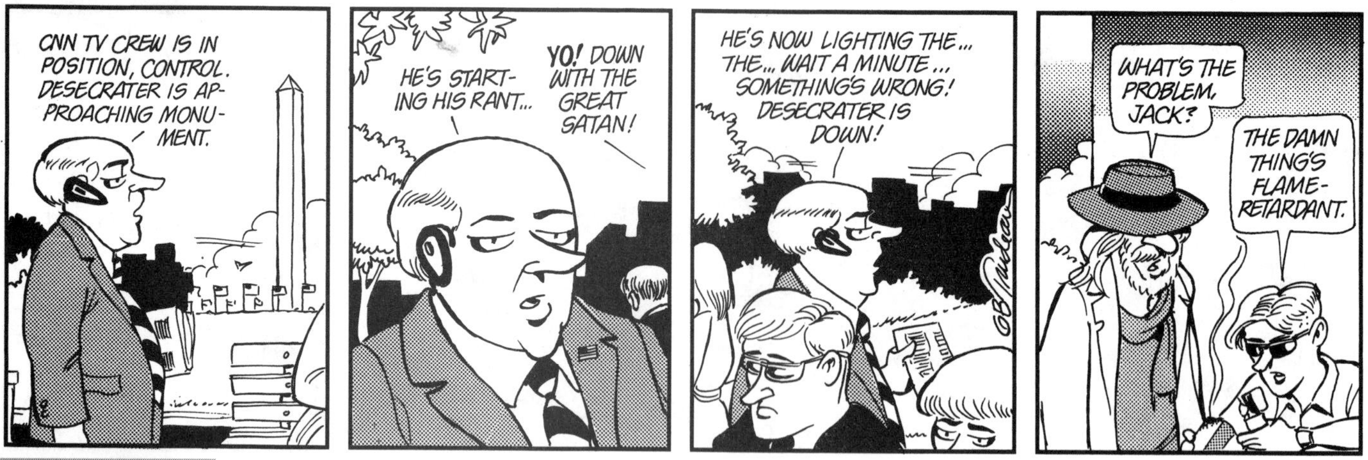
CNN TV CREW IS IN POSITION, CONTROL. DESECRATER IS APPROACHING MONUMENT.
HE'S STARTING HIS RANT...
YO! DOWN WITH THE GREAT SATAN!
HE'S NOW LIGHTING THE... THE... WAIT A MINUTE... ...SOMETHING'S WRONG! DESECRATER IS DOWN!
WHAT'S THE PROBLEM, JACK?
THE DAMN THING'S FLAME-RETARDANT.

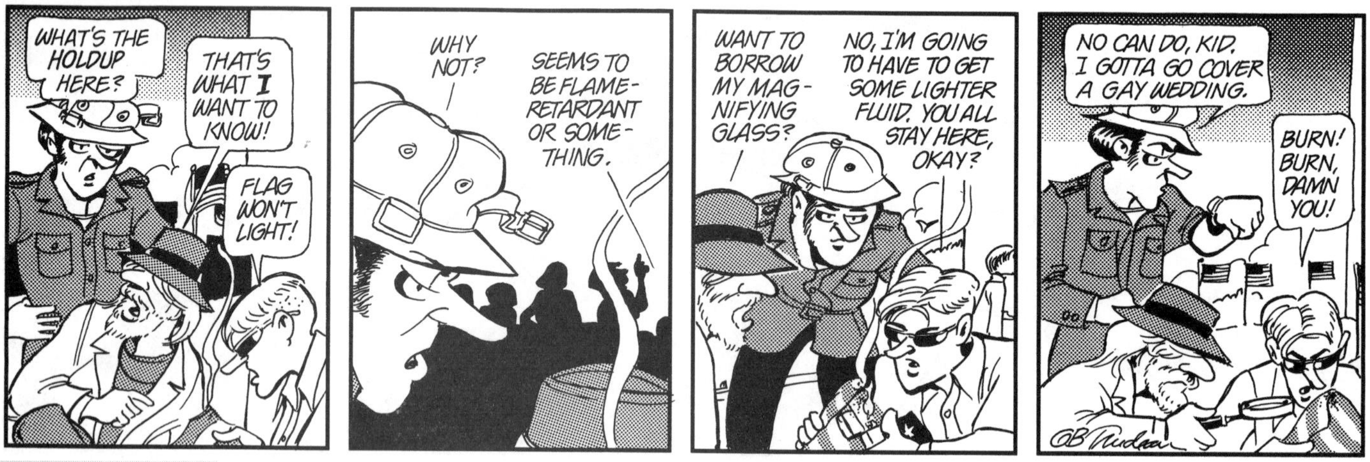
WHAT'S THE HOLDUP HERE?
THAT'S WHAT I WANT TO KNOW!
FLAG WON'T LIGHT!
WHY NOT?
SEEMS TO BE FLAME-RETARDANT OR SOMETHING.
WANT TO BORROW MY MAGNIFYING GLASS?
NO, I'M GOING TO HAVE TO GET SOME LIGHTER FLUID. YOU ALL STAY HERE, OKAY?
NO CAN DO, KID. I GOTTA GO COVER A GAY WEDDING.
BURN! BURN, DAMN YOU!

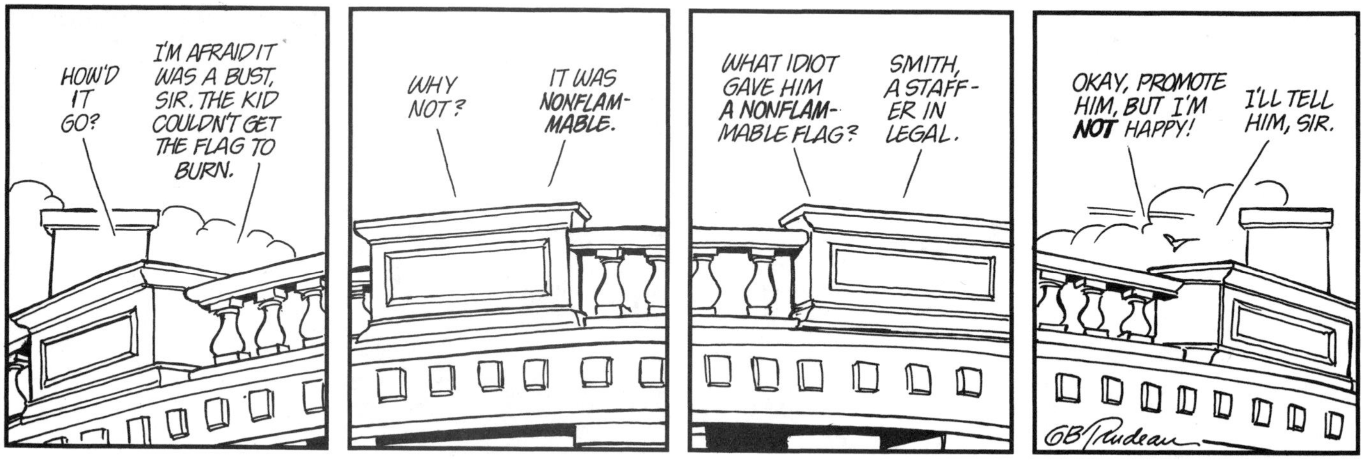
HOW'D IT GO?
I'M AFRAID IT WAS A BUST, SIR. THE KID COULDN'T GET THE FLAG TO BURN.
WHY NOT?
IT WAS NONFLAMMABLE.
WHAT IDIOT GAVE HIM A NONFLAMMABLE FLAG?
SMITH, A STAFFER IN LEGAL.
OKAY, PROMOTE HIM, BUT I'M NOT HAPPY!
I'LL TELL HIM, SIR.

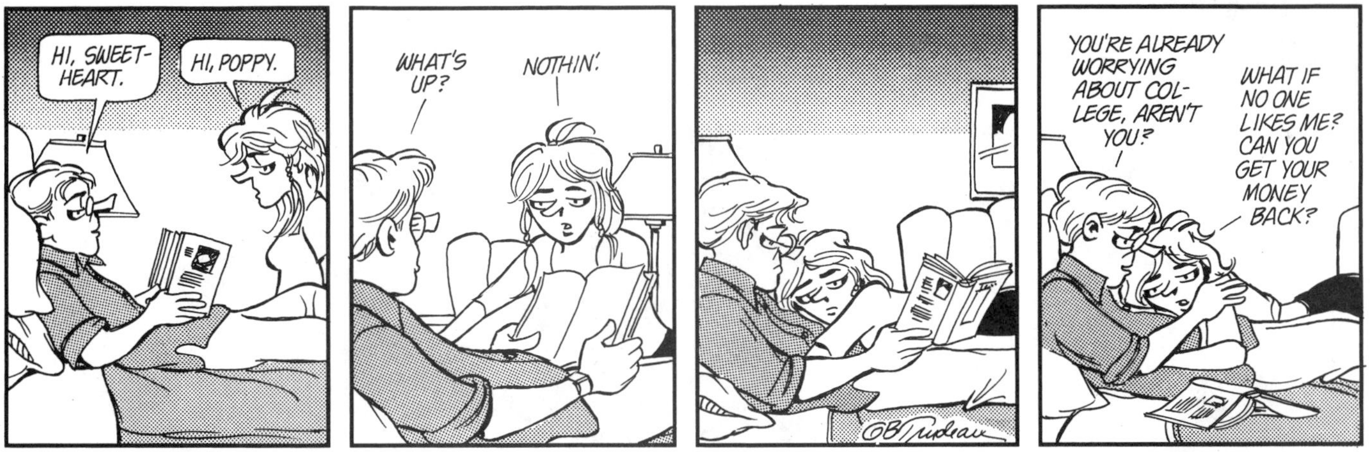
HI, SWEET-HEART.
HI, POPPY.
WHAT'S UP?
NOTHIN'.
YOU'RE ALREADY WORRYING ABOUT COL-LEGE, AREN'T YOU?
WHAT IF NO ONE LIKES ME? CAN YOU GET YOUR MONEY BACK?

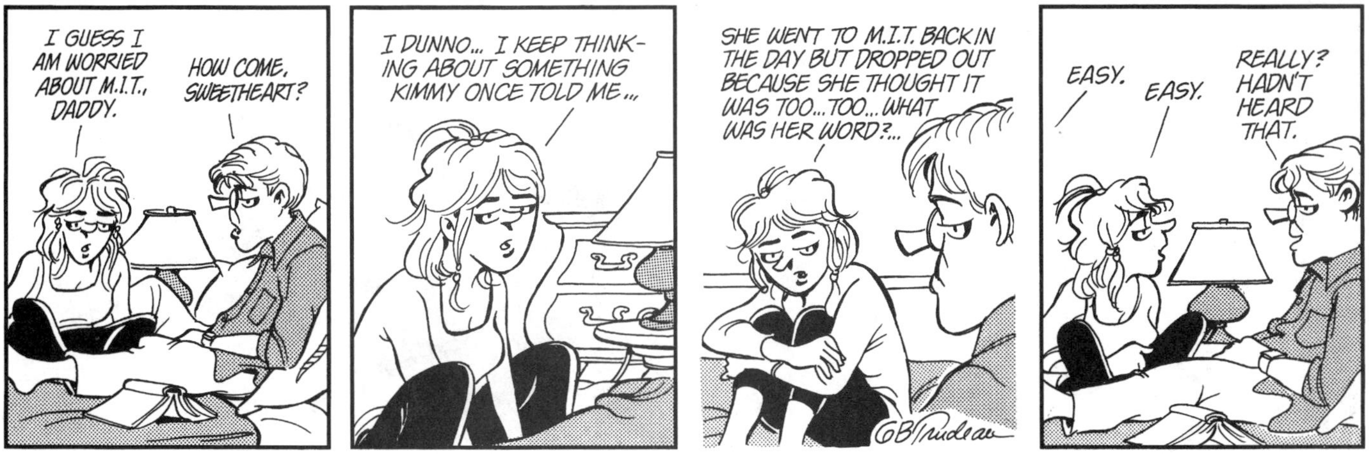
I GUESS I AM WORRIED ABOUT M.I.T., DADDY.
HOW COME, SWEETHEART?
I DUNNO... I KEEP THINK-ING ABOUT SOMETHING KIMMY ONCE TOLD ME...
SHE WENT TO M.I.T. BACK IN THE DAY BUT DROPPED OUT BECAUSE SHE THOUGHT IT WAS TOO...TOO...WHAT WAS HER WORD?...
EASY.
EASY.
REALLY? HADN'T HEARD THAT.

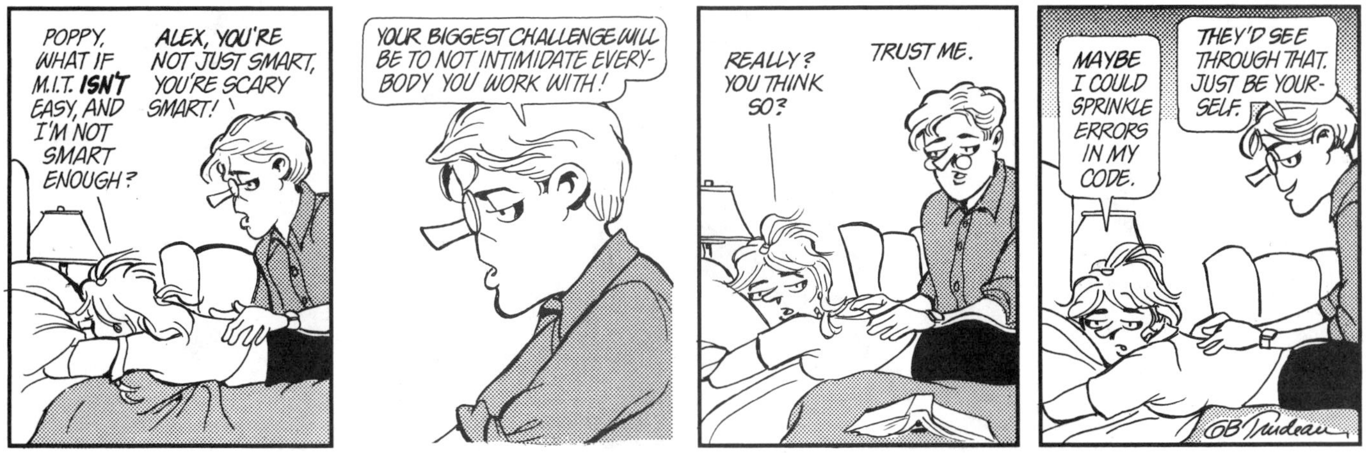
POPPY, WHAT IF M.I.T. ISN'T EASY, AND I'M NOT SMART ENOUGH?
ALEX, YOU'RE NOT JUST SMART, YOU'RE SCARY SMART!
YOUR BIGGEST CHALLENGE WILL BE TO NOT INTIMIDATE EVERY-BODY YOU WORK WITH!
REALLY? YOU THINK SO?
TRUST ME.
MAYBE I COULD SPRINKLE ERRORS IN MY CODE.
THEY'D SEE THROUGH THAT. JUST BE YOUR-SELF.

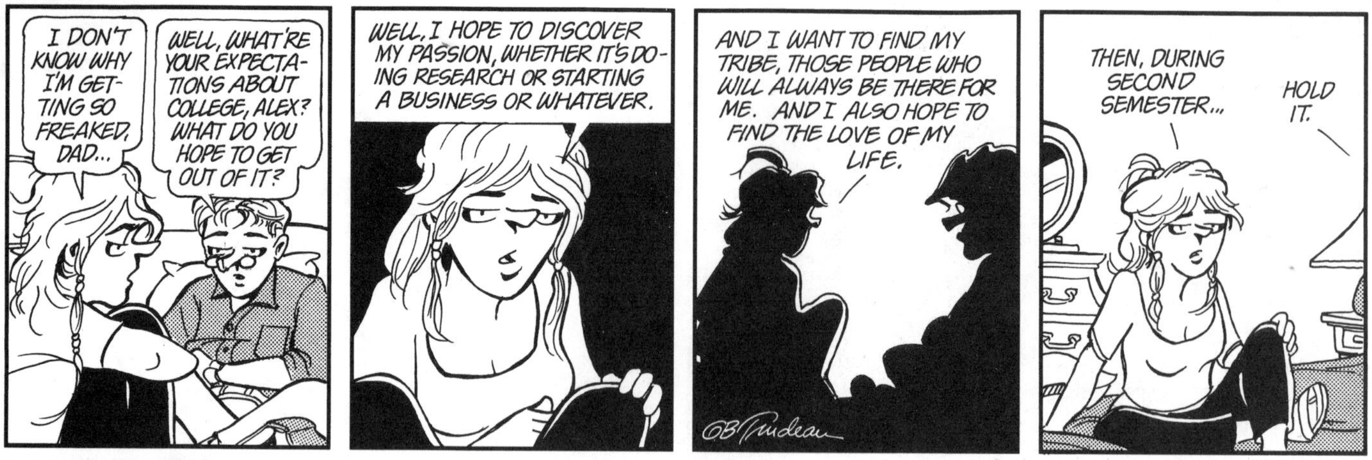
I DON'T KNOW WHY I'M GETTING SO FREAKED, DAD...
WELL, WHAT'RE YOUR EXPECTATIONS ABOUT COLLEGE, ALEX? WHAT DO YOU HOPE TO GET OUT OF IT?
WELL, I HOPE TO DISCOVER MY PASSION, WHETHER IT'S DOING RESEARCH OR STARTING A BUSINESS OR WHATEVER.
AND I WANT TO FIND MY TRIBE, THOSE PEOPLE WHO WILL ALWAYS BE THERE FOR ME. AND I ALSO HOPE TO FIND THE LOVE OF MY LIFE.
GB Trudeau
THEN, DURING SECOND SEMESTER...
HOLD IT.

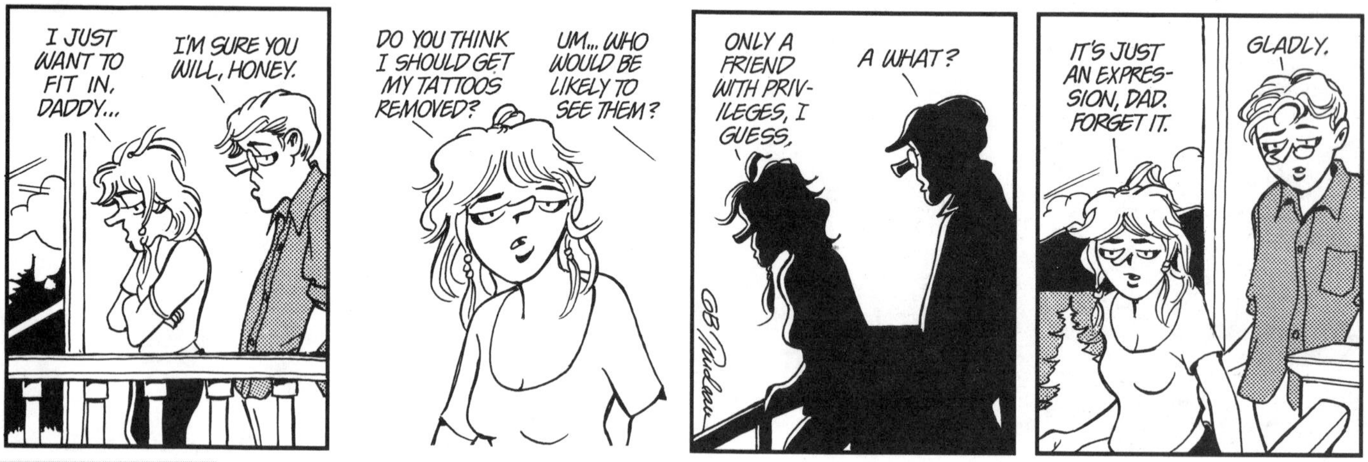
I JUST WANT TO FIT IN, DADDY...
I'M SURE YOU WILL, HONEY.
DO YOU THINK I SHOULD GET MY TATTOOS REMOVED?
UM... WHO WOULD BE LIKELY TO SEE THEM?
ONLY A FRIEND WITH PRIVILEGES, I GUESS.
A WHAT?
GB Trudeau
IT'S JUST AN EXPRESSION, DAD. FORGET IT.
GLADLY.

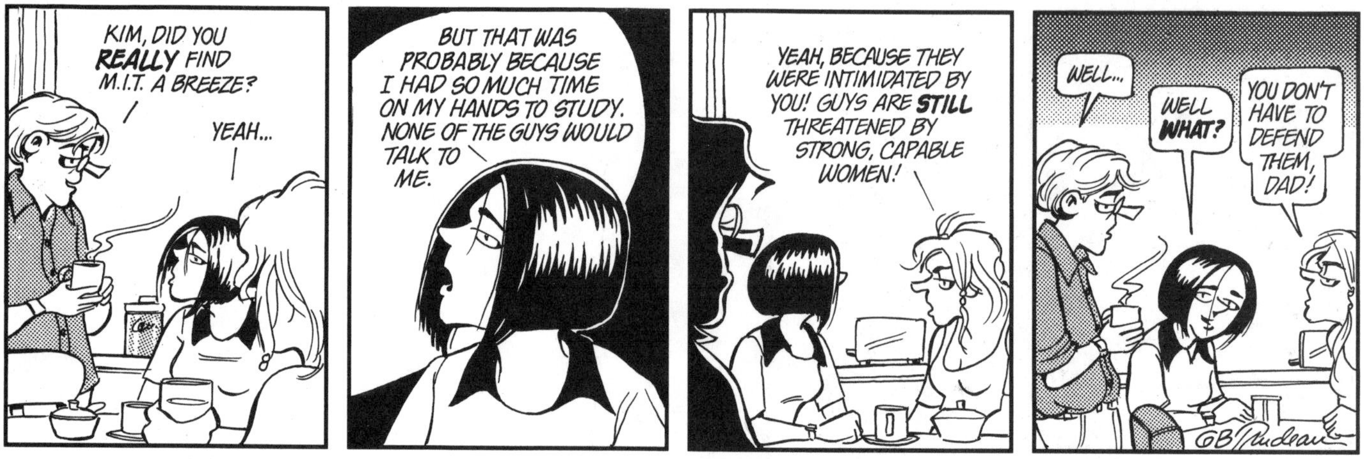
KIM, DID YOU **REALLY** FIND M.I.T. A BREEZE?
YEAH...
BUT THAT WAS PROBABLY BECAUSE I HAD SO MUCH TIME ON MY HANDS TO STUDY. NONE OF THE GUYS WOULD TALK TO ME.
YEAH, BECAUSE THEY WERE INTIMIDATED BY YOU! GUYS ARE **STILL** THREATENED BY STRONG, CAPABLE WOMEN!
WELL...
WELL **WHAT?**
YOU DON'T HAVE TO DEFEND THEM, DAD!
GB Trudeau